Business Education and Training: A Value-Laden Process

Volume IX: Instructed by Reason

Editors
Samuel M. Natale
Anthony F. Libertella

University Press of America, Inc.

Lanham • New York • Oxford

Oxford University Centre
for the Study of Values
in Education and Business

Copyright © 2003 by
University Press of America,® Inc.
4501 Forbes Boulevard
Suite 200
Lanham, Maryland 20706
UPA Acquisitions Department (301) 459-3366

PO Box 317
Oxford
OX2 9RU, UK

Copublished by arrangement with Oxford University Centre
for the Study of Values in Education and Business

ISBN 0-7618-2578-9 (clothbound : alk. ppr.)
ISBN 0-7618-2579-7 (paperback : alk. ppr.)

For
Juan Ignacio Chemes

Keep Ithaka always in your mind.
Arriving there is what you're destined for.
But don't hurry the journey at all.
Better if it lasts for years,
so you're old by the time you reach the island,
wealthy with all you've gained on the way,
not expecting Ithaka to make you rich.

Constantine P. Cavafy

Contents

Preface*

In 1988 Professors Samuel M. Natale (Adelphi University) and Richard Pring (University of Oxford) bestrode a lovely idea, the establishment of the Oxford University Centre for the Study of Values in Education and Business. This idea became an exemplary intellectual enterprise, which is still going strong and is alive and well judging by its latest progeny, the Sixth International Conference on Social Values, convened at Oxford, July 3-5, 2002.

The proceedings of this cognitive feast are contained in the readable, sometimes inspiring, and often instructive papers constituting these two volumes. The authors' insights into business and education are scholarly and practical, appropriate for the tastes and appetites of academicians and practitioners alike. Not surprisingly, some of the papers are brilliant, enlightening, and pleasurable to read as indeed they were when we first heard them presented last year.

The conference's dual audience of scholars and practitioners is a model that deserves widespread emulation since, at the end of the day, or if you will indulge another cliche, with the bottom line in mind, knowledge bereft of its applications in the worlds of work, nonprofit agencies, and governments, is really hollow and a luxury that the world cannot afford, while practice in the absence of solid and sound and replicable theory and empirical underpinnings may well be of questionable value. And so it is commendable that the organizers of this seminal conference were equipped to walk with grace both sides of the street, the scholarly or academic and the applied or practical. These pacesetting organizers—Samuel M. Natale, J. W. Sora, and Geoff Hayward— served the conference's participants well by providing a forum for esoteric and utilitarian constituencies, the combination of which makes it possible to serve the ultimate constituency, society at large.

According to Natale (2002), the conference's "underlying premise is the belief that all knowledge is consilient." Indeed, no less an academic luminary than Edward O. Wilson (1999) devoted an entire book to the proposition that there is unity among variegated disciplines and learned fields, that things go together, that theories and principles and concepts from one field correspond with those in another field, that, as it were, there is a "theory of everything" (Wilber 2000), a common thread that weaves together the stuff, the fabric, and the ideas extant in all of knowledge. Now it would be an exaggeration to exclaim that this conference was indeed consilient, but it would be no exaggeration to assert that Natale's premise of consilience was a noble aspiration.

---

* Many thanks to Professor Frank Dumont (McGill University, Montreal) for his eagle-eyed grammatical sleuthing and his astute editorial guidance, both of which tuned the timbre and elevated the tone of the preface.

After all, the sufficiency of consilience would not be possible sans the necessity of striving for consilience. Thanks for the striving, Sam—you did good!

The Conference's Setting

The city of Oxford. Oxford, in existence since AD 912—over one millennium ago!—was one of the largest towns in England at the time (1066) of the Norman conquest. It lies within a prosperous agricultural region, at the confluence of the Thames and Cherwell rivers.

Oxford has strong links with its most celebrated tenant, Oxford University, but also with the surrounding countryside. It is punctuated with delightful gardens; charming abodes famously described by scores of celebrated English novelists, poets, and playwrights; imposing—even snazzy—estates of the sort featured in the recent film, "Gosford Park"; painterly and engaging street patterns; and fashionable young men— on their way up, to be sure—nattily attired in derby hats and striped trousers briskly tramping the streets with their trusty black umbrellas, intent on making their way in the world with a stiff upper lip.

The city is generously sprinkled with museums, churches, quaint kiosks hawking everything but the kitchen sink, and tempting stores that will certainly imperil your charge cards.

The University of Oxford. The university has been referred to cryptically and paradoxically as being "everywhere and nowhere." How can this be? Well, notwithstanding the contradiction in "everywhere and nowhere," it is true, the University of Oxford nestled in the interstices of the city of Oxford is indeed everywhere and nowhere. Here is an Oxford College sandwiched between a hotel and a cluster of stores. There an Oxford College situated insouciantly between an automobile repair shop and a "Bear and Boar" pub. Look again and you will spot an Oxford College between a book store and a bank or beauty parlor. And next to an apothecary is an Oxford College cheek and jowl with an Indian restaurant whose exotic odors irrepressibly permeate the atmosphere. The idea is, simply, that Oxford University is not a single or cohesive site, a mall, as it were, with adjacent laboratories, libraries, and classrooms. It is, rather, a helter-skelter mishmash of medieval fortresses or castles catering to the mind, where students, learn, live, eat, play, and, it's a certainty, engage in hanky-panky. The university's collection of 39 colleges is dispersed audaciously and with historic panache in every nook and cranny of Oxford the city.

The university started up in the 12th century, a couple of hundred years before Christopher Columbus was born. By the year 1200 Oxford was offering a regular course of study. Of its 39 colleges , 9 are for graduate work. The first college (University) was established in 1249, 600 years before gold was discovered in California; the most recent college (Manchester) ordained in 1996.

The Conference Itself

The conference consisted of some 45 papers, 6 panels, and 89 participants, offering a delectable smorgasbord of ideas and research from disciplines and professions including education, political science, psychology, public administration, management science, international relations, corporate governance, economics, and ethics and values.

The participants hailed from 20 countries, among which were the United Kingdom, several European nations, America, and Taiwan. The conference offered an opportunity for colleagues and friends to meet biennially, and for the formation of new colleagues and friends, in order, as Oxonians, say, to "have a chat." (An Oxonian, for naifs like thee and me, is a student, graduate, or professor from Oxford. Thus, Bill Clinton, inter alia, is an Oxonian.)

The sessions were small, clubby, chummy, many of them incredibly rewarding intellectually and fulfilling socially. Tea was served in the mid-mornings and mid-afternoons. .

All the sessions took place at the university's Department of Educational Studies, located on a street, Norham Gardens, which conjured up in my fanciful mind images of houses, white gates, and front lawns populating the novels of Agatha Christie describing the settings in which Hercule Poirot held forth with his "little gray cells" and where beguiling butlers lurked behind drawn curtains and peered noiselessly through revealing keyholes.

The theme of the conference was "Higher education in the 21st century: leadership, governance, and entrepreneurship," and embraced these topics: the expansion of higher education, entrepreneurship, the changing rationality of higher education, leadership, governance, and communication. But do you know what? Some of these topics were not represented in the papers and panels that were on the program, while some of the papers and panels addressed other issues, but this shouldn't matter as long as everyone was having a good time. I know that I did.

Bon appétit.

Robert Perloff
Joseph M. Katz Graduate School of Business,
University of Pittsburgh

References

Natale, S. M. personal correspondence, October 25, 2002.

Wilber, K. (2000). A theory of everything: an integral vision for business, politics, science, and spirituality. Boston: Shambhala.

Wilson, E. O. (1999). Consilience: the unity of knowledge. New York : Alfred Knopf.

Acknowledgments

The editors wish to thank President Robert Scott of Adelphi University for his personal and professional support of this project.

A dept of special gratitude is owed to Professor Richard Pring who for fourteen years was a staunch supporter and energy source for the work both of the conference and the academic volumes which emerged from them.

Dr. Geoff Hayward remains the mainstay of the conference with his willing insight, organizational and administrative skills and, especially his scholarly contributions to the ongoing research work of Oxford University Centre for the Study of Values in Education and Business (OXSVEB).

We wish to acknowledge the generous gift and support of SKOPE which provided a grant to assist in the conference development and execution.

Finally, and most critically, the authors owe the deepest gratitude to Dorothy Albritton of Majestic Wordsmith for her keen eye, professional work and generous heart in preparing these volumes for publication. To her and her professionalism, we are deeply grateful.

SMN
AFL

Chapter One

Cultural Adaptations for Hispanic Students in Higher Education

Susan Elizabeth Morey

Introduction

This nation of immigrant heritage believes that all children, whatever their circumstances, deserve a chance to learn, and rise, and succeed. I mean every child, not just a few, not just for those whose parents may speak English. We want educational excellence "para todos que viven in este país" (for all who live in this country).

President George Bush, October 12, 2001

By virtue of their mission, all institutions of higher learning are in continual transformation as the clientele and the communities around them change. Central to this transformation is the role of college faculty and university leaders in recognizing the forces of change and in introducing reforms or interventions that adapt the college or university to these changes.

Several trends are now becoming evident among colleges and universities nationwide that serve a newly emerging Hispanic population. Hispanic Americans, or Latino Americans as preferred by most, have experienced rapid population growth, nearly doubling in 14 years, from 14.6 million in 1980, to over 30 million in 1994 (Bureau of Census Report, 1994). By the year 2030, the U.S. Bureau of the Census projections suggest that Latino students age 5 to 18 will number almost 16 million—25 percent of the total school population. Obviously, this projected increase in the number of Hispanic children in the USA provides critical challenges to the nation's education systems.

Projections for the year 2050 predict that Hispanic Americans in general will comprise 25 percent of the total population of this country with the three largest groups of this burgeoning, ethnic population composed of Mexican Americans, Puerto Rican

Americans, and Cuban Americans. In addition, the Census projections say that Latinos will constitute one-fifth of the workforce by 2020. Hence, the lack of preparation of this workforce will undeniably affect the wealth of the nation. What has not been assessed or examined are which strategies for change are most effective, and what resources are required to maintain exemplary learning environments that effectively integrate linguistic and cultural factors in post-secondary education for this population.

Statement of the Problem

As the Latino population has continued to grow, their educational attainment on average has continued to lag behind the rest of the nation (Educational Standards, Assessment, and Accountability: A New Civil Rights Frontier, 2000) and the participation rate of Hispanics in post-secondary education remains extremely low. It is known that the participation rates are under 20% for post-secondary education and with the completion rates little more than 50% (Carter & Wilson, 1993). As absolute numbers in the population increase, the absolute numbers of Hispanics participating in post-secondary education will likewise increase, presenting the "illusion" of participatory success. These numbers may mask a "decline in access and choice for college age Hispanics" (Orfield, 1988, p. 20).

In 1996 only 9% of Hispanics had attained 4 years of college compared to 22% of non-Hispanics. Hence, post-secondary Hispanic student enrollment, retention, and graduation rates are not keeping pace with the Hispanic American presence in the general population. In 1996, Hispanics also represented only 4% of post-graduate students, while Whites represented 73% and Blacks 6%. (NCES, Digest of Education Statistics, 1998).

In the United States, educational attainment has traditionally been regarded as a key to economic prosperity. Ample evidence now exists of a strong relationship between low-income, low educational attainment, and low economic productivity—conditions readily evident among most Hispanic communities throughout the United States and Puerto Rico. More than 26% of Hispanic families were classified as living below the poverty level in 1998. In 1999, the Hispanic unemployment rate was 7%, nearly three full percentage points higher than for non-Hispanics (U.S. Department of Commerce, Bureau of the Census).

In addition, a shortage exists in Hispanic teachers, counselors, and administrators in the educational system. Consequently, there are few school professionals who are linguistically, culturally, and socially empathetic to the needs of Hispanic students which leaves Hispanic students without mentors to guide them toward college or toward technical and professional careers. Hispanic students like other American students need instructors who can challenge them academically and set high expectations. Educators must understand campus conditions for Hispanic students before they can enhance the academic experience of those students.

As a consequence of not understanding their students' native language, culture, and socio-economic realities, many teachers have low expectations for their Hispanic students, which contribute, as does the lack of Hispanic staff, to attrition. This teacher insensitivity to cultural and linguistic diversity can often influence a student to become alienated from the school system.

One can conclude from the statistics that the systems are failing the Hispanic population: the employment system, public school systems, and the system of higher education, all of which are intertwined. Pascarella and Terenzini (1991) stated that a bachelor's degree remains "a major, if not *the* major prerequisite for entrance into the more lucrative managerial and professional positions" (p. 575). More than half of all new jobs created in the 21st Century will require education beyond high school, and some say nearly one-third will require a college education (Hearing Before the Select Committee on Children, Youth and Families, 1989). The limited participation rates and decidedly low proportion of baccalaureates awarded to Latinos suggest that a significant portion of the group will be denied opportunities that are associated with this level of education.

Retention and completion rates also would suggest that more is needed to insure equity, access, and student success. Most believe that creative plans and multiple solutions are needed to improve educational opportunities for Latino youth as they make their way through the educational system to higher education (ENLACE: An Initiative of the Kellogg Foundation, 1999).

Rational for the Study

As data previously cited show, Hispanic American education is definitely in crisis. Some problems that affect Hispanic student achievement found throughout the literature are: culture shock, difficulties with English, typically starting school at a grade level below Anglo-American peers, lack of teacher role models, a standardized testing system that often discriminates, significant numbers of placements in vocational and special education tracks, and lack of attention to different learning styles by teachers.

It is also important to note that over 40% of the Hispanic American college-students are attending one of the 195 Hispanic Serving Institutions (HSIs) in the United States and Puerto Rico. These colleges and universities, formerly all White-serving institutions, are accredited, degree-granting public or private non-profit institutions of higher education with 25% or more total undergraduate Hispanic full-time student enrollment; or they are serving a large number of Hispanic students due to their overall size (NCES, 1997).

Indeed, the Hispanic Serving Institutions (HSIs) provide Hispanic students with some cushion in meeting the challenges mentioned above as more comfort and less isolation exists for these students when there are more Latinos on campus. One might think that the sheer numbers of Hispanics should make their needs more visible and thus the interventions easier to implement. A correct assumption in theory, but the question arises as to whether Hispanic Serving Institutions really rise to the educational challenge. The evidence is mixed. These universities are more likely to be receptive to assisting Latinos, but prior to their new status, they had no experience or infrastructure in place. In most cases the faculty is the same, the curriculum is the same, and the student services are the same.

Statement of the Purpose

The purpose of this study was threefold. First, was to uncover the cultural adaptations and interventions that two Hispanic Serving Institutions (HSIs) of higher education are using to meet the needs of their Hispanic students. Second, it was to discern how these interventions have evolved to meet the needs of specific Hispanic populations. And lastly, it was to describe each university's experience for potential emulation by other institutions.

This study focused solely on cultural and perception elements that played a role in the educational experience of Latinos. The two ENLACE universities selected for the study were the University of South Florida (USF) in Tampa, Florida, and Northeastern Illinois University (NEIU) in Chicago, Illinois. The two universities were chosen, because their adaptations address the cultural needs of the two major Hispanic population groups, Mexican-American and Puerto Rican-American students, as well as other Hispanic groups from Latin and South America and the Caribbean. Also, the universities represent a large public research university of 35,000 and a smaller urban university of 11,000 addressing the non-traditional students. The cultural interventions were examined and compared in light of the goals to raise the admission, retention and graduation rates of their Hispanic American students in post-secondary education.

Research Background

The objectives of this dissertation were further warranted by national policy events. In 1996, the President's Advisory Commission and the White House Initiative on Educational Excellence for Hispanic Americans recommended that colleges establish retention programs targeting Hispanics, and that the campus climate be improved to ease the transition to college life and counteract students' feelings of isolation. In addition, four-year institutions were challenged to examine their agreements and other initiatives with community colleges to facilitate the transfer of Latino students. Some additional recommendations from the 1996 Presidential Advisory Commission and the White House Initiative on Educational Excellence for Hispanic Americans that informed this study were as follows:

1. Long-term, strategic plans must be developed through collaborative approaches with the public and private sectors at the local, state and national level to monitor and to ensure a high standard of educational attainment among Hispanic Americans.
2. Support must be developed for Hispanic graduate students in targeted fields especially mathematics, the sciences, health related professions, the humanities, and in fields of anticipated faculty shortages.
3. Special initiatives and resources need to be committed to HSIs.
4. To address these issues and policy areas, effective educational models must incorporate high quality standards, equitable financial support, and diverse language and cultural knowledge.
5. A national professional development program for college and university faculty must be launched which focuses on increasing the participation and success of Hispanic students.
6. Collaborations between businesses and higher education institutions must be facilitated in order to provide mentoring relationships for Hispanic undergraduate students.

Also of importance were the following research areas of socio-cultural interest to this study that were identified by the 1996 President's Advisory Commission:

1. Identify cultural factors and interventions that influence and predict Hispanic student's decisions to remain or leave post-secondary education.

2. Determine which strategies for change are most effective and what resources are required to maintain exemplary learning environments that effectively integrate linguistic and cultural factors.

One organization that came to the forefront in response to President Clinton's "Call to Action" in 1996 was the W.K. Kellogg Foundation (WKKF). The WKKF initiated a program focused on assisting communities to strengthen the educational pipeline for Latino youth known as ENLACE, or "Engaging Latino Communities for Education." This initiative was designed to be a comprehensive community based collaborative effort among HSIs.

According to the W. K. Kellogg Foundation, the Presidential Commission on the Educational Excellence of Hispanics, and the National Council for Community and Educational Partnerships, what HSIs provide is not enough. Hence, to supplement the work of the HSIs, the W.K. Kellogg Foundation committed 28 million dollars.

Kellogg did a prior "needs" assessment and their assessment showed that targeting HSIs can produce the maximum positive impact to the academic success of Hispanic students, in part because of their larger numbers at those institutions. Also, the goal of the WKKF was to create prototypes that promise best practices at HSIs that can then be models for other institutions.

The W.K. Kellogg Foundation previously conducted exploratory research and relied upon an advisory group of national Hispanic leaders to help frame the initiative, provide guidance, and identify best practices, potential partners and resources. They learned that sustainable educational improvements required changes along the entire educational pipeline (ENLACE: An Initiative of the W.K. Kellogg Foundation, 1998). The Foundation identified institutions that could bring together diverse organizations, which in turn could pool their resources to design long-term community and institutional structures.

The HSIs selected by the Foundation were eligible for a one-year grant of $100,000. Upon completion of the planning phase, the 16 competed for implementation grants of up to $2 million, of which 13 were funded for a four-year period. In addition, the structures and partnerships had to demonstrate an ability to impact system change over the time of the grant.

The final phase will focus on disseminating the impact of the efforts as well as on institutionalizing success through programs, practices, and policies. All cognizant of important Latino culture elements, ENLACE activities must link with other national education agendas and rely on leaders and change-makers who are at the forefront of the policy issues for counsel. These institutions are now completing their second year of funding. In all, ENLACE will be carried out in the three phases over a period of five years.

The W. K. Kellogg Foundation's overall goals were designed to attempt to unite the institutions, organizations and communities that previously had been working in relative isolation, into a single-minded partnership that will improve the academic success of Hispanic American students. The two institutions of higher education chosen for this study are both ENLACE grantees. Their positions in the forefront of educational change provide unique cultural models of adaptations in serving their Hispanic populations.

Participants

The University of South Florida (USF) is the second largest university in Florida with 35,000 students and is one of the top 20 largest universities in the USA. It is also among the top 40 universities in the country for educating Hispanics according to the 2001 Hispanic Outlook for Higher Education. Additionally, USF ranks at the top, classified by the prestigious Carnegie Foundation for its excellence in research. In 1988 USF also began a program for at-risk migrant children to complete their high school equivalency.

Northeastern Illinois University (NEIU) is a fully accredited, non-residential public university serving the Chicago metropolitan area. Total graduate and undergraduate enrollment is approximately 11,000. In addition to offering traditional programs in the arts, sciences, business, and education, NEIU has a strong commitment to innovative, non-traditional education and has been a leader in the development of special programs for Latino adult learners. Satellite campuses, El Centro de Recursos Educativos and the Center for Inner City Studies, enhance the University's ability to serve the entire metropolitan area of 1.5 million Latinos and the non-traditional student.

Potential Benefits of the Study

This study which examined and compared two of these 13 ENLACE institutions representing Puerto Rican American, Mexican American and other Latino student populations helped to inform the Kellogg Foundation, the Hispanic community, NCCEP, The White House Commission on the Educational Excellence of Hispanic Americans, Hispanic national associations, IDRA, and the President's 2010 Alliance. This study also contributed to the search for appropriate culturally sensitive models of educational support for this large ethnic minority.

Educators must understand campus conditions for Latino students before they can enhance the academic experience of those students. This study provides one basis for that understanding, as it pertains specifically to Hispanic students' cultural experiences on two different campuses. How this information translates to other campuses will be for representatives from other campuses to evaluate and apply.

Literature Research

There is a growing body of research on the education of Hispanic Americans. However, this information is generally "demographic" in nature and offers raw data on retention and graduation rates, or descriptive data of approaches that target specific parts of the educational pipeline and work in relative isolation. However, few studies exist that identify interventions that influence and predict Hispanic students' decisions to remain or leave post-secondary education.

No evidence exists of what strategies for change are most effective, nor what resources are required to maintain exemplary learning environments that effectively integrate linguistic and cultural factors in post-secondary education. Hence, this study is an important contribution to the scholarship about increasing the achievement level, the successes of Hispanic American college students, and the different cultural adaptive models of higher education that are being explored today.

Research Questions

The presence of a cultural group can offer significant contributions as well as challenges to the greater community of a college. Identifying what affects the Hispanic students' campus life, academic life, and what keeps them enrolled, is of obvious importance to any institution with minority students, to those Hispanic students enrolled, and to potential future students. With the "geographic location and proximity to home" identified as important factors in the Hispanic student's choice of college (Carnegie Foundation for the Advancement of Teaching, 1988), the proximity of the university to this population would also suggest that the university may be in a position to capitalize on a potentially important new enrollment base.

Some basic questions come to the forefront in response to this stated problem. Are the two Hispanic Serving Institutions in the study serving their new Hispanic populations well, but perhaps differently? Do they draw out the voices and minds of those they work with and for the new community they serve? Does the inherent culture of the Hispanic American student play a crucial role in the admission, retention, and graduation from such a college or university, which has undergone the necessary changes?

Understanding the university environment through the cultural experiences of Latinos on campus should be considered by any university in designing adequate responses to low participation and persistence rates. Maintaining the status quo, taking enrollment and current participation of Hispanic students for granted, and doing things the way they have always been done is no longer a viable option (Berry, 1991). Knowing what happens to Hispanics after they enter college and what effect these experiences have on their academic achievement is important (Duran, 1983), as well as on their perceptions of the collegiate experience.

The specific research questions of this study were as follows:

1. What culturally relevant interventions and adaptations are being made at the universities in addressing Hispanic student needs?
2. How does the Latino population view these cultural adaptations and interventions?
3. What patterns emerge in the interventions being used by the two HSIs serving predominant Hispanic student subgroups (Puerto Rican, and Mexican)?

The central question that guided this inquiry was how does each ENLACE HSI of higher education provide a positive, culturally-based educational experience for its Hispanic students to impact admission, retention, and graduation rates of these students? The ENLACE grant they received allowed the two institutions to develop and design further cultural adaptations and interventions to build upon the implementations in place before receiving the grant.

Methodology

Data collection was accomplished through in depth interviews with each ENLACE Director, the Coordinator of the campus ENLACE Program, knowledgeable faculty and staff and Latino students, examination of college catalogs, Interim Reports for the ENLACE grant given to the researcher by each university and U.S. Census data.

Document analysis was used to provide historical background, policies of the universities, and future plans. Interviews were used to gather qualitative information from participants from each university. In addition a 50-item questionnaire was administered to 48 Latino students on each campus for further inquiry which added a quantitative dimension to the study.

This study examined differences across campuses in the following areas: (1) family and community support, (2) faculty and staff issues, (3) language issues, (4) ethnic identity issues, (5) "other" student interactions, (6) classroom interactions, and (7) university support.

Conclusions and Implications

The Research Questions:

1. *What culturally relevant interventions and adaptations are being made at the universities in addressing Hispanic student needs?*

The overall vision for this cultural paradigm for Latino success in higher education consists of a seamless interaction between elementary, high school and college, between the schools and the community, and between the families and the students. The researcher found that the new cultural paradigm for a successful college experience for Latino students in these two universities provided in varying degrees the development of a positive Latino(a) self-identity through curricular, co-curricular and community efforts:

- preparation for college through outreach programs to middle/high schools and mentoring by older university Latino students and/or Latino staff and faculty
- dissemination of information about college to high schools through recruitment efforts and through Spanish language communication and special programs for parents
- emotional support on campus for Latino students through mentoring
- Spanish/English language usage and university outreach to parents
- academic support in college through transition programs, remedial courses, career counseling, and academic clubs
- Hispanic programs and events for the general student population of the university and the community
- significant presence of Latino university faculty and staff
- participation by Latino students on committees and in decision-making groups involved with Latino issues on campus
- recognition of bilingualism and biculturalism as assets for every college student
- accommodation of class scheduling in recognition of the "struggle" Latino students endure between work, study and family
- education of non-Latino university students on the contribution of Hispanic culture and history to the United States by integration throughout the curriculum
- implementation of major areas of study in Latino studies such as a Latin American and the Caribbean Studies program.

- provisions for "cultural awareness" training for all faculty and staff at the university to end the stereotyping of migrant students and other ethnic subgroups and enhance learning
- creation of Latino social organizations such as fraternities, sororities, and clubs
- encouragement of multicultural events and activities involving all groups on campus

2. *How does the Latino population view these cultural adaptations and interventions?*

The study found that Latino and Latina students felt that through the many cultural adaptations on both campuses they were slowly becoming part of the American dream that their mothers and fathers sought and expected for them. These findings differ significantly from previous research. Arias (1995) found that Latino students were "ignored, unappreciated, and disenfranchised" from the educational processes in general and found support chiefly among other Latinos and Latino groups.

At USF the institutional structure of campus life itself illustrated the dominance of an Anglo culture which did foster racial/ethnic clustering. Although aware of this ethnic/racial hierarchy in the society there, many Latino students took comfort in the presence of Latino support programs and African American and Latino student organizations on campus. To the Latino students this symbolized the University's openness to racial/ethnic differences and made students feel that they were in a safe environment. However, this bonding with other minority groups often challenged the complete integration of Latino students into campus life.

At NEIU many students did not feel the need for strong attachments within their own subgroups and/or within other ethnic groups except for activism purposes. Pascarella et al. (1996) found that first-year students' openness to diversity was positively affected by the perception of the institution as racially non-discriminatory. The openness and multicultural sharing at NEIU was accepted by most of the students. The size of the Latino group that was almost equal in size to the Anglo population of students could have contributed to this phenomenon.

Mezirow stated that in an adult's life certain dilemmas are so dramatic that we cannot handle them in the usual way. "We undergo significant phases of reassessment and growth in which familiar assumptions are challenged and new directions and commitments are chartered. Feire believes that as a human being learns, he feels more in control of his life and environment. This empowerment rises out of deeper knowledge of the *self*. Feire's position is that people can change those around them and eventually change society as a whole.

Both philosophies are evident in this research of Latino student issues in higher education. All of the students in the study said that college had influenced them positively in many ways, but their expectations that college would help them understand themselves more as Latinos and Latinas were never met. They considered attending and continuing in college as an achievement in itself. The decision to attend college was often a difficult decision for Latino students due to parental ambivalence and the expectation that they would have to earn money to supplement the family income.

Education as a vehicle for creating social change was another shared value for all the students. They expressed a strong desire to remain tied to Latino communities through their careers. They also said they wanted to be influential in creating a new and positive

Latino (a) image for the majority society and especially for the Latino youth and community.

Education as a vehicle for a better life was also important to all the students on both campuses. They concluded that an education would help them have a more financially stable life than their parents, although no one spoke of being rich. Inequity and marginalization were experienced by the Latino students as well. The university Latino populations reflected the perception that the universities were not sharing the power of decision-making with the Latino minority. Policy decisions affecting the content and curriculum and the hiring of faculty, administrators and staff have been and still are in the hands of Anglo males at these universities.

The Latino students did not see themselves represented in the courses, the course content, the faculty, the staff or the administration. They saw themselves mainly in the co-curricular activities, usually sponsored by and attended by Latinos. Although these co-curricular activities were a positive reform on both campuses, the students were very clear that it was not enough and maintained the Latino culture in a marginal status. Although the students were succeeding in finding positive ways and creative ways to support each other in their college experience, the universities were not serving them in a consistent way.

The Latino students perceived the creation of two Latina sororities and two Latino fraternities at USF as very positive and showed that their presence as a group on campus was important to the university. The creation of the Latin American and Caribbean Studies program at USF further added to their worthiness as a group.

The university outreach to the Latino community and schools also was important to the students at both USF and NEIU. This served to validate their importance in a dominant Anglo society. The students who were linked to a particular Latino support group or transition program targeting Latino students felt the most supported and had the highest comfort level. Having faculty/staff members who were Latino, albeit a small group, at both universities also affected the students positively. These staff and faculty became their mentors and continued their support throughout the year.

All of the students expressed varying degrees of social consciousness and commitment to provide mentoring to younger Latinos, to advocate for change, to join in with other minorities, and to become role models in their own communities. This was somewhat surprising as these same students had not experienced mentoring from the previous generation. It was interesting to find that they perceived no real connection to Latino professionals of today; and they saw these professionals as too quiet and not actively helping other Latinos succeed.

The desire to have more Latino faculty/staff at each university was tremendously high for all students. The lack of cultural understanding and discriminatory actions by some professors played a significant role in this demand. As well, the desire to understand their own culture and history and to see it reflected in the curriculum permeated all discussions with students.

Tierney (1992) argued that student independence can be developed while maintaining strong family ties; and Nora and Cabrera (1996) stated that it was important for Latino students to maintain such ties that are part of their cultural heritage. However, the students at both universities suffered the role stress of being a student, a family provider, and family caretaker.

The Latino students appreciated the flexible scheduling at NEIU and the satellite campus locations. The daycare on campus at NEIU for children of the Latina student parents was important to them as well. In this way they were able to juggle their many responsibilities at home, work and school. These adaptations, however, were not available to Latino students at USF who had to adjust to a normal campus schedule. The students at USF also felt unhappy about missing Latino activities on campus due to their work schedules off campus.

Spanish language usage was prevalent on both campuses. The freedom to speak their own language with their friends, to hear some faculty/staff speaking Spanish and to see bilingualism encouraged at both universities was confirming to all students. They felt free to be themselves and interact with others. They also were beginning to see that their bilingualism and bi-culturalism was in fact an advantage in the workplace due to the globalization taking place in the surrounding communities. The silencing of their language was a thing of the past.

It was significant that all students on both campuses felt that they were capable of succeeding at their university and very much needed the support of the university to meet this goal. They expressed gratitude for the programs and staff involved and for the vision inspired by their mentors. These programs no doubt will help the Latino students at both universities to become whole individuals who can tap into their bicultural positivity and become socially committed individuals to their families and their community.

3.   *What patterns emerge in the interventions being used by the two Hispanic Serving Institutions serving predominant Hispanic student subgroups (Mexican and Puerto Rican)?*

The study did indicate that the Latino support programs and minority support programs were growing at both universities; and therefore no longer were marginal entities. Rather than being an advocate for only those students who had difficulties during their experience at college they served to support the entire Latino population on campus. The research also showed that the students were beginning to find comfort and nurturing experiences in the wider college community outside the confines of these support programs.

These ENLACE universities were also no longer ignoring the historical, socioeconomic and political contributions of the Latino population to the U.S. society. Both universities have begun programs on Latin American and Caribbean studies, Mexico, and other Hispanic areas of the world. Northeastern Illinois University in particular placed strong emphasis on Spanish language acquisition and the bilingual student and on encouraging bilingualism and biculturalism among its student population. USF had begun to recognize this agenda due to the globalization in Tampa.

The data collected in this study also confirmed many of the factors that had been previously explored by other researchers. The Latino students often felt unprepared for the demands of college, female students faced greater obstacles because of their gender, and they had little help from their families. Regardless of these difficulties, these students were continuing to persevere. In addition, they all expressed a desire to learn more about their own Latino culture and history.

Another finding was that the student's attempts to explain to their families the rigors of a higher education were significant. However, all students said they received overwhelming emotional support from their parents in going to college. However, because they had difficulty with this communication the "struggle" to survive the college experience was often intense.

It was also interesting to discover that more Latino students are being mentored by faculty, staff and older Latino students than previously uncovered in other research. These students expressed very positive feelings about having a mentor, being recognized on campus by someone besides their peers, being able to speak Spanish with someone in authority, and having someone to confide in during times of stress or decision-making. And, more and more faculty were being trained in workshops on "cultural awareness" on both campuses, participating in Hispanic activities, serving as mentors and becoming generally aware of the large Latino population and its culture.

The outreach from both universities to partner organizations was significant. The mentoring of middle and high school students, changes in admission structures, counseling and communication with parents and students prior to admission, transition courses in the summer between high school and college, and academic support programs all served to enhance the success of the Latino students. These supports are proving successful in the short run as shown by the Latino student confidence in their desire to persevere to graduation from college. The high retention rates are also beginning to show a real impact for those students who are tied to these support programs

All of these findings suggest a fundamental shift toward a new paradigm in higher education for Latino students which incorporate adult education theories and bi-culturalism as central philosophies. Adult educators by definition concern themselves with the *whole* individual, not merely his or her academic performance.

The monocultural university institution as it has existed until today was a rigid structure where academic expectations and institutional processes superseded all personal considerations. This new institutional bi-culturalism, however, provides a framework to reassess and restructure higher education to better serve a growing Latino population. In the study, the Latino students expressed some anxiety in being able to maintain the "best of both worlds" in their lives, and not subjugating or sacrificing one for the other. Hence, it was very important to them that their bi-cultural identity be supported by societal structures including higher education.

Recommendations for Practice

This study found that Latinos at USF and NEIU are being served better and in different, more culturally appropriate ways in an effort to address Latino recruitment, retention, and success issues. Some conclusions are offered with accompanying recommendations:

1) Given the fact that Latinos will represent the largest non-white group in the United States in ten years, it is recommended that the focus on a multicultural curriculum be continued. It is concluded from this study that the Latinos at the two universities have more positive self-images than found in previous studies. This positive self can be further developed if children grow up with positive role models throughout their school years and with curriculum that illustrates the contributions of the Latinos to the world and the United States. This curriculum must contain culturally diverse authors and perspectives with cultural awareness included. And, textbooks need to be more culturally and gender inclusive.

2) It is recommended that the university outreach to Latino parents and the Latino community be continued and enhanced through community partnerships. Collaboration between teachers in the early grades and parent groups to communicate the benefits of a higher education and the subsequent career opportunities for both genders is important.

These universities have made great strides in this area, but have much work to do. The cultural attributes of the Latino parent group that often keeps them away from the schools need to be overcome with cultural awareness and Spanish language usage. Latino parents need more understanding of their children's academic and emotional development and the role that they, as parents, play in that development.

3)   One of the findings of the study concluded that the students did not have a college education as a goal when they were in high school. However, because of the outreach efforts from the university, the high school counselor or an older Latino student they were given new direction. It is recommended that this outreach to provide information, applications and counseling to Latino students in high school be continued and expanded. College information in Spanish disseminated to parents through the high school and workshops in Spanish and English have proved successful in both universities.

4)   Due to the "struggle" that many of the students say they have between family, work and school, it is recommended that admissions offices and other staff and faculty offer frequent programs for the parents of incoming freshmen Latino students. The Latino students have special needs in dealing with the obstacles they face daily. An emotional support structure is needed that would address the additional demands placed on the Latino students. Discussions both on campus and at satellite off-campus locations near the Latino communities could include workshop topics offered by students and their parents.

Both universities have made significant inroads in this area using Latino faculty and staff that have been facilitating these experiences quite successfully. However, due to the lack of Latino staff at the universities these people have been overwhelmed by the needs of the community, and working in small programs in relative isolation. More Latino staff and faculty would both serve as role models and help facilitate these programs.

5)   Both universities have developed cultural awareness and teaching enhancement workshops for faculty and staff to enhance their sensitivity to their students. The results of the Questionnaire indicated that much needs to be done in understanding the cultural attributes of the various Latino subgroups with respect to eye contact and personal space issues. However, these workshops are not mandatory due to union and other policy regulations. These workshops help faculty to develop materials with a Latino focus to incorporate into their curriculum. It is highly recommended that these workshops be continued and expanded.

Incentives and other recruitment options for these courses need to take place to increase the number of faculty who are not indifferent and insensitive to their ethnic students. Unfortunately, the Latino faculty and staff reported that there were an inordinate number of indifferent faculty members on staff at both campuses.

6)   It is also recommended that the ENLACE grantees continue to offer Latino activities and programs that are open to the whole university and the community. It is vital that the entire university student and faculty population begin to understand this large ethnic community present on their campus. This cultural understanding on the part of the general student population will also serve as a sense of pride and enhanced self-esteem for the Latino students.

Conclusion

These universities—rather than addressing interventions in the same old way— have introduced a revolutionary look. They are demonstrating through their programs how educators can help Latinos and Latinas become socially committed and responsible American citizens who are blessed with two cultures, two languages and multiple ways of living.

The two universities studied offer the higher education community two different models, an urban multi-ethnic teaching university serving a non-traditional population and a large predominantly white research oriented university. Both, ENLACE grantees, are attempting to address the goals of raising the admission, retention and graduation rates of the Latino student population in the United States. The ENLACE grant from the W.K. Kellogg Foundation has served as a catalyst to each university to develop new partnerships and strengthen existing ones among higher education institutions, communities and businesses in order to increase opportunities for Latino youth to enter and graduate from college.

The two universities though are in different stages of understanding campus conditions for Latino students and implementing the necessary support programs. They are beginning to determine strategies for change that are most effective in integrating linguistic and cultural factors. They are collaborating with businesses and other educational institutions to provide mentoring relationships for Latino youth. They are beginning to implement professional development programs for university faculty to increase the participation and success of Hispanic students. And, most importantly they are both attempting to hire more Latino faculty and staff to provide role models for this burgeoning new population even though the number of educated Latino faculty in the United States is small.

The Latino students deserve more than simple access to higher education. They like all users deserve a quality education that meets and exceeds their expectations. These universities are attempting to empower Hispanic youth, giving them educational opportunities and teaching them to succeed. By doing this, they are treating the language and culture of these new young Americans as an asset, not a perceived deficit that will certainly help all of American society. By increasing the educational pipeline of Hispanics the entire nation will benefit.

For the nation to continue as a leader in the global economy it must take rigorous, proactive approaches to educate and train all of its youth. Much still needs to be done, but these two models offer educators a place to begin. This large segment of American society will undoubtedly play a crucial role if America is to compete successfully in the world economy. It is in schools that the most effective seeds of citizenship are sown.

Our workforce and our schools will be enhanced by this newly educated population of Hispanic Americans. The knowledge of the experiences and outcomes of these two institutions can be used by other colleges and universities to identify areas of strengths and weaknesses that they must strive to enhance or correct. In doing so, institutions in general will establish themselves in a more solid position to capture a rapidly increasing market segment, that of the Hispanic college student.

U.S. Secretary of Education Richard W. Riley (2000) stated:

> It is time for us to empower Hispanic youth by giving them educational opportunities, teaching them to succeed, expecting more, and holding schools and communities accountable for their success. When we achieve this, when we transcend stereotypes, and overcome the tyranny of low expectations, and when we treat the language and the culture of young Americans as an asset, and not a perceived deficit, then we will be able to guarantee everyone the key civil right for the 21st century—a quality education (p. 16).

References

Arias, B.I. (1995). Latino adult students in higher education: a new paradigm for success. (A Doctoral Dissertation: Northern Illinois University) Ill.

Bennett, C., & Okinata, A. (1990). Factors related to persistence among Asian, Black, Hispanic and White undergraduate students at a predominantly White institution: Comparison between first and fourth year cohorts. *The Urban Review*, 22(1), 33-60.

Cabrera, V. V. (1998) Factors influencing first-generation Mexican-American college students' persistence at the University of Texas at Austin. (Doctoral dissertation, the University of Texas at Austin) *Dissertation Abstracts International*, 60, 07A.

Chapa, G., & Valencia, R.R. (1993). Latino population growth, demographic characteristics and educational stagnation: An examination of recent trends. Hispanic Journal of Behavioral Sciences, 15, 165-180.

Cruz, L. (1999). The influence of mentors on Hispanic college women. (Doctoral dissertation, Texas Tech University). Dissertation *Abstracts International*, 60.08B.

Gomez, J. G. (1998). Bicultural functioning of Hispanic and Latino college students. (Doctoral dissertation, University of Minnesota). *Dissertation Abstracts International*, 59. 07A.

Halcon, J. & de Luz Reyes, M. (1991). Trickle down reform: Hispanics, higher education and the excellence movement. The Urban Review, 23(2), 117-135.

Hanish, J. M. (1997). Latino students: Issues on a predominantly white campus. (Doctoral dissertation, University of Iowa). Dissertation *Abstracts International, 58*, 05A.

Kavanaugh, P.C., & Retish, P.M. (1991). The Mexican-American ready for college. Journal of Multicultural Counseling and Development, 19, 136-144.

Mezirow, J. and Associates (1990). Fostering Critical Reflection in Adulthood: A Guide to Transformative and Emancipatory Learning. San Francisco, Ca.: Jossey-Bass.

Morell Thon, C. (1998). Job satisfaction of Hispanic faculty in higher education. (Doctoral dissertation, University of Virginia). Dissertation *Abstracts International*, 5907A.

Morley, K. M. (2000). Fitting in by race/ethnicity: the social and academic integration of diverse students at a large predominantly white university. (Doctoral Dissertation: University of Massachusetts) Mass.

Murguia, E., Padilla, R. V., & Pavel, M. (1991). Ethnicity and the concept of social integration in Tinto's model of institutional departure. *Journal of College Student Development, 32*, 433-439.

National Center For Education Statistics, (1995). The educational progress of Hispanic students. U.S. Department of Education, Washington, D.C. Office of Educational Research and Improvement.

Nicolau, S., & Ramos, C. L. (1990). Together is better: Building strong relationships between schools and Hispanic parents. Washington, DC: Hispanic Policy Development Project.

Nieves-Squires, S. (1991). *Hispanic women: Making their presence on campus less tenuous*. Washington, DC: Association of American Colleges.

Pascarella, E. T., & Terenzini, P. T. (1991). *How college affects students*. San Francisco: Jossey-Bass.

President's Advisory Commission on Educational Excellence for Hispanic Americans (1996) *Progress report to the Secretary of Education*. Washington, DC: U.S. Department of Education. *A comprehensive approach*. Washington, D.C.

President's Advisory Commission on Educational Excellence for Hispanic Americans (1998) *Progress report to the President of the United States*. Washington, DC: U.S. Department of Education. *Our nation on the fault line*. Washington, D.C.

President's Advisory Commission on Educational Excellence for Hispanic Americans (1996). *Our Nation on the Fault Line: Hispanic American Education*. Washington, D.C.: US Department of Education.

Riley, R. (2000). "Excellence for all. The progress of education for Hispanic Americans and the challenges of a new century." Speech delivered at Bell Multicultural High School, Washington D.C.

Tierney, W. (1998*). The responsive university*. Baltimore Md.: The John Hopkins University Press

Tinto, V. (1987). *Leaving college: Rethinking the causes and cures of student attrition*. Chicago University of Chicago Press.

United States Department of Commerce, Bureau of the Census (1993). *Hispanic Americans todav: Population characteristics* (Current Population Reports, pp. 23-183). Washington, DC: U.S. Government Printing Office.

Verdugo, R.R. (1995) "Racial stratification and the use of Hispanic faculty as role models: theory, policy, and practice." Journal of Higher Education, p. 669.

Villafane, A. (1998) First generation Hispanic student's failures and successes at 4-year liberal arts institution. (Doctoral dissertation, Walden University). *Dissertation Abstracts International*, 59.10A.

Chapter Two

Declining Participation in an Expanding System: The Case of Construction-Related Higher Education Courses in the United Kingdom

ALISON FULLER

Introduction

The UK higher education system has expanded significantly during the past twenty plus years and currently has nearly two million students (Uden 1996, Fuller 2001). However, although the overall number of students has increased dramatically, some subjects have experienced declining take up. This chapter identifies construction-related courses as an area which has been struggling to recruit students during a period when more and more young people are being encouraged to progress to higher education (HE). In contrast, participation in subjects such as Business Administration and Computer Science has grown rapidly. The discussion includes an analysis of some of the reasons underlying such uneven patterns of participation.

In terms of recruiting highly qualified staff, the construction industry is facing a stark scenario. Recent research has shown that if current rates of decline were to continue, no students would be entering civil engineering or construction courses by 2012 (Fairbrother 2002). This chapter discusses the problematic relationship between the industry and higher education (HE) and identifies how the government's policy on expanding young people's participation is relevant to this and other sectors' recruitment difficulties.[1] It goes on to suggest reasons for the decline in applications and links these to changes in the characteristics of the student population as well as issues more directly linked to construction. The chapter argues that in order to meet their higher level skills shortfall, industries such as construction must think more critically about "who" to target. It concludes that the challenge for sectors which have become unpopular with HE students, is to develop recruitment strategies that appeal to people with a wider variety of personal characteristics, prior educational attainment and work experience.

Following the Introduction, section two of the chapter outlines the national HE policy background. Section three provides a brief statistical account of participation and demand in construction-related courses and in two competing subject areas. Section four outlines some of the underlying reasons for trends in take-up. Section five identifies and discusses who "struggling" industries might target to meet their requirements for a more highly skilled and qualified workforce. The chapter concludes by suggesting that solving recruitment difficulties will require a more flexible response from the Government, industry and higher education.

The Policy Context

The UK government is committed to expanding take up of HE and has put this commitment in concrete terms by setting a target of 50 per cent of 18 to 30 year olds to have experienced HE[2] by 2010. There are two major and by now, well-rehearsed, rationales behind the national push to expand HE. The first is economic. The government argues that technological developments including those in information and communication technologies as well as the need for increasing customisation of services have generated a need for a larger proportion of the workforce to be qualified to HE level. The argument is that an advanced industrial country such as the UK has to compete on the basis of "added value" and not simply on cost. Countries with lower labour costs can produce more cheaply but are less likely to have the sophisticated technology, knowledge and skills which enable their companies to produce goods and services to high specifications. At the same time, low and semi-skilled jobs in manufacturing and primary industries have been lost over the past thirty years or so reducing the demand for those without or with few qualifications. In contrast, recent research has shown an increased and continuing demand for more highly educated and qualified staff and, particularly, for those with management, professional and higher level technical skills (NSTF 2000).

The government acknowledges that productivity in the UK is lower than in many of the country's competitors (eg USA, Germany and France) and seeks to address this through raising skill and qualification levels in the workforce as a whole but especially for those adults with no or few qualifications (PIU 2001). Fostering lifelong learning has been high on the national policy agenda for the last few years (see for example DfEE 1998). Although it is orthodoxy in political and policy maker circles, that an increasingly highly qualified workforce is necessary to maintain and improve the UK's economic position, some commentators argue that the case has been overstated. Keep and Mayhew (1998), for example, counter by showing that much of the UK economy does not depend on high skills and that their requirement by employers is patchy. This suggests that the increasing demand for higher level qualifications is as much a feature of credential inflation, where employers use qualifications as a way of filtering people in the selection process rather than because they have a genuine occupational need for more highly educated, skilled and qualified people (Dore 1976, Collins 1979).

The second rationale relates to social justice and the government's pronounced determination to improve opportunities for disadvantaged groups (see for example Hayton and Puczuzka (eds.) 2002). Education (including at HE level) is considered the prime vehicle for helping people to climb the socio-economic ladder. The government places "opportunities for all" as one of its core political values. However, the policies that flow from this, can also be seen as expedient: by encouraging more young people to participate the policy coheres with the economic analysis that a more highly skilled and qualified population will increase the economic success of "UK plc."

In national terms, the debate on HE expansion has focused mainly on how a larger proportion of the youth cohort can be attracted into university in order to ensure that the government's 50 per cent goal is met. This attention has given rise to a long line of initiatives such as Aimhigher and the Excellence Challenge[3] which are designed to increase the number of young people from disadvantaged backgrounds entering HE and reports identifying the barriers to widening participation and possible ways to dismantle them. In a recent document, the Institute for Public Policy Research (Piat 2000), argues that the key obstacle to the participation of more "working class" young people is their relatively weak attainment of entry level qualifications, particularly, A levels. Consequently, the report calls for more investment in schools to raise the "staying on rate" and educational attainment of this group so that more are qualified to enter HE at 18+. The columns of the HE (and often national) press provide ample evidence of the ongoing debate on the need for further financial support for those who overcome the odds and proceed to HE (see for example The Times Higher, 18 January 2002).

The government is also attempting to increase participation by encouraging access to HE via the "work-based route." In this regard, the new Foundation Degree is being marketed as a bridge between work and HE and is the suggested next step for leavers from the Advanced Modern Apprenticeship Programme[4] who have attained level 3 qualifications but are capable of progressing to HE level study (Cassels 2001). In addition, the availability of places to study more flexibly in HE, for example, on part-time courses or by distance learning, is being increased, as a way of facilitating the participation of those in work or with other commitments. The Open University, which only offers part-time provision, has been a big institutional winner in the race for the additional cash that is attached to the expansion of part-time places.

The brief references I have made to government initiatives and to more flexible modes of attendance encapsulate the thrust of national policy which is to increase the proportion of young people entering HE by a twin strategy of widening participation in terms of the socio-economic and ethnic background characteristics of students and widening access in terms of diversifying entry routes and qualifications. Although young people's (18 to 21 year olds) participation has increased to over 30 per cent and overall participation to around 40 per cent, the government and providers are still concerned that those from lower socio-economic groups and certain ethnic minority backgrounds are under-represented.

Overall, it is important to remember that public funds are allocated for the provision of student places in HE. Institutions are rewarded financially when places are filled. Patterns of student demand, then, are clearly related to how much money Higher Education Institutions (HEIs) receive through the public purse routed, in England, via the Higher Education Funding Council and from tuition fees. In short, when providing institutions are successful in attracting students they benefit financially. To encourage HEIs to recruit from disadvantaged groups, the government pays more for places which are filled by students living in deprived areas: the so called "post code premium."[5] Clearly there are implications attached to funding issues with student demand broadly dictating the flow of money to institutions and to departments. As a side effect of this approach, subject areas struggling to recruit will become short of the funds needed to invest in course and staff development and are likely to get caught in a vicious circle of decline which contrasts starkly with popular subject areas where success breeds success.

There has been very little overt opposition to the UK government's policy of expanding HE through widening participation, nor to the 50 per cent target. However, recently there have been signs of a "wobble" in the consensus. Barry Sheerman, chair of the Commons Parliamentary Education Committee has said that the target has "no rational basis" and is worried that the push for numbers is distorting the system. Those responsible for promoting "lifelong learning" are concerned that the emphasis on young people's take up inevitably distracts from the task of encouraging older adults' to return to study (Tuckett 2002, Times Higher 12 April). Voices from industry are also starting to question the policy. For example, John Gains the chief executive of the construction company "John Mowlem" and president of the Construction Federation has argued that young people are being encouraged to go to university without the benefit of adequate information about the alternatives (The Guardian Education, Jan 22nd, 2002). In another article, (The Daily Telegraph, Jan 25th 2002), he points out that the government's emphasis on increasing participation in HE deflects attention and public money from other, arguably more important questions, such as the shortfall in young people training in trades such as plastering and plumbing. In some similarity, the chairman of the Motor Industry Training Organisation has made the point that raising the proportion of young adults pursuing HE can limit the pool of people entering the labour market at lower levels and through programmes such as Modern Apprenticeship. These issues are relevant for the construction industry which has forecast an undersupply in managers and professionals and also in a number of trades including "roofers," "plasterers" and "floorers" (CITB 2001-2005 workforce planning brief). While the focus of this chapter is on the relationship between industry and HE, it is worth remembering that changes in patterns of recruitment in one area of the system will have knock on effects in others.

Patterns of Participation and Demand

Changes in the organisation of work, together with global economic and technological trends have been well rehearsed in the academic (see *inter alia* Brown et al 2001; Castells 1996; Ashton and Green 1996) and policy literatures (NSTF 2000, CBI 1989). Although there has been a debate in the academic community about the implications of these changes for skills (see for example, Keep 1999), there is a strong consensus, at least amongst policy makers, that they require the workforce to be increasingly highly skilled and well-qualified. In line with UK industry more widely, forecasts by the construction sector have highlighted an increasing requirement for highly qualified staff. The workforce planning brief 2001-2005 states:

> With the decline in higher education provision, the shortage of managers, professionals and civil engineers in the industry is expected to worsen. Shortages will be particularly acute for managers, where strong growth is expected. (CITB p. 30).

In addition, the CITB found that the sector was short of IT skills, both technical capability and in the ability to manage IT effectively. There may be other "pull factors" which are increasing employers' demand for more highly qualified staff and which, if increased or intensified, could be used to drive up participation. These include the impact of national and European regulation on the industry in areas such as environmental management and health and safety. Another pull factor could be through the supply chain where the largest and most influential companies may increasingly require all their suppliers to meet set quality specifications. This process has already had significant impact in the automotive industry where firms such as Ford are dictating quality terms to their sub-contractors and, thereby, indirectly generating employer and employee demand for higher level qualifications (e.g., Brown, A. et al 2001).

In their recent paper, Gann and Salter (1999) outline the case for (increasingly) high skills in the construction sector. Drawing on the work of Gibbons et al (1994) on shifts in the mode of knowledge production, they argue, firstly, that contract and service specifications are becoming broader and more complex, thus placing more demand on the capabilities of professionals and managers. Secondly, that demands for knowledge and skills in new areas such as environmental protection and working on contaminated land have emerged and are not being sufficiently catered for by university providers. Gann and Salter suggest that HE provision for the "built environment" should adapt to ensure that students acquire the interdisciplinary knowledge and new skills needed to meet the requirements of the contemporary construction industry.

Trends in Participation and Demand for Places

The Higher Education Statistics Agency figures show that the overall number of students enrolled in HE has increased by 6 per cent to 1,856,330 during the period 1996/97 to 1999/00. During the same period and in contrast, take up of courses in civil engineering has fallen by 17 per cent and take up of building and construction by 15 per cent (Fairbrother 2002). Reports have also highlighted the steep decline in applications and take up of places on construction related courses in HE (see Gann and Salter, 1999; Fuller, 2002a; Fairbrother, 2002). The most recent paper by Fairbrother shows that applications for "built environment" degrees (including civil engineering, architecture, and building and construction courses) fell by 35 per cent between 1994 and 2000 whereas, applications in all subject areas increased by 9 per cent. Applications for "civil engineering" and "building/construction" were down by 43 per cent and 45 per cent respectively. Architecture fared relatively better with applications down by 11 per cent.

However, while applications are down, acceptances as a proportion of applications have been rising. The proportion of successful applicants for built environment courses for the year 2000 was higher (87%) than the proportion for all subject areas (71%) (Fairbrother, 2002). Nearly all (97%) of those applying for places on building and construction courses were accepted by the year 2000 (ibid). The high level of acceptances is likely to be an indicator that HEI admissions tutors are relaxing entry requirements in an effort to maintain course numbers. Indeed, Gann and Salter's study found that "new entrants tend to have lower grades than in the past" (1999, p. 11). Overall, the trend data indicate a decline in the number of qualifications gained in built environment courses at first degree level (-8%) and more severely at "other undergraduate" level (-41%) during the late 1990s (Fuller 2002a).

Comparing Participation and Demand

The following statistics compare trends in participation in architecture, and building and planning courses with those in "computer science" and "business and administrative studies" which have both seen increases in take up in recent years. Table One shows figures for first year full-time, first degree undergraduates students participating in the three subject areas mentioned for the years 1994/95 and 1998/99. Following a first degree full-time still constitutes the most popular form of participation in HE in the UK.

Table 1
First Year Full-Time Students Following First Degrees
in Three Subject Areas—1994/95 and 1998/99

United Kingdom

Subject area	1994/95	1998/99	% change
Computer Science	13470	19003	+41
Business and administrative studies[1]	33498	40777	+22
Architecture, building & planning	8855	7990	-10

Source: Derived from HESA 2000 and 1995, Table 1b (Fuller 2002a)
1. The subject area business and administrative studies includes the specific subjects Business & management studies; Operational research; Financial management; Accountancy; Marketing & market research; Industrial relations; Catering & institutional management; Land & property management; Transport & other business and administrative studies, and balanced combinations within subject area.

Business and administrative studies is the most popular choice of subject area with around five times more students entering HE than for construction related courses and with twice as many as computer science. The percentage change figures show the substantial increase in take up there has been for computer science and business and administrative studies first degrees in recent years. These two subjects have clearly benefited from the expansion of HE and the increasing demand for higher level qualifications associated with changes in technology and the organisation of work: whereas, as we have seen, construction-related courses have not.

The important point for the construction industry to take from the above statistics is that it is drawing on a relatively small and shrinking pool of people pursuing industry specific qualification. In contrast, the statistics for subject areas such as business and administration studies, and computer science, as well as for HE as a whole, show that the overall pool of people qualified at HE level has grown substantially.

Reasons Underlying Trends in Participation

Some explanations for the decrease in demand and participation in construction related courses in HE have been widely aired. For example, representatives from universities who have been meeting to discuss the crisis in recruitment to construction-related courses, concluded that "the industry has a grave problem with image" (Action Points, 18 July 2001). Other reports have identified reasons such as the industry's "poor reputation" and "weak information provision" for the decline in numbers pursuing undergraduate programmes (see for example, Gann and Salter 1999). Gann and Salter suggest that in the absence of good quality information about courses and the industry, student choices are largely based on perceptions of the industry rather than facts. While this may be true, it is worth asking how much difference the provision of "good" information could, by itself, overcome the image problem that has been strongly associated with discouraging students (especially school leavers) on to construction-related courses. Fairbrother suggests that the narrowly based nature of most construction related courses deters young people from applying. He comments:

> Part of the issue is that the industry is attempting to attract its new blood into the same old silos. (2002, p. 14).

In addition to such industry specific factors, I suggest that there are a number of broader reasons underlying the changing pattern of participation in HE which can help explain why a subject area like construction is struggling to recruit students. Firstly, it is important to consider the changing nature of the cohort proceeding to higher education. As McNair (1993) and Fuller (2001) have pointed out, until recently in the UK, only a small minority of young people followed A level courses and proceeded to university. The typical university entrant twenty years ago was 18 years old, male, white and was pursuing a full-time degree course. The expansion of the system that has taken place since, and particularly since the early 1990s, means that universities are attended by a much wider variety of student. Furthermore, and in contrast with the past, HE now appears to be viewed as a continuation of full-time schooling, by many young people and their parents. The "staying on rate" beyond the end of compulsory schooling at 16 years old currently averages 70 per cent nationally. Post-compulsory participation in A levels or general vocational qualifications is seen by the majority as a taken-for-granted next step on an extended educational pathway which eventually leads to full-time entry into the labour market during people's early to mid twenties. Progression in to HE and attainment of higher level qualifications appears to be increasingly viewed by young people as a way of keeping options open while they refine their career ideas. For this group, some clearly vocationally-oriented courses, such as in construction, may appear too specialised and as limiting employment prospects to one sector. Qualifications in computing or business administration are more likely to be perceived as generic.

Alison Wolf (1997) has analysed trends in young people's take up of qualifications over the past twenty or so years. She shows that increases in individual demand have been greatest for general academic and educational qualifications. Her analysis indicates that the rise in "staying on" in full-time education at 16 has led to a large increase in the numbers taking A levels and continuing with their general education. In contrast, new vocational qualifications such as the advanced level General National Vocational Qualification have been far less popular. Wolf shows that increasing numbers of those attaining A levels are then proceeding to HE rather than entering the labour market at 18. She argues that from the individual's perspective the decision to pursue widely recognised advanced and then higher level general qualifications is a rational response by young people (and their parents) to the uncertainties and competitiveness of the contemporary labour market. She recognises that there has been some credential inflation but this merely reinforces the need for individuals to gain the sorts of higher level qualifications, such as degrees, which employers' recruitment practices show they are demanding for the most attractive sounding positions.

Drawing on Wolf's argument I would suggest that from the school leaver's perspective, it is probably sensible to pursue a strategy which enables them to achieve three positive aims a) attain a higher level of general education including generic analytical and organisational skills; b) allow more time to consider careers—keeping options open; and c) gain qualifications such as degrees which have wide currency in the labour market. This line of reasoning can be used to help shed light on why subject areas such as computer science and business and administrative studies have prospered in recent years and in comparison with construction. Business and administration and computer science (Information Technology) skills are relevant across industry. Attaining qualifications in these areas appears to open up the possibility for the recipient to work in any sector. Given the fluctuating fortunes of different industries at different times, such an option would appear a better bet or risk to young people embarking on their career, than opting for a subject area which appears to qualify them for only one sector, such as construction, which is also known to be cyclical.

Given that the number and calibre of school leavers applying and taking up places in construction related HE courses is in decline, the onus is on the industry to think flexibly about recruitment and workforce development. In particular, it needs to clarify whom it wants to target to address the shortages that have been identified. However, I would argue that sector policy makers should be wary of letting national policy concerns and initiatives overly influence the industry's approach to promoting HE level study. In particular, how appropriate is the emphasis at national level, on the proportion of young people and, particularly, school leavers entering HE to the specific requirements of the construction industry? This chapter questions whether a strategy which prioritises the recruitment of young people is the most effective way of increasing the numbers of the workforce qualified to HE level in sectors which are struggling to fulfil their high skill requirements.

Identifying Targets

It is one of the purposes of this chapter to encourage policy makers and employers to think critically about the relationship between industry and HE, and to clarify the role university provision can play in helping sectors to meet higher level skills shortfalls. In the case of construction, the industry is actively seeking to increase workforce skill and qualification levels and is working with universities to try and reconstruct the relationship in order to stimulate student demand (Fuller 2002a). The approach, hitherto, appears to revolve around two themes a) prioritising increases in the number of school leavers entering (construction-related) HE, thus mirroring the national policy approach to expansion and b) adopting a catch all strategy which identifies the wide range of groups which the industry could pursue without sufficiently weighting, or differentiating between, them. For example, how helpful is it to identify broad categories such as women or mature students without a more fine grained analysis of who the industry wants to attract? Could more clearly defined "targets" be identified and, if so, what sort of support package would employers and the industry need to offer to compete successfully with other sectors? This section identifies some of the challenges involved in increasing the numbers of school leavers taking up places on construction-related HE courses. It goes on to identify a number of other groups who may be attracted to the industry but who, if recruited, could place new demands on both providers and employers.

Earlier in the chapter, I drew attention to the UK government's target that 50 per cent of young people (under 30) should experience HE by 2010. It is becoming increasingly clear that the main route to achieving this goal (see for example, Margaret

Hodge, The Guardian 14, Jan 2002) is to increase the participation rate of young people from lower socio-economic backgrounds. As the government makes progress in this area and succeeds in increasing the numbers of young people entering HE, then the sector might benefit if some of these additional students opt for construction-related courses. However, the following list of summary issues highlights some of the problems associated with locating school leavers at the centre of an industry's relationship with HE.

- There appears to be weak student demand for specific (narrow) courses. Even if the overall participation rate increases there is no guarantee that more students will opt for courses, such as in construction, which are perceived as being narrow. Many students see participation in HE as a way of keeping career options open.

- As young people's demand for some vocationally specific courses weakens, institutions are having to lower entry requirements to try and maintain numbers. Struggling students are more likely to drop out of their courses and require more support (including financial) from their departments or sponsoring employers.

- The retention challenge: an industry such as construction has to find ways of ensuring that students who have followed relevant courses enter and stay in the sector. This issue is particularly crucial for those employers who attract pupils into courses and jobs by offering generous sponsorship and career development packages.

- Creating "modern" provision: increasing the availability of courses in new areas of employer demand and, in particular, in new interdisciplinary provision where areas such as construction are combined with other subjects (e.g., business administration, economics, IT). The provision of broader-based vocationally orientated degrees may help attract younger students who want to keep their options open. However, developing new courses is expensive and risky as graduates of the new provision still might not enter the industry and those that do are likely to graduate with fewer technical and industry specific skills, thus, increasing employers' training costs.

Other Targets

Mid-career employees is an important source of demand for HE. Currently, more than four out of ten (44%) of all students are aged 25 or over and most of these participate in part-time courses while working (Brennan et al 2000, Fuller 2002b forthcoming). In construction, Gann and Salter found that only 45 per cent of those working in professional occupations are qualified to degree level. This finding suggests that many employees obtained their professional level positions before qualifications grew in importance and when the opportunities for progression to HE from school were much fewer. In addition, there is also potential to encourage ex-apprentices, already qualified to intermediate level and with industry experience, to upgrade to higher level qualifications. Continuing professional development, training and qualifications for existing staff could, therefore, provide part of the answer to solving the higher level skills gap. Another approach could focus on recruiting those already qualified to HE level (in other subjects) and who are equipped with potentially transferable skills, for example in management and IT. Targeting those with generic skills and experience but without a specific occupational background would generate other training requirements. Such individuals would need the support and opportunity to gain industry awareness and the specific technical and professional skills and qualifications required by their employer. Targeting those who already have relevant higher level professional and technical qualifications reduces the burden for employers to provide specific skills but, given the ways and pace in which industry is changing, it does not address the growing need for generic skills in management and IT which skills forecasts have identified.

For illustrative purposes, I offer two short vignettes which help illustrate the issues associated with targeting non-traditional groups. Importantly, the vignettes indicate the relevance of individual backgrounds and aspirations to recruitment and highlight the point that key characteristics for recruitment could be less associated with fixed factors such as qualifications held, age, gender, ethnic background, than with areas such as motivation, dissatisfaction with current situation, and willingness and ability to learn. The first vignette relates to someone currently working in another sector but who could become a recruitment target, for example, for the construction industry. The second vignette refers to an existing employee who, as yet, does not have HE level qualifications but who has the potential to become more highly qualified.

Vignette One: Peter

Peter is 27. He graduated from university five years ago with a good degree in Geography. After leaving university he travelled for a year. On his return he needed a job quickly to start paying off his debts and gained a position with a rapidly expanding chain of DIY stores. Peter quickly progressed to assistant manager and then to store manager a position which he has held for the past three years. Peter enjoyed his early years with the company. He quickly gained self-confidence in his ability to work with and then to manage other people and developed a range of other skills in stock control, the effective presentation of goods and customer relations. He also developed an interest in DIY using the store's discount system to good effect in making improvements to his first home.

However, over the past couple of years Peter has grown increasingly bored and feels that the job is no longer a challenge. He is not interested in gaining further promotion (to area store manager) as he sees this as a less interesting job than his current one. Overall, Peter feels that if he doesn't change career soon he will become stuck. Although he realises he might have to take an initial pay cut to embark on a new path, this would be acceptable if the opportunity provided him with the opportunity to gain new skills and qualifications which he could use to expand his career prospects.

> **Vignette Two: Jill**
>
> Jill is 44. She works in the planning office of a local authority. She has worked as a town planner for fifteen years and loves her job. However, she has become increasingly worried in recent years that her younger colleagues are more highly qualified than she is and that, as a consequence, she is being passed over for promotion. Many of Jill's colleagues are educated to degree level whereas she left school at 18 with A levels. Jill has learned her job through experience and through attending training courses, funded by her employer. Jill's two children are now at university and she feels able to give her career a higher priority than before.

The above vignettes highlight the point that industries struggling to meet their higher level skill and qualifications' needs can look beyond the traditional 21 year old university graduate. In particular, sector policy makers may need to think harder about a number of questions including: how important is age; and, what are the relative merits of recruiting people with industry-related HE qualifications in comparison with those who have other attainments in other subjects and skills and, or experience gained in employment contexts which could be applicable? Below, I identify three, non-traditional, groups which industries, such as construction, could target and which can also be seen to point up the limitations of national and sector policy makers' emphasis on the recruitment of young people to higher education and to jobs.

Strategy One: To attract people who have HE level qualifications in non-industry specific areas, but who have potentially transferable skills and experience (e.g., in IT, business development or project management). The industry and providers may need to develop opportunities for such people to acquire specific technical and professional skills as well as industry recognised qualifications. Some "generic" subject areas such as business and administrative studies are producing an over-supply of graduates who are subsequently under-employed and which sectors such as construction could consider targeting (Fuller 2002a).

Strategy Two: To attract experienced employees from other sectors, who are currently not qualified to HE level but who have the potential to achieve it and the experience and character to be of value to the industry This strategy would also entail the provision of appropriate conversion and upgrading opportunities in HE and support for those following this route to higher levels. The development of work-based and flexible attendance routes through HE could be particularly appropriate for this group.

Strategy Three: To upgrade the skills and qualifications of staff currently employed in the sector. This could include encouraging staff, such as recent ex-apprentices, to progress to part-time higher level courses, as well as supporting older experienced employees working in "professional occupations" but who do not hold degrees, to pursue the relevant higher level qualifications while they are working in the industry.

Final Remarks

This chapter has fulfilled a number of functions. It has provided a review of the current national policy context and patterns of participation which form the backdrop to the creation of new relationships between an industry like construction and HE. It has documented the downward trend in young people pursuing construction-related courses in comparison to "rival," and all subject areas and has used the findings to shed light on why an area such as construction is struggling to attract more of the overall growing cohort of university entrants in to its area. Having outlined and discussed "the problem," the chapter has also considered ways forward. In particular, it has focused on the issue of target groups. The analysis suggests that sector policy makers, employers and university providers need to work together to clarify "who" the industry can successfully target and to develop provision more closely aligned with the preference of most contemporary students for broadly-based courses and the requirements of the industry for more graduates with interdisciplinary knowledge and skills.

The chapter emphasises that options other than increasing the number of young graduates should be seriously considered. The identification of target recruits is not an end in itself, their pursuit carries resource implications which centre on the availability of provision and the financial and learning support employers individually and collectively may have to offer. The key issue revolves around attracting more diverse people in to HE in an era when participation is at an all time high but when, as I have illustrated using the case of construction, there is low demand from "traditional" students for some vocationally-specific courses.

References

Ashton, D. and Green, F. (1996) *Education, Training and the Global Economy*, Aldershot: Edward Elgar

Brown, A., Rhodes, E., and Carter, R. (2001) Supporting Learning in Advanced Supply Systems in the automotive and aerospace industries, Paper presented at oint ESRC/ SKOPE conference *Context, power and perspective: confronting the challenges to improving attainment in learning at work*, University College Northampton, November 8-10, 2001

Brown, P., Green, A. and Lauder, H. (2001) *High Skills*, Oxford: Oxford University Press

Cassels, J. (2001) *The Way to Work*, London:DfEE

Castels, M. (1996) *The Information Age: Economy, society and culture iii, end of millennium*, Oxford: Blackwell

CITB *Construction Workforce Development Planning Brief 2001-2005*

CITB *Business Plan 2000-2004*

CITB Research (July 2000), *Managing Profitable Construction: the skills profile*

CITB/DTI/CIC/ICE *Making Connections: action points arising from the meeting with Vice Chancellors*, 18 July 2001

Confederation of British Industry (1989) *Towards a Skills Revolution—a youth charter*, London: CBI

Construction and the Built Environment Foundation Degree National Task Group (September 2001) *Market Research Report, first draft*, CITB (prepared by RBA Associates)

Collins, R. (1979) *The Credential Society: An historical sociology of education and stratification*, New York: Academic Press

Daily Telegraph (25 January, 2002)

Department for Education and Employment (1998) *The Learning Age: A renaissance for a new Britain,* CM3790, London: DfEE

Dore, R. (1976) *The Diploma Disease: Education, qualification and development,* London: George Allen and Unwin

Fairbrother, J. (2002) *Rethinking Construction Innovation and Research: A review of government R and D Policies and Practices,* London: DTLR

Fuller, A. (2002a) *Construction and Higher Education: preparing the ground for a "modern relationship"* unpublished discussion paper for CITB: Kings Lynn

Fuller, A. (2002b in press) "Widening Participation: Describing and explaining the growing importance of HE for mature students." In Hayton, A. and Puczuska, A. eds. *Access, Participation and Higher Education: Policy and Practice,* London: Kogan Page.

Fuller, A. (2001) "Credentialism, Adults and Part-time Higher Education in the United Kingdom: an account of rising take up and some implications for policy, *Journal of Education Policy,* Vol. 16, No. 3, pp. 233-348.

Gann, D and Salter, A. (May 1999) *Interdisciplinary Skills for Built Environment Professionals: A scoping study,* London: The Ove Arup Foundation

Gibbons, M., Limoges, C., Nowotny, H., Schwartzman, S., Scott, P., and Trow, M. (1994) *The New Production of Knowledge: the dynamics of science and research in contemporary society,* London: Sage

The Guardian Education, 14 and 22 January 2002

Hayton, A. and Puczuska, A. (eds.) (2002 in press) *Access, Participation and Higher Education: Policy and Practice,* London: Kogan Page

HESA (2000) *Students in Higher Education Institutions: Reference Volume,* 1998/99, Cheltenham: HESA

HESA/GSS (1996) *Higher Education Statistics for the United Kingdom,* 1994/95, Cheltenham: HESA

Keep, E. and Mayhew, K. (1998) Was Ratner Right/ Product market and competitive strategies and their links with skills and knowledge, *Economic Policy Institute Economic Report,* 12, 3, April.

Keep, E. (1999) Employers' attitudes towards training, *STF Research Paper,* 15, Sudbury: DfEE

McNair, S. (1993) *An Adult Higher Education:* A vision, Leicester: NIACE

National Skills Task Force (2000) *Tackling the Adult Skills Gap: upskilling adults and the role of workplace learning,* Sheffield: DfEE

Performance and Innovation Unit (November 2001) *In Demand: adults skills for the 21st century,* London: Cabinet Office.

Piat, W. (2001) *Opportunity for Whom?* London: IPPR

Times Higher (18 January 2002; 12 April 2002)

Uden, T. (1996) *Widening Participation: Routes to a learning society—a policy discussion paper,* Leicester: NIACE

Wolf, A. (1997) Growth stocks and Lemons: diplomas in the English market-place 1976-1996, *Assessment in Education: principles, policy & practice,* Vol 4, No. 1 pp. 33-50

Notes

1. This paper is based on a discussion document prepared for the Construction Industry Training Board and entitled *Construction and Higher Education: preparing the ground for a "modern relationship,"* 2002.
2. The use of the terminology "experienced HE" is interesting as it hints that a wide interpretation of what counts as HE will be applied when the government assesses progress on meeting the target. HE institutions (HEIs) offer broad and diverse provision including the opportunity to gain professional certificates and diplomas (e.g., certificate in marketing, diploma in management), as well as conventional and well-known qualifications at sub-degree (e.g., HND), first degree and higher degree levels and non-credit bearing courses.
3. The Aimhigher initiative was launched by the DfES in mid-January 2002 and is a campaign to encourage more children from disadvantaged backgrounds to consider HE. The Excellence Challenge was launched by the government in September 2000. It is a three year programme with a 190 million pound budget.
4. The Advanced Modern Apprenticeship is a government supported work-based training programme leading to intermediate skills and qualifications which are categorised as level 3 in the UK qualification system.
5. An article in the THES shows that the postcode premium has its flaws. Firstly, not all students applying from these postcodes come from disadvantaged backgrounds and secondly, the premium applies to all students from these postcodes who take up places including older students taking postgraduate courses and who already have first degrees (THES January 18 2002)

Chapter Three

Emerging Archetypal Perspectives on University Governance: New Conceptual Understandings About the Role of Universities

BRUCE CUTTING

ALEXANDER KOUZMIN

Governance within modern tertiary institutions is complex, multiform and varied and needs to be refocused within the context of changes to menetype dynamics. This chapter seeks to re-position the debate about effective university governance by refocusing critical debate around nine issues: education as an economic commodity; the emergence of mass universities; commercial subservience to industry; changes in organizational governance; knowledge creation processes; the institutional impact of new technology; life time learning; post-graduate management training; and learning in learning organizations.

> The evolution of the intellect, Comte asserted,
> determines the main course of social evolution
> (Mills, 1956: 301).

Introduction

Universities are organizations of human creation that exist within a society, which, in its turn, is also a creation of many human minds.[1] The principle trinity of *menetypes* (as depicted in Figure 1)[2] used by humans to position themselves and operate in the world is that captured in the increasing level of abstraction associated with the thinking in terms of themselves as an individual, themselves as part of, or in relation to, a group and, then, as part of a society (depicted in Figure 2). As such, it may be helpful to understand the changing governance of universities in the context of the way human thinking is changing; in particular, the way one's thinking about society, about the organizations that go to make up that society and about one's particular role within all that.

A society and the organizations within it are so because people believe or cognitively accept that they are so.[3] That is, individuals are thinking and speaking of organizations or groups as though they were a single entity with personal characteristics. Moreover, they will tend to think and speak of organizations out of particular mindsets that reflect some kind of inner beliefs or implicit assumptions formed through the societal thinking within which they are formed.[4] "An institutional fact cannot exist in isolation but only in a set of systematic relations to other facts" (Searle, 1995: 35). That is, each individual has these particular sets of beliefs and knowledge operating at three levels of abstraction: namely, what it is to be an individual, a group or a society. This is essentially what is meant that man is a social animal. It means that one is able to, and moreover cognitively looks to, think on these three levels of abstraction and think of oneself as an individual, as a member of a group and as a member of society. However, it is cognitively impossible to think simultaneously in terms of each perspective equally, but rather one of the three levels of thinking is given predominance at a particular time.[5] It is this cognitive differentiation and necessity to focus on particular perspectives that results in the different types of society on the highest level, and different types of organization on the lower levels of abstract thinking (and different personalities on the lowest level).

It is seen, therefore, that the modes of thinking in terms of the individual, the group and society constitute a core differentiation in the cognitive framework of the intellect.[6] This chapter discusses the emerging changes in governance of universities: first, in terms of the way one thinks of them as part of society; secondly, as operating organizations in their own right; and thirdly, from the perspective of the changing demands on their individual participants—principally, the staff and students.

Tertiary Institutions in Society

The legitimacy and dynamics of universities and other tertiary institutions as entities are determined by the nature of the society they find themselves in.[7] This follows, in principle, from the cognitive law of procession that decisions and beliefs adopted at the higher levels of abstraction (namely, society), flow down automatically to inform and shape the thinking and actions at the lower levels (namely, the thinking and action about groups and, then, as individuals). Therefore, it is necessary to understand the nature of society before analysing the dynamics of tertiary institutions as particular organizations (and this discussion of society and organizations will, of course, focus mainly on the experience of the Western industrialized society). In what way, then, do individuals structure their thinking about their society? One's thinking about society has been most usefully considered to comprise three interrelated sectors of activity; namely the economic, the social and the political (as depicted in Figure 3).[8]

Essentially, all conscious social action within the society can be explained in terms of the inherent pattern of these three principle *menetypes* (and their *sub-menetype* systems) of the social catallactic system (Cutting and Kouzmin, 2001a). How then does one fit higher education and universities within this societal framework? The essence of higher education can be understood from an appreciation of what particular "good" is to be served and the purpose, process and the nature of knowing pursued by post-secondary education.

First, the tertiary education sector is about contributing to the understanding and formation of the way society knows and understands itself and this endeavour is characteristic of the institutions in the society's social sphere (*menetype #B*). Secondly, the traditional university is focused on the pursuit of objective truth and scientific method, which guides it in the accumulation, refinement and dissemination of knowledge and meaning within society (embracing a *sub-menetype #B* orientation within the social sphere). Thirdly, it is part of the whole educational system that is focused on preparing and moulding individuals for their place and life in society, perhaps working in one particular sphere but being mindful of participating in the whole.

This *philosophical* orientation clearly places the overall value of the tertiary education sector, and universities in particular, within the social sphere of society, as opposed to serving the political or economic spheres. This philosophical fact has immediate implications:

- With the primary focus on serving the interests of the social sphere, tertiary education necessarily eschews the way of thinking exemplified in the economic sphere. This is cognitively necessary in their endeavour to enhance their primary pursuit and teaching of knowledge about objective truth—academics would conceive this practice in terms of them staying above the undignified commercial fray. On the other hand, the tertiary education sector would naturally look towards the political sphere (in a secondary supporting role) to help define their identification of desired educational outcomes for the community and to provide the necessary resource support rather than relying on the imperative of the economic sphere. In this sense, any charging of fees would be in terms of requiring students to pay their way through "membership fees" to participate in the academic fraternity and process, rather than in terms of setting a price as though education was an economic commodity.

- In keeping with the dynamics of the philosophic trinity of *menetypes*, the tertiary education sector would move more naturally and constructively in the direction of political sphere activity rather than that of the economic sphere, which can be regarded as the shadow of the academic world. The academic thinking in terms of commercial, market-oriented activity would therefore be under-developed and any steps into the commercial world would most likely seem rather clumsy. In this sense, then the overall formation of society is undermined to the extent that there is a growth in the corporation-specific universities (such as the one instituted by McDonalds) because it represents a shift of the principle spirit of such education from the *menetype #B* social orientation to the *menetype #A* economic orientation. The outward manifestation will be the further breakdown of the national community spirit into separate competitive corporate communities, each espousing a different "good" and perspective on life.

- It is acknowledged that (as with any trinity of *menetypes*) thinking perspectives from all of society's spheres are in play, but there is a focus and a hierarchy of influence of such thinking that is captured in the dynamics of the trinity of *menetypes*. Processes can therefore be implemented within tertiary education institutions to take account of, and exercise the thinking from, the political and economic spheres, but the eventual development of such thinking will be dependent on the significance of the role they play in the institution's decision-making processes.

In keeping with this notion of contributing to the overall "good" of society by the educational formation of its citizens and groups, the role of post-secondary education can be differentiated and understood as contributing to the formation of the society's skills, knowledge and meaning and commitment as follows (as depicted in Figure 4).

- *Skills Formation (sub-menetype #A)*. This is the most concrete aspect of learning or personal formation and is about advancing human practical usefulness. Basic skills (reading, writing, arithmetic and basic social etiquette) are taught in formal primary and secondary education. The contribution of post-secondary education is to teach those skills applicable to specific services or contributions within the community and is focused in sympathy with the productive "good" of the economic sector (through the connection of the same *menetype #A* spirit). The focus is on teaching the individual how to apply a particular field of knowledge for the material good of society and therefore incorporates the specific trade and vocational training. The measured success of this learning is that the individuals are then competent to carry out particular roles/tasks within the workforce—that is, "the criterion of success is not what a man knows or is but what he later does" (Embling, 1974: 29). In essence, this aspect of learning constitutes more the philosophical basis of the technical and further education colleges or the British polytechnics.[9] However, to the extent that the skills required by a particular component of the workforce are more complex or benefit from continuous direct development of their knowledge base, they are taught in universities. This is learning to support practical achievement and would include a focus on basic processes in industry. Such learning would therefore benefit from close collaboration with industry to identify the skills required and the best methods to combine a set of skills to achieve particular material ends.

- *Knowledge Formation (sub-menetype #B)*. This is a more abstract aspect of learning which involves an education in cognitive processes to discover, refine and disseminate knowledge. This teaching of knowledge and how to generate more knowledge, or the training of the intellect, has long been regarded as the traditional role of universities.[10] It is the stimulation of intellectual curiosity and the associated process of cognitive reversion (Cutting and Kouzmin, 2001a) that takes this aspect above the concrete and the practical into the sphere of meaning. In essence, this captures the core spirit of tertiary education to strive after objective truth and clarity, to pursue knowledge for its own sake rather than for its usefulness,[11] which, however, is expected to flow from a knowledge of the truth as a matter of good process. Such education embraces research to equip and encourage individuals, organizations and societies to continually pursue knowledge and its refinement in the dispassionate objective way that has been captured in the notion of the modern scientific way— rather than merely doing what works for the desired purpose. In essence, it is about cultivating first a belief in knowledge legitimately formulated by others;

secondly a confidence that by following the proper scientific processes or inquiry, they could themselves generate more understanding and add to the store of valid knowledge; and thirdly, the accumulation of such a store of validly developed knowledge is of inherent value to society. The spirit of this aspect of learning is captured by a paraphrase of the Embling (1974: 29) quote above, "the criterion of intelligent learning is not what a person does or is, but what they know."

• *Commitment Formation (sub-menetype #C).* The most abstract (or prescinded) aspect is the formation of personal or group commitment. There is also ultimately a contribution to the overall societal commitment by the formulation, development and promulgation of the big ideas. [12] This education is about socializing the whole person in teaching them the necessity and importance of making decisions and equipping them with the wherewithal and guidance to make life decisions.[13] For instance, the first life choice or commitment required of the individual by the tertiary institution is in selecting their course or the particular focus of their study, which will necessarily influence their later choice of a career. They are then encouraged to make a choice to believe in the particular school of thought or knowledge that is promulgated through their academic lectures. In some cases, students are encouraged to test something out for themselves and are then more enthusiastic to commit to some knowledge they know as opposed to believe (because some trusted authority said it was so). They also make a choice for their group of personal and social contacts. The social sphere is about formation of society and its accepted hierarchy and way of operating and, over time, the universities have played a significant role in building and sustaining that social hierarchy through its "elite culture" (Embling, 1974: 28-29) and lasting associations. To the extent there has been a move to democratise or move to the mass universities, there has been an attempt to diminish or redirect this contribution that universities make to the formation of social hierarchy.

Commitment formation involves the inculcation of personal knowledge where the individual takes on "deliberate intellectual commitments (and) accept(s) these accidents of personal existence as the concrete opportunities for exercising personal responsibility. *This acceptance is the sense of (one's) calling*" (Polanyi, 1958: 322, emphasis in original)—or the pursuit of what is to be made real for oneself. This cultivation of the ethic of personal responsibility also extends to an influence on cultivating a sense of organizational and societal responsibility. It is about instilling a sense of what should be valued, an appreciation of the necessity and ability to make sensible judgments and decisions and how to work with others to bring something worthwhile about. It is about how to exercise power and control over the knowledge and potential knowledge that is being accumulated.

It is seen, therefore, that the *raison d'être* of the university can be understood primarily as contributing to the social sphere formation of the individual (and to a lesser extent, the formation of institutions and society) and that the understanding of this formation can be differentiated in terms of the formation of skills, knowledge and commitment—which is seen to constitute a trinity of cognitive *menetypes*. There are a number of immediate implications flowing from the dynamics of this cognitive reality.

- Though there are always elements of all aspects of personal formation in higher education, it is a cognitive reality that there cannot be an equal focus on all three aspects of personal formation at the same time—there is necessarily a focus on one particular aspect of the formation trinity that will then define the secondary formation perspective and the third aspect which is to be actively downplayed. For instance, the traditional concept of the university is taken to have a focus principally on the formation of knowledge and meaning—on the pursuit, refinement and dissemination of knowledge in the form of the objective truth (Embling, 1974; West, 1998), which is *menetype #B* spirit through and through. This aspect of knowledge formation is actively supported by the formation of personal commitment to a particular school of thinking, to a group of colleagues who will continue to support one another in their endeavour to live out their chosen role and standing in society. As a way of being open to the knowledge that they are to learn and come to master in a way they are able to expand that knowledge, it is helpful if they remain above the fray and be objective, and so the doing of it or the development of practical skills is put on hold or downplayed. In this *menetype #B* mode, there is a concentration on pure science or the search for Truth with a capital "T" (Jackson, 1999: 91), rather than applied technology. In the same way, to sustain the objectivity of knowledge formation, the academics will eschew the mundane prosaic thinking and practices of the *menetype #A* economic sphere.

  On the other hand, where there is a concentration on the technical skills or technology (sub-*menetype #A*), the acquaintanceship with knowledge formation is used as a secondary support and the personal formation is regarded as unnecessary or inappropriate as all is needed is that they develop the practical skills and competency to get the job done—"they would accept the obligation to have regard to the needs of the individual but within a limited sphere based primarily on material interests" (Embling, 1974: 30). Because of the *type #A* oriented thinking, the formation of skills is most attuned to the thinking of the *menetype #A* economic sphere and therefore is most responsive to industry in a practical way in what skills should be included and how to teach them.

- Where there is a movement of cognitive focus towards higher levels of abstract thinking within the trinity (clockwise movement around the trinities of *menetypes*), the formation system is evolving and the changes are usually seen as constructive as it calls upon the secondary supporting role to take a higher profile. On the other hand, the movement of cognitive focus to the next lowest level of abstract thinking (anticlockwise) is normally seen as destructive as it plays into the hitherto repressed aspect of thinking that is normally under-developed and the resultant actions are more primitive and awkward as a consequence. For instance, an institution with the traditional notion of knowledge formation would be seen as improving if it placed more emphasis on the personal commitment formation of the students aspiring to enter a particular profession because they would be creating better citizens and more effective members of the professional group. On the other hand, any move into purely commercial enterprises would be seen as crass and diversionary because it would undermine the perception of objectivity and integrity of the knowledge formation. Hence, it would be regarded as entirely inappropriate were the academics to benefit from any commercial connection to their students as it would undermine their objectivity in teaching and in awarding academic marks and awards.

Each of the aspects of the formation trinity concentrates on developing a different style of personal thinking. First, the skills formation phase accentuates an outward oriented thinking where there is a concentrated conscious effort to marry explicit knowledge with concrete practical instances. It is what the individual does that is important and, therefore, the questions are more about what available knowledge is needed in this situation to achieve what is intended. The thinking sequence most encouraged, therefore, is that of cognitive procession from general principles to specific knowledge to practical application or an anti-clockwise movement around the individual's personal cognitive trinity. Secondly, the knowledge formation phase includes a more inward-oriented thinking which concentrates on a personal assimilation of relevant knowledge. The individual is trained to question phenomena and test out the adequacy of particular aspects of knowledge rather than just to blindly do. It is what an individual thinks that is important and, therefore, the questions are more about the why and how of a situation. The thinking sequence most encouraged therefore is that of cognitive regression from experience to understanding to general principle or a clockwise movement around the individual's personal cognitive trinity. Thirdly, the personal commitment phase attempts to marry both inward—and outward—oriented thinking to act appropriately in the particular situation. There is encouraged an attitude of power or control over the available knowledge and skills to further one's personal cause or that of the group or society. The questions are, therefore, more about the what that is to be achieved, how the various resources are to be brought together to make it happen and who is responsible or who benefits. This is the most abstract and fluid of the thinking and changes to suit the particular situation.

Trends in Societal Thinking

The ways of abstract thinking about organizations and society, in particular, are never static and there has been much observation and discussion about the dramatic shifts in thinking that have been occurring in Western society. It is worthwhile to make some cursory remarks about the implications of this broad societal shift in thinking at this point, but to save the discussion of particular shifts in tertiary education until the later discussion of specific issues.

- The nature of capitalism has changed over time. Much was made of the shift in the early part of the twentieth century from the entrepreneurial capitalist society to a managerialist perspective which, in essence, represents an evolutionary shift from a *menetype #A* consumer market mindset to the *menetype #B* managerial production processes (Berle and Means, 1991/1933; Burnham, 1941; Schumpeter, 1950; Galbraith, 1967). The more recent shift in thinking to the so-called knowledge society has been termed post-industrial, post-modern or the new information age. In fact, it can be understood as a shift from the *menetype #B* managerialist mindset to the more abstract *menetype #C* politicist mindset where there is a recognition of the validity of different personal and group perspectives as opposed to universal objective truths (Cutting and Kouzmin, 2001c). The focus is on a grasp of the reality that presents itself in the particular situation rather than the universal concepts that are at play.

This involves a shift from concern with the rules and procedures of process and order to a greater focus on core values the ethics of particular (political) stances to the favour, or not, of particular groups. There has been a shift of focus from the more scientific questions of "how does it work" or "what are the universal laws at play," to more like "what is really happening here" and "what is the appropriate response." In effect, the central importance of knowledge has been down-played because there is so much of it that is readily available, and more is becoming available all the time, that it's availability is now taken for granted. The question now is what knowledge should be applied to this particular situation and so the central importance is on the ability to assess the situation and commit to a particular solution—one just has to harness the knowledge and skills that are the most appropriate. This is particularly evident in large corporations where the managers ability to cope with corporate politics has become more important than their ability to think in terms of orderly scientific management principles (Cutting, 2001; Cutting and Kouzmin, 2001c).

The shift in societal thinking captured by the notion of globalisation captures the same shift from the *menetype #B* mindset, of having a central focus on the organization, its processes and position (legal and social) within society, to a more *menetype #C* mindset of organizational politics where one nation-like corporations are positioning themselves and competing or aligning with other nation-like corporations on a world market. This clearly represents a shift upwards in the level of abstract thinking that is captured in the notion of moving from a managerialist mindset to a *politicist* mindset.

- The societal thinking at this level necessarily impacts on the lower levels of thinking and, therefore, the managerialist phase of societal thinking was manifested in the post-secondary educational formation trinity as a focus on the *menetype #B* knowledge phase—that is, a focus on the creation, refinement and propagation of knowledge for its own sake. Thus, the managerialist mindset valued and called forth the traditional concept of the university to pursue knowledge for its own sake on the assumption that society would benefit from more knowledge whatever it was. It was taught that if one followed the scientific process taught in universities to solve real-life problems then one could have confidence that the most beneficial outcome would result from the good intellectual process. The primary expectations of the product coming out of tertiary education has now shifted in accordance with the shift in thinking from the managerialist mindset to the *menetype #C politicist* mindset.

Graduates are now assumed to have the knowledge or know how it can be readily accessed rather than developed. They are expected to have the nous to assess and choose the appropriate stance and available knowledge applicable to a particular situation and then to decide what actions will contribute to the immediate good of their group. The stress is on resource coordination and positional power to enable one's group to prevail and prosper in a particular turbulent environment. Knowledge has become just another resource available to be used and good scientific process is no longer the most highly regarded approach in tackling problems. Rather, it is more important to assess and choose a particular stance and strategy and act and if it doesn't work then one needs the ability to assess that and choose something different that has a better chance of working.

This is to be taken as a fact of life because it is turbulent times where everything is constantly changing and there is not time to trust in a scientific process to establish the particular truth or universal concepts at play—principally, because the reality of the environment is changing so fast that the answer to the scientific process would be inappropriate by the time it is realized. Moreover, the predominance of the *menetype #C* politicist mindset encourages the continuation of the turbulent environment because they like treating everything as in the moment and making immediate, in-the-moment value judgments about the reality being faced at the present. In this ever-changing environment of reality they naturally focus thinking on appropriate positioning against threats and towards opportunities rather than developing logically ordered processes (which are more appropriate to the stable environments that one can control in the spirit of everything else being constant).

In terms of the education formation trinity, then, the shift to focus on the *menetype #C* commitment phase means that the predominate focus should now be on personal commitment formation with a secondary focus on the skills needed to thrive in the new so-called "knowledge society." In other words, it is now of primary importance in the selection of budding corporate executives as to who the person is and will their personal commitment profile fit in, then, of secondary importance, it is what the person is able to do.[14] What they know in terms of scientific or management facts and their ability to pursue knowledge of the truth is now of lesser importance as long as the individual knows how to access it or buy it in if they assess it as being useful. It is a question, therefore, whether the many changes in tertiary education actually support this shift in society's needs and expectations?

• What does calling this the new "post-modern" world the "knowledge society" or "information society" mean when the importance of the pursuit of knowledge is actually downplayed in favour of what fits? The sense of this descriptive tag is that knowledge is now in *abundance* and taken as a given and it is the *manipulation* and *application* of this knowledge that is the predominant focus. Corporations now form more around the available abstract knowledge rather than physical assets—a learning organization or society is taken to mean a system for developing the skill of applying the knowledge to solve particular problems rather than the search for knowledge *per se*. Life-time learning is taken to mean keeping abreast of the "latest" or most appropriate technology to enhance the personal capacity to make the right judgments and decisions, rather than the pursuit of knowledge for its own sake. It is somewhat the same manner as the way the managerialist age was also being termed as the "consumer" age, principally because a large range of consumption goods had become so readily available that the focus had shifted onto developing the managerial processes to make them more efficiently, cheaper and better. During that management phase, the entrepreneurial aspect of creating new products was also approached scientifically in formally managed research and development programs. Now that a vast range of knowledge and production processes are readily available, the focus has shifted onto the selection of the most appropriate mix of physical and intellectual resources that are needed to conquer the particular challenges at hand in a way that furthers the lot of the power group.

In keeping with this shift, research and development has been transformed from the formal, logically-managed processes to so-called "skunk-works," where the creative ideas are expected to arise from the tension of debate on conflicting approaches to a problem. There is more focus on developing networks and alliances to accumulate the power necessary to survive and thrive within the vast sea of readily available abstract knowledge (as opposed to ownership of physical resources or production processes). The corporate society (Galbraith, 1967) has truly arrived in the sense that the individual's personal commitment to the corporate group that bests controls and manipulates the knowledge and other available resources is now seen as more important to survive and thrive in this new politicist age. And the newly acquired *menetype #C* mindset suggests that if that personal commitment to this particular corporate group does not work out then it is appropriate to shift their political allegiance and make a new personal commitment to another corporate group or strategy that does work. This is in contrast to the former behaviour of the now devalued *menetype #B* "duty-bound" attitude that encourages individuals to persist in their continued loyalty as a "company man" in the belief that it will always pay off in the long run if everybody involved is logical and well intentioned.

Universities as Organizations

Governance within modern tertiary institutions is complex, multiform and varied. However, the essential nature and dynamics can be understood by extending the pattern of differentiation encompassed in the hierarchically-ordered trinities of inter-acting mindsets, to analyse the way that the educational institutions operate as autonomous organizations. A full explanation of the intricacies of this methodology is explained elsewhere (Cutting, 2001; Cutting and Kouzmin, 2001a) but this discussion will necessarily be cursory and focus on the changes that flow directly out of the above-mentioned changes in societal thinking. Also, to assist in the later discussion of the issues, it is helpful as a benchmark to focus principally on the nature of governance in the traditional universities which, by their pursuit and propagation of the knowledge of objective truth, carry the most accentuated *menetype #B* orientation in support of social sphere aspirations. However, the analysis could be easily extended to other tertiary institutions by identifying the particular focus in each of the trinities of mindsets.

- Like any other organization, the governance of a university can be understood in terms of the principle trinity of organizational governance which captures the dynamics and interaction of the participant, culture and authority spheres (as depicted in Figures 5 and 6).[15]

As an outcome of an analysis of the university governance in terms of these hierarchical trinities of organization within the influence of the social sphere of the trinity of societal thinking, the following observations can be made.

- The governance of the university flows directly as a consequence of everybody's commitment to the role of the university in society and so is focused on the pursuit, refinement and dissemination of knowledge and understanding. Creating a studious environment and pursuing objective processes is paramount and, therefore, the predominant focus of traditional universities has been on the *menetype #B* culture phase of governance. This reinforced the spirit of the social sphere and was accentuated particularly by the spirit of the scientific/managerialist age, which encouraged emulation of the *type #B* emphasis on belief in legitimate knowledge, logical, ordered processes to convert accepted principles into action and sound scientific research processes which lead to the evolution of more knowledge. In the main, universities concentrated on the transference of formal, explicit knowledge, but to the extent that the university operated primarily on implicit assumptions or belief in the academic process,[16] the primary orientation of the university was to instil a culture or environment conducive to the scientific mind (which is *menetype #B*).

Reliance on a mindset predominantly oriented by the culture mindset means that the university relied on everybody's belief in the academic process to guide and order their behaviour. The spirit of knowledge and knowing was pre-eminent and everything else had to be subservient to this end. The exercise of the authority sphere was a secondary support to sustain the academic environment and, therefore, would have been experienced as much looser than say in a private corporation or Government agency. In keeping with the dynamics of the organizational governance trinity, the least focus was on the participant sphere. The simple approach of awarding tenure provided the so-called academic freedom and obviated the need to carefully define the academic's role. There was considerable freedom in the particular subjects that made up the courses and almost complete freedom within each particular subject as to what was taught and how it was taught- in many cases the material remained the intellectual property of the individual academic and, therefore, could change quite dramatically with a change of personnel. Little attention was given to the personal development of individual academics as great reliance was placed on collegial peer pressure and the knowledge publication and legitimisation processes to maintain an orderly standard of behaviour and professional progression. Individual entrepreneurship across the ordered disciplines was not encouraged as all advancement and propagation of knowledge was best done within the established academic system to ensure its integrity and truth. Much freedom was also given to the student and their role was defined only to the extent they enrol in classes and gain a pass grade—the behavioural requirements for that pass grade varying widely from subject to subject. There was minimal attention to the students" personal progression except where the academic staff took an interest in particular students.[17]

• Within the authority sphere[18] there was a natural inclination towards order and so the centralised administration had to have a sound management orientation to process the many students in an ordered manner. This was in keeping with the core *menetype* to *#B* spirit which fosters a sense of belonging and adherence to the necessary administrative rules to teach and recognize the attainment of students and to encourage a proper balance between teaching and research. The secondary political orientation was the other aspect of the authority sphere which was manifest and this aspect was *accentuated by the university structure of essentially independent faculties* (or fiefdoms). In fact, the faculty arrangement sometimes took on such a strong political orientation (because professors were regarded almost as "gods" or autocratic rulers of their own kingdoms) that the presence of central management was despised (in keeping with the dynamics of the cognitive trinity).

At the executive level, the professors would come together as a council of equals (with some being more equal than others depending on their political alliances) to the extent that the experience of authority in the university as political became stronger than the central management ethos. There has been a continual tension between these two mindsets but the expression of authority in the highest corridors of University Councils and executive committees was decidedly more politically oriented in keeping Michels (1962) iron law of oligarchy (Cutting, 2001). As the political orientation has come out of the primary *menetype #B* spirit of belonging and order, the nature of such politics tended to be more that of consensus or collegiality[19] —but it did not have to remain that way. Entrepreneurial leadership by the Vice-Chancellor was not seen as appropriate because the professors had their academic freedom through the system of tenure and they were not inclined to follow a charismatic leader anywhere they did not want to go themselves. Executive governance in the university was principally an exercise of power and the Vice-Chancellor had diminished power over the tenured academics.

The shift from the *menetype #B* managerialist mindset to the *menetype #C* politicist mindset has been accompanied by an evolutionary shift in attitudes about the acceptable orientation of governance in organizations (Cutting, 2001; Cutting and Kouzmin, 2001a; 2001b).[20] An evolutionary shift in thinking is in the direction of cognitive regression, or in a clockwise direction around the phases of the trinity of *menetypes*. This shift has also been evident in university governance. Universities are still operating essentially to promote the good of the social sphere but there is a much greater responsiveness to the dynamics of the political sphere through everybody's desire to develop the "knowledge" nation. A greater shift has come about at the level of organizational governance. There has been a deliberate shift to mass tertiary education where it is more a matter to maximize justice so that everybody has a chance to participate rather than to maximize knowledge for its own sake.

As a consequence, the emphasis seems to have shifted from the culture sphere to the authority sphere as it has been seen as necessary for the executive to take charge to implement the substantial change being urged on them from the political sphere. It is no longer seen as paramount to create an academic way of doing things or to pursue knowledge of the truth for their own sake. It now seems more important for the executive to "manage" the university so as to maximize the value of their resources as any good corporate body would do. This translates to maximizing the number of students relative to the staff and other resources, which leads to an exercise of power in the decision-making process to abandon the pursuit of knowledge in those areas where there is not a sufficient market to pay for its dissemination.

Such decision-making is expressing judgments on the value of one academic area over another and, as such, are seen as political and short-sighted; sometimes done in the name of university survival and sometimes done purely as an exercise of power to favour some areas of study over others—or in favour of some professors, as individuals, over others. The spirit of collegiality has turned into a need to build alliances and power to protect one's position and so governance in the authority sphere has evolved to where the dynamics of the political phase are clearly dominant. Moreover, as the political orientation has taken hold in being the predominant mindset throughout the corporate life of the university, the leadership phase has begun to rise anew in secondary support. As a consequence, the calls for the vice-chancellors to become more like entrepreneurial leaders have become more prominent and the justification of academic tenure has been seriously undermined. The movement towards an open market for full-paying students including an increased reliance on foreign fee-paying students is exaggerating this move away from a focus on the university as an institution of knowledge seekers.

Universities Serving Individuals

Tertiary institutions are there to serve the "good" of the citizens and, therefore, will respond to the changing collective needs of individual participants. Individuals" societal thinking and active participation in Western capitalist democracies is focused principally on the economic sphere and so it is that the knowledge transmitted in the tertiary sector is essentially focused on enhancing the citizen's participation in the workforce. It is useful to round out this preliminary analysis of the governance of universities by looking at the way changing workforce needs are dictating the way universities operate or should operate. To generate some insight on how universities should approach the teaching of skills, knowledge and commitment it is helpful if each of the phases of society's education process is further differentiated from the perspective of the personal learning process.

From the perspective of the individual citizen, personal learning can be understood if differentiated into three phases of personal knowledge acquisition of increasing abstract quality; namely explicit knowledge, implicit knowledge and personal judgment. This trinity of personal learning is applicable to each of the education phases of skills, knowledge and commitment as follows (as depicted in Figure 7).

- *Explicit knowledge* (*menetype #A*) is that which can be transmitted overtly through the written or spoken word and embraces the cultivation of belief in manual instructions, a body of legitimatized knowledge or a code of behaviour (or codified decision limits).
- *Implicit knowledge* (*menetype #B*) is more abstract knowledge that is acquired by some inner process of assimilation to gain insight, understanding or meaning around the explicit knowledge (Polanyi, 1958; Nonaka and Takeuchi, 1995). It could embrace the acquisition of practical know-how from the master, intellectual insights from the spirit of inquiry or an appreciation of the unspoken mores of one's group.
- *Personal judgment* (*menetype #C*) is an even more abstract personal capability which embraces the weighing up of personally acquired explicit and implicit knowledge in light of one's experience of the particular situation to make a decision about what is possible, a judgment about what is logically true or an assessment about the reality of what is right or wrong.

There are a number of observations that follow from acknowledging the reality that these three inter-acting phases of personal learning constitute a *trinity of menetypes*,

- In the sense that explicit knowledge is the concrete accepted expression of knowledge or ordered information that is taken on as a belief from trusted external sources, it is like a consumer commodity that is picked up by the individual for particular applications. Explicit knowledge can therefore be mass marketed through the written word or formal coursework for large numbers. In contrast, implicit knowledge is a more intuitive expression of knowledge that is conveyed to the individual through a process that encourages personal appropriation of the rationale or meaning conveyed in the knowledge. Implicit knowledge requires a structured production process of learning such as supervised practical application to learn skills, structured problem solving to learn the process of scientific thinking or an induction process to grasp the mores of a particular group. Personal judgment is a more abstract personal art that can only be conveyed through a more sustained value-oriented (or feeling-oriented) state of being. There is a sort of infusion of this abstract knowledge into the individual and this is best achieved through a master-apprentice, professor-pupil type or mentoring type relationship.

- An individual would have great difficulty to trying to learn or take on all the three types of knowledge at the same time. There has to be an explicit or implicit choice to focus on acquiring a particular type of knowledge, which means eschewing one of the other forms of knowledge for the time being. For instance, to take on as much explicit knowledge as possible one would find it easier to avoid wasting time with the diffuse dialogue with a mentor but perhaps look to testing it out and acquiring some implicit knowledge along the way. To effectively inculcate implicit knowledge, it is necessary to consciously put to one side any thinking on the dictates of explicit theories or facts and go through the recommended cognitive processes while taking some notice of the mentor. When in a master-pupil relationship, it is necessary to suspend the formal, logical learning processes and to be ready to pick up on the way of thinking and the school of thought of the master while looking at how to order the explicit knowledge into such a world view.

- Given that it is necessary to focus on particular aspects of learning at different times, the sequence in which that occurs is cognitively significant. The sequence of cognitive procession is the way of indoctrination into a particular school of thought or group thinking. For instance, if the individual is first mentored about which beliefs are right or wrong and then on the conceptual framework of meaning that flows from the belief or conceptual system passed on by their mentor, it is natural that the individual would then take on the explicit knowledge that is helpful within that particular belief system and reject the rest as superfluous or irrelevant. The sequence of cognitive regression is the way to individuality and independent thinking or personal knowledge, which is likely to be in conflict with the personal knowledge of others. For instance, if one approaches the acquisition of explicit knowledge quite openly but puts it on intellectual hold while going through a process of learning how to learn by applying it to the explicit knowledge already acquired, one would be much more discerning about which advice of the mentor to take on and which to let slip by or be able to make a personal judgment of how much and how long to give oneself over to the influence of such a mentor. In reality there is always some oscillation between the learning processes of cognitive procession and reversion but it is easy to identify particular instances where one or the other has been predominant to produce a particular intent or result.

Managerialism captured the notion essentially associated with Taylorism (Taylor, 1996: 66-79) that the managers had to develop their thinking to understand the whole system and its interaction with the environment, while the workers could stay focused as an individual as long as they did what they were told by the managers. Growing corporations brought in new intellectual challenges for the top managers as they had to deal with multiple bureaucracies of production/administration or fiefdoms of autonomous power and they had to further develop their thinking to higher levels of abstraction. With this development, there was an accompanying politicization of the executive and management echelons of these corporations.[21]

In the new information or knowledge era, all managers are being asked to develop their thinking to higher levels of abstraction. Workers are required to develop their thinking as well because they are being asked to "manage" the automated or informational systems using essentially a similar cognitive-level thinking as managers used previously with people systems. Managers, in their turn, have to manage these new operators who are now managing systems in their minds as much as through the information systems and so the governance relationships become more personal and political. Similar to the political arena, then, "authority is located in the process of creating and articulating meaning, rather than in a particular position or function" (Zuboff, 1996: 559). To put it another way, managers are required to govern over a harmonious polity of "cognitive citizens" who need to be enthusiastic about being educated and about educating themselves—or in the rhetoric of the day, managers are required to be *coaches* to a *learning team*.

Some fifty years ago, Berle and Means (1991/1933), Burnham (1941) and Schumpeter (1950) were reporting the shift to a managerialist society. What is now being reported is a further evolutionary maturing of capitalism in the shift to a politicist society (Cutting, 2001; Cutting and Kouzmin, 2001c).[22] In keeping with the evolution of this age of politicism, the movement towards the *menetype #C* orientation has been replicated in the shift of what is now important in the individual participants' trinity of personal knowledge. The focus is clearly moving onto the personal judgment and commitment phase—or "just do it" as the slogan goes. Individuals and corporations are now encouraged to learn by committing themselves to the most appropriate strategy. If it does not work or if the situation changes, then do something different or, perhaps, change the persons involved, particularly if the individual's replacement is necessary for the power network to maintain its hold. When the focus has shifted to the commitment mode (as it has in this age of politicism), there is support from a secondary focus on the body of knowledge that is actually available to decide what would be the most useful to apply to the current situation. In this phase of continual decision and commitment, scant regard is paid to the impact of those decisions on the style or culture of the individuals or organizations (but rather whether the available knowledge is used to earlier and better effect than their rivals).

This focus on the *menetype #C* commitment phase of knowing or the ability to make decisions is the reason why it is seen as important by employers that the individuals are already largely educated, trained and competent before they are appointed. They need to be well versed in making decisions and going with it as well as being conversant with the range and depth of knowledge and technology available. In the current corporate decision-making milieu, it is regarded as less important to have a deep understanding of the knowledge detail of technology or associated processes, rather just how to use them. This lack of concern for the deeper knowledge of how it works or the processes that are necessary to work towards a desired outcome, is the Achilles" heel of the corporate executive and while it might not seem important in many circumstances, corporate executives should be encouraged to take time to learn, even though it essentially could be regarded just as some personal and group "cognitive slack."

This need for individuals to be well versed in operating in the commitment phase with a secondary grasp of how to make effective use of the available explicit knowledge has implications for the training and development of individuals aspiring to be corporate executives and/or members of the corporate boards. First and foremost, they need to be competent to make decisions in a political environment and in doing this they need to learn to be reasonable. Next, they need to acquire access to what knowledge is available and useful in their spheres of operation and so they need to learn how to be perceptive and discerning about what could be useful or not. Lastly, they need to have an understanding of the way people need to work together and the importance of corporate culture and to do this they need to learn to be intelligent.

And what is it that the community's leaders, or the elite "ruling class" (Mosca, 1939), do? "We must judge men of power by the standards of power, by what they do as decision-makers" (Mills, 1956: 286). However, (Mills 1956: 145) observes that those in the power elite do not invent their own ideas and avoid overt decision-making, but choose sound advisers to assist decision-making within the group. Therefore, in the shift to the managerialist corporations there has been a shift from personal decisions of a particular entrepreneur or their proxy to a group decision-making process where power is brought to bear to decide and commit to the most appropriate course of action.

Organizational dynamics have provided a learning experience in the past and will continue to be the principal place of learning, but now the individual is required to make a much greater inner cognitive effort to pull it together better and faster. The key is a personal desire to know and fuelled by this desire each individual needs to go on the journey of question and dialogue, both externally and internally—why, how, what, is that right? This is helped by new work situations as "when work becomes synonymous with responsiveness to data, it engenders inquiry and dialogue" (Zuboff, 1996: 555). However, it really calls for an understanding of how one knows and learns, particularly if the individual is required to coach others to more sophisticatedly appropriate personal understandings.[23]

Learning and contributing to a learning environment are now regarded as a core competence required of managers. "It would assume shared knowledge and collegial relationships" (Zuboff, 1988: 558). This is much akin to the operation of the higher education fraternity as they husband and develop their body of knowledge. It also categorizes a stable political-type environment where knowledge alliances are built up and there is mutual trust in the integrity of the knowledge shared—but always in a spirit of questioning and personally testing the relevance and usefulness of that knowledge. Organizations are still struggling to know how to provide such an environment and could really do with a hand up—and that does not mean the introduction of the next round of management fads being peddled by the stalking consultant set (Micklethwait & Wooldridge, 1996). But what is needed to help them get there?

Issues in Higher Education

In the light of the natural evolution of the community's governance thinking from the era of managerialism to the era of politicism, what can be made of the moves to:

- generate income by making education a commodity for purchase in the economic market place;
- democratize education by developing mass universities available to any in the community who qualify to attend; and
- generate income by developing commercial relationships with private industry.

In the light of the natural evolution of organizational governance from the managerialist mindset to the politicist mindset, what can be made of the moves to:

- amalgamate and reorganize universities into efficient economic corporations;
- redirect the research effort from pure science to technological innovation; and
- reorganize teaching methods to take advantage of the latest IT/ communications technology.

In the light of the natural evolution of personal governance and education needs of individuals in the workforce, what can be made of the moves to:

- provide access to life-time learning and market such opportunities to the workforce;
- tailor the learning experience to coincide and reinforce participation in the workforce; and
- meet the challenge of developing a knowledge community.

Education as an Economic Commodity

First, it would be inappropriate and counter productive to require higher education institutions to operate in the economic sphere like a private corporation. Not only would the educational institutions have organizational difficulty in making the adjustment to a mindset that had previously been their institutional shadow[24] but, more importantly, their contribution to the maintenance of a sound social fabric by educating the individuals as citizens first and as part of the workforce second. It is clear that private corporations in the economic sphere have looked naturally towards the social sphere (as its secondary cognitive perspective) for support in providing adequately equipped and ably trained citizens to participate in industry, and to provide intellectual assistance in overcoming particular problems, but private corporations have not really been looking for educational institutions to become one of them. For higher education "to become one of the natives," so as to speak, would, in effect, reduce the value of their external objective perspective to the corporate sector and derogate them to the status of just another conniving business consultant (Micklethwait and Woolridge, 1996).

Secondly, universities need financial resources to exist and so there has always been provision for charging fees. However, such fees are not primarily to make a profit but rather to fund the cost of the individual's membership and activity in the academic community, in much the same way as other institutions in the social sphere require membership fees (or donations). In some ways also, the fees served to sustain the existing social hierarchical stratification because even from the early days, the fees were set so high ostensibly to support the relatively high academic to student ratio, that only those social elite families who could afford the fees were able to send their members to universities. To require dependence on fees for their income and to stimulate an economic market for the provision of education, is to drive societal thinking to regard tertiary education as an economic commodity. Education is, in some respects akin to the provision of a service but the purchase of a learning experience is, in essence, different to the purchase of personal cleaning or valet services or an amusement experience. To the extent that the learning experience moulds and develops the individual's thinking at the organizational and societal levels, it is not private but rather there is a direct concern to the broader society. Moreover, this movement of thinking about education to the *menetype #A* perspective will heighten the focus on the *menetype #A* formation learning of skills and downplay the importance of the formation of personal commitment. This is a retrograde step for universities and downgrades their ability to contribute effectively to the formation of citizens, vocational groups and societal life in the social sphere.

Thirdly, the phenomenon of private corporations sponsoring their own universities is the logical end point of this movement of tertiary education from the social sphere to the economic sphere. It should be clear in these cases how the social sphere function of citizen formation has been usurped by the economic imperative which naturally gives the "McDonald's way of life and thinking" pre-eminence over the development of a healthy national community culture. To subject the educational spirit and ethos to the economic imperative is a cognitive distortion and undermines any concept of knowledge society or a learning nation. Learning then becomes more akin to indoctrination on how to act efficiently and effectively in accordance with the prescribed set of beliefs—without any question of whether those beliefs are sound and for the best, even for the individual let alone the society. As a consequence, creativity and innovation become very utilitarian. The effects of such a constricted learning experience would be akin to the restrictive experience of medieval learning when the church exercised control of all knowledge and learning.

Mass Universities

With the advent of the great advancements in technology, the operation of the community as a whole has required an increase in all citizens" capability to think at higher levels of abstraction. It is necessary and advantageous that that most people in the community are given the basic skills and knowledge to participate. The aspiration that "all Australians should have access to some form of post-secondary education" (West, 1998: 16), which repeats the earlier similar suggestion for Americans by the Carnegie Commission (Embling, 1974: 22), is a step forward for the nation in raising the general level of intellectual knowledge and capabilities of its citizens. However, the move to mass higher education necessarily alters the nature of that education. To cater for such numbers, the teaching knowledge naturally becomes focused on the more efficiently transmitted explicit knowledge and technological skills and this trend is exacerbated by the greater use of on-line education. The capacity for dialogue and mentoring interaction between educator and student is of necessity diminished. This, in turn, diminishes the opportunity for students to develop their critical thinking processes and their personal judgment/commitment frameworks within the higher university experience. The clear focus is on explicit knowledge acquisition which is recognized in the acquisition of an awarded degree that can be used as a commodity to gain employment—rather than regarding it as a learning experience to develop one's intellectual capabilities.

The encouragement for institutions to focus on efficiency and throughput, and to build a globally competitive higher education industry, also dilutes the potential learning experience offered by the institution. It is one thing to take on an international orientation to better educate the nation's citizens to operate in the more globalized economy. It is a completely different thing to be so driven by economic necessity to provide knowledge as a commodity to people of a different nation, language and culture that such foreign thinking students make up a substantial proportion of the total student population.25 This not only shifts the higher education more into the economic sphere but it also necessarily requires a principle focus on the explicit content of education and an avoidance of exercising the student's thinking at higher levels of intellectual reasoning because of the conflict and incompatibility of cultural thinking in the diverse student population. There is a conscious repression of debate about societal values and mores and so the student's personal judgment/commitment formation is stunted.

University curricula have been modified and expanded in a pragmatic way to attract more students into the system and to respond to the demands of the workforce dynamics. Coincident with this expansion of the curricula, the higher education has taken on a much more practical bent (courses in media, leisure and nursing) and a greater focus on skills development or vocational-related training at the expense of the pursuit of knowledge for its own sake—as witnessed by the demise of many science and humanities faculties because they are not able to attract sufficient students. This reinforces the emergence of a more economically-prosaic attitude in higher education and a greater concentration on marketable commodity of explicit knowledge. However, not all degrees so attained are necessarily good commodities, even in the job market.26 Nevertheless, there is the potential that the elevation of such practical-oriented courses to university status could lead to the intellectual development of the associated profession—as would seem to be happening in the case of nursing, where it seems only a matter of time before they are allowed to take on some of the role previously preserved for the exercise of doctors such as diagnosing and prescribing for low-level illnesses.

Commercial Subservience to Industry

There is no doubt that the whole of society benefits if private industry (in the *menetype #A* economic sphere) has access to the knowledge of the higher education institutions in the social sphere. This is not only of benefit in a practical sense, it is also in keeping with the people's cognitive appreciation of the order of things within a well-operating society. Private industry should benefit from their employees" education, from the knowledge and understanding that flows out of the higher education system and from the specialized advice that industry receives from particular academics. In fact it has been argued elsewhere (Cutting, 2001; Cutting and Kouzmin, 2001c), that large private corporations should be required to include more direct advice from the social sphere's higher educational sector in its corporate decision-making processes. However, this shift would only be positive from a societal perspective if the thinking and advice of the academic remained rooted and informed by the social sphere/learning ethos that is the prerogative of higher educational institutions. To the extent that the higher educational institutions go commercial and become partners for economic profit, their capacity to contribute to a healthy learning experience by the community is correspondingly diminished. It is helpful to partner industry in research projects where there is a joint interest in a particular field of study, but it is deleterious to the academic spirit to search for areas of research to establish partnerships as a matter of economic necessity.

It is also deleterious to run academic courses after the spirit of the economic market as has seemingly been done with the prolific expansion and charging for the Masters degrees in business administration, public administration and management. Many universities run the courses as a cash-generating business by charging what the market will bear and running it as marketably attractive and efficient as possible. The academic result is an overdue concentration on the explicit knowledge formulation (*menetype #A*), with a saturated program of management theories, techniques and facts with little serious focus on the development of the individual's rational thinking processes and values framework. Courses are so packed with information transfer and re-assembly that little time is left for the serious reflection and dialogue of issues of importance that might develop the individual's personal judgment/commitment capability—which, it would be argued, is the principal need of aspiring corporate leaders in today's politicist organizational governance regime. As a result, the demand for MBAs and MPAs are suffering or will suffer the same fate as any other mass-produced, similar-looking commodity that fails to satisfy the real hidden desire or need of the market place.

The closer partnership between higher education and industry has resulted in a trend to vocationalize the range and content of the academic courses to better prepare students participate in the workforce. As a consequence, the democratization of educational opportunity and the shift of higher education governance towards the economic imperative might seem very good to better equip the workforce of the future, but it has diminished its capacity to produce healthy independent thinkers as potential leaders of tomorrow's society. Some attention is needed on how potential leaders are to receive an adequate education of how to think in a way to extend society's knowledge in all respects and to develop their decision-making faculties in the more politicized nature of governance in all spheres of society. The fulfillment of this need would seem to fly in the face of the so-called democratic trend to efficient mass universities but there is a need to maintain some elite universities that provide the face-to-face academic environment and personal experience (as suggested by Keohane (1999, 63), invoking Trow. That is, the universities still need to be allowed to perform their social sphere contribution to society's hierarchically-structured leadership formation which, of course, will be seen as contributing to sustaining the economic divide between the haves and the have nots— because only the haves will be able to afford the relatively high fees set by the economic market place for education. Perhaps, the high membership fees for the more elite higher education stream will continue to operate as they did in the past when they were more a means to sustain the social hierarchical divide rather than merely set in response to the economic marketplace.

The acknowledgement of the value for lifetime learning is also a somewhat rudimentary societal response to this need for individuals to have more access to the means of personal judgment/commitment formation. However, the concept of lifetime learning has to be developed into something more than merely helping participants in the workforce to keep up with technology, to retrain to change careers or to provide an interesting leisure diversion but, rather, there is needed a focus on educating the person to think in better ways and to develop the capacity to contribute effectively to the governance of others. Otherwise, the individual's personal judgment/commitment formation at the higher levels of abstract thinking will be left to the corporate processes of on-the-job training which, of course, would be necessarily constrained. It has been argued elsewhere (Cutting, 2001; Cutting and Kouzmin, 2001c) that corporations need help in the formal continuing education of their aspiring executive leaders.

Changes in Organizational Governance

First, as explained above, higher education institutions have been subject to the same shift in governance mindsets as others in the Western society; namely a shift from the managerialist mindset to the politicist perspective. It could be argued that the governance in tertiary institutions has long been more political than managerial and is partly the reason why the academic institutions" executives now seem much readier to embrace the next movement to entrepreneurial activities as a secondary support to bolster their political power vis-à-vis the professors in their fiefdoms. This political organizational environment has been enhanced where there has been institutional amalgamations and has been the underlying rationale of some brutal internal restructuring—which, in turn, re-entrenches the political style of authority. Their long-time practice of decision-making through the political orientation of governance puts the higher education institutions in a good position to play a more significant role in society's political and economic decision-making—again, this would only be productive as long as academics remain essentially true to the social sphere's academic mindset. It would be helpful to society for the academics to take a lead in promoting a rational political/economic debate on the value, truth and good of the particular directions that are being taken in knowledge and technology.

Secondly, there is conscious acknowledgment and support for the political decision-making processes of higher education institutions. Such processes are generally well-defined with constitutions, governing boards and plenty of committees at all levels to stimulate, interpret and streamline the internal political dialogue on the many governance issues. Moreover, such education institutions are, in the main, like private corporations of moderate size in that they are large, well-resourced and well-capitalized organizations that need to balance external environmental pressures and internal organizational imperatives. Keen judgment and wise commitment is called for in the decision-making process. Therefore, universities are well positioned to be role models and mentors to the large private and public organizations on how to provide for and conduct the politicized corporate decision-making processes in an appropriate and effective way. To do this, universities themselves need to go about their business of corporate governance in a conscious, open and publicly accountable way. In particular, they need to demonstrate and proclaim how all stakeholder interests can be taken into account in the corporate political dialogue, reflection and decision-making in a reasonable, appropriate and accountable manner. This would be a tremendous gift to the proper governance of society and could be a particular help to private sector corporations that are globalized and operating at the highest levels of abstract practical reasoning in their politicist decision-making processes but have not yet consciously developed the appropriate processes to recognise and build on this political orientation (Cutting, 2001, Cutting and Kouzmin, 2001c). Moreover, a more open acknowledgment of this expertise of orderly politicized corporate decision-making could see academics as a more attractive addition to private sector corporate boards, where they could effectively promote the interests of the social sphere of society (Cutting, 2001).

Thirdly, the more conscious political orientation of university decision-making has seen the rise of the secondary entrepreneurial spirit. This has found expression in the call for universities to develop a vision and mission statements and for more leadership from the Vice-Chancellor. Such leadership is still to be contained within, and subject to, the political milieu of institutional executive decision making rather than treating the university as their own kingdom after the manner of the early capitalist entrepreneurs. This would raise the danger that the entrepreneurial leader might get too caught up in the spirit of economic entrepreneurship and take the university too far down the commercial corporation route with the inevitable undermining of the institution's academic culture. The other danger, of course, in the politicist mindset is that the Vice-Chancellor (or Chancellor as has happened in some cases) is not inspired by a grand vision for the university but is merely accumulating such political power to their office that they are tempted to assume almost despotic political powers which then evoke the predictable and understandable reaction and eventual rejection. This is particularly evident where dramatic reorganizations are embarked upon or even the inevitable re-reorganizations as the university organization tries unsuccessfully to be all things at once.

Knowledge Creation Processes

First, new knowledge of truth is born of the spirit of inquiry, dialogue and reflection. Technological innovation is born more out of the application of the knowledge of truth through the entrepreneurial energy and opportunity, creativity and risk. Pure knowledge creation has been more the product of formal university-promoted processes of scholarship and technological innovation of formal government and industrial research processes. Then there are the serendipity inventions discovered by the creativity of individuals. The advancement of knowledge by the academic process of scholarly publication has long been characterized by the *menetype #B* spirit of probing the understanding of the parts with the oversight support of the *menetype #C* network of colleagues with their unwritten tacit mores of acceptance or rejection. The prevalence and perhaps dominance sometimes of the *menetype #C* political spirit has entrenched the protection of particular schools of thought to the exclusion of the fresh cross-discipline flow of ideas. This system of academic networks within disciplines has worked well to encourage and nurture many fledgling academics to advance through their careers but have excluded others who do not seemingly fit in. The nature of this system of academic dialogue could be transformed in particular by the move to market-oriented education and research and the impact of the much more powerful communications capability offered by the internet and successive technology. There is more room now for the intellectual entrepreneur to create and acclaim their own new intellectual product and capitalise on it in terms of commercial profitability or simply the acclaim of fellow citizens. This will shift the value and importance for academics from the cultivation of their networks of academic colleagues to the creative marketing of their new ideas. This will have a profound effect on the nature and direction of the dialogue on new ideas.

The trend to regard both tertiary education and new ideas as commodities is resulting in technological innovation being valued over pure knowledge with the consequence that the notion of Intellectual Property is displacing the spirit of free academic dialogue. It is therefore difficult to see how cash-strapped universities will continue to support their academics financially while they produce scholarly papers and intellectual property that is then made freely available to others who work in institutions that are competing with each other to attract students and industry's research dollars. The notion of a return on this intellectual capital is growing and is predominant where the pursuit of useful technological knowledge has pre-eminence over the pursuit of the knowledge of truth for its own sake. One obvious response in keeping with this trend is the Australian funding of coordinated research centres that are subject more to rules of commercial intellectual property than the free dialogue on new ideas characteristic of academic networks.

There is the pressure or trend to conduct the academic dialogue via the freely available Internet rather than the refereed academic journals. At first blush, this trend towards a seemingly free inter-change of ideas on the Internet might seem to run counter to the trend of protecting and capitalizing on the individual academic's intellectual property. However, on further reflection the trends can be seen to mutually supporting, as through the use of the Internet rather than the academic journals, the individual academic retains control and commercial power over the presentation and dissemination of their new knowledge. Therefore academics are becoming more commercially discerning about how they handle new knowledge and more effort will go into creativity and attractiveness of marketing rather than the need to establish the refereed bona fides of the new knowledge. The acceptance of this trend to use the Internet as a publishing medium is underwritten by the general shift from the managerialist to the politicist mindset, which debunks the pursuit of the absolute truth in favour of accepting the reality of particular knowledge applicable to a particular situation. That is, scientific rigour is no longer the criterion of accepting knew knowledge but, rather, it is whether it fits the particular reality and is useful (economically, in the main). In summary, the scholarly discipline of the academic networks are likely to shift their attention from nurturing the advancement of the body of knowledge to having more of a focus on collaborating to capitalize on the marketability of their shared intellectual property. Thus, again, the economic imperative is supplanting the social endeavour and specific initiatives are necessary to arrest this nugatory direction of tertiary education policy so as to require universities to retain some influence in moulding the society's social sphere thinking in a constructive way.

Institutional Impact of New Technology

Teaching in tertiary education has traditionally been face to face or, more accurately, one face to many. For some time now, distance education has been conducted successfully and more recently there has been the advent of on-line education which is guaranteed to grow and perhaps become the dominant mode, at least for the adult workforce with pressing needs for ongoing training and little time and availability to do it on campus. The use of IT and communications technology substantially depersonalizes the learning experience. As a consequence, the focus of education necessarily is re-oriented towards explicit knowledge formation, its capture and manipulation for particular gain. There is an abundance of explicit knowledge transferred and so the individual is taught the skills to access the relevant information and to use it to best effect in particular situations. In effect, the process of learning becomes more skewed towards knowledge identification and manipulation rather than knowledge discovery through the hard inner intellectual work of cognitive regression. The questions have changed from why and how to what and who; the dialogue has been refocused from the wonder of discovery to the excitement of application and the mobile phone and continuous availability ensure there is no time put aside for reflection. However, it is conceivable that coursework based on sophisticated IT software and a limited amount of face-to-face contact, could stimulate the individual to develop their powers on intellectual regression but it is unlikely to be the main aim or outcome of the course. In particular, it would be difficult to conduct a socialization of the individual's personal judgment and commitment except perhaps to a limited extent through some business modeling or gaming software—but then only if there is some effective means of debriefing with real people. It would seem, therefore, that higher education will become more and more focussed on the *menetype #A* technological skills and explicit knowledge. Again, this might be great for educating the mass workforce but it is not helping much in personal formation that is so necessary to the leaders of the future.

The logical end-point of the university's use of powerful communication technology is to move all higher education on-line so that university campuses are no longer needed—students can study from home or work and even use the Internet chat rooms or interactive digital TV to substitute for tutorials. This would seem equivalent to yester-year's concept of the paperless office which has been a long time coming and may never be wholly true, but it is likely to progress far enough to reap the consequences. In such a distributed educational institution, the transmission of knowledge and the practice of critical thinking may be more efficient but organizational and personal governance will be less cognitively effective as it will be focused more on externalities and explicit measurables. Moreover, the experience of group learning processes will also be diminished. The ability for the individual to think effectively at the group and societal level will have to be learnt elsewhere, either at the workplace or in social groups. If the student is not called to think at the group level in an effective way within their university education, then it is going to be more difficult for the individual to think consciously at the societal level. The effectiveness of the university educating the individual in the social sphere thinking will therefore be greatly diminished. The nature and quality of life-time learning opportunities will take on much more importance in the education of society's future leaders. If some group educational opportunities are not sustained or provided within the tertiary education system (to identify with a university as an identified group of people rather than a main server), then there will be an inevitable fracturing of society and make it much easier for those who do happen to attain leadership positions to exercise power over all the other more mass-thinking but intellectually isolated individuals of the community.

This form of isolated on-line learning would appeal to the preferred style of learning of some but not others. It would probably be effective for those individuals (essentially *type #B* oriented) who naturally internalize their world and readily question what they perceive against their conceptual framework and, in so doing, exercise their powers of intellectual reversion. Such logical thinking people will readily assimilate the knowledge and enhance their powers of critical abstract thinking. However, these are the very people who would probably most need to develop their personal interactive skills and their ability to reach personal judgments and commit to particular courses of action under pressure of group interaction with other people. Their ability to make it in the world would be severely hampered by the lack of such opportunities in their tertiary education.

Another set of individuals (essentially *type #A* oriented) would consciously miss the human interaction and real-life dialogue because they actually need such discursive interaction and argument to help come to grips with the key principles and their applications. To help such oral-discursive people the on-line problems would have to be particularly creative and allow for substantial interaction to allow the individual to argue their case. The other (*type #C* oriented) individuals would have even more difficulty in picking up on a logically- ordered explanation of seemingly irrelevantly detailed knowledge. The biggest challenge with such individuals is to avoid boredom as they much prefer action or things happening around them. They will tend to concentrate on developing their awareness of the range of knowledge available and the skill to identify and retrieve the relevant usable knowledge. They will work out how to use it as a resource and how it can be harnessed to enhance one's position and power.

Given that general societal- and organizational-level thinking have moved more to the *menetype #C* politicist mindset, it is clear that this latter aspect of knowledge identification, dissemination and use is becoming the most important attribute for aspiring executives to acquire. Further, as a result of the distributed mode of learning the acquisition of such skills is becoming very utilitarian and peculiar to the particular needs of the individual rather than, say, what the education system thinks is important. This seems to be a real "divide and conquer" policy direction which will enhance the power of the corporate political bosses who rule over an ever more fragmented workforce (in the same way as feudal lords ruled over a very geographically-fragmented fiefdoms).

Life-Time Learning

As alluded to above, it is helpful to discuss life-time learning in terms of the on-going educational needs of the aspiring corporate executives and board members in the more *menetype #C* politicized corporate world. It is of primary importance that the individual is a practical decision-maker at the strategic level for the corporation. They need to see the reality of the situation that the corporation is in, recognize the problems and the challenges and have some appreciation for what is required to put the corporation in the right position to survive and flourish. The skills are those that Porter (1995) associates with the need to focus on developing the corporation's competitive positioning strategy by scanning the environment (in terms of the Five Forces model) to assess the threat of new entrants, threat of substitutes, bargaining power of buyers and bargaining power of suppliers (Porter, 1995: 87). This is an essentially *menetype #C* approach to developing corporate strategic intent and is the reason that Porter's ideas have been so successful and popular with practitioners.[27] Secondary in support, they need to be innovative in seeing the opportunities inherent in the corporation's competitive situation.

This is a practical knowledge at a very high level of cognitive abstraction or complexity that comes essentially from the doing and giving it a try, but they need to have this competence when they are actually appointed to the corporate board. "Most people do not score very high on cognitive complexity. They may act in complex ways, but they are typically led—and argue that they lead themselves—by a few dominant ideas" (Golembiewski, 1989: 91). Potential corporate executives and board members need to develop their thinking to handle practical decision-making in highly abstract and complex issues. This can only be done through practice and so needs to be built mainly into the individual's career experience of dealing with similar issues but at lower levels of complexity. This is why there is pressure for the lower levels of the corporation to reflect the same power dynamics (*menetype #C*) as the top. For instance, it would be helpful if the individuals had a chance to serve on organizational boards at the lower divisional levels of the corporation (Cutting, 2001; Cutting and Kouzmin, 2001c).

Of continual concern is the need to develop the individual's capacity to think through issues logically because the immediate relevance and pay-off may not seem to be there—because reward goes to decisions that are practical and are seen to work rather than what is the continuation of a logical process that may or may not be relevant. Thus there is a need to acknowledge that individuals each need to build up some "cognitive slack" by acquainting themselves with some of the detail of how things work. This is achieved by a combination of personal analysis, on-the-job training and the continuing use of formal education.

Post-Graduate Management Training

Individuals need to be well practiced in the particular style or culture that is in play at the corporate-executive level; namely the political collaborative approach (*menetype #C*) of working in networks. This requires an acknowledgment of the essentially political nature of the decision-making process, an admission of the importance for the individuals to develop and practice their political skills and that support structures are put in place to help them do that. The practice of mentoring is an obvious mechanism in this regard but there needs to be a more overt acknowledgment of what it is about and that it can be a primary mechanism for the individual to be actually introduced into the networks that matter.

At the secondary support level the individual needs to develop market-oriented creative capabilities and this continues to be best done by placing the individuals in organization leadership positions that offer the necessary autonomy and commercial challenges that demand an entrepreneurial approach. Managers would benefit from some coaching on how to be more effective entrepreneurial leaders—principally, on how to cultivate and develop followers to provide effective support in their commercial endeavours and, then, how to be able to coach these followers to enhance their capacity to think at higher levels of complexity.

While developing these necessary strengths it is also important for the individual to recognize the value and place of using a regimented approach in hierarchies (because the practice and value of thinking in these terms has been repressed in the move to the more practical, politicized *menetype #C* mindset). The development of an understanding of the logical, hierarchical orientation could be regarded as irrelevant to the prevailing management culture and it thus needs to be promoted in the sense of building in some "cognitive slack." The hierarchical approach has had primary relevance and value in physical production processes but it will also make a future comeback in the increasing need for order and regimentation of the Internet or communication equivalent of tomorrow. Protocols and procedures for use of these seemingly infinite information channels will become more and more important as there is an increasing focus on the efficiency and security of use.

Learning in a Learning Organization

The type of knowledge-creation skill that is most valued in the world of practical decision-making (*menetype #C*) is practical know-how—that is; the learning that comes from the doing. What is required is a grasp of those aspects of the vast reservoir of knowledge that are most appropriate in the particular circumstances and how that knowledge could best be used. This is a cognitive approach that requires a continual assessment of whether a particular approach or process is working or getting the desired results and if it is not then doing something else that fits the circumstances better. This is done by lining up the menu of available options against what might have worked well or not in similar past experiences or by simply taking advice from somebody they trusted to know what to do in these particular circumstances. Thus, the learning of the individuals comes primarily from the relevance and challenging complexity of their career positions on the way up. This on-the-job learning could be enhanced by greater conscious dialoguing on the lessons of their experience either with a mentor or by deliberately building in some dialogue or *evaluation slack* into the organizational processes.

The knowledge-creation skill requires the individuals to be more pro-active rather than reactive in the selection of novel ways of employing the available knowledge. Cognitively, this involves some more innovative thinking and rather than going with what worked or what would work better than last time, the individual needs to envision something different—or call on somebody who can. Learning in this case would be to practice the art of imagining better futures or empathizing with what others would think as being a better world, such as what would the consumers be impressed with or what would inspire the admiration of other corporate executives. In essence, the individuals should try and show themselves to be a bit more of a practical leader by having followers who actually believe in them and their capacity to find a better way.

There is also a challenge to keep in mind why something works or why it would be better, because there is a tendency to repress this aspect of knowing. The wane in industrial and academic support for pure science reflects the necessary repression of the reasoning or "know why" orientation to knowledge creation to make way for the vocational aspects; or the doing it. There is a need for individuals to push against this apathy towards pure reasoning and take some opportunities to think logically through the reasons why something works or should work. It is a necessary part of learning if the individual wants to truly be able to think at higher levels of complexity and abstraction and not just operate out of half-understood ideas.

The above analysis of the learning needs of corporate executives and board members suggest a few critical mechanisms that need to be put in place, such as the following.

- Corporations should openly acknowledge that individuals need to develop skills in political decision-making and put in place organizational processes to aid the learning -such as value-based management; lower-level subsidiary corporate boards; realistic mentor programs; and in-house training that simulates decision-making in the real world.
- The higher education sector should develop on-going executive learning packages that focus more on the know-how aspect of knowledge and use teaching methods that convey such practical knowledge more effectively. This would mean more experiential training in realistic simulations of the corporate decision-making world geared to raise the individual's capacity to think at higher levels of complexity and abstraction. This means that there has to be some working through the logic of why things are or why they work but in a supporting role to the main focus on increasing capacity for practical thinking (as opposed to the way formal education has made the teaching of logical systems, processes and methods the core of management education).

• Corporate boards can stimulate continued learning (and the corporation) by designing processes that require managers to extend beyond the reactive practical thinking (*menetype #C*) as encompassed in the normal board consideration of CEO proposals. There is a need for an on-going dialogue that encourages managers to focus their thinking more in the innovative mode (*menetype #A*). This would be achieved by requiring managers to champion new policy initiatives within the context of board deliberations. Group and personal learning could also be stimulated by exercises that simulated a corporate board confrontation with realistic scenarios as suggested earlier (De Geus, 1997; Cutting, 2001; Cutting and Kouzmin, 2001c).

This learning on the job, so as so speak, or individual experiential education is offered in contrast to the "school for directors" (Ward, 1997: 181: Dror, 1971: 2, 218), which is often recommended at the end of the day for one sector or another of the power elite.[28] Such schools would only serve their purpose if focused on teaching individuals how to think at higher levels of abstraction and complexity (and how to lead others to do likewise), rather than the traditional effort to convey a body of explicit knowledge. Certainly, there is a need for something like a Master of Governance to replace the Master of Business Administration (Cutting, 20001). That is, the learning should be a combination of both individual and group that takes place within the corporate or industry setting; as far as is practical. However, the content and delivery should be guided by the spirit of the tertiary education sector (within the society's social sphere), rather than be sponsored by the individual commercial organization (such as McDonalds) in the economic sphere.

Conclusion

Society thinking is shifting, organization thinking is shifting and individual thinking is shifting in perceptibly patterned ways. The thinking about tertiary education in society needs also to change but it needs to shift in ways that are supportive rather than blindlessly mimicking what organizations in other sectors are doing well. It would seem that the trend to become commercialized mass-universities seems to run counter to what is actually required of the social sphere-oriented universities in the wholesale shift of societal thinking from "managerialism" to "politicizm"—where there is now greater preference for the more politicized *menetype #C*—oriented approach to governance of society and organizations within it.

In essence, while there is a need for many to be better educated, it should not be at the expense of diminishing the capacity of the tertiary education sector to grow society's leaders of the future. The over-whelming conclusion of the analysis of this paper is that, perhaps, at this time, more than ever, there needs to be a consciously accepted hierarchy within the tertiary education sector?—not the mass flattening out that Australia has experienced in the recent past. There needs to be a greater focus on the development of tomorrow's leaders by educating them better in the more appropriate and useful ways to consider and make decisions and to be able to coach others in doing likewise.

This call to focus on more personalized, quality education within the all-encompassing move to mass higher education, could seem to run counter to the so-called spirit of democratization and smack of elitism. However, society, and all that have preceded, speaks of the need for effective leadership and some degree of cohesion if there is to be maintenance of effective governance. Universities have in the past, and more than ever today, been called upon to contribute to society by not only nurturing and propagating knowledge, but also by growing and moulding the leaders of tomorrow— and then assisting them in the life-time need for continual self- and group-development.

In short, there is a need for the tertiary education sector to focus on the qualitative needs of effective governance and not just on the quantitative needs of supplying a competently-trained workforce for the new, more advanced technological society. Finally, there needs to be a consciously modelled effective governance (in the emerging, more politicized spirit of politicism) in order to achieve the necessary social standing to be effective intellectual leaders in the new knowledge society.

Notes

1. The basic insights on the philosophy of mind and human governance that underpin such a philosophical framework are as follows. First, all human affairs and the experience of those affairs at each of the levels of the individual, the group and the society have their genesis and fulfillment in the human mind. In particular, an organization is such only because the participating individuals are able to think of it in such a way.

    Secondly, any view of reality is only ever a partial view and the power of that partial view in experiencing, understanding and knowing that particular reality, is critically dependent on the cognitive framework employed by the individual. It is argued elsewhere (Cutting and Kouzmin, 2001b) that human intellectual power comes from the way one is able to structure one's reality in terms of hierarchical trinities of differentiated perspectives, each ordered in terms of their respective level of abstraction. In such a way, one is able to think of an organization or a society basically in the same way as one thinks of an individual, except that the thinking is at higher levels of abstraction.

    Thirdly, humans have the capability to think in any of all possible ways, as the limits of their potential to know are infinite (Proclus, 1963: 149). However, if one tries to think of all perspectives at once, one would be pulled in all directions and so get nowhere—and probably be overwhelmed. Differentiation and choice is the key. One chooses a particular perspective, and in so doing, other conflicting perspectives need to be consciously repressed. Through constant use over time (namely, because it works for the individual), the dynamic of this predominant cognitive perspective makes for the development of one's personality. In a similar way, but at a higher level of abstract thinking, individuals also consciously or unconsciously take on a cognitive orientation in the development of their concept of organization and society and the result of this is their perceived culture.

    With each separate character (or culture) that is manifest in an individual, organization or society, comes a patterned set of perspectives, motivations and predictable ways of behaving. This is well captured in the explanatory dynamics of the Enneagram (Riso, 1987; Palmer, 1991) and Jungian (Jung, 1971; von Franz and Hillman, 1971; Myers, 1980) typologies as understood in the terms of the insights provided by the synthesised philosophy of mind identified and employed by the authors (Cutting, 2001, Cutting and Kouzmin, 2001b).

2. The explanatory power of a system of cognitive differentiation has been captured in a philosophical conceptual framework, which can be explained (Cutting, 2001; Cutting and Kouzmin, 2001a) in terms of a trinitarian hierarchy of *menetypes* (i.e., "numbered" *ideal types* that are ordered within their group) that interact together to give way to the concept of something more (the fourth, or something beyond the particular trinity of focus). The order within any trinity of these *menetypes* can be understood as follows (as depicted in Figure 1):

- *Menetype #A*—the first level of cognitive abstraction capturing the externally oriented, concrete perspective.
- *Menetype #B*—the second level of cognitive abstraction capturing the internally oriented, imaginative perspective.
- *Menetype #C*—the third level of cognitive abstraction capturing the prescinded perspective that can be some kind of compromise between the dialogue of the other two perspectives, but can more gainfully lead to transcending the particular conflict and rising to a new level of understanding.
- *Menetype #D*—the other, capturing all that has not been made conscious in the patterns of the three principle perspectives of the trinity, including that which is more than (or operating at higher or lower levels of abstraction than that of the particular trinity).

The value-added in recognizing the existence or manifestation of a hierarchy of such trinities of *menetypes* is that the human mind processes thinking about them in a particular way that can be defined and predicted. The principles and dynamics of the hierarchy of such trinities of abstraction are explored elsewhere (Cutting, 2001, Cutting and Kouzmin, 2001b), but the essential aspects can be summarized as follows—which perhaps can be understood by thinking about the oft-used (Thompson et al, 1991; Kooiman, 1993; Rhodes, 1997) trinity of markets (*menetype #A*), hierarchies (*menetype #B*) and networks (*menetype #C*) in reference to Figure 1.

> It is not possible to think at all three levels at once as they take the mind in essentially different directions. There is normally then a focus on a particular cognitive orientation. Focus on a particular perspective or *menetype* cognitively defines the secondary *menetype* as the next highest level of abstraction (in the sequence #A-#B-#C-#A etc.) and the third *menetype* thinking is cognitively repressed.

> There is much meaning in the direction and movement of thinking between the three *menetypes*. In particular, there is the dynamic of cognitive reversion (going against the arrow in Figure 1) or evolutionary, inner-directed learning, the dynamic of cognitive procession (with the arrow) or revolutionary, externally-directed learning, and the process of combining both dynamics.

> The outcome, manifestation and evolutionary change of phenomena and the way one thinks about them, need to be understood holistically in terms of not only the conscious structure and dynamics of the trinities of

abstraction, but also the unconscious other that is also operating in a similar but complementary manner.

It should be emphasized that this is not the first time this type of approach to sociological analysis has been used. For instance, Mooney (1947) used such an approach based on the hierarchy of trinities in his classic, *The Principles of Organization*. More recently, Handy (1978) also essentially captured the manifestation of this line of thinking in his *Gods of Management*. For his understanding, he drew on work inspired by the 19th century philosopher, Hamilton (1859). Hamilton grasped the significance of the trinitarian mode of analysis from that used by Aquinas (1952) and other Scholastic philosophers. Of course, like seemingly most other ideas, this thinking had its origins in Plato and Aristotle but was most clearly enunciated in the writings of the two Neoplatonists, Plotinus (1952) and Proclus (1963). This trinitarian structure of analysis has also been used intuitively by many other great thinkers over the intervening centuries. Weber (1949; 1962), in particular, could be said to have used such a conceptual framework to great effect to underpin and inform his employment of sociological analysis. Weber's (1949; 1962) trinity of "authority types" (charismatic, rational-legal and traditional) is well known, but the concept of an inter-related three factors or aspects seems not to be used to good effect in many other areas of his work. Hegel (1952) also framed much of his analysis and discussion in the trinitarian framework, as exemplified by the structuring his analysis of the *Philosophy of Right* in terms of a hierarchy of trinities.

3. "Aristotle adopted Plato's famous principle, 'the state is the soul writ large,' and 'the soul is the state writ small.' In our contemporary context, we would say that a culture sets the conditions for developing the character of its people, or a culture is the people writ large . . . Plato and Aristotle were both aware of this mutual relation between particular souls and their social order. Plato's famous maxim that the state is the soul writ large also implies that the soul is the state writ small. The social order does not necessarily determine the character of its members, but it certainly does set the conditions and disposes them to behave in socially approved and disapproved ways" (Flanagan, 1997: 202; 211).

    As Boulding (1993:188) observed, "Another important artefact consists of organizations—families, corporations, churches, states, professional societies and so on. These exist primarily as images in peoples' heads, though they may be embodied in part in buildings, homes, or in documents and charters, even though these are important mainly as symbols and evidence of the existence of the organization in the minds of people. The 49th parallel is quite invisible from outer space and exists only in the minds of humans as a boundary. . . . Similarly, a corporation exists only in the minds of humans in a common belief in its existence, the evidence of which may also be embodied in charters and legal documents, shares of stock, bonds and so on. A share of stock is not the paper it is written on, but is a belief in the minds of the right people that governs their images of the future and their behaviour and decisions."

4. It is also worth noting, at this stage, that while thinking at the level of society represents the highest level of abstraction in the intellect, there is a whole higher level which has been called the spirit of man. The workings of the spirit sphere of the mind is beyond the workings of the intellect (which encompasses the cognitive

operations of perceiving, understanding and reasoning to reach conscious
commitment) and dwells on higher things in different, even more abstract ways. It
is in accordance with the principle of cognitive procession (Cutting and Kouzmin,
2001a) that spiritual beliefs have the power to influence and frame the thinking in
the intellect about society, the group and the individual. In these terms it can be
seen how astute and correct Weber (1930) was to focus on the way man's changing
spiritual values helped frame the development of the modern capitalist society.
After the same manner, an individual's thinking at the higher level of abstraction
that treats society as a single entity, in its turn, affects the individual's way of
thinking at the organizational and personal levels.

   Miller (1969: 275) quotes the historian Edward P. Cheney as saying, "These
great changes (the Protestant Reformation, the American Revolution and the
development of parliamentary government) seem to have come about with a certain
inevitableness; there seems to have been an independent trend of events, some
inexorable necessity controlling the progress of human affairs." The "inexorable
necessity" driving human affairs has been termed as the collective unconscious and
is the thinking of individuals at the level of society, albeit in an unconscious way
for the vast majority.

5. Aquinas (1952) discusses this point in terms that when talking about, say, a lot of
   people who are of course different, the human mind does not think of all the
   separate individuals at once but thinks of them as a collective of one species,
   understood as one intelligible entity.

> From this it is evident that many things, in so far as they are distinct,
> cannot be understood at the same time; but in so far as they are joined
> under one intelligible aspect, they can be understood together. Now
> everything is actually intelligible according as its likeness is in the intellect.
> All things, then, which can be known by one intelligible species, are
> known as one intelligible thing and, therefore, are understood
> simultaneously. But things known by various intelligible species are
> apprehended as different intelligible things. . . . The intellect can, indeed,
> understand many things as one, but not as many; that is to say, by one but
> not by many intelligible species. . . . Therefore it is impossible for one
> and the same intellect to be perfected at the same time by different
> intelligible species so as actually to understand different things. . . .
>
> But a man is the master of a free subject by directing him either towards
> his proper welfare or to the common good . . . first, man is naturally a
> social animal and so in the state of innocence he would have led a social
> life. Now a social life cannot exist among a number of people unless
> under the headship of one to look after the common good; for many, as
> such, seek many things, but one attends only to one. . . .
>
> It is impossible for one man's will to be directed at the same time to
> diverse things, as to so many last ends. . . . Therefore, just as of all men
> there is naturally one last end, so the will of an individual must be fixed
> on one last end (Aquinas, 1952; 301, 457; 513; 613).

6. There are three insights that can be interpolated from an understanding of the cognitive dynamics associated with capturing the thinking about the individual, the organization and the society in terms of a trinity of *menetypes*.

First, one's commitment to a particular concept of society flows readily and involuntarily into framing one's conceptions of how an organization should be and then how one personally should be (in keeping with the concept of cognitive procession explained in Cutting and Kouzmin (2001b) and as depicted by going with the arrows in Figure 3). It does not work so easily going in reverse (i.e., going against the arrow in Figure 3), where one has to labour under cognitive tension to question what is this so-called organization one is experiencing in the light of one's knowledge of the individuals who make up that organizations and so on to conceive of the truth of the society in light of one's knowledge of the individuals and organizations of which it is comprised.

"It is Max Weber's contention that although social science is value-neutral, values embraced by a society are themselves criteria which indicate what issues are relevant to a particular form of human associated life during a certain historical period. . . . The so-called science of organization, as we now know it, is entrapped within the unchallenged assumptions derived from, and reflective of, the market-centered economy. . . . As Adam Smith acknowledges, the market society necessarily transforms the individual into a job holder: 'Where the division of labor has been once established,' he says 'every man lives by exchanging, or becomes in some measure a merchant, and the society itself grows to be what is properly a commercial society'" (Ramos, 1981: 24-25; 73; 89). This is put the other way around in Sutton (1993: 8, quoting Worthy), "Governance . . . is concerned largely, though . . . not exclusively, with relating the corporation to the institutional environment within which it functions." That institutional environment is principally the society within which it operates and institutions will have different cognitive orientations in different societies.

Secondly, no individual can think at all three levels at once. There is an irreconcilable cognitive tension when trying to inform a line of thinking with the three countervailing perspectives of being simultaneously an individual, a member of an organization and a member of a society. For instance, what one needs to do to survive as an individual may be in conflict with the loyalties owed as a member of an organization or with the responsibilities of being a good citizen (i.e., when one either emigrates or sacrifices one's needs in subjugation to the needs of the state). One, therefore, chooses to accord an importance in thinking at one particular level of the individual, the group or the society and that determines how important one holds thinking at the other two levels—namely, the next highest level is secondary and the lower level is consciously repressed. For instance, the so-called "company man" focuses thinking at the level of the group. Consequently, it is relatively easy for him to see what the organization needs to be doing as a good corporate citizen but he is not so prepared to focus on what he should be doing to be a balanced, healthy individual himself (because he tends to repress the thinking of himself as an individual human with his own personal/individual needs and aspirations).

Thirdly, there are similar subsets of cognitive trinities supporting each of the three levels of abstractive thinking. Essentially, one tends to think of each of the individual, the organization and the society as though they were a unit or a real individual. One is inclined to say that the organization did this or that the nation did that and, even, personal characteristics are attributed to them, such as referring to the organization as being a tough, inward-looking or irresponsible. This is a natural outcome of the similarity of cognitive explanatory patterns used to categorize in one's mind the notion of another individual, an organization or a society, albeit at increasing levels of generality accorded to the higher levels of abstracted thinking. *The implication of this is that the explanatory patterns of the Enneagram and Jungian typologies, used to explain the motivation and thinking of individuals, can also legitimately be adapted to explain the way one thinks about the dynamics of organizations and societies. Institutional archetyping is a cognitive reality.*

7. As Gordy (1993: 101) notes, "Corporate legitimacy cannot be abstracted from its context, from its interrelationships with politics, economic developments and cultural milieu." The nature and dynamics of the organization will therefore be quite different as to whether it is serving the "good" of the political, economic or social sphere of the society.

8. This is a very common and accepted differentiation. For example, just to mention a couple, it was referred to in Burnham (1941: 74) and Galbraith (1967: 49). More specifically (as depicted in Figure 3):

> The notion of the economic life (*menetype #A*) of a society captures the concrete material aspects the communal experience; principally those experiences involving an *explicit, materialistic* exchange between different parties. Essentially, it captures the external expression of the consumer wants in the market of exchange of goods and services and anything else that can be formulated in an external. It is about the individual and collective will to do—achievement is the driving motivation and it is continuous and never ending. The measure of performance in this *menetype* is external success; for instance, the show of great production, consumption or wealth—the more, the better. As a result, production and consumption are taken well beyond the level of basic needs. "He saw deeply into the role of work that it continued long after they had become rich" (Tocqueville, 1966: lxxvii). The individual's thinking on the economic sphere of a society is further differentiated in terms of the *sub-menetype* trinity of consumption, production and market exchange.

> The social life (*menetype #B*) is less tangible and comprises more the imaginative framework of the desired way of personal life, civic life and artistic fulfillments. Essentially it captures the inner life of a society that goes to make up what is called its culture or way of coming together and interacting as a society. The measure of performance in this *menetype* is the degree to which citizens have an inner sense of belonging and security within the group (as opposed to danger from outside foes). Loyalty and ordered living are the driving motivators and there is constant peer pressure on one another to live a life that supports the ordered life of the whole group. The individual's thinking in terms of the social sphere of a society can, therefore, be further differentiated in terms of the *sub-menetype* trinity of living standards, associative arrangements and aesthetic life.

> The political life (*menetype #C*) of a society is the least tangible, most abstract (or prescinded) form of exchange in the social catallactic system.

It is characterized by an endless and largely indeterminate myriad of interlocking webs of personal and group alliances. The manifestations of the political system such as the promises, the policies, the spending programs and the edicts and laws that emanate continuously are certainly visible and tangible—for the moment anyway! However, though there are many claims, nobody can really get a detailed grip on how such decisions come about and then get modified—sometimes not even the players themselves really know. It is characterized by a trading in power *that can be assembled in a particular situation. The overall measure of* performance in this *menetype* is whether the "good" of the community is being served by such conscious concentration of power and the level of trust that is assessed, or "felt," to exist throughout this catallactic system. The individual and personal measure of success is the degree of power that one "feels" can be brought to bear. The personal, group and national survival are high priorities in exercising the political catallaxy and it is where the values of the society have greatest conscious impact in the making of decisions. The nature and dynamics of the individual's thinking on the political sphere have been well expounded by Montesquieu (1952) and comprise the *sub-menetype* trinity of the Executive, the Judiciary and the Legislature.

9. "The British polytechnics are the most difficult to classify. If they had all adopted the philosophy of E. E. Robinson whose ideas are set out at length in his book and in numerous articles and speeches, the difference from universities would be substantial for stress would indeed be laid on usefulness and involvement. The interpretations of this concept of higher education have some affinities with the views of the (Carnegie) Commission; education must be student-centred and community-orientated, courses must be of a variety and pattern to suit student and social needs; research and consultancy should be directly aimed at the solution of practical problems; the criterion of success is not what a man knows or is but what he later does; academic disciplines have no validity in themselves, they can be seen only as a convenience of courses and not of their substance. But few of the polytechnics would follow this extreme pattern" (Embling, 1974: 29).

10. The purposes of universities has been broadly interpreted from the literature as follows:

- tackle new intellectual horizons and explore reality in new ways so as to overcome the limitations of existing knowledge and skills in the application of that knowledge (*menetype #A*);
- develop the personal and group understanding both internally within the university and externally in society by developing processes to produce and disseminate the existing body of knowledge (*menetype #B*);
- deliberate on the emerging new understandings and knowledge, decide which is true and real and articulate the agreed new knowing about reality (*menetype #C*); and
- equip individuals with the knowledge and thinking processes to contribute positively and effectively to the economic, social and political life of the society (the whole as transformed to something more than).

This summary of the purposes of higher education reconciles with the discussion in the *West Final Report* (1998: 45-46) of the *Review of Higher Education Financing and Policy*.

"(T)he Vice-Chancellors have put out a more pragmatic statement of the purpose, distinctive nature and value of universities.
Universities:

- discover, preserve, refine, apply and disseminate knowledge;
- have a commitment to free inquiry and to being a critic and conscience of society;
- develop intellectual independence in their graduates, together with a set of cognitive and social capacities which support active participation of graduates in society;
- have staff whose active engagement in scholarship and research both enriches the nation in itself and ensures that students at both the undergraduate and postgraduate level learn from those at the forefront of knowledge, whether rhetorical or applied;
- are committed to making the best possible use of the emerging technologies to ensure Australia provides high quality education to its domestic and international students wherever they are located; and
- meet international standards of teaching, research and scholarship.

. . . The Higher Education Council describes the purposes of higher education in a 1992 report as:

- the education of appropriately qualified Australians to enable them to take a leadership role in the intellectual, cultural, economic and social development of the nation and all its regions;
- the creation and advancement of knowledge; and
- the application of knowledge and discoveries to the betterment of communities in Australia and overseas.

. . . More recently, The Dearing Review Committee stated that the purpose of higher education in the UK is to:

- inspire and enable individuals to develop their capabilities to the highest potential levels throughout life, so that they grow intellectually, are well equipped for work, can contribute effectively to society and achieve personal fulfillment;
- increase knowledge and understanding for their own sake and to foster their application to the benefit of the economy and society;
- serve the needs of an adaptable, sustainable knowledge-based economy at local regional and national levels; and
- play a major role in shaping a democratic, civilised and inclusive society.

Our own [The West Review] assessment is as follows:

The threefold purpose of universities has ever been to preserve, transmit and expand the domain of human knowledge. Universities have been the living repositories of the accumulated knowledge of the ages, as well as places in which each new generation can be inducted into the process of constructive dialogue with the best that has been thought throughout history. However, the explosion of knowledge has made impossible any continuing consensus as to the task of the university in relation to some presumed canon of privileged knowledge. There is just too much to choose from. The purpose of the modern university, therefore, must be to open the mind, to strengthen and discipline the cognitive powers and sensibilities of the mind, to refine the mind and to create efficient and effective independent learners and knowledge builders (West, 1998: 45-46).

11. "Newman's idea of the university, then, was the idea of it as a place where Truth is made known—Truth with a capital 'T.' And his book derives much of its power from this Platonic background. . . . The philosophy behind the Anglican monopoly at Oxbridge was based on the same Platonic foundations on which Newman built his Idea of a University. Here is the argument: the University exists to reveal the Truth; the Truth is Divine; when it is known or revealed it is our duty to defend it; and that duty lies most heavily upon those who have the most power—notably the power of government" (Jackson, 1999: 91, 103). The concept of "truth" has evolved and is different—particularly from the post-modernist perspective—but the core idea is of the university's role is still understood.

12. For instance, "practical men, who believe themselves to be quite exempt from any intellectual influences, are usually the slaves of some defunct economist" (Keynes, 1936: 383-384). The collective belief in a coherent set of such big ideas of economists, philosophers or psychologists—or (more powerful still) religious beliefs—helps build a coherent society.

13. "They accept that the university has the function of 'socializing' the students into the patterns of academic life by inculcating 'the virtues of hard work, of postponed gratification, of integrity of one's personal performance, of respect for the facts, of cognitive rationality, of independence of mind' (Carnegie Commission, page 19) but there are other environments which contribute to the total socialization of the individual—the communications media, the peer group, the Church. . . . What can be hoped say the (Carnegie) Commission is that the individual institution will in its own way provide an environment which will help the student to develop for himself 'an overall ethical orientation, competency in social situations, and a sense of identity, of autonomy, of personal integrity' (Carnegie Commission, page 18)" (Embling, 1974: 26).

"Martin Trow offered a definition of these goals twenty years ago that remain helpful today. What do our finest colleges and universities attempt to do which sets them apart from mass-provider or convenience institutions. First of all, says Trow, élite higher education seeks to socialize students, not merely to train or inform them; that is to shape qualities of mind, feeling and character. In the second place, this kind of education is carried on through a relatively close and prolonged relationship between teacher and student. It depends on the creation and survival of the social and physical settings within which that kind of relationship can exist. Finally, although the specific content of the curriculum in these institutions may vary widely, this type of education tries to convey to students that they can accomplish large things in the world, they can make important discoveries, lead great institutions, influence law and government" (Keohane, 1999: 63).

14. The spirit and value of this personal formation by experience is captured in the notion of élite higher education: "In this sense, brand name or élite education is clearly distinguished from the transmission of skills or knowledge through a fleeting, impersonal relationship between teacher and student or across the distant learning of the Web. It is also distinguished by a commitment to adding value and satisfying several specific goals. These features run directly athwart the mass-market, consumer-oriented, low-cost distance learning trends that have been described above. Yet, the elements in élite education retain an immense appeal to potential students and their families: not just the brand name, but the provision of experience that can never be fully replicated through a virtual substitute. On this basis, I am confident that for the foreseeable future there will be a steady market for the richly-varied and intensive undergraduate education that a small number of places provide, as a rite of passage for young American adults" (Keohane, 1999: 63).

This provision of a tailored, effective learning experience needs to be continued throughout the career of the ever-emerging potential leaders of the future. They would get the basics in their early formal higher education but the concept of whole-of-life learning needs to be given some meaning in training the potential leaders to think appropriately and effectively and to cultivate the sense of principles and value to ensure that their personal decision-making and action framework is adequate and robust and in keeping with the needs of the organization and society.

15. These three principle *menetypes* are taken to embody an explanation of the nature of conscious organizational thinking within the particular catallactic system that comprises the organization.

- The *participant sphere (menetype #A)* is the external, concrete face of any grouping and encapsulates the execution of the collective will of the group and the vehicles for any action taken. This aspect captures the decision or action outcome of the interplay between the roles assigned to individuals and the inner character orientation of the particular individual concerned (as depicted in the lower, left-hand sphere of Figure 7).

- The *culture sphere (menetype #B)* captures those explicit and implicit, stated and un-stated understandings within the minds of the individuals within the group that guide or inform the day-to-day operations inside the organization. These internal understandings are manifested in the formal and informal organization structures and processes of the group and the nature of the decision-making processes adopted to reconcile these often-competing interests (as depicted in the lower, right-hand sphere of Figure 7). This is the phase of thinking, in particular, which regards the organization as a whole or as a separate entity apart from the individuals (although the thinking of the organization in terms of individuals as participants is essentially repressed, it is still existent but usually in a more unconscious way).

- The *authority sphere (menetype #C)* encapsulates the collective discernment of value of how the group is operating that reconciles the visible, external actions of individuals with the internally generated and acknowledged *modus operandi* of the way it should be done. The responsibility to assess and commit the organization to a particular course of action based on the competing viewpoints has to be invested in designated individuals who are given a tacitly approved legitimate authority of some sort. Just how this legitimate authority is distributed and how it operates can be explained in terms of the dynamics of political, management and leadership power (as depicted in the top-most sphere of Figure 7). There is always one or other of these possible patterns of authority in operation—either it is collectively discerned as right by the organization, thereby making it legitimate authority, or it is regarded as undesirable or out of kilter with the prevailing mindset and there is dynamic tension within the organization.

16. This training of the intellect still figures prominently in conservative and liberal (as distinct from radical) conceptions of higher education. . . . It is not the mere acquisition of knowledge that matters: it is the development of intellectual curiosity, the ability to assess the value of evidence objectively and impartially, to determine relativities, to distinguish what is important. This for many people is still the ideal which transcends all other objectives for it gives to the university a role of superiority and significance" (Embling, 1974: 18).

17. It is interesting to observe that the rudimentary beginnings of universities had a primary focus on the participant sphere with the principal focus being on the school of thought propounded by the individual professors and the academic/personal progress of the individual students (which was feasible because of the small numbers). "At all levels of education, the personal relationship between master and pupil was regarded as crucial. Beyond the walls of the classroom, students of Bologna or Paris would have identified more easily with their nation, their college, their hall, their confraternity, to whichever of these they may have belonged, than with the university, which to them was little more than a fee-exacting mechanism" (Dunbabin, 1999: 30).

18. The individual's thinking on the *authority sphere* can be framed in terms of the dynamics of interaction of the following trinity of *sub-menetypes*.

   • **Leadership power** (*sub-menetype #A*), which is the expression of the collective will to achieve the practical "good" which essentially is the replacement of the current organizational reality with a new organizing reality that is potentially better. If this vision or image of the "good" is captured and articulated effectively, individuals in the group can acknowledge it and sign up to become followers and be led in the expectation that it is the answer for their own "good." This is the generic expression of Weber's (1949; 1962) charismatic leadership and is found most purely expressed in the creative entrepreneur in the private sector.

   • **Management power** (*sub-menetype #B*), which is the collective acceptance of the authority of an incumbent of an official position in a hierarchical structure to interpret the rules and logical order of actions to decide on what to do next. There is an inner search for the "true" way or the path of correct processes that will naturally lead to good outcomes. This encapsulation of the implicit notion of cause and effect in the rationality of actions involves a higher level of abstract (or imaginative) thinking than does delivering the practical vision (or the "good"). The implicit understanding is that this allegiance to hierarchical authority facilitates orderly and efficient processes and everything progresses smoothly by degrees. This is the generic expression of legitimate authority equivalent to the concept of Weber's (1949; 1962) legal rationality and is found most purely expressed in the diligent and loyal bureaucrat in the public sector.

- Political power (*sub-menetype #C*), which is the exercise of power that accumulates to an individual directly to effect the acceptance of a decision or action that impacts on the collective in a particular situation. The power stems from the collective willingness of the other individuals to compromise their personal agendas to the dictates of the acknowledged boss in the current political reality—that is, a recognition that one has to subjugate one's will to another in this instance to ensure support or protection at some time in the future. This represents an expression of a value assessment on the "reality" of the situation and that it is right to accede to the particular person's authority. This cognitive act requires thinking at an even higher level of abstraction again because it is difficult to articulate why or the logical cause and effect of doing so—it is just the right thing to do in this set of circumstances. This is the generic expression of authority in keeping with Weber's (1949; 1962) traditional rationality and is most evident in the career politician (as their vocation).

These three principle *menetypes* are taken to embody an explanation of the nature of conscious organizational thinking within the particular catallactic system that comprises the organization. Although the frame of reference includes an understanding of the stance of those within the organization to the objects and events outside, it does not go into a detailed objective analysis of how they see and differentiate their external environment. However, a similar framework could be constructed or interpolated to capture their subjective perspective of the world outside their organization.

19. This is similar to the phenomenon of collegiality in the decision-making of a pure democracy. A pure democracy (as opposed to the modern capitalist democracy) has a primary focus on life in the social sphere and so the political sphere supported this collegial life of the community of citizens. The difference with the modern universities is that although they are operating predominantly in the social sphere of the society, the society is predominantly oriented to the economic sphere (capitalist democracies such as the United States of America) or the political sphere (many of the Asian countries and some of the European).

20. Throughout the managerialist age, the principal focus of universities was on the knowledge production processes to increase the individual's grasp of existing knowledge. Greatest importance was given to adhering to the ethic of clarity of thinking or the unrestricted desire to know. This effort was supplemented by a growing collaboration with industry, at the group level, to develop and apply the existing knowledge to group processes for the benefit of operating firms, which happened to be mainly in the economic sphere. With the major focus on the knowledge production processes there was always difficulty in entertaining new research that challenged existing paradigms. Progressive expansion of knowledge

was encouraged but it had to be in an ordered, controllable manner. This was supported by the operation of the political networks of academics focused on sharing, testing and culling the continual offerings of potentially new knowledge. There was an increasing focus on reinforcing the collegial collaboration of the academic community to support the main game of propagating and sharing the body of knowledge.

As the politicist age has emerged there has been an increase in the importance and value of new knowledge ready for use and the associated political orientation of academic networks that deliberate and decide on that new knowledge. The principal question focuses on what to make of the dynamics of change in this highest level of university decision-making where the political-type academic networks effect an assessment of, and secure an assent to, emerging new knowledge. These academic networks have been geared to maximize the sharing of knowledge and the basic coinage is trust—trust that the work and research of others can be believed and incorporated into the general body of knowledge. Although everything is tested and debated, this basic trust is necessary so that each academic doesn't have to reinvent the wheel. The whole fabric of a subject area is built up on the back of the works of others.

It has been important for academics to get themselves accepted into networks— within their own university, with other universities nationally and internationally within their particular discipline of study (such as a particular science, politics or business). Moreover, professors are renowned for managing as though they are ruling their own fiefdoms, which reflects their preference to operate more informally than by rule-bound processes. University administrative rules are normally looked on as burdensome and circumvented at many an opportunity. Within the Governance Framework, university life has put a primacy on the *menetype #C* network aspect and represses the hierarchical rule-bound influence. Further, it has encouraged the development of the secondary *menetype #A* market orientation by placing importance on the participants getting published in the academic marketplace of conferences and journals—"publish or perish" has long been the mantra. However, academics have found that they can more easily get published if they belong to strong networks and are well-regarded by at least some of their peers.

21. "As Eells and Walton point out, 'In the economic sphere, rights are now more clearly attached to men rather than to things—something that has always been true in the political sphere. The result is that, from an economic point of view, society has passed from a private property system to a corporate power system.' . . . Finally, it seems appropriate to quote from Mary Parker Follet, who, handicapped by the lack of a vocabulary not yet invented, suggested that a 'right and proper' decision, an authoritative decision, must always be based on the 'law of the situation'" (McNulty, 1993: 162).

Now, with the new information or knowledge era, even the lower-level managers are saying "it is a different kind of decision making now . . . I have to make the larger decisions and I have to have the information to make those decisions" (Zuboff, 1996: 555). "While efficiency was the hallmark of deterministic industrial-era technology, reliability is the hallmark of stochastic, continuous technology associated with the post-industrial era" (Weick, 1996: 563), who then goes on to describe this shift in the nature of decision-making demands on the manager as going from *structure* to *structuration*. "Structuration is defined as 'the production and reproduction of a social system through members' use of rules and resources in interaction'" (Poole, as quoted by Weick, 1996: 566). If the understanding of "rules" is taken as more the implicitly understood rules as the context would seem to suggest, then what is being described is a political process (*menetype #C*), where trust, reliability and dependability are the key driving principles. "Related to all three characteristics (complexity, dynamics and diversity) of the modern world is the "politicizing" of the administrative apparatus as a strategy" (Kooiman, 1993: 257).

22. The timing quoted by Burnham (1941: 68) is uncanny in terms of the growth and maturation of managerialism, to the point it can begin evolving into politicism. "This transition is *from* the type of society which we have called capitalist or bourgeois *to* a type of society which we shall call *managerial*. This transition period may be expected to be short compared with the transition from feudal to capitalist society. It may be dated, somewhat arbitrarily, from the First World War, and may be expected to close, with the consolidation of the new type of society, by approximately fifty years from then, perhaps sooner."

23. Managers for their part "realized that the abstraction of work necessitated a fundamental re-appraisal of their methods of supervision and evaluation" (Zuboff, 1996: 551). Most are finding these new intellectual demands personally difficult. Many are not getting the opportunity as they get "down-sized." The higher education sector had grown to be effective in providing a solid foundation to get aspiring managers to the level of thinking required in the managerialist world. It is not so evident they are equipped to help educate them to the next cognitive level of abstraction—it might even be said they are going in the wrong direction as humanities courses are being scaled back just when our managers need to be more aware of human relations and how humans think and learn.

24. This tendency to adopt a primitive and un-sophisticated approach to the economic perspective previously repressed to the institutional shadow is clearly evident in the reported experience of Australian universities as they try to become more self-financing and market-oriented.

"The commercialization of universities, initiated by the Dawkins reforms in the late 1980s, has changed higher education beyond recognition. Driven both by the government-imposed need to seek much of their funding from outside sources and a shift in the culture of universities to conform with the demands of the marketplace, academics find themselves in a new world of moral ambiguity. A series of scandals involving soft marketing, plagiarism and academic freedoms show how far universities have drifted from the moral certainties of the past. The clumsy and, at times, vindictive, treatment of academic whistleblowers by the new class of university administrators indicates how power has shifted away from those who have the knowledge to those who hold the purse strings" (Hamilton, 2001: 26).

"Brutal, but clear. The view from one of the nations top education bureaucrats this week was that Australia's universities could either sink or swim in the shark-infested waters of the free market. There would be no bail-outs and no softening of approach, despite some startling facts about its failure . . . Gallagher, who was speaking to a conference held at the Australian National University was joined by Labor Senator Kim Carr and several prominent academics and politicians.

Gallagher and Carr are usually combatants, sitting on opposite sides of the table in Senate inquiries, but this week they agreed on one point at least. Education department figures show that Australia's universities raised $1.5 billion from outside sources (not including student fees and charges) last year. This is exactly what federal Education Minister Dr. David Kemp and the Government want them to do . . . Carr wanted to know how much money the universities had spent in order to raise the $1.5 billion. Gallagher said the figure had not been published because the department did not know what it was. The sum would be difficult to calculate and universities themselves probably didn't know exactly what they were spending in pursuit of the commercial dollar. But he agreed it would be substantial, *likely more than $1.5 billion they eventually raised.*

In fact, in a paper Gallagher presented to the Organization for Economic Cooperation and Development last year, 'The Emergence of Entrepreneurial Public Universities,' he wrote that one university claimed it spent, on average, 92c to earn $1. Staff costs probably were not factored in and this university was doing well. 'For all the effort universities have been making to grow their earned income, the impact on the bottom line for many is apparently adding little, if at all, to surpluses'" (Jackson, 2001: C2, *emphasis added*).

Such an economic performance after more than 10 years of trying is less than acceptable and it is doubtful whether any truly commercial organizations would be allowed to languish that long. What we are dealing with is an attempt to put a square peg into a round hole and it is not going to work until the peg is shaved and made round—and when that happens the ability of the universities to provide anything that would resemble education will be greatly stripped to the bare bones of marketing and transferring knowledge and/or entertainment.

25. "Yet the potential contribution of foreign students to the experience of American students is often over-stated. For students from other countries enrolling in US colleges and universities to pursue their academic goals helping American students gain international knowledge and competence is typically only a small part of the foreign student's agenda, if at all. Moreover, the striking disjunction between American under-graduates and foreign students is not conducive to much interaction. The majority of foreign students pursue graduate degrees in the sciences and engineering. Over 60 per cent come from Asia; their English may be difficult to follow; and their customs and cultures can seem intimidatingly different to American under-graduates . . .

The numbers of foreign students enrolling in American colleges and universities promises to increase, especially at the graduate level. As various Asian countries— China, India, Taiwan, South Korea—produce a growing number of first-degree recipients and continue, significantly, to send the best of these students into graduate study programs in Europe and the United States, and assuming that the US share of foreign students worldwide remains at approximately 35 percent, or even goes up, *foreign graduate students at US universities will out-number American students.* Whether this contributes to any important degree to American students' international education will be determined by the motivation, inter-cultural expertise and staffing efforts of the US host institutions" (Burn, 1996:159; 161, *emphasis added*).

The ability of university education to pass onto students an experience that contributes to their understanding and learning in the context of their own society as per the function of the universities within the social sphere is severely diminished by the dilution of cultural interaction between citizens. As a consequence, the potential of their own citizen-students to contribute to the strengthening of the country's social, political and economic life will be severely dampened. It is a matter of judgment whether the other dubious economic and globalization benefits from the presence of foreign students really compensates for this diminution of the country's ability to fully educate its own potential leaders.

26. One anecdotal experience that casts doubt on the educational value of this strategy is the instance of a newspaper editor's advice to a young, would-be-journalist. The advice went along the lines that if the person really wanted to improve their chances of gaining employment as a journalist then the idea would be not to undertake a university course in journalism but, rather, to acquire some in-depth knowledge (explicit and implicit) on the particular area of interest such as sport or politics and then try to get in on the ground floor of journalism as a specialist researcher or assistant writer in that area. This underscores the continuing greater value of on-the-job training of these practical trades (including nursing).

27. De Wit (1997: 11), in the context of a book reporting a conference in Porter's honour, hones in on the reason for the popularity of Porter amongst the corporate executives: "Porter considered that his primary target group to be practitioners: 'This book is written for practitioners; that is, managers seeking to improve their businesses' . . . the importance of Porter's contributions to business managers is illustrated by Shell's CEO Herkstroter's contribution," who gave Porter big accolades for the impact of his generic competitive strategy approach with executive decision-makers. "He is a profound thinker on matters about which Shell feels strongly. It is particularly those of his ideas that have found practical application in the hard-nosed world of business, that I wish to recall here. Who can doubt that he has had an impact?" (Herkstroter, 1997: 19).

28. There are, in fact, proposals to develop such schools for directors: "There is the foreign service school that produces an elite corps for the State Department, so there could also be a school that would produce qualified directors" (C. Vance, quoted in Ward, 1997: 181). The comment here is that the foreign service school produces polished bureaucrats and perhaps diplomats who advise the foreign policy leaders on the National Security Council, who invariably have not been processed through the foreign policy school.

    In addition, Dror (1971: 218), in his continual concern to improve the inner mind of government and the quality of its leaders, recommended the establishment of a school for political leaders. He then developed these thoughts into another article titled "School for Rulers" in which he reasons: "Four premises serve as a foundation for this assertion: One, Rulers matter a lot; two, Rulers must know a lot, in addition to meeting other criteria; three, as a matter of fact, nearly all Rulers lack essential knowledge, in particular policy-cogitation competence; and four, carefully designed learning institutions are needed to supply Rulers with required knowledge and can do so" (Dror, 1991: 2).

References

Aquinas, T. (1952), *The Summa Theologica: Volume I* (translated/revised by Sullivan, D. J.), Encyclopaedia Britannica Great Books, Chicago.

Berle, A. A. and Means, G. C. (1939), *The Modern Corporation and Private Property,* Macmillan, New York.

Boulding, K. E. (1993), "Business in the Ecosystem of Power," in Sutton, B. (ed.), *The Legitimate Corporation: Essential Readings in Business Ethics and Corporate Governance,* Blackwell Business, Cambridge, pp. 183- 200.

Burn, B. (1996), "Preparing For Global Citizenship in US Universities: Curriculum Reform and International Exchange," in Muller, S. and Whitesell, H. L., *Universities in the Twenty-First Century,* Berghahn Books, Providence, pp. 153-162.

Cutting, B. A. (2000), "How the Enneagram and Jung are One," workshop given at the Annual Enneagram Conference on Ancient Wisdom for the New Millennium, Brisbane, April.

Cutting, B. A. (2001), *Refounding Governance: Transforming the Science to Master the Art,* unpublished draft thesis under examination, University of Western Sydney, Sydney.

Cutting, B. A. and Kouzmin, A. (1997a), "Beyond Weber, We Can See Clearly Now: Explaining the Dynamics of Governance in the Maturing Westminster System," paper presented at the 1997 International Conference of the International Institute of Administrative Sciences (IIAS), Quebec City, July, pp. 1-24.

Cutting, B. A. and Kouzmin, A. (1997b), "From the Chaos to Patterns of Understanding: An Ontological Understanding of Good Governance Based on a Synthesis of Weber's Concept of "Ideal Types" and the Enneagram Typology," paper presented at the 1997 National Conference of the American Society for Public Administration, Philadelphia, July, pp 1-13.

Cutting, B. A. and Kouzmin, A. (1998), "The Emerging Patterns of Power in Corporate Governance: A Hermeneutic Analysis of Institutional Archetyping and its Capacity to Improve Corporate Performance," paper presented at the Tenth Annual International Conference of Socio-Economics, Vienna, July, pp. 1-21.

Cutting, B. A. and Kouzmin, A. (1999a), "Formulating a Metaphysics of Human Endeavour and Social Action: Synthesizing the Work of Aquinas, Lonergan and Jung to Construct a Cognitive Formwork of Social Development," paper presented at the Australian Lonergan Workshop, Sydney, April, pp. 1-23.

Cutting, B. A. and Kouzmin, A. (1999b), "Formulating a Metaphysics of Governance: Explaining the Dynamics of Governance Using the New JEWAL Synthesis Formwork," paper presented at the Inaugural PAT-Net Regional Symposium, Sydney, July, pp. 1-21.

Cutting, B. A. and Kouzmin, A. (1999c), "From Chaos to Patterns of Understanding: Reflections on the Dynamics of Effective Decision-Making, *Public Administration,* Volume 77, Number 3, pp 473-508.

Cutting, B. A. and Kouzmin, A. (2000a), "The JEWAL Synthesis Formwork of Knowing and Governance: Making Sense of the Psycho-Philosophic Voices," paper presented at the 13th Annual Conference of the Public Administration Theory Network, (PAT-Net), Fort Lauderdale, January, pp 1-29.

Cutting, B. A. and Kouzmin, A. (2000b), "The Emerging Patterns of Power in Corporate Governance: Back to the Future in Improving Corporate Decision-Making," *Journal of Managerial Psychology*, Volume 15, Number 5 pp. 477-507.

Cutting, B. A. and Kouzmin, A. (2001a), "Formulating a Metaphysics of Governance: Explaining the Dynamics of Governance Using the New JEWAL Synthesis Framework," *The Journal of Management Development*, Volume 20, Number 6, pp. 526-564.

Embling, J. (1974), *A Fresh Look at Higher Education: European Implications of the Carnegie Commission Reports*, Elsevier Scientific Publishing Company, Amsterdam.

Flanagan, J. (1997), *Quest For Self Knowledge: An Essay in Lonergan's Philosophy*, University of Toronto Press, Toronto.

Galbraith, J. K. (1967), *The New Industrial State*, Oxford and IBH Publishing, Calcutta.

Golembiewski, R. T. (1989), "Strategy and Structure: Developmental Themes and Challenges," in Rabin, J., Miller, G. J. and Hildreth, W. B. (eds.), *Handbook of Strategic Management*, Marcel Dekker, New York, pp. 91-121.

Gordy, M. (1993), "Thinking About Corporate Legitimacy," in Sutton, B. (ed.), *The Legitimate Corporation: Essential Readings in Business Ethics and Corporate Governance*, Blackwell Business, Cambridge, pp. 82-101.

Hamilton, C. (2001), "Whither the Future of the Australian University in the Age of the Market," *The Weekend Australian*, 21 July, p. 26.

Hamilton, W. (1859), *Lectures on Metaphysics and Logic: Volumes I-IV*, William Blackwood and Sons, Edinburgh.

Handy, C. (1978), *Gods of Management*, Souvenir Press, London.

Hegel, G. W. F. (1952), *The Philosophy of Right* (translated by Knox, T. M.), Encyclopaedia Britannica Great Books, Chicago.

Herkströter, C. A. J. (1997), "Business Level Strategy: Lessons From Shell," in van den Bosch, F. A. J. and de Man, A. P. (eds.), *Perspectives on Strategy: Contributions of Michael E. Porter*, Kluwer Academic Publishers, Dordrecht, pp. 19-24.

Jackson, C. (2001), "Universities Told to Swim or Sink," *The Canberra Times*, 28 July, p. C2.

Jackson, R. (1999), "The Universities, Government and Society," in Smith, D. and Langslow, A. K. (eds.), *The Idea of a University*, Jessica Kingsley Publishers, London, pp. 91-105.

Jung, C. G. (1971), *Psychological Types (Collected Works: Volume 6)*, Routledge and Kegan Paul, London.

Keohane, N. E. (1999), "The American Campus: From Colonial Seminary to Global Multiversity," in Smith, D. and Langlslow, A. K. (eds.), *The Idea of a University*, Jessica Kingsley Publishers, London, pp. 48-67.

Keynes, J. M. (1936), *General Theory of Employment, Interest and Money*, Macmillan and Company, London.

Kooiman, J. (ed.) (1993), *Modern Governance: New Governance—Society Interactions*, Sage Publications, London.

McNulty, M. S. (1993), "A Question of Managerial Legitimacy," in Sutton, B. (ed.), *The Legitimate Corporation: Essential Readings in Business Ethics and Corporate Governance*, Blackwell Business, Cambridge, pp. 153-164.

Michels, R. (1962), *Political Parties: A Sociological Study of Oligarchical Tendencies of Modern Democracy* (translated by Paul, E. C.), The Free Press, New York.

Micklethwait, J. and Wooldridge, A. (1996), *The Witch Doctors: Making Sense of the Management Gurus,* Random House, New York.

Miller, A. S. (1976), *The Modern State: Private Governments and the American Constitution,* Greenwood Press, Westport.

Mills, C. W. (1956), *The Power Elite,* Oxford University Press, New York.

Montesquieu, C. De. (1952), *The Spirit of Laws* (translated by Nugent, T.), Encyclopaedia *Britannica Great Books: Volume 38,* William Benton, Chicago, pp. 1-315.

Mooney, J. D. (1947), *The Principle of Organization,* Harper and Brothers Publishers, New York.

Mosca, G. (1939), *The Ruling Class: Elementi di Scienza Politica,* McGraw-Hill Book Company, New York.

Myers, I.B. (1980), *Gifts Differing,* Consulting Psychologists Press, Los Angeles.

Nonaka, I. and Takeuchi, H. (1995), *The Knowledge-Creating Company: How Japanese Companies Create the Dynamics of Innovation,* Oxford University Press, New York.

Palmer, H. (1991), *The Enneagram,* Harper Collins, New York.

Plotinus (1952), *The Six Enneads* (translated by Mackenna, S. and Page, B. S.), *Encyclopaedia Britannica Great Books: Volume 17,* William Benton, Chicago.

Polanyi, M. (1958), *Personal Knowledge,* Routledge and Kegan, London.

Porter, M. E. (1995), "How Competitive Forces Shape Strategy," in Mintzberg, H., Quinn, J. B. and Voyer, J. (eds.), *The Strategy Process* (College Edition*)*, Prentice Hall, Englewood Cliffs, pp. 87-102.

Proclus (1963), *The Elements of Theology* (translated by Dodds, E. R.), Clarendon Press, Oxford.

Ramos, A. G. (1981), *The New Science of Organizations: A Reconceptualization of the Wealth of Nations,* University of Toronto Press, Toronto.

Rhodes, R. A. W. (1997), *Understanding Governance: Policy Networks, Governance, Reflexivity and Accountability,* Open University Press, Buckingham.

Riso, D.R. (1987), *Personality Types: Using the Enneagram For Self-Discovery,* Houghton Mifflin, Boston.

Schumpeter, J.A. (1950), *Capitalism, Socialism and Democracy* (Third Edition), HarperPerennial, New York.

Searle, J. R. (1995), *The Construction of Social Reality,* Allen Lane, The Penguin Press, London.

Taylor, F. W. (1996), "The Principles of Scientific Management," in Shafritz, J. M. and Ott, J. S. (eds.), *Classics of Organization Theory* (Fourth Edition), Harcourt Brace College Publishers, Fort Worth, pp. 66-79.

Thompson, G., Frances, J., Levacic, R. and Mitchell, J. (eds.), (1991), *Markets, Hierarchies and Networks: The Coordination of Social Life,* Sage Publications, London.

Tocqueville, A. de (1966), *Democracy in America* (translated by Lawrence, G.), Harper and Row, New York.

von Franz, M-L. and Hillman, J. (1971), *Lectures on Jung's Typology*; Spring Publications, Texas.

Ward, R. D. (1997), *21st Century Corporate Boards,* John Wiley and Sons, New York.

Weber, M. (1930), *The Protestant Ethic and the Spirit of Capitalism* (translated by Parsons, T.), Unwin University Books, London.

Weber, M. (1949), *The Methodology of Social Sciences* (translated and edited by Shils, E. and Finch, H.), The Free Press, New York.

Weber, M. (1962), *Basic Concepts in Sociology* (translated and edited by Secher, H.P.), The Citadel Press, New Jersey.

Weick, K. E. (1996), "Technology as Equivoque: Sensemaking in New Technologies; in Shafritz, J. M. and Ott, J. S. (eds.), *Classics of Organization Theory* (Fourth Edition), Harcourt Brace College Publishers, Fort Worth, pp. 561-577.

West, R. (1998), *Learning For Life: Final Report of Review of Higher Education Financing and Policy,* Government Publishing Service, Canberra.

Zuboff, S. (1996), "In the Age of the Smart Machine: The Limits of Hierarchy in an Informed Organization," in Shafritz, J. M. and Ott, J. S. (eds.), *Classics of Organization Theory* (Fourth Edition), Harcourt Brace College Publishers, Fort Worth, pp. 547-560.

Figure 1   **Figure 2**
The Trinity of Cognitive Abstractions   The Principle Trinity of the Intellect

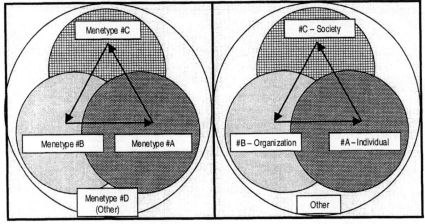

Figure 3
The Cognitive Trinity of Societal Life

Figure 4
The Trinity of Societal Education

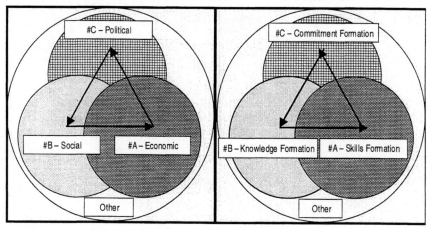

Figure 5
The Trinity of Organization

Figure 7
The Trinity of Personal Learning

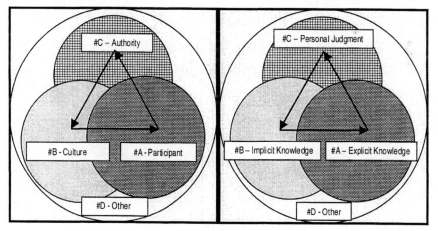

Instructed by Reason

Figure 6
The Trinitarian Hierarchy of Organization

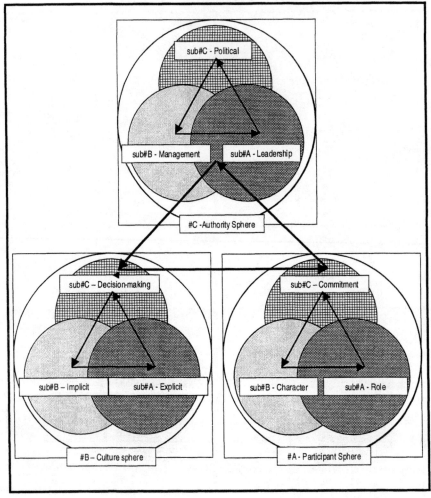

Chapter Four

Proposed Ethics for Managing Endowments of Eleemosynary Institutions

Richard N. Ottaway

Introduction

The purpose of this article is to develop and propose a set of ethical guidelines for the managers of endowments of eleemosynary institutions, such as churches, hospitals and universities. Endowment trustees and managers take at least three sets of actions where these ethics can be used: how the money is raised, how it is invested and how it is spent. This chapter will look at how the money is invested. The process of development of the proposed ethics will be to examine the investment actions of mainline Protestant churches, particularly the Episcopal Church. The ethics will be abstracted from their actions to critique the ethical management of endowments of eleemosynary institutions.

A new source of endowment gifts came available to universities following the case of A.P. Smith Pump and Valve Company vs. Barlow in 1953 when the Supreme Court of New Jersey ruled to allow corporate gifts from profits be given to eleemosynary institutions. A new model for the ethics of endowments was launched in 1971 when "the Episcopal Church filed the first social issue shareholder resolution—with General Motors on the issue of its involvement in South Africa—by a religious institution. ("Proxy Voting and the Mission of the Church," 2000)

A prior question for democratically governed churches, like the Episcopal Church, is what do the members want? Although no empirical evidence exists for the Episcopal Church, a survey of the membership of the United Church of Christ gives some indication of the attitudes of church membership.

The office of Corporate Social Responsibility of the United Church of Christ surveyed 5961 congregations in 2000. ("Investment Issue Survey," 2000) They received 1136 responses for a response rate of 19%, a respectable rate considering that the respondents had little to gain from filling out the questionnaire. Pastors, or lay leaders of these congregations, completed the questionnaires. Four interesting findings give some confidence that church members in general support their national church investment activities described in this chapter.

The first finding is that 52% of the pastors responded that their congregations understand the term Corporate Social Responsibility, meaning an integration of business operations and values. The second point is that the pastors believe that 58% of the congregations understand the definition of Socially Responsible Investing (SRI) to be "the integration of social (including environmental), or ethical criteria, or personal values into the investment decision-making process." This means that the rest of the answers are based on an understanding of the topic. The third finding of interest to our work is that 56% of the respondents strongly or somewhat *disagree* that the church should use financial return as the only criterion for investment decisions. The fourth finding relevant to our discussion is that 62% of respondents strongly or somewhat agree that churches should invest in community development initiatives and other socially responsible efforts even if it means a lower rate of return. These findings add credibility to the socially responsible investing (SRI) policies set and actions taken by national churches.

The Case of the Episcopal Church

The Episcopal Church is recognized as a leader among religious institutions in setting policy and taking action on social and ethical issues. Following the proxy resolution in 1971, the SRI Committee was established to coordinate the national church's shareholder activities. The Episcopal Church was one of the founding members of the Interfaith Center on Corporate Responsibility (ICCR) in 1972, a coalition today of 275 religious institutions that "merge social values with investment decisions." ("About ICCR") We will examine how the Episcopal Church at the national level creates policies and takes actions as "an important part of the church's social and economic witness." The fiscal and social actions, our concerns in this chapter, can be divided into three categories of ethics: fiduciary ethics, ethics by rules and ethics by principles.

Key to any institution dealing with ethical issues in its investments is its governance structure: Who is enabled to act by whom? How is fiscal and social policy set and carried out? The governance of the Episcopal Church rests on an elected bicameral General Convention held every three years and an Executive Council elected by that Convention, which meets several times a year in the interim. The House of Bishops is composed of all the Bishops, active and retired, in the Church. The House of Deputies, is composed of elected clergy and lay delegates from each of the church's 113 dioceses. These delegates are elected at annual diocesan conventions that are composed of all clergy serving in that diocese and delegates elected by each parish. Diocesan and General Conventions can pass resolutions to set the doctrinal, fiscal and social policies of the Church, local policy when originating in the Diocesan Convention and national policy when originating in General Convention.

Fiduciary Ethics

The delegates at the General Convention and members of the Executive Council act as fiduciaries for the members of the Episcopal Church. "Fiduciary relationships are relationships of trust and dependence in which one party acts in the interest of another.

. . . Fiduciaries, that is, are bound to act in the interests of those who depend on them even if these interests do not coincide with their own." (Moore, 1990) Fiduciary relationships are composed of agents acting on behalf of principals. They form the core of relationships in business and many professions. Employees are agents of shareholders. Physicians are agents of patients [although health management organizations are creating some issues that in professional relationship.] Public officials, appointed or elected, are agents of the public.

The national Episcopal Church, mainly through funds in the Domestic and Foreign Missionary Society (DFMS) acts as fiduciary for donors. The Episcopal Church Pension Fund (CPF) acts as fiduciary for the parishes paying funds in and clergy who receive pension payments from the earnings of the investments. The CPF manages a portfolio of about $6B with about 35% of it in fixed income. Many of the remaining funds are invested directly in the common stock of corporations. Annually the SRI, working directly under review of the Executive Council, and the Committee on Social and Fiduciary Responsibility in Investments of the CPF, draw up a list of corporations they want to influence by presenting the shareholders a resolution to act on. An average of 250 shareholder social resolutions are filed annually in America. "In 1998, the Episcopal Church filed such resolutions with 14 of the companies in which it holds common stock. . . . Many resolutions lead to dialogue between the company and the proponents of the resolution. In most years, for example, the Episcopal Church withdraws two-thirds of the resolutions it files after successful dialogue with the company yields an agreement on the social issue in question." ("Proxy Voting and the Mission of the Church," 2000)

The shareholder resolutions, based on policy resolutions passed by either the General Convention or the Executive Council, usually fall within seven categories:

- *Corporate Governance*, discouraging golden parachutes for executives, encouraging more independent directors on corporate boards, favoring board review of executive compensation and separation of the offices of Chairperson and Chief Executive Officer.
- *Environment*, endorsing the adoption of CERES Principles, formerly known as Valdez Principles, and calling for action against global warning.
- *Equality in Organizations*, requesting more revealing of equal employment opportunity data, promoting more inclusive boards and calling for non-discrimination in all corporate actions.
- *Fair Lending and Responsible Use of Capital*, aimed at fair and equal access to credit and lending for low-income people and forgiving debt of impoverished economies.
- International Operations, *endorsing corporations that operate in countries that protect human rights, promoting a global living wage and encouraging corporate codes of conduct.*
- *Militarism*, asking for adoption of ethical criteria for the manufacture and sale of arms, requesting reports of foreign military sales and reduction of dependence on military contracts.
- *Specific Products and Services*, promoting responsible sale and use of alcohol, ask for drug price help for needy, supporting the WHO code of breast-milk substitutes and oppose manufacture and sale of tobacco products. ("Doing Good and Doing Well")

The SRI Committee recommendations for shareholder resolution filings for 2001-2002 named ten corporations, including Target, Harley Davidson and Wells Fargo, that were filing of previous resolutions. Often companies will agree to dialogue after a second or third filing of a proxy resolution. Two companies, Boeing and Lockheed Martin, are proposed for a filing against weaponization of space. The Committee recommends that two companies, BP Amoco and Talisman Energy, be divested because of direct operations in Sudan. ("Report from The Social Responsibility in Investments Committee," 2001)

Staff and volunteers carry out the shareholder activity. At the national headquarters of the Episcopal Church are a director with an assistant, plus a part time consultant, and the administrative support services of the Executive Council. The SRI Committee is composed of volunteers. At the CPF the Committee on Social and Fiduciary Responsibility in Investments is composed of eight trustees, with Amy Domini as Chair.

The principles that appear to be operative in the Episcopal Church's fiduciary ethics are: 1. There are governing bodies that are enabled and actually pass resolutions that set ethical policy on which actions can be based. 2. The institution has staff and resources committed to monitoring the investments, preparing lists of targeted companies, preparing the resolutions, conducting the dialogues and finally, if need be, presenting the resolutions at annual shareholders meetings. 3. An alignment of the governing body, or bodies, and the work of the staff and volunteers results in changed behavior in corporations in which common stock is owned.

Although the Episcopal Church is recognized as a leader among religious institutions in fulfilling its fiduciary responsibility, the United Methodist Church, Evangelical Lutheran Church of America, Presbyterian Church USA, Mennonites (through the Mennonite Mutual Aid Association which serves about twenty-five Anabaptists denominations), American Baptist Church USA, and United Church of Christ have comparable programs.

Ethics by Rules

Lawrence Kohlberg (1973) identified three levels of moral development: pre-conventional [before the person accepts the moral expectations of society], conventional [when the person accepts the rules or norms of society as the way to live], and post-conventional [those persons who live by principle regardless of the rules]. Lynn S. Paine (1994) has applied Kohlberg's work to institutions. Based on her study of Sears auto service centers, she identified two organizational ethics strategies: compliance strategy, with an emphasis on making and keeping the rules, and integrity strategy, with an emphasis on principles like obligation and aspiration. Following the thought of Paine, conventional behavior can be divided into ethics of rules and ethics of principles.

Corporations, for profit and not-for-profit, are creations of the State and federal, state and local governments have rules that govern and regulate their actions. Institutions create endowments from money and other valuables received as gifts and converted into securities. This process is regulated by rules such as tax laws or the Securities and Exchange Commission. Socially responsible investing is also regulated by rules. For instance, one must own $2000 worth of shares in order to propose a shareholder resolution in that company. Within these rules socially responsible investing is based on principles.

Ethics by Principles

There are two broad categories of activities where endowments are guided by principles: what to invest in and where to spend the investment income. Each of these categories can be guided by the ethics espoused by the institution owning the endowment. This chapter explores the first category, what to invest in.

The Social Investment Forum, a non-profit association of 600 financial professionals and institutions "promoting the concept and practice of socially and environmentally responsible investing," suggests that "Three key SRI strategies have evolved over the years: Screening, Shareholder Advocacy, and Community Investing . . ." ("Introduction to Socially Responsible Investing") We will discuss these three strategies.

Socially Screened Investment Funds

Socially screened investment funds were pioneered by Amy Domini. (Domini, 2001) The point of a socially screened fund is that the stocks in the portfolio are selected for both their financial and social value. In May 1990 she set up The Domini Social Index (DSI), composed of 400 stocks similar to the Dow Jones or Standard and Poor's indexes. The following year she set up the Domini Social Equity Fund tracking the DSI. At first these funds were shunned by many investors for fear that they would not perform as well as traditional funds. With assets of over \$2B, today it is the largest and oldest socially screened investment fund in the US. Her fund has out performed the Dow and the S&P for ten years. Domini Social Equity Fund averaged 20.83% growth per year and the S&P averaged 18.70%, as of May 2001. This is a performance achieved by "fewer than a third of other mutual funds." (Roosevelt, 2000) Since then all funds have declined in shareholder value. Some think that screened funds might decline more than the market due to the dot.com bubble bursting. But that has not yet been proven. Referring to the DSI, Savides reports, "Being weighted in technology, it fell 12.1 percent through Dec. 31, while the S&P 500 was down a marginally better 11.9 percent during that period." (Savides, 2002)

Now virtually every investment company, 150 or more funds, offers a socially screened fund as an option. Sue Schaefer of Commonfund, estimates that 10% of mutual fund assets are in socially screened funds. ("Socially Responsible Investing," 2000)

Generally speaking the financial performance criterion is like a gate. If the stock does not perform well financially, it will not be included regardless of its social importance. (Van Buren, 1995) Most commonly used screening criteria are avoiding investments in companies that manufacture alcohol or tobacco, or engage in gaming. "You won't find any 'booze, butts, or bets' in her portfolios," referring to Amy Domini's funds (Roosevelt, 2000) Social Investors Forum lists 12 screening criteria: alcohol, tobacco, gambling, defense weapons, animal testing, products/services, environment, human rights, labor relations, employment/equality, community investment, and community relations. ("Introduction to Socially Responsible Investing") Shareholder Action Network, a project of Social Investment Forum, names the leading four screens for 2002: global warming and renewable energy, predatory lending and executive compensation, vendor standards (sweatshops), and protecting human rights. ("Shareholder Action Network Focus for 2002") The 2002 list reflects the current concerns over globalization and international issues affecting politics and investments.

Screening can be very complex. If the company has many product divisions, some kind of explanation will be required as to why a stock is included or excluded. Sometimes it is based on the percent of total sales that product represents. Usually a fund screens for several criteria. The number of screens varies from one or two, like Calvert World Values Fund, to a lengthy list like Calvert Social Balanced fund, which screens for all twelve listed above. The verdict may be as extreme as "no investment" or "not screened for this concern." But often a fund will take a middle ground, using phrases like "seeks company with strong labor relations track record." ("Introduction to Socially Responsible Investing")

Shareholder Advocacy

The cornerstone of shareholder advocacy is using the share ownership options like the annual proxy vote. The Episcopal Church pioneered using their proxy power to influence corporate behavior. Now most national religious groups and their pension funds have an active social responsibility program for their investments. The Interfaith Center on Corporate Responsibility (ICCR) was formed in 1972 to assist religious institutions with their proxy activity. The ICCR has 275 member institutions with a $110B portfolio, it assists religious organization introduce over 100 of the 250 social proxy resolutions introduced annually.

The model for proxy activity used by most ICCR members consists of six steps. It begins with the passing of a resolution by the governing body of the group. The group's investments are reviewed in light of the resolution and, thirdly, companies are targeted that do not abide by the resolution. A resolution is introduced, often through the ICCR, to the shareholders by proxy. The fifth step is an attempt to open a dialogue with target companies. If the dialogue fails to move the company in the direction of compliance with the resolution, the last step is to have the resolution appear on the notice of the annual meeting and proxy statement mailed to all shareholders. Representatives from the church group will appear at the annual meeting to question the company officers in public and speak in favor of the resolution.

What are the successes or results of shareholder advocacy? This is a persistent question because there are few clear wins in the exercise. The divesting of companies with operations in South Africa in the 1980s is still a big win. Many shareholders who are not normally active in advocacy were active in that campaign. But influencing corporations is slow: the Episcopal Church shareholder resolution was in 1971, but the big action did not come until the 1980s. It is interesting to note that divesting is not now the preferred advocacy campaign because the shareholder loses influencing power in divestment. Many groups, like the ICCR, prefer remaining a shareholder in order to enter into dialogue with companies. The most evident success is the number of proxies that are withdrawn because the target company has made an effort to move in the direction the proxy sponsor wants. The Episcopal Church has about three-quarters of its proposed resolutions withdrawn because the company has moved in the desired direction. Some of these are easy fixes, like "minority representation on the board." But many of them are serious, honest discussions valued by both sides, which probably would not have happened without the shareholder resolutions.

Advocacy on environment issues shows some impressive gains. GE being forced to clean up the PCBs from the Hudson River is often sighted, particularly with current White House stands on environmental issues. A quick scan of the status of this year's voting to date (Spring, 2002) at annual meetings shows support of "Reduce greenhouse gas emissions" resolutions up dramatically: ChevronTexaco—withdrawn, Eastman Chemical—29.4%, ExxonMobil: 20% [up from 7% last year], Occidental Petroleum—19%. Support for pharmaceutical price restraint is still around 3 or 4% in most cases, as is support against weaponization of space. ("Companies, Resolutions, and Status—2002")

Another example of shareholder advocacy that illustrates how results take time is the Independent Monitoring Working Group that was established as the result of dialogue with Gap. The group began work in 1995 and consisted of three Non-Governmental Groups (NGOs), including ICCR, and Gap. The final report was made May 24, 2002, detailing the accomplishments toward "fair, productive and harmonious conditions" in Gap's manufacturing plants in Central America. ("Independent Monitoring Working Group Final Report On Independent Monitoring in Central America")

Community Investments

The third area where ethical decisions can be made about investing institutional funds is commonly called "alternative investments" or community investments. In 1977 Congress passed the Community Reinvestment Act (CRA) that mandated that "All banks and savings and loans have a 'continuing and affirmative' obligation to help meet the credit needs of their communities, including low-and moderate-income areas. The 1988 General Convention called on the Episcopal Church, in all dioceses and parishes to establish a ministry of community investment and economic justice for the economic empowerment of the disadvantaged and to utilize community controlled economic development programs to achieve this end." (Community Investing, 1999:44, 6)

Traditional banks experienced a crisis in the early 1970s when deposits moved to various mutual and money market funds with checking accounts at stock brokerage houses, like Merrill Lynch cash management accounts (CMAs). Loans to community development projects and low-income housing were hardest hit by this shift. Local banks engaged in "redlining," drawing a red line around poor areas where they refused to make loans. Congress responded to this by passing the CRA, which requires all banks to be evaluated on their community investment performance. Since 1990 the report of that evaluation is a public document. Local community development financial institutions (CDFIs) were the main recipients of the money flowing to the depressed areas. At first the response was slow with only about fifty CDFIs in existence by 1994.

That all changed in 1994 when Congress created the Community Development Financial Institutions Fund which "was created to provide the availability of credit, investment capital, and financial services in distressed urban communities." ("CDFI Fund Overview") On February 15, 2002 the Department of the Treasury listed 553 certified CDFIs in the country. For example, there are 10 in New Jersey and 25 in North Carolina. To be certified a CDFI must be "a legally existing entity, having a primary mission of promoting community development, principally serving and maintaining accountability to eligible target market(s), being a financing entity, providing development services and not being either a government entity or controlled by a government entity. Certification does not constitute an opinion by the Fund as to the effectiveness or financial viability of the certified organization." ("Community Development Financial Institutions Fund")

There are basically four types of CDFIs, although new government funds are constantly becoming available for specialized programs: community development banks and community development credit unions (deposits insured by the FDIC), community development loan funds and community development venture capital funds (not insured by the FDIC). "Though still small by capital market scale, more than 550 CDFIs manage more than $6.5B in assets today" with no losses of investor capital. (Pinsky, 2001)

The government is the largest investor in CDFIs. Religious institutions and socially motivated groups (mission-motivated investors) are the second. For example, The Social Investment Forum has launched a "1 % in Communities" campaign to encourage socially motivated investors to put 1 % of their portfolios in below-market community investments. CDFIs also borrow from traditional banks and insurance companies. Individuals contribute with deposits and CDs. "These CDFIs finance business start-ups and expansions, housing, and social and cultural institutions, ranging from childcare to community arts facilities. Business finance ranges from microenterprises to mid-sized enterprises. Housing finance includes single and multi-family rental as well as homeownership." (Pinsky, 2001)

The Episcopal Church has set up community development centers in many communities across the country. There are five in Northern New Jersey. They act as a non-profit conduit to borrow from CDFIs. They use other sources, including donations, for development projects such as housing or daycare centers. They also help prepare applicants to get these funds. The Church Pension Group is actively seeking investment opportunities in CDFIs.

Summary of Four Ethical Principles For Managing Endowments

The examination of the Episcopal Church indicates that it uses four ethical principles for managing endowments: (1) fiduciary ethics where the social actions taken in the market place are rooted in resolutions enacted by elected representatives, (2) socially screened mutual funds, (3) shareholder advocacy and (4) investments in Community Development Financial Institutions.

The church examined in this case, the Episcopal Church, is run by democratic processes, which makes fiduciary action easy. Non-democratically run churches, such as the Roman Catholic Church, have other ways to fulfill their fiduciary responsibility. For instance, many Catholic monastic groups and managers of Catholic college endowments are very active in carrying the Catholic principles of justice to the market place. For instance, Sister Patricia Daly, a Dominican Sister, has been executive director of the Tri-State Coalition for Responsible Investment for over twenty years. Her group invests for the pension funds of religious groups and she is well-known for her shareholder activism. The famous Jack Welch of GE sent her a note when he retired. (Goldsmith, 2002)

Funds invested in mutual funds, the second principle, can now be invested in socially screened funds to articulate a social belief in the action of the market place and fulfill a fiduciary obligation to church contributors and pensioners. The operative word in social investing today is "and." Many fund managers used to argue like "Tom Herndon, Executive Director of the Florida Board of Administration, which manages the state and local retirement funds, said social concerns do not enter his calculations. 'We're not activists for any particular social cause. Our purpose is to try and maximize our return on our investments for a given amount of risk.' Otherwise, he said, 'It's a slippery slope. It's tobacco today, and tomorrow it's alcohol and entertainment. . . . Eventually you get to a point that your stockholdings are fewer in number than the ones you exclude.'" (Goldsmith, 2002) He represents the old view that the investor's choices are to go for profit maximization *or* social causes, sometimes referred to as the choice between "Doing Well **Or** Doing Good." Today a growing number of investors believe that one can "Do Well **And** Do Good." The Episcopal Church's website for explaining its proxy voting guidelines is titled: "Doing Good and Doing Well."

The shareholder advocacy principle is proxy action by direct owners of shares. Religious groups are leaders shareholder advocacy. Of the 250 social proxy resolutions filed each year, from 100 to 150 are filed by religious organizations through the ICCR. The current round of annual meetings shows a marked increase in the number of shareholders who are voting with the activists. The resolution at the ExxonMobil meeting about green house gases got a 20% approval, up from 7% last year. (Goldsmith, 2002)

The third area of investing, and the fourth principle, that is an option for socially-motivated investors is community investments. This is new to many investors and institutions. But with the Federal funds available to Community Development Financial Institutions (CDFIs), it is a growing option. These are an important part of community development. Religious and socially motivated groups are the second largest sources of these funds. There are some groups calling for a percent of endowments to be invested in these FDIC insured institutions.

References

"About ICCR." www.iccr.org

"CDFI Fund Overview." www.cdfifund.gov/overview/index.asp

"Community Development Financial Institutions Fund," www.minoritybank.com/cdfi.html

"Community Investing: An Alternative for Religious Congregations Seeking a Social as well as a Financial Return." (1999) The Episcopal Network for Economic Justice.

"Companies, Resolutions, and Status—2002." www.iccr.org/products/proxy_book02/rezstatus_chart.hmt

Doing Good and Doing Well. www.episcopalinvestments.org

Domini, A. (2001). SOCIALLY RESPONSIBLE INVESTING: Making a Difference and Making Money. Dearborn Financial Publishing, Inc. Chicago.

Goldsmith, R. (2002, June 23). "Nun keeps 'nudging' for corporate reform." *The Sunday-Star Ledger*, pp. 1, 23.

"Independent Monitoring Working Group Final Report On Independent Monitoring in Central America." www.iccr.org/news/press_releases/art_imwg.htm

"Introduction to Socially Responsible Investing." www.socialinvest.org/areas/sriguide

"Investment Issues Survey." (2000) United Church of Christ Foundation.

Kohlberg, L. (1973). The Claim to Moral Adequacy of a Highest Stage of Moral Judgment, *Journal of Philosophy*, 70, pp. 630-646.

Moore, J. (1990). What Is Really Unethical About Insider Trading?" *Journal of Business Ethics*, 9, March.

Paine, L. S. (1994). "Managing for Organizational Integrity." *Harvard Business Review*. March-April.

Pinsky, M. (December, 2001). "CDFIs Look Ahead After 25 Years of Community Development Finances" www.brook.edu/dybdocroot/es/urban/capitalxchange/article9.ntm

"Proxy Voting and the Mission of the Church." (January, 2000). Peace and Justice Ministries of the Episcopal Church.

"Report From the Social Responsibility In Investments Committee." (September 19, 2001). www.episcopalchurch.org/peace-justice/sri.html

Roosevelt, M. (2000, October 16). "How Green Is Your Money?" TIME. Vol. 155. No. 16, p. 79.

Savides, S. (2002, Jan 14). "Over time, social funds hold their own." *Christian Science Monitor*. P. 16. Boston, MA.

"Shareholder Action Network For 2002." www.shareholderaction.org

"Socially Responsible Investing." (Winter 2000) CFQ. www.commonfund.org

Van Buren, H. (1995). "Business Ethics For The New Millennium." *Business & Society Review*, no. 93: 51-55.

Chapter Five

The Values of Business Education and Working Life from a Gender Viewpoint

ANNA-MAIJA LÄMSÄ

PIRKKO TURJANMAA

AILA SÄKKINEN

Introduction

A t the end of 1999, the Finnish Government fixed new national guidelines for higher education up till the year 2004. The guidelines define education as a crucial factor in our strategy for the future, aiming at the well-being of all citizens and cultural diversity, sustainable development, and prosperity. A watchword in the Finnish higher education policy over the next few years is "educational equality." Moreover, in order to meet the needs of the different regions of the country, the guidelines expect the institutions of higher education to pay special attention to better regional responsiveness through intensified cooperation with local businesses and industries. And finally, the academic curricula and degrees are to be developed to meet the specific needs of working life. (Ministry of Education, 2000.)

If the aim is to develop education to meet the needs of working life, it makes sense to explore the values that these needs are derived from. In the context of business education, then, we should study the value basis of business life and its relation to the values of business education. It is also important to know how the values of the business world stand with respect to issues like equality and cultural diversity. Some scholars have criticized the fact that that educational and working life contexts rarely meet in research (Tynjälä et al., 1997); that is, studies of values in educational settings have mostly been conducted separately from studies of values in a working life context. This chapter represents an attempt to take the criticism into consideration and to integrate these two perspectives.

The emphasis given to equality and cultural diversity in the educational policy leads us to approach the topic from a gender viewpoint. Gender is a core question in any discussion on equality, and is also related to cultural diversity. We believe that the use of a gender viewpoint can lead to a higher degree of sensitivity to the values implicit in business education and its practices. Martin (2000), for example, says that if scholars fail to investigate the workings of gender in their research, they will contribute to the perpetuation of inequality—whether intentionally or not.

Katila and Meriläinen (1999) contend that most of the contemporary Western academic organizations claim to be gender-neutral. Based on an empirical study in a Finnish business school, however, they argue that instead of gender neutrality, the social reality in the academic environment of the business school was gendered, so that the masculine was taken as the norm, the feminine marking a difference.

We base the present study on ideas reported in an earlier paper (Lämsä et al., 2000), in which we suggested that business education might induce a change in students' values towards the masculine. In the said study, however, our sample was not well-balanced in terms of sex, which is why we wanted to reinvestigate the issue in more depth. The focus here is on the effect that business education has on the values of business students. Additionally—and in contrast to the earlier study—this chapter explores the values of prevailing in the business world by asking how they are defined by Finnish entrepreneurs. Our aim is to compare the values of students and those of entrepreneurs, and discuss how they are related. This type of knowledge is useful if we want to assess the value basis of Finnish business education from a gender viewpoint. "Values" here refer specifically to "feminine" and "masculine" values.

We conducted our empirical survey among Finnish business students and entrepreneurs, with the objective of finding answers to the following questions:

- Are there differences between the values of women and those of men?
- How do the values of business students change in the course of their education?
- How are the values of students and entrepreneurs related to each other?

The remaining part of this chapter is divided into four sections. In Section 1 we describe our theoretical background, followed by an overview of the study method in Section 2. Section 3 presents the empirical results. The contribution of the study is then discussed in Section 4.

Theoretical Background

Our theoretical framework is based on the concepts of "feminine" and "masculine" values, and "gender." Moreover, we draw upon socialization theories, particularly on the ideas of social constructivism (Berger and Luckmann, 1966).

"Feminine" and "masculine" are quite vague as concepts. Masculine values are defined as those ascribed to men in our socio-cultural environment and feminine values, correspondingly, as those ascribed to women (Alvesson and Billing, 1997). In other words, the members of this culture know what "being a man" or "being a woman" amounts to (Jansz, 2000). Although we accept that men's values are often masculine and women's are often feminine, it would be simplistic to assume that such a connection is either direct or self-evident. These are socio-cultural concepts which people learn in the course of their lives. In other words, when something is labelled as masculine or feminine, it does not necessarily relate to the characteristics of actual men or women but, rather, is culturally associated with the categories of "male" and "female" (Fondas, 1997).

Scholars have suggested that there is no single form of masculinity and femininity. Instead, they claim, it is possible to distinguish a variety of masculinities—paternalism, authoritarianism, careerism, and so on (Collinson and Hearn, 1994). Similarly, there are a variety of femininities: women can be categorized as "iron women," "victims," "mothers," "pets," and so on (e.g., Kanter, 1977; Lämsä and Tiensuu, 2002). In this chapter, we apply the well-known masculine-feminine dimension suggested by Hofstede (1980, 1990). According to him, this is a fundamental socio-cultural dimension, which expresses the extent to which the dominant values in a particular cultural context are masculine or feminine. Hofstede considers the masculine-feminine dimension as a major feature of a particular culture—say, an occupational culture.

A feminine value basis refers to characteristics that emphasize ideals such as interdependence, the importance of other people, of caring and nurturing, fluid sex roles, and the idea that people work to earn a living, "work to live." The stress is on equality between men and women. Participation and cooperation are seen as a source of motivation in working life. Sympathy with the less fortunate, good relationships with other people, and an emphasis on the quality of life are other crucial elements. A masculine value basis, on the other hand, stresses the importance of financial success, the possibility to earn a lot of money. Big is beautiful. Outstanding performance is greatly appreciated, and sex roles are differentiated: men are expected to be assertive and women to be caring and nurturing. Independence, not interdependence, is the ideal. Ambition and money are the driving force in working life, and the successful achiever is admired. Performance is what counts. People do not "work to live," they "live to work."

There are several ways in which business education and business life can be understood as gendered. The concept of gender can, accordingly, have diverse meanings. Joan Acker (1990) systematizes the insights of previous researchers into occupations, working life, and gender in her article "Hierarchies, Jobs, Bodies: A Theory of Gendered Organizations." She argues that neither working life nor business education should be regarded as gender-neutral but, rather, as environments where gender is created and maintained. In this chapter we follow the idea that working life in the business world is gendered in such a way that gender-typing, particularly in managerial and entrepreneurial jobs, has come to be seen as masculinized. Several writers have noted that current business theory as well as business education are based on masculine values as the accepted norm of behaviour (e.g., Aaltio-Marjosola, 1994, 2001; Alvesson and Billing, 1997; Billing and Alvesson, 1987; Calas and Smircich, 1996, 1999; Derry, 1996; Erikson and Pietiläinen, 2001; Hite and McDonald, 1995; Katila and Meriläinen, 1999; Lämsä and Sintonen, 2001; MacLellan and Dobson, 1997; Martin, 2000).

Some theorists claim that the asymmetrical cultural evaluations of the categories of "male" and "female" have promoted the idea that femininity is of lesser value as compared to masculinity (Fondas 1997). Other scholars have pointed out that, although gender is an inescapable part of business life, it should not be a source of hierarchy or inequality (Gherardi, 1994; Irigaray, 1993). To the extent that gendered features are differently valued and evaluated, what inevitably follows is inequality (Britton, 2000).

Moreover, we stress the view that both masculine and feminine characteristics need to be recognized and valued in the business world, not only to eliminate the prevailing inequality but also because of the increasing diversity of the workforce (Rollinson and Broadfield, 2002). In Finland, for example, more than half of all business students are females. Also, partly as a result of the Equality Act and the high educational level of Finnish women, the number of female professionals entering positions of power in today's business world is increasing, albeit only slightly slowly. Women are encouraged nowadays more than ever to choose occupations in technical fields, which have traditionally been a men's domain. This poses a challenge both to business schools and business firms: how to make themselves more accommodating to diverse types of people with differing values. The gender viewpoint draws on the idea that there should be social space, not only for masculine, but also for feminine values in education as well as in working life.

Social constructivism sees the socio-cultural environment as a resource by means of which people understand their own and others' behaviour (Berger and Luckmann, 1966). Socio-cultural definitions such as masculinity and femininity are typically perceived as law-like and self-evident by those who live in a particular cultural context, since such definitions are collectivized and even reified through socialization processes (Phillips, 1991). From a gender viewpoint, this means that in the course of life women learn values that are feminine and men values that are masculine. Psychologically oriented theories emphasize the role of "primary socialization," that is, people's experiences of early childhood with their parents (Chodorow, 1978; Gilligan, 1982). In other words, an individual's development process in early childhood is understood as something which brings about different identities in males and females as a result of this parental influence. These theories can be criticized for overemphasizing the role of primary socialization, although to some extent they might explain women's keener interest in social relations as compared to men's (Billing and Alvesson, 1994).

"Secondary socialization" refers to the internalization of institutional or institution-based values (Berger and Luckmann, 1966). In other words, the establishment of differences between the genders is attributed to the outside world. By accepting socially accepted roles and rules, people incorporate the prevailing feminine and masculine value basis. Women and men learn to live up to the expectations of how they should behave. They encounter various socialization agents, such as school and occupational expectations, and through these are provided with models for suitable behaviour (Billing and Alvesson, 1994, p. 43). Following this line of thought, we might expect the practices of business education and of working life in the business sector to act as socialization agents and to play an important part in the secondary socialization process of business students and entrepreneurs.

Method

Sample

Our survey sample consisted of 178 persons, of whom 38 were entrepreneurs and 140 business students (see Table 1).

Table 1
Description of the Sample

Group	Total number (n)	Female (%)	Mean age (yrs)
Students beginning their studies	69	58	21.7
Students ending their studies	71	61	25.4
Entrepreneurs	38	47	37.6
Total	178	57	26.6

The gender distribution in the sample was 57% female and 43% male. The share of women among the entrepreneurs was 47% and among the business students 59%. The ages of the entrepreneurs varied from 25 to 53 years, while the students were between 19 and 27 years of age. The entrepreneurs' lines of business covered transportation (33%), private service sector (17%), wholesale and retail industry (17%), and hotels, restaurants and tourism (13%). Their entrepreneurial experience varied so that 33% had been entrepreneurs for over 10 years, 47% from 3 to 10 years, and 20% less than 3 years. The students in the sample were undergraduates of a typical Finnish business polytechnic. The sample was so divided that 49% of the students were just beginning their studies, while 51% were nearing the end of their studies. The students also differed as to their work experience: 17% possessed no work experience whatsoever, whereas 20% had gained more than 3 years of experience in working life. The surveys with the students were conducted in classroom settings, and with entrepreneurs in connection with training events on a voluntary and anonymous basis.

Questionnaire

Hofstede et al. (1990, p. 287) argue that it is possible to measure people's cultural values quantitatively on the basis of their answers to written questions. In our survey we used a two-part questionnaire (Lämsä et al., 2000). The first part consisted of 14 statements for measuring Hofstede's (1980) dimension of masculine vs. feminine values. The second part asked about background factors such as sex, age, phase of education, line of business, and work experience.

The part concerning Hofstede's masculinity-femininity dimension was measured as a continuum with pairwise comparisons. At the level of observable variables, this meant using a questionnaire consisting of pairs of statements or characteristics from which the respondent had to give priority to one over the other using a scale from 1 to 5 (1 is the most feminine characteristics and 5 is the most masculine characteristics). The pairwise comparison might, for example, be expressed in the following form (Lämsä et al., 2000; cf. Laurila, 1995; Hosseini and Brenner, 1992):

Please estimate the relative importance of the statement on the left compared with the statement on the right.

	Very Important		Equal		Very important	
Caring for others	1	2	3	4	5	Financial success
Employees participate in decision- making	1	2	3	4	5	Managers make the decisions

The masculine vs. feminine dimension—referred to as the "masculine-feminine index" in this article—was compiled as a mean from the individual statements.

Results

The results of the study are illustrated in Figure 1. A two-way ANOVA method (presented in Table 2) was used to test the means of the masculine-feminine index in the three groups (students beginning their studies, students ending their studies, entrepreneurs) according to two factors: 1) phase of secondary socialization, and 2) sex of the respondents in each group.

Figure 1
Means of the Masculine-Feminine Index by Two Factors:
Secondary Socialization Phase and Sex of Respondents

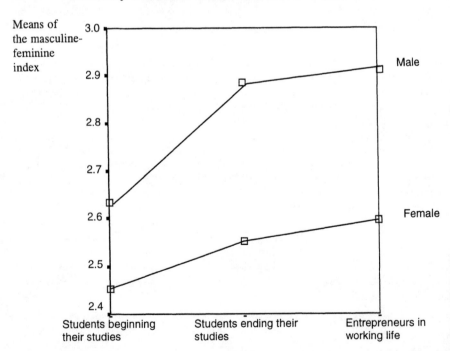

Table 2
Two-way ANOVA

Dependent variable: Masculine-feminine index

Source	Sum of squares	df	Mean square	F	Sig.
Corrected model	5.057	5	1.011	7.667	.000
Intercept	1241.417	1	1241.417	9411.963	.000
Phase of socialization	1.609	2	.804	6.099	.003
Sex	3.216	1	3.216	24.385	.000
Phase of socialization and sex, interaction	.231	2	.116	.877	.418
Error	22.686	172	.132		
Total	1269.161	178			
Corrected total	27.743	177			

R squared = .182 (adjusted r squared = .158)

Figure 1 shows that both the phase of socialization and the sex of the respondents had an effect on the masculine-feminine index. This effect is statistically significant, as indicated by Table 2. However, there is no interaction between the two factors: the curves in Figure 1 are similar, but at a different level ($p = 0.418$, Table 2).

Our first research question was: Are there differences between the values of women and those of men? Table 2 indicates that there was a significant ($p = 0.000***$) difference in the orientation of men and women. Figure 1 shows that femininity is clearly associated with females and masculinity with males. This result is consistent with our earlier finding (Lämsä et al. 2000, p. 209) and, for example, also supports Gilligan's (1982) argument that women are socialized into feminine and men into masculine values. Women tend to prefer values such as caring, nurturing and collaboration with others, while men favour competition, independence, and financial success.

Our two other research questions asked: How do the values of students change in the course of business education? How are the values of students and entrepreneurs related to each other? A general finding is that the phase of socialization does, indeed, have an effect on the masculine-feminine index ($p = 0.000***$). To investigate the change in values during education, we performed a multiple comparison of the means of the index according to the respondents' phase of socialization, using Tukey's test. The test showed a statistically significant ($p = 0.031*$) difference between students at the beginning and those at the end of their studies. Moreover, as illustrated in Figure 1, there was a change in a masculine direction. Thus, it appears that the social practices, rules, and expectations of business education affect the values of the students so that the masculine model becomes increasingly common as they pursue their studies. This finding confirms our earlier suggestion that values may change in a masculine direction in the course of business education (Lämsä et al. 2000, pp. 210-211).

Figure 1 further shows that entrepreneurs had more masculine values than business students as a whole. Tukey's test confirmed that the values of students who were only beginning their studies differed significantly from the value basis of entrepreneurs ($p = 0.003**$). The corresponding difference between entrepreneurs and business students ending their studies, on the other hand, was not statistically significant ($p = 0.484$).

These findings suggest that the value basis of entrepreneurs has taken masculinity as the norm of behaviour. The results further indicate that the institutional practices of business education act as a source of secondary socialization. These practices affect both female and male students, so that their values shift in a masculine direction in the course of education. Thus, the values of business education and working life seem to converge in favour of the masculine value basis of the latter.

Finally, an issue worth noting is the natural imbalance with regard to the age of the respondents in the sample: the entrepreneurs were considerably older than the students (see Table 1). To see if this affected the results, we investigated whether there was a dependency between age and the masculine-feminine index. However, there was no dependence either in the graphical presentation (scatterplot) or the correlation coefficient ($r = 0.045$). Thus, age was not an intervening variable.

Discussion and Conclusions

The results reported here seem to indicate that business education in Finland is quite well in agreement with the guidelines of the Finnish higher education policy, to the extent that education certainly does appear to draw upon the values of working life. In other words, the findings suggest that the values of business education correspond closely to the ideals valued in business life. With respect to the masculinity and femininity of the value sets of students, our earlier study (Lämsä et al. 2000, p. 209) indicated that business students tended to be more masculine in their orientation than their non-business counterparts. Those results together with our present findings imply that the socialization process of business education reinforces an already internalized value basis among students who have chosen this line of study. Hence, we argue that current business education is adaptive rather than critical or transformative in nature, and affirms the dominance of masculine values. This argument is consistent with the study by Katila and Meriläinen (1999), who suggest that although business education often claims to be gender-neutral, in its practices it tends to prioritize masculinity. Our study shows that gender is part of the very conceptualization of business education: it affects learning processes and institutional practices and also has an impact on the kind of professional competence that business students develop during their education.

According to the gender approach adopted in this chapter, there should be social space not only for a masculine but also for a feminine value basis. If we consider the results from this viewpoint, they imply that the values of working life should not be taken as a self-evident and given basis for the development of business education but, rather, that they merit critical reflection. We propose that scholars as well as teachers and those responsible for business education development should acknowledge the presence of the gender aspect and realize the need to reconsider its importance in the social construction of education.

But then, all this raises the crucial question: What are the mechanisms by which educational practices and processes produce such one-sidedness of masculinity instead of giving equal space to both masculinity and femininity. We suggest this as a topic to be investigated in future research. For example, it would be important to study systematically how school textbooks, curricula, and symbolic and material practices of teachers, school managers, and students "produce" gender. By so doing we might be able to reveal the often concealed and taken-for-granted assumptions of masculinity as "normality" in such practices and processes. We think that qualitative research methodology would offer particularly suitable tools for investigating this topic.

Doing away with the cultural asymmetry between femininity and masculinity would require that both business education and business life patterns should be more attuned to a feminine value basis than what is generally the case (Alvesson and Billing, 1997). A transformation towards that direction would allow, not only women, but also men to "do" gender in a more flexible way than what is possible today. For example, the leading newspaper in Finland reported recently (Pölkki, 2002) that research shows that young well-educated, well-earning women in Finland as well as in Sweden are increasingly—even alarmingly—suffering from stress. There are probably several reasons for this phenomenon, but one reason may be that the dominant masculine value basis, which admires the successful and independent achiever and emphasizes dedication to work, contributes to young women's efforts to act up to such standards. The expectations and demands of working life together often with the family responsibilities of a young wife can be a heavy burden to bear. Thus, the values prevalent in working life may force young women to exceed the limits of their own well-being, and we then have to ask whether a better acceptance of feminine values would ease the situation. We propose that the issue would merit further study in the future from this perspective.

As we see it, any change towards doing away with the assymmetry between femininity and masculinity calls for critical and transformative thinking and acting. For example, the assumptions inherent in business education and practices need to be revealed, questioned, and discussed. Such a change may be slow and difficult to carry out, since the social world is easily perceived as an objective reality which is taken-for-granted, natural, and not often called into question. However, it is important to note that the "objectivity" of the social world is humanly produced and constructed and, thus, also open to change (Berger and Luckmann, 1966). Before such a change can occur, the learning processes of business education should provide the with tools for adopting diverse perspectives of understanding. We feel that this kind of learning is not based on cognitive processes alone, but also on emotional experiences which enable the learner to grasp new relationships between things. Thus, we find it important to study and develop learning principles and methods which stress the connection between cognition and emotion, whereby students' experiences of social reality can be expanded, encouraging them to imagine alternative perspectives to business life.

Moreover, following Fondas' (1997) suggestion that the ongoing "feminization" of managerial language may be a significant conceptual development in management and business thinking, we believe that the institutionalization of feminine concepts— both in educational settings as well as in working life—could promote a change. The institutionalization of new concepts is not an easy process, however. The process requires new concepts, and their development is probably at least partly a matter of creativeness. And additionally, we feel that there is probably the question of power at the core of such a process.

The results of this study reveal an interesting feature in the formal guidelines for Finnish higher education. On one hand, the major emphasis on the needs of working life as a starting point for education in fact shifts the responsibility for the value basis from which such needs arise to the constituents of working life. As our study shows, these values may be one-sided, biased, and not even easy to recognize. On the other hand, the stress cultural diversity and equality is a clear contention of what are considered "good" values in education. Thus, the content of educational values is explicated. However, viewed from the viewpoint of business education and gender, the values are contradictory: on one hand, they favour masculinity and the needs of a "masculine" business world, while at the same time, they call for equality of diverse value bases, of masculinity and femininity. It is important to reveal this contradiction, since it helps us to see that educational policy needs to draw upon a wider societal value basis than today's business world often has. Once this contradiction is made visible, it is possible to discuss and explore the topic in depth.

Finally, we recognize that the gender viewpoint is not an easy one since gender itself is not fixed as a concept. We emphasize that the field of this study and the validity of the adopted viewpoint are constrained to their societal and historical context; in other words, the ideas and results of this chapter are historically and culturally situated. The diversity of different types of masculinities and femininities should, in our view, be investigated in the future, also in relation to the unidimensional definition of masculinity and femininity applied in this study. This would give us a broader understanding of the concept of gender in the contexts of business education and working life.

References

Aaltio-Marjosola, I. (1994). "Gender Stereotypes as Cultural Products of the Organization." *Scandinavian Journal of Management, 10*(2), 147–162.

Aaltio-Marjosola, I. (2001). *Naiset, miehet ja johtajuus*. Porvoo: WSOY.

Acker, J. (1990). "Hierarchies, jobs, bodies: A theory of gendered organizations." *Gender & Society, 4*(2), 139–158.

Alvesson, M. & Billing, Y. (1997). *Understanding Gender and Organizations*. London: Sage.

Berger, P. & Luckmann, T. (1966). *The Social Construction of Reality. A Treatise in the Sociology of Knowledge*. Harmondsworth: Penguin Books.

Billing, Y. D. & Alvesson, M. (1989), "Four Ways of Looking at Women and Leadership." *Scandinavian Journal of Management, 5*(1), 63–80.

Billing, Y. D. & Alvesson, M. 1994, *Gender, Managers, and Organizations*. New York: De Gruiter.

Britton, D. M. (2000). "The Epistemology of The Gendered Organization." *Gender & Society, 14*(3), 418–434.

Calas, M. & Smircich, L. (1996). "From 'The Woman's Point of View': Feminist Approaches to Organization Studies." In S. R. Clegg, C. Hardy and W. R. Nord (eds.), *Handbook of Organization Studies*. London: Sage, 218-257.

Calas, M. & Smircich, L. (1999). "Past Postmodernism? Reflections and Tentative Directions." *Academy of Management Review, 24*(4), 649-671.

Chodorow, N. (1978). *The Reproduction of Mothering*. University of California Press, Berkeley, CA.

Collinson, D. & Hearn, J. (1994). "Naming men as men: implications for work, organization and management." *Gender, Work and Occupation, 1*(1), 2-22.

Derry. R. (1996). "Toward a Feminist Firm: Comments to John Dobson and Judith White." *Business Ethics Quarterly, 6*(1), 101-109.

Erikson, P. & Pietiläinen, T. (2001). "Yrittäminen ja sukupuolen moniuloitteisuus—haaste tutkimukselle ja koulutukselle." *Aikuiskasvatus, 4*, 295-305.

Fondas, N. (1997). "Feminization unveiled: Management qualities in contemporary writings." *Academy of Management Review, 22*(1), 257-282.

Gherardi, S. (1994). "The gender we think, the gender we do in our everyday organizational lives." *Human Relations, 47*(6), 591-610.

Gilligan, C. (1982). *In a Different Voice.* Harvard University Press Cambridge, MA.

Gomez-Mejia, L. R. (1983). "Sex Differences During Occupational Socialization." *Academy of Management Journal, 26*(3), 492-499.

Hite, L. M. & McDonald, K. S. (1995). "Gender issues in management development: implications and research agenda." *Journal of Management Development, 14*(4), 5-15.

Hofstede, G. (1980). *Culture's Consequences: International Differences in Work Related Values.* Beverly Hills, CA: Sage.

Hofstede, G. (1990). "Motivation, leadership and organization: Do American theories apply abroad?" In D. S. Pugh (ed.), *Organization Theory Selected Readings*, 3rd edition. Harmondsworth: Penguin Books.

Hosseini, J. C. & Brenner, S. N. (1992). "The stakeholder theory of the firm: A methodology to generate value matrix weights." *Business Ethics Quarterly,* April (2), 191-249.

Irigaray. L. (1993). *je, tu, nous. Toward a culture of difference.* New York: Routledge.

Jansz, J. (2000). "Masculine identity and restrictive emotionality." In Agneta H. Fischer (ed.), *Gender and Emotion. Social Psychological Perspective.* Cambridge: Cambridge University Press, 166-186.

Kanter, R. M. (1977). *Men and Women of the Corporation.* New York: Basil Books.

Katila, S. & Meriläinen, S. (1999). "A Serious Researcher or Just Another Nice Girl? Doing Gender in a Male-Dominated Scientific Community." *Gender, Work, and Organization, 6*(3), 163–173.

Laurila, J. (1995). *Moral Issues in Business: Top Managers' Perceptions of Moral Issues in Stakeholder Relations.* School of Business and Administration, Series A1: Studies 41. University of Tampere, Finland.

Lämsä, A-M, Säkkinen, A. & Turjanmaa, P. (2000). "Values and Their Change During the Business Education—A Gender Perspective." *International Journal of Value-Based Journal, 13*(3), 203-213.

Lämsä, A-M. & Sintonen, T. (2001). "A Discursive Approach to Understanding Women Leaders in Working Life." *Journal of Business Ethics, 34*(3-4), 255-267.

Lämsä, A-M. & Tiensuu, T. (2002). "Representations of the woman leader in Finnish business media articles." *Business Ethics: A European Review, 11*(4), 355-366.

Martin, J. (2000). "Hidden Gendered Assumptions in Mainstream Organizational Theory and Research." *Journal of Management Inquiry, 9*(2), 207-216.

MacLellan, C. & Dobson, J. (1997). "Women, ethics, and MBAs." *Journal of Business Ethics, 16*, 1201-1209.

Ministry of Education (2000). Higher Education Policy in Finland. http://www.minedu.fi/julkaisut/Hep2001/Edusys/3HEPolicy/index.html. 14.5.2002.

Phillips, N. (1991). "The Sociology of Knowledge: Toward an Existential View of Business Ethics." *Journal of Business Ethics, 10*(10), 787-795.

Pölli, M. (2002). "Nuorten naisten stressi lisääntyy." *Helsingin Sanomat* 6.2.2002, A7.

Rollinson, D. & Broadfield, A. (2002). *Organizational Behaviour and Analysis. An Integrated Approach,* 2. ed. Harlow: Prentice-Hall.

Tynjälä, P., Nuutinen, A., Eteläpelto, A. Kirjonen, J. & Remes, P. (1997). "The Acquisition of Professional Expertise—a challenge for educational research." *Scandinavian Journal of Educational Research, 41*(3-4), 475-494.

Chapter Six

Uncovering the Values Driving Business Practitioner and Student Strategies: The Case for Pathfinder Pragmatic Inquiry

F. Byron Nahser

Business conduct and strategies are in the headlines today. And we are fascinated. Of course, the main headline is the stupendous collapse of the American stock market—an estimated $7.9 trillion lost in equity value since March, 2000.

With so many Americans watching stock portfolios shrink and jobs disappear, of course we are interested. And we have a lot to get our attention. Collapsing companies, greedy executives bailing out at the top, insider trading, fraudulent accounting practices, failed mergers, huge losses incurred chasing wildly optimistic technology forecasts. What is the real story behind the disastrous business headlines we see every day? What are the lessons to be learned as we examine the evidence of our recent experience? How are we to run our businesses? What are the lessons of all this?

The Premise

The premise of this account of the current state is that we have to look at the oldest question about human behavior: why actions were taken; what was the motivation. We see the crime; what was the motive. All the headlines tell a story of individual and groups of executives making decisions. On what basis were the decisions made?

What values are driving the behavior? Clearly, it isn't the values that are printed on the wall of virtually every corporation mentioned in the headlines.

These are not abstract, theoretical ideas, but flesh and blood people weighing the options and alternatives based on some end in mind . . . some motivation—call it beliefs, goals, intent, what-is-important, virtues, purpose—values drive all action? Just like any good mystery story, we may see the result, but what was the motive. If not, maybe the confusion lies in the word: Values. Motivation, beliefs, goals, purpose.

This chapter will set the context for the argument that values do have a vital role in the conduct of business, not just in compliance, but in the very heart of the business purpose—service to the market and to society. Business may not be driven by "love," but certainly we are coming to the realization that ignoring others and focusing on the enrichment of the few has led to catastrophic results.

Surely, there are loopholes and regulations need to be passed, as they have been in the past when scandals of this dimension have occurred. Just consider all the changes in the anti-trust era at the turn of the century and the government regulation that occurred after the 1929 stock market crash and the onset of the depression. But, there is a level of focus that cannot be overlooked: the decisions made by the business leaders.

We will make the case for the need to re-evaluate the motives—the values as we will call them—driving business behavior today and offer a way to help executives align their personal values with the values of the corporation, and the marketplace, within the context of society.

The reason why we place such emphasis on the personal motivation of individuals is that this, ultimately is where change must happen. And this time offers us a rare chance to look at these motives.

This is not an idle opportunity. It only comes along once every several generations. The first in American history was the so-called "Gilded Age in the late 19th Century with the rise of the "robber barons" and the resultant regulation of the "trust busters." Later there was the "roaring twenties" and the Great Depression hang-over from the party and the New Deal. Post World War II prosperity led to the Great Society development. What will result from our current situation and how will it happen?[1]

The Decisions Made

When you look at the stories behind the current business headlines, there are three themes:

1.   Individual ethical breaches
2.   Company wide cultural values issues
3.   Disastrous strategic decisions.

Individual Ethical Breaches

Let's take the ethical issues first. This is the "few bad apples" theory. While all the cases aren't outright fraudulent as Dennis Kozlowski skirting the New York sales tax by shipping paintings to his plant in New Hampshire and then back to avoid $1 million in sales tax or the Rigas family members using Adelphia as a personal bank,
We have our attention. but the moral foundation on which business is based?

Company Culture—Values and Vision

Every one of these companies had a mission and values statement. Arthur Andersen was one of the early leaders in establishing ethics programs. Enron values statement would bring tears to your eyes stating the importance of the individual to reach their full potential. But there seemed to be an understanding of how things were done at the company which condoned broad breaches of behavior. While the attitude clearly began at the top, these weren't cases of just one or two people, but a culture which understood what was valued above all else. And where breaches occurred, it wasn't the interests of the stockholders, much less the interests of the customers and society.

Strategic Decisions

The word "synergy" came to the fore often during the '90s. To take one of the more visible examples, AOL, at the height of the dot.com bubble merged with Time Warner with AOL taking the lead. Now, with the stock depressed, veteran Time executives are taking over and going back to some of the basics of the business, mainly quality content. In the words of many executives close to the situation, they admit that they got away from serving the customer. Add Vivendi and Bertlesmann ex-CEOs to the casualty list in moves to bring various media together.

Or look at the so-called Third Generation of telephone service that seized Europe in the bidding for licenses, dramatically over-reaching the market need. Is this an ethical problem? No, just one of over optimistic market forecasting. The venerable Corning bet the company on the fibre optic market making acquisitions funded by the sale of more traditional and stable long-term Corning businesses. The market responded with great enthusiasm driving the stock go from under $20 a share in 1998 to over $100 in 2000. When the bubble burst, the stock plummeted to under $2 in August 2002. No hint of fraud or overly generous compensation. Just a bad bet, based on one view of the core competencies of Corning and a misreading of the market opportunities. But a more reasonable one than the thousands of dot.com smoke dreams where there was no chance of ever making a profit.

The Purpose of Business

This attention globally has raised questions about the American business model making it once again important and useful to raise perennial questions about the underlying purpose of business which were drowned out in the rush for the stock market bubble inflated by dot.com mania, technology convergence and acquisition conquests.

We measure success in business by the valuation of the company. So, not surprisingly, the motive behind these three stories was the promise of financial gain through increased stock evaluations. This began as a worthy effort because the market does offer, in the long run, a very efficient way to evaluate companies.

Take "pay for performance" which grew out of a reaction to the evidence that executives during the '50s and '60s were paid well whether their corporations did well or not. Why not pay them for how well the company did measured by how well the investors in the company did, i.e., by the stock price. Make the managers shareholders, the simple and compelling logic went. That way their decisions would not be in conflict with the good of the company. So, the sensible idea of stock options programs for executives was implemented with a vengeance. We have now seen that did little to change the focus from self-interest of the senior executives. It merely shifted the mechanism for fulfilling their measure of success: money.

When we talk about this being an opportunity to re-examine our purpose in business, we can look at it from the perspective of the three stories behind the headlines: personal values, corporate values and strategy issues.

Investment in Core Competencies—the Essence of Strategy

Underlying that question is the basic question of investment. If business has any purpose in society it is the function of funneling investments of human, material and financial capital to those projects that are deemed to be in the best interests of the future needs of society. It is about change and innovation. As Peter Drucker has said, "It is the purpose of organization and, therefore, the grounds of management authority: *to make human strength productive.*" He goes on to say: "The principle underlying this is . . . *'personal strengths make social benefits.'*"[2]

How do individuals as well as companies determine what they are to do? All investment decisions must be considered in the competitive context. Consider the popular so-called SWOT analysis: the strengths and weaknesses of the company and the Opportunities and Threats in the marketplace.

Therefore, the discipline of Strategy, which is being more and more driven by marketing considerations, focuses on investment choices which create the points of product differentiation that will give the corporation a "sustainable competitive advantage." One leading strategist has gone so far as to say that the fundamental role and purpose of strategy is to "induce your competitors not to invest in those products, markets, and services where you expect to invest the most. . . ."[3]

My 40 years experience in advertising has shown that these investments must translate into core competencies which help the organization fill customer's needs better than the competition. The sum total of these features and benefits are well summarized in the meaning in customers' minds as the "brand."

Relationships—The Heart of Marketing

Love is the extremely difficult realization that something other than oneself is real.
— Iris Murdoch: *The Sublime and the Good*, 1959.

Serving something or someone. The "other"—the central figure in this chapter—through my work in the advertising business. Behind the ubiquitous presence of the advertising veil, lies the powerful (and some would say seductive) pursuit of meaning. Advertising is designed to define and support a brand—the sum total of the meaning of the product or service—its philosophy. The activity of *branding* is coming to be seen as the critical component of business strategy, since the purpose of business is to create and serve a customer. In earlier days, marketing was looked on as structuring a one-time exchange between the buyer and the seller. Marketing worked with the so-called "four Ps"—product, price, place and promotion—and adjusted these elements to come up with an optimum exchange. Today, marketing's role has been raised to a much higher level. It is responsible for the *relationship* with the customer to determine their needs and then respond with a flow of ideas and products for the long-term benefit of the relationship over time. (This change of view can also be seen as the familiar move from the mechanical view of nature, which is highly structured and to be manipulated like a machine, to the organic or biological view of nature as a living entity with a wide range of choices, responses, relationships, and interdependencies. I will come back to this thought later in this chapter). Or, in the terms we are using for this chapter, the company must consider the needs of the "other," whether for love or profit, and then make the necessary choices and investments to deliver what the market needs.

Marketing Relationships—Three Targets

Elements of strategic relationships in Pragmatic Pathfinder Inquiry may be shown as:

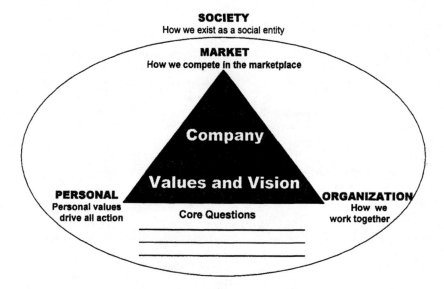

This framework shows how values and vision need to be aligned for a successful organization to bring the three key elements of personal, corporate, and market values into alignment—within the context of the broader society which supports the overall effort.

How to reflect on—uncover—the values and vision driving these three elements is the subject of the rest of the chapter. The vision of the company grows out of these values and is the basis for making strategic investment decision.

How to Think About Values

How do you decide? Based on a philosophy or belief, as people have always decided what to do. The result of this search for values to drive business decisions is cropping up all over business, e.g.: Victoria's Secret has a corporate philosophy stated inside their provocative catalog. Jaguar Corporation has a philosophy. If you check, your local dry cleaner will most likely give you a copy of their Mission Statement. And recently, while visiting Seattle, I walked into the Pike's Place Brewery, and, after a casual look at that most American of products—the six-pack of beer—I was shocked and pleased to see these words begin the copy on the side of the carton: "Micro-brew is a philosophy."[4] Clearly, philosophy has come of age. However, from the evidence, these values are not driving business behavior.

How to connect the values to performance. Too often, values, as defined by ethicists, has been a constraint—"don't" as opposed to the source of motivation to "do."

This chapter will make the case that all the searching for deeper meaning to drive motivation—what we are calling values—in business will be greatly enhanced by the application of that unique, and often maligned and misunderstood philosophy: Pragmatism. (Pragmatism means far more then the usual "do whatever works" or "action unguided by principle.") There is a reality out there—a truth; an "other"—with which I must be in touch and understand, and perhaps even love. Pragmatism, as I will be using the term, is the method of inquiry which helps determine a "belief" or "truth" in terms of the consequences which result from embracing that belief or truth. As William James asked: "What is the *cash value* of the idea?" (I find this turn of the phrase to describe Pragmatism particularly engaging for business people.) Or John Dewey would say something like: "If this is what we believe, then this is the action we should take." Pragmatism, therefore, involves an "other."

Pragmatism holds great promise for the type of strategic investment inquiry suggested above. The founder of Classic American Philosophy, Charles Sanders Peirce, states the case quite dramatically:

> A certain maxim of Logic which I have called Pragmatism has recommended itself to me for diverse reasons and on sundry considerations. Having taken it as my guide in most of my thought, I find that as the years of my knowledge of it lengthen, my sense of the importance of it presses upon me more and more. If it is only true, it is certainly a wonderfully efficient instrument. It is not to philosophy only that it is applicable. I have found it of signal service in every branch of science that I have studied. My want of skill in practical affairs does not prevent me from perceiving the advantage of being well imbued with pragmatism in the conduct of life.[5]

Allowing for the fact that Peirce was trying to impress his audience at Harvard, his alma mater which had rejected him, this is high praise for a simple insight that ideas and beliefs are the action and consequences which result *from* those visions and beliefs.[6] While simple, it has profound implications for pursuing the truth. Yet, this original meaning has traveled quickly down the slippery slope to the much maligned "do whatever works" stance. This is far from the original intent of these earnest members of the canon who urged the most rigorous and challenging thinking and feeling to come to the best beliefs to guide actions.

Peirce has said that the truth was approached in the movement between ideas and the reality in the form of constant testing. His basic model was Scientific Inquiry where you establish an hypothesis and then go out to test it, continually modifying your hypothesis, based on the evidence. He called this "abduction" in distinction from "induction"—constantly collecting facts and evidence—and "deduction"—applying a conclusion, law, or truth.

How to Practice Pragmatic Inquiry

Since the meaning of Pragmatism today has degenerated into a simple "do whatever works (for *me*)," it is well to begin by stating that the major breakthrough of pragmatic thinking established the relationship between one's ideas and the "other" in the outside world. Modern thought, for example, can be characterized as either falling to one extreme of individual, subjective interpretation or to the other extreme of worship of objective science.

Peirce's successor, Josiah Royce, noted these two extremes as two categories of knowledge—*perception* and *conception*—which he saw as dominating the greater part of the history of philosophy. *Perceptions* are what we see; the signs or evidence around us which we take in through our senses. *Conceptions* are ideas, especially our beliefs, which filter what we see. Royce took from Peirce the realization that there is a third category of knowledge, different from *perception* and *conception,* called *interpretation* that brings perception and conception together and compares them. In Royce's words, interpretation "surveys from above. It is an attainment of a larger unity of consciousness."[7] Reality must then be understood as a "sign" which needs to be interpreted, not as a thing in itself. It is to be known, understood, and judged true by the *activities* that keep it going as a sign. Royce's insight overcomes the centuries-old debate between realism—something out there—versus nominalism—the construction of reality in our own minds. The Pragmatists say it is both; it's the constant interaction between the two that make up the pursuit of truth.

Intuition

We have now seen how Pragmatism corrects the individual's subjective orientation at one end of the spectrum and focuses on the movement between the individual and the outer reality of the "other." Pragmatism's emphasis on intuition also corrects the orientation to fact and the rational at the other end of the spectrum. The following quote states the problem:

> The status of intuition has declined over the last century, perhaps with the increasing emphasis on formal logic and explicit data and assumptions of science.
>
> —Oxford: *Companion to the Mind*

The Pragmatists all realized the great importance of being able to think and listen to other sides of your intelligence. Peirce called it musement: "Enter your skiff of musement and push off into the lake of thought and leave the breath of heaven to swell your sail. With you eyes open, awake to what is about, or within you, and open conversation with yourself, for such is all meditation."[8] This important idea of musement brings the intuitive to what too often is considered a very utilitarian form of logic.[9]

William James put it equally poetically: "Dive back into the flux itself if you wish to know reality, that flux which Platonism in its strange belief that only the immutable is excellent, has always spurned; turn your face towards sensation, the flesh-bound thing which rationalism has always loaded with abuse."[10]

We now apply intuition and interpretation to the "flux" of our experience, the center of Pragmatic Pathfinder Inquiry.

The Heart of the Inquiry: The Evidence of Experience

We all know how easy it is to say what our values are. But the only way is to ask: what is the evidence of experience.

- How have the values worked in your life?
- What is the evidence of your experience?
- What decisions have you actually made?

When the work is done in a group, we find that the use of "interpretation" is particularly important. Each person has a different view of the reality the corporation faces. But the image is of a cable where each strand is important as opposed to a chain where the line of reasoning is only as strong as the weakest link. We always remind participants in a group that "everyone has a piece of the truth."

At the Personal level, we have used PPI in helping individual executives and leaders of corporations determine the direction of their careers and how they can articulate their leadership beliefs and structure the Vision, Purpose, and Strategy statements of their corporations. Students of business schools have a particular need to reflect on their careers. They too often have moved into career decisions, either guided by outside influences or by narrow monetary interests, but not by a clear grasp of Vision, Beliefs, and Values to drive their decisions.

Begin—Doubt, Problem

One of the major features of scientific thinking is the testing of hypotheses. The way scientists go about their business is to set up a theory, called an hypothesis, and then design tests to prove, or, more accurately disprove it. We seldom look to prove ourselves wrong, but this element of pragmatic inquiry is invaluable, and leads us to the second feature of Pragmatic Inquiry, learning.

Not the scientific method as understood.

The word, *Pragmatism*, therefore, needs a dramatic redefinition. Several elements of Pragmatism help correct and expand the truncated definition and which guides PPI. I will suggest three:

Falsification

Many people today claim that the most scarce commodity is time to reflect.

Pierce, the founder of Pragmatism, attributed this not to a lack of time but to a more fundamental problem: "Few persons care to study logic because everyone can see themselves to be proficient enough in the art of reasoning already. I observed that this satisfaction is limited to one's own ratiocination and does not extend to that of other men."[11] But it is doubt or uncertainty that begins the process: "The irritation of doubt causes a struggle to attain a state of belief. I shall term this struggle, inquiry. . . ."[12]

Learning—Explore

John Dewey embraced that idea. Dewey, who focused on the logic of inquiry, said "all learning is a continuous process of reconstruction of experience."[13] Looking at experience in this way, we need to ask what assumptions were behind the experiences— challenge these assumptions, and look for clues as to how we might develop and change these assumptions and beliefs. Keeping in mind that Pragmatism states that beliefs are seen in light of their consequences, then this idea has considerable importance in pursuing the truth and modifying beliefs for future action.

Know More

We are all familiar with this format. We don't know much about something so people tell us about it.

Reformat/ReFrame

We know something and then we re-think it to put a different meaning on it.

Transformative

Here the idea takes over us. We see that we cannot do other than to see ourselves as part of a larger story.

Narrative—Interpret

Reflection on Experience

This focus on consequences and action leads naturally to the idea that truth is not told once but is always in the making. This relationship with an "other," as told through the experiences forming into a plot, tells a great deal about the set of beliefs and assumptions that are guiding the storyteller as well as the people in the story. Their beliefs have been driving the action.[14] The simple reason for this is that only by knowing the underlying beliefs and direction of the story can we determine such things as success, failure, danger, alliances, and practice of virtues.

This brings us to the central feature of Pragmatic Inquiry: it leads people to reflect on their own experience and see what assumptions and beliefs are behind it and what clues they can get as to where the narrative of their lives might go . . . *based on their vision and beliefs in connection with the "other."*

A good place to conclude this discussion of the thee basic elements of *Pragmatic Pathfinder Inquiry* is to relate the definition of philosophy by Alfred North Whitehead, the last member of the canon of Classic American Philosophers. He gave an address at the Harvard Business School in 1934 entitled: "On Foresight." In the talk, he encouraged the students to be looking ahead, constantly testing the environment, and going from the general to the specific, all of which he felt were indications of philosophical thought. He concluded his statement with this definition of philosophy:

We have now examined Pragmatism and the three major elements which have guided the development of the *Pragmatic Pathfinder Inquiry*. We will now consider how Pragmatism has been put to work through the *Corporantes Pathfinder Notebook*.

There are many other features and aspects to this rich philosophy, but, since the framework for this discussion is to help individuals and corporations determine the investment they need to make for future action in developing a relationship with the "other," these three strike me as the most helpful. They offer strong medicine to remedy the traditional narrowness and traps of business thinking characterized before:

Now that we have some general background on business strategy and levels of inquiry which corporations and individuals have to go through to determine their choices of investments, we will turn to three elements of Pragmatism which help structure and facilitate the application of pragmatism to practical inquiries.

Putting Pragmatic Pathfinder Inquiry to Work
with the Corporantes Pathfinder Notebook™

As I mentioned before, we have the Inquirers consider the three elements of relationship with the "other." The inquiry process can begin at any point and then move to the other two.

Below is the Spiral outlining the steps in the Corporantes Pathfinder Pragmatic Inquiry process:

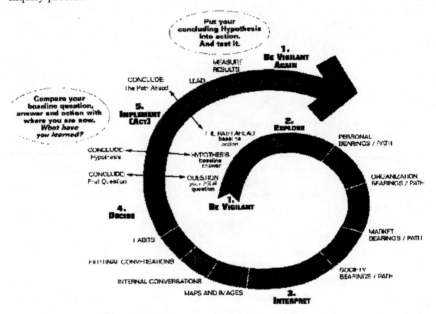

Copyright: Corporantes 1999

A brief explanation of the name, *Corporantes Pathfinder Notebook* and *Pragmatic Pathfinder Inquiry*, and how they developed might be of help. We have considered the key elements of Pragmatic Inquiry. We have added "Pathfinder" to suggest the narrative aspect of the inquiry. As we have worked over twenty years with students and executives in hundreds of settings, we have developed a notebook. We've also used Pathfinder—again to suggest the narrative idea of people finding the way they have to go and Corporantes is a play on the Latin "corpus" (the present participle "forming into a body" which individuals and executives do as they inquire together).

The inquiry begins with a question. In business, this is easy because generally there is some crisis which begins the inquiry. With students, while it may seem easy to have students reflect on their careers, it is actually more difficult because they often have a lot invested their choices and certainly don't want to start rocking the boat with job interviews and graduation in view. This is especially true with MBAs who see a pot of gold at the end of the rainbow. In any case, it is critical to have inquirers in a stance of uncertainty—of interpreter—when they begin the investigation. It is then important to have them state what their preliminary beliefs, assumptions, and answers are now, which frees their minds to explore other alternatives.

The exercises are then organized in five steps: **Begin, Explore, Interpret, Hypothesize** and **Act!** Here is an outline of the inquiry:

Begin!

- As we move forward, what question, issue, doubt, problem, situation, do we face?
- Why is the question important?
- What is our preliminary answer now?
- Why is the question or issue important—what actionable steps will we be able to take when we get an answer? (This will sharpen the question and make it actionable.)
- What actions do you now think should be taken?

Explore!

Corporate

Bearings
- Our thoughts regarding where the corporation and its products and services are now.

Path
- Retrace how the corporation and products have developed.
- What has been learned?
- Decisions made and not made.
- And where do we want to head in the future?

Market

Bearings
- Our thoughts regarding where the market situation, the customer, the industry, and this society are now.

Path
- Retrace important events and decisions and how the market, etc., have developed and where they seem to be headed in the future.

Personal

Bearings
- Your thoughts regarding your personal situation. In terms of your individual career or your career within a corporation now.

Path
- Retrace your experience with the issue or problem that the corporation faces or, if you are contemplating your career, the path—reflect on the path you have been on and where it seems to be heading.

Society

Bearings
- Where is society now and how does it impact your question or issue?

Path
- Where has society been in relation to your question and where would you like to see it go?

Interpret

Maps and Images

- This covers various drawing exercises in what the situation looks like, what it should look like and what action plan should look like.

Internal Conversations

- Explore the inner voice and well as what you think others might say.

External Conversations

Compare your ideas with others and ask questions and get their opinion.

Habits

- Explore known and unknown habits, strategies, or tactics, which lead or limit our progress. On what assumptions are they based? What needs to change?

Hypothesize!

Create a vision (purpose, mission, values, and beliefs) for your corporation and for your involvement with that corporation, or for your own career.

Act—The Path Ahead

Put your vision and beliefs to the test in action. What actions will the corporation take and what actions will you take.

How to Conduct the Inquiry

A Pragmatic Pathfinder Inquirer works much like a healthcare practitioner works with clients—surveys the symptoms, collects test information from many sources, probes for causes, formulates an hypothesis, takes action in recommending a healthful regiment, and monitors the results.

Central to this inquiry is to treat the corporation and one's career as living entities with talent, character, a service to provide, and a path to follow. As in any exploration, we urge inquirers to be open to surprises, capture vague impressions, feelings and memories, and look for patterns and connections; be willing to entertain new explanations and ideas you don't now believe in. In a word, use intuition—the right brain—as well as the more rational left brain.

Keeping notes on an ongoing basis as ideas, facts, and impressions present themselves is an important part of the practice of Pragmatism. With enough entries in the CPN, Inquirers discover their own interpretation of the evidence they have collected. This gives a way to:

- Explore and interpret the reality in which they operate.
- Respond to the reality.
- Improve their habits and thought.
- Think more intuitively.
- Understand their unique, sustainable role—individually and as a corporation—to serve the needs of society.
- Think together as a group and make the best use of different perspectives and talents.

The result is a simple statement of logic:

If this is what we have discovered and believe in,
then this the action we need to take.

Conclusion

Attention

At the beginning of this chapter I pointed out the service which all the headlines about business is providing us. Business now has our attention and that is the first step in the inquiry. It must have a problem or some issue you want to think about. This is also the time-honored beginning of reflection and what we pay attention to does determine who we are.

Alfred Whitehead in his famous talk before the Harvard Business School talked about *Foresight* and said that business' purpose was to be thinking ahead and making investments in behalf of society. It was in that talk where he had his famous quote about:

A great society is one in its men (and women) of business think greatly of their function.

He concluded his talk with a definition of philosophy:

Philosophy is an attempt to clarify those fundamental beliefs that finally determine the emphasis of attention that lies at the base of character.[15] The behavior of the community is largely dominated by the business mind.

Whitehead's emphasis on character is what becomes clear as we reflect on one's experience because the fundamental beliefs that one holds determine the action which exhibits one's character.

Relationship—Mechanical to Organic

Many business thinkers are looking at and taking seriously the importance of moving from the mechanical point of discovery to a biological or organic point of view. Under the mechanical theory, scientific inquiry was to determine the truth of how something actually operated. This gave rise to the spectacular success of science and mathematics to explain the great Newtonian machine of the universe. As we move from that to the more organic model, we need to look on development models and the best come to us from biology. An image I often use with executives and students is to consider a cell or organism, and how it needs to relate to its environment. It is constantly taking in data and interpreting it to determine a better way to engage the environment and survive and thrive. This model rings true with business people who are constantly in contact with the marketplace and need to take in information and modify their behavior.

Narrative—Drama

A second model, in addition to the organic model, is to see this process of relationship and movement as the unfolding of a drama. So-called "arts-based management studies" is springing up and seizing the imagination of the theory laden and passion starved executive. For instance, the Cranfield School of Business outside of London is using drama, such as Shakespeare's *Henry V* or *Julius Caesar*, as the theme for students to study lessons of management.

> Charles Osgood—what is this an example of? (chunk up) vs. principle and give an example (chunk down)

This was first suggested by Fr. Oliver Williams and John Houck of the University of Notre Dame, has been to encourage business people to write their own stories. They have focused on "character traits the endure over time, [that] display what it means to be a Christian in the business world. Christian beliefs give shape to a person's lifetime story."16 Other people's stories will surely be shaped by different beliefs. But the point is the evidence of beliefs will be revealed through the story.

The CPN has the advantage of students writing their own dramas and learning the lessons from their own experiences, something the pragmatists and those encouraging storytelling in business would applaud.

The final word is that the story of business and people's individual careers needs the awakening to "the extremely difficult realization that something other than oneself is real." That to me is the major connection between business strategy and deeper questions of business purpose.

This is an attempt to show the constant movement of an "other" manifesting itself in this world.

Maybe the story of which you are a part, you see the larger picture. It begins with a Divine spark, which we embody in a spirit, or a soul, or life force. This is then expressed in our psyche, our temperament, personality, inclinations. The psyche then finds expression in a career which, along with "others," forms an organization to serve some market need.17 This market exists within a larger society which lives by prevailing ideas and beliefs. Then images emerge at the so-call global consciousness level, which is not nearly as vague a concept as you might think. Major examples include the movement from the machine age to the information age, the awareness of the ecological crisis and interdependence of the planet, rise in the respect for the feminine, concern for rights in ethnic conflicts, third world labor issues building to the wider issue of global, political, and economic justice. Others go so far as to see this global consciousness as an expression of the emerging of a Divine Consciousness.

Whether *Pragmatic Pathfinder Inquiry* as practiced through the *Corporantes Pathfinder Notebook* can awaken the beginning of "love" or not, as we all search for relationships with others, is a story which each one of us tells through the evidence and activities of our own lives.

Notes

1. Fogel Robert William, *The Fourth Great Awakening*, University of Chicago Press, Chicago, 2000.
2. Consider the words of John Paul II concerning corporate purpose from a spiritual development perspective stated in *Centesimus annus*: "the purpose of a business is not simply to make a profit, but is to be found in its very existence as a community of persons who in various ways are endeavoring to satisfy their basic needs, and who form a particular group at the service of the whole of society."
3. Bruce Henderson. *Strategy*. BAT Press, Boston, 1985, p. 10.
4. Philosophy could even be called "hot" as indicated by a recent article in *Elle* magazine one of the most sophisticated women's fashion publications. In an opening section of their Fall Fashion issue, they had an article entitled "The Philosopher" is describing philosophy as the new way to get in touch with your life and the choices you might make using Socratic dialogue, logic, and reason. September, 1999, p. 170.
5. Christopher Hookway. *Peirce*. Routledge, Inc., London, 1992, Cover.
6. William James said: "The ultimate test for us of what a truth means is, indeed, the conduct it dictates or inspires."
7. Josiah Royce. *The Problem of Christianity*. University of Chicago Press, Chicago, 1968, pp. 273-300.
8. James Hoopes. *Peirce on Signs*. Chapel Hill, NC; University of North Carolina Press, 1982, p. 264.
9. This has been especially important in my work in advertising where ideas need to incubate. Plato says much the thing in the Phaedrus #270. Socrates says: "Every great art must be supplanted by leisurely discussion, by stargazing, if you will, about the nature of things."
10. *William James Writings 1902-1910*. The Library of America, pp. 745 and 746.
11. Charles S. Peirce. *The Philosophical Writings of Peirce;* Justus Buchler New York: Dover Publications, Inc. 1955, p. 5.
12. Ibid. p. 4.
13. John Dewey. *Experience and Education*. Macmillan Publishing Co., Inc., Old Tappan, N.J., 1963, p. 89.
14. So truth appears to always be in movement or may even be considered as a verb as in the Hebrew definition of truth which means something like "a consciousness sitting in a great and loving lap learning about the world." So it really exists. Pragmatic truth is not things made, but things in the making.

15. Alfred North Whitehead. *Adventures of Ideas*. The Free Press, New York, 1967, p. 98.

16. Oliver F. Williams, John W. Houck. *Full Value*. Harper & Row, San Francisco, 1978, p. xvie.

17. I have had a long-standing conversation with my old Marketing Professor, Philip Kotler, at the Kellogg Graduate School of Management, Northwestern University. In our conversations, I have asked him just how far we can stretch the marketing relationship concept. After some discussion, he looked me and queried: "You mean to the level of *I-Thou*?" We were referencing the reflections of Martin Buber. We both feel that as marketing continues to evolve, it must reflect authentic relationships and not the manipulative models that often rule today." Professor Kotler is suggesting, as an example, that we move from the "hunter" model of markets to the "farming" model.

Chapter Seven

Paying for Tuition at the Higher Educational Level, a Contribution to the Ethical Debate

Cécile Deer

Introduction

In the wake of the British government's decision to introduce means-tested tuition fees for British and other EU students and to replace maintenance grants by loans, the debate concerning the funding of higher education continues. In spite of the repeated pledge made by the current Labour cabinet that fees will remain stable and that no top-up fees will be tolerated, pressure has been mounting for higher education institutions to be given some leeway for charging tuition fees at higher rates that those set at government level and in some instances to be given the right to charge at whatever level people are prepared to pay for their university and their course. This is still a controversial issue, but many university representatives and academic staff are now eager to increase the income of their institution in this way, thereby reducing dependence on dwindling unit costs from central government funding.

Views differ regarding the best way a differentiated fee policy could be implemented. Most claim, however, to have the problems of access and equity in mind. The economist Nick Barr, for instance, working from the assumption that free tuition is unaffordable in the mass system of higher education that Britain now has, comes to the conclusion that universities should be allowed to set their own fees because a central funding council can no longer do so adequately. The solution he puts forward is based on income-contingent loans, whereby tuition fees are not paid up front by the poor student but are repaid later by the rich graduate he or she becomes.[1] This is presented as a fairer deal than the current situation as it removes the subsidy that middle-class students enjoy. On the public choice side, there is the voucher school of thought whereby government funding for students to universities would be given directly to individual students to pay their fees.[2] This plan is presented as highly equitable in social terms: students, as fully-fledged customers, would be in a stronger position to demand higher standards and improved facilities and, by the same token, the universities would become more independent from the State. Finally, a number of pamphlets from the Institute of Economic Affairs have adopted a Malthusian approach and argued not only that freely-set fees would reduce student numbers, but also that this is what Britain needs. Artificial demand, rampant credentialism and unemployable graduates are the terms of the debate as expansion diminishes the added value of a higher education both for individuals and society.[3]

The aim of this chapter is not to assess in detail the specific fairness or unfairness of options such as variable fees, vouchers, grants and/or loans. The discussion will focus on the moral assumptions underpinning the current debate, which, had it taken place twenty years ago, would certainly have provoked a major outcry both within and outside academia.

Nothing New Under the Sun: Adam Smith's Approach of Market Rules in Education

In the utilitarian tradition, if each man is entitled to take into account his losses and gains when satisfying his own interest, so too is society. Any nations—and by extension any society—is said to be well organized, and *a fortiori* just, when its institutions deliver the highest total sum of satisfaction for all individuals.

In line with this understanding, some of Smith's observations concerning education would be familiar to those who follow the debates surrounding higher education in Britain, in particular the one concerning the Phoenix-like binary divide. Well-endowed universities are described as having become "sanctuaries for exploded systems and obsolete prejudices" [WN 781][4] while improvements have been made in poorer institutions because they have had to become more responsive to public demand (he does concede, however, that the former have managed to attract the wealthiest students!) [WN 772]. Similarly, his position on the funding of education would find a resounding echo:

> The institutions for the education of the youth may . . . furnish a revenue sufficient for defraying their own expense. The fee or honorary which the scholar pays to the master naturally constitutes a revenue of this kind. Even, where the reward of the master does not arise altogether from this natural revenue, it still is not necessary that it should be derived from that general revenue of the society, of which the collection and application is, in most countries assigned to the executive power. [WN 758-59]

Ultimately, Smith asked the question which is at the heart of the current debate concerning tuition fees in higher education, namely if education should be a public responsibility at all [WN 781]. The answer he offered was clearly a recipe for a two-tier system of education: on the one hand, there should be public provision for the "common people" in order to foster socio-political stability and technical dynamism [WN 784] but for the middling ranks, as a public form of education would prevent fair competition through an induced lack of profitability or lack of competitiveness for any private providers, the role of the state should be to indirectly render the study of science and philosophy[5] almost universal—though not pay for it—by imposing probation for entrance to the professions.

As a matter of principal, the Smithian understanding holds that education should not be entrusted to the public sector, where there is little incentive for teachers to over-exert themselves [WN 759]. Teaching, with its salaries, endowments and the privileges of graduation, is likened to trading with a bounty which works against proper and useful private provision. This is why the very idea of an academic salary is deemed to be as "directly in opposition to duty as it is possible to set it." Stemming from the belief that Man is naturally lazy and that his interest "vulgarly understood" is to neglect his duty, it leads naturally to the conclusion that, in order to ensure that teachers are effective, they have to be directly dependent upon deserving "the affection, gratitude, and favorable report of those who have attended upon their instructions" [WN 760]. Moreover, as the teacher/student relationship is considered to be a private exchange, the institutional setting in which this exchange takes place should have no impact on the financial reward to which a teacher is entitled. No advocate of tuition fees has gone so far as to reintroduce this radical utilitarian logic.[6,7] In the various ideas for reform that have been put forward, higher education is and remains institutionally-based, with the universities and their various departments allowed to fix fee levels for whichever courses they offer. Market purists could swiftly identify this as a tangible cause of market failure.

In balance, a number of Smith's opinions also depart from the strict supply and demand approach. In particular, he recognises that without public subsidies certain important subjects would simply not be taught [WN 765].

> Were there no publick institutions for education, no system, no science would be taught for which there was not some demand; or which the circumstances of the times did not render it, either necessary, or convenient, or at least fashionable to learn [WN 780].

This concern is echoed in *The Theory of Moral Sentiments,* where he justifies public funding for mathematics by suggesting that necessity, convenience or fashion may not be the sole justifications for the kind of knowledge imparted at a higher level. He also concedes that rivalry and emulation can occasion the greatest exertions [WN 760], a clear hint that non-pecuniary rewards may be worth taking into account in order to understand individual motivation. Although Smith denounces the modern philosophy of his time for treating the duties of human life as chiefly subservient to the happiness of a life to come rather than to the happiness and perfection of a human life [WN 771], his own theory of moral sentiments is closely related to this perspective. The way in which he justifies this suggests a further reason for studying unrelated to market-led demand which is that "education can mend the heart" [WN 772]. Here again Smith identifies a key dimension of education that university reformers in Britain have to address.

How are we to relate Smith's general propositions for optimizing education at a higher level to today's utilitarian school of thought to which the proponents of differentiated fees more or less avowedly belong? Their shared understanding is that efficient social interactions are best achieved when they stem from an accumulation of unhindered profit-maximizing individual actions. This originates from a sentimental conceptualization of human activities (as opposed to the rational one preferred by the social contract philosophers) which owes much to the notions of sympathy and of the impartial spectator expounded in Adam Smith's *Theory of Moral Sentiments*. The approach is characterized by the essentially speculative dimension of human interactions. Individuals seek admiration and approval from others, without which they cannot fulfill their whole selves. In the particular case of higher education, this applies to the motivations of academics, to those of the students and even to those of their families.

The added-value accruing to each social agent taken individually does not arise from other specific social agents but from the characteristics of the whole that they have contributed to shape. The pursuit of material well-being *and* moral excellence are both part of the picture. The collective context allows individual to define himself, but remains nothing more than a collection of individual actions. A causal loop unites the individual and the collective and, together, men produce something that goes beyond their own individual experience.[7]

This represents an exteriorization of the norm which can be a source of freedom. The self is freed from the influence of others while its individual actions contribute to the shaping of society. This is what Nicholas Barr feels able to say about income-contingent loans in that they would set young adults free and this measure is presented as fundamentally progressive in social terms.[8] *De Profundis In Loco Parentis*. Freedom consists of being dependent from an exterior force—the "invisible hand"—which lies beyond each individual but which individuals produce together. In this context, the heuristic path to establishing a definition of justice is an inductive one and may be deduced from what an impartial observer would approve of. The basic structure of society is taken as given and may be efficient in its own right which, in turn, justifies that certain members of a society be deprived of their well-being for the good of all the remainder. The intrinsic risk of reforms and actions based on this approach is that the liberating exteriorization it purports to bring might degenerate into unrecognized forms of alienation.

Internal Limitations of the Utilitarian Perspective on Tuition Fees: A Popperian Criticism and Game Theory

From a utilitarian perspective, the payment of tuition fees and, more particularly, differentiated tuition fees have been socially and therefore morally justified by the idea that the main beneficiary of a higher education is the individual.[9] It should therefore be considered as a private investment right rather than welfare provision which the collectivity has a duty to provide. In particular, the following arguments have been put forward:

- With a higher qualification, one is likely to earn considerably more during one's lifetime.
- Graduate income is likely to rise more rapidly than non-graduate income.
- A degree protects against unemployment and opens up greater job opportunities.

Regarding the impact of a higher education for individuals, the use of past experience to infer such future trends is dubious, especially in the long term.[10] Paths of action cannot be rationally justified upon such inherently flawed inductive premises. In Lange's own terms:

At the individual level, the possession of a university degree is beneficial as long as there is a large number of potential competitors for jobs in the labour market who do not possess the same formal credentials. As higher education continues to expand, however, this advantage will become less pronounced [Lange, 1999].

This statement has been empirically proven.[11]

Let us suppose, therefore, as most supporters of fees do, that action is future-oriented towards goals and aspirations and that the choice of a higher education is solely motivated by future financial rewards.[12] This means that we consider students to be active decision-making agents, eager to avoid risks and able to evaluate realistically the material benefits of a higher education. Most ineffectual behaviour will implicitly disappear as individual choices will be tuned to the completion-rate of expected rewards.[13]

One senses that this line of reasoning has its limitations but, in order to avoid using an over-deterministic approach such as the one used by the reproduction school of thought,[14] we may formalize it using a Prisoner's Dilemma model according to which, in order to achieve their best interests, certain individuals should choose to do one thing, while others do the opposite. If we consider that students are rational decision-makers then the most appropriate model to formalize the likely behaviour of an individual student would be a two-person game against Nature.[15] This would provide a mock-up for the decision process involved in the choice of staying on, or not, in higher education when the other player is neither an individual, nor an identifiable group of individuals. It would show that the advent of mass higher education combined with tuition fees (differentiated or not) brings a real case at a personal level for deciding against staying on. At this stage we need to remind ourselves that the government is both introducing tuition fees in higher education *and* pushing for greater participation. If it succeeds, then even if the relative private returns for staying in higher education decrease,[16] a high proportion of students can be expected to choose to stay in post-compulsory education.

Risk avoidance means that the greater the participation rate in higher education, the riskier it becomes to opt out. What this ultimately shows is that assessing the range of risks which a student faces is as important as assessing the level of expected returns. However, it is because the utilitarian approach to higher education has little to say about the former that it may be considered to have its limits, as we will now discuss.

The Justification of Tuition Fees on a Social Contract Basis

As we have seen, differentiated tuition fees have been justified mainly on utilitarian grounds, that is on the common good that would not fail to accrue to society if students taken individually were encouraged by their introduction to evaluate the potential risks and rewards of staying on in higher education. However, we run into a problem if we cannot agree on what can and should be taken into account in the measurement of such risks and rewards. This is very much the case for a value-loaded activity such as education. However, there is an alternative moral framework to the one adopted by those who use market mechanisms to justify tuition fees, one that attempts to account for the initial conditions of individuals and their likely attitude towards external risks and opportunities. This may be found, in particular, in John Rawls's *Theory of Justice*.

Rawls's theory is based on a revised social contract, where the role played by the state of nature in the traditional theories is replaced by an egalitarian situation at the point of origin. This provides the foundation for the principles of justice for the basic structure of society. As the original "contract" is "signed" between free and equal individuals who are also rational and disinterested, it may be expected to take place in fair and morally acceptable circumstances. In particular, no one would willingly sustain protracted personal losses for the sake of the collectivity. Benevolence would be an alien concept and nothing would indicate that utility would be the prevailing principle of human interactions, since it is incompatible with the conception of social cooperation among equals for mutual advantage.

Rawls establishes a key distinction between the *concept of justice* and the *conception of justice*. The *concept of justice* is an adequate equilibrium between competing demands argued along the lines of the constitutive principles in the distribution of rights and duties and in the adequate distribution of social advantages. This would correspond very much to the kind of arguments developed by the proponents of market-determined tuition fees. The *conception of justice* consists of an ensemble of principles that aims to determine the pertinent elements that are to be taken into account in order to define the equilibrium.

Two initial principles of justice follow. The first one holds that each person should have an equal right to the most extensive basic liberty compatible with a similar liberty for others. The second one holds that social and economic inequalities need to be arranged so as to be:

a)   reasonably expected to be to everyone's advantage
b)   attached to positions and offices open to all.

From this it ensues that all social values, be they liberty and opportunity or the basis of self-respect *via* income and wealth, should be equally distributed *unless an unequal situation turned out to be to everyone's advantage*.

How may these rules be applied to the case in point? To what extent do the different options proposed regarding tuition fees in English and Welsh higher education satisfy such principles of justice? The subtlety lies in the four possible interpretations of the combined terms "everyone's advantage" and "equally open to all."

The first one, which Rawls calls *natural aristocracy*, would apply to an open system, at least from a legal point of view and bears some similarities to Smith's approach. Its ultimate goal is to avoid a situation where, if less were given to those above, then less would be had by those below. For this purpose, social contingencies should be subject to minimal interference and social advantages limited to those with a potential for furthering the good of society in general, and of its poorer sections in particular. Closer to today, it explains the intellectual positions of certain free market thinkers such as James Tooley, who has even revived the deeply controversial idea of IQ tests for entrance at university to select those apt to benefit from a higher education.[17]

The second interpretation, *natural liberty*, would be consistent with the kind of approach adopted by Thomas Lange, for whom market mechanisms should be brought to bear via income-contingent loans and realistic tuition fees. Here, *"everyone's advantage"* is understood as an *efficiency principle* applied to basic social institutions and *"equally open to all"* as careers being open to talents. An efficient social configuration is one which cannot be altered to better the situation of at least one person, without worsening the situation of at least another one. Inefficiency may be identified when the situation of at least one person could be improved without harming the situation of another one. The rationale is that if those who are able—and willing—to strive for success can do so, then this leads to a form of social distribution that is *inherently* just. The problem is that countless configurations may be considered as efficient depending on the vantage point adopted. For example, many consider that British higher education in the not-so-distant past, with the participation rate at 5%, had an efficient configuration, whereas others believe that an efficient configuration would be one which would see Britain among the top countries in terms of participation rate. However, with regard to this model, nothing is said about the morally unacceptable influence of natural and social contingencies.

The third system is *liberal equality*. The introduction of tuition fees as proposed by Barr and Hills, but also by Lange and Tooley, is consistently formulated along these lines with a central proposition consisting of market-determined tuition fee levels combined with income-contingent loans. Clearly, liberal equality seeks to remedy the obvious social shortcomings of natural liberty. The emphasis is on "fair" equality of opportunity, which neutralizes the influence of social background. Opportunities should exist for all those who are of comparable abilities, providing they show the same willingness to grasp them, and social institutions should steer the free market in this direction. In this picture, it is not surprising to find that education plays a central role, the axiomatic being that it should contribute to fair equality of opportunity. Perfect liberal equality, however, is unachievable. Even if social contingencies could be fully neutralized, it would mean that social distribution would be a function of the natural distribution of talents, which is also unacceptable on moral grounds for it is impossible to secure equal chances of achievement and culture in such a way.

Rawls's final notion is that of *democratic equality*. Fair equality of opportunity remains a valid principle but the impact of natural contingencies in social distribution should be kept under control. *Given a social configuration coherent with equal liberty and fair equality of opportunity, it is just for those above to entertain higher expectations only if this will improve the expectations of those below.* Do the current reforms proposed for higher education, and in particular tuition fees pass the test?

The answer comes in two parts:

First, have the expectations of the least advantaged been maximized by the introduction of tuition fees? The answer to this is "no." It is enough to look at the recent drop in the number of mature student applications. Given that the expectations of the least-advantaged are not being maximized, the next stage is to ask whether their prospects would fall if higher education remained free or tuition fees nominal. There the answer would vary according to whether it is articulated along the line of *access*, *standards* or *aggregate social impact*. This brings to the fore what has not yet been clearly defined, that is to say who exactly would be better off if universities were allowed to set their own fees. Even if participation in higher education is being actively encouraged, it seems unlikely that the greatest beneficiaries will be the least well-off, who rarely gain access to higher education. In very broad terms, two social groups might be said to emerge as overall winners:

- the first is the academic profession and, in particular, that part of it which would be able to build upon a national and even international competitive advantage.

- the second is the generation which has already enjoyed free higher education and will not have to pay for the higher education of those who follow them.

At this point, the discussion would need to shift towards two main areas of possible contention. One would deal with the norm-based behaviour in the current sphere of academic activities, and in particular with the moral value of its economic and cultural implications. The other would be a reflection on *justice between the generations*. There is scope for a far-reaching moral debate concerning Nick Barr's statement that student loans are "wrongly" considered to be public spending as if they were grants, when in effect a significant part would be repaid. After all, it is certainly not by chance that Plutarch, Mandeville, Montesquieu and Smith have upheld the law of Solon, whereby "children were acquitted from maintaining those parents in their old age who had neglected to instruct them in some profitable trade or business" [WN 777].

As far as norm-based behaviour within academia is concerned, I would simply quote Smith in the *Theory of Moral Sentiments*:

> Every independent state is divided into many different orders and societies, each of which has its own particular powers, privileges, and immunities. Every individual is naturally more attached to his own particular order or society, than to any other. . . . He is ambitious to extend its privileges, and immunities. . . . Upon the ability of each particular order or society to maintain its own power, privileges, and immunities, against the encroachments of every other, depends the stability of that particular constitution. That particular constitution is necessarily more or less altered, whenever any of its subordinate parts is either raised above or depressed below whatever had been its former rank. . . . All those different orders and societies dependent upon the state to which they owe their security and protection . . . are all subordinate to that state, and established only in the subserviency to its prosperity and preservation. . . . It may often, however, be hard to convince (them) that the prosperity and preservation of the state require any diminution of the powers, privileges, and immunities of his own particular order or society. . . .

However, Smith also admits that such partiality may sometimes be usefully unjust for:

> It checks the spirit of innovation. It tends to preserve whatever is the established balance among the different orders and societies into which the state is divided; and while it sometimes appears to obstruct some alterations of government which may be fashionable and popular at the time, it contributes in reality to the stability and permanency of the whole system [TMS 230-31].

Conclusion

As Rawls himself recognises, when a moral theory is used to help define a point of view from which to judge social policies, a proposed solution may not be entirely satisfactory without there being a better one at hand. I believe that this is currently the case for the introduction and financing of tuition fees in British higher education. The degree to which the new arrangement, and any future ones, may be deemed just or unjust depends on whether certain expectations are excessive and to what extent these expectations depend upon the violation of other principles of justice, in particular, fair equality of opportunity. For this purpose, a key notion to keep in mind is that whenever an individual gains relative to another, further benefits that accrue to him/her become less valuable from a social point of view. It goes without saying that the level at which tuition fees are set is a key factor in this matter as is their financing through a combination of scholarships, vouchers and income contingent-loans. Free higher education is inherently inequitable, but the income-contingent loans solution is also based on a flawed conception of equity. At this point it is interesting to recall the disagreement between Adam Smith and Jeremy Bentham regarding money-lending rates where Bentham saw no reason to fix a limit as this would be a means of selecting the most entrepreneurial people.

If "justice is the first virtue of social institutions, as truth is of systems of thought,"[18] then we may feel that those who today advance utilitarian arguments to justify the introduction of tuition fees are not telling the whole truth. The moral validity of their reasoning holds because of the narrowness of its scope. Lange warns, for instance, that if full-cost tuition fees are not introduced then Britain may end up—like Germany—with probably the best qualified unemployed workforce in Europe.[19] Not only does he negate the time dimension of any educational process but he also contradicts himself as he has previously written that labour demand cannot be accurately forecast. Moreover, like others, his central assumption is that there is a direct causal link between educational choices and employment opportunities. Even liberal free-market philosophers such as Adam Smith or Friedrich Hayek tell a different story. Social exclusion is for them the result of the externality, of the invisible hand that men create together which ultimately bears little more than a remote relation to direct personal responsibilities. The question Lange should have asked is therefore whether Britain wants the *least* qualified unemployed workforce as opposed to the *best* qualified one.

Adam Smith came closer to an accurate description of the current development in British higher education when he wrote that:

> Society may subsist among different men, as among different merchants, from a sense of its utility, without any mutual love or affection; and though no man in it should owe any obligation, or be bound in gratitude to any other, it may still be upheld by a mercenary exchange of good offices according to an agreed valuation [TMS 86].

In the new era heralded by the technical revolution in information technology, the real problem of social justice in higher education will not be access to knowledge, but access to a real "higher" educational experience. Ultimately, we may wonder if there is any room for social justice in the arena of global competition which the universities have entered.

Notes

1. N. Barr and I. Crawford (1997) *The Dearing Report, the government response and a view ahead* (Submission to the House of Commons Select Committee on Education and Employment).

2. G. Hills (1999) *From Beggars to Choosers: University Funding for the Future* (London, Politeia).
3. T. Lange (1999) *Rethinking Higher Education* (London, Institute of Economic Affairs).
4. References to Smith's work are as follows:
    WN—A. Smith (1775, 1981) *An Inquiry into the Nature and Causes of the Wealth of Nations* (Indianapolis, Liberty Fund).
    TMS—A. Smith (1759,1982) *The Theory of Moral Sentiments* (Indianapolis, Liberty Fund).
5. Science is the great antidote to the poison of enthusiasm and superstition [WN 796].
6. D. Hague (1991) *Beyond Universities: a New Republic of the Intellect.* Hobart paper 115 (London, The Institute of Economic Affairs).
7. J. Tooley (1997). *The Debate on Higher Education: Challenging the Assumption.* Studies in Education. n. 5. (London, Institute of Economic Affairs).
8. N. Barr and I. Crawford (1997) *The Dearing Report, the government response and a view ahead* (Submission to the House of Commons Select Committee on Education and Employment), p. 27.
9. By their early 30s male graduates earn 30% more and women 46% more on average that those who have gone from sixth form straight into a job.
10. L. C. Thurow (1972) *Education and Economic Equality.* The Public Interest.
11. M. Bee (1991) What do Graduates Earn? The Starting Salaries and Earning Prospects of University Graduates. 1960-1986? *Higher Education Quarterly*, 45, 1 pp. 78-90.
12. Young people do not choose a given salary but entrance into a particular segment of the labour market and a range of return into which they would fall at some stage.
13. A. Coleman (1982) *Game Theory and Experimental Games* (London, Pergamon) Chapter 4.
14. P. Bourdieu et J. C. Passeron (1977:1970). *Reproduction in Education and Society.* London: Sage.
15. D. Turner (1992, 3rd ed.). Game Theory in Comparative Education: prospects and propositions in Schriewer, J. and Holmes, B., *Theories and Methods in Comparative Education.* Berne: Peter Lang.
16. OECD (1998) *Education at a Glance: OECD Indicators: 1998.* (Centre for Educational Research and Innovation) p. 361.
17. J. Tooley and A. Seville (1997). *The Debate on Higher Education: Challenging the Assumption.* Studies in Education. n. 5. (London, Institute of Economic Affairs), p. 34.
18. J. Rawls (1973). *A Theory of Justice.* Oxford: Oxford University Press, p. 3.
19. T. Lange (1999) *Rethinking Higher Education* (London, Institute of Economic Affairs), p. 51.

Chapter Eight

Perspectives on Cults as Affected by the September 11th Tragedy

Herbert Rosedale

Introduction

I am the President of the American Family Foundation,[1] a not-for-profit organization in the United States dedicated to the Study of and education of the public about destructive cults. We have been in existence for about 20 years, and I have been President of the organization for over 10 years. For this period of time, I have in effect led a double life. I have been a member of a law firm principally engaged in corporate practice. I have dealt with the representation of large, public corporations, as well as individual entrepreneurs, and I have carried on that work separate and apart from my commitments to the American Family Foundation.[2]

Our organization does not have a formal membership, but consists of professionals such as doctors, lawyers, educators, religious leaders and care givers who are involved with and contribute different perspectives regarding destructive cults. We examine groups based upon their behavior and not their beliefs, and, accordingly, extend our concerns and analyses to many different kinds of groups, including religious, political, self help, occult and self improvement organizations.

Over the years, our analytic approach has been devoted to three goals: (1) providing information about these groups so as to deter people from making ill informed choices of affiliation; (2) treatment of people who have suffered harm from their involvement in destructive groups and (3) education of professionals who analyze and deal with such groups. Our financial support comes solely from individuals and private charitable foundations. We do not receive any governmental aid directly or indirectly. Our existence and delivery of message has not been without controversy. Representatives of cultic groups picket our meetings and threaten our supporters. Critics who support limitless religious freedom for activists and blind themselves to the harm religious activities can cause to other individuals and societies, call us religious bigots. Those who favor unrestricted freedom of expression without regard to responsibility for adverse social consequences or the abuse by the powerful of less well endowed elements in society, such as women and children, claim that we seek to abridge the rights of individuals to express themselves freely associate, and carry out actions without restriction of any kind.

Our supporters have no single political or ideological base. We do not draw our support from the left or the right. Indeed, over the course of our existence, both extremes have been harshly critical of our views. That is not surprising because we tend to criticize zealots of all stripes and praise and support individual critical thought, self respect and respect for the rights others.

One would have thought that the events of September 11th would have brought greater attention to our perspective and given our voice greater attention, but we sadly note that those who confine their examinations to the channels of their narrow perspective continue their mode of analysis disregarding those horrific consequences and ignore views beyond their own narrow field, still remain transfixed counting the number of angels sharing the space on the head of a pin.

But, regardless of those moribund pendants, I believe the events of September 11th have given new urgency to examining cultic activities in societies around the world. We hear this from many sources using language expressing a sense of commonality, but often tenuously parsing words so as to strain shared meaning out of them. Many voices express fervent opposition to "cultic" terrorist groups.[3] Some focus only on a single group, others include those that include those which use the trappings and language of religion to attract membership others use patriotic, psychological, self help or other social themes as their emblems.

World leaders and many professionals insist that current campaigns against Osama bin Laden and his cohorts are not campaigns against religious practitioners of Islam any more that campaigns against the horrors committed by Jim Jones were directed against Christian evangelism or continued prosecution of Aum is directed against any eastern religion's believers.

Since September 11th, I believe that we have become more aware of the cynical use of the language and trappings of religion and should be more opposed to what has been the highjacking of religion to assert claimed protection for actions which if clearly labeled, would be recognized as indefensible.

Likewise, in recent prosecutions of violent groups which harm people and property in claimed defense of environmental or animal rights does not constitute persecution of all adherents of those causes, rather it fastens responsibility for excesses committed in the name of those causes.

Often interpretation of cultic phenomena requires sensitivity to cultural diversity and history. The limits of acceptable individual action in a state and the borders between individual rights and the concerns of state sovereignty involving the welfare of its citizens may differ sharply based upon ethnic considerations, history and policy.

Putting differences aside, it is remarkable how there has been in the main a rallying around condemnation of terrorism evidencing once more an almost universal repugnance towards zealots' assertions that to achieve their perceived desirable ends and goals, they have has the right to ignore the suffering they cause to those who stand in their way. While there has been, of course, no consensus on definition of the term terrorism or clear agreement on condemnation of all violent action no matter what its motivation, there appears to be a growing consensus that there are limitations to individual or group actions destabilizing society through violence.

We need examine cultic phenomena from a three-fold perspective. First the relationship between a cult leader and the members of his or her group, second, relationships between group members and those in the society who are not members of the group and finally, society's role in establishing relations among varying groups, a number of which may claim to represent the unique source of ultimate truth.

What I propose to do, therefore, in this chapter is to outline these three areas of analysis from the perspective of students of destructive cultic activities developed over the past generation. In doing so, I believe we will find striking analogies to the current situation existing in China both with regard to its perception of the need for regulation of leaders and practitioners and supporters of Falun Gong as well as the appearance on horizon and past experience with other groups that threaten the rights of citizens and stability of the society as a whole in China.

Please bear in mind that in my making this analysis, this is a general observation, and I am only a lawyer—not a psychiatrist, psychologist or an historian. In particular, my knowledge of China's history is superficial but even such surface investigation has demonstrated the connections I described herein.

Relationship Between a Leader and Members

It has often been observed that an essential element of cultic attraction and organization is the presence of a charismatic and omnipotent leader.[4] Mere existence of a division in role between leader and member is not a cultic indicator but an organizational one. It is, however, expansion to the extreme that is the concern. Initially, it is common for a leader to attract members through assertion of idealistic goals which attract people seeking to achieve a change in the social fabric or to overcome a preconceived injustice or seemingly intractable economic or social disparity. Sometimes projected goals focus on ameliorating secular defects in current society but, in other instances, they propose rejection of a materialistic approach to life and hold out the aim of spiritual gratification.

These assertions initially often portray the current society as imbued with corruption and uncertainty and offer a simplistic view of a perfect or vastly improved society without focus on the complexity of methods needed to achieve idealistic results.[5] The leader stressing the goals to be achieved, asserts his omniscience and perfection of his vision. In order to enhance the gulf between leader and follower, the leader emphasizes the need for full and complete obedience and requires its continued demonstration through acts of subjugation and destruction of individual initiative and critical thought by the member. Through ritual denigration and humiliation and required increased commitment to prove unquestioned loyalty, the leader emphasizes alienation of the individuals from other existing ties and increases involvement of the membership in group activities and commitments. Members' obedient actions are performed not through choice, but at increasing levels of dictated performance proving dedication. Connections with outside non-members are severed whether they be friends, family or professional associations or, if they are maintained, they are maintained only on a constricted basis with a secondary level of commitment. The extent of the area of domination expands so as to encompass all areas of the members' lives.

Increases in the distance between the leader and the membership continue both with respect to power and control. Whereas, originally the group was ostensibly involved in a value-oriented task of achieving beneficial social ends, in a destructive cult, exposure to the lure of power leads the leadership to increase the gulf between it and the members and to expand the area of control asserted over them. Whatever beneficent aims originally attracted the members to the group, they are subsumed in an aura of obedience with the power of the leader growing in its scope and absolute infallibility. The membership role is reduced to that of a claque and remnants of individual members' critical thought and questioning become signs of disloyalty and deficiency. The area of controlled activity expands far beyond the achievement of purposes of the initial recruitment and is measured by those which reinforce the leader's aura of power and control.[6]

All of the aspects of the members' behavior are placed within the leader's control and are subsumed in the group's agenda. While, perhaps, continuing to profess ideals, in fact, the organization becomes rigid, inhumane and feeds the ego of the leadership divorcing it from the idealism that was used for initial recruitment purposes.

Structurally, therefore, the development of a destructive cult highlights the cynicism in the use of ideals which initially made the group attractive. Slogans embodying them were formulated to respond to perceived social needs and deficiencies but the substance is disregarded as soon as the member is attracted and connected within the group. At that point, the group exists not for achievement of the goals used for recruitment but for the aggrandizement of the leadership. Members become merely a faceless cadre of individuals having lost human distinction, simply filling roles to enhance the leader's ego. In this analysis, it does not matter whether the attraction initially is framed on a spiritual or secular basis. Those ideals are merely used as recruitment slogans only to attract a member, they do not later maintain their position as ideals to be striven for. That is why in dealing with religious groups which become destructive cults, the content of their religious beliefs is secondary and focus on them is a distraction.[7] These religious beliefs are repeated and promoted solely to enhance the leader's goals and they may deviate significantly from those urged by other proponents of the same religion. That deviation is evident, for example, in xenophobic and racially bigoted Christian militant groups such as the Aryan Nation in the United States as well as extremist Islamic groups in the Middle East and Asia. It is likewise why, in a secular area, the content of dogma and doctrine may shift with the prevailing wind so as to continue to form a basis for the attraction of new members, and assertion of the leader's control over members.[8]

We also observe two additional elements. First, that the information made available to initial recruits is far less complete as to the degree of control and compulsion than that given to members as they progress in the membership.[9] Secondly, we often see great deviance in the leadership between the professed goals and idealism and the cynical amassing of trappings of wealth and power.

The common element identifying the destructive cult is not only the cynical use of idealistic goals to recruit without sincere devotion to their achievement, but the growing distance and differentiation between leadership and members so that the leaders become more and more powerful and the members more and more subjugated—even in groups professing egalitarian organization.[10] Yet another key element is the distinction between the recruitment agenda put forth to attract new members, and the discipline and control asserted over members. The discontinuity between the initial assertions and ultimate commitment is deliberately concealed from members. Initial recruits into Falun Gong as an exercise vehicle promoting health are no more told of ultimate suicidal conformity requested than were members of Heaven's gate told they could look forward to castration and mass suicide.

While we always have been aware of the increasing authority asserted by destructive cult leaders over the membership, the occurrence of mass tragedies always serves to bring it back again into sharper focus. Many pose the question of how a sensitive or intelligent person could have been led to commit inexplicable and inhumane acts such as suicide or participate in genocide, mass murder and torture.[11] But, historical illustrations show how past leaders lost their restraint in zeal to exert unlimited power. A long line of religious zealots tyrants and gurus of all stripes start out as reformers, social do-gooders or critics and wind up inciting their followers to commit the most despicable acts to further their power and achieve their ends. Historical analysis gives cultural verification to these otherwise unbelievable narratives, even as in different cultures, different paths are taken.[12] Psychological studies over the past generation have also confirmed the ability of leaders, bearing the trappings of authorized control to induce followers to abandon moral restraints in their actions.[13]

As illustrations of some of these cultic trends, Rajneesh, the Eastern leader preaching simplicity and love amassed a fleet of expensive autos while many followers, lured to his city in the northwest United States, froze to death in unheated portions of the group's facility. Jim Jones as head of his commune induced parents to feed poisoned Kool-Aid to their children so as to avoid his apprehension by American authorities following the trail of complaints. In Uganda, a church was nailed shut and followers incinerated inside by a leader consumed with megalomania. Indeed, induced suicide to serve the ends of the leader occurred not only in China, but in the Ukraine Canada and Switzerland in connection with the deaths relating to the Order of Solar Temple and in the United States with regard to Heaven's Gate. An excellent personal analysis of this transformation is provided in the book written by Nansook Hong (*In the Shadow of the Moon*), the ex-wife of the eldest son of the Reverend Sun Myung Moon, in which she illustrates the transformation and corruption in the development of the Unification Church. The Nuremberg trials and trials of Japanese war criminals after the end of WWII illustrated inhumane behavior performed to carry out the orders of all powerful leaders. With a brief examination, Chinese history shows us groups and leaders transforming themselves in this manner, including such groups as the Yellow Turbans, the Tai Peng and the Boxers, in each instance showing leaders utilizing millenarian or idealistic recruitment tactics and turning their movements into politically and socially destabilizing uprisings.[14] Likewise, illustrative is the Japanese movement of Sokka Gakki (NSA). In the United States, it holds itself out as an exercise group, in Japan, it is a political party with strong ambitions to exercise political domination. Members shift back and forth between various countries and are subject to varying degrees of control. We can also gain insight into these issues through political analyses from George Orwell's 1984[15] to studies of the history of certain Stalinist leaders by Arthur Koestler and others.[16] Now, certain Islamic fundamentalists adopt terrorist tactics and eliminating humane restraints on prospective actions to achieve their ends. Chemical, biological, nuclear—all weapons are acceptable vehicles to be used.

Lord Acton summed it up well when he reflected that power corrupts and absolute power corrupts absolutely. We are continually reminded of the threats that a destructive cults pose when we examine the unlimited lengths to which destructive leaders ask their followers to go and the disregard they have for each individual's worth and rights of their followers. After the tragedy of September 11th, the world has seen the scope of the potential tragedy that zealot members can create. We know that both Aum and Osama bin Laden strove to obtain nuclear weapons to enhance their power. I personally was involved in the examination of Aum's efforts in this regard. While not all terrorist groups are in all respects similar to cults, there are certain characteristics that both share in the exercise of unrestricted power by leadership over members of the group and their willingness to sacrifice members as well as innocent human beings to achieve the goals of the group—which ultimately are the glorification of the leader.

The Relationships between Members and Non-Members

A second critical indicia of a destructive cult is the degree to which the group sharply distinguishes itself and its members from all non-believers. In doing so, it establishes an "us against them" world view, used to build the bonds between members through concentration of common activity, shared secret language and symbolic behavior and an air of elitism so that while believers and participants are claimed to be favored or specially blessed non-believers are stripped of elements of humanity and respect.[17]

Development of this distinction is reinforced internally by practices that seek to allow members of the group immediate identification and special lines of communication. Groups re-define language so that terms have "sacred" or secondary meanings to members that are not readily evident to outsiders. Some groups go so far in this effort as to create their own dictionaries. They may also adopt special forms of dress distinct in appearance by color or enforce or hair styles that will identify members in the group. These both serve to identify members to other members and foster isolation from non-members through their distinctive behavior patterns.

In addition, the group may encourage or require behavior which violates non-members' norms. Encouraging sexual relations with children, fostering interracial marriages, adopting polygamous practices all serve to isolate the group and estrange its members from their families, friends and associates. The group will also substitute career and esthetic evaluations causing rejection by its members of commonly held values shared with non-members.

The distinction is often reinforced by cutting off communication and social interaction between members of the group and non-members. Such interaction may be presented by the group as a threat to purity of members of the group or a diversion which could cause them to lose their intense focus group loyalty or commitment.

Of course, some non-destructive groups encourage or require separation of their members from the rest of society who are non-members. If that separation recognizes respect for non-believers and honors their distinct existence in an pluralistic society, that separation may pose no problems. It is when the separation is combined with dehumanizing non-believers that the destructive elements of cults appear. In some group destructive behavior towards non-believers is fostered. The Church of Scientology for example expressly recognizes and supports harsh treatment of non-believing critics even if they are spouses or family members of believers. Other groups recognize that its proper to deceive and lie to non-believers if for the purpose of enriching the believer's group or achieving their view of beneficent ends. This conduct may embrace criminal activities as well. Of course, engaging in such conduct also tends to isolate the members because through commission of antisocial acts which may well be immoral as well, they reinforce feelings of separation and guilt tying them to other members and preventing and inhibiting free transition out of the group. Groups often use information confidentially obtained about such conduct to intimidate and threaten a potential defector, particularly where disclosure would have adverse effects on the individual's career or relationships outside the group.

There are instances where groups have engaged in what Robert Lifton in his study of Nazi doctors calls "doubling."[18] In those situations, group members in order to justify their heinous behavior towards non-members, internally create two schizophrenic lives. Doing so, they suppress guilt about feelings concerning the heinous acts they have committed towards non-members and live a separate life free of contacts with such non-members fulfilling roles as loyal group members while minimizing the internal impact of inflicting harm on non-members. Of course, this doubling dulls their moral sensibilities and the ethical strictures of the people involved while providing them with a false world in which they can deny the existence of their guilt by suppressing accountability for their behavior. As an analogy, consider those who have incited the suicide of group members as well as those who inflicted harm in the name of enforcing group discipline on members or on non-members.

In addition to that, there are other situations in which in order to carry out assignments, members are sent out into communities of non-members and instructed to suppress indicia of their membership. To conceal their affiliation, they engage in behavior they would not permit to members. Recently, we have seen that with respect to the "sleepers" who are sent out by terrorist groups who engage in activities that are inconsistent with the rules of the groups. But those activities, of course, are instructed, insincere and manipulative. The ultimate purposes are kept and contacts maintain secretly to the group are strong and evident of their real world. An illustration of this recently appeared in the Al Qaeda terrorist's final letter to his German girl friend, expressing in cryptic terms his farewell to her and his devotion to his murderous mission.

Another aspect of the member, non-member relationship deals with questions concerning non-violent interface. In some instances, members of groups who believe they have the ultimate truth tolerate non-believers and confine their efforts at conversion or proselytization to adoption of conduct as an exemplar, demonstrating by their actions consistent with their beliefs the value of their doctrine. Destructive groups, however, do not take such a benign view. In their perspective, non-members do not have essential human rights and their failure to accept and follow the beliefs and practices of the group has deprived them of human status. Such a view can be used to justify ethnic cleansing and other barbaric practices denying human rights and dignity to non-believers.

We have seen this in recent tribal and cultic conflicts in Africa and to a certain extent, in Bosnia and Kosovo. In a recent work dealing with Aum Shinrikyo, Robert Lifton has commented on how in the view of that cult was manifested in the apocalyptic goal of "destroying the world in order to save it" and their action in killing innocent non-believers was viewed as altruistic murder benefiting both the victims and their perpetrators.[19] A similar view may be seen in other apocalyptic cults who through deceit and manipulation induce members into mass suicides for the purpose of accelerating an eschatological aim of bringing about ultimate world salvation. In a less dramatic way, it is common for members to deceive non-members for the benefit of the group using fraudulent misrepresentations and engaging in the concealment of material facts. We may even see this in commercial cult-like groups dealing with pyramid schemes and direct sales tactics which have in recent times been the subject of governmental regulation in China.[20] After September 11th there has been more focus on the use of emotion laden language calling for elimination of non-believers. That happens often after horrific catastrophes. To the extent we believe in a pluralistic world in which diverse groups will co-exist, and some will believe that they possess ultimate truth, establishing a relationship among believers and non-believers, as an essential element in preserving societies that are pluralistic as fostering respect for the ultimate divergence of individuals.

During the course of their lives people may move in and out of groups with strong commitments. A society which recognizes the reality of change and growth must support people's right to leave groups as well as join them.[21] A group which is dedicated to the total control and demands complete loyalty of its members may place significant difficulties and costs in exit. It is a function and responsibility of society and those concerned with cult activities to ease transition by providing support and understanding for people who leave such groups. This is just as important as activities devoted to deterring people from entering into the groups or abusing them while they are members. Exiting a group is difficult and people who emerge form an abusive group need to be viewed in a manner similar to those who are recovering from inflicted psychological and emotional harm and should not be viewed as intellectually or emotionally deficient people who have made voluntary mistakes and need to suffer the consequences of their poor choices.[22] The results of destructive cults practice in retaining members do not immediately disappear when the member leaves. While some have criticized processes used in counseling members leaving the group and analogized them to the deceptive and coercive recruitment process used by the groups themselves, but, of course, that analysis is fatally flawed. People who are recruited into destructive cults are put into an environment of enforced conformity where exit is made difficult. People who are counseled and chose to leave the group still have the option open to return to the group if they so desire.

The September 11th tragedy has caused us to focus not only on the leaders and committed members of terrorist groups, but upon the process used in separating members of those groups from the rest of society and inculcating them with hate. In viewing the relationship between members and non-members of highly committed groups, I would hope that the focus of September 11th has caused us to emphasize study of processes by which we can ameliorate the effects of such inculcation and provide alternatives and to aid people in obtaining more free transition in and out of committed groups and emphasize that societies will always consist of believers and non-believers of all kinds, who we teach each to live tolerantly with each other.

Relationships between the Group and Society

The third facet of analysis with respect to a destructive cult is mutual relationships between groups and societies in which they exist. There never is an identity of membership of all citizens and members of any single group. Even if it did exist for a moment, it would not persist. Rather there are always citizens of a state who are not members of any one particular group. The group may focus on its own membership and make demands of them with respect to behavior, lifestyle and obedience, but government in a society owes its obligations to all citizens of the polity, not only those who are members of any single group, no matter how numerous or dominant.

Society in upholding the interests of its members has obligations to them which may or may not be inconsistent with the duties or obligations of members of any single group within it. A totalistic group may require its members to engage in certain kinds of behavior. Those may be different than behavior engaged in by non-members in the society. In some instances, tolerance may find those differences acceptable because they do not violate or infringe upon any of the society's essential concerns. However, in situations involving certain destructive groups, it may well be that the behavior required of members is inconsistent with society's obligations to all members of its polity.

For example, society may require of its citizens certain conduct relating to maintaining health and control of infectious diseases. In such circumstances members of a group are not free to jeopardize the lives of non-members by refusing to adhere to such regulations by refusing to be vaccinated, for example.[23] Society may be concerned with preservation of each individual's human rights and their right to live and so may enact restrictions and procedures regulating euthanasia and suicide. Observance of such restrictions may be enforced even if contrary to practices of a group. Society may establish recognized rights for those lacking parity of power such as women and children and these may be inconsistent with strictures placed upon them by certain groups. The group could require child marriage, it could turn a blind eye to sexual and psychological abuse and it could prohibit or limit health care and education.[24] The fact that the group prohibits or mandates certain practices does not mean that the state must abstain from action protecting rights of its citizens affected by them. Society may establish rules dealing with wages and conditions of employment.[25] These bind groups who may otherwise impose child labor, slavery and unhealthful practices on their members.[26] The fact that a group is tolerated with the state does not give it the freedom to regulate its member's behavior without limit. The state owes obligations to all of its citizens independent of their group membership.

This relationship here is a mutual one, it is not one predicated solely upon a state's abdication from regulation. Since September 11th, many countries have recognized the necessity of consideration of the needs and rights of victims of zealots, the provision of food and shelter to those whose needs were subordinated to the zealot's cause. In Afghanistan we have observed an imposed recognition of women's rights, regardless of the persistence of various groups' restrictions on their education and lifestyle. This shift of focus, hopefully, will restore a balance in assessment of human rights, taking into account rights of non-members of groups as well as members.

"Human rights" advocates often focus solely on the rights of members of groups as if any limits on their rights constitutes an abridgement of human rights generally, but that is only half the story. In order to protect human rights, one must look at the whole society and include consideration of the rights of all members of society not just rights of members of a particular group. Additionally society must not ignore practices of members of groups that violate human rights and must protect the compact between the state and all of its citizens.

Members of a group may be induced through various pressures to engage in conduct that violates social norms. To the extent that human rights are non-forfeitable—(such as those involving slavery)—the apparent consent of members to their abridgement is not a bar to state regulation protecting them.

Here again, the role of the society is a reciprocal one—while observing restrictions respecting the liberty of the individual group member, it need not stand silent in the face of abrogation of non-members' or members human rights by the group.

Conclusion

Analysis of these issues did not arise with the terrorist incidents in September 2001. However, the worldwide attention to the utilization of religious dogma as purported justification and encouragement heinous acts has caused us to look again and sharpen our focus in our concerns about destructive cults and the threats posed by them. The outpouring of shock and revulsion at terrorist activity has been offset by a like outpouring of zealot incitement against perceived wrongs and promotion of terror as an acceptable means to achieve religious ends.

We have likewise been treated to many illustrations of the mind control carried out by religious "educational" institutions training terrorists and suicide bombers and have been appalled by the chorus of proponents of religious wars. If we needed graphic evidence of the chilling effect of mind control in removing moral restraints on horrific behavior we certainly have it now.

We have seen efforts to build coalitions dedicated to restraints on such activities and discrediting those who proclaim themselves as heroes and martyrs for a violent cause. What has become evident and what is most needed is an understanding that destructive cults transcend the social boundaries of mutual respect and have no regard for the human rights of those who disagree with them or even members of their own group. We must strive to recognize individual rights and to protect them in a society that allows flourishing of divergent groups and gives respect to individual differences but does not dehumanize any of its members as a means of achievement of any group leader's aims. This is an opportunity to seize the attention focused on the elimination of the horrific consequences of terrorism and expand its focus to shared concerns about the dangers posed by destructive cults.

A Word on Human Rights and Cults

We often see these two terms linked in learned discussions and in glaring headlines. Since cults are well sponsored academically and since there are ample cult financial resources to devote to public relations when these two terms appear together, it is a pretty good bet that the discourse that follows deals only with the rights of cult members and not the rights of people who are not cult members or other citizens.

This limitation was recently brought home to me in the reports issued after the Chairperson of the United Nation's Commission on Human Rights visited China and came away with pronouncements on human rights issues. I found in them some recognition of increase in dialogue, but still a narrow focus on complaints about treatment of individual Falun Gong members. I did not see anything about the human rights' violations of Falun Gong member families, and I did not see anything about any concerns related to destructive practices of Falun Gong and the harm suffered by Falun Gong members. Unfortunately, this one-sided view is not unique. It has ample historical precedent and has seldom been critically commented on.

When German government agencies decided they would investigate the Church of Scientology because they thought its practices posed a danger to the rights of German citizens, a well-financed claque quickly formed to criticize the German government as violating human rights. Indeed, John Travolta, a movie star and high profile member of the Church of Scientology, was able to get an appointment with a senior national security official in the American government to discuss these alleged human rights concerns.

When a delegation supposedly objectively investigating the position of the German government and the alleged human rights abridgements of members of the Church of Scientology conducted an inquiry, they met with paid supporters of the Church of Scientology as well as some of its members but refused to meet with representatives of the German government who were prepared to explain the basis for their concerns. When the French adopted legislation expressing their concern about destructive cults' abridgement of human rights of French citizens, the claque again enlisted some of its most vocal supporters. Press releases and articles flooded the media out proclaiming the end of liberty and civil rights in France and grave threats to religious freedom throughout the world. Lobbying pressure intensified in the United States to the point where a leader in the French government finally issued a statement saying that they understood of the close connections between Scientology supporters and senior persons in the American government and the United Nations and they did not believe that French legislation indicated any abandonment of the French commitment to liberty, equality, fraternity or human rights.

More recently we have seen terrorists whose horrific actions have been criticized and condemned seek to apply language claiming their religious persecution to assert a moral equivalency of the destruction of the World Trade Center and infliction of far more than 3,000 deaths and repression they claim to suffer through religious and economic persecution.

On an even more recent event, I contrasted the national reactions relating to the Chinese Government's treatment of certain Falun Gong protestors in Beijing.

While certain governments, such as Sweden focused their comments solely on alleged mistreatment of protestors and members of Falun Gong. In contrast, Pravda featured an article discussing the causes for Chinese concern about the abuses of Falun Gong and the suffering of a number of immolated Falun Gong members including a 12-year old girl earlier. A recent article in a Spanish magazine also featured discussion of harm to Falun Gong members and their families.27

Human rights are important because they are based on the inherent humanity of each individual and the necessity for respect accorded to each person but they are also important on an overall social level. Why is there no public inquiry as to why the Chinese government is concerned with Falun Gong? In the few instances where this is discussed, it is political analysis that is primarily featured. Why is there no examination of Chinese history and the recognition of the destructive and destabilizing apocalyptic consequences of groups led by a leader possessing the power to compel total obedience from all followers and launch them on a mission to bring a new order into society. Certainly, the Tai Peng and Boxer Rebellions in China provided insight into a perceived threat of that kind and the adverse social consequences that flowed from it. Why isn't there recognition of the background in Chinese society of family values and the common social goal of preserving families as opposed to allowing outside influences to destroy them? What about the tradition of individual critical intellectual integrity?

Certainly all members of Falun Gong possess individual rights which should not be abridged but that does not mean they are free to engage in whatever conduct they desire without heed for the rights of those they will affect. Nor does it mean that an organization having an adverse impact on the rights of other citizens who are not members of the group, or having an impact on the members of the group in areas in which the state has an established right to protect the life, liberty and happiness of all its citizens must be immunized from state action. Threats to freedom by destructive cults, religious or not are not entitled to benign neglect. Human rights is a matter of mutual concern on a "micro" level dealing with individual rights and on a "macro" level dealing with social responsibility and relationships in a society administered by a responsible government.

We need more balanced, thoughtful media coverage of these issues, free from a knee-jerk reaction contrasting a tiny new religion with a powerful state. We need an objective perspective on human rights extending to all members of society and criticizing all infringements of civil liberties, with consideration given to the rights and obligations of all citizens of society, and the responsibility of all to observe its laws and regulations.

Notes

1. The history of the American Family Foundation is set forth in the *Cultic Studies Review*, Vol. 1, No. 1 2002. This is a publication of the American Family Foundation ISSN 1539-0152, pages 3-21.

2. I am counsel to Jenkens & Gilchrist Parker Chapin LLP in New York City and a member of its Corporate Department. I have been part of that firm and its predecessor for over 40 years. I have served as a director of two NYSE companies. I have no familial involvement or friends involved in destructive cultic groups. My interest stems from concern about the importance of issues intellectually as a lawyer and member of our society. When representing individuals who have been involved with destructive cults, I have generally acted on a pro bono basis and (with rare exception), receive no compensation for the legal services rendered or counsel offered.

3. In recent months, I participated in a number of programs offered in New York City on the issue of cults and terrorism. Presenters in each did not have uniform analysis, nor did they agree on the boundaries that could be drawn defining "cultic" terrorist groups.

4. In the American Family Foundation publication, *Recovery from Cults: Help for Victims of Psychological & Spiritual Abuse*, the Executive Director of the American Family Foundation, Michael Langone, and I included a definitional essay dealing with the benefits and detriments in using the term "cult." This volume, a publication of the American Family Foundation, is a guide containing not only information that may be helpful to various inquirers but a reference list of books, videos, articles and reprints relating to cultic issues. I also suggest for those unfamiliar with the general area a broad introduction in *Cults in our Midsts*, Margaret Thaler Singer with Janja Lalich, forward by Robert J. Lifton, San Francisco: Jossey-Bass Publishers, c. 1995. A broad contemporary overview can be found in *Misunderstanding Cults*, edited by Zablowski and Robbins, University of Toronto Press, 2001.

5. This phraseology stresses the absence of a necessary religious basis in the nexus of the organization. The cult phenomenon can be understood in different times and societies from a political, idealistic, philosophic or social view. Political analysis stretch back to studies of totalitarian organizations such as *Behemoth the Structure & Practice of National Socialism 1933-1944*, 2nd ed./Franz Leopold Neumann, New York, NY: New American Library, [1983] c. 1977 and George Orwell, *1984:*

A Novel, with a special preface by Walter Cronkite; and an afterward by Erich Fromm. New York, NY: New American Library, [1983] c. 1977. Historic analysis can relate to communal movements such *Without Sin: the Life & Death of the Oneida Community*, Spencer Klaw. New York: Allen Lane, c. 1993. See also *On the Edge: Political Cults Right and Left*, Dennis Tourish and Tim Wohlforth. Armonk, NY: ME Shaarpe, c 2000.

6. Analysis of a degree and scope of control asserted over members is discussed in Laxer, *Take Me for a Ride*, Outer Rim Press, 1993, dealing with Dr. Frederick Lenz, a/k/a Zen Master Rama and *Captive Hearts, Captive Minds: Freedom & Recovery from Cults and Other Abusive Relationships*, Madeline Landau Tobias and Janja Lalich. Almeda, CA: Hunter House, c. 199.

7. There is no mention here of the voluminous works of cult apologists who catalog the content of new religious movements and purport to be neutral about negative aspects. My view focuses on actions not beliefs, a distinction derived from the religious freedom provisions of the First Amendment of the U.S. Constitution. Interpretations of this provision clearly set forth that while beliefs are privileged, to the degree actions involve others, they are not free from regulation and restriction in order to protect the rights of parties affected by the believer's action. See e.g., *Sherbert v. Verner, 374 US 398.*

8. A good example has been the history of the New Alliance Party, a group labeled by the FBI as a cult. The Anti-Defamation League traces the history of this group and its founders Fred Newman and Lola Falani, a politician, through its affiliation with such diverse allies as Louis Farrakhan and Lyndon LaRouche. It shifted its name and is now operating through a social therapy group, a theatre, and the Independent Political Party, See New York Post article, *Extremist Politician Shadow World*, July 22, 2002. Likewise, illustrative of such a shift is the Unification Church's switch from vehement anti-Communist rhetoric and activities combating left wing groups in the Third World to its embrace of the regime in North Korea and its involvement in China. Then again, these can be compared with the actions of Nazi Germany with respect to their alliance with and subsequent invasion of Soviet Russia.

9. This has also been set forth in deceptive recruitment tactics of certain cultic groups. Thus, for years the Unification Church recruited members using as a front The Collegiate Association for the Research of Principles. The solicitors acting on behalf of Hare Krishna claimed they were raising money for drug rehabilitation centers which never existed. The Church of Scientology used as its initial introduction a personality test and offered to improve communication and business skills rather than presenting a religious ideology.

10. Illustrations drawn here from hierarchies in political organizations such as the Communist Party are appropriate. Likewise, the study of the Oneida Community illustrated the destructive gap that grew between the leaders and the members.

11. Despite numerous studies profiling cult members and pointing out that intellectual idealists are often most susceptible to cult recruitment, its amazing to see the proliferation of recent expressions of shock and incredulity related to the intelligence and social position of the terrorists involved in the destruction of the World Trade Center.

12. In recent times, there have been numerous articles characterizing the structure and ethics of North Korea society to a cult as well as studies of cultic proliferation in societies going through destabilizing trauma such as the former Soviet Union, Serbia and Bosnia and the proliferation of Islamic Fundamentalists.

13. Recent publicity recognized the anniversary of the studies by Stanley Milgrim showing the socially outrageous behavior engaged in by volunteers acting under the purported direction of an authority figure in violation of their moral inhibitions. While no one doubts the validity of the conclusions of those studies, it would be very difficult to replicate them now given boundaries of social experimentation.

14. A recent study entitled *Bad Elements, Chinese Rebels from Los Angeles to Beijing*, Buruma, Random House 2001, cites the history in China of millenarian cults and secret societies into which exploded in mass violence. The Yellow Turbans were a faith healing sect that roiled China after the end of the Han Dynasty for 20 years, the White Lotus were an apocalyptic group which plagued society at the end of the Mongol Yuan Dynasty followed by a martial arts master and herbal healer named Yong Lun who rebelled against the Manchu rulers of the Qing Dynasty at the end of the 19th Century, who, in turn were succeeded in the early 1900s by the Boxers who believed their sacred spirit made them impervious to foreign bullets. Subsequently, the Tai Ping Rebellion sought to establish God's heavenly kingdom their leader claimed to be a brother of Jesus Christ and their crusade left millions dead.

15. Orwell's, *1984: A Novel.*

16. Arthur Koestler, *Darkness at Noon,* translated by Daphne Hardy; introduction by Vladimir Bukovsky, wood engravings by George Buday. London: The Folio Society, c. 1980. See also Eric Hoffer, *The True Believer, Thoughts on the Nature of Mass Movements,* New York, NY: Harper & Row, c. 1951.

17. See Margaret Thaler Singer with Janja Lalich, forward by Robert J. Lifton *Cults in our Midsts*, San Francisco: Jossey-Bass Publishers, c. 1995 and Ronald M. Enroth, *Churches that Abuse*, Grand Rapids, MI: Zondervan, c. 1992.

18. Robert J. Lifton, *The Nazi Doctors*, Medical Killings & Psychology of Genocide, New York, NY: Basic Books, c. 1986.

19. *Destroying the World in Order to Save It: Apocalyptic Violence & the New Global Terrorism*, Robert J. Lifton, New York, NY: Metropolitan Books, c. 1999..

20. See e.g., *Behind the Smoke and Mirrors*, Carter, Back Street Publishing, 1999. (A study of Amway marketing.)

21. See Zablocki, *Towards Demystifying and Disinterested Scientific Theory of Brainwashing* in *Misunderstanding Cults: Searching for Objectivity in a Controversial Field*, edited by Benjamin Zablocki and Thomas Robbins, University of Toronto Press, 2001, page 159.

22. See e.g., *Recovery from Cults*, edited by Langone.

23. The law in the United States is well settled that a member of a religious group cannot, based on religious beliefs, deny medical treatment to a minor even though they may refuse it themselves. A recent case in the Commonwealth of Massachusetts involved the criminal charge of murder against a leader of a group who permitted starvation of a minor (*Commonwealth v. Ribidoux*, Superior Court, Bristol, MA BRCR00-00358).

24. A recent prosecution in Utah found a practitioner of polygamy guilty of a crime where one of his multiple wives was a minor at the time of the marriage (*State of Utah v. Greene*).

25. The balancing of the state's interest and religious beliefs has led to balancing requirements relating to the required level of mandatory education, affixing warning signals to the horse drawn vehicles using the public roads, compulsory vaccination of children and recital of the Pledge of Allegiance, among others.

26. The Tony Alamo Foundation was found guilty of violating minimum wage laws by requiring its members to "volunteer" their services in its businesses, a group known as the Commune or the "12 Tribes," admitted violating child labor laws in utilizing minors in their factories operating machinery used in the construction of furniture.

27. Patsy Rahn, an American scholar has published a paper called *The Falon Gong: Beyond the Headlines* reprinted in the Cultic Studies Journal of the American Family Foundation, Vol. 17, pages 168-186, which contains a study of Falon Gong that goes beyond the simplistic cult offered by its proponents. Likewise, the Chinese government has recently supported publications of a number of works publicizing the lesser non aspects of the Falon Gong, and the beliefs and views of its founder which are homophobic and require complete subversion of the individual to the dictates and directions of its leaders. Likewise, since the beginning of this paper, there has been more discussion about the tactics of Chinese government used in treatment of Falon Gong members and their re-education. Although I have not yet seen any reports by independent observers, it is notable the Chinese report a large measure of success in re-education although not uniform and have committed some of those people who go through the process and still remain loyal to the Falon Gong to talk to the media.

Chapter Nine

Global or Provincial?
Different Models of Part-Time Degree Studies at Major Universities in England and Wales and their Accessibility for Prospective Students

JAN THOMAS

Introduction

The introduction of part-time programmes at universities and colleges is usually led by the basic idea to attract special groups of students who could otherwise not be convinced to start (or to continue) academic degree studies. The underlying benefit of these part-time programmes is the fact that enrolled students are enabled to continue their job, to finance their studies and to care for their children besides their studies.

Part-Time Programmes at British Universities

In contrast to Germany or Austria, British universities offer a wide range of part-time options. In numerous study programmes, there is the choice to study either full-time or part-time. Unfortunately, however, traditional timetables are usually not tailored according to the needs of part-time students. For this reason, personal timetables of part-time students often resemble an irregular patchwork. Only few jobs and professions fit into the gaps of a daily changing lesson-plan. There may be, for example, two classes on Monday mornings, and another one around noon, then there are two seminars on Tuesday evenings in combination with a fortnightly tutorial in the morning and so on. Similarly, it will be very difficult to combine personal child care with such an irregular schedule.

Despite these difficulties, though, there *are* students who do complete such part-time studies successfully. After having completed their degree, these students will most necessarily be experts in organisation and time management as well. In other words: this model of part-time studies is a very demanding and strenuous one.

Obviously, most part-time studies in Great Britain do not yet utilise all advantages of more sophisticated models of part-time instruction. They could, for example, simply be made more attractive by merging the hours of attendance into one comprehensive time block. In fact, such advanced part-time models can be found at some English and Welsh universities.

With the following survey, I would like to show the basic principles and ideas of such advanced models of part-time instruction. Subsequently, I will point out which groups of prospective students might be attracted by them.

The following overview will be restricted to Master's level programmes at major British universities. Their normal duration in full-time mode usually takes one year. In their part-time mode, these programmes can be completed in two or three years. Corresponding studies leading to a first Bachelor's degree have a duration of 3 to 4 years already in their full-time version. A part-time option often exceeds six years or more and consequently has its own disadvantageous dynamics.

"One Day a Week"

One method by which part-time studies can be made more attractive would be to concentrate seminars and lectures on one day every week. It would also be possible to use one afternoon and the following morning, or weekends for teaching purposes.

Such a programme is offered by Regent's Park College, a Permanent Private Hall of the University of Oxford with their Master of Theology in Applied Theology.[1]

All lessons are regularly placed on Fridays during term. In addition, there is one study-week every year. The course programme has a duration of two years, followed by one or two further years for the completion of a Master's thesis.

By its nature, this programme is attractive for a broad group of working adults and parents. If the workload can be concentrated on the other days of the week, it would still be possible to continue full-time work. Part-time options with 3/4 oder 2/3 arrangements would be even more convenient. It should also be possible for parents to arrange a full-day childcare for one day a week within the described part-time study type.

Contact Hours

If the overall number of contact hours in this part-time model and the ones described below are counted together over the full programme length, one will not find a big difference to the number of contact hours in a conventional full-time programme.

Besides, an implementation of distance learning options (paper-based or e-learning) can bridge the time gaps between different modules or between the days of attendance. Although not generally realised, distance learning modes may also give the option to reduce the contact hours in number or in length.

Study Weeks

Another model uses study weeks for instruction. Usually, three of these weeks are spread over one year. This is quite a common model of part-time instruction, realised, for example, by the University of Oxford (Master of Science in Evidence Based

Healthcare[2]), the University of Cambridge (Master of Studies in Applied Criminology and Management[3]), the University of Nottingham (Modular MBA[4]), the Institute of Education, University of London (MBA in Higher Education Management[5]), and the University of Wales in Lampeter (several MA and MTh in Theology[6]).

This part-time study mode requires the investment of paid or unpaid leave days or of educational leave, but it reduces organisational efforts to the level of a one-week vacation trip.

In practise, these programmes show a few differences concerning the flexibility within a year of studies. Some universities offer a strict pattern of dates for their modules which have to be attended (London, Cambridge), others provide a variety of study modules per year, so that the students are given the choice to attend more modules in one year and less in the next one, or vice versa (Nottingham). This arrangement makes it easier to spread the studies over more that two years as well.

The attractiveness and flexibility of a part-time programme also depends on the modular sequence and inter-relation: Are the modules self-contained or does the content of one module build upon the knowledge of an earlier one? In the latter case, a sudden absence in one module might cause a problem with admission to the next modules. Conscious of such problems, the University of Wales in Lampeter who—for didactical reasons—organises its study-weeks in this way, does very clearly advise prospective students not to choose the modular option in case, an absence at any module can be foreseen. As will be seen later on, Wales-Lampeter offers several other participation modes, so that all in all the limitation of flexibility in one mode will still not make the programme unattractive as a whole.

Summer Schools

One of the most well-known and long-established ways of part-time university level instruction is the summer school model. The University of Cambridge International Summer School,[7] for example, will celebrate its 80th anniversary in 2003.

Several British universities use this model to offer courses to worldwide audiences, who are prepared to pay rather high course fees to be admitted to these programmes. But, in most cases, as in Cambridge, it is not possible to study for a degree through summer schools.[8]

The University of Nottingham is exceptional in this respect: It runs a programme that offers a Master of Arts degree in Educational Leadership[9] only through summer schools. The coursework for this degree can be completed in two (or in some cases more) summer periods.

With this programme, Nottingham makes attendance possible for a wide target group. Although all students have to dedicate most of their summer holidays for a period of two years, the traditional holiday time in summer eases an educational project as well.

Some Thoughts on International Audiences

Looking upon the presented part-time models more closely, it turns out that the first two modes of attendance, the "traditional model" and the "week-day option" still have the usual, local catchment area in mind. Students attending these programme need to live in the surrounding area of the campus and only the weekday-model might widen the catchment area marginally.

A participation across the country's frontiers can usually not be realised, even if low-budget airline carriers are considered.

The other part-time programmes, however, may very well attract a European or even international audience.

The (costs for) travel expenses are reduced through a limited number of modules and the summer school model finally minimises these costs. In fact, in most cases the international reputation of a University is reflected by its internationally accessible part-time programmes.

Why then does Regent's Park College of Oxford University choose a part-time mode which makes their Master's programmes virtually "provincial"?

In this case, the answer is to be found in the idea of the college as a community. Though Regent's Park College is ready to make concessions to cater for their part-time students, it is still intended that a community life does happen at least every Friday, and maybe over one or the other following weekend.

Mixed Modes

Additional flexibility can be obtained by offering different modes of instruction and attendance within one and the same study programme, giving the option to create a mixture of personal choice.

As already mentioned, the University of Wales in Lampeter offers such a model. Since Lampeter is a small village in a rural surrounding without direct access to an airport, the University can minimize the disadvantage of their geographical location by offering the most flexible way of studying for a Master's degree.

In a wide range of MA and MTh programmes within the Department of Theology the organisers offer three modes of instruction:

- 3 modules per year in Lampeter and a few other locations in Wales
- single modules via distance learning
- full-time study at Lampeter for one term (trimester).

All these option may be combined individually. While not all of the courses are offered in all modes, a number of courses offer at least two of the options mentioned above. The University of Wales also welcomes students who only choose one option to complete their studies.

Some Thoughts on the Implementation of Part-Time Programmes

Apart from the growing attractiveness for audiences, it should be pointed out that a sophisticated part-time mode may also simplify the allocation of resources within the teaching institution. If (as in most cases) the modules are run during the summer break or between the terms, it will most probably be much easier to reserve instruction rooms for an additional programme than it would be during term. The same is true concerning the provision of accommodation for participants.

But the model of part-time studies will not only be attractive for organisers and students. Besides, a modular part-time programme might also enable a university to hire internationally well-known instructors—and not to forget: to finance them.

In fact, such tendencies can be observed in the University of Oxford's Master's programme in International Human Rights Law.[10] It does not only attract an internationally mixed group of participants, but it also recruits its faculty among specialists from all over the world.

Undoubtedly, such a teaching post may also be very attractive for scholars committed to children and family life. For both groups, students and instructors with children, it would be most desirable, if those organizers responsible for planning part-time programmes would also take care of arranging professional child-care options during all modules.

In this context, the time length of part-time modules is a most relevant factor. Longer modules do necessarily increase the problem of finding convenient child-care options for students and lecturers. Providing accompanying child-care opportunities, therefore, belongs to the most urgent requirements which need to be fulfilled by the universities.

Notes

1. http://www.rpc.ox.ac.uk/rpc/postgrad.htm [Retrieved August 31, 2002]
2. http://www.conted.ox.ac.uk/Courses/Health/htmlfiles/master/masterfr.htm [Retrieved August 31, 2002]
3. http://www.crim.cam.ac.uk/courses/management/ [Retrieved August 31, 2002]
4. http://www.nottingham.ac.uk/business/mba/N19M.htm [Retrieved August 31, 2002]
5. http://ioewebserver.ioe.ac.uk/ioe/schools/leid/docs/MAHigherEdMan.pdf [Retrieved August 31, 2002]
6. http://www.lamp.ac.uk/trs/postgraduate2002/taughtmasters.html [Retrieved August 31, 2002]
7. http://www.cont-ed.cam.ac.uk/IntSummer/ [Retrieved August 31, 2002]
8. Nevertheless, most participants will have their courses at Cambridge Summer School converted into credit points accepted by their local universities at home. Therefore, both Cambridge and Oxford give detailed advice concerning the credit point value of their summer school courses. There are special, integrated arrangements with certain universities from overseas as well.
9. http://www.nottingham.ac.uk/education/courses/maelss.htm [Retrieved August 31, 2002]
10. http://www.conted.ox.ac.uk/HumanRightsLaw/index2.html [Retrieved August 31, 2002]

Chapter Ten

Integrative Partnership: Rationale and Model

Yi-Ying Huang

Introduction

With the convenience from various modern vehicles, technical media or the world wide web, partnerships among human beings and related organizations are established almost everywhere in the past century: the partnership between different nations, military units, political clans, commercial or noncommercial organizations, research teams, societies, etc. All kinds of participants in the system can be a partner, such as a teacher, a student, a parent, a policy enactor, a researcher, or a classroom, a family, a school, a community, a nonpublic instructional media center, etc. The search for establishing and facilitating partnership has become the request or policy for most participants and organizations. Obviously, there must be important reasons for human beings and their organizations to develop and maintain partnerships. Studies on the essence of partnership, perspectives behind partnership development, and the purpose of the existence of partnership, however, are far less than those on case application, benchmark construction and strategy evaluation. What is partnership? In what kind of circumstances or conditions will partnership exist? Why partnership? What do human beings want from partnership? And, what kinds of partnership should human beings develop? Without clarifying the essence of "what" and digging into the questions of "why," the study on the approach of "how" will implicitly take the existence and necessity of partnership for granted. Thus, in order to develop ways to facilitating partnership with a rational basis, it is imperative to clarify the substance of partnership, and discuss the kind of partnership that should be constructed and developed.

The existence of partnership is based on the connections established between partners. The kinds of connections that a partner continues to construct in the partnership will influence the maintaining possibility and growing state of such partnership. It is claimed that participants should develop the kind of partnership with integrative connections. Thus, the purpose of this chapter is to explore and justify the kinds of connections each partner develops to not only keep the partnership persistent but also make it much more integrative.

First, the necessity of integrative partnership is justified through analyzing the "what" and "why" of partnership. Then, explained is a model on the "how" of partnership with four kinds of correlated connections proposed for developing much more integrative partnership: (1) the partner-with-partner connection (PPC), (2) the partner-with-partnership connection (PIC), (3) the partner-with-self-as-partner connection (PSC), and (4) the partnership-with-world connection (PWC). Finally, presented is the implication on partnership research.

Why Partnership with Integrative Connections

Partnership development becomes a global phenomenon or movement, where the forms of partnership are various. To claim that the participants in the micro- or macro-system should develop the kind of partnership with integrative connections, it is important to clarify the essence of partnership and then justify the necessity of integration in partnership.

Without Connections, Without Partnership or Partners

According to Collins Cobild Dictionary (Birmingham University International Language Database, 1988), "partnership" is a relationship, in which two or more people, organizations or countries work together as partners; or (2) a business owned by two or more people. "Partner," in the same dictionary, indicates someone with whom one (1) has a romantic or intimate relationship; or (2) shares the ownership; (3) is doing something; and "partner" also can be an organization with which another organization or country has an alliance and agreement. Obviously, the meanings on "partnership" and "partner" all relate to a kind of bond, chain or inosculation. It is reasonable to claim that without the existence of "connections," there is no "partnership"; and that without "partnership," there are no so-called "partners." Connections then can be identified as the essence of partnership. The individuals, who look for partnership, must establish connections with the others, and those, who want to maintain and develop the current partnership between each other, must strengthen and make much more connections. Connections have different characteristics; to further explore the kind of connections that the partner should develop, the purpose of partnership is reflected upon as follows.

Why Partnership:
The Human Being vs. Systems Paradigm Perspective

Every existence has its own unique reasons or values of being existing in the universe, and so does "partnership." Practically speaking, the connections in partnership are established by and reflect the partners' inner needs to obtain something from the others and exchange what the self can provide. For example, according to findings in the studies of "enneagram" (Rohr & Ebert, 1990), the fundamental drives, with which human beings interact with the world, are the inner need (1) to be perfect, (2) to be needed, (3) to succeed, (4) to be different, (5) to perceive, (6) to be safe, (7) to be joyful, (8) to be righteous, and (9) to be peaceful. However, most human beings in the century chase economical efficiency and are used to make partnership bring profits for their own goods with the least time and resources than just obtain what they fundamentally need. The reasons for the existence of partnership from the previous viewpoints are partner-centered or human-centered. Such perspectives, where the human beings look forward to satisfying their personal needs while regarding themselves as the masters of the existence or the world, are argued to be too idealistic, untrue and not promising.

From the systems paradigm perspective (Bertalanffy, 1973; Briggs & Peat, 1984 & 1989; Gleick, 1987; Hayles, 1990; Jantsch, 1992; Morgan, 1986; Pagels, 1982; Prigogine & Stengers, 1980 & 1984), connections, either explicit or implicit to the human being, naturally exist in the complex system, such as the world, the educational system, the human race, a government, a supermarket, or a person. Elements or subsystems are dynamically correlated. Besides, every existence, regarded as, or comprised in, a complex system rather than an inorganic or insulated object, has its own reason for existence— Existence itself is its own measure. To every entity, the simple reason to exist is to facilitate the existence of the whole system in order to help keep the entity itself, as a participant in this larger system, persistently existent. Without concerning the whole, the partners' partner-centered or human-centered perspective will finally put themselves in danger. The collapse of a much larger system will soon or later influence the continuing growth of its involving and interrelating participants, including the human race. If human beings transit their attention of the existence as insulated and controlled object and the self as the measure of all existences to the systems paradigm point of view, then the consciousness of "what do human beings want from partnership?" will transit to "what does partnership want for itself from its partners?" The answer flowing out from the systems paradigm perspective is: Partnership asks partners to make the kind of connections first maintaining the whole system itself and furthermore increasing the energy of the whole system for its continuing evolution and renewal.

Partners usually develop the kind of connections, which help obtain the energy they want and need. But, no matter what kind of connections is developed, the maintenance and growth of partnership consume energy. The increase of entropy, of which value is unavoidably generated as the time goes, will decrease the quality of the useful energy in a system, is unavoidably generated in the operation of making connections. That is to say, the whole system obtains energy from its partnerships but loses some at the same time. The more entropy, the more disorderly the system becomes. The more disorderly, the more possible the system collapses. It is obvious that the human-being partners had better to establish the kind of connections, which can produce more energy than entropy so as to make the partnership dynamically persistent and growing. What kind of connections can the partner develop in order to generate more energy and help decrease entropy? According to Huang (1998, 2000, 2001a & 2001b), the more integrative a system becomes, the higher the degree of dynamical orderliness and the less the entropy generated. In other words, the connections loosely structured will produce more entropy than energy. Thus, it is suggested that human beings develop the kind of partnership with integrative connections.

Connections in Partnership: Loose or Integrative

In a system there exist explicit connections, which are easy to be described or pointed out, such as contracts or treaties. There are also abundant connections that are implicitly intertwined within and usually are not easy to be identified, such as a kind of "seeing" between the self and the inner self, the interdependence between human beings and other races on the earth, or the "Tao" (evolution rules, in Chinese interpretation) emerging from the interactions between existences. Explicit connections are those decided by certain purpose, and existing and working between partners. Implicit connections are relatively those operating behind explicit ones and have the potential of emerging themselves in the future. Human beings "make" those connections under different states. The state of connection making influences the degree of integration and thus influences the amount of entropy generated. Table 1 explains different states of connection making in the partnership system.

As mentioned, there exist explicit and implicit connections in the partnership system. When human beings contact those connections, which have already existed or will form the states of connection making are as follows.

State 1—Encounter: Unaware or Aware

Human beings, or the partners, may or may not be aware of those connections in their partnership. Awareness manifest the implicit connections and makes them become much more explicit. The partners' awareness of explicit and implicit connections increases the degree of integration in the partnership system. The partners' unawareness, a state of disconnection, generates entropy.

State 2—With Awareness: Unrecognized or Recognized

The connections being aware of may or may not be internally recognized. The partners' recognition of the connections being aware of increases the degree of integration in the partnership system. Unrecognition generates entropy.

State 3—With Awareness and Recognition: Meaningless or Meaningful

The connections being aware of and recognized may or may not be meaningful to the partners. The meaningless connections, though being aware of and recognized, still generate entropy. But, the meaningful ones increase the degree of integration in the partnership system.

State 4—With Awareness, Recognition and Meaningfulness: Passionless or Passionate

The partners may or may not be passionate to the connections that they are aware of, recognized, or regard as meaningful. The making of passionless connections consumes energy and produces more entropy in the whole partnership system.

State 5—With Awareness, Recognition, Meaningfulness and Passion: Not Practicing or Practicing

The partners may or may not practice what they are aware of, recognized, regard as meaningful, or fill with passion. Without personal experience, the partners cannot thoroughly understand the practical aspect of the connections. The disconnection between "knowing" and "practicing" usually increases entropy in the whole partnership system.

Table 1
States of Human Beings' Connection Making

	State 1	State 2	State 3	State 4	State 5	State 6
Human	Unaware					
Beings	Aware	Unrecognized				
		Recognized	Meaningless			
V.S.			Meaningful	Passionless		
				Passionate	Without	
Explicit					Practicing	
Connections					Practicing	Not for
and						Coevolution
Implicit						For
Connections						Coevolution

State 6—With Awareness, Recognition, Meaningfulness, Passion and Practice: Not for Coevolution or for Coevolution

The more explicit or implicit connections the partners are aware of, recognize, feel meaningful, passionate and practically experience, the much higher degree of integration the partnership system obtains. However, from the systems paradigm perspective as discussed earlier, entropy will still be generated in the disconnection between this partnership system and those much larger systems involving the former as a participant. That is to say, the partnership system can be much more integrative and thus obtain much more energy by searching for coevolution or making connections between the larger systems and itself.

Table 2 inductively describes the characteristics of partnership with loose connections and that with integrative connections.

Table 2
Characteristics of Partnership With Loose or Integrative Connections

Loose Partnership	Integrative Partnership
With The Connections:	With The Connections:
*Established by those other than the self	*Constructed by the partner him/herself
*Partners are unaware of	*Partners are aware of
*Partners are unrecognized	*Partners are internally recognized
*Meaningless to partners	*Meaningful to partners
*To which partners are passionless	*To which partners are passionate
*Formally coupled	*Perceptionally cohesive
*Partners haven't personally experienced	*Partners have personally experienced
*Partners haven't practiced yet	*Partners have been practicing
*Not for coevolution	*For coevolution

The studies on the evolution of systems claim that if the amount of entropy generated in one system is far less than the amount of energy obtained from the integrative connections within or from the environment, this system will be able to keep dynamically renewing itself. The importance of developing integrative partnership is distinct. In the following, presented is a model of developing four correlated connections for much more integrative partnership.

Developing Four Correlated Connections for Much More Integrative Partnership

According to the justification on the significance of integrative partnership, the model is constructed based on the previous argument on states of connection making and characteristics of integrative connections. There are four correlated connections in this model regarded as fundamental and elemental for integrative partnership: (1) the partner-with-partner connection (PPC), (2) the partner-with-partnership connection (PIC), (3) the partner-with-self-as-partner connection (PSC), and (4) the partnership-with-world connection (PWC). The application of this connection-making model can help partners (1) make the implicit connections explicit, and (2) reclarify the substance of the explicit connections, which partners usually do not apprehend thoroughly. Through questioning, reflection, sharing and searching for possible answers, partners in this model develop four kinds of connections for much more integrative partnership. The partners will share when their drives, personal capabilities, and chances between one another happen to emerge at the same time, even they view, define and respond to things differently. In the following explanation about the model, "I," "me" or "we" in the questions indicates the self, or a system as one partner, symbolized by "Partner1" and "Partner3" in the figures. "Partner2" in the figures represents another partner or plural partners.

The Partner-with-Partner Connection

Participants in the same system share the ownership and thus are partners to each other. Those linked because of a formal or juristic agreement are also called partners to each other. In either case, however, the connections between the partner and the others, which make the partnership possible, may not be clear. The connections implied within the partnership should be manifested. Meanwhile, the substance of those explicit connections should be further explored in order to create more opportunities for recognition.

PPC in Figure 1 indicates the partner-with-partner connection. Themes for reflection and sharing that help partners to make such connections are: (1) With what do I connect Partner 2? (2) What connections do I possibly not see or pay attention to? (3) What is the substance of those connections? In a school system, for example, the principal, teachers and parents of students are partners to one another. Connections with each other are developed through digging into questions such as: Are the professional and practical knowledge on education the connection between the other partners and me? Or, the care on students, the seller-customer relationship, the private friendship, the political and economical interest? What else are implied? If (for example) "the care on students" is one of the connections between the other partners and me, what on earth is the "gut" of such "care"? What do I know about "the care on students"?

Figure 1
The Partner-with-Partner Connection

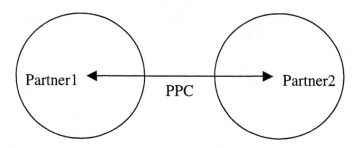

The Partner-with-Partnership Connection

While making clear the partner-with-partner connection to increase the opportunities for awareness on partnership, the partner further search for his/her internal connection with PPC, that is, the personally recognized meanings towards such partnership.

PIC in Figure 2 indicates the partner-with-partnership connection, the connection usually implicit but influencing the way through which the partnership operates. Themes that help develop such connections are: (1) Why do I need to connect with Partner 2? (2) How do I connect with Partner 2? (3) Why does PPC exist? Meanings, generating from searching for the "why," strengthen the connections that are meaningful to the self, and weaken those that are meaningless. That is, the development of PIC will encourage the spontaneity of the partner's participation in the partnership and meanwhile facilitate such spontaneity marching towards the evolution direction of this partnership system. And, the system's dynamical orderliness will then be enhanced.

Figure 2
The Partner-with-Partnership Connection

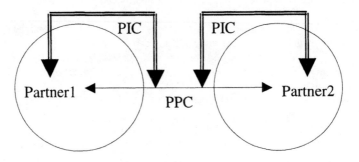

The Partner-with-Self-as-Partner Connection

PSC in Figure 3 indicates the partner-with-self-as-partner connection, the connection bond with the deep inside of the partner him/herself. Such connections usually hide unconsciously or subconsciously, for example, the weakness of the self, the kernel of the belief system, the worldview. Themes that help develop such connections are: (1) Why does or doesn't such partnership mean to me? (2) Why does such PIC exist? (3) Why do I connect with Partner 2 in such ways? To make partnership much more integrative, it is imperative for the partner to dig into the "why-why" connection in the partnership while developing PPC (the "what" connection) and PIC (the "how" and "why" connection). Digging into the "why-why" connection means inquiring the "origin" of meanings, that is, the self—the subject, who constructs meanings. The partner gets much more acquainted with the inner self each time when reflecting on the "why-why" connection, which facilitates self-renewal. The partner's self-renewal will bring new energy into the partnership, increase the degree of integration and meanwhile inspire change in the partnership system.

Figure 3
The Partner-with-Self-as-Partner Connection

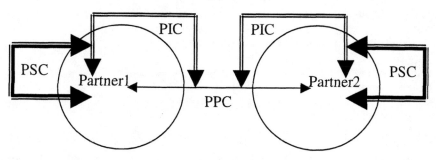

The Partnership-with-World Connection

Searching for PSC facilitates the renewal of the partner him/herself. However, it is quite possible that the operation of such self-renewal is still on the dimension of being egocentric, shortsighted or human-being-centered. To facilitate the kind of change inspired by the partner's self-renewal in the partnership system, not to deaden but dynamically maintain and renew the partnership in the long run, a perspective transition from human-being-centered to systems-centered and existence-itself-centered is the key.

PWC in Figure 4 indicates the partnership-with-world connection, concerning the coevolution of the world (or all larger systems participated) and the partners comprised. The construction of PPC, PIC and PSC makes the "I" with "Partner 2" one "we" partner (Partner 3). Themes that help develop PWC are: (1) How does such "we" as one coparticipate in the coevolution of the world? (2) What does "we" connect the world with, and what is possibly not see or pay attention to? (3) What is the substance of those connections?

Figure 4
The Partnership-with-World Connection

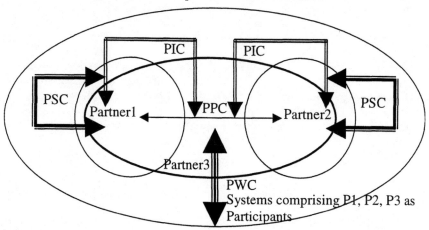

Connections Between the Four Kinds of Connections

The inquiry for developing PWC, obviously, will further restart the search for the "what," "how," "why," and "why-why" connections (PPC, PIC and PSC) in the partnership system. Taking the partner-with-partnership connection as the cognition basis, the partner will look at the partner-with-partner connection in another way. From the viewpoint of the partner-with-self-as-partner connection, the partner will be able to give the partner-with-partnership connection a new interpretation. And, built on the partnership-with-world connection, the partner will find out different choices of renewing the original operation of the partner-with-self-as-partner connection. With the attention on the partner-with-partner connection, the partnership-with-world connection will be further explored explicitly and clearly. The four kinds of connections in the model are justified as not only correlated but also circulative. It is now claimed that developing the four kinds of connections will make the partnership much more integrative and help establish a mechanism for its persistently renewing.

In addition to presenting the model for facilitating integrative partnership, it is also concerned to provide an appropriate context helping make integrative connections. To construct such a context requires at least the following efforts: (1) increasing ways for informal as well as formal interactions between partners; (2) providing partners with opportunities to experience explicit and implicit connections in the partnership system; and (3) creating a culture with trust, which respects plural opinions and the partner's personal timing of making those connections.

Implication on Partnership Research

In this chapter, the concern on awareness, recognition, meaning, and the inner self of the partner is evident. It does not mean that the economical profit and efficiency cared by most human beings is not worth noticing. Inversely, how to pursue the most and meanwhile persistent profit from the partnership is deeply cared and reflected upon. The necessity of developing partnership with integrative connections, which facilitates a kind of ecological profit or profit for the whole, is claimed and then justified from the systems paradigm perspective according to the studies on the evolution of complex systems. The more integrative the partnership system evolves, the more energy generated to help maintain and renew the dynamical orderliness in the partnership system. The issue not further explored in this chapter, yet necessarily paid attention to, is the hegemony implied in partnership. Each partner owns more than one role in the system, composed by subsystems and linked with other systems. As long as interactions with the human-being partners occur, there exists hegemony. The image, right, power and responsibility of each role are socially and culturally constructed from the human-centered perspective. That is, hegemony is born inevitably when participants make connections with the human-being partners. The substance and the operation of hegemony in different types of partnership and in the previous model for making the four correlated connections will be further inquired in the near future.

References

Bertalanffy, L. V. (1973). *General system theory: Foundations, development, applications*. New York: George Braziller.

Birmingham University International Language Database (1988). *Collins Dictionary*. London: William Collins Sons.

Briggs, J., & Peat, F. D. (1984). *Looking glass universe: The emerging science of wholeness*. New York, NY: Simon and Schuster.

Briggs, J., & Peat, F. D. (1989). *Turbulent mirror: An illustrated guide to chaos theory and the science of wholeness*. New York, NY: Harper Collins.

Gleick, J. (1987). *Chaos: Making a new science*. New York, NY: Penguin.

Hayles, N. K. (1990). *Chaos bound: Orderly disorder in contemporary literature and science*. Ithaca, NY: Cornell University.

Huang, Y. (1998). Curriculum Integration: The search for meaning and model construction. *The Proceedings of the National Science Council, Part C*, 8(4), 616-633.

Huang, Y. (2000). Teacher Change Through Experiencing and Reflecting on Curriculum Integration: A case study. *Journal of Education and Psychology*, 23, 237-280.

Huang, Y. (2001a). Probing Activity Curriculum and Integrated Activity Curriculum From Systems-theory Viewpoints: Essence, Rationale and Prospect. *Applied Psychology Research*, 9, 215-251.

Huang, Y. (2001b). Changing schools from loosely coupled elements to a perceptionally integrated system through facilitating curriculum integration. *Journal of Education and Psychology*, 24, 99-133.

Jantsch, E. (1992). *The self-organizing universe: Scientific and human implications of the emerging paradigm of evolution*. New York, NY: Pergamon.

Morgan, G. (1986). *Images of organization*. Beverly Hills, CA: Sage.

Pagels, H. R. (1982). *The cosmic code: Quantum physics as the language of nature*. New York, NY: Simon and Schuster.

Prigogine, I. (1980). *From Being to Becoming: Time and Complexity in the Physical Sciences*. San Francisco, CA: W. H. Freeman.

Prigogine, I., & Stengers, I. (1984). *Order out of chaos: Man's new dialogue with nature*. New York, NY: Bantam.

Rohr, R., & Ebert, A. (1990). *Discovering the enneagram: Ancient tool for a new spiritual journey*. New York, NY: Crossroad.

Chapter Eleven

Corporate Control Through Corporate Culture: Prospects and Problems

DAVID P. BOYD
THOMAS M. BEGLEY

Corporate Culture as a Control Mechanism

Jaeger (1982) has postulated two "ideal types" of control styles. The first "type" is a bureaucratic model that expresses control through knowledge (Dougherty & Course, 1995). Superiors direct subordinates and monitor their compliance. Rules pertain to process as well as product (Ouchi, 1979). As today's managers enact corporate strategy, they are fully cognizant that this kind of command-and-control governance no longer holds sway. Geographic dispersion as well as employee predilection militate against such ostensible forms of control.

With the decline of hierarchical control, management increasingly relies on a second "type" of control style. Unlike formal bureaucratic control, informal social control flows from a firm's implicit culture. Corporate culture has been defined as "the set of shared behaviors, artifacts, values, beliefs, and assumptions that a corporation develops as it learns to cope with the external and internal aspects of survival and success" (Peters & Waterman, 1982, p. 103).[1] Cultural control emphasizes employee commitment to the values espoused by the corporation (Baliga & Jaeger, 1984; O'Reilly & Chatman, 1996). If organizational members internalize these key tenets, "shared cognitive approaches" (p. 74) guide and even govern their actions (Adler & Jelinek, 1986). Since corporate culture can operate more extensively than most formal systems, it is a more powerful mechanism than traditional controls (O'Reilly & Chatman, 1996). By calling upon "a higher order concept of almost indisputable essence" (p. 98), management can increase organizational performance even as it lessens organizational command (Laurent, 1986). Moreover, the absence of perceived hierarchical mandate promotes a sense of autonomy. The reduction in formalization paradoxically heightens a centralization that is "internally derived" (Baliga & Jaeger, 1984, p. 29). By dispersing power, management accrues more.

The purpose of this chapter is to examine the concept of corporate culture. Specifically, how important is it, and what core values drive it? The chapter concludes with an assessment of this reliance on corporate culture, citing organizational benefits as well as potential pitfalls.

To explore these issues, we conducted in-depth interviews with 46 senior HR managers from 33 high technology firms headquartered in the United States.[2] This sample comprises the major firms in software, hardware, and services. Respondent revenues ranged from $3 billion to $88.4 billion.[3] We chose the technology arena for its economic impact and timely appeal; we were also mindful that such focus would permit more robust extrapolation about the sector.

Central Role of Core Values

Most HR executives in the present study drew upon corporate culture to further company goals. They often advanced their agenda through explicit links to corporate values. By referencing this fit, HR sought to rationalize systemic and programmatic change. As an HR director at Xerox observed: "You have to take advantage of the culture to the extent you can. Culture is like a gravitational pull. You can either fight it or take advantage of it." Commenting on the directional utility of Gateway values for decision making, an HR executive stated: "You always go back to the values to find out what's the right thing to do."

In terms of sheer number of values, sample firms invariably perceived less was better. One firm, for example, devoted more than a year of effort to crafting a policy that would encompass all aspects of computer usage in the workplace. The Herculean task of considering Internet, intranet, and extranet proved daunting. The task force finally took a six-month reprieve and returned fortified with a simple but strong conviction: business computers should be used exclusively for business purposes. Rather than bureaucratic monitoring to ensure compliance, the company would rely on the principle of rectitude that girded cultural norms. Subsequent events confirmed the strength of those informal controls. In the few instances of violation, peers admonished their colleagues and infractions then ceased (Boyd & Begley, 1998). By framing context rather than managing content, companies like Unisys allow their work force to focus on strategic effort. Echoing this sentiment, our Texas Instruments respondent observed that "if you focus on less, you will control more" while her Intel counterpart declared that "if you talk too much, people stop listening." A Compaq executive also found that "if the policy repository is too extensive, then employees will not use it." All Compaq policies are meant to be "baseline," elucidating and emphasizing the corporate culture.

While shielding employees from information overload, this emphasis on a few seminal values hardly dispels complexity. As opposed to the rigid and slow characteristics of the bureaucratic model, the cultural approach allows interpretive latitude and flexible application. The old and new forms of behavioral influence are juxtaposed in Figure 1. Under the old system, managers merely found the page that listed the relevant policy or procedure. In the new system, managers need to ascertain whether a policy exists in the relevant area and also understand its connection to the larger values of the company. A flexible approach based on principles/values/guidelines requires more thought and time than the rules and regulations approach. Our Analog Devices respondent spent most of his time assisting managers with policy interpretation. His counterpart at Qualcomm also indicated that much of her time is spent on policy interpretation. Yet if properly developed and disseminated, corporate values themselves become a source of competitive advantage. According to the vice president of HR at Lotus Development: "If people understand the philosophy behind what we are trying to accomplish, then tactically they can go off and implement the right set of practices." At Texas Instruments a vice president argued that the company's values-guidelines-policies foundational model for decision making presented a much more powerful pathway to consistent decisions and rational justification than was possible under the previous rule-based control system.

As potent a force as corporate culture might be, our respondents did not consider it to be immutable. They were ready to alter its complexion especially if traditional views no longer accorded with the company's situation. An HR director at Microsoft highlighted the malleability of corporate culture when she discussed a process to define the cultural pillars of the company: "There are elements of the old we need to retain and other elements we need to discard. There are also new pieces we need to create." A Hewlett-Packard HR manager explained that even the vaunted "HP way" was under review due to internal questions about its ongoing relevance. Some "HPers" opined that certain time-honored cultural elements failed to address performance prerequisites for the current, competitive environment. One Hewlett-Packard senior manager has been quoted as saying: "The Hewlett-Packard Way is not jobs for life. It's jobs for performers. . . . We're a business, not a philanthropic enterprise" (McGovern & Hope-Hailey, 1997, p. 198).

Corporate Culture in High Technology Firms

In view of corporate culture's increasing importance as a behavioral determinant, it becomes instructive to locate the primary values that underlie it. As Gateway's vice president succinctly stated: "Values are not simply depicted on a poster in my office. If you don't value the values, you will have a short career at Gateway." General Electric's Jack Welch also considers compliance with values as the pre-eminent prerequisite for continued employment. Absent such values, you will not make it at the company even if you make your numbers (Bartlett & Wonzy, 2000). Such turnover may actually enhance cultural permanence since estranged employees leave the organization (Delacroix & Swaminathan, 1991).

Due to intense competition in the relatively nascent high technology sector, bureaucratic legacy systems seldom clutter the landscape. From Silicon Valley to Route 128, stories echo the centrality of corporate culture to organizational effectiveness. The cultures of these various companies may have distinctive elements. Intel's "only the paranoid," for example, contrasts with the people-centered emphasis of Hewlett-Packard's "HP Way." Nevertheless, several common elements characterize the corporate culture of high technology firms, especially when viewed from the outside. We divide values related to corporate culture into "credo" and "conduct" values. Credo values present end-state conditions that are worthy of emulation and toward which corporations claim to strive. These transcendental "shoulds" of corporate culture are most often expressed as guiding principles in vision and mission statements. Conduct values are the means-state qualities that define a desirable mindset. These action-oriented values are highly prized in day-to-day pursuits. Figure 2 presents this values classification based on our set of high technology companies.

As Figure 2 illustrates, high technology corporate values are far from warm and fuzzy. Instead, the value that surpasses any other in importance, relevance, and emphasis is results-driven performance. It is the rubric that subsumes other corporate values. Results-driven performance primarily reflects an instrumental orientation since U.S. corporations measure themselves by financial indices such as revenue and earnings growth. Wall Street pressures have caused companies like Analog Devices to yield some of their original liberal, people-first principles.

Components of the performance credo value include productivity, merit, competitiveness, innovation, commitment, and integrity. For example, Cisco's high-energy environment stresses "productivity above all else. The work ethic is severe" (Business Week, 2000). A Cisco executive epitomized this attitude when she said: "Our culture is a web-based culture, and we seek the fastest productivity in the industry." In such firms, the mentality is "execute or exit." As EMC's president notes: "If you don't make your numbers, you get pushed off the island" (Lyons, 2000, p. 149). At GE "no sharp knife stays in a drawer" (Stewart, 1999, p. 136). Conversely, merit-based rewards await those who do make the numbers. This technology milieu respects contribution more than position. The winning cycle links individual contribution to personal compensation, thereby abetting corporate performance (James, 1998). Some companies have implemented pay-at-risk systems that link a portion of annual compensation to the attainment of individual, unit, or corporate goals. Unlike other incentive systems, which leave base salary intact, pay-at-risk systems can lower the base in the event of target shortfalls. Taking a different tack, a vice president at 3Com described HR's innovative efforts to develop a flexible pay package, called "out-of-cycle incentives," that allowed managers to exercise autonomy in making incentive-related decisions outside the annual review process. They could thereby recognize meritorious performance in timely fashion.

A spirit of competitiveness prevailed across our sample. Intel, for instance, promulgates a siege mentality among its employees and "takes no prisoners." In the market for computer storage, EMC shows similar aggressiveness as it seeks to thwart upstart rivals like Network Appliance. EMC positions Chameleon, its new network attached storage device, as a "Net App killer." Using identical verbiage, IBM originally touted its Shark storage product as an "EMC killer." Insiders have described Microsoft's extreme task orientation in similar terms; in the war zone of daily activity, "brushes with death are the only way to win" (Nocera, 2000). Reverence for innovation is ubiquitous, epitomized by an Intel manager who calls himself "a transformational virus" (U.S. News and World Report, 1995). Innovation, in turn, presupposes a focus on product quality and customer utility. Yet this creative context comes at a cost since autonomy is coupled with accountability. Though the values approach eschews bureaucratic thinking, it does not abrogate structural control. In their study of Hewlett-Packard, McGovern and Hope-Hailey (1997) found that bureaucratic controls over employee performance could co-exist with a corporate culture predicated on innovation and empowerment. As noted by an IBM vice president: "We can get rid of the bad cholesterol while keeping the good cholesterol." Several respondent companies use forced ratings that require managers to distribute pay recommendations across the entire categorical spectrum. The goal is to recognize top performers and remove lesser ones. Individual empowerment thus in no way negates the demanding corporate culture. While there may be an egalitarian, round table ethos, employees undergo Darwinian drama to sit at the table. "There is no hand holding," says a Sun insider (Business Week, 2000).

Commitment is included in this list because it is usually phrased as commitment to excellence and corporate success, not as commitment of company to employee or employee to company, much less to some higher cause beyond financial metrics. In this value set, integrity is an exception to the single-minded focus on performance. This value is further manifest in related terms such as honesty and respect for people. Respondents claimed that integrity is the most likely value to be honored in the breach. Corporate legends recount situations where profits were purposely foregone in order to preserve moral foundations.

The main conduct values emphasized in high technology companies concern timely delivery of product. Competition occurs in Internet time. An atmosphere of perceived crisis helps generate the sense of urgency (Kotter & Haskett, 1992). In such a combative arena, time to market is the first measure of effectiveness. Need for speed compelled respondent actions. This nimbleness is prompted by fear (Economist, 1997). In reviewing the product transition from defense to semiconductors, for example, our Texas Instruments respondent emphasized that now "backlog is only as good as the hour you are looking at it." Survey participants considered rapid enactment more important than any increment coming through iteration. As one noted: "The world is moving at such a rapid pace that if you wait to get it all right, it is probably obsolete." A Hewlett-Packard executive pithily pronounced: "The 80% solution becomes the core strategy."

In the service of speed, flexibility and adaptability were watchwords. Such entrepreneurial thinking assumes a penchant for risk-taking. Technological problems were seen as personal opportunities (Economist, 1997). GE, for example, endorses a stretch concept that rewards success more than it penalizes failure. Under his tenure Jack Welch wanted the right gene pool which he defined as those who "break glass" (Stewart, 1999, p. 130). Respondents' willingness to push against barriers extended to colleagues who were "in the way." Open discussion and constructive criticism were bastions of the task-driven culture. These companies encourage creative dissent as part of the exploration process. Most companies expressed strong antipathy toward stultifying systems. A Cisco executive epitomized this attitude when she said: "We are not bureaucratic. We just do it." Due to this premium on velocity, our sample companies found little time to engage in benchmarking. There were, in the words of a Unisys executive, few "touchstones to the outside."

Consequences of Cultural Control

What are the advantages and disadvantages of this reliance on corporate culture? As a concept, should it be espoused or eschewed?

An obvious advantage is that shared norms allow standardization, thereby limiting complexity and facilitating administration. Pressure for such uniformity came from a range of constituents in our sample companies. Internally, corporate culture is viewed as an essential tool to further consistency and control across the theater of operations. Managers want baselines for advising employees around such issues as performance expectations and reward systems. For their part, employees wish to minimize confusion and redress any perceived imbalance in resource distribution across countries. Externally, customers expect companies to manifest the same "look and feel" everywhere. No matter where they dealt with the company, customers demanded similar products, similar service, and similar pricing. They became frustrated when, for example, a company's globally dispersed units reacted in different fashion to the same problem. Using terminology of the trade, an Oracle executive concluded that clients want his company "to be the server."

While the concept of corporate culture affords pragmatic advantages, its philosophic premises may be more suspect. Cultural control is achieved through the value congruence of organizational members. Socialization processes therefore attempt to ensure such congruence. An executive at Cisco, having described the protracted process of assessing prospective employees, claimed that it produced eventual economies since the predilection of recruits coincided with the value structure of the company. When hiring for HR overseas, Cisco "overlays the company culture on nationals." Mentors help all new Cisco hires learn the culture and imbue its results-orientation. In the non-sales area, each recruit meets straightaway with a boss to set five or six goals that need to be accomplished in the first 90 days. Executives at Oracle described a values survey regularly used in lieu of the more traditional employee attitude survey. The instrument queries the extent to which the unit and the company itself support values Oracle claims to hold most dear. A portion of management's annual compensation is tied to the survey results. In our study there were numerous instances where such indoctrination smacked of unilateral imposition. Cultural conduits were one-way communication channels. EMC, through its own University, goes so far as to require corporate citizenship modules complete with self-paced CD-ROMs.

Another pitfall is the nature of the corporate culture itself. Though many corporate cultures tout adaptiveness as a hallmark, such permeability can prove elusive in multinational settings. The corporate suite wants commonality so it can manage effectively. Our EMC respondent acknowledges that "if EMC homogenizes, it has the power to leverage." In much the same language, "Lotus starts with the position of consistency and then we argue our way from there." "The Teradyne process transcends any particular country" while Hewlett-Packard "optimizes at the company rather than the country level." Slavish devotion to cultural tenets often fostered the notion of a supra-culture that blends "the various values of the worldwide workforce into a single value system that embodies the organization's vision" (Schell & Solomon, 1997, p. 35). An IBM vice president saw no dissonance between the company's professed penchant for a "borderless mindset" and his admission that "the leverage points drive toward centralization." Companies such as GTE believe that the same attributes are responsible for driving business success, regardless of geographic locale. To the extent a company disseminates HR programs and policies worldwide, it presumes that employees should universally espouse the values on which they are based. Yet in the coinage of Palick and Gomez-Meiga (1999), corporate culture cannot protect a firm from "the "entropic forces of cultural diversity" (p. 597).

Corporate culture thus runs the risk of being both prescriptive and parochial. Our sample firms invariably averred that core values were non-negotiable. If subsidiaries are not culturally proximate, however, cultural control is more likely to appear normative than neutral (Baliga & Jaeger, 1984). As a result, when educational interventions are unilaterally forced through the corporate chain, the change effort may fail. Instrumental compliance is not indicative of internalization (Willmott, 1993). Silence should not be construed as consensus. Moreover, excessive efforts toward homogenization might incite organizational members to display counter-cultural activism. Beer, Eisenstat and Spector (1990) see the genesis of successful change as incremental wins on the periphery rather than mechanized imposition from the center. AT&T regards values as "an expression of choice and self-control whereas rules tend to control and constrain freedom of choice."

A question arises, however, as to who chooses the values. To some this cultural form of control smacks of Orwellian omniscience. Through moral manipulation of the workforce, corporate culture "contains possibilities to ensnare workers in a hegemonic system" (Ray, 1986, p. 287). According to such writers, as a doctrine corporate culture subjugates employee autonomy to managerial imperatives. By defining centrist values and excluding all other values from their purview, such "monocultures" inhibit critical reflection. The result can be a "hypermodern neo-authoritarianism which, potentially, is more insidious and sinister than its bureaucratic predecessor" (Willmott, 1993, p. 541).

Is U.S. Culture Especially Ethnocentric?

Although all countries are inherently ethnocentric, American culture seems particularly so (Trice & Beyer, 1993). Two scholars on culture have observed: "Overseas Americans feel confident that their ways are the best ways and often demonstrate messianic zeal about imposing them on other cultures and then fail to understand why they encounter resistance and resentment" (Hall & Hall, 1990, p. 149). Numerous respondents expressed concern about the "colonialist" tag and were aware of the danger inherent in the "tendency to forget about other countries" voiced by a Motorola executive. Yet several executives expressed a firm belief in the international efficacy of American management systems. A Seagate executive represented this position when he observed that HR managers from other countries often adopted the approaches used in the company's U.S. operations because "the U.S. has the most highly developed policies and systems."

Why do many Americans fail to question the rationale behind their ethnocentric efforts? A frequently cited factor is lack of exposure to other countries and consequent insensitivity to cultural dimensions. A French CEO commented: "European companies have an advantage in managing culturally; they know there's not one best way because they're in such a diverse market. By contrast, because of the size of their market, the U.S. thinks they have the best way" (Rosen, 2000, p. 195). Others are not so kind. One author, for example, blamed "an ingrained inability on the part of Americans to learn from other cultures" (Hampden-Turner, 1991, p. 96). As a result, a MediaOne vice president concluded: "We are not particularly culturally adept. We know how to do business the American way."

In sum, substantial evidence supports the argument that many U.S. companies are very ethnocentric in their approach overseas. Despite the Japanese reputation for ethnocentricity, research indicates that American companies are even less sensitive to local conditions and less able to combine global and local thinking than Japanese companies (Kriger & Solomon, 1992; Yuen & Kee, 1993). The prominence of U.S. companies in the world economy draws attention to the specific features of U.S. ethnocentricity. An exportive orientation toward corporate culture fuels the perception that most U.S. companies are oblivious to local ways.

To facilitate recognition and removal of cultural obstacles, companies may pursue a variety of action steps. For example, there are common calls to broaden the international composition of the board, rotate employees overseas for developmental assignments, and even require international experience for promotion to executive ranks (Ashkenas, Ulrich et al., 1995). Based on our field interviews, however, four approaches hold particular promise for addressing cultural gaps: cultural audits, inclusive management, communities of practice, and socialization processes.

Conducting a Cultural Audit

Geographical distance from overseas facilities creates difficulties for many United States-based executives. This separation might distort their judgment about the state of international operations, especially in a subjective area such as human resources. When physical barriers combine with cultural distance, there is paramount need to obtain systematic feedback on value clashes. As a first step, multinationals should diagnose the extent of potential disparity through a cultural inventory. This audit compares a company's corporate culture with the dominant cultures of the primary countries in which the firm operates. It will indicate whether international HR has avoided "the trap of universalism" (Laurent, 1986, p. 97). Even companies with an explicitly ethnocentric orientation need to determine which battles to fight and which to avoid.

A starting place is to target countries where the company has a substantial number of employees. The categorization of HR systems into corporate philosophy, policy, and practice offers an initial framework. The first step in a cultural audit is to identify the company's key values, its central HR policies and programs, and the practices that enact them. The second step is to identify values, policies, and practices commonly used in each target country. The third step is to assess the degree of fit across the respective sets. To what extent are the principles, policies and practices of the company compatible with those of the host country? The focus should be on congruence with those factors that are instrumental to corporate success. Figure 3 categorizes degree of fit between those success factors and corporate-national compatibility. By plotting the position of major HR components on this graph, executives can pinpoint areas where a company's emphasis on cultural consistency might clash with national culture, most notably areas that fall within the "danger zone." [4]

An additional question concerns the auditors themselves. If possible, the potential biases of either headquarters executives or local managers should be avoided. The ideal candidate would be familiar with the corporate culture as well as the culture of the host country. In select instances, HR executives in regional offices might serve as effective auditors for countries beyond their bailiwick. Their experience would render them cognizant of the corporate culture and the tensions inherent in reconciling it with national culture. At the same time, their distance from the country under scrutiny could provide the desired objectivity. In certain companies, the realities of corporate politics might preclude managers from performing such a role. External or internal consultants might then be engaged.

Inclusive Management

To avoid difficulties that can arise from potential cultural clashes, companies can accentuate a few programs deemed pivotal to corporate success. By explicitly identifying specific programs as essential, headquarters can set the stage for dialogue with subsidiaries. Such dialogue elucidates reasons for a program's centrality, thus bolstering the rationale for compliance. If a company limits subsidiary adherence to a small number of programs, it gains a greater chance of cooperation. With allowance to preserve many values central to their own culture, local managers may then more willingly yield on the small set of vital corporate values. Moreover, simple communication can go a long way toward dispelling resistance. Managers who provide input into the decision-making process are more likely to support and implement the final decisions reached (e.g., Kim

& Mauborgne, 1993). Participation at the country level also opens the possibility of creative solutions to cultural exigencies.

3Com's policy loop, for example, extends some discretion to provide a "local overlay on the corporate mandate." The company recognizes that "people typically do not implement policies that they feel are stupid." Hence it is important to tie the knots locally. In the words of Gateway's Vice President of Global HR: "If locals have some flexibility, they will take off their parochial hats." Similarly, Honeywell's HR Manager of Global Mobility declared: "If you want to have global policies, you have to have global input." When contemplating a policy change, Xerox builds a case and involves people in solving the problem. As the company's Director of HR Effectiveness asserts: "We first indicate what is wrong with A and then why we are looking for B. This inclusiveness brings both ideas and buy-in." In one of our sample firms, the communications group had installed a dedicated line so field personnel could express their preference on any proposed change.

Even with a limited number of essential programs, cultural clashes are inevitable. In those instances, executives can weigh the relative centrality of corporate and national culture. If core corporate values are at stake, the company should gauge employee adaptability. For example, as previously noted, Oracle sought to establish the primacy of performance over seniority in Japanese compensation and promotion decisions. When managers conducted an anonymous employee survey to determine the effects of this experiment, they discovered that older employees predictably preferred seniority. However, younger employees were pleased with the accent on performance, a finding that ran counter to the prevalent societal norm.

When culture clash occurs, it is sometimes possible to accommodate both corporate and national inclinations. An IBM HR vice president observed that most commentators view the worldwide Web as a means to standardize systems such as performance appraisal. Yet the Web also permits low cost customization of HR systems. When IBM was designing a performance appraisal system, it considered dimensions reflective of its win/execute/team core values to be universally mandatory. Within these dimensions IBM allowed customization of particular components according to country, divisional, or functional needs. The number of items rated as well as their effect on pay differed from country to country.

Communities of Practice

When Lou Gerstner assumed the helm at IBM, he allegedly commented that he had never seen an organization so focused on "internal plumbing." He halted internecine warfare by casting competitors as the common enemy. It was they who were taking business away from IBM. Colleagues were not the culprit and could be the solution. Gerstner's rationale for teamwork has found international extension through the concept of communities of practice (CoPs). CoPs provide an interactive forum for cross-site and cross-country groups. One firm took as the starting point a principle enunciated by Lawrence Bossidy, CEO of Honeywell: "Whoever can contribute value . . . needs to be encouraged to collaborate with others to make things happen, without waiting for some central authority to give permission" (Ashkenas et al., p. xix). When corporate and national culture clash, the best place to respond is where the clashes are occurring. Imposed central models hamper the flexible mentality and speedy response that our respondents repeatedly cited as critical conduct values. Rather than hierarchy, HR might rely on networks of connectivity dispersed across many divisions, locations, and functions. Unlike formal work groups that produce a product, project teams that accomplish a task, or informal networks that collect information, CoPs have no tangible deliverable; they exist to build and exchange knowledge. Members are bound by "passion, commitment, and identification with the group's expertise" (Wenger & Snyder, 2000, p. 142).

Many respondents proclaimed the efficacy of informal groups in a global setting. While virtual teams create opportunities for learning and sharing without a gatekeeper, formal committees typically "want to sit in a room." MediaOne finds such teams an ideal way to share best practices that are not yet policies. Through their emergent, organic structure, such communities can leverage "social capital," simultaneously reducing rework and increasing innovation (Lesser & Storck, 2001). Despite varied nomenclature, the rudiments of this community concept have been evident for some time in several organizations. Hewlett Packard has utilized "learning communities" while Xerox has formed "family groups." In 1995 IBM Global Services extensively applied the model and institutionalized a whole series of "knowledge networks" focused on organizational competencies (Gonglia & Rizzutto, 2001).

While these organizational forms require senior support, the executive sponsorship must be manifest as cooperation rather than co-optation. By first specifying the knowledge domain, organizational superiors can acquaint the virtual team with managerial priorities. In the words of 3Com's HR Vice President: "There is a clear need to identify what needs to be done as opposed to what would be nice but is less critical." To provide this focus, Unisys situates each driver or "owner" of a new policy in an appropriate "center of excellence," thereby assuring concentration on the issue at hand.

Management's second role in a CoP is to preserve and perpetuate the tacit knowledge spontaneously generated by member interaction (Brown & Duguid, 2000). While the community focuses on sharing knowledge and sparking innovation, management helps husband this intellectual capital. The firm must have access to the knowledge developed in dialogue. An internal Web site would then be one means for ongoing engagement with an expanded audience. By having all HR centers of excellence report directly to HR rather than their business units, Motorola ensures knowledge distillation. NCR has also seen the need to tie network "substructures" to their functional parent since a process like compensation tends to get disconnected from a related activity like staffing. For their part, members must be alert to the danger of excessive group solidarity. Should a community become overly exclusive and exclusionary, its aims may no longer align with the larger organization. Team members must accept the corporate credo and march to the beat of a common drummer. Only then will strategic intent inform CoP discussion.

Informational infrastructure allows CoPs to communicate easily and electronically. IBM communities have utilized customized collaborative space such as Knowledge Café, a Lotus notes and Domino application for internal use. NCR's globally dispersed networks galvanize around roles and defined skill sets. Using a proprietary net technology called "Round Table" to facilitate interaction, members complement voice communication with concurrent data on the Web. NCR deploys this model for global compensation processes and now seeks to replicate it in performance management, career management, and staffing. Such process mechanisms engage a broad purview of people to help in design, dissemination, and deployment. As a result, there are no surprises in the field and staff overhead is minimized.

Socialization Processes

Increasing size and scope can lead to cultural dilution. The HR Vice President of SCI Systems remarked on such contrarian behavior when he observed that "new people with their new ways can chop up a lot of the sacred cows for hamburger." To prevent clash with local mores, the most expeditious approach is to hire people who fit into the overall corporate culture. An Oracle Vice President of HR frames the challenge as a "need to find and develop the people who will make us their future." The organization must be attractive to those graduates who will prove "loyal" and "functional." Similarly, our Gateway respondent observed that "it all goes back to whom you source." Company prospects undergo a grueling interview because Gateway is not in a "forgiving industry." As a consequence, there has to be consensus on a hire. No person on the interviewing team outranks another. Moreover, assessment requires inclusion of a representative from outside the applicant's immediate department. This arduous process insures that Gateway employees will not be pitted against their internal value set. The firm has the option to select compatible candidates, but prospects can also disengage of their own accord if they are uncomfortable in the corporate setting.

Preservation of cultural values assumes special importance when a company is seeking to integrate acquisitions. Compaq affords an example when it acquired Digital and Tandem. Unlike the mature phase of these heritage organizations, the "Compaq Way" depicted a culture that was decentralized and fast-paced. In the words of the HR manager: "We didn't want someone to go through volumes of policies to find out what they needed to do." While Compaq expects consistent employee behavior, it also accords business units flexibility since they are the revenue-generating aspects of the business. Enculturation becomes the channel to effect this purposeful action. Especially in a cross-cultural context, philosophic boundaries can ensure strategic unison. As Lotus' Senior Vice President of HR indicated: "You are a Lotus employee no matter where you sit."

For its part, EMC has a common induction process around the world that takes place over the employee's first 90 days and socializes newcomers into the company's "language." IBM's new employee orientation is called "Becoming One Voice." In place around the world, it consists of a core curriculum that includes "the IBM heritage." IBM has also come to realize that exclusive focus on employee selection can adversely affect retention. IBM's perspective now includes present as well as prospective hires. To be the employer of choice, you must look to the outside but you must also "re-recruit the people who already work for you."

All the above examples show how training can perpetuate corporate culture. Yet training can also smooth the interface of corporate and national culture. Even in a virtual world, Lotus emphasizes the importance of in-person contact since philosophy is conveyed mainly through discussion. Given the spatial separation of worldwide employees, companies must create occasions for cross-cultural socialization. For example, GTE developed a global enrichment series by contracting with the University of South Carolina. Targeted mainly toward upper-level and middle-level managers, the program provided five-day intensive sessions "to move the organization toward 10 on a global scale." According to the Director of International HR, "it is a big task, it is a large population, and there are different levels of international understanding."

A Surplus of Exported Culture

In summary, corporate culture achieves control through values rather than hierarchy. Peer control obviates the need for bureaucratic control. All our participants were keenly interested in values but not as a way of balancing occupational pursuits with other life perspectives. The notion of values had nothing to do with contemplative meditation or stress reduction. Rather than offering refuge from the storm, these firms deliberately create stormy seas. As their overarching value, they focused on performance. HR departments inculcate this orientation through socialization and training and then reinforce it through performance assessment.

Although our study was limited to high technology firms of a certain critical mass, we suspect that in the United States this Silicon Valley culture may be rampant far beyond the Valley. Further, despite the relative nascency of some of our sample companies, age of firm was not a major distinguishing factor in relation to stage of internationalization or HR orientation. To compete in the technology sector, companies must internationalize very rapidly. The youngest companies in our sample professed no less need for global positioning than did the oldest, nor did they profess higher levels of U.S.-centricity.

Given the centricity of corporate culture, it is not surprising that U.S. companies export their performance orientation and expectations. Such values are so ingrained in American companies that they may not always be recognized as idiosyncratic. Once exported, however, these foundational values become more explicit and questionable. Undeniably, some benefits accrue from this attempt to propagate value-based management systems. When the corporate ethos conflicts with local mores, however, companies may be in danger of carrying cultural control too far.

The recommendations presented here permit HR executives to move away from a top-down approach while still advancing corporate vision and strategy. By allowing decision making at the level where information exists, our suggestions reduce the likelihood of culture clash. Such an approach depends on a small set of directional values, globally dispersed communities of practice, and a continuous process of sensitive socialization. By recognizing local sensibilities, firms can successfully diffuse local strengths.

References

Adler, N. J. & Jelinek, M. 1986. Is "organizational culture" culture bound? *Human Resource Management*, 25(1): 73-90.

Ashkenas, R., Ulrich, D., Jick, T., & Kerr, S. 1995. *The boundaryless organization.* San Francisco: Jossey-Bass.

Baliga, B. R. & Jaeger, A. M. 1984. Multinational corporations: Control systems and delegation issues. *Journal of International Business Studies*, 15(2): 25-40.

Bartlett, C. A. & Wozny, M. 2000. *GE's two-decade transformation: Jack Welch's leadership.* Boston: Harvard Business School Publishing.

Beer, M., Eisenstat, A. & Spector, B. 1990. Why change programs don't produce change. *Harvard Business Review*, (November/December): 158-166.

Business Week. 2000. The truth is in the vault. *Business Week*, (August 14).

Delacroix, J. & Swaminathan, A. 1991. Cosmetic, speculative, and adaptive organizational change in the wine industry: A longitudinal study. *Administrative Science Quarterly*, 36: 631-661.

Dougherty, D. & Course, S. 1995. When it comes to product innovation, what is so bad about bureaucracy? *Journal of High Technology Management Research*, 6, 1: 55-76.

Economist. 2000. The real meaning of empowerment. *Economist*, (March 25): 75-77.

Economist. 1997. Silicon Valley. *Economist*, (March 29): 5-20.

Edstrom, A. & Galbraith, J. 1977. Transfers of managers as a coordination and control strategy in multinational organizations. *Administrative Science Quarterly*, 22: 248-263.

Garvin, D. A. 2000. *Learning in action: A guide to putting the learning organization to work*. Boston: Harvard Business School Press.

Gonglia, P. & Rizzutto, C. R. 2001. Evolving communities of practice: IBM global services experience. *IBM Systems Journal*, 40(4): 842-862.

Hall, E. T. & Hall, M. R. 1990. *Understanding cultural differences*. Yarmouth, ME: Intercultural Press.

Hampden-Turner, C. 1991. The boundaries of business: The cross-cultural quagmire. *Harvard Business Review*, 69 (Sept.-Oct.): 94-96.

Jaeger, A. M. 1982. Contrasting control modes in the multinational corporation: Theory, practice, and implications. *International Studies of Management and Organization*, XII(1): 59-82.

James, J. 1998. *Success secrets from Silicon Valley*. New York: Time Books/Random House.

Kim, W. & Mauborgne, R. 1993. Making global strategies work. *Sloan Management Review*, 22:11-27.

Kotter, J. P. & Heskett, J. L. 1992. *Corporate culture and performance*. New York: The Free Press.

Kriger, M. & Solomon, E. 1992. Strategic mindsets and decision-making autonomy in U.S. and Japanese MNCs. *Management International Review*, 32: 327-343.

Laurent, A. 1986. The cross-cultural puzzle of international human resource management. *Human Resource Management*, 25: 91-102.

Lesser, E. L. & Storck, J. 2001. Communities of practice and organizational performance. *IBM Systems Journal*, 40 (4): 831-841.

Lyons, D. 2000. Boom. *Forbes*, (October 2): 146-153.

Malone, M. 1995. Killer results without killing yourself. *U. S. News and World Report*, Special Supplement, (October 30): 1-6.

McGovern, P. & Hope-Hailey, V. 1997. Corporate culture and bureaucratic control. In S. Sackmann, Ed., *Cultural complexity in organizations*: 187-206. Thousand Oaks, CA: Sage Publications.

Nocera, J. 2000. I remember Microsoft. *Fortune* (July 10): 114-136.

O'Reilly, C. & Chatman, J. A. 1996. Culture as social control: Corporations, cults, and commitment. In B. Staw & L. L Cummings (Eds.), *Research in organizational behavior*, 18:157-200. Greenwich, CT: JAI Press.

Ouchi, W. G. 1979. A conceptual framework for the design of organizational control mechanisms. *Management Science*, 25(9): 833-848.

Palick, L. & Gomez-Meiga, L. 1999. A theory of global strategy and firm efficiencies: Considering the effects of cultural diversity. *Journal of Management*, 25(4): 587-606.

Peters, T. & Waterman, R. 1982. *In search of excellence*. New York: Harper & Row.

Ray, C. A. 1986. Corporate culture: The last frontier of control? *Journal of Management Studies*, 23(3): 287-297.

Rosen, R. 2000. *Global literacies*. New York: Simon & Schuster.

Schell, M. S. & Solomon, C. M. 1997. Global culture: Who's the gatekeeper? *Workforce*, 76(11): 35-38.

Senge, P. M. 1990. *The fifth discipline: The art and practice of the learning organization*. New York: Currency/Doubleday.

Stewart, T. 1999. See Jack run: See Jack run Europe. *Fortune*, (September 27): 124-136.

Trice, H. M. & Beyer, J. M. 1993. *The cultures of work organizations*. Englewood Cliffs, NJ: Prentice Hall.

Wenger, E. C. & Snyder, W. M. 2000. Communities of practice: the organizational frontier. *Harvard Business Review*, 78 (Jan-Feb): 139-145.

Willmott, H. 1993. Strength is ignorance; slavery is freedom: Managing culture in modern organizations. *Journal of Management Studies*, 30(4): 515-552.

Yuen, E. & Kee, H. 1993. Headquarters, host-culture and organizational influences on HRM policies and practices. *Management International Review*, 33: 361-383.

Notes

1. In this chapter, we follow the practice in the literature of referring to corporate culture as a unitary construct. However, we acknowledge that substantial cultural variation may occur within companies as well as across countries. Company subcultures have received increased attention in recent years (e.g., Schein, E. 1999. *The Corporate Culture Survival Guide*. San Francisco: Jossey-Bass). In citing characteristics of dominant cultures in our sample, we aim to avoid turning modal differences into stereotypes.

2. We followed a semi-structured interview format. The average interview lasted 70 minutes. Both authors took extensive notes and audio-taped sessions. Analysis followed the template approach presented in B. F. Crabtree and W. L. Miller, (Eds.), 1992. *Doing Qualitative Research*. Newbury Park, CA: Sage. After coding responses into thematic constructs, we continued categorical revision and refinement as we developed the data. We then qualitatively interpreted emergent patterns.

3. The authors began by conducting an in-depth examination of corporate values in one high technology multinational. This pilot stage included over twenty hours of interviews with the executive responsible for worldwide HR policies, interviews with six managers involved in the process, and questionnaire surveys of five additional HR executives in Asia-Pacific, Canada, Europe, Latin America, and the United States. Fortified by a literature review, these sessions guided direction of subsequent interviews. The interview set was comprised of 39 HR executives in 32 publicly traded high technology multinational enterprises. All were headquartered in the United States. Of those interviewed, 21 were vice presidents, 7 directors,

and 11 managers. Executives were identified through a combination of convenience and snowball sampling. FY 2001 size of companies ranged from 10,200 to 316,000 employees.
4. This figure is an adapted version of one presented by Harris, P. R. & Moran, R. T. 1996. *Managing cultural differences*. 4th ed. Houston, TX: Gulf.

Figure 1
Hierarchical and Culture-Based Forms of Behavioral Influence

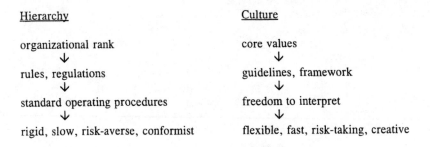

Hierarchy   Culture

organizational rank   core values
         ↓   ↓
rules, regulations   guidelines, framework
         ↓   ↓
standard operating procedures   freedom to interpret
         ↓   ↓
rigid, slow, risk-averse, conformist   flexible, fast, risk-taking, creative

Figure 2
Values Emphasized in High Technology Corporate Cultures

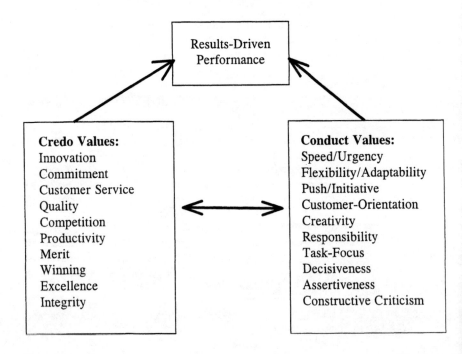

Results-Driven Performance

Credo Values:
Innovation
Commitment
Customer Service
Quality
Competition
Productivity
Merit
Winning
Excellence
Integrity

Conduct Values:
Speed/Urgency
Flexibility/Adaptability
Push/Initiative
Customer-Orientation
Creativity
Responsibility
Task-Focus
Decisiveness
Assertiveness
Constructive Criticism

Figure 3
Compatibility of Corporate Culture Components with National Culture

Specific Corporate HR Component: _____

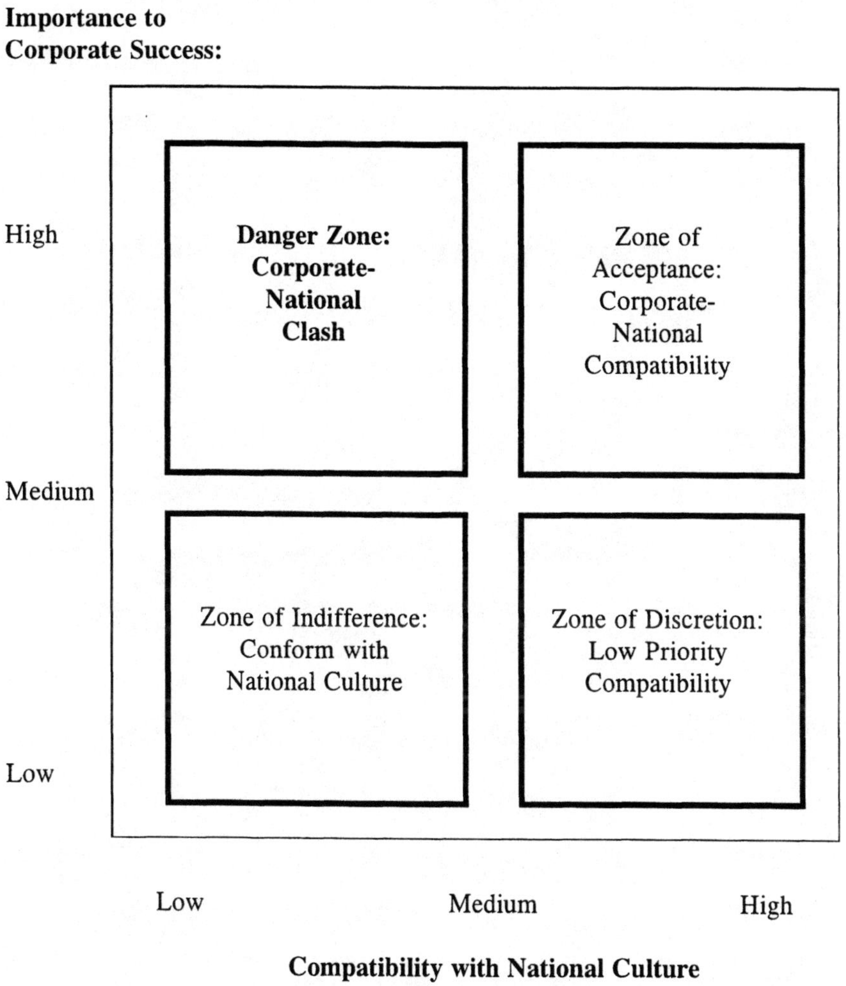

**Importance to
Corporate Success:**

High	**Danger Zone: Corporate- National Clash**	Zone of Acceptance: Corporate- National Compatibility
Medium		
	Zone of Indifference: Conform with National Culture	Zone of Discretion: Low Priority Compatibility
Low		
	Low Medium High	

Compatibility with National Culture

Chapter Twelve

Walking the Humanities into the Marketplace: A Communicative Call

RONALD C. ARNETT

I do not know if one can speak of a "phenomenology" of the face, since phenomenology describes what appears. So, too, I wonder if one can speak of a look turned toward the face, for the look is knowledge, perception. I think rather that access to the face is straightaway ethical. You turn yourself toward the Other as toward an object when you see a nose, eyes, a forehead, a chin, and you describe them. The best way of encountering the Other is not even to notice the color of his eyes! When one observes the color of the eyes one is not in social relationship with the Other. The relation with the face can surely be dominated by perception, but what is specially the face is what cannot be reduced to that . . . the face is what forbids us to kill. (Levinas, 1985, pp. 85-86)

. . . An anthropological definition of good and evil . . . revealed to the human person's retrospection, his cognizance of himself in the course of the life he has lived. We learn to comprehend this anthropological definition as similar in nature to the biblical tales of good and evil, whose narrator must have experienced Adam as well as Kain in the abyss of his own heart . . . neither intended nor able to provide any criterion over and above that, either for the use of theoretical meditation concerning the entities "good" and "evil" nor, certainly, for the use of the question of man, who is not spared enquiry and investigation into what in the sense of design, good and what evil. . . . (Buber, 1952, p. 131)

W hy introduce *Walking the Humanities into the Marketplace* with quotations from Emmanuel Levinas and Martin Buber? The question reveals disconnect between the humanities and the marketplace—disconnect encouraged by "true believers" (Hoffer, 1951) in the purity of the humanities and those unduly committed to the pragmatics of the marketplace. The humanities seldom offer comment on the marketplace, unless in critique, instinctively choosing William James's stance: "There is no more fiendish behavior than to act as if another did not exist" (as quoted in Watzlawick, Beavin & Jackson, 1967, p. 86). This chapter chooses an alternative route, suggesting that difference between humanities scholarship and the marketplace offers the possibility of texture, insight, and challenge to taken-for-granted assumptions, when the two realms learn from one another.

Plato in "Phaedo" suggested: ". . . those who have purified themselves enough by philosophy live without bodies . . ." (trans. 1954/1999, p 94). This chapter suggests a goal for the humanities contrary to purification. This chapter suggests the importance of engagement with difference, with the unknown. Engagement in the marketplace is this chapter's charge for the humanities—a marketplace often termed alien and sinister, pejoratively understood as a place of "mere" exchange and profit. When the humanities invite learning within the protective walls of the academy, significant insight emerges in isolation and retreat. Additionally, another form of learning transpires in action, in engagement, in ongoing life within the public square.

This chapter suggests that one of the tasks of rhetoric/communication is to engage the humanities and the marketplace. The marketplace, understood as the gathering of multiple voices, functions as audience and as actor—consuming ideas, learning, and persuading.

Introduction

This chapter suggests that the humanities encounter the marketplace, learning from a place of perceived "radical alterity" (Levinas, 1961/1969, p. 192). Engaging the unfamiliar opens the possibility for insight not only into the standpoint of the Other, but also into oneself. The above suggestion assumes a basic hermeneutic presupposition—we learn from difference, from the meeting of competing cultures, in this case, the humanities and the marketplace. In a humanities situated academy, there is no public space more alien than the marketplace. Learning from contrary cultures begins not only when different ethnic, racial, and affective cultures meet, but when an academic humanities culture opens a window to the marketplace. Such meetings offer opportunity to see differently, to learn, and upon occasion to find points of temporal agreement, learning from one another. If the humanities do not embrace such engagement, the culture of the marketplace, by force of number and by its centrality to daily life, will make the humanities increasingly irrelevant.

Engagement between the humanities and the marketplace is an essential rhetorical task of the 21st century. Otherwise, by default the market increasingly narrows questions and issues, limiting the texture and understanding in the 21st century. This chapter calls for more than a marketplace of economic exchange, but a return, a revisiting of the "marketplace of ideas." The humanities and the marketplace jointly offer a "marketplace of ideas."

Unlike the sciences and the social sciences, the humanities do not tender implementation strategies that immediately augment efficiency in the market. The humanities put forward historical, literary, and philosophical content that enriches and embeds market decisions within ideas that deepen decision-making beyond supply and demand of material exchange. The humanities and the marketplace together form the "marketplace of ideas" (Jefferson, 1939). The exchange of ideas is a natural complement to the exchange of goods, each with the possibility of enriching human life, providing interpretive insight into the exchange of goods, services, and ideas.

Barnes's discussion of Aristotle's study of animal life is analogous to this chapter's walk into the marketplace. The marketplace is akin to a little known and feared creature that is off-putting to visitors. Barnes's suggestion assists rationale for the "why" of the humanities meeting of the marketplace.

> Thus, we should not childishly complain against the enquiry into the less worthy animals; for in everything natural there is something marvelous. Heraclitus is reported to have said to some visitors who wished to meet him and who hesitated when they saw him warming himself at the stove: "Come in, be bold: there are gods here too." In the same way we should approach the study of every animal without shame; for in all of them there is something natural and something beautiful. (Barnes, 1991, p. 180)

This chapter shifts the taken-for-granted position of the humanities on the marketplace, a "hermeneutic of suspicion," (Arnett, 1994, p. 238) to a stance of engagement and learning. We learn both from closer examination of the familiar and from encounter with the unknown. Learning propelled by close examination of the familiar underscores precision, which opens doors for application and implementation. Learning that emerges as a by-product from encounter with the unknown invites paradigmatic questioning, paradigmatic shifts, and innovation. Difference permits us to meet and learn from the unexamined ideas of the Other, while, additionally, discerning and clarifying our own presuppositions through learning by contrast. This chapter suggests that difference invites additive learning through engaging an alien marketplace, inviting paradigmatic questioning.

A Marketplace of Learning

The differing commitments of the humanities and the marketplace permit the possibility of learning from the unknown, the Other. Meeting difference by engaging different cultures requires learning about the Other's standpoint, which provides insight into previously taken-for-granted assumptions about the Other and oneself. The humanities and the marketplace function as parallel cultures, presenting opportunity for mutual insight and learning. Like in C.P. Snow's published Rede lecture, "The Two Cultures and the Scientific Revolution" (1959/1993), the two cultures of the humanities and the sciences, the humanities once again encounter an alien voice—this time in the guise of the marketplace.

Recently, Edward O. Wilson returned to the theme of the humanities and the sciences in his book, *Consilience: The Unity of Knowledge* (1998). One may disagree with Wilson's Enlightenment grounding of ideas, but his call for learning is ever present and noteworthy. He states:

> We are entering a new era of existentialism, not the old absurdist existentialism of Kierkegaard and Sartre, giving complete autonomy to the individual, but the concept that only unified learning, universally shared, makes accurate foresight and wise choice possible. (Wilson, 1998, p. 325)

Wilson outlines this historical moment as another era in which the term "existentialism" assists understanding. Wilson suggests revisiting the idea of existentialism with new eyes.

Wilson's endorsement of the Enlightenment project, which assumes rationality and universal knowledge, is far afield from postmodern consideration. Yet, if one alters the above quotation with the following adjustments, Wilson's call for learning enters postmodern conversation. "We are entering a new era of existentialism, not the old absurdist existentialism of Kierkegaard and Sartre, giving complete autonomy to the individual, but the concept that only **temporally** unified learning, universally shared **situated within public, temporary agreed-upon narrative structures** universally shared, makes accurate foresight, **insight and agreement** and wise choice possible." Wilson's "new" existentialism situated within constant learning is historically appropriate. Wilson's new existentialism addresses the postmodern issue of multiple narrative and virtue structures (MacIntyre, 1981/1984) without falling into a postmodern vocabulary that too quickly polarizes readers. Existential living in time of confused narrative and virtue structures requires an ongoing and pragmatic commitment to learning. Using language more akin to Wilson's project, taken-for-granted knowledge unresponsive to ongoing learning becomes imprudent and anachronistic.

The popular term used to emphasize ongoing learning in the marketplace is "knowledge worker" (Amar, 2002; Drucker, 1999; Horibe, 1999). Wilson's commitment to learning calls into question such a vocabulary, pointing to a "learning worker." Perhaps the only way to invite another to ask what you "know" in a time of narrative and virtue contention is to model an unending commitment to learning. Ongoing learning signals a willingness to engage this existential moment of seemingly constant change, giving temporal rationale for asking another "What do you know?" The "knowledge worker" finds his or her knowledge "sought after" when an ongoing display of learning offers reason to gather more information. The ongoing learning invites communicative space for engaging learning in a constructive way, creating shared paths to new knowledge and providing a "why" for the Other to ask and learn.

This historical moment of narrative and virtue confusion requires the humanities to explore alternative conceptions or varied textures for understanding life together, and challenge to profits require businesses to re-examine what types of learning cultures nourish organizational health (de Geus, 1997; Isaacs, 1999; Senge, 1990; Senge et. al., 1999; Slater, 1999). As a culture shifts, how one makes a profit also changes. A humanities insight into the texture of human life assists knowledge of long-term shifts within a culture, while offering a modest check on popular material culture.

The metaphor of "learning worker," unlike the implications of a "knowledge worker," more aptly fits Wilson's new version of existentialism. The independence of the "knowledge worker" is too close to being a contemporary market version of Camus's *L'Etranger* (1942). This new existential moment that Wilson suggests requires more than existential confidence in the self; this moment calls for understanding an existentialist commitment to learning beyond the scope of self-judgment.

Life situated in the ongoing existential moment offers muddy, blurred vision as the natural form of everyday clarity. Decision-making without agreed-upon guidance requires action without the illusion of complete knowledge, understanding the lack of narrative background agreement. Temporal learning becomes the mantra of our time, beginning with the meeting of difference, adding texture with knowledge not previously encountered.

Learning From Difference

This chapter leans on Wilson's insistence about learning, without accepting his confidence in the Enlightenment hope for unified knowledge. The Enlightenment offered hope for unified knowledge that seems far distant as we consider complex issues in the Middle East, the events of September 11, 2001, and the ongoing threats of terrorism. Unified knowledge for such a complex time appears outside our reach.

Perhaps our learning task for the twenty-first century is both more pragmatic and more humble than universal agreement—constant learning/discernment together, searching for temporal public agreement on historically situated issues. Constant learning questions paradigmatic assumptions, grounding knowledge within metaphors such as public, temporal/historically situated, and engaged. Unlike earlier existentialist thinking that counted upon the self, we must discover temporal agreement together in public interaction, learning from different cultures and perspectives, ideas dissimilar from our own. *La différence*, not unified knowledge, is the metaphor in an era of narrative and virtue contention.

One can locate numerous examples of narrative contention today, making the case for the difficulty of decision-making in this historical moment. The exchange between Michel Foucault and Maoist militants in 1971 foreshadowed postmodern narrative and virtue contention. Maoist militants wanted to establish a people's court to judge the police. Foucault disagreed:

> . . . This judicial system, and the ideology which is associated with them, must become the target of our present struggle . . . re-employing a form like that of the court, with all that is implied in it—the three-party place of the judge, reference to a law or to impartiality, effective sentencing—must also be subjected to the very rigorous critics; and, for my part, I cannot see using this form as valid except in a case where one can, in parallel with a bourgeoisie trial, conduct an alternative trial which can expose as lies what is taken as truth in the former, and its decisions as an abuse of power. Apart from this situation, I can see thousands of possibilities on the one hand for anti-judicial guerrilla operations, and on the other hand for acts of popular justice; but neither of these involves using the form of the court. (1980, p. 36)

The key to the above quotation is that Foucault forewarned us about a form, traditional structure, a particular response to difference—one that disregards what "is," arguing for alternative configurations. Deconstructive hermeneutics questions what "is." Wilson, on the other hand, suggests something more akin to a constructivist hermeneutic, forgoing the call for replacement for the commitment to learning. Such learning, however, does not necessitate agreement, but learning from difference.

The humanities provide a space for deconstructive insight. This chapter suggests that additional room for a constructivist hermeneutic that seeks to know the different, not destroy or overturn it, but to engage the different, is necessary. A constructivist hermeneutic works with the assumption that additive change, not just substitutional change, can make a difference in human life together.

This chapter and Wilson's suggestions do not go the length of Foucault's project—intentionally. This project calls for recognition of differences and learning from diversity, with the assumption that learning what one did not know changes people and positions.

Of course, learning from the Other does not ensure change, but such action does open up knowledge about previously marginalized ideas and persons. This chapter does not suggest that walking the humanities into the marketplace offers alternative structures, but recognizes the necessity of contrasting structures (humanities and the marketplace). Contrasting structures engaged can open the door to learning. Moving from radical structural change to recognition of the necessity of learning from difference moves the conversation from the metaphor of change (a rhetoric of telling) to the metaphor of texture (a rhetoric of learning, learning from the Other).

From Acknowledged Difference to Textured Understanding

Learning that is temporal and focused upon the Other, not the self, calls forth a humanities that learns from difference—finding texture, breadth, and additional insight in meeting of the unknown. Textured learning requires encountering difference and "interpreting otherwise," asking questions that open up the taken-for-granted, seeking to learn from the unknown and the unexpected. For the humanities today, the marketplace is a public sphere" that offers difference, the possibility of textured learning.

Calvin Schrag contends that the major task of the humanities is to discern "texture," the depth and substance of a phenomenon, its sense of meaning. He includes the irrational in the ongoing texture of life. For many in the humanities, the irrational is the market, and for many in the market, the irrational rests within the humanities. He suggests

> . . . recovery of the texture of everyday life as the proper operational field for interpretive understanding . . . metaphorical extension of the meaning of "text" so as to encompass the "texture" of everyday life as a "context" of meaning-formations. . . . The irrational remains as a positive feature of the texture of world experience and needs to be comprehended within development process. It is not at all like a textual "error" in literary corpus that can be set aside as an adventitious intrusion because it has no bearing on the intended meaning of the author. The irrational is not an adventitious intrusion upon the meaning-fabric of man's personal and social existence. Its significance needs to be articulated as part of the context of personal behavior and social goals. (Schrag, 1980, p. 107)

Schrag is wary about the task of "correcting" or "righting" irrationality. Such wisdom seems helpful as one meets the marketplace from a humanities perspective. Interpreting otherwise suggests that various forms of irrationality will be with us forever. Certain forms of irrationality that destroy human life need contending voices. However, we must resist the temptation to eliminate much of what we perceive as irrationality, to do so places paradigmatic shifts and creative new ideas at a disadvantage. Additionally, within difference we discover alternative insight. Such is the ground of imperialism, whether propelled by the right or the left. Learning depends upon difference, not similarity, which offers increasing texture to our understanding of human life.

Using a communication/rhetoric vocabulary, Schrag applies the metaphor of communicative *praxis* (1986) to open the texture of communicative life. He offers a textured understanding of communication that highlights theory-informed action. Communication that engages the humanities and the marketplace invites textured understanding and learning. Schrag's communicative *praxis* portrays a model of textured learning that enhances the hermeneutic value of communicative encounters with difference, in this case the marketplace.

Schrag's communicative *praxis* rests upon four basic prepositional guidelines/ metaphors: *about* the topic, *by* a given communicative agent, and *for* a given other or audience, and *within* responsiveness to a given historical moment. Schrag employs the first three metaphors explicitly, with the fourth (*within*) assumed. Schrag's constituent parts of communicative *praxis* are embedded, or situated, *within* content, *within* the temporal needs of a person/audience, *within* the narrative ground that shapes embedded agents and *within* the historical moment. Schrag decenters subjectivity, embedding subjectivity within narrative life, debunking universal claims, embedding content within historicity and narrative limits. Communicative *praxis* lives ". . . within the play of 'conversation' . . ." (Schrag, 1986, p. 2). Embedded *within*—conversation about ethics in communicative action in a postmodern culture recognizes a multiplicity of narrative structures, the limits of individual agency, and the power of the historical moment.

Conceptualizing communication/rhetoric as a connecting link between the humanities and the marketplace permits communicative *praxis* to function as an interpretive key— ever cognizant of the ongoing interplay of communicative content (*about*), communicative agents (*by* and *for*), and historical situation (*within*). The preposition of *within* situates communicative *praxis*, contrasted with a universal or foundational perspective in spheres of action, such as the marketplace. The particular view of communication/rhetoric recognizes the postmodern argument of multiplicity, embeddedness, and limits, stressing the interplay of a given communication content, communicative agents, and historical situation within a given setting.

In the interplay of Schrag's communicative praxis, the prepositions *about, for*, and *by* situated *within* a historical moment and a sphere of action become conceptual keys to learning from difference. Communicative *praxis* analysis permits one to see and learn from texture discerned in the meeting of difference. "Communicative praxis is both a discursive and nondiscursive affair, implicating and constituting the self as once speaking and acting subject, texturing the genealogy of self-formation as an adventure both in discourse and in action" (Schrag, 1997, p. 75). Such learning acknowledges the pragmatic reality of a multiplicity of positions, understanding the construction of momentary communicative clarity on the run, in motion, discerned without a safety net of control— without controlled content, controlled agents, and a controlled historical situation. Without an assumed metanarrative (agreed-upon content), similarity of communicative agents (taken-for-granted agreement upon social practices), and ideological assurance about a tradition-informed present, a particular communication ethic begins in the interplay of discernment of theory and ideas, differing perspectives of communicative agents, and recognition of temporality, moving communication to action. Communication understood outside of universals, collective agreement, and individual agency points to particularity in response to content, participants, and the historical situation. The marketplace as a place of economic activity and idea exchange offers a place to learn texture from communicative *praxis*. One must engage the *by*, the *about*, the *for*, and the *within* of difference.

Such learning from the marketplace seeks to understand the *by, about, for, and within* of difference—information that moves the market closer to a learning place: "a marketplace of ideas," (Jefferson, 1939) a public space where understanding, insight, and learning emerge. Without such engagement and learning, we find economic forces shaping life within a taken-for-granted paradigm. If one hopes for change and seeks decision-making beyond concern for bottom-line issues, engagement with the marketplace is essential. The marketplace is a significant/major component of public life; to ignore such a sphere can relegate humanities learning to private life alone. Beyond the repetitive acts of critique of the marketplace, we can meet a sphere that removes us from insular conversation to private discourse that masquerades as public discussion. Such solipsistic exchange offered under the illusion of public discourse is a form of Sartreian "bad faith" (1943/1956, pp. 86-116). The marketplace calls us to the public sphere, not to a private substitute for idea exchange.

Public space is not a place of uniformity, but a place of difference. When one engages conversation with those primarily in agreement, excluding contrary and differently textured voices, public space becomes what Maurice Friedman called a "community of affinity" (1983, pp. 133-151). Acknowledging the multiplicity of theories/ ideas, agent standpoints, and rapidity of change invites construction of communication with public admission of presuppositions and assumed social practices, and the particularity of situatedness of engagement in particular public places, such as the marketplace.

Communicative *praxis* in the marketplace permits one to learn differently, from an alien Other, from a place often unfriendly to the humanities. Communicative *praxis* opens the particulars, revealing the texture of ideas in a given setting. Communicative *praxis* within the marketplace provides opportunity for textured insight, attentiveness to temporality, and an opportunity for a humanities basis for communicative action to learn from radical alterity called the marketplace.

Rhetoric and Radical Alterity

A humanities/marketplace project assumes a form of rhetoric based upon responsiveness to the Other, not what Levinas calls misplaced rhetoric of eloquence, (1961/1969, pp. 70-72; 1990, pp. 277-288) imposition upon the Other. Communicative *praxis* does not seek to tell, but to discern the *about*, the *by*, and the *for—within* a given setting. One enters the marketplace with guiding prepositions that permit one to learn.

Levinas does not offer kind words about rhetoric; he only witnessed eloquence, telling as imposition upon the Other. Perhaps, he might have seen different possibilities with a learning rhetoric, a responsive rhetoric, a rhetoric that bears the weight of the Other. Schrag's communicative *praxis* works at learning and response, rejecting Levinas's aversion to telling; the humanities can interpret otherwise with a learning and responsive rhetoric, engaging the marketplace, seeking to understand the pragmatic learners of a world of difference. The task of a learning and responsive rhetoric is not to make the Other "right, correct, or like me," but to engage and learn from him or her.

As the following Hasidic tale suggests, the engagement of a responsive rhetoric seeks to learn from difference, even the difference of the marketplace. The people of a great Rabbi felt much pain; they then asked their Rabbi for help. The Rabbi offered the comment, "Pray." The people went home and prayed for a number of weeks only to return, still in pain, still asking the Rabbi for guidance. This time the Rabbi stated: "Study." Weeks later the people returned and stated, "We prayed and we studied and our pain remains. What are we to do?" This time the Rabbi stated: "Give me a moment. I will find my cloak. Sometimes when prayer and study are not enough, we must walk into the marketplace to find answers. In the marketplace, together and with prayer and study, we might find answers." Sometimes prayer and study do not suffice; we must see differently to understand and to move us to new insights. The Rabbi recognized the necessity of difference to find novel answers. He walked into the marketplace.

Without the marketplace, new possibilities go unnoticed. The alien marketplace makes us question and look anew. Such is the place where a responsive rhetoric finds its soul—taking the humanities into the marketplace to learn. Unlike Plato's purified soul, the soul of a responsive rhetoric tainted with ongoing engagement of the humanities and the marketplace walks into the marketplace to learn.

Engagement with the marketplace is not novel from a humanities tradition. Adam Smith, as a rhetorician, penned *The Wealth of Nations* (1776/1994), and Karl Marx, completing his Ph.D. in 1841, published *Das Capital* (1867/1992). These two major figures brought intellectual power to the marketplace. Marx wrote in London, hoping to complete his work before the revolution began in England. Marx wrote in response to a world aptly pictured in the novels of Dickens—capitalism unrestrained, oppressing the vulnerable, the weak, and the young. Smith, on the other hand, offered a competing version of capitalism. His version embraced liberation, not oppression, as the primary metaphor. He understood the new owners of production as liberators from the class structure that maintained aristocratic power. Smith offered us a picture of liberation and Marx a picture of oppression. Both views of capitalism rest in data that one can marshal to promote a given position. The two together, Marx and Smith, provide an ongoing dialectic played out on the world stage. The collapse of the Soviet Union offered a lull in this ongoing fight, not an end to the controversy. To engage the marketplace as Other does not presume agreement with either Smith or Marx, but more pragmatically and modestly a willingness to encounter the marketplace of ideas.

The point of the above is to suggest a simple reminder—the marketplace is not simply a place of capitalism. The marketplace is the home of competing visions of the good life, visions that affect people, the audience in a given historical situation. Capitalism, socialism, fascism, communism, are efforts to control the marketplace. One cannot equate a given view with the marketplace. However, a given position privileged in the marketplace at a given time in history offers power and influence, but not the final answer. To engage the marketplace does not necessarily presuppose capitalism or socialism as the only form of exchange. To engage the marketplace is to meet the audience of given historical moment, people working to make a living within given structures at a given time. To ignore the marketplace is to ignore our largest rhetorical audience, an audience that historically transforms societies. The American Revolution, the French Revolution, and rebellion against imperialism throughout the world serve as powerful examples.

Rhetorical encounter with the marketplace, from the perspective of this chapter, begins with assumptions contrary to a world of inevitable progress—a world of temporal learning. A learning rhetoric lives by engaging moments, not grand schemes. Failure to understand, to engage, and to learn from "radical alterity" (Levinas, 1961/1969, p. 192) typified a modern world of increasing nationalism, industrialism nourished by division of labor, and the Enlightenment hope for unified knowledge ever progressively pursued. Levinas, writing against the Nazi effort to unify knowledge, witnessed the political limits of the Enlightenment project—the project perverted with ethnic hatred and uninational standpoint called for an alternative. Radical alterity, not unified knowledge, propels a world of difference, a world in which the Other offers opportunity for learning. Levinas's commitment to difference places him in favor with postmodern scholars looking for an alternative to modern presuppositions of unified knowledge

(Derrida, 1997/1999). Such scholarship understands the inevitability of "taint"; each interpretive perspective, each standpoint, comes with a tainted, not a pure, perspective. Communicative *praxis* reminds us of the necessity of learning from radical alterity, from the Other. We enter a given sphere to learn, not to tell.

A Responsive Rhetoric/An Ethic of Learning

Levinas provides a phenomenological reading of the construction of the "I," which is illustrative of this learning framework, a responsive rhetoric. Simply put, life begins with the Other that calls the "I" into existence. For Levinas, one must engage a phenomenological sense of responsibility for the Other—"I am my brother's keeper" (Cohen, 1998, p. xii). One protects the Other out of primordial knowledge that without the Other there is no "I." The "I" learns from the presence of the Other.

Pushing Levinas beyond the notion of a human face to an entity called the marketplace is, at best, far from traditional application of the horizon of his work. However, if one views the marketplace as a form of radical alterity for the humanities, one can offer a phenomenological reading of the marketplace. What if one suggested that the humanities accept the responsibility of being "my brother's keeper" for the marketplace? Without the marketplace, would there exist something called the humanities? Were not early teachers in Classical Greece hired to "educate" the young? (De Romilly, 1988/1992, p. 1) Did not early bards such as Homer move from place to place talking about ideas and citing poetry and saga for supportive and rewarding listeners? (De Romilly, 1988/1992, pp. 31-32) Is the marketplace, the Other for the humanities, the very entity that makes the "I" of the humanities possible? The humanities found construction and life within the marketplace of ideas; from Egypt to Greece, to Rome, to all of Europe, awareness of differing cultures throughout the world educated the "I." The "I" of the humanities finds augmentation, texture, and interpretive complexities in one encounter after another with alien others. Insight comes from the different, from what one does not know.

The alien Other typifies the relationship between the humanities and the marketplace, making the humanities and the marketplace potential dialectical companions capable of inviting textured insight. Learning emerges from the novel, the different, seldom from the routine, the same. Differences between the humanities and the marketplace invite conversation capable of invoking learning—learning from radical alterity. Focus on difference moves communication from a universal and agent-centered investigation to communicative ethics *praxis* embedded in action with communicative content altered responsive to changes in a given historical situation.

Radical alterity and rhetoric of responsiveness and learning does not suggest agreement, nor does it imply the nobility of the Other, or the learning of only "good" ideas. The opening quotation from Martin Buber suggests the constant interplay of good and evil that accompanies us as we enter conceptual ground of ambiguity and difference. Buber reminds us of the ongoing drama of good and evil (Buber). There is no "pure" place without the possibility of evil's existence. The humanities can avoid the evil of the marketplace by bracketing its existence, which lessens opportunities for learning from the different, while failing to recognize evil in one's own house. Any humanities academic would be hard pressed to find a department or a college dedicated to the humanities in which some form of evil to or by colleagues, students, or outsiders is conspicuously absent. Evil lives alongside good, making escape from evil merely a bracketing of one's willingness to name it. For instance, Rudy Henry Wiebe's novel *Peace Shall Destroy*

Many (1962), offers the tale of a fictional Mennonite community in Canada refusing participation in the World War II, only to find interpersonal violence and evil guiding their daily lives.

Buber is correct in his assessment of the unity of good and evil. We cannot escape evil; good and evil live intertwined together. Good ideas have unknown evil consequences and evil actions offering possibilities for good. Life is too complicated to disentangle good and evil—each is intricately tied to the other in each setting, in each moment, in each act of perception and action. The opening of the door for conversation and interplay between the humanities and a radical form of alterity, the marketplace, simply acknowledges the necessity to walk into multiple places, not knowing which may actually offer more good or evil to the human community at a particular time, in a particular place. Levinas presupposes that the Other calls us to responsibility, not to purity or the ability to judge what is and is not pure. The call for Levinas is learning and responsibility, not amusement at the Other's limitations or infractions.

The marketplace, never a place of purity or of goodness, as the Other, calls us to responsibility—not to inquire of the Other's purity, but to learn and respond. Buber, responsive to Nazi efforts to unify knowledge, rejected Gandhi's pleas for the use of Jewish nonviolence (1983, p. 305). Buber understood that all of life, not just the market, meets us in the interplay of good and evil, questioning the legitimacy of purity and peace. Clearly, the marketplace fits such a description—a place of good and evil. For Buber, such places offer human opportunity—a place where "great characters" (1947/1965, pp. 113-114) find their direction, their calling.

Failure to engage the ambiguity of good *and* evil keeps one outside of conversation with soiled places—places that exude a force of radical alterity. Perhaps this insight into radical alterity permitted Gandhi to call forces of opposition, at times, friends (Erickson, 1969). Such insight permitted Buber to call for saving the life of Adolph Eichmann (Hodes, 1971, pp. 112-115). Such insight permitted Martin Luther King, Jr. to speak well of the Director of the Federal Bureau of Investigation, J. Edgar Hoover, under the worst of circumstances (Garrow, 1986, pp. 360-363). Each recognized that a world of good *and* evil guides decisions; we cannot miss engaging radical alterity, even when in supreme disagreement.

Michael Hyde's call for a rhetorical turn to the practical places action and application at the centerpiece of *The Call of Conscience* (2001). He calls upon the conscience of the communication discipline, asking: "How can we make a difference with communication ideas and methods?" Hyde takes philosophy into everyday communicative life, discussing euthanasia within the philosophies of Levinas and Heidegger. Hyde, like Littlejohn and Pearce (1997), follows a related call for communicative engagement with everyday decision-making. Each assists communicators to make a difference, implying transformation of communicative partners and the historical situation. The marketplace is a place of radical alterity where difference can inform, shape, and educate communicative partners.

Working to make a difference in the midst of communication quandaries (Rawlins, 1983) requires one to recognize differences inherent in theory, interpretation, and in context or setting. Difference announces the necessity for attentiveness to the historical moment and social-cultural limits as one seeks a decision in a moment of quandary, benefiting from the insight from multiple theories that recognize the pragmatic linkage of theory with changing audiences and contexts. The marketplace is the premiere unknown context for the humanities.

Walking the Humanities into the Marketplace was the rhetorical task of Hermes, who interpreted the gods to the people. A major communicative task of the 21st century is to interpret the humanities to the marketplace. Without such conversation, we leave the market to its own devices. Human life without some form of marketplace is beyond the scope of imagination. The market has traditionally provided opportunities for the meeting of difference and the sharing of provincial skill and resources, which enriched the Other. Erasing the marketplace, is akin to erasing the Other, attempts to do so only momentarily eclipse the necessity of the marketplace of life together and for the support and textured development of the humanities.

This chapter accepts the marketplace as human fact. Conversation about the existence of the market is akin to questioning the rising of the sun. The question is not the existence of the market, but its temporal nature and action. We must learn from the marketplace, if we are to shape the future of the marketplace; communicative *praxis* and a responsive, learning rhetoric brings the humanities into an alien world of radical alterity, calling the "I" of the humanities to learn from and protect the Other of the marketplace.

References

Amar, A.D. (2002). *Managing knowledge workers: Unleashing innovation and productivity.* Wesport, CT: Quorum Books.

Arnett, R. C. (1994). Existential homelessness: A contemporary case for dialogue. In R.

Anderson, K. N. Cissna & R. C. Arnett (Eds.), *The reach of dialogue: Confirmation, voice, and community* (pp. 229-245). Cresskill, NJ: Hampton Press, Inc.

Barnes, J. (1991). Aristotle. In *Founders of thought: Plato, Aristotle, Augustine* (pp. 85-191). Oxford: Oxford University Press.

Buber, M. (1952). *At the turning; Three addresses on Judaism.* New York: Farrar, Straus & Young.

Buber, M. (1965). *Between man and man* (R.G. Smith, Trans.). New York: Macmillan. (Original work published 1947)

Buber, M. (1983). *A land of two peoples: Martin Buber on Jews and Arabs.* P. R. Mendes-Flohr (Ed.). New York: Oxford University Press.

Camus, A. (1942). *L'Etranger.* Paris: Gallimard.

Cohen, R. A. (1998). Introduction. *Otherwise than being or beyond essence* (A. Lingis, Trans.). (pp. vi-xvi). Pittsburgh, PA: Duquesne University Press.

de Geus, A. (1997). *The living company.* Boston: Harvard Business School Press.

de Romilly, J. (1992). *The great sophists of Periclean Athens* (J. Lloyd, Trans.). Oxford: Clarendon Press. (Original work published 1988)

Derrida, J. (1999). *Adieu to Emmanuel Levinas* (P-A. Brault & M. Naas, Trans.). Stanford, CA: Stanford University Press. (Original work published 1997)

Drucker, P.F. (1999). *Management challenges for the 21st century.* New York: HarperBusiness.

Erickson, E. (1969). *Gandhi's truth: On the origin of militant nonviolence.* New York: W. W. Norton.

Foucault, M. (1980). *Power/knowledge: Selected interviews and other writings, 1972-1977* (C. Gordon, Ed. & Trans.). New York: Pantheon Books.

Friedman, M. (1983). *The confirmation of otherness in family, community and society.* New York: The Pilgrim Press.

Garrow, D.J. (1986). *Bearing the cross: Martin Luther King, Jr., and the southern Christian leadership conference.* New York: William Morrow & Company, Inc.

Hodes, A. (1971). *Martin Buber, an intimate portrait.* New York: Viking Press.

Hoffer, E. (1951). *The true believer: Thoughts on the nature of mass movements.* New York: Harper & Row.

Horibe, F. (1999). *Managing knowledge workers: New skills and attitudes to unlock the intellectual capital in your organization.* New York: J. Wiley.

Hyde, M. S. (2001). *The call of conscience: Heidegger and Levinas, rhetoric and the euthanasia debate.* Columbia, SC: University of South Carolina Press.

Isaacs, W. (1999). *Dialogue and the art of thinking together: A pioneering approach to communicating in business and in life.* New York: Currency.

Jefferson, T. (1939). *Thomas Jefferson on democracy.* S.K. Padover (Ed.). New York: Mentor Books.

Levinas, E. (1969). *Totality and infinity: An essay on exteriority* (A. Lingis, Trans.). Pittsburgh, PA: Duquesne University Press. (Original work published 1961)

Levinas, E. (1985). *Ethics and infinity: Conversations with Philippe Nemo* (R. A. Cohen, Trans.). Pittsburgh, PA: Duquesne University Press.

Levinas, E. (1990). *Difficult freedom: Essays on Judaism* (S. Hand, Trans.). Baltimore: Johns Hopkins University Press.

MacIntyre, A. (1984). *After virtue: A study in moral theory.* Notre Dame, IN: University of Notre Dame Press. (Original work published 1981)

Marx, K. (1992). *Capital: A critique of political economy, volume 1* (B. Fowkes, Trans.). London: Penguin. (original work published 1867)

Pearce, W. B. & Littlejohn, S. W. (1997). *Moral conflict: When social worlds collide.* Thousand Oaks, CA: Sage.

Plato. (1999). Phaedo (H. Tredennick, Trans.). In E. Hamilton & H. Cairns (Eds.), *Plato: The collected dialogues including the letters* (pp. 40-98). Princeton, NJ: Princeton University Press.

Rawlins, W. K. (1983). Individual Responsibility in Relational Communication. In M. S. Mander (Ed.), *Communications in transition* (pp. 152-167). New York: Praeger.

Sartre, J. P. (1956). *Being and nothingness: A phenomenological essay on ontology* (H. E. Barnes, Trans.). New York: Simon & Schuster. (Original work published 1943)

Schrag, C. O. (1980). *Radical reflection and the origin of the human sciences.* West Lafayette, IN: Purdue University Press.

Schrag, C. O. (1986). *Communicative praxis and the space of subjectivity.* Bloomington, IN: Indiana University Press.

Schrag, C. O. (1997). *The self after postmodernity.* New Haven, CT: Yale University Press.

Senge, P. M. (1990). *The fifth discipline: The art and practice of the learning organization.* New York: Doubleday/Currency.

Senge, P. M. et al. (1999). *The dance of change: The challenges of sustaining momentum in learning organizations.* New York: Doubleday/Currency.

Slater, R. (1999). *Jack Welch and the ge way: Management insights and leadership secrets of the legendary ceo.* New York: McGraw-Hill.

Smith, A. (1994). *An inquiry into the nature and causes of the wealth of nations.* E. Cannan (Ed.). New York: Modern Library. (Original work published 1776)

Snow, C.P. (1993). *The two cultures.* Cambridge: Syndicate of the University of Cambridge. (Original work published 1959)

Watzlawick. P.W., Beavin, J. H. & Jackson, D. D. (1967). *Pragmatics of human communication: A study of interactional patterns, pathologies, and paradoxes.* New York: W. W. Norton.

Wiebe, R. H. (1962). *Peace shall destroy many.* Toronto: McClelland & Stewart.

Wilson, E. O. (1998). *Consilience: The unity of knowledge.* New York: Knopf.

Chapter Thirteen

Advertising: Storytelling in the Marketplace of the 21st Century

S. Alyssa Ritz

The Storyteller (1936/1968) by literary critic Walter Benjamin laments a crisis in our ability to exchange experiences—a crisis in the art of storytelling. Benjamin critiques the rise in value of information qua information, and the subsequent focus on "abbreviation" (1936/1968, p. 93) and "prompt verifiability" (p. 89) over the craft of telling and retelling experience. Information processed in this way does not draw on the function of memory, making it increasingly difficult to weave shared "webs of significance" (Geertz, 1973) between people across generations and cultures.

Benjamin believes that the work associated with storytelling is reaching its end as "the epic side of truth, wisdom, is dying out" (1936/1968, p. 87). This understanding of truth and wisdom is embedded in the interplay of story and lived experience, and stands in opposition to the discrete view of communication as information. In *Volume 2* (1985) of Paul Ricoeur's *Time and Narrative* Ricoeur considers Benjamin's critique as an indictment of advertising and its impact on contemporary culture. "Perhaps we are at the end of an era where narrating no longer has a place [. . .] because human beings no longer have any experience to share. And he [Benjamin] sees in the rule of advertising the sign of this retreat of narrative, a retreat without return" (p. 28).

While not explicitly a sphere that Benjamin associates with the capacity for storytelling and narration, the marketplace is a vital part of human expression and experience, and, therefore, a factor that impacts how our lives are shaped. In light of Ricoeur's claim that the art of telling stories precedes "the art of narrating in all its forms" (p. 28), it is not a stretch to say that even the marketplace exists in some capacity because of stories. According to Benjamin's critique, advertising's role in the marketplace is to provide information that is "understandable in itself" (Benjamin, 1936/1968, p. 89) for dissemination in the moment. In this surrender to "abbreviation," it would seem that advertising's ability to be associated with the craft of storytelling—a craft that draws from the past, speaks to the present, and is attentive to the future—is a stretch, at best.

Working from the presupposition that the marketplace is a defining factor in human existence—texture in our webs of significance—Benjamin's critique provides a catalyst for investigating the possibility of a relationship between advertising and the craft of storytelling. It permits us to inquire into the role and relationship between advertising and the marketplace, as well as how it impacts the broader scope of human interaction. Benjamin's critique makes it possible for us to investigate alternative avenues of creative possibility for the field of advertising in the today's marketplace.

Introduction

Recognizing the necessity and place of the market in everyday life, as well as advertising's role in it, this essay accepts the challenge implicit in Benjamin's critique and pursues a story-centered framework for understanding and situating advertising in the marketplace of the 21st century. To this end, it seeks to move characterizations of advertising and those involved in the discipline beyond that of "witnesses" and "artisans" (Ricoeur, 1984, p. 28) in the retreat and possible loss of narrative. Instead of accepting this view—essentially a view of advertising as purely discordant, or disrupting lived experience (Ricoeur, 1984)—this essay asks how a story-centered approach to advertising offers an alternative view of its role in the marketplace and life in general.

A necessary point of departure is the idea of storytelling and narration. Narration is made possible when stories are not just told, but lived and believed. A storyteller's life, according to Benjamin, is the life of a craftsman. Much like the characterization of a craftsman by Aristotle in the *Nichomachean Ethics*, Benjamin identifies the storyteller as having the capacity to counsel others in practical matters. The work of a storyteller is thus deeply connected to practical wisdom, or *phronesis* (Aristotle, vi 1140ab, pp. 88-9). Benjamin writes, ". . . one can go on and ask oneself whether the relationship of the storyteller to his material, human life, is not in itself a craftsman's relationship, whether it is not his very task to fashion the raw material of experience [. . .] in a solid, useful, and unique way" (1936/1968, p. 108). The material of experience can be crafted only in relation to a particular situation. A situation permits counsel and the possibility of "a proposal concerning the continuation of a story which is just unfolding" (Benjamin, 1936/1968, p. 86). Counsel, for Benjamin, is "woven into the fabric of life" (1936/1968, p. 86) in the form of practical wisdom gained through life's experiences. When this counsel is "storied" to others, believed, and lived out, a narrative is born.

Advertising's ability to counsel—to move "story" to narrative—requires greater distinction between advertising as merely prophesying and perpetuating a culture of commodification and advertising as the means to building and communicating meaning through the story of a brand. Benjamin's lament that advertising is subverting experience and practical wisdom comes to the foreground in the view of advertising as promoting a form of "secular religiosity" (Carey, 1989, p. 114). Advertising, as such, accommodates the sacred to the secular to promote products, ultimately enabling and perpetuating a culture of commodification. With a focus on style and consumption, advertising speaks from the pulpit of the marketplace, functioning as both prophet and high priest in a highly individualistic call to consumption.

When focused on building and communicating the story of a brand, however, a more holistic, interactive understanding of the relationship between product, organization, and audience guides the role of advertising. Seeking "fit" more than accommodation and serving as a part within the larger whole of the brand building process, the focus of advertising is on communicating meaning. Advertising to build brands is more than just implementing strategic integrated communication; it is, in the communicative terms of Calvin Schrag (1986) a story *about* a product, *by* an organization, *for* a particular target in a given historical moment.

The distinction between advertising as perpetuating a culture of commodification or as communicating meaning through the story of a brand adds depth to a discipline often regarded in terms of creativity and finance. In the first two sections of this chapter, these two approaches are discussed in order to provide a background from which to suggest a constructive connection between advertising and storytelling. The final section of this essay then situates advertising in relation to storytelling through the philosophical insights of Paul Ricoeur and Calvin Schrag. It is this author's belief that Ricoeur's conceptions of time and narrative taken together with Schrag's conception of "communicative praxis" (Schrag, 1986) permit a story-centered framework for advertising to emerge.

Advertising and a Culture of Commodification

Benjamin's lament at the passing of "epic" truth that leads people in the way of wisdom points to a structural weakening of tradition and to a zeitgeist that venerates individualism. Alexis de Tocqueville (1835/2000) wrote that individualism leads people to forget their ancestors while simultaneously separating them from their contemporaries. According to de Tocqueville, individualism keeps people in the "habit of always considering themselves in isolation [. . .] fancy[ing] that their whole destiny is in their hands" (1835/2000, p. 484). It perpetuates the search for and conception of identity in discrete, isolated units of experience in which no one experience is more valuable than any other.

Individualism appears today in its most extreme form—emotivism, or decision-making based on personal preference (MacIntyre, 1981/1984). Culturally, this approach to life removes experience from the public realm to privatized spheres of knowing. Emotivism perpetuates a self "under siege [. . .] a self exist[ing] in a state of continuous construction and reconstruction" (Gergen, 1991, p. 7). Jean Baudrillard (1983) identifies this condition as "the ecstasy of communication"—a world of stimulation that models a "'real' without origin or reality: 'the hyperreal'" (pp. 126-34). Without tradition, then, the self lives by stimulation through discrete, illusory moments of communication that provide no boundaries and no guidelines.

The overt rejection of tradition by many postmodern scholars is, however, tempered by an attitude of resignation and ironic regret at the passing of a more confident era (Weedon, 1987). When seeking to reconcile this abandonment and/or loss of traditional forms and to fill and stabilize the self, sociologist Robert Bellah (1985) and his colleagues say that we have been "improvising alternatives [to tradition, especially traditional forms of religion]" (p. 291). One very visible and pervasive means of substitution is through privileging the "marketplace as a lived tradition" (Penaloza, 2000, 1). In so doing, the bold promotion of a consumption-oriented lifestyle through advertising is foregrounded as way to order and establish meaning in life. As an alternative to the traditional forms like religion, advertising instead promotes consumption and a culture of commodification as a substitute for meaning and value once found elsewhere.

A culture of commodification perpetuates communication as information, fragmentation, narcissism (Lasch, 1979), and emotivism (MacIntyre, 1981/1984) as by-products of the promise of salvation through consumption. Charles Davis refers to this cultural trend as the "redivinization of the temporal" (1994, p. 149). He contends that commodification is a response to the very human need for "faith" in something as a guide for existence, and in the context of the marketplace, this faith is co-opted from traditional religion into a form of secular religiosity. Thus, the marketplace serves as a secular temple through which advertising communicates temporal claims at truth, the promise of the good life, and hope (Heilbrunn, 1996)—"80 proof" or on sale for one week only.

In *All Consuming Images: The Politics of Style in Contemporary Culture*, Stuart Ewen's commentary on style frames the search for truth and the promise of the good life based on commodification and consumption. He says

> Style today is a preoccupation of nearly all sectors of society [. . .] [it] is an intimate component of subjectivity, intertwined with people's aspirations and anxieties. [. . .] A sense of rootedness or permanency is elusive in the world of style, and it is perhaps this quality, more than any other, that locates style in the modern world. [Style] speaks for the rise of a democratic society, in which who one wishes to become is often seen as more consequential than who one is. [It also] speaks for a society in which coherent meaning has fled to the hills, and in which drift has provided a context of continual discontent. (Ewen, 1988, p. 3, 22-3)

Ewen argues that out of late nineteenth century industrialization emerged a consumer society "filled with mass-produced status symbols" (1988, p. 68). Equating productivity with work (what one does) shifted to equating productivity with possessions (what one has). Citing Roland Barthes (1983), Ewen argues that the substitution of commodities for tradition reflects a longing for wholeness and the good life, or, according to Barthes, the dream of identity. Style then becomes one way of substantiating meaning in one's life. Ewen suggests that although the diversity of images (style) has created new possibilities that are both individual and cultural, meaningful ways of ordering our lives can only come about through the reconciliation of image and reality.

The reconciliation of image, identity, and meaning in a culture driven by commodification is the subject of Douglas Kellner's essay "Popular Culture and the Construction of Postmodern Identities" (1992). Kellner (1992) contrasts the fragmentation, instability, and flux of postmodernity with the anthropological folklore claims that, ". . . in traditional societies [modernity], one's identity was fixed, solid, and stable. Identity was a function of predefined social roles and a traditional system of myths which provided orientation and religious sanctions to one's place in the world, while rigorously circumscribing the realm of thought and behavior" (p. 141).

The key to Kellner's investigation of popular culture is his treatment of the role of advertising as "social texts" created in response to "key developments" during the historical moment in which they appear (1992, p. 162). Advertising, according to Kellner, brings discord and disruption to stable, fixed conceptions of identity, generating, instead, a multiplicity of coexisting values (1992, p. 171). He understands advertising today as emergent from an affluent image and style conscious culture that makes it possible to constantly restructure one's identity.

In a culture of commodification, goods (products) serve as bridges to a life and identity that is never fully owned but always coveted (Kertzer, 1988, p. 102). The collective vernacular of these social texts in a consumption-oriented context works to supplant the "terminal values" in our culture (Heilbrunn, 1996)—values that are a means to a given end in our culture—with values aimed at immediate gratification. The outcome is akin to seeking instruction from the Cheshire cat; the bridge of goods is never complete, and it always appears just a step or two ahead of the consumer, offering glimpses of a way to something more promising but never delivering. Driven by a focus on accumulation, this culture makes it increasingly more difficult for meaning to be established or shared, and for relationships to develop between the individual and the community (Heilbrunn, 1996).

James Twitchell (1992) claims that advertising has facilitated the cannibalization of "high" culture by low culture to the point where the "high" forms are now so familiar that they have become banal. The loss of an "aura of ritual" in the process of secularization (Twitchell, 1992, p. 47) has left the individual with a conception of salvation—identified by Benoit Heilbrunn (1996) as traditionally being a terminal value—that is spurred on by the hope and possibility of attaining some *thing* infinitely stable in a temporal, changing, and contingent world. Salvation through consumption promoted by a culture of commodification converts the symbols once revered as sacred to idols on the marketplace road to truth, the good life, hope. Advertising, as prophet and high priest, delivers these illusions in an age when the "sizzle" and not the steak is what nourishes us (Kertzer, 1988, p. 103).

Advertising and the Story of a Brand

The possibility of advertising as counsel and not prophet or high priest speaks to the challenge implicit in Benjamin's critique. Twitchell and others point to the problematic outcomes that follow Benjamin's claim that we have lost our ability to pass on experience— to evoke memory, share our experiences with others, and anticipate what the future will bring beyond discrete moments of communication that provide "sizzle" or information only.

While a culture of commodification offers a multiplicity of values and identities via advertising, some suggest that its symbolic processes invite a sense of cultural stability through the rituals and myths used to "package" its secular goods as sacred. David I. Kertzer (1988) refers to symbolic processes in general as ". . . action wrapped in a web of symbolism. . . . Human reality . . . must be fashioned by individuals out of the culture into which they are born and the experiences they have. . . . There is a continuous interaction between the ways people have of dealing with the physical and social universe and the actual contours of that universe" (p. 9, 4). Humans interact with symbols to generate and sustain meaning in reality; symbols "instigate social action and define the individual's sense of self" (Kertzer, 1988, p. 9).

Thus, when engaged as a part within the larger whole of the marketplace, the social text of advertising "affects not only [one's] view of the product, but also [one's] view of society, of social power and of social relations" (McAllister, 1996, p. 55). On the one hand, advertising as the marketplace alternative to tradition in postmodernity stands in opposition to the "residual traditional and modern values and practices" (Kellner, 1992, p. 171), pointing to a quest for virtue and the good life centered in what a person accumulates. Advertising aimed at communicating the story of a brand, however, offers realistic hope for leveraging the power of symbols through storytelling in order to communicate meaning and reclaim a sense of shared experience that spans beyond marketplace transactions.

Seeking "fit" over accommodation, advertising's role in the process of building and communicating the meaning of a brand is as a part within a larger whole. Viewed as such, advertising must maintain a healthy tension between two necessary elements: fidelity to the reality of the product—its "affordances" or what distinguishes its functions (Grassel, 1999), and creative inspiration geared to stimulate customer connections that run deeper than product function and recognition. Generating meaning comes from a well-established vision (Kapferer, 2001) and an understanding of communication as gestalt (Jones, "Gestalt," 1999), not just information, image, and style.

In *Brand Leadership* (2000), David Aaker and Erich Joachimsthaler quote Charlotte Beers of J. Walter Thompson as saying, "You cannot win the hearts of customers unless you have a heart yourself" (p. 33). Communicating the story of a brand must begin with the brand itself. This includes identifying the *raison d'etre*—or the purpose of the brand. According to Kapferer (2000) in *Strategic Brand Management*, without a sense of "internal necessity" or purposeful existence, there is no potential for leadership (p. 49). Vision clarifies the purpose and mission for an organization and its brand identity. It establishes the "why" behind a brand's existence, and knowing the why makes it possible to communicate the purpose to others.

Contrary to the focus on image in a culture of commodification, vision purposes to invest meaning in and through the life of a brand over both the short and long term. It is, by design, focused on content *and* delivery, not just information qua information, or the mere communication of information. When substantiated by a sound vision, advertising is able to not only write the history of the brand (Kapferer, 2001, p. 117), but to communicate meaning within the spirit of what Ricoeur terms "discordant concordance" (1984, p. 42). Wrought with reversals, surprise, and often tragedy, the marketplace is an arena where change—many times unforeseeable—is the only constant.

Within this atmosphere of change, advertising has the ability to establish and maintain "communities of memory" (Bellah, 1975) capable of being sustained over the long term. Doing so requires brand fidelity and a clear message, which, in the spirit of Ricoeur (1984), is made visible in concordant communication practices. For Ricoeur, the search for concordance is a "part of the unavoidable assumptions of discourse and communication" (1984, p. 28). It is characterized by "completeness, wholeness, and an appropriate magnitude" (1984, p. 38). These three characteristics suggest a commitment to the affordances of the brand and the nature of the organization, as well as a commitment to "the intelligent use of action" (Ricoeur, 1984, p. 40). In the spirit of Ricoeur's understanding of concordance advertising demonstrates responsiveness to the story of what it represents.

In order for advertising to communicate a message characterized as concordant it must be situated as a part within a larger whole. Concordance, according to Ricoeur, permits "creative imitation" (1984, p. 31) because it focuses on connections with people's lives, which are embedded in experience. The impact of this is a communicative gestalt where both the background story of the brand and the foreground needs of a target audience drive the advertising. As such, advertising cannot simply be about just selling or great creative ideas; it is about connecting to lived experience in such a way as to help people shape and communicate meaning, as well as engage each other and the marketplace.

James Carey in *Culture as Communication: Essays on Media and Society* (1988) argues that we live *in* communication. The model, according to Carey, "is not that of information acquisition, though such acquisition occurs, but of dramatic action in which [a participant(s)] join a world of contending forces as an observer at play" (1988, p. 21). Calvin Schrag's theory of communicative praxis brings texture to Carey's insight by positing communication as being *about* something, *by* someone, *for* someone in a given historical moment. The emphasis, for Schrag, is on the interplay of these three within a given context and when applied to advertising, the interplay invites the perpetuation of the brand through the telling and retelling of its story. The emergent texture extends customer experience beyond a discrete encounter with the product to involvement in a larger community.

When acknowledged as situated "within" the discourse and communication of the marketplace, advertising as communicative praxis is able to negotiate discordance and bridge audience and text together to ". . . extend the reach of expressive meaning beyond intentions and the conscious appropriations of rules by particular speakers and actors [advertising alone]" (Schrag, 1986, p. 47). Communicative praxis encourages interpretation and interaction; it permits purposeful action that seeks to reclaim the relationship between texts, in this case advertising, and the social practices, or habits of those engaged in the marketplace.

Advertising that communicates the story of the brand points to the possibility of establishing a community of memory and discourse through which the vision of an organization might be conveyed so as to invite people to be participants or characters in its unfolding story. For an invitation to be understood and responded to by the customer, the story must be clear. Advertising as communicative praxis provides this clarity as it recognizes the *about* of communication—the vision and why of an organization and its brand(s); knows its role as communicator and chronicler of the story of the organization, and more specifically a given brand (*by*); and understands the *"who"* or target audience to whom its messages are directed. The praxis orientation speaks to the embeddedness or context sensitive nature of advertising in the marketplace, and offers the promise of "a shared project and a joint endeavor by a community of investigators and interpreters" (Schrag, 1986, p. 190). It permits the story of a brand to unfold, uniting brand, organization, and audience in the experience of a given historical moment. Meaning may thus be derived from what Schrag calls the "intertexture" or play of advertising between and within not only the participants engaging the context of the marketplace itself, but also participants as they engage the marketplace with other lived traditions. Communicative praxis invites advertising to be responsive and accountable as a storyteller in a given historical moment.

Advertising as Storyteller

Paul Ricoeur works from the assumption that narrative is an inescapable part of our existence. While he comments on Benjamin's concern, Ricoeur is quick to follow up by asserting that stories are always with us, and, therefore, the possibility of narrative always exists.

> [. . .] it is necessary to have confidence in the call for concordance that today still structures the expectations of readers and to believe that new narrative forms, which we do not yet know how to name, are already being born, which

will bear witness to the fact that the narrative function can still be metamorphosed, but not so as to die. For we have no idea of what a culture would be where no one any longer knew what it meant to narrate things (Ricoeur, 1985, p. 28).

Ricoeur states that narrating proceeds from the art of telling stories, yet he recognizes that we are working with "sedimented deposits of tradition" (1985, p. 28)—tradition that is not immune to the effects of time. We cannot assume that people are engaging life with similar backgrounds or expectations; while our lives are storied, they are done so with different texture. For Ricoeur, it is in the action of narrative and time that time itself—past, present, and future—is co-present and, therefore, meaning is capable of being communicated from story to story, one person to another, from one generation to the next.

Just as with Benjamin who understood that the storyteller is not isolated—that his stories come from experience, which he then shares with others (1936/1968, p. 87)— advertising happens in the intersection of various stories told in both the marketplace and across other traditions. Ricoeur's understanding of the interweaving of history and fiction makes it possible to understand the craft of storytelling as a possibility for advertising. He distinguishes storytelling from a chronicle of events, and instead points to the capacity of stories to organize and communicate through themes and motifs (1984, p. 164). As the "first-order entities" (1984, p. 181) of history—the primary people involved in events, or, in the case of advertising, the brand and the organization—are "put into relief" (1985, p. 71) differently by time, distance, and alternative contexts, fidelity to the brand can be pushed to the background in favor of fiction, or creative innovation. An unrestricted focus on creativity alone becomes a form of chronicling in which images are substituted for events.

Storytelling weaves together innovation and the brand/organization to reach a particular audience, yielding advertising that is appropriate, creative, and a "fit" within a given historical moment. Advertising's ability to partake in the craft of storytelling emerges from the interplay of history and fiction through what Ricoeur calls a "reciprocal overlapping" (1988, p. 192) and Schrag alludes to in terms of a "temporal imprinting" (1997, p. 20). According to Schrag (1997)

> Narrative provides the ongoing context in which the figures of discourse are embedded and achieve their determinations of sense and reference. Narrative supplies the horizon of possible meanings. . . . The horizon of narrativity thus suffers a temporal imprinting, emerging from a past and advancing into a future, recollective of stories that have become part of a tradition and anticipative of accounts, both fictive and factual, yet to be rendered. Narrative comprises the continuing context, the expanding horizon of a retentional background and a protentional foreground, in which and against which our figures of discourse are called into being, play themselves out, and conspire in the making of sense. (Schrag, 1997, pp. 19-20)

In midst of the overlap and/or temporal imprinting, stories communicate meaning across distance and time. They reflect the current moment, but not exclusively. Stories build on expectation, memory, and attentiveness (Ricoeur, 1984); they are communicative praxis in action. As they come to be believed and lived out, their reach moves them into a place where the meaning derived from their symbols, themes, and motifs narrate people's actions and behavior.

The advertising industry faces a challenge from Benjamin's critique that advertising is responsible for our inability to exchange experience—for our crisis in the art of storytelling. Shifting to a role as counsel and not prophet or priest, advertising viewed as a part within a larger whole is responsive and able to address the marketplace with texture and agility, understanding that the marketplace is one of many lived traditions that form human experience. When tied to communicating meaning, advertising as storytelling reflects an understanding of the brand that, according to Jean-Marie Dru (2002) is "less a set of values or associations that create differentiation for a product and more a living business idea that lies at the center of everything a company does" (p. 64).

The craft of storytelling in advertising evolves from of a "living business idea." The brand and organization are the real starting point for countering Benjamin's critique. It is through fidelity to brand purpose and organizational vision that advertising can extend a creative invitation for people to participate in a story.

References

Aaker, D. & Joachimsthaler, E. (2000). *Brand leadership*. New York: The Free Press.

Barthes, Roland. (1990). *The fashion system*. New York: University of California Press.

Bellah, R. (1975). *The broken covenant: American civil religion in a time of trial*. New York: Seabury Press.

Bellah, R., Madsen, R, Sullivan, W. M. Swidler, A., & Tipton, S. M. (1985). *Habits of the heart: Individualism and commitment in American life*. Berkeley, CA: University of California Press.

Benjamin, W. (1968). The storyteller (H. Zohn, Trans.). In H. Arendt (Ed.), *Illuminations* (pp. 83-109). New York: Schocken Books. (Original work published 1936)

Carey, J. (1988). *Communication as culture: Essays on media and society*. New York: Routledge.

Davis, C. (1994). *Religion and the making of society: Essays in social theology*. Cambridge: Cambridge University Press.

de Tocqueville, A. (2000). *Democracy in America* (H. C. Mansfield & D. Winthrop, Trans. & Eds.). Chicago: University of Chicago Press. (Original work published 1835)

Dru, J. M. (2002). *Beyond disruption: Changing the rules in the marketplace*. New York: John Wiley & Sons, Inc.

Ewen, S. (1988). *All consuming images: The politics of style in contemporary culture*. New York: Basic Books.

Geertz, C. (1973). *The interpretation of cultures*. New York: Basic Books.

Gergen, K. (1991). *The saturated self: Dilemmas of identity in contemporary life*. New York: Basic Books.

Grassl, W. (1999, April). The reality of brands: Towards an ontology of marketing. *The American Journal of Economics and Sociology* [On-line Infotrac], *58*(2).

Heilbrunn, B. (1996). In search of the hidden go(o)d: A philosophical deconstruction and narratological revisitation of the eschatological metaphor in marketing. In S.

Brown, J. Bell, & D. Carson (Eds.), *Marketing apocalypse: Eschatology, escapology and the illusion of the end*. London: Routledge.

Jones, J. P. (1999). Gestalt: How brands are influenced by multiple communications. In J. P. Jones (Ed.), *How to use advertising to build strong brands* (pp. 51-54). Thousand Oaks, CA: SAGE Publication.

Kapferer, J. N. (2001). *Strategic brand management*. United Kingdom: Kogan Page.

Kellner, D. (1992). Popular culture and the construction of postmodern identity. In S. Lasch & J. Friedman (Eds.), *Modernity & identity* (pp. 141-77). Oxford: Blackwell.\

Kertzer, D. I. (1988). *Ritual, politics, and power*. New Haven: Yale University Press.

Lasch, C. (1979). *Culture of narcissism: American life in an age of diminishing expectations*. New York: Norton.

McAllister, M. P. (1996). *The commercialization of American culture: New advertising, control and democracy*. Thousand Oaks, CA: SAGE.

MacIntyre, A. (1984). *After virtue: A study in moral theory*. Notre Dame, IN: University of Notre Dame Press. (Original work published 1981)

Penaloza, L. The commodification of the American west: Marketers' production of cultural meanings at the trade show. *Journal of Marketing 46* (4).

Ricoeur, P. (1984). *Time and narrative: Volume 1*. (K. McLaughlin & D. Pellauer, Trans.). Chicago: University of Chicago Press. (Original work published 1983)

Ricoeur, P. (1985). *Time and narrative: Volume 2*. (K. McLaughlin & D. Pellauer, Trans.). Chicago: University of Chicago Press. (Original work published 1984)

Ricoeur, P. (1988). *Time and narrative: Volume 3*. (K. McLaughlin & D. Pellauer, Trans.). Chicago: University of Chicago Press. (Original work published 1985)

Schrag. C. O. (1986). *Communicative praxis and the space of subjectivity*. Bloomington, IN: Indiana University Press.

Schrag, C. O. (1997). *The self after postmodernity*. New Haven, CT: Yale University Press.

Twitchell, J. B. (1992). *Carnival Culture: The Trashing of Taste in America*. New York: Columbia University Press.

Weedon, C. (1987). *Feminist practice and poststructuralist theory*. New York: Basil Blackwell.

Chapter Fourteen

Rhetoric and the Marketplace: Recalling Adam Smith's Model of Rhetorical Studies

Joseph W. Sora

The Humanities and the Marketplace

Humanities academics are currently experiencing a dramatic crisis of purpose that one might argue has its roots in higher education's adoption of "corporate-style management and accounting techniques" (Nelson, 1999, p. 89). In 1987, humanities departments employed nearly 523,000 full-time professors and 270,000 part-timer faculty; by 1995, the number of full-time academics in the humanities had increased to 551,000, a 5% increase; while the number of part-time humanities faculty had increased to 381,000, a 41% increase (National Center for Education Statistics, 1999, p. 230). The connection between increased part timer hiring and an adherence to corporate models within the university is oft made. As Paul Delaney (2000) notes, "universities are differentiating more and more ruthlessly among disciplines on the ground that universities must be responsive to the market . . . [Administrators] argue that computer scientists will bring in additional research funding into the institution, whereas Chaucerians will not" (p. 91). The hiring of additional part-timers in lieu opening tenure lines would seem to be one manifestation of that differentiation.

In the corporate-university, the humanities are on shaky ground because "unlike medicine . . . engineering and computer sciences, which can raise substantial funding for the University, the humanities are, from the perspective of efficiency and the market, quite superfluous" (Mignolo 1243). Paralleling the rise of part-timer hiring in humanities disciplines, Sheila Slaughter (1997) notes that from 1983-1993 full professor salaries in Computer Science rose 74.8% to over $74,000, while the average salary of a full-time English professor, over that same ten-year period, rose only 52.3% to $57, 000 (p. 58).

Computer scientists have a far better chance of participating in the development of a technology that might contribute to a university's or corporation's fiscal health through the sale of that technology. Chaucerians and other humanities academics are generally not privy to the same opportunity and it would seem that decreased tenure-track offerings and lower salaries are the consequences of inhabiting a corporate-university that employs bottom-line oriented "corporate-style management and accounting techniques."

Deplorable hiring rates and lower salaries for humanities academics point to a discrepancy between what humanities academics do and the values of the corporate or marketplace-oriented context in which they work. Andrew Delbanco (2000) argues "to an extent never before known or imagined . . . the institutions in which we work have become saturated by market values. We have offices staffed by professional advertisers . . . we hawk our wares in glossy brochures, we furnish fast-food malls and coffee bars" (p. 1207). Higher Education's saturation by corporate values is a symptom of the unprecedented "global reach" the corporate world has attained in this historical moment (Bleich, 2002, p. ix). "Fast-food malls and coffee bars" in our universities are a tangible representation of that reach. As William Greider (1995) writes, "modern capitalism driven by the imperatives of global industrial revolution" is the engine fueling "the drama of a free-running economic system that is reordering the world" (p. 11). Major trans-national corporations are spearheading that system, accounting for 51 of the world's 100 largest economic units. 200 corporations account for over a quarter of all economic activity on the globe. The odds are that our students will work for a major corporation and humanities academics are compelled to wonder if the apparent devaluation of the humanities within higher education, as reflected in diminished tenure-track offerings and salary discrepancies, reflects a greater disconnection, i.e., between the humanities and the marketplace our students are likely to enter upon graduation.

Robert Scholes (1998) argues that such a disconnection does in fact exist, remarking the "gap, between the values of the humanities and those of the powerful worlds of business and public life has only increased. . . . And our inability to deal with it has been a contributing cause to our present state of confusion" (p. 18). It is a safe assumption that "the powerful worlds of business" will continue to dominate universities just as corporations will continue to spearhead the free market's global presence and it is an equally safe assumption that we need to find a way "to deal with" corporate power and presence if we are to assert our value to a liberal education. To turn our backs on the "powerful world of business," to consider ourselves separate, perhaps even above, the corporate contexts is to ignore the reality of our own corporate-university employers as well as the world our students will enter.

Assuming then that humanities academics feel the need to look around, both for our own benefit and the benefit of our students, we might ask the question David Downing (2002) posed in reference to English faculty: "How, as . . . scholars and teachers, can we act as agents to engage the economic and technological shifts our discipline[s] face[]?" (p. 2). Seemingly, and as suggested by diminished tenure-track offerings and lower salaries, the economic and technological shifts that define the market-oriented context do not require the engagement of humanities academics because a concern for those texts that represent interests beyond sustaining growth and profit are, quite simply, not perceived as necessary in the quest to attain marketplace success. Adam Smith, however, did not agree. He firmly believed that the marketplace need be engaged by those capable of effecting the social, political, ethical, and moral concerns that inhabit the texts humanities academics teach, discuss, and write about.

From 1748 to 1751 and throughout his formal academic career, Adam Smith gave a series of lectures on Rhetoric and Belles Lettres. He continued lecturing on Rhetoric and Belles Lettres when he was appointed chair of logic at Glasgow University in 1751 (Lothian, 1971, p. xii). While there is no record of Smith's earlier lectures in Edinburgh, student notes of his lectures at Glasgow are regarded by scholars as an enhanced version of the original Edinburgh lectures (Lothian, p. xvi). From Franklin Court's reading of these lecture we see a model of rhetorical studies that regards literary texts as a dynamic medium embodying meanings, insights, and concerns that Smith believes need to be brought to the market. The ability to bring these concerns to the market is conveyed to the student in Smith's concern for enabling the student to incorporate components of the author's style in his own writing. Smith taught the text for those political, social and ethical meanings an exclusive concern for the marketplace was not likely to foster. He also offered that text as a model of composition. In this fashion, students were taught to effect the social and political concerns manifest in the text that was under discussion. In light of the apparent disconnection between humanities scholars and the "powerful worlds of business and public life," recalling Smith's model of rhetorical studies presents a means by which present-day humanities scholars might engage the marketplace through the student and, consequently, better bridge the gap between the humanities and those contexts that lay outside university walls.

Adam Smith's Model of Rhetorical Studies

The underpinnings of Smith's model of rhetorical studies can be found in Smith's *Theory of Moral Sentiments*. Smith opens *The Theory of Moral Sentiments* remarking, "how selfish man may be supposed, there are evidently some principles in his nature, which interest him in the fortune of others" (p. 1). According to Smith, man has the potential to achieve an "interest . . . in the fortunes of others." We are not inherently atomized individuals because even though Smith believed "we have no immediate experience of what other men feel . . . the very appearances of grief and joy inspire us with some degree of the like emotions" (p. 2, p. 5). Simply witnessing, rather than actually experiencing, "grief and joy" is sufficient to induce those same feelings within the reader. A belief in the ability to feel the "grief and joy" of another without physically experiencing that "grief and joy" underscores Smith's notion that a "Moral Sense" develops through our encounters with those we admire (Court, 1992). As Smith writes, "it is the great leader in science and taste, the man who directs and conducts our own sentiments, the extent and superior justness of whose talents astonish us with wonder and surprise, who excites our admiration and seems to deserve our applause" (p. 21). We encounter such "talents" in the books written by those "great leader[s]" and, in doing so, our own "sentiments" are accordingly molded.

Texts are therefore not regarded by Smith as artifacts having little or no meaning for our individual characters. We are, according to Smith, deeply affected by the concerns of "those great leader[s]" that are revealed in their texts. As Court (1992) writes, for Smith "texts no longer repeated a static world of similitude, resemblance, and their representations" but instead functioned as the cornerstone of "an on-going dialectical progression" in which "a student's sense of self-identity and difference from others would give way to a sense of identity with others," being those authors under discussion (p. 23). The student encounters the text that "excites [his] admiration" and, consequently, his or her initial "self-identity" is necessarily changed as it incorporates the interests exhibited by those authors in their various texts. As the author's interests alter the student's initial "self-identity" a new identity is realized, being one that embodies the insights and understandings of the text at hand (Court, p. 23).

It follows then that for Smith reading is a meaningful act with great significance to both the reader's identity and the actions he or she purports out of that identity. For this reason Smith discussed texts by Thomas Swift, John Milton, Demosthenes, and Racine that, while they lack an explicit marketplace orientation, nonetheless reveal the concerns and insights that Smith hoped would positively shape the student's identity and behavior in the marketplace. For example, in the eighth lecture, Smith praises Thomas Swift as "a plain man" who issues "writings [that] are adapted to the present time, either in ridiculing some prevailing vice or folly, or exposing some particular character" (p. 38). Smith understands the relationship between Swift's writings and present age to lay in a precise, hardnosed critique of the age in which he lives. While Swift's critique conflicts with Smith's assessment of "present taste, which delights only in general and abstract speculations," Swift's writings nonetheless engage "the present time" with "propriety and precision" (p. 38, p. 37). According to Smith, Swift's ability to confront the vices and follies of his age springs, in part, from Swift's "complete knowledge of his subjects" (p. 38). To support this assessment, Smith recalls Swift's *A Treatise for Good Manners and Good Breeding* and argues that "it would have been impossible for anyone who had not given such attention to allege so many particulars" as concerns the "rules for behaviour" that are portrayed in Swift's work (p. 38). Smith's treatment of Swift suggests that Smith believed Swift's work insightfully engages the "present time" by offering a valuable critique that, while it may conflict with the nature of "present taste," unabashedly and intelligently discusses the vices and follies of the present age.

In Smith's estimation, Swift's ability to provide such a critique suggests a "general character" that Smith believed worthy of making a contribution to a student's identity. Linking an author's character to his writing suggests that Smith understood an author's text to reflect that author's "general character." Swift the man is thus upheld as a model of ethical behavior that, in accords with Smith's notion of the "Moral Sense," Smith believes can be realized within the student's identity and therefore the actions that reinforce that identity. As Court writes, Smith believed by discussing authors such as Swift as representative of a preferred mode of behavior Smith believed he "enforced the code of conduct and standard of judgment that his lectures professed" (p. 28). While I am not arguing that humanities academics should teach authors as examples of ethical behavior to be emulated, the fact that Smith understands a correlation between an author's "character" and his text suggests that Smith believed in a potential relationship between text and behavior, both in the case of the author and his text as well as the student and the text. Since "author and his style were held to be inseparable," style or text and student character might achieve a similar union in the development of the student's "Moral Sense" as the student adopted those interests or concerns Smith understood as part of the texts under discussion. Within Swift's text such values and standards manifest in the writing of an informed critique that demonstrates an interest in bettering the age, in practical terms, rather than conforming to public "taste." Since Smith firmly believed that the marketplace needed individuals capable of effecting such an impartial critique and Swift was a logical object of discussion.

Smith, however, was not content with simply placing students in contact with those "general character[s]" he deemed valuable. He was equally committed to providing the student with a means of effecting the concerns and insights that spring from those authors he discussed. Thus Smith combines his theoretical discussion of Swift's text with an explicit concern for imparting writing skills, noting, that Swift's ability to engage his time is successful because Swift adopts a "plain style" that "paints . . . each thought in the best and most proper manner, and with the greatest strength of colouring" (p. 39). Seemingly, Smith has left literary analysis to argue for a particular writing style. Theory has been supplemented with a concern for action.

Smith's interest in teaching a particular writing style runs throughout the lectures on Rhetoric and Belles Lettres. For example, Smith quite clearly places the burden of honest expression on his students remarking, "our words must be put in such order that the meaning of the sentence shall be quite plain, and not depend upon the accuracy of the printer or reader in placing the points or laying the emphasis on certain words" (p. 3). To illustrate how meaning can be obfuscated Smith uses the example of Alexander Pope, stating "Mr. Pope often errs in both these respects: as, first, in that line, 'Born but to die, and reasoning but to err.' The sense of this line is very different in these cases, when we put the accent in both members on *but*, or in the one on *born* and in the other on *reasoning*" (original emphasis, p. 3). Smith is telling his students to avoid the vagaries evidenced in this example of Pope's language because such ambiguity prevents a clear written expression.

In advocating Swift's plain style and criticizing Pope's style for breeding ambiguity, Smith reveals his interest in teaching a type of writing that he believes more appropriate to the extra-academic contexts Swift engages. In other words, Smith has a clear agenda in deeming a particular writing style worthy of praise. In what Smith deems the plain style, "No word can be passed over without notice" and the reader is compelled to read such "works with more life and emphasis than those [of] most authors" (p. 34). As Swift's writings demonstrate, the plain style lends itself to an effective critique of the present age by avoiding those "general and abstract speculations" that Smith believes undercut the clarity of that text. Thus, Smith is urging a particular style because he believes it has the greatest chance of being heard and understood and therefore of attaining the practical engagement with the age that Smith believed so valuable.

Notions of (L)iterature

Smith's ability to teach texts as offering a type of writing the student could in fact attain was made easier by virtue of the fact that literature had not yet attained a capital "L." In other words, at the time Smith was lecturing there was not yet a gulf between published writings student writing. In contrast, many disciplines in the humanities uphold a yawning gap between student writing and professional or published writing. James Berlin (1996) notes that in the academy this gap is reflected in the separation of writing into two camps—rhetoric and poetics (p. 2). Rhetoric is the "production of spoken and written texts," or composition; poetics is the "the interpretation of texts" or "what most college and university professors of English think of as 'English'" (Berlin, 1996, p. 1; Scholes, 1998, p. 2). This separation between student writing and Literature is, however, hierarchical. As Berlin writes, "the ruling tendency in the English department since its inception some one hundred years ago has been . . . all that is important and central in the study of discourse falls within the domain of literary texts and all that is unimportant and marginal falls within the realm of rhetoric" (p. 3). In other words, as Scholes remarks, "reading is actually called literature, while [student] writing is just writing" (p. 160). Such a hierarchy suggests that in the current academic there is little relationship between authorial writing and student writing and it follows that students are rarely led to any relationship between what they read (poetics) and what they write (rhetoric).

Smith, however, was teaching long before a concept of literature as separate from student writing had emerged. When Smith taught, the word "literary" had only recently "appeared in the sense of reading ability and experience" (Williams, 1977, p. 47). Since "literary" in the 18th century implied simply "a specialization of rhetoric or grammar," it did not connote "a rule" that indelibly separates certain works from student writing (Williams, p. 45). Lecturing without any concept of a separation between literature and student writing meant that Smith could treat particular works as reflecting not only those insights and concerns he wished to impart but also a style of writing his students could in fact effect. Rather than teach rhetoric and poetics as separate endeavors, Smith could simultaneously express his interest in both, thereby granting the student an insight into that author's concerns as well as the tools to effect those concerns in their own writing.

The Student in Smith's Rhetorical Model

It's important to note that Smith's lectures on Rhetoric and Belles Lettres were not presented exclusively to traditional students. According to Court, Smith's students "were the sons of the newly emerging mercantile class" who "constituted the majority of his enrollments both at Edinburgh in the 1740s and later . . . at Glasgow University" (p. 20). It follows then that Smith had the present and future marketplace roles of his students in mind when he devised his lectures. Smith's envisioned the culmination of his pedagogical efforts taking place in the extra-academic lives his students would engage after their coursework. He believed that "doctrinaire support for individualism and free-market capitalism would encourage a corresponding change in behavior manifested especially in an increase in problems associated with the unrestrained ambition and unchecked greed that was the ultimate outcome of free-market competition" (Court, p. 21). To circumvent the problems stemming from a myopic market-driven world-view, Smith projected an equal interest in both the theoretical and practical values of text. Even though such texts as Swift's *A Treatise of Good Manners and Good Breeding* and Pope's *The Rape of the Lock* lack an explicit marketplace orientation, Smith understands them as texts that offer valuable political and social meanings as well as great relevance to a student's writing. As we've seen in the example of Swift, Smith teaches his students to both uncover the relationship between Swift's text and the extra-academic world (a relationship based on the critique it offers) and to incorporate the sinews of that relationship—the style of the writing itself—within their writing. In attributing to text the potential to mould and inform a student's writing, Smith professed a model of rhetorical studies he believe absolutely vital to the health of the marketplace. If he hoped to "eliminate the spectre of self-serving corruption that threatened the dream of *laissez-faire*" he had to be concerned, first and foremost, with the activities his students would engage as future participants in the surrounding cultural context, and the marketplace specifically, that lay outside the lecture hall (Court, p. 21).

Smith's lectures on Rhetoric and Belles Lettres thus answer the call of some literary critics and rhetoricians who feel that academics can bridge the chasm that separates the humanities from the "powerful worlds of business" by more fully considering the role of the student in the classroom. The students, not the University, nor the community of academics with whom Smith worked, nor even the authors under discussion are at the center of Smith's pedagogical efforts. Robert Scholes (1998) recently declared that humanities academics are "responsible to our students . . . for helping them . . . understand their world and survive in it, and secondarily some grounds for criticizing and trying to improve it" (p. 83). Echoing Scholes' call to give students a basis from which they will effect business, Wayne C. Booth (1998) believes we should try to "change students in ways that we are sure will be most useful to them." (p. 42). For both Scholes and Booth, and Smith as well, the student, and his or her life outside the university, is viewed as playing a pivotal role in curricular design. The student's actions outside the university function as the ultimate goal of academic effort and, for this reason, one might believe that the student is being understood as the real bridge between the humanities and the marketplace.

Myopia and the Marketplace

William Greider (1995) likens our version of the marketplace to "a wondrous new machine [that] plows across fields and fencerows" and lacks "any internal governor to control the speed and direction . . . sustained by its own forward motion, guided mainly by its own appetites" (p. 11). The problem with such a machine, the problem anticipated by Adam Smith when he provided the earliest articulation of that very machine, is that without "any internal governor," the marketplace has the potential to function as a "controlling mechanism" (Court, 1992, p. 21). As Court describes Smith's assessment of the burgeoning 18th century marketplace: "in such an atmosphere, conventional moral and social concerns could easily be subordinated in the name of competition to more immediate economic realities" (p. 21). While Smith in *Wealth of Nations* persuasively argued for the inability of the state to manage the growth of the market, he did not argue for a completely unfettered economic system. In place of the "old, centrally directed mercantile system" Smith posited "leaders who would be ethical as well as educated— sober, prudent people, who as active borrowers, investors, and managers in a free market could be trusted to promote the interests of the market fairly and equitable and to practice high standards of political behavior" (Court, p. 21). The recent fall of Enron and WorldCom's accounting scandals suggest that such high standards of political behavior are not always evident in actions directed toward attaining marketplace success—that in fact there has never been a greater need for the leaders Smith envisioned.

As the free market becomes a galvanizing global text in the wake of Communism's fall, the consequences of allowing its shortcoming to go unaddressed are infinitely significant. Gerald Graff (1979) once described "the modern corporation as able to appropriate . . . any type of values and any type of culture" (p. 117). When applied to the university, Graff's assessment of the flexibility of the modern corporation fails to account for the grumbling and outright protest that often accompanies the modern corporation's inability to appropriate all values. The capitalist system is in fact more selective than Graff would have us believe. It throws its dollars only toward those "cultures," those "values," those texts from which it might gain financial reward. As noted, tenure for humanities academics does not represent one such value. And neither does nationalism for that matter. As a text, national prejudices and fears represent "the most dangerous myth of modern man, as the World Managers see it" because economic interests can be subjugated below national or political interest (Barnet, 1974, p. 54). Consumerism, "a mark that . . . no benefit . . . that would not be subject to cost-benefit analysis . . . could be imagined" has no need for national interests, a set of values that survive despite cost-benefit analysis (Readings, 1996, p. 46). The pure consumer is interested only in "national prejudices and fears" to the extent that they can be transformed into a commodity and sold. The citizen, the human being has other concerns and interests in other texts that are not reflected within the text that is the free market but that are nonetheless a vital component of the human Story.

Does the marketplace's inability to accommodate explicitly non-market oriented concerns mean that national, social, political, ethical and moral impulses go away in a market context? Certainly not as these values exist as viable texts with which the market must reckon and in which humanities academics typically traffic. Smith's lectures on Rhetoric and Belles Lettres offer a means by which the student might use non-market texts expressing such political, ethical and moral concerns as grounds for generating a responsible critique that could function in extra-academic settings. William Greider warns that unless "the global economic system" learns to account for those texts that are not readily accomodated by the marketplace, "weary political and class conflicts are sure to ripen, leading toward the same stalemate between markets and society in which fascism arose and flourished nearly one hundred years ago" (p. 246). In many ways, the September 11th 2001 attacks can perhaps be read as a culmination of exactly such political reactions. At the very least, the events of September 11th suggest that free market is functioning in ignorance of a variety of political and social texts that are ceasing to go unheard. Perhaps a corps of professionals with the experience of reading, discussing and writing about those social, political, and cultural texts the market does not readily incorporate into its activity would go someway toward alleviating that ignorance.

While fewer tenure-track lines and lower salaries for humanities academics suggest a devaluation of the humanities in the current market-oriented context, Adam Smith believed that humanities academics has a vital role within the free market. He lived that awareness in his lectures on Rhetoric and Belles Lettres, teaching those texts that embodies a variety of non-market concerns that he believed need be brought to the marketplace if that market were to succeed. In doing do, he demonstrated the inherent viability of the humanities within higher education.

The marketplace will not survive without a faculty of critique that can reveal to it that those social and political concerns that humanities academics commonly engage but that are ignored by the marketplace. One might believe it is the special duty of the humanities to engage the marketplace by guiding our students in bringing to the market that which it was never designed to see. From a conception of text as a living entity with genuine meaning to a student's work life and his or writing, the humanities and Rhetorical Studies in particular, can aid students in gaining the grounds for establishing a critique that will enable the marketplace to accommodate those social and political facts that underlay dramatic unrest. In doing so, the Humanities can effect an agency that is of global necessity.

References

Barnet, R. J., & Muller, R. E. (1974). *Global reach: The power of the multinational corporations*. New York: Simon & Schuster.

Berlin, J. (1996). *Rhetorics, poetics, and cultures: Refiguring college English studies*. Urbana, IL: National Council of Teachers of English.

Bleich, D. (2002). Foreword: It's about time we go "beyond English." In D. B. Downing, C. M. Hurlbert, & P. Mathieu (Eds.), *Beyond English, Inc.: Curricular reform in a global economy* (pp. ix-xiv). Portsmouth, NH: Boynton/Cook.

Booth, W. C. (1998). The ethics of teaching literature. *College English,* 61(1), 41-55.

Court, F. (1992). *Institutionalizing English literature: The culture and politics of literary study, 1750-1900.* Stanford, CA: Stanford University Press.

Delaney, P. (2000). The university in pieces: Bill Readings and the fate of the humanities. *MLA Profession 2000,* 89-96.

Delbanco, A. (2000). What should PhD mean? *Conference on the Future of Doctoral Education in PMLA,* 115, 1205-1209.

Downing, D. B. (2002). English incorporated: An introduction. In D. B. Downing, C. M. Hurlbert, & P. Mathieu (Eds.), *Beyond English, Inc.: Curricular reform in a global economy* (pp. 1-22). Portsmouth, NH: Boynton/Cook Pub.

Graff, G. (1979). *Literature against itself: Literary ideas in modern society.* Chicago: University of Chicago Press.

Greider, W. (1997). *One world, ready or not: The manic logic of global capitalism.* New York: Simon & Schuster.

Mignolo, W. D. (2000). The role of the humanities in the corporate university. *Proceedings from the Conference on the Future of Doctoral Education in PMLA,* 115, 1283-1285.

National Center for Education Statistics. (1999). *Digest of education statistics.* Washington, D.C.: GPO.

Nelson, C., & Watt, S. (1999). *Academic keywords: A devil's dictionary for higher education.* New York: Routledge.

Readings, B. (1996). *The university in ruins.* Cambridge, MA: Harvard University Press.

Scholes, R. (1998). *The rise and fall of English.* New Haven, CT: Yale University Press.

Slaughter, S., & Leslie, L. L. (1997). *Academic capitalism.* Baltimore: Johns Hopkins University Press.

Smith, A. (1963). *Lectures on rhetoric & belles lettres* (J. M. Lothian, Ed.). London: Thomas Nelson and Son. (Original work published. . . .)

Smith, A. (199-?). *The theory of moral sentiments, or, an essay towards an analysis of the* principles by which men naturally judge concerning the conduct, first of their neighbours, and afterwards of themselves: To which is added, a dissertation on *the origin of languages* (6th ed.). Charlottesville, VA: Ibis. (Original work published. . . .)

Williams, R. (1977). *Marxism and literature.* Oxford, England: Oxford University Press.

Chapter Fifteen

Two Sides to the Story: Women's and Men's Views on the Difficulties Women Face in Accessing Directorships

ALISON SHERIDAN

GINA MILGATE

Introduction

With women representing only 3 per cent of board members of publicly-listed companies in Australia, the views of the "lucky" few as to why so few women sit on corporate boards is an important source of information to help us understand the factors contributing to the gendered nature of the corporate board room. To this end, a survey of Australian women directors was carried out in 2000 (Sheridan, 2001). Although this most senior level of management in Australia is still very much the domain of men, the board members responding to the survey were clearly well-qualified women with considerable experience and expertise to bring to their boards. It seemed to many of these women, however, that there were barriers continuing to limit women's opportunities to access public boards, including the tendency for "like to promote like." From the responses of these board members, it seemed this was not in the best interests of the companies. Seventy percent (70%) of respondents believed the current mix of professional experiences and backgrounds of board members was not adequate and could be enhanced through the inclusion of a greater variety of experiences and backgrounds. Further, while many viewed a strong track record in one's own field and a good understanding of general business principles as important in accessing board membership, many others highlighted the importance of business contacts; or "who you know not what you know." What many of the respondents suggested was that the current criteria for board membership may need to be reframed (Sheridan, 2001).

The findings of this study of women board members generated considerable interest in the financial and popular press at the time of their release (Batt, 2001; Walsh, 2001). A number of talk back radio programs also picked up on the research as a topical social issue in a context of several high profile corporate collapses and increasing criticism of board members' roles in these failures. A number of comments were made to the effect "but surely this is only half the story", with one of the common questions asked by interviewers about the research being "what do the men say?". The study reported here sought to report the "other half of the story"—in particular, to answer the questions "do men believe the current mix of professional experiences and backgrounds is adequate?" and "do they perceive there to be barriers limiting women's access to this most privileged level of management?" Together, women's and men's views may help us to understand the climate in which debates about the need to bring about change in board membership are being held. From the research reported here it seems there are significant differences between the views held by women and men and these differences are explored in the context of increasing scrutiny of board members performance.

Method

Data Collection

The study was based on a survey of male board members of publicly-listed companies in Australia. The sample was drawn from the public reports submitted to the Australian Stock Exchange (ASX). While the ASX requires all publicly-listed companies in Australia to submit reports annually, including details of their board members, the ASX does not make this data freely available in an aggregate form. The details of board members of publicly-listed companies were purchased through Ian Huntley Publishing (who acquire the data from the ASX annually and collate it) in 2000. While each of the publicly-listed companies reported all board members' names, the level of detail about board members provided to the ASX in the public reports varied considerably between companies.

The data from the public reports indicated there were 1299 publicly-listed companies in Australia as at 30 March 2000 and there were 7341 board positions associated with these companies. The average board size is between 5 and 6 members with a range of 3 to 15 board members. From the publicly-reported information and the additional information concerning each of the companies provided on the ASX web-site, it was possible to identify that 6409 (87.3%) of the board positions were held by men and 251 (3.4%) were held by women (see Table 1). Six hundred and eighty one (681) (9.3%) could not be identified as being held by either men or women as the biographical information provided in the public reports was insufficient.

Table 1
Board Positions by Gender, March 2000

Board members	Number	Percentage
Men	6409	87.3
Women	251	3.4
Not identifiable	681	9.3
Total	7341	100

The gender composition of 1082 (83%) of the 1299 companies could be fully identified. It was not clear what the exact gender composition of the remaining 217 (17%) companies was because the information concerning the board members supplied to the ASX was not sufficiently detailed. Eight hundred and fifty seven (857) of the companies (66%) had all male boards while 225 (17%) had boards with women on them. In none of these mixed boards, however, did women make up a majority of board members. Of the 225 companies with women board members, 183 had one woman board member, 28 had two women board members, four had three women board members and there were no companies with four (4) or more women board members. As such, the gender composition of Australian publicly-listed boards is not unlike that reported in the US (Collingwood, 1996) and Israel (Talmud and Izraeli, 1999). Collingwood's (1996: 16) comment that "a female director is still likely to be the only woman in the boardroom when the meeting comes to order" while written about the US situation, could be equally applied to public companies in Australia.

The database was revisited in 2001 to identify a random selection of men on boards to survey. From the 6409 board positions held by men, 500 names were randomly selected to survey. As the list had been generated 18 months earlier, and board memberships can change on a regular basis, a manual check was carried out of the names of the men against the current details of the relevant boards on the ASX web site. Following this manual check, the sample was reduced to 468, as 32 of the men were no longer board members of the relevant companies. In December 2001, a slightly modified form of the survey that had been conducted of women 18 months earlier was sent to the 468 men. The adaptations to the survey included removing the questions specifically asking respondents "as a woman. . .".

Response

In an effort to maximise the response rate, respondents were not required to identify themselves on the survey. Of the 468 questionnaires sent out, 38 were returned because the men were no longer members of the company's board (although their names still appeared on the ASX public files), so the sample size was reduced to 430. The original mailing was followed by a reminder letter one month later. It may be that in some cases the company did not forward the mail to the directors, but we could not quantify this. Forty seven (47) participants responded, representing a response rate of about 11%. This compares with the 31% rate achieved in the similar survey of women board members conducted 18 months earlier. While a response rate of 11% is very low (Miller 1991), this was not particularly surprising. A survey of men, about the barriers women face in accessing board positions, is unlikely to generate the same level of interest and engagement with men as it did with women. While the response rates varied significantly between the two samples, the actual number of respondents was the same.

In seeking to examine whether the two groups' responses were similar to questions concerning the adequacy of board composition and whether there are barriers to women's entry into boards, tests of the significance of difference between two independent proportions, or z tests, were conducted (Ferguson & Takane, 1989). Where statistically significant differences were found, these are reported.

Results

Personal details

As seen in Table 2, the age, marital and family status of the respondents varied between the two groups. The women responding were, on average, younger than the men and the range of ages for women was greater than that for men. Men were more likely than women to be married and with children. As well, men were more likely than women to hold university qualifications. With respect to the respondents' primary occupations, men were more likely to be full-time employees, part-time employees or business owners than women. Women, on the other hand, were more likely to be consultants than men. Eight of the women and six of the men were not in paid employment. The distribution of incomes was fairly similar between the two groups.

Table 2
Characteristics of Respondents

	Women (n= 47)		Men (n = 47)	
Age				
Range (years)	28-75		38-71	
Average (years)	45		53	
	n	%	n	%
Married	36	77	41	87
Children	35	74	40	85
University qualifications	37	80	45	96
Primary occupation				
Full-time employee	15	32	20	43
Part-time employee	0	0	3	6
Consultant/outside contractor	11	24	8	17
Business owner	12	26	15	32
No other paid employment	8	17	6	13
Income				
< $100 000	4	8	6	13
$100 000-$300 000	22	47	21	45
$300 000-$500 000	13	28	7	15
$500 000-$1 000 000	5	11	4	8
> $1 000 000	0	0	2	4

Respondents also provided details about the nature and frequency of directorships they held. As can be seen in Table 3 men, on average, held more directorships than women on publicly-listed and other companies, while women held more directorships on not for profit organisations.

Table 3
Average Number of Board Memberships

Boards	Women (n= 47)	Men (n = 47)
Publicly-listed	1.68	1.83
Other companies	2.32	2.72
Not for profit	1.13	0.49

The respondents indicated their backgrounds and experiences in terms of three broad categories; the professions, not-for-profit or public sector and business. With respect to the professions, nineteen (40%) men had accounting credentials and expertise, while only five (11%) of the women did. In the finance sector men accounted for almost twice as many women with thirty (64%) and seventeen (36%) respectively. In the area of general management thirty-three (70%) were men and twenty-five (53%) were women. Nine (19%) of men were represented in the product/operations management field, while four (9%) were accounted for by women and in the engineering/science profession ten (21%) were men and seven (15%) were women. Eight (17%) women and only three (6%) men cited experience in the public sector. Three (6%) of women and one (2%) man had professional experience in the area of medicine/health, while nine (19%) women and seven (15%) cited experience and qualifications in law. In the areas of human resources seven (15%) women and four (9%) men cited experience while in marketing/ sales, and fifteen (32%) women and eleven (23%) men cited experience. Seven (15%) women were in public relations, with only 3 (6%) men only represented in this field. In the areas of education and not-for-profit management, both groups had similar representation were with seven (15%) women and five (11%) men citing experience in these areas. Twelve (26%) women and six (13%) men cited experience in the "other" category.

Table 4
Backgrounds of Respondents

	Women		Men		z
Background	n	%	n	%	
Professions					
Accounting	5	11	19	40	3.311*
Law	9	19	7	15	-0.549
Medicine / Health	3	6	1	2	-1.022
Not for profit or public sector					
Education	7	15	7	15	0
Government	8	17	3	6	-1.604
Not-for-profit management	5	11	5	11	0
Business					
Engineering/science	7	15	10	21	0.804
Finance	17	36	30	64	2.682*
General management	25	53	33	70	1.697
HR	0	0	4	9	2.044**
Marketing/sales	15	32	11	23	-0.922
Product/operations management	4	9	9	19	1.494
Public relations	7	15	3	6	-1.338
Other	12	26	6	13	-1.573

*p < 0.01
**p < 0.05

Respondents were asked about the entire pool of current board members and whether the mix of professional experience was adequate. There were significant differences between the two groups' responses. While 25 (53%) men said the current composition of boards was adequate, only fourteen (30%) of women agreed with this. In contrast, thirty two (68%) of women said the boards composition wasn't adequate, with only twenty-one (45%) of men agreeing here.

Table 5
Adequacy of Board Composition

	Women		Men		z
	n	%	n	%	
Yes	14	30	25	53	2.303**
No	32	68	21	44	-2.288**

*p < 0.01
**p < 0.05

Respondents were asked their views on why more women were not directors of publicly-listed companies in Australia. While respondents were given eight reasons to choose from, they were not limited to these responses as space was left at the end of the question for them to add any other reasons they deemed relevant. As can be seen in

Table 6, there were significant differences between the two groups with respect to the attribution to the following reasons; companies are not looking to put women on boards; companies don't think women are qualified for board service; companies are afraid to take on women who are not already on boards; and there are not enough qualified women.

Table 6
Reasons for Low Numbers of Women Directors

	Women		Men		z
	n	%	n	%	
Companies don't know where to look	21	45	18	38	-0.809
Companies not looking to put women on boards	19	40	8	17	-2.974**
Companies don't think women are qualified for board service	19	40	5	11	-3.876**
Companies afraid to take on women who are not already on boards	23	49	10	21	-3.589**
Qualified women not making it known they're interested in board service	8	17	13	28	1.44
Companies concerned women will have a "women's issues" agenda	13	28	7	15	-1.710
Not enough qualified women	18	38	31	66	3.94**
Qualified women not interested in board service	4	9	4	9	0

*$p < 0.01$
**$p < 0.05$

The qualitative responses from the two groups also highlighted some interesting differences in perspectives. While the most of the male respondents focused on the shortage of experienced and/or committed women, the female respondents tended to focus on the nature of the processes. It seems the women responding were less likely than the men to believe the lack of women on boards is because the women themselves are not making their interests known. Rather, the women were more likely to attribute the reasons for low numbers of women directors to factors relating to the company's resistance to women board members.

> *Directorships of public companies are very much given through the old boys network. It's a complete gravy train. Many older male directors are completely out of touch with modern business. 8% female directors is atrociously low—there's a pool of very capable women being wasted while a bunch of old farts who belong to the same old club hand out directorships like lollies to their mates. Many are on more boards than they could really contribute to.* (Female Respondent 14)

Boards still selected to create the right team—a woman is less likely to be "known" and part of the team (Female Respondent 9)

Not part of the "boys network" (Female Respondent 39)

There are not enough qualified women for board service relative to the pool of men (Male Respondent 10).

I am the MD of a mineral exploration company and there is a shortage of suitably qualified female geologists and mining engineers. This will not change until more women take up these professions. (Male Respondent 22)

Change in women's priorities required (Male Respondent 30)

One of the male respondents did nominate men's lack of interest in sharing the role with women.

Many men simply do not want women on boards (Male Respondent 19).

The directors were asked whether they believed there is currently a sufficient pool of women from which to select for boards. As can be seen in Table 7, once again there were significant differences between the responses of the two groups. While the majority of women believed there was a sufficient pool of women from which to select, the vast majority of men disagreed. That the majority of women believed there was a sufficient number of appropriately qualified women available for board service is consistent with their earlier responses that there appear to be impediments at the company level to women's access to board positions, while the men's response was consistent with their earlier response that the reason there were so few women on boards was that there are not enough qualified women.

Table 7
Sufficient Pool of Women

	Women		Men		z
	n	%	n	%	
Yes	26	55	6	13	-4.353*
No	10	21	34	72	4.961*
Don't know	10	21	7	15	-0.804

*p < 0.01
**p < 0.05

Respondents were asked about their experience on boards and whether men were comfortable with women directors. There were no significant differences between the responses of the two groups. Seven (15%) of women and five (11%) men indicated they were all comfortable, while twenty (43%) men and fifteen (32%) of women indicated most are comfortable with women on boards. Twenty one (45%) of women agreed that some men are comfortable and some are not, while seventeen (36%) of men also indicated this. For both groups, three respondents (6%) felt that most male CEOs and directors are not comfortable with women, and none of the respondents agreed that no CEOs were comfortable with women.

Table 8
Male CEOs Comfort with Women Directors

	Women		Men		z
	n	%	n	%	
Yes, all are	7	15	5	11	-0.618
Yes, most are	15	32	20	43	1.066
Some arc, some not	21	45	17	36	-0.841
No, most are not	3	6	3	6	0
None are	0	0	0	0	0

*p < 0.01
**p < 0.05

One of the questions added to the survey of men was designed to ascertain whether men perceived there was a need for more women directors. While 53 per cent of the male respondents had indicated they believed the current composition of boards was adequate (as per Table 5), 68 per cent indicated they believed there should be more women on boards. This inconsistency in their responses is one that we shall be taking up in the discussion.

Table 9
Need for More Women Directors

	Men	
	n	%
Yes	32	68
No	2	4
Don't know	13	28

Discussion

It seems from the findings reported here that men and women on the boards of publicly listed companies have disparate views on the adequacy of the current composition of boards and the reasons for women's low representation. These differences in views deserve attention, as while the women view the need for changes to the composition of boards as important, this is not well recognized by the men surveyed. While women seem to be promoting the value of diversity to the performance of boards, the men seem to be promoting the value of homogeneity of board membership and the importance of maintaining current selection criteria. The differences between the two groups can be understood with reference to the work of Conger, Lawler and Finegold (2001) who highlight the tensions in seeking to balance the value that a diverse range of perspectives can bring to board performance with the recognition that many board members recognise the highly interdependent nature of board interactions and the importance of the team working well together.

Understanding the differences between the two perspectives—diversity vs. homogeneity—can be enhanced through reflections on the writings surrounding masculinity and identity politics. As Collinson and Hearn (1996) note, in a gender, hierarchical and class sense it is men in management, and we would argue men in board positions particularly, who most closely resemble hegemonic masculinity—or the dominant masculinity. It is the successful claim to authority that marks hegemony (Connell, 1995). As part of the dominant group, there is no questioning by these men of the structures that sustain that hegemony. They take as given their right to be there and deny (or perhaps simply lack awareness) that such privilege is occurring or is related to gender (Martin, 1996). The following comments illustrate some of the claims by respondents that reflect this unquestioning acceptance of the current practices.

> *It's really about the right people for the right job, not about "more women."*
> *Hence the challenge is to ensure they (women) have the characteristics and*
> *skills sought.* (Male Respondent 25)

> *I do not believe in having the "token" woman, black, minority group member.*
> *Business in Australia is about survival on the world stage—not tokenism. There*
> *are no barriers to skilled performance.* (Male Respondent 38)

There appears to be no questioning by these men of how "skilled performance" has been defined within the organisational context.

In terms of change management, one of the key determinants of the success of a change process is the perception by those affected that change is necessary. In the case of women's representation on boards, while there is considerable discussion in the popular press about the need for changes to board selection processes, and evidence is accruing about the value of bringing an array of perspectives to board discussions (Conger et al, 2001), this doesn't seem to be a view held by those who have the power to execute change—the men on boards. It seems that if change is to be achieved, we will need to educate board members about the benefits of change. For any change process to be successful, it has to be "owned" by those affected by it (Patrickson and Bamber, 1995) and this is no different for a change process designed to bring about changes to the gender composition of organisational structures (Kirton and Greene, 2000). Despite the majority of these men responding that there should be more women in board positions, their other responses support the existing evidence that managers continue to make decisions on the basis of stereotypes, that men in powerful positions have a predilection for people in their own image and they have strongly sex-typed views of the job requirements (Liff and Wajcman, 1996).

In the context of board positions, the notion of merit deserves scrutiny. It seems that the majority of men responding to this survey did not question the current criteria for board memberships—which it seems from the extant literature is previous experience in senior level management positions, preferably at the CEO level, in other companies with similar profiles (Conger et al, 2001). The structures and processes within organisations that privilege men in attaining the most senior positions are well documented in the gender and management literature (see for instance, Martin, 1996; Collinson and Hearn, 1996; Maier, 1999). The gendered dimensions to these processes are largely invisible to those who benefit from them—white, anglo-saxon, able-bodied, heterosexual men. "It is in the very nature of the phenomenology of power that those . . . who have it experience its workings the least aware of it" (Shotter, 1992: 40).

In seeking to bring about change, education about the gendered processes that reinforce the current composition of boards and the benefits to be gained by organisation in having more diverse boards will be a necessary first step in raising awareness, and perhaps commitment to, bringing about change. Such a recommendation, however, has at its core the assumption that board members are primarily interested in the well-being of the organisation. Recent corporate experiences in Australia suggest this may be a fallacious assumption. Considerable debate within the popular press has focused on the apparent self-interest driving some high profile board members' actions (Sexton, 2002). One of the male respondents supported this concern when they noted that one of the factors they believed contributed to the poor functioning of a board they were involved with was "the company's interests put behind personal interests" (Male respondent 30).

Conclusion

Previous research on women's views on the barriers they face in accessing board positions prompted questions about what men think. Men's perspectives are important, as they make up the vast majority of board members and represent the "gatekeepers" for board positions. We wanted to find out whether men saw the need for changing board composition, as recognising the need for change is an important precursor to change (Patrickson and Bamber, 1995). It seems, however, that the majority of men responding to the survey believed that the current composition of board is adequate. This research confirms existing work on masculinity and identity politics that those who are part of the hegemonic group do not question the structures that sustain that hegemony (Martin, 1996; Edley & Wetherell, 1996; Collinson & Hearn, 1996). The low response rate from the men surveyed further confirms how little interest those in privileged positions were prepared to direct to reflecting on factors affecting women's access to this most privileged level of management.

References

Australian Bureau of Statistics (1999) *Labour Force Australia* (Cat No. 6203.0), Australian Government Publishing Service, Canberra.

Batt, C. (2001) Still no room at the top, *The Age*, 3 February, 2001, p. 4.1

Burke, R. (1996) "Why aren't more women on corporate boards? Views of women directors," *Psychological Reports*, Vol. 81 No. 3 (Part 1), pp. 812-814.

Burke, R. (1997) "Women on corporate boards of directors: A needed resource," *Journal of Business Ethics*, Vol. 16, pp. 909-915.

Collingwood, H. (1996) "Party of one: Women in the boardroom," *Working Woman*, Vol. 21 No. 2, p. 16.

Collinson, D. and Hearn, J. (1996) "Men at 'work': multiple masculinities/multiple workplaces," in Mac and Ghaill, M. (ed.) *Understanding Masculinities, Social Relations and Cultural Arenas*, Open University Press: Buckingham.

Connell, R. W. (1995) *Masculinities*, Polity Press, Oxford.

Conger, J., Lawler, E. and Finegold, D. (2001) *Corporate Boards, Strategies for Adding Value at the Top*, Jossey-Bass, San Francisco.

Edley, N. and Wetherell, M. (1996) "Masculinity, power and identity," in Mac an Ghaill, M. (ed.) *Understanding Masculinities, Social Relations and Cultural Arenas*, Open University Press: Buckingham.

Kirton, G. and Greene, A-M. (2000) *The Dynamics of Managing Diversity: A Critical Approach*, Butterworth Heinemann: Oxford.

Liff, S. and Wajcman, S. (1996) "'Sameness' and 'difference' revisited: which way forward for equal opportunity initiatives?" *Journal of Management Studies*, 33(1), pp. 79-94.

Maier, M. (1999) "On the gendered substructure of organization: Dimensions and dilemmas of corporate masculinity," in Powell, G. (ed.) *Handbook of Gender and Work*, Sage Publications, Thousand Oaks.

Martin, P.Y. (1996) "Gendering and evaluating dynamics: Men, masculinities and management," in Collinson, D. and Hearn, J. (eds.) *Men as Managers, Managers as Men, Critical Perspectives on Men, Masculinities and Managements*, Sage Publications, London.

Miller, D. (1991) Handbook of Research Design and Social Measurement, Sage, London.

Patrickson, M. and Bamber, G. (1995) "Introduction," in Patrickson, M., Bamber, V. and Bamber, G. (eds.) *Organisational Change Strategies, Case Studies of Human Resource and Industrial Relations Issues*, Longman, Australia, Melbourne.

Sexton, E. (2002) "When blame is the name of the game," *Sydney Morning Herald*, 30 March.

Sheridan, A. (2001) "A view from the top: Women on the boards of public companies," Corporate Governance, 1, 1, pp. 8-14.

Shotter, J. (1993) *The Cultural Politics of Everyday Life*, Open University press: Milton Keynes.

Talmud, I. and Izraeli, D. (1999) "The relationship between gender and performance issues of concern to directors: correlates or institution?", *Journal of Organizational Behavior*, Vol. 20, No. 4, pp. 459-474.

Walsh, P. (2001) Few women break the glass ceiling, The Courier Mail, 16 January, p. 23.

Note

1. The authors thank Professor Ronald Burke, York University, Canada for permission to use his survey in Australia.

Chapter Sixteen

Can Professors Learn in the Classroom? Team Teaching Conflict Management Skills

DOROTHY M. CALI BALANCIO
DIANA D'AMICO JUETTNER
ARTHUR LERMAN

C an professors learn in the classroom? Collectively, with over 80 years of college teaching experience, our answer is an unequivocal yes. We, a sociologist, a political scientist and lawyer, set out to teach conflict management skills to college students using an interdisciplinary approach. The three of us were willing to be open and vulnerable to each other's ideas and teaching styles as we developed a program to team teach conflict management skills. We used traditional teaching methods as well as collaborative group learning. Our dialogue was often the catalyst for discussion and problem solving where one-dimensional topics became three-dimensional. Three professors would not only be lecturing but would be debriefing assignments and role-plays, participating in small groups with students, and commenting on student papers. We quickly discovered that we learned from our students as well as from each other as we modeled collaborative learning. We chose to use collaborative learning because it is an instructional approach that encourages students and faculty to work together to create knowledge.[1] Through our students' journals, we discovered that they learned more from our interaction with each other than from the textbooks, activities, lectures, classroom discussions and role-plays.

This chapter describes the use of an interdisciplinary, team-teaching, collaborative-learning approach to successfully communicate conflict management skills to each other and to our students. First, we will focus on our team's formation and then the development of the relationship. Next, we will discuss the team teaching aspects of our course and how it was successfully implemented. Finally, we will present our thoughts for the program and its future.

Formation of the Team

Three faculty members from law, political science/history and sociology, came together to discuss the needs and benefits of including conflict management skills in the curriculum. During our initial discussions, we discovered that each one of us was including various forms of conflict management in our courses and we were interested in teaching collaborative ways to handle conflict from an interdisciplinary perspective.[2]

Our sociologist included conflict management in her courses because of the brutal murder of her son days after his 21st birthday. She wanted to equip young people with the competencies to find a non-violent way to resolve conflict. Our political scientist included conflict management in his political science and history courses because history and political science are about finding democratic-peaceful ways to manage conflict and everyone's well being. Our legal studies professor included these skills to show students that the legal system provides varied forms of resolving conflict. An intricate litigation process isn't always the best approach.

Since our shared and complementary goals were one of the factors that brought us together, we decided to work together to provide a team-taught interdisciplinary course for our students. The formula for forming an effective collaborative team consists of four stages: choosing the team members, dividing the work, establishing guidelines of responsibility, and terminating the relationship.[3] Since we came together voluntarily, we fulfilled the first criterion. Next, we divided the work with each of us doing the part we enjoyed or had the skills to complete. Then, we slowly developed guidelines and continue to modify them after every course. Our guidelines are in continual negotiation in order to find ways to meet evolving individual needs. We have not reached the last step of terminating the relationship because we are still developing the curriculum for the program.

Development of the Relationship

Even though our disciplines are interrelated and conducive to integration, our teaching styles are quite different. Our next goal was to decide how to integrate our teaching-styles. Integrating our teaching styles became an initial priority.

Before our program began, only our attorney was committed to collaborative group learning. She was using all types of classroom techniques: lectures, discussions as well as project centered collaborative learning groups. She found that small collaborative groups were an important way to attract and hold student's interest, and that students who were reluctant to speak in the larger classroom environment would blossom and reveal talents that would have gone unnoticed unless they had been able to work in small groups.

At the outset, however, our political scientist felt that whole-class discussions were generally adequate for engaging students. Our sociologist used a wider variety of techniques such as: lecture, classroom discussion, and videos to motivate students. She was reluctant to use collaborative learning because she was concerned about the negative impact on students if they shared personal stories in the classroom. It was only after our political scientist and our sociologist began taking courses at International Center for

Cooperation and Conflict Resolution, Teachers College, Columbia University,[4] that both were inspired to bring collaborative learning into their classrooms.

All three professors were now not only convinced of the importance of collaborative learning, but they were convinced that, in terms of conflict management, it was essential. At this point, it became easier to integrate our teaching styles because conflict management training stressed the skills necessary for successful team teaching and collaborative learning. For example, the following guidelines for conflict management, listed by two leading scholars in the field, could easily be mistaken for collaborative learning guides:

> . . . Distinguish clearly between interests and positions [often a party in dispute insists on a position that does not effectively represent his or her underlying interests]. . .

> Explore your interests and other's interests to identify the common and compatible interests that you both share. . . .

> Define the conflicting interests between oneself and the other as a mutual problem to be solved cooperatively. . . .

> In communicating with the other, listen attentively and speak so as to be understood; this requires the active attempt to take the perspective of the other and to check continually one's success in doing so. . . .

> Be alert to the natural tendencies to bias—misperception, misjudgments, and stereotyped thinking—that commonly occur in oneself as well as the other during heated conflict.[5]

Conflict management skills became the framework for our entire team teaching relationship.[6]

Aspects of Team Teaching and Collaborative Learning

Goals

The program focused on clear measurable goals. We realized that poorly focused and unrealistic goals would lead to fuzzy results and failure. As time went on, we became better at setting forth our specific competency goals and providing workable plans to get there. In addition, we made sure the goals for each course were relevant to both our students and us.

As part of the goals, each student was required to submit a journal summary, participate in classroom activities, be part of a group project and produce a paper that evaluated how the group worked. The journal summary was to include reactions to classroom activities with relevant references from assigned readings to be handed in every three weeks. These journal summaries evolved into dialogue journals. Before the journal is submitted, another student in the class reviews it. The reviewer was instructed to critique it in the following way: 1. nothing negative should be said about the journal entries; 2. comment must end in a question; and 3. reviewer must date and sign the comment. The owner of the journal is encouraged to respond to the question(s) posed by the reviewer. The goal is to promote dialogue among students as well as between students and the instructors. Then, all journals are read by the instructors, and feedback is given throughout the course.

Classroom participation included participation in class discussion and role-play situations. The group project required each group to analyze a conflict of interest to the group. The group was to present its findings at the end of the semester in oral and written form. Finally, each student was required to write an analysis of the highlights of conflict and cooperation within his or her group.

One student, who has a dream of becoming a diplomat or foreign-service officer, reflected in her journal about the usefulness of two of the assignments.

> . . . (W)riting the journal papers was very helpful in organizing and reviewing what I learned from the class. The final group project was also helpful in making students learn how to cooperate and study as a group.[7]

Not all students were happy making and keeping a journal for the course. In fact, one student was so resistant that he called his assessment of the assignment, "Not my Journal, My Summary." In spite of the fact that he did not like journals and proceeded to tell us why, we discovered that his insight into the materials for the course was outstanding.[8] We found this feedback very helpful when evaluating the effectiveness of the assignments that were required.

Another goal was to evaluate the dynamics of three professors working in the classroom at the same time to teach conflict resolution skills. One of us would present an idea while the other two would expand and interject references from the readings and other supporting materials. Some students found this confusing while others found it challenging and stimulating. To keep information straight, one student kept notes by professor.[9] Another student reflected as follows:

> The things that stick mostly in my mind are the techniques I learned when the professors were negotiating in the classroom. I have copied these techniques and used them on my job . . . my job deals with the public and I have found that the skills I have learned have become increasingly helpful in many situations.[10]

For example, the course outline for the first semester delineated the parameters of the student's final group reports. However, in our enthusiasm, each professor was interpreting the written instructions differently. Upon noticing the confusion of our students, we were reminded of the conflict management literature's insistence on clarity, and discussed our own thoughts on the assignment and brought consensus to the class. This was a great way to illustrate the importance of being aware of the difference between "intent" and "impact." There were three very different interpretations of the instructions by the professors and more than fifteen different ways it impacted the class.

Strengths and Limitations of the Relationship

Each of our individual profiles of strengths and limitations were assessed to identify what needed improvement. Our sociologist contributes great energy and enthusiasm and has the ability to interject new ideas at the spur of the moment, even if it disrupted the planned lesson. Her enthusiasm and burning commitment, motivated by the loss of her son, provided the class with valuable unplanned interventions that inspired many students to bring non-violent conflict resolution into their own lives. One such example is expressed as follows:

> . . . I appreciate my professors' hard work and, specifically, the sharing a personal tragedy. This motivated me to realize that, even in a time of deep emotional pain, there are other ways to resolve conflict other than hating the wrong doer.[11]

Our political scientist is "low key," wanting to move forward in an orderly fashion; however, experience has taught him the wisdom of flexibility. Our lawyer shared most of this penchant for orderliness tempered by flexibility contributing great patience to the mix. This provided her with the opportunity to mediate the clashes that occurred from time to time by balancing our sociologist's spontaneity with the need to cover the required competencies by the end of the course.

Team Support

It was realized that team support was invaluable and we needed to further develop our collaborative-teaching skills. As our first course in conflict management progressed, we realized that change is slow as we slipped numerous times into our own methods of teaching. What we did not realize at the time was that this was not an unusual occurrence. Fortunately, we did not see this as a sign of defeat. From this we learned to encourage each other and help to prepare ourselves to challenge our students for the next semester by working through some of the rough spots in the course.

We realized that continued application of the team teaching approach required sustained practice in and out of the classroom. A single semester, a single course was a beginning, but not sufficient in itself. Unless an individual can relate his/her own personal goals to the conflict management program, then he/she would not be motivated. Effectiveness of our team required each one of us to believe why it was important to be collaborative. We lectured, debriefed assignments and role-plays, and commented on student papers. Agreeing on course requirements and student evaluation criteria became a major learning event for all of us.

After several semesters, we began to develop a comfortable relationship with each other that respected and validated our self worth personally and professionally. We learned to negotiate our differences. This became evident in our relationship with our students as well as with one another. A perfect illustration is when the 2001 Student Commencement Speaker highlighted how she learned practical ways to cope with life's challenges from her experiences with her fellow students and us in our basic conflict management course.[12]

Feedback

While we were aware that constructive feedback is necessary for effective teaching, we quickly learned that feedback relating to our team members' and students' strengths and weakness carries an emotional charge. Skilled feedback is motivating and stimulating. Inept feedback is upsetting. Understanding how emotions play a part in adult learning is as important a component as the "rationalist doctrine" that is used in most formal education efforts.[13] We were convinced that it was important for us to include emotional learning techniques in our teaching.

We incorporated the emotional intelligence competencies of self-awareness, self-regulation, motivation, empathy, and improving relationships into our teaching.[14] These emotional competencies came together through the development of our relationship in the classroom.

By sharpening our personal competency of self-awareness, we came to better recognize our emotions and their effects. By knowing our strengths and limitations, we were able to develop a sense of self-worth and to articulate our capabilities and help our students to develop theirs. The students' dialogue journals contributed to the self-awareness of our team by revealing those assignments that were working in the classroom.

We strengthened our personal competency of self-regulation, i.e., we improved our ability to keep disruptive emotions in check. This enabled us to develop trust in the relationship. We took responsibility for personal performance, adaptability and innovation. Our commitment to offering dispute resolutions courses was such a priority that we took them on as an addition to our regular teaching load.

Our personal competency of motivation was deepened. As we struggled toward our goal, the experience of striving and the tangible progress we experienced deepened our motivation to continue.

Our ability to handle relationships with the social competency of empathy was improved. We began to better sense each other's feelings and perspectives. We took an active interest in each other's and the students' needs and concerns. We actually developed a heightened ability to sense others' developing needs and to bolster their abilities. We were able to anticipate, recognize and meet their needs and cultivate their opportunities. The following is a student account of how this jointly taught conflict management training helped bolster her emotional intelligence competencies:

> I feel like I have increased my knowledge in so many different areas, but most importantly in the area of self-awareness. . . . Being able to understand others . . . will help to give me a better understanding of life. I have enjoyed this journey of learning, and I know that it has enjoyed me. Thanks. My group was astonishing. . . . I feel that we not only encouraged each other, I feel that we were able to form lasting friendships within the group.[15]

The final emotional competency had us improving relationships using social skills. We put into place effective tactics for persuasion, communication, conflict management, collaboration and team building. We succeeded in inspiring and guiding students and each other, leading to initiating and managing change. We also nurtured instrumental relationships and built bonds among ourselves, with other faculty and students. A pre-law student expressed his feelings about the course and how he incorporated conflict management skills in his life.

> I can better handle myself at times of disagreements and arguments, and I know that my fists aren't my only way to win an argument. I feel I have a basic understanding of conflict and the techniques to establish cooperation. . . . The negotiations were very cool because I got to see first hand how conflicts originate and conclude.[16]

We used the emotional intelligence competencies[17] to provide feedback to our students as well as each other. We were sensitive that our students were at different levels of readiness to receive the "critiqued" messages. We learned to assess for readiness, and if someone was not yet ready, readiness was made an initial focus. Because of our own experiences, we knew that feedback carries an emotional charge. However, our "ongoing performance feedback" encouraged and enhanced communication with our students. For example, our political scientist found himself slowing down the pace of the course to accommodate the sudden awakening of a very shy student by allowing him to discuss some points of importance to him even though it slowed the pace the faculty team had set for that day. The other members of the team quickly became aware of the unplanned pedagogical shift and supported him whole-heartedly. Emotional bonding continued as we interacted in the classroom, in our workshops for staff, students and faculty, in planning sessions for these activities, as well as in the skill development workshops, seminars and courses we attended.

Communications based on this feedback helped us design the direction of the new changes in the program as the semesters progressed. Our "progress reviews" were welcome from the students, the administrators as well as from each other. The Provost provided support by giving us the opportunity to develop the curricula for additional team taught courses.

Tailoring the Program

As we focused on goals, the relationship, team building and feedback, we continued to tailor the program meet our needs, circumstances, and motivations. We designed the specifics of our courses and program to fit within our respective disciplines as well as within our interdisciplinary courses. We relied on the conflict management guidelines set forth by Coleman and Deutsch,[18] and the emotional intelligence competencies, encapsulating them with the following precepts learned at the Harvard Negotiation Project.

> Separate the people from the problem;
> Focus on interests, not positions;
> Invent options for Mutual Gain; and
> Insist on using objective criteria.[19]

This student who is a native of Ghana, middle child of seven, mother, wife reflected on how she used these skills.

> . . . This course has made me become more open minded and understand more about problems that face the world today. Furthermore, it has given me a greater sense of maturity that has also helped me in dealing with my family issues. . . . I have learned to separate the people from their positions . . . and to focus on interests not positions. . . . We have worked together to create options that will satisfy both parties, and to negotiate successfully with different people.[20]

Development of Listening Skills

Since a key factor in resolving conflict is keen listening skills, we devoted a number of classes to developing listening skills. By developing our student's listening skills, we also sharpened our own. In our classes, we outlined the components of communication and the barriers to effective listening. We focused on listening, an active response versus hearing, a passive response. When someone listens effectively, he/she is able to reach a clearer understanding of the issue. Once there is a clear understanding, it enables the person to respond appropriately. To respond appropriately is to enhance communication.[21] One student expressed how he applied these skills in the workplace.

> The information, theories and techniques have not only helped me professionally, but also as an individual. I have noticed great improvement in my interactions with clients, supervisors, colleagues and family members. One area where I have been able to implement many of these techniques is in my role as union delegate. My success rate, in winning cases, for unfair suspensions and terminations, has increased tremendously, since the beginning of the course. Prior to taking this course, I was losing many cases because of poor mediation skills and my personal desire of always wanting to win every case regardless of how the parties felt at the end. . . . I attribute my success rate to a new way and style. . . . This new style allows me to take the focus off the people's position and refocus on the underlying interests of the parties. I now look at many things from different perspectives. It helped me to learn how to listen and to listen to learn. . . . I understand and better relate with individuals.[22]

Modeling Collaborative Learning

Models for the behavior, we were teaching, were provided by our guidelines for conflict management, our emotional competencies and the Harvard Negotiation Project precepts. These were not simply taught as abstract concepts, but were embodied in our own behavior. We became living models of the behavior, we wanted the students to emulate. We promoted professional disagreement and conflicting viewpoints by taking opposing views on subjects. We encouraged our students to voice a logical opposition to our position as well as encouraging them to try new things. Our students became critics of our teaching techniques as well as the course literature. We organized role-plays from which students learned to respect their positions and confidently articulate their points of view. A very shy student noted that

> I haven't ever been very good in dealing with conflicts with other people. I'm always shy, therefore, I never state my opinions and I keep them inside. . . . As the course went on, I felt that I was getting better at speaking my opinions, and backing up my thoughts and ideas. I felt that it was a lot easier to discuss my points when I had a plan right there in front of me. It was easier that way because I knew what I was supposed to be arguing for and I had the goal that I had to meet. Also, I think that it was easier for me to do it in class because I knew that the people who were against me were just following their preparation sheets too.[23]

Future of the Program

A human resource management supervisor summarized her experience in our conflict management course as follows:

I have spent many years in Human Resource Management and I can attest that 90% of my department's job consists of resolving conflicts. Conflicts between employees and the company, conflicts between managers and subordinates, conflicts between co-workers, conflicts between departments, conflicts between owners and principals of the company—the list is just endless. Although I have participated in numerous seminars relating to my profession, I have never received any education on the topic of conflict resolution. . . . I feel that theories I have studied and the actual experience I have had with classroom role-play have made me better able to work effectively in the future toward the peaceful resolution of personal and professional conflicts. I feel the group project drove home to me the need to work together to achieve a common goal even if the members of the group come into the group with dissimilar goals, values and ideas.[24]

The program being developed at Mercy College in Conflict Management has provided significant pedagogical results as well as student acceptance. Even though we have been working at this project for about 3 1/2 years, we continue to have extensive enthusiasm to develop and extend the program. Our goal is to offer our basic course, Managing Human Conflict, at all of our campuses and extension centers and launch a graduate program in Behavioral Studies with a Specialization in Conflict Management. This fall, classes in conflict management will be offered at the undergraduate and graduate levels. We have peaked the interest of our colleagues in the other disciplines so that courses evaluating conflict in Shakespearean literature and art history are being contemplated for future offerings.

Fortunately, for the future of the program, we have the support of the chairs of the Social and Behavioral Sciences and Civic and Cultural Studies Divisions, the Provost and the President. The administration's support includes flexible scheduling permitting us to teach together and financial support for the development of our conflict management skills. Without real support from the administration, the program's long-term efforts will not be successful. We are encouraged that the administration recognizes that our goals and objectives fit within the college's mission. A contributing factor for this support is based on a survey that was sent to the business community and municipal officials asking for the issues effecting workplace productivity. The number one issue reported was conflict management. Our courses have been developed to provide our students with the fundamental conflict management skills necessary to be productive in the workplace and in their daily lives. We learned from our training, our students and each other that this is a program in progress—always evolving.

Notes

1. Stage, F., P. Muller, & J. Kinzie, 1998. "Creative learning centered classrooms: what does learning theory have to say?" *ASHE-ERIC Higher Education Report v. 26,* No. 4, p. 37, Washington, D.C.: The George Washington University, School of Education and Human Development.
2. Austin, A., R. Baldwin, 1991. "Faculty Collaboration: Enhancing the Quality of Scholarship and Teaching," *ASHE-ERIC Higher Education Report No. 7,* p. 6,

Washington, D.C.: The George Washington University, School of Education and Human Development.
3. Id at iv.
4. The International Center for Cooperation and Conflict Resolution at Teachers College, Columbia University, New York, New York is one of the programs where our political scientist and sociologist were trained.
5. Coleman, P. & M. Deutsch, "Introducing cooperation in conflict resolution into schools: a systems approach," as part of a book edited by D. Christie, R.V. Wagner & D. Winter, *Peace Conflict and Violence: Peace Psychology for the 21st Century*, Upper Saddle River: New Jersey, Prentice Hall, 2001, pp. 230-231.
6. Members of our team have also trained at Cornell University's School of Labor Relations, New York University's School Law, Marywood University's Conflict Resolution Resource Center, Strauss Institute for Dispute Resolution at Pepperdine University School of Law.
7. Excerpt from student #1's journal, Fall 2002 program.
8. Excerpt from student #2's journal, Fall 2001.
9. Student #3's journal submitted in the stated format, Spring 1999.
10. Excerpt from student # 4's journal, used the skills at his workplace, Spring, 2002
11. Excerpt from student #5's journal (nurse, wife, mother of three) Spring, 2002.
12. 2001 Commencement Speaker, student #6, Spring 2001.
13. Dirkx, John M. "The Power of Feelings: Emotions, Imagination, and the Construction of Meaning in Adult Learning, *New Directions for Adult and Continuing Education*, No. 89, Spring 2001, Jossey-Bass, A Publishing Unit of John Wiley & Sons, Inc., pp. 63-4.
14. Goleman, Daniel. *Emotional Intelligence*. NY: Bantam Books, pp edition-1997. Particularly "Part Five: chapter 15. 'The Cost of Emotional Literacy' and chapter 16. 'Schooling the Emotions,'" Goleman, Daniel. *Working with Emotional Intelligence*. NY: Bantam Books, 1998. (Particularly chapter four: "A New Model for Learning")
15. Excerpt from student #7's journal, Spring, 2002.
16. Excerpt from student #8's journal, Spring, 2002.
17. *See* note 13.
18. *See* note 5.
19. Fisher, R. & W. Ury. *Getting to Yes*, Penguin Books, 1991, pp. 17, 40, 56, 81. These principles were expanded upon in an intense program taken by our attorney and sociologist at the Harvard Negotiation Project, Harvard Law School, Cambridge, Massachusetts.
20. Excerpt from student #9's journal, Spring, 2002.
21. Brown, Hezekiah, Workshop Handouts, Dispute Resolution Certificate Program, Labor-Management Program, New York State School of Industrial and Labor Relations, Cornell University, New York City, April 1999.
22. Excerpt from student #10's journal, pre-law student, substance abuse counselor, former police officer, elected community leader, Spring 2002.
23. Excerpt from student #11's journal, Spring 2002.
24. Excerpt from student #12's journal, Fall 2001.

Chapter Seventeen

Building Strategic Technology Alliances for Teaching and Learning

Ronald Black

Introduction

Higher Education exists as a community of scholars dedicated to the creation and dissemination of knowledge and the preparation of future leaders in a global society. For many students there are significant barriers to full participation in this teaching and learning experience. Technology is intended to break down the barriers of time and space and enable more of our students to participate and collaborate with faculty and other students. Certain critical thresholds must be met in order to use technology to communicate, collaborate, and transform teaching and learning. Technology will not replace faculty or the hard work that teaching and learning requires. We must use technology to expand teaching and learning options. Technology can help the learner to get connected to information and learning communities; expand participation in the teaching and learning process; improve access to learning materials, experts, and peers; and provide new channels for active learning. These new teaching and learning options will require a substantial investment in ongoing faculty development and technology enhancement.

Technology by itself does not improve or cause changes in learning. Online learning environments have many capabilities and the potential to widen options and opportunities available to teachers and learners. The key to changing conditions for improving learning is how these options and opportunities are implemented. The value of technology for higher education is proportional to the need for that technology to impact on educational objectives. The current use of technology involves the restructuring and the re-development of new teaching and learning models that match the unique capabilities and features of the technology media. To carry out this complex paradigm shift and address higher education's challenges we must develop effective partnerships and collaborative efforts internally and externally.

There is a major need for most colleges and universities to confront the intense local and national competition, to enhance academic programs to meet the challenges of this competition, and to develop new teaching and learning strategies to meet the demands of a global marketplace. A report prepared by the Business-Higher Education Forum at the American Council on Education suggests that competitiveness in the global market has resulted in an increase in higher education and business alliances. As cited by Rosemary Gonzales in the online document concerning higher education and business partnerships (1999), "the main motivation to develop strategic alliances and partnerships varies according to the needs of both organizations involved. However, there do appear to be common factors that prompt the creation of alliances. These factors include workforce development, financial benefits, sharing experts, political gain and prestige" (p. 2).

A primary factor contributing to higher education's enrollment paradigm is that traditional teacher-centered pedagogy and curricula no longer meet current and future student expectations. Students who enroll in colleges today have completed courses using multiple technologies including video conferencing, personal computers and on-line learning tools in high school. Many of the high schools and colleges that they have attended have extensive technology infrastructures and include technology throughout their curriculum. These students expect technology to be an integral part of the curriculum. The limited use of applied technology in the curriculum has created differences of opinions between faculty and students concerning course delivery.

Each partner bases strategic technology alliances upon a strong commitment to mutual decision-making, investment, risk, and reward. The relationship includes executive level participation, shared technology resources, and the development and implementation of mutually beneficial and innovative academic programs. Colleges must take advantage of the geographic reach and functional capabilities of today's most sophisticated, interactive technologies including the Internet, multimedia, and electronic courseware applications. Alliance projects must focus on the learning environment, enabling the college to design, develop, deliver, and manage distributed learning in a way that complements rather than competes with traditional curriculum.

Vendor Branding

As geography becomes less and less important, the way colleges and universities will compete may be determined by brands that will add values or belief systems to educational programs to permit institutions to carve out a niche in their market. There are some indicators that the market for education will become increasingly branded. Branding may be a key tool in the institutional arsenal to gain competitive advantage (Riley, 1998, p. 13). At many colleges, this branding approach may include an executive level master of business administration degree program (EMBA). This dynamic technology-based EMBA can be taught at the vendor's location throughout the world. The executive MBA will reflect the collaborative relationship between business and academia. The curriculum's focus is designed to help mid-level executives build valuable skills that will enable them to leverage the academic material generated, analyzed, and distributed via technology. With this focus the student will gain valuable experiences that will empower them to advance the goals of their organization and advance their career. Each course in the EMBA will contain online courseware projects, electronic bulletin boards, E-mail and on-line chat in addition to lecture based classes and leadership seminars. The courses will be team-taught using the college's faculty and vendor professionals and executives. In addition, a speaker series made up of senior executives from leading technology vendors will participate in a monthly speaker series. This session will be in the form of a dinner business meeting on the evening before allowing a forum for questions and answers between the speaker and the student. All of the courses will use e-business strategies as the basis for instruction. The diagram below indicates the three-pronged approach to the EMBA, including student-centered instruction, executive leadership series, and Internet learning applications.

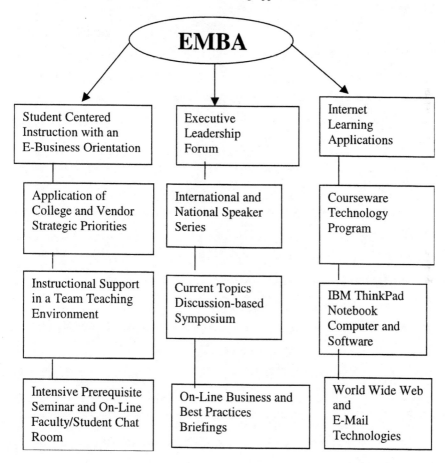

There is a dangerous mismatch between what today's student needs from higher education and what it is receiving. This disparity has led colleges and universities to evaluate and develop partnerships to ensure their ability to compete in a global economy. Many colleges have as a strategy to embark on a program to maximize the advances in information related technology to enhance operations, decision making, and instruction and to build bridges with government, business, and other educational institutions, nationally and internationally, that adds perspective and breadth to their programs, maximize resource utilization, and enhance the reputation and exposure of our institution.

Jose-Marie Griffiths, Chief Information Officer at the University of Michigan wrote in a recent article in IBM's higher education quarterly magazine called Multiversity, "The global information revolution, including an integral relationship with and dependence on technology, is propelling organizations to develop new models of partnership." He goes on to state: "The initial models consisted of little more than handouts, gifts, given and then left to the recipients to use as they saw fit" (1999, p. 15).

As stated earlier, colleges exist as a community of scholars dedicated to the creation and dissemination of knowledge and the preparation of future leaders in a global society. Colleges have recognized that for many of its students there are significant barriers to full participation in this community. The changing demographics are placing new demands on the college. Students are more diverse. In addition to ethnicity as a sign of diversity, students are older, balancing life and career priorities, and prefer to attend the college on a part-time basis. Students are being more selective about which institutions they attend. They expect to participate in a learning environment that fosters measurable improvement in their skill development. Dolence and Norris write: "Today's learners are becoming increasing impatient, their dealing with world-class service providers in other settings have conditioned them to expect just-in-time services" (p. 11). Technology is intended to break down the barriers of time and space and enable more students to participate in the college experience. However, certain critical thresholds must be met in order to use technology to communicate, collaborate, and transform teaching and learning to meet the diverse needs of the current and future student.

At many colleges today the use of technology is very limited in liberal arts and other academic programs. The tenth national survey of desktop computing and information technology in higher education revealed that more college courses are making greater use of technology as an instructional resource (Green, 1999). The Campus Computing Survey is the largest continuing study of the use of information technology in American higher education. The 1999 study was conducted during the summer, 1999. The survey focuses primarily on the use of computing and information technology resources to support and enhance instruction and scholarship. The survey respondents were typically chief academic computing or information technology officers at their institutions.

The study reported that assisting faculty efforts to integrate information technology into instruction remains the single most important information technology issue confronting colleges and universities over the next two or three years. Two-fifths (39 %) of the 530 two and four year colleges and universities participating in the survey identify "instructional integration" as their single most significant technology challenge. This is up from 33.2 % in 1998 and 29.6 % in 1997. In order to meet these demands significant human resources will be needed to provide the training, development and support of instructional technologies. College administrators have only realized recently that major technology challenges involve human factors that include assisting students and faculty in their efforts to utilize new technologies in ways that will support teaching and learning, instruction and scholarship.

The 1999 survey data suggest that despite some dire predictions on both sides of the issue, the real future of technology in higher education is not about a winner take all competition between high-tech and high-touch. Rather, the survey data suggest that what lies ahead for most students and faculty is some kind of hybrid learning experience in which technology supplements, both the content and discourse that have been part of the traditional experience of going to college (p. 4).

The survey indicated that the percentage of classes using e-mail jumped by a fourth this year to 53.4 % compared to 44 % in 1998 and just 8 % in 1994. As a matter of fact, Nova Southeastern University pioneered the use of e-mail for instruction in the early 1980s through its patented electronic classroom technology. This software called ECR was developed by Nova and used in their distance learning courses in the School of Business, School of Computer Science and School of Education throughout the 1980s and 90s. ECR was the first to pioneer chat room strategy where the instructor and student could ask each other questions.

Table 1
Percentage of College Courses Using E-mail, by Sector from 1994 to 1999

College and University Sector	1994	1995	1996	1997	1998	1999
All Institutions	8	20	24	32	44	53
Public Universities	10	30	32	48	55	62
Private Universities	14	32	48	59	60	61
Public 4-Year Colleges	12	28	32	39	48	54
Private 4-Year Colleges	10	22	29	34	50	59

Note. Percentages have been rounded to the next highest number. From "The Tenth Survey of Computing and Information Technology in Higher Education," by Kenneth C. Green, 1999

Similarly, but not surprising, the percentage of college courses with World Wide Web pages has also increased dramatically in recent years. As shown in table 2 below, more than one-fourth (27.8 %) of college classes now have individual web pages, up from 22.5 % in 1998 and just 6.2 % in 1995. As with e-mail, the actual numbers of classes with Web pages vary by sector, highest in private universities and lowest in community colleges. These differences notwithstanding, the data also document significant gains across all types of institutions since 1995. The survey also indicated that three-fifths of the faculty makes daily use of the Web.

Table 2
Percentage of College Courses with Web Pages by Sector from 1995 to 1999

College and University Sector	1995	1996	1997	1998	1999
All Institutions	6.2	10	12	22.5	27.8
Public Universities	10	12	17	32	34
Private Universities	8	17	27	33	34
Public 4-Year Colleges	10	12	18	25	28
Private 4-Year Colleges	5	10	15	23	28

Note. Percentages have been rounded to the next highest number. From "The Tenth Survey of Computing and Information Technology in Higher Education," by Kenneth C. Green, 1999.

However, these fairly common uses of technology in the classroom still do not capitalize on the real power of technology to make available real-world situations, aid visualization, facilitate learning communities, support collaborative thinking, or provide continual feedback to the student. Internet-based virtual learning centers will create new ways of teaching in which exchanges among students are as important as the exchange with the teacher. Just as corporate employees will learn to work in more collaborative ways, so instruction in many cases will take on a teamwork approach. (Martin, 1999, p. 233).

Alliances between higher education and business have occurred for decades, mostly in the research and development area. Sean Rush, an executive in IBM's higher education division predicted in a speech that, "strategic alliances would be essential for higher education in order to compete in a global marketplace" (1999). Strategic alliances are a logical and timely response to intense and rapid changes in economic activity, technology, and globalization, all of which have cast many corporations into two competitive races; one for the world and the other for the future (Doz & Hamel, 1998). At the 81st annual meeting of the American Council of Education, Elson Floyd, president of Western Michigan University stated, "Universities and private industries must form strong collaborative relationships and we must strengthen our college curricula to meet the workforce needs of businesses and corporations" (1999).

The recognized leader of technology throughout the world is IBM. During the first half of the twentieth century, under the leadership of Thomas J. Watson, Sr., IBM grew into a major corporate power, creating and building new markets for accounting machinery. Thomas J. Watson, Jr. assumed the presidency in 1952 and built on his father's success. The younger Watson ushered IBM into the age of computers, leading the company to a position of dominance unmatched in business history (McKenna, 1989).

IBM began its formal relationship with higher education 50 years ago when Nicholas Murray Butler, president of Columbia University and Thomas J. Watson, Jr., President of IBM, jointly announced the formation of the Watson Scientific Computing Laboratory at Columbia University (Pugh, 1994, pp. 127-129). Throughout the years IBM has provided significant support to higher education through investments, research grants, curriculum, software tools, and consulting services.

Brands, Partnerships and Alliances

Specific projects in strategic technology alliances can be based upon the marketing value and emotional loyalty of the vendor's brand. Vendors have spent billions of dollars creating positive feelings toward its brand, both in the form of advertising and in skillfully designed products and services. Throughout the years, technology vendors have created banner brands that have added value to the products and services that its loyal customers continue to purchase. The attributes of a banner brand that determines its impact on buyer predisposition include (a) recognition, the level of brand awareness; (b) reputation, the confidence one has that a product bearing a particular brand will live up to the producer's claims; (c) affinity, the extent to which the brand is an integral part of the customer's sense of self; and (d) domain, the breadth of the brand's potential catchment's area in terms of plausible product scope. Multiplied together, recognition, reputation, affinity, and domain determine a brand's share of mind (Hamel & Prahalad, 1994). The stretching of the technology vendor's brand to academic programs is expected to communicate a universal message about product integrity and quality, based upon the recognition that the vendor and the college have formed a strong strategic technology alliance.

The strategic technology alliance establishes a partnership between technology vendors and colleges that will pool each organization's resources and cut costs through the sharing of those resources such as training, consulting and providing joint educational opportunities. In an article on partnerships in Business Week's Frontier magazine J. Trent Williams, a principal at Regional Technology Strategies, Inc., a Chapel Hill, NC based research firm that advises companies and local governments on how to set up partnerships states, "These days, you need to be too good at too many things to do it yourself." The article also reports that on national level almost one out of five businesses has used strategic alliances as a way to expand. The results of a PricewaterhouseCoopers survey of 436 chief executive officers showed that 43% of the companies that launched breakthrough services and products did so with outside collaboration (Fromartz, 1999, p. 2).

James W. Cortada defines partnerships in a Multiversity article as "a legal relationship between two or more persons contractually associated as joint principals in a business." He goes on to state "partnerships invariably reflect a sincere commitment to the success of the partners. This is reflected in personal and emotional involvement and the allocation of sufficient resources by all parties" (1998, p. 2). The point is that partnerships and alliances are agreements in which there is equality of expectations, investments of time, funding, and commitment to make them work.

Francis Hesselbein, president and CEO of the Peter F. Drucker Foundation for Nonprofit Management states: "The day of the partnership is upon us. Leaders who learn to work with other corporations, government agencies, and social sector organizations will find new energy, new impact, and new significance in their organization's work (Beckhard, Goldsmith & Hesselbein, 1997, p. 83)." Partnering will belong to those institutions that are comfortable and competent in building long-term relationships. When they are effective in building long-term partnerships, we create competitive immunity. Competitive immunity means having such a powerful relationship with each other at all the connecting points that the relationship and the institution are immune from its competition (Wilson, 1994). Often long-term alliances allow companies insight into competencies that are deeply buried within the fabric of a partner.

Thompson, the French consumer electronics firm, learned much from JVC, its partner in VCR production, about the subtle interplay of hard technology and process improvement skills that combine to produce a world-class manufacturing competence. When the relationship began, Thompson knew next to nothing about how to make a VCR. Five or so years later Thompson was able to start production of VCR's in Singapore, more or less free of JVC's help (Hamel & Prahalad, 1994).

Businesses are witnessing an explosion in alliance activity, driven by combined forces of rapid technological innovation, globalization, intensifying competition and the blurring of industry lines. In the past two years, more than 20,000 alliances have been formed worldwide. (Harbison & Pekar, 1998). Powerful forces are driving the formation of strategic alliances between firms in the world economy. The movement toward globalization has opened many new opportunities to companies, triggering a desperate race for the future by major global suppliers of everything from credit cards to telecommunications. These features make alliances essential (Doz & Hamel, 1998).

On the Alliance Analyst web page dated December 6, 1999, titled, Peter Drucker, Nonprofit Prophet, the author explains that alliances and nonprofits are a convergence of interests for Peter Drucker, the eighty-something father of management theory and inventor of such concepts as empowerment, knowledge workers, and the flat organization. In 1993, he argued, "Today, businesses grow through alliances, all sorts of dangerous liaisons and joint ventures, which, by the way, very few people understand." In 1998, he added, "The greatest change in corporate culture, and in the way business is being conducted, may be the accelerating growth of relationships based not on ownership but on partnership, joint ventures, minority investments cementing a joint marketing agreement or an agreement to do joint research; semi-formal alliances of all sorts." During November 1999, Drucker devoted his annual conference to alliances. In his opening remarks, he called alliances "the central tenet for survival of the sector." He urged nonprofits to make alliances the bottom timber of their strategies and use partnerships with the private sector as sources of revenue (1999, p. 1).

The establishment of partnerships between government, business, and learning institutions appears fundamental to the development of technology in support of life-long learning. The public and private sector partnerships provide the synergy required to develop innovative, large-scale technical solutions and innovations in their use in the academic arena. Clearly, the development and growth of partnerships in education and learning will benefit the development of effective systems and break down the artificial barriers between disciplines (Lee, 1997). Colleges are placing greater emphasis on developing partnerships with business and industry and conducting contract training through continuing education and shadow colleges. These initiatives are usually long-term, self-supporting and free of bureaucratic red tape. College leaders have also used economic development projects, particularly those that are developed in partnership with area businesses, to enhance the institutions image and utility (Honeyman, Wattenbarger & Westbrook, 1996)

Strategic Alliances in Higher Education

Higher education is currently faced with the challenge to connect people of all ages to the learning process in new and different ways. Employers are seeking new ways to train their employees with the assistance of colleges and universities. Alliances can meet both of these needs. Alliances and partnerships are based on resource sharing. It is difficult for colleges and universities to keep pace with rapidly changing technologies and new expectations in the workplace.

Alliances between higher education and business and industry have occurred for decades, mostly in the research and development area. The types of partnerships established between business and industry and higher education institutions vary greatly depending on the needs of the parties involved. For example, partnerships included fairly standard alliances for contract training, research initiatives, and cooperative education. On the other hand, very unusual alliances were created to build athletic facilities and entertainment complexes; indeed, creativity and need appear to be the only limitation to the type of partnership developed (Gonzales, 1999, p. 1).

A model for strategic technology alliances in higher education is outlined in the book titled, "Reinventing higher education" edited by Diane Oblinger and Richard Katz in a chapter written by J. C. Henderson and M. R. Subramani titled, "The shifting ground between markets and hierarchy: managing a portfolio of relationships" (1999, p

114). The eight step model for college and university relationships with industry includes (a) focus, (b) leverage, (c) capability development, (d) planning horizon, (e) accountability, (f) information behavior, (g) information mechanisms, and (h) risk management. The strategy behind the model is to identify and include management procedures that involve both organizations in the process of alliance development and implementation. Involvement by personnel from each organization serves to develop a better alliance and often ensures a "buy-in" from everyone involved in the outcomes.

Strategic alliances and partnerships in higher education consist of many different initiatives. The American Council of Education Network (ACEnet) highlights a number of partnerships and alliances on their Business-Higher Education Forum web pages.

Table 3
Comparisons of Two Business/Higher Education Partnerships

	Purdue University and Caterpillar	University of Massachusetts and GE
Purpose	Purdue and Caterpillar have signed a master agreement that is the basis of the partnership.	UMass and GE signed a partnership agreement to further the educational, outreach, and research objectives.
Type of Partnership	student internships, recruitment, faculty/business collaboration.	Corporate college articulation agreements, distance learning courses, student/employee recruitment.
Description	Caterpillar wants access to leading Edge research and researchers.	The GE/UMass partnership encompasses research, education, service, and task-oriented projects.

Source. American Council of Education.

The table above compares the purpose, type and description of strategic partnerships in place between Purdue University and Caterpillar; and the University of Massachusetts and General Electric. This table indicates the significant differences that can exist between business and higher education partnerships and alliances. The Caterpillar/Purdue partnership focuses on research and faculty involvement as compared to the GE/UMass partnership that focuses on academics, training, and recruitment (American Council on Education, 1999). The research has shown that no two partnerships or strategic alliances are alike. The main lesson learned by comparing these partnerships and alliances is that traditional colleges and universities are going to have to listen and work together with those companies that employ their students or the companies will become higher education's greatest new competitors. Developing academic programs collaboratively strengthens the strategic technology alliance insuring that each organization will not become competitors.

Some critics are warning that there is a failure of higher education to prepare students for jobs of the 21st century. Even employees already in the workforce do not have the right skills for corporate needs of the future and nothing is being done to teach them. Because of the constantly changing job skills needed in our high-tech society, most college graduates will not be able to compete adequately by the year 2000 (Vella, 1995). A significant question that must be asked is whether or not alliances between higher education and business and industry will force shifts in the relationship to address the skill failure. The question is even more complex by the fact that higher education, having become increasingly dependent on federal and state government aid, are now battered by government regulations and declining enrollments among youth (Fetter, 1995). In the face of declining resources, institutions are turning toward corporations in search of sympathy, political allies, and new resources to enhance enrollments, perhaps without thinking through the consequences of these alliances. Colleges and universities seeking a competitive advantage are forming substantive alliances with the business community in this new competitive environment. Strategic partnerships and structural alliances are replacing the more formal goal of collaboration and cooperation. This is especially advantageous for those seeking a foothold in the burgeoning adult-learning marketplace.

Technology Transformation in Higher Education

According to a study released by KPMG, LLP (1999), one of the leading professional advisory firms in the world, titled "Transforming Higher Education: At the Gateway of the Knowledge Economy," higher education must transform to meet the needs of the emerging knowledge economy. The study analyzes trends and provides a perspective on how colleges and universities can operate in the new century. According to the study, the changes facing higher education are, (a) an increasing diverse student body, in terms of age, race, gender, work, background, needs and interests; (b) students who are no longer mastering bodies of knowledge for a single career are acquiring the skills needed to access information, solve problems, and communicate; (c) students who are less likely to be learning at the workplace, home, or on the road; and (d) students, parents, employers, and policymakers are increasingly evaluating education in terms of a return on investment. Higher education will see revolutionary changes in the next decade, the study states, requiring institutions to reassess market position, and embark in new directions. Universities are often at the leading edge in the use of technology for research. Academics have been slower to apply leading technology in the classroom, and slower still to apply it to the administrative side of the institution. The challenge of the future is to explore and use the power of technology in teaching students and running the operation.

The Internet is fundamentally changing relationships, blurring the lines between buyers and sellers, competitors and partners, employers and employees, and teachers and students. It is a new economic order, based on a new currency called knowledge, which fundamentally changes the playing field. The result is new rules of competition, with new requirements for workers, new challenges for management, and new demands for higher education. The figure below reflects the changing rules of competition as they relate to jobs, education, and success.

Although these observations have greater acceptance today, the world is just beginning to experience their impact. The integration of technology into a world economy is changing the rules that have guided us through the industrial age, creating a very different environment. For higher education the challenge is to prepare people to adapt to this ever-changing environment (KPMG, 1999).

The debates are growing more intense about higher education's ability to respond to the needs of the knowledge economy. Consultants Michael G. Dolence and Donald M. Norris estimate that a new campus would have to be opened every eight days in order to meet the demands of the full-time equivalent enrollment of one-seventh of the workforce at any point in time. The solution they see will not be more college campuses

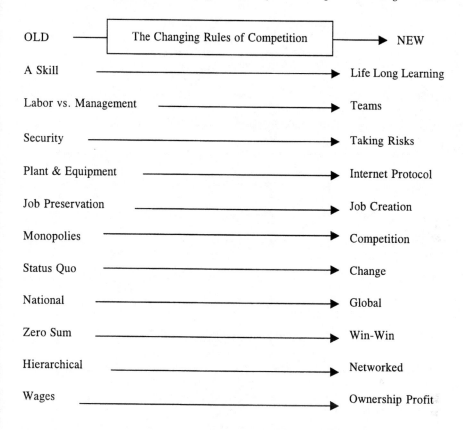

OLD	The Changing Rules of Competition	NEW
A Skill		Life Long Learning
Labor vs. Management		Teams
Security		Taking Risks
Plant & Equipment		Internet Protocol
Job Preservation		Job Creation
Monopolies		Competition
Status Quo		Change
National		Global
Zero Sum		Win-Win
Hierarchical		Networked
Wages		Ownership Profit

but a variety of providers and new types of facilitators, learning agents, and intermediaries with far greater competition and choice (1995). They continue to stress the transformation from teacher-centered strategies to learner-centered strategies. Learner-centered strategies are built around learner objectives, accommodate learner restraints, are self-paced and self-motivated, and provide for individual learning styles.

Massey and Zemsky cite a similar challenge for higher education (1995). They observe that the demand for technology-based teaching and learning programs will grow over the next decade as an economical means of providing continuous education, and that information technology will change the teaching enterprise. Jane Marcus of Stanford University discusses the development of conceptual models based upon factors affecting faculty adoption of technology as part of an article by Steven Gilbert in Change Magazine (1995). In her model, technology adoption is considered a function of available resources, the perceived value of the innovation, and communication with other early adopters. Her research provides evidence in support of the model, indicating that social/contextual variables are as important as resources in encouraging adoption of technology.

A significant technology transformation in higher education is the methodology used to help students get the education they need to remain competitive in a rapidly changing world. The transformation of teaching and learning and the creation of learning communities will be driven by the rapid change of skill sets required, the cost of education and training, and the explosion of adult learners. In the future, there will be a blurring of the lines between the 18-21 year old student to an adult population that will be pursuing degrees in non-traditional ways, seeking professional certification or getting training to improve job skills. These students need greater flexibility if they are to be able to handle their course work while working.

Net-based virtual learning centers have created new ways of teaching in which exchanges among students are as important as the exchange with the teacher. The best way to teach adults online is to form learning communities, to get students working together in collaborative groups. This capitalizes on the strength of technology (Martin, 1998). Using technology for teaching and learning is an adventure with unpredictable outcomes. What we can predict with certainty, however, is the fascination that technology holds and the fact that its mastery will be indispensable for productive and fulfilling lives in the twenty-first century (McKeachie, 1994).

Sean Rush and Diana Oblinger from IBM provide answers to the question, "How can we transform our students, ourselves, and our institutions? The answer is embedded in the philosophy of a future compatible campus. That is, (a) we must redefine learning, (b) we should expand our options with technology, (c) our institutions must be learning centered, (d) we must renew administration, and (e) we need to leverage partnerships" (Oblinger & Rush, 1998).

IBM's Role in Higher Education

IBM has a strong history of and commitment to improving education throughout the world. They believe that no organization can succeed in an unsuccessful community and no community can be successful without an educated population. Throughout the years, IBM has provided significant support to higher education. For example, in the 1980s, IBM supported the Advanced Education Projects. In phase 1, they invested $175 million and worked with 19 colleges and universities to develop instructional and research materials to help establish an advanced educational computing environment. The result was more than 3,300 curriculum development projects, spanning the full range of disciplines, from liberal arts to engineering. In phase 2, IBM made the software available to everyone in higher education.

In an article written in the IBM Research Magazine, Joe Sehee of IBM's Research Division explains that the division began staging monthly "jam sessions" as a way to foster breakthrough thought, and setting the stage for future technological innovation. Typically involving 8 to 25 people, and lasting from one hour to a full day, these sessions provide participants with a scenario to ponder. The idea is to generate insights that might not surface through more traditional problem solving. On July 7, 1998 they hosted their biggest session when they brought together 700 students with 200 researchers in each of its eight labs around the world for eight hours of brainstorming. The session was dedicated to how technology will change the way we live, work and learn in the year 2000. The morning session examined the ways in which technology will continue to fundamentally reshape our lives, global society, commerce and learning. In the article, IBM Fellow Gerd Binnig states, "The student's imaginations really took off, and the group effect, how they inspired each other to consider new ideas, was really something to see" (Sehee, 1998, p. 48).

More recently, IBM is working with California Polytechnic University to create a new model for access to education called education-on-demand. Faculty are developing computer-based multimedia courseware to increase student access to learning. In 1998, IBM created the Reinventing Education grant program as its centerpiece of the company's global commitment to education. The program has as its genesis in IBM's tradition of good corporate citizenship and its commitment to contributing to an enriched civic society. Through this grant, IBM has set out to raise student achievement and enhance academic productivity through partnership and broad-based systematic change driven by technological innovations in instructional delivery methods.

IBM is very active in the research community, also. The IBM Shared University Research (SUR) program is designed to establish or enhance a strong IBM technical presence at research universities throughout the world. IBM reports on their higher education web page that there are approximately 40 universities participating in the SUR program with over $110 million in equipment provided to the institution. This program also connects the university researchers with IBM personnel from the research, development and solution provider communities.

In a press release from Seton Hall University in New Jersey titled, IBM-Seton Hall University alliance will set new direction in higher education, the president of Seton Hall states, "Seton Hall is teaming with IBM because IBM offers the very finest resources for instructional technology. IBM's vision for integrating technology into the higher education experience so closely matches our own goals for incorporating technology into the learning environment that we decided to formalize the collaboration with the signing of this agreement" (Seton Hall University, 1997). IBM became interested in an alliance with Seton Hall in 1995 when consultants from IBM's Global Education Industry Unit assisted a university committee in completing a five-year plan for information technology. Sean C. Rush, general manager, IBM Higher Education states in the press release: "Seton Hall is among the leaders in incorporating information technology in higher education. By working in collaboration with Seton Hall we can share the strengths of both organizations and work together to meet our goals" (Seton Hall University, 1997). The Seton Hall University and IBM strategic technology alliance has been recognized as the leading model for strategic technology alliances throughout higher education.

Summary

The plan for creating a strategic technology alliance has to be unique to a college's culture. Colleges and universities who have developed strategic alliances with business and industry have determined that the critical elements to alliance development includes planning, transformation, and the appropriate use of technology to create a mission that is more productive and personal to each organization. Strategic technology alliances and partnerships between higher education and industry take many forms. All of the models demonstrate common themes of collaboration between each organization, internal and external variables and how the strategic technology issues facing higher education may capitalize on the industrial resources. The collective skills, vision, and ongoing dialogue between each organization will help sustain the transformation of technology in higher education throughout the early decades of the 21st century. Technology has changed the way we live, work, and educate. It has created a networked world and a global community. As a result people need lifelong skills. Institutional, national, and global competitiveness ultimately depends on people. Individuals will be more competitive if they have the right set of skills. The challenge is how to incorporate those 21st century skills into the fabric of educational institutions. These projects include new student-centered academic pedagogical methodologies, electronic learning, and Internet based courses for using various modes of academic courseware, student mobile computing, and technology enhancement initiatives. An alliance's collaborative projects must be designed to improve new student enrollment, increase retention rates, integrate technology for teaching and learning, streamline administrative processes and enhance the college's ability to offer credit-bearing executive management and technology education. It is clearly evident that strategic alliances between business and industry and higher education are unique with different focuses and content.

Issues relating to collaborative practices and enhanced strategies using the Internet will force colleges and universities to take a fresh look at how academic programs are delivered in the 21st century. Higher education institutions are faced with the critical need to support the technology investment to ensure that they continue to be responsive to societal expectations. In order to meet these technological demands, higher education must develop effective partnerships with business and industry. Strategic technology alliances are designed quite differently at public colleges and universities than those at private colleges and universities. Public institutions require purchase orders, legal agreements and approvals from state boards of regents where private institutions only required senior administrator approvals. Most public institution alliances with technology vendors are mainly created to save money on capital technology investments. One major private university formed a strategic technology alliance in 1995 that included the development of a five-year strategic technology plan that included using the vendor's hardware, software and consulting teams. This alliance included providing all students with a laptop computer. They have also centered all technology-based courses on courseware solutions. In addition, they have re-organized their technology organization based upon recommendations from the vendor that includes a large student support services department.

Most public and private institutions use strategic technology alliances to include specific projects centered on academic programs, mobile computing and the technology infrastructure to support these projects. Each project will usually have a separate statement of work reflecting the mission and goals of the alliance.

A model for the development of a strategic technology alliance with technology vendors may be based upon Henderson and Subramani's model in Reinventing Administration, a book edited by Diane Oblinger and Richard Katz. They created an eight-step model for creating and managing the processes in different types of relationships. This model includes the following issues: (a) focus, (b) leverage, (c) capability development, (d) planning horizon, (e) accountability, (f) information behavior, (g) information mechanisms, and (h) risk management.

A strategic technology alliance must include value creation, accountability, and measurement to achieve specific strategic outcomes visionary trust, belief that direction is appropriate, and trust to share strategic direction. These outcomes are based upon the current thinking on alliances (Doz & Hamel, 1998) that stress a new perspective in the development of strategic technology alliances as compared to conventional wisdom of the past. The values expressed in a strategic technology alliance between colleges and technology vendors provide an operational foundation based on the premise that strategic technology alliances will uphold the collaborative efforts to provide a significant return on investment for each organization.

An important strategy point for any development project is the definition of what is to be accomplished or developed in the project. It is important to define how a college views strategic alliances and partnerships and how the vendor views the significance of the college's place in higher education. Over the years, college administrators and faculty have considered strategic alliances as a way to raise money for scholarships or obtain gifts-in-kind from business and industry. Other administrators have considered an alliance as a way to get free consulting and technical services. While many others simply have no operational definition of strategic alliances. It is important to offer college and vendor administrators a definition of a strategic alliance that provided a starting point for the development of the alliance document of understanding while, at the same time, not limiting anyone's creativity in approaching this important partnership. Alliances between business and industry are strategic not tactical, focus on long-range goals, and features tight linkages among partners with specific emphasis on cooperation and collaboration. This definition expresses the realization that the college will benefit in increased enrollment, better retention, enhanced and new academic programs, and structured administrative technology processes as a result of this technology partnership.

Higher education must pay specific attention to partnerships and alliances and the opportunities they provide to each organization. During the development of a strategic technology alliance we cannot overlook the value, direction, economics and strategy of partnerships and alliances between colleges/universities and business and industry. Many colleges and universities have invested heavily in technology over the past ten years with specific emphasis on the implementation of web-based courses. Unfortunately, these investments have failed, or are failing, due to the lack of direction, vision and project management. These projects were not focused on specific academic and administrative technology goals and in most cases are not meeting the needs of the students. The literature provides validation that collaborative project management between the institution and business and industry will be successful.

Current conditions in higher education continue to proliferate the need for strategic alliances between business and industry and higher education. The alliance provides an opportunity to leverage the resources of each organization and develop innovative and exciting collaborative academic programs focusing on teaching and learning. The alliance will add value to each organization's strategic initiatives and priorities. By working collaboratively an alliance will form the basis for a long-term relationship between the institution and the vendor. A relationship that will enhance the teaching and learning environment, enabling the college or university to design, develop, deliver, and manage distributed learning in a way that compliments rather than competes with traditional modes of delivery.

A strategic technology alliance that is based upon a strong commitment to mutual decision making, resource investment, risk, and reward by each partner will enhance on-campus academic programs and extend the college's reach to students anywhere at anytime.

References

Alliance Analyst. (1999). Peter Drucker, non-profit prophet. [Online]. Available: http://www.alianceanalyst.com/Drucker.html. [1999, December 6].

American Council on Education. (1999). 81st Annual meeting special issue: Education leaders advocate partnerships with business community organizations. [Online] Available: http://www.acenet.edu/hena/issues/1999/03_01_99/partnerships.html. [1999, September 24].

American Council on Education. (1999). Business-Higher Education Forum: The Purdue-Caterpillar Partnership. [Online]. Available: http://www.acenet.edu/about/progra...F/coops/student-intern/purdue.html.

American Council of Education (1999). Business-Higher Education Forum: GE.Umass Partnership. [Online]. Available: http://www.ac enet.edu/about/programs...F/coops/corp-college/ge_umass.html. [2000, January 7].

Beckhard, R., Goldsmith, M., & Hesselbein, F. (Eds.). (1997). *The organization of the future: The circular organization.* San Francisco, CA: Jossey-Bass.

Bolman, L. G. & Deal, T. E. (1997). *Reframing organizations.* San Francisco, CA: Jossey-Bass.

Bowie, N. E. (1994). *University-business partnerships: An assessment.* Lanham, MD. Rowman & Littlefield Publishers, Inc.

Brown, D. G. (1999). *Always in touch: A practical guide to ubiquitous computing.* Winston-Salem, NC: Wake Forrest University Press.

Conference Board. (1996). *Strategic Alliances: Gaining a competitive advantage.* New York, NY: The Conference Board.

Cortada, J. W. (1998). How to make partnerships work. [Online]. Available: http://www.hied.ibm.com/multiversity/Spr98/partners.html.

Dolence, M. G., & Norris, D. M. (1995). *Transforming higher education: A vision for learning in the 21st century.* Washington, DC: Society for College and University Planning.

Doz, Y. L. & Hamel, G. (1998). *Alliance advantage, the art of creating value through partnering.* Boston, MA: Harvard Business School Press.

Ewell, P. T. (1995). (Ed.). *Student Tracking: New techniques, new demands.* San Francisco, CA: Jossey-Bass.

Fenton, M. B. & Natale, S. M. (Eds) (1997). *Education and value conflict.* Lanham, MD: University Press of America, Inc.

Fetter, J. (1995). *Questions and admission.* Palo Alto, CA: Stanford University Press.

Frayer, D. A. (1999). *Creating a campus culture to support a teaching and learning revolution.* [Online]. Available: http://www.educause.edu/ir/library/html/cem9923.html.

Fromartz, S. (1999, April 21). *Power partnerships. Business Week Frontier.* [Online] Available: http:://businessweek.com/smallbiz/news/columns/99-17.f3626060.htm. [1999, December 14].

Gilbert, S. J. (1995, March/April). An online experience: Discussion group debates why faculty use or resist technology. *Change Magazine.* 42-45.

Gonzales, R. (1999). *Best practices: Developing higher education and business/industry partnerships.* [Online]. Available: http://www.acenet.edu/calec/partnerships/practices.html. [1999, September 24].

Green, K. C. (1999, February). *The ninth national survey of desktop computing and information technology*. Campus Computing Project, 4.

Griffiths, J. M. (1999, Summer). "From handout to handshake to hands on." *Multiversity*, Summer. 14-21.

Hamel, G. & Prahalad, C. K. (1994). *Competing for the future*. Boston, MA: Harvard Business School Press.

Harbison, J. R. & Pekar, P. J. (1998). *Smart alliances: a practical guide to repeatable success*. San Francisco, CA: Josey-Bass.

Henderson, J. C. & Subramani, M. R. (1999). The shifting ground between markets and hierarchy: managing a portfolio of relationships. In R. N. Katz & D. Oblinger (Eds.), *Renewing Administration: Preparing colleges and universities for the 21st century*. (pp. 99-125). Bolton, MA: Anker Publishing Company.

Honeyman, D. S., Wattenbarger, J. L., & Westbrook, K. C. (1996). *A struggle to survive in the next century: Funding for community colleges*. Thousand Oaks, CA. Corwin Press, Inc.

Hunt, K. B. (1997). Higher education alliances. Journal of Excellence in Higher Education, Spring 1997. [Online]. Available: http://www.uophx.edu/Joehe/spring97/introduction.html.

Katz, R. N. & Oblinger, D. G. (Eds.). (1999*). Renewing administration: Preparing colleges and universities for the 21st century*. Bolton, MA: Anker Publishing, Company, Inc.

Katz, R. N. & Rudy, J. A. (Eds.). (1999). *Information technology in higher education: Assessing its impact and planning for the future*. San Francisco, CA: Josey-Bass.

Kobulnicky, P. J. (1999). Critical factors in information technology planning for the academy. [Online]. Available: http://www.educause.edu/ir/library/html/cem9924.html. [1999, September 23].

KPMG, LLP. (1999). *Transforming higher education: At the gateway of the knowledge economy*. New York, NY:KPMG, LLP.

Lee, A. (1997). Lifelong learning, workforce development and economic success. [Online] Available: http;//www.lifelong-learning.org/alee.htm. [1999, December 3].

Martin, C. (1998). *Net future*. New York, NY: McGraw-Hill Publishing Company, Inc.

Massey, W. F. & Zemsky, R. (1995). *Using Information Technology to Enhance Academic Productivity*. Washington, DC: EduCause.

McKeachie, W. J. (1994). *Teaching Tips: Strategies, research, and theory for college and university teachers*. Lexington, MA: D. C. Heath and Company.

McKenna, R. (1989). *Who's afraid of big blue?* Reading, MA: Addison-Wesley Publishing Company, Inc.

Oblinger, D. G. & Rush, S. C. (Eds.). (1998). *The Future Compatible Campus*. Bolton, MA: Anker Publishing Company, Inc.

Pugh, E. W. (1994). *Building IBM: Shaping an industry and its technology*. Cambridge, MA: The MIT Press.

Riley, C. (1998-99, Winter). Will colleges and universities become brands? *Planning for Higher Education*. 12-20.

Robinson, M. & Daigle, S. (1999, Fall). Are universities ready for partnerships? *Planning for Higher Education*. 3-9.

Rush, S. (1999). *The learning revolution.* Speech presented at 1999 Dowling College Convocation, Huntington, NY.

Sehee, J. (1998, number 4). Seeing 2020. *IBM Research.* 47-48.

Seton Hall University. (1997). IBM-Seton Hall University alliance will set new direction in higher education. [Online]. Available: http://www.shu.edu/compute/ibmalliance.html.

Wilson, L. (1994). *Stop selling-start partnering.* New York, NY: John Wiley & Sons, Inc.

Vella, J. (1995). *Training through dialogue: Promoting effective learning and change with adults.* San Francisco, CA: Jossey-Bass.

Chapter Eighteen

Leadership and Ethics in the 21st Century

FAITH M. PEREIRA

Preface

All through history we see that nations and empires that were hitherto thought to be invincible, were totally destroyed by some destructive, subversive elements, very much like the fifth columnists. Today the economic empires of the western world seem to be on the edge of a precipice. As in the days of classical literature, it can be seen that even the mighty can fall if they use the ruse of the ancient Greek army with their Trojan horse. Despite the warnings of Cassandra, the gigantic hollow wooden horse, filled with armed soldiers, was taken within the battlements of Troy. This ruse of espionage won the battle for the Greeks against the mighty Trojans. Those fully armed Greek soldiers sprang out of the belly of the wooden horse, and caught the country by surprise.

So too, our mighty economic empires of today can be caught unawares by the Trojan horse that houses a network of unethical, false and corrupt values that can sabotage our entire western economic system, with its progress and growth. This may turn out to be the Achilles heel that can bring about the destruction of the hitherto formidable Western world and its economy.

Strange as it may seem, ethics can make or break a person, a nation, or an entire system. In fact leaders are more liable to be judged by ethical codes than most other people. Leaders live in the proverbial *fish bowl*, and the whole world is waiting to evaluate their every action. Past successes and power are no deterrents to the searching eye of scrutiny that drags them down. We have seen this happen again and again, in country after country. The general public will pardon a million mistakes made by their friends and buddies, but will hesitate to forgive their heroes.

Recently we read that the never ending list of giant operations and corporations like Enron, Harkin, Haliburton, World Com, Quest, Christie's, Sotheby's, Xerox, Arthur Anderson, Adelphia, ImClone, Global Crossing, Tyco, Perot Holdings, Merrill Lynch, Bristol-Myers-Squibb, the Telephone companies, and even the Red Cross, United Way and Religious personnel, have betrayed their people and their customers, in spite of their global reputations. Thus proves to us that those materialistic *idols have feet of clay*. Unethical issues are now noted in corporations, with CEO's and their exorbitant salaries and bonuses, while thousands of their people are laid off; financial managers advising clients to invest in stock that they themselves are selling, because of poor performance; pharmaceutical companies maintaining their very high prices of life-saving drugs, and also preventing the manufacture of the less expensive *generics*. These and the many more examples of today make the phrase, *ethical leaders*, the *oxymoron de jour*.

Introduction

At the mere mention of the word LEADER, one usually visualizes and thinks of the typical leader: a tall, dark and handsome man. However, as we turn the pages of history we note that not all leaders were tall; not all were dark and handsome; and not all were men. We believe that leaders are dynamic, successful, powerful people who lead religions, armies, nations and corporations.

Leadership is a complex phenomenon that requires different definitions that have undergone metamorphosis over time: starting with the antiquated autocratic Theory X leader, and blossoming into what we have today, when leading is considered to be the process that influences other people to act to achieve specific objectives.[1] Managers and supervisors are now seen more as coaches, facilitators, and integrators of team efforts.[2] Leaders today must move away from the "hierarchical command—and control—to more of a collaborative philosophy."[3]

Of the essential functions of management, leadership is the most challenging—because leadership involves the most unpredictable ingredient: *people*. We are all so different from one another; we are all so different in the different stages in history; and different too, in different situations. If we add in a change in the conventional culture, the task of leadership is rendered even more difficult, complex and challenging. Most of the mistakes leaders make today, are the result of a lack of understanding of the *backstage* culture[4] of the people in the countries under consideration. This problem is further enhanced as we note today, the multicultural nature of the workforce, the customer, the suppliers, and the competition. This diversity in the workforce demands new recruiting initiatives[5] in the private and public sectors too. These multiracial identifications might affect government programs too.[6]

Faced with all these obstacles we wonder if they are insurmountable! Are we doomed for disaster? Will we ever be able to climb the mountain of obstacles? Will we ever be able to work within the new system, and turn those obstacles into opportunity? Perhaps we can.

Let us recall the popular serial on space travel called **Star Trek**. It grabbed the attention of most people, young and old. Think back to the scenes when Captain Kirk and his crew were faced with unforeseen challenges—invasion from another planet. At first they felt totally inadequate as all their weapons and know-how could not handle such situations.

Now let us flash back to that scene when Captain Kirk and Mr. Spock are standing on the Bay of their spaceship Enterprise. Do they have any answer to this new challenge? Yes. If they are *energized* from their spaceship, they can—in an instant, find themselves landing in the galaxy or planet of their choice via a new medium, the *energizer*. That was the answer to a brand new challenge; and from then on, they would use it to reach new frontiers.

Leadership today is faced with similar new challenges emerging from the new millennium. Our most recent technological advances have suddenly ripped through the barriers of the past. Thanks to new *Technology*, **instant communication**, together with **instant feedback,** we now find ourselves in a totally different orbit—a veritable *quantum leap* in communication, so essential in leadership. This is a lot similar to the much-mentioned quantum leap in the science of evolution. Hence the *leadership of yesterday* is at a distinct disadvantage. This calls for fresh thinking from all of us, if we are to come up with a leadership concept that is relevant in the new millennium.

We will not need the services of "Scottie" to *beam* us back to the 20ᵗʰ or an earlier century, for now there is no turning back—unless we want to be turned into *pillars of salt* in a world we once knew. We all need to be *energized* into a totally different and dynamic way of leading, educating and working with our subordinates, superordinates, peers and customers.

In the British Royal Family, the next leader of the Empire will be the eligible Hanovarian member who will be subject to intensive and extensive *training*. In the Catholic Church, leaders are *elected*. In corporations, promotions to positions of leadership are mainly rewards for past superior technical performance,[7] in the area in which they have their education and training. Scarcely any attention is paid to ability in **leadership**. This therefore is the area that demands much attention. Working with and through people does not *come naturally* to everyone. **Team work and group projects** should be encouraged in Business classes, to prepare the leaders of tomorrow to face the challenges they will soon encounter.

Graduation, often referred to as *Commencement*, must initiate an incentive in all the new graduates to aim at enhancing their leadership skills, to ensure success as they enter the corporate world. The ground rules for managing people are changing dramatically. Learning to be a good leader must be an on-going process. In today's working world, organizations have to be adaptive to be competitive in the long run. In an attempt to cope with change, jobs are becoming more flexible. Today, the diverse interests and backgrounds of potential employees,[8] result in firms using alternative ways of designing work positions. Skills that are valuable today may be obsolete tomorrow. Hence the dire need for innovation and technological change. Flatter organization structures used today mean that there are fewer positions for promotion. Individuals may therefore look for advancement opportunities outside the firm. At the same time, increased competition for talent means that some individuals may be lured away to work for other firms.[9, 10]

In our technologically sophisticated and complex society, success is the result of the joint efforts of a large number of talented people working together to successfully complete major projects. Success will only be materialized with the creative, synchronized effort of leaders and subordinates. Neither would experience success without the other.[11]

In the *Journal of Accountancy*, June 1999, William A. Cohen details his *"rules,"* which can be followed by anyone who wants to become a leader. (Appendix I).

It is believed that CEO's who are *charismatic leaders*[12] tend to exert a positive influence that eventually permeates the hierarchical layers of the organization. An environment that is seen as being volatile may enhance the impact of charismatic leadership further. In corporate cultures that involve anticipation and adaptation to environmental change, one will note over time, enhanced performance and progress at different levels in the firm.

In their efforts to develop leaders, leadership talent and ability within their corporations, companies used to invest in leadership development programs, in both upper and middle management; however, the concentration is mainly at upper management levels. Two major problems arise from that fact:

(i) Will those *trained* managers ever be given the opportunity to utilize and put into practice, the theories and new ideas they have just learned?

(ii) As we realize that the winds of change are taking on cataclysmic proportions today, what should be the *optimal* set of issues and basic skills that are required in this 21st century? In the new millennium?

Strong leadership was a way of life in the past; but obviously, as is the case with *production orientation*, in the world of marketing, it is indeed a product of its time, and must make way for a newer and more current *modus vivendi*—referred to as *customer orientation*.[13] In leadership, a more modern management style will certainly be a great help.

In this age of the *Consumer*, the shrinking global village, combined with market, technological and political complexities having rapid rates of change, the *charismatic leader* may soon be an anachronistic figure in the 21st century—and may even be counterproductive today. Bennis[14] cites examples of such situations: (Stalin, Hitler, Chainsaw Al, et al); he states that "what should be clear by now is that post bureaucratic organization requires a new kind of alliance between leaders and the led . . . almost anything but pyramids with their obsolete Top-down leadership."[15]

Bennis believes that the New Leader will not be surrounded by *similar* and *Yes-people*. Instead, cultural differences and diversity may result in success and survival in the long run. This cannot be the demise of leadership, as we know it. He states that rather, "it clearly points the way to a new, far more subtle and indirect form of influence for leaders to be effective. . . . Leaders will have to learn an entirely new set of skills that are not understood, not taught in our business schools, and, for all of those reasons, rarely practiced."[16]

In an attempt to influence their followers, leaders must be ethical, socially responsible, fair, flexible, firm initially, and have faith in those followers. They must always aim at achieving the corporate objectives, and hope to have those objectives meet the objectives of their people.

We now realize the importance of *team leadership* and a spirit of camaraderie in a multicultural workplace (that includes minorities of all kinds). To retain and satisfy our qualified technocrats or *knowledge workers*,[17] all leaders must make a quantum leap into the new *modus vivendi* as we plan to succeed in the years ahead. Obviously, prejudice of every stripe must be *stripped out* of our vocabulary, if we sincerely believe in our effort to achieve success as leaders in the 21st century.

Leadership & Lifelong Learning—
in our Dynamic Environment

Because we realize that we cannot complacently continue with our *old ways of leading*, we must make some changes. However, we find that it is not easy to "embrace change and mobilize others to do the same."[18] We believe that *the only permanent thing in life is CHANGE.* We cannot fight it, so let us join it and realize that we can rejoice in the fact that we will be participants in this new *phase of change.* We note that resistance to change is not uncommon, mainly because in order to adopt **change**, we must strip ourselves of our old ways, as we face the forces of change. This is not easy.

Reacting to change is often witnessed in our dynamic environment. However, being *proactive* and anticipating change, will provide a valuable weapon in the hands of the leader, especially if accuracy, speed, success and decisiveness[19] are to be the desired way of life.

Perhaps Steve Jobs, chairman of Apple Computer and Pixar, said it best, "The best way to predict the future is to invent it . . ." and obviously, keeping up and coping with change, will always position the corporation ahead of the competition. The latter is thus thrown into an abyss of frustration. True Leadership lies in knowing all aspects of one's job, and constantly trying to reinvent the system within which one works.[20]

Technological advances have taken us to new heights: From black & white TV's, to color, to large screen, to projection screen, to HDTV; (not excluding the use of fiber optics/ A/V discs.). Another example is the basic black telephone that underwent metamorphosis, culminating in the sophisticated equipment we use today: international conference calls, ultimately leading up to A/V telephones perhaps; permitting major business transactions, without the hassle and inconvenience of travel. Even the cloning of humans is not a far-fetched idea today.

Because we realize that we live in a dynamic world, with technological advances so far ahead, that yesterday's science fiction is today's reality; the leaders of the future must be *constantly learning* to keep up with the new technologies, in every phase of technological advance. It must be stated here, that whereas we have experienced meteoric advances in technology, sociologically, we seem to be crawling cautiously behind. We therefore must learn how to cope with these advances morally, legally, or emotionally, in any cultural setting.

Education for these leaders must be a commitment of lifelong learning. Many leaders of today lament their inability to locate and train successors. They believe that the latter lack discipline, principle and "what it takes" to become a productive leader. Leadership seems to present a potent challenge for corporations of the future. There seems to be a chasm between what the leaders of today are doing, and what their followers expect them to do.[21]

The aim of leadership education is to produce citizens for a society in which democracy prevails. This normally was achieved in the past by developing the leadership potential of an individual. However, in the 21ˢᵗ century we will have to address the concerns for the obvious outcomes of an industrial society: environmental changes, drug abuse, etc. What is needed is a new approach to leadership, and appropriate education to achieve it. In the future leadership education must shun the past concepts and cliches of control and command, and replace them with words like mutual and dynamic.

"The content of leadership education in the future will cover three broad categories: the evolution of social change and development, the processes that influence social development, and the dynamics of human nature in change processes. . . . Leadership is democratic, and democracy relies upon a cultural orientation towards citizenship for its existence."[22] Leadership in the 21ˢᵗ century will be more democratic and no longer in the static state it was in the past. This will be the wave of the future.

We realize that change has come to stay; so for the leaders of the 21st century, change is the challenge that all leaders must face. Seeing it as an obstacle would be a mistake. Instead, leaders must look upon the challenge of change as an opportunity that will lead them to the *promised land* of **success**. It has been said that "change and leadership go hand in hand"; and change challenges and ruffles routine processes, resulting in a state of discomfort. This is why people have a hard time accepting change and the accompanying challenges and opportunities.[23]

The Importance of Ethics & Values in
the Leaders of Today &Tomorrow

The leaders of the future must have multidirectional talents; be able to adapt to change and challenges; master their computer skills, with easy access to the worldwide network. They must be visionaries who will always equip themselves with alternative plans: B & C, just in case plan A does not work; they must have universal appeal—and be comfortable in all cultures and *protected* groups.[24] They must, above all, be leaders of exemplary character, setting a stellar example to all around them, despite our fragile humanity.

The winners of the future will be the corporations that can constantly innovate and customize their marketing mix to meet the specific needs of their customers. The market of the future is dynamic and unpredictable—and only customer-oriented corporations will be the ones that will succeed. Managers must concentrate on the future, and only use their experiences of the past to prevent a recurrence of those past mistakes.

Mass production, mass transportation and mass communication are all conducive to worldwide involvement and competition. In this atmosphere of the *global village,* rather than *generic* management, true dynamic leadership is what the outstanding corporation needs. "To give significant competitive advantage, a leader must provide his or her organization with some key elements: strong moral integrity and certainty of purpose and beliefs, dedication to the corporate vision and purpose, high levels of creativity and innovation, comfort with ambiguity and experimentation, strong drive and optimism, dedication to building service and other corporate competence, strong social/team skills and persuasiveness, and emotional stability and intelligence."[25]

In environments that are highly complex and dynamic, *true* leadership is absolutely essential. It involves, *inter alia*, self-confidence, commitment and motivation. Leadership development includes study and knowledge, based on an appropriate academic background, specifically suited to the industry or institution, life experience, personality, the corporate culture and context, and other variables. Today corporate programs are coordinating training exercises specifically to meet the goals and values of the corporation.[26]

In this new century, the primary duty of leadership is to be more altruistic, serving the needs of society at large, and not just those of individual corporations and their executives; the community, and not the selected elite. Leadership must, in other words, take on a *macromarketing*, and not a *micromarketing* approach,[27] incorporating complexities associated with "social processes and the pluralistic nature of global society."[28]

Even as we look ahead, we cannot ignore the risks and problems that face us. Our technological advances with all their advantages also have some disadvantages. They increase our vulnerability to Internet abuses: pedophilia, pornographic literature, pervert meetings, computer hacking, illegal financial transactions, breaking into top government secrets, shootings in schools, etc. A proactive leader, aware of these risks and obstacles, will attempt to anticipate them and be better prepared to face future problems, including, *inter alia*, human and/or civil rights; downsizing and outsourcing, while we face a shrinking pool of qualified technocrats or knowledge workers.[29]

A socially responsible and ethical leader will not accept a multimillion dollar bonus, at a time when the company is *downsizing* its workers, and when financial data reveals rather poor economic performance. Leaders must set high moral and ethical standards to earn the respect of their people.

> While management is needed to create consistency and stability, leadership is a process of change that occurs when change is needed. . . . As the "reality" of leadership changes, so must the "reality."[30]

In an attempt to compare the leadership of today with that of tomorrow, one must realize that whereas leaders performed as individuals in the past; team leadership will be absolutely essential in the future. How similar this is to *space travel* of the future—where the success of the mission is due, not just to the pilot alone, but to the entire team of technical experts at the *ground control room*, who assist the pilot. In the closest of collaboration, with excellent **team work**, they monitor the movements of the spaceships on their screens, set the commands for every stage of rocket launching, correction of the path of the space ship, and its landing too. Leaders of tomorrow will have to be able to deal with and depend on people from a global perspective: hailing from different countries and cultures; each having a specific set of values, likes and dislikes. Above all, the leaders of the future must also be intelligent and diligent, have high ethical standards, be concerned about human and civil rights, be the unbiased, socially responsible leaders, the inspiration for all followers to emulate.

The ENRON, WORLD COM, and all the other scandals mentioned earlier, have had an indelible impact on almost everyone everywhere. Leaders must realize they have a responsibility, not just to protect, multiply and maximize their *own* personal profits; they have an **obligation** to take care of their subordinates, shareholders and the corporation itself. Financial gains are not the sole monopoly of top management and their friends. Corporate success is the resultant component of the efforts of *everyone* in the organization. Hence they all have a rightful claim on the corporate gains, and no *leader* should even attempt to use illegal or fraudulent means to conceal financial or other facts from their own people, their stockholders, or even the general public. Good ethical business practices always win in the end, creating a positive impression on the business and the local communities.

References

Beach, D.S., *Personnel: The Management of People at Work*, 5th Edition, (New York: Macmillan Publishing Company, 1985).

Bennett III, R.H., Harriman, J.H.P., & Dunn, G., "Today's Corporate Executive Leadership Programs: Building for the Future," *Journal of Leadership Studies*, Summer-Fall 1999.

Bennis, Warren, "The End of Leadership: Exemplary Leadership Is Impossible Without Full Inclusion, Initiatives, and Cooperation of Followers," *Organizational Dynamics*, July 1999 v 27 il.

Bohlander, G., Snell S., & Sherman, A., *Managing Human Resources*, 12th Edition, (Cincinnati, Ohio: South-Western College Publishing Co., 2001).

Drucker, Peter F., "Knowledge Worker Productivity: The Biggest Challenge," *California Management Review*, Winter, 1999, v 41 1 2, Article #3.

Fulmer, R.M., Gibbs, P.A., & Goldsmith, M., "Developing Leaders: How Winning Companies Keep On Winning," *Sloan Management Review*, Fall 2000, v 42 il.

Harari, O., "The Spirit of Leadership," *Management Review*, April 1999.

———, "Why Do Leaders Avoid Change?" *Management Review*, March 1999.

Perreault, Jr., W.D., & McCarthy, E.J., *Essentials of Marketing: A Global Managerial Approach*, 8th Edition, (New York: McGraw-Hill Higher Education, 2000).

Roepke, R., Agarwal, R., Ferratt, T.W., *Aligning the IT Human Resource with Business Vision: The Leadership Initiative at 3M [1,2]*, *MIS Quarterly*, June 2000, v 24 I 2.

Rost, J.C., Barkeer, R.A., "Leadership Education in Colleges: Toward a 21st Century Paradigm," *Journal of Leadership Studies*, Winter, 2000, v 7

Sappal, P., *The Wall Street Journal*, March 20, 2001.

Schmitt, E., *The New York Times*, March 20, 2001.

Terpstra, V., & David, K., *The Cultural Environment of International Business*, 3rd Edition, (Cincinnati, Ohio: South-Western College Publishing Co., 1991).

Walman, D.A., & Yammarino, F.J., "CEO Charismatic Leadership," *Academic of Management Review*, April 1999, v 24 i2.

Notes

1. Beach, D. S., *Personnel: The Management of People at Work*, 5th Edition, (New York: Macmillan Publishing Company, 1985), pp. 332–333.
2. Bohlander, G., Snell. S., & Sherman, A., *Managing Human Resources*, 12th Edition, (Cincinnati, Ohio: South-Western College Publishing Co., 2001), p. 684.
3. Roepke, R., Agarwal, R., Ferratt, T.W., "Aligning the IT H.R. with Business Vision: The Leadership Initiative at 3M [1,2]," *MIS Quarterly*, June 2000, v 24 i2 p. 327.
4. Terpstra, V., & David, K., *The Cultural Environment of International Business*, 3rd Edition, (Cincinnati, Ohio: South Western College Publishing Co., 1991), pp. 9-10.
5. Sappal, P., *The Wall Street Journal*, March 20, 2001, p. B18.
6. Schmitt, E., *The New York Times*, March 20, 2001.
7. Bohlander, et al., op. cit., p. 277.
8. Ibid., pp. 20–27 & 111–112.
9. Ibid., pp. 274–308.
10. Fulmer, R.M., Gibbs, P.A., & Goldsmith, M., "Developing Leaders: How Winning Companies Keep On Winning," *Sloan Management Review*, Fall 2000, v 42 il p. 49.

11. Bennis, Warren, "The End of Leadership: Exemplary Leadership Is Impossible Without Full Inclusion, Initiatives, and Cooperation of Followers," *Organizational Dynamics*, July 1999 v 27 il p. 71.
12. Walman, D.A. & Yammarino, F.J., "CEO Charismatic Leadership," *Academy of Management Review*, April 1999, v 24 i2 p. 266 (2).
13. Perreault, Jr., W. D., & McCarthy, E.J., *Essentials of Marketing: A Global Managerial Approach*, 8th Ed., (New York: McGraw-Hill Higher Education, 2000), pp. 29-40.
14. Bennis, W., op. cit.
15. Ibid.
16. Ibid.
17. Drucker, Peter F., "Knowledge Worker Productivity: The Biggest Challenge," *California Management* Review, Winter, 1999, v 41 1 2, Article # 3, p. 79.
18. Harari, O., "The Spirit of Leadership," *Management Review*, April 1999, p. 33.
19. Ibid.
20. Ibid.
21. Bennett III, R.H., Harriman, J.H.P., & Dunn, G., "Today's Corporate Executive Leadership Programs: Building for the Future," *Journal of Leadership Studies,* Summer-Fall 1999, p. 3.
22. Rost, J.C., Barkeer, R. A., "Leadership Education in Colleges: Toward a 21st Century Paradigm," *Journal of Leadership Studies,* Winter, 2000, v. 7 il p. 3.
23. Harari, O., "Why Do Leaders Avoid Change?" *Management Review*, March 1999, p. 35.
24. Bohlander G., et al., op. cit., pp. 46-48 & 150-156.
25. Bennett, et al, op. cit.
26. Ibid.
27. Perrault, et al., op. cit., pp. 7-11.
28. Rost, et al., op. cit.
29. Drucker, Peter F., *California Management Review*, Winter, 1999, v 41 1 2. Article # 3, p. 79.
30. Rost, et al., op. cit.

Appendix I

Dowling College Library
General BusinessFile ASAP

Journal of Accountancy, June 1999 v187 i6 p8(1)

The eight universal laws of leadership. (management skills)

Full Text: COPYRIGHT 1999 American Institute of CPA's

Great leaders are made, not born, according to William A. Cohen. A West Point graduate and retired major general in the U.S. Air Force Reserve with an MBA and a PhD in management, Cohen knows something about leadership--whether it's on the battlefield or in the boardroom. Here he shares his rules, which anyone can follow to become a leader.

[] Maintain absolute integrity. If your staff doesn't trust you, they won't follow you. When the situation is calm, you may not notice or care if others trust you. But in tough times, when you need support the most, key people may hesitate to support you if they don't think you're trustworthy.

[] Know your stuff. No one cares if you're good at office politics. People want to follow the competent, so, although political savvy may get you promoted, it will not earn you the respect of those you want to lead. Only your knowledge and skills can do that.

[] Declare your expectations. Determine where you want to go and promote your goals, objectives and vision.

[] Show uncommon commitment, If you're not committed to your goals, no one else will be.

[] Expect positive results. Winners expect to win. Those who "think positive" will rack up more wins than those who don't.

[] Take care of your people and customers. If you take care of them, they will take care of you.

[] Put duty before self. You have a responsibility to your mission and your staff. Sometimes one comes before the other, but both always come before your personal interests or well-being.

[] Get out in front. Set the example. Get out of your office and talk to your people. See and be seen. Sitting in your office all day issuing commands is not leadership.

Article A54882573

Chapter Nineteen

Corporatizing Education
Taken to Another Degree

RALPH PALLIAM
ZEINAB SHALOUB

Introduction

For well over a century, the American higher education system has set world standards for academic excellence and equitable access for all citizens. The Morrill Act of 1862, which created the land grant university, guarantees that all citizens who can profit from higher education will have access to it. Today, however, there are signs that this far-sighted social contract may soon be broken. Higher education sectors throughout the world face challenges unprecedented in its history, and it is floundering in its response. The term university, within the context of higher education, refers to a heterogeneous conglomeration of institutions, large and small, public and private, denominational and secular. Historically, one thought of universities as distinct from colleges, with the university term reserved for those institutions with substantial advanced programs in research and doctoral education and the college name reserved for the essentially undergraduate institution focused on baccalaureate instruction. Today, however, the enthusiasm for applying the term university to modest undergraduate and other types of institutions reflects more an aspiration than the reality of advanced studies. It comes as no surprise therefore, that the current focus of higher education policy and legislation is on structural changes in governance (Rochford, 2001). In response to constrained fiscal conditions and increased competition, many institutions have positioned themselves strategically to function in a market oriented entrepreneurial environment to maintain a competitive edge, as trends in innovative universities bears out (Clark, 1998). Due to the nature of higher education, governance ought to be seen as specialized form of management rather than a specialized form of ownership. Academics contend that the new form of governance of higher education should be consistent with the idealogy of governance used in the corporate sense. (Whitehead and Moodley, 1999; Clarke and Newman, 1997; Exworthy and Halford, 1999). This idea comes from the notion that the providers of education are under an obligation to render an account of their actions. From a corporate perspective, there are various justifications put forward for this duty to render accounts including the notion of social contract. Accountability is the essence of corporate governance. The excuse that corporate governance has scandalously desecrated its sacred covenant with society may not be acceptable since it has started to purge and revive its lost moral order. (Palliam and Shalhoub, 2002). Accountability in higher education is an issue that has not yet been adequately addressed due to the universality of higher education.

Accountability and the Social Contract of Universities

Taxpayers have commissioned the various governments of the day to provide meaningful education to their citizens. This mandate is passed over to chancellors, presidents and rectors and other higher education administrators. The single most important concern of this mandate is the issue of accountability. The necessity for proof that taxpayers' funds are being expended in a cost-effective manner, to a good end, and with tangible and visual benefits to those being served, escaped higher education for many years. Colleges and universities have a basic obligation to answer to the public authority (government officials and boards of trustees), as well as to students and their families, the media and the general public (Grantham, 1999). Academia has been an institution in itself, distinct in its mission, its values, and its structure from the larger society. From time immemorial academia fed graduates into the formal and informal society, law, diplomacy, clergy, politics, civil bureaucracy and business. It also served as a socializing, civilizing, and even moralizing agent for the students who passed through it. All these were done as essentials of the mandate.

A historical survey of higher education would suggest that the general characteristic of the 18th century mandate was philosophical reasoning. The 19th century mandate was one of industry and the 20th century was a period of profound scientific and technological revolutions. For the most part, the contribution of institutions towards society during this period was conceptualized within a techno-economic paradigm in terms of economic development by addressing the research and manpower demands of business and industry (Subotzky, 1999). The 21st century can very well be thought of as the period of continuous learning, not merely for the sake of learning, but acquiring new knowledge and skills for the purpose of continually improving the quality of life. In this age of learning, colleges and universities, communities, and governments must develop, promote, and maintain unfettered access to both information and learning; make such access practical and ubiquitous; and produce powerful, lifelong learning by and for their constituencies. The central finding is that the new mandate of the 21st century, in which costs and demand are expected to rise much faster than funding, is unsustainable.

In the light of tight budgetary controls, the public authorities are increasingly interested in value for money and quality of services offered by higher education institutions. Governments and research councils are expecting higher education institutions to increase performance, and are rewarding them accordingly. This comes at a time when the level of education needed for productive employment is increasing, the opportunity to go to college will be denied to millions of Americans unless sweeping changes are made to control costs, halt sharp increases in tuition, and increase other sources of revenue. (Deem 2001). Since money is the abiding preoccupation of higher education stakeholders these days, questions are being raised about the purpose of universities, funding, ownership, governance, regulation and management. It can be expected that institutions of higher education will be scrutinized to a greater degree by a public that has become more critical of higher education. Since the public's trust in academic institutions has eroded, the institutions' ability to obtain funding can threaten institutional missions. Within this context, Marchese (2000) focused attention on the rise to prominence of for-profit providers in higher education. Great universities are determined by the quality of life they accord to its faculty; the quality of service provided to their customers; and the quality of their products and their placement in the marketplace (both formal and informal). Should universities excel in these areas, the image of the university is enhanced. Each of the activity that makes a great university entails the raising of private sector funds through enterprising activities. The movement towards the "entrepreneurial" university, serving corporate interests and the private good is inevitable and ubiquitous (Subotzky, 1999).

Emergence and Prevalence of Entrepreneurial Universities

Mangan (1998) reported that there are a growing number of presidential searches looking for leaders who can bridge business and academia and to cultivate corporate contacts. They are better at translating the academic environment to the outside world. Mangan's article makes clear that what was once part of the hidden curriculum of higher education has now become an open, and defining principle of education. As universities increasingly model themselves after corporations, it becomes crucial to understand how principles of corporate culture intersect with the meaning and the purpose of the university, the role of knowledge production and social practices. The emergence of the "market" or "entrepreneurial" university, which increasingly serves private sector interests is gaining particular focus (Dill, 1997; Orr, 1997; Slaughter and Leslie, 1997; Tierney, 1997). This has changed, not only the epistemological and organizational forms of knowledge production and dissemination, but also the role of the state in relation to higher education (Orr, 1997; Kraak, 1997; Scott, 1997). It would be an appropriate time for universities to lead the way to a sustainable future. Leading universities to a sustainable future is corporatizing or enterprising a university.

The implications of the entrepreneurial university are well documented (Subotzky; 1999). These include amongst others:

- changes in the form, focus and dissemination of knowledge involving:
- the commodification of knowledge;
- research increasingly funded by non-statutory, private commissioned sources;
- new forms of quality and evaluation, including performance indicators;
- the emphasis on science and technology; and
- the transfer of technology through business-university research partnerships, consortia and specialist units, leading to proprietary intellectual rights.
- changes in the control and governance of higher education, involving:
- increasing stakeholder influence and the changing role of the state in relation to higher education;

- alternative funding sources—bidding for state funding and contracts on the basis of institutional competition, entrepreneurialism and managerialism.

To fulfill its mandate, universities need to function increasingly as market or market-like organizations, which is what defines "academic capitalism" (Slaughter and Leslie, 1997). These authors show that, against the backdrop of global markets, the indicators of academic capitalism are: the development of national policies that target faculty-applied research, the decline of the grants as a vehicle for state subsidy and the concomitant increase in faculty engagement with the market. In industrialized countries, common conditions arising from the emergence of a global market are reduced fiscal allocations for social welfare and education, and increasing allocations for building corporate competitiveness. This impacts directly on the shaping of research and teaching priorities towards the commercialisable science and technology fields and away from the social sciences, humanities and education. Noticeably, there are shifts from basic and curiosity-driven research to commercial or strategic research. In the countries studied by Slaughter and Leslie (US, Canada, Australia, UK), national policies shaped higher education strongly towards academic capitalism, using the rhetoric of maintaining global market shares, creating national wealth, increasing the number of higher paying jobs, and building prosperity. Increased access and participation rates were encouraged with reduced costs, higher fees and a change from student grants to loans. Preference for departments close to the market was exhibited with a shift towards entrepreneurial research. In most cases, higher education planning was being integrated into national planning process which emphasize economic development. Financing patterns changed accordingly towards market-like behaviors, with institutions, which are largely dependent on state funding, focusing on maintaining and expanding revenues in an increasingly competitive environment. Increased funds were accrued from market activities, private gifts, grants and contracts and other competitive sources. Expenditure on instructional activities declined and that on research, public service and administration increased.

Furthermore, Slaughter and Leslie track the way in which the advent of the global economy has impacted on faculty behavior. Management strongly encourages entrepreneurial activities among faculty: developing income-generating products and marketable services, consulting, business linkages, inter-disciplinary partnerships and knowledge production in ongoing enterprises, and producing income from technology transfer activities which provide intellectual property. The authors report that these measures are generally positively regarded by applied scientists and faculty in professional schools, especially the external links, heightened prestige and added monetary benefits. These faculty saw entrepreneurial work as "extension of the research in which they were traditionally engaged or, in the case of intellectual property, as a justifiable extension of that work" (Slaughter and Leslie, 1997: 20). Junior, post-doctoral fellows and graduate students generally held less favorable views towards academic capitalism. The greatest resistance has come from faculty.

Market pressures are also changing academic epistemology. Faculty engaged in academic capitalism were reconceptualizing knowledge in such a way as to value entrepreneurial research more highly, especially that on the leading edge of science and technology and innovation. The combination of the professional norm of altruism and income-generating market-like activities are somewhat in tension. The distinction between basic and entrepreneurial research appears to be blurred and merit is being more widely interpreted beyond traditional publications to incorporate entrepreneurial activities. If axiological issues are in question, there would be no doubt that issues of epistemology should surface.

Similarly, in tracing three ways in which globalization has impacted on higher education in Australian universities (corporatization, accountability and decision-making), Currie and Vidovich (1998) identify the wholesale assimilation of efficiency paradigm. This is based on performance indicators, quality assurance exercises and quality audits, which they interpret as the tightening of central governmental control. Their research shows that, as a result of managerialism, academics feel excluded from decision-making and that the academic function of the university has been made secondary to managerial imperatives. Through globalization, market and business practices have been inserted into universities with what these authors regard as "serious negative ramifications." The focus on increased accountability is perceived by many faculty as a growth in bureaucratic procedures. Decision-making has become increasingly non-participatory as a direct result of increasing managerialism. There has consequently been a perceived decline in collegiality. Faculty expressed a sense of frustration and alienation arising from increased student loads and other income generating activities, from reduced time to contribute towards new knowledge, reflect and exchange ideas.

Polster and Newson (1998) identify growing infringements on professional autonomy of faculty as a result of globalization and managerialism. This is manifested in the form of reduced participation in decision-making, being pressured to secure partnership funding, the erosion of intellectual property rights and the marginalisation of the public sphere. Towards a strategic response, these authors propose asserting "a more robust and public-serving notion of autonomy." This is not to be construed as a retreat into the conventional ivory tower notion of autonomy, but rather to interpret autonomy in terms of "actively and continually responsive to the public interest" (Polster and Newson, 1998: 6). In this way, the negative effects on the profession of globalization can be counteracted and the contribution of higher education towards the public, rather than the private, good can be asserted. The entrepreneurial university is characterized by closer university-business partnerships, by greater faculty responsibility for accessing external sources of funding, and by a managerialist ethos in institutional governance, leadership and planning (Subotsky, 1999). It thus entails increasing market-like behavior among both management and faculty. In citing West (1994), Giroux (1994) considers the corporatizing of American education as reflecting a crisis in vision regarding the meaning and purpose of democracy at a time when market cultures, market moralities, and market mentalities are shattering community and eroding civic society. Such crisis also represents a unique opportunity for faculty to expand and deepen the meaning of democracy. No great university can exist without an economy that supports it.

Criticisms against Corporatizing

McClane (1998) critically examines in the midst of the universal confusion of balanced budgets, America's economic competitiveness and the government support of science, whether universities should imitate industry. He concluded: "as an institution, the university has existed much longer than industrial corporations. Universities represent a vital model for society, presenting well-tested models for the difficult process of discovering ideas and transmitting these ideas to a new generation. This process, slow and unpredictable, does not fit the corporate model of 'competitiveness.' It also does not fit the confusing agitation of government bureaus or the troubles created when politicians pretend to understand scientific priorities." Within this context McClane (1998) questions the proposal that science should support industry, and explicitly that universities should seek and provide research results useful to industry. This paradigm is extended into a proposal to "manage" universities as one would manage an industrial corporation. This is the difficulty that is experienced by academics worldwide in convincing the likes of McClane that centers of economic activity and intellectual activity are not mutually exclusive.

A new generation of university faculty, realizing the monetary difficulties of colleges and universities, is bridging the gap between the worlds of academic scholarship and economic activity. If one accepts the notion that most of the highest growth and highest income areas of a country are linked to the application of intellectual capital rather than physical capital, then universities have a unique role to play within this emerging environment. Globally, universities are forced by financial realities to play a larger role in the economic and social growth of the communities in which they exist. This responsiveness to rapidly changing market conditions significantly alters the role of universities that are being challenged to become more responsive to the needs of several constituencies. Higher education has to emerge from its myopic absorption with outmoded objectives. Historically universities were major cost centers of the government of the day. The engagement or preoccupation of faculty was teaching, classical research and community service. Classical research (research for the sake of research) is becoming a luxury that universities can ill afford in the light of many social, political and economic evils. In Africa, it is argued that 1 out of 100 graduates will find a job in the formal sector. Ninety-nine graduates out of one hundred would have to find jobs in informal sectors. Currently, these graduates of institutions are blind to deterioration of housing, illegal dumping or environmental pollution in the neighborhood, lack of public services in the neighborhood or inequitable access to city services, redlining (the unwillingness of local banks to make loans in the neighborhood), loss of neighborhood stores and shopping areas, lack of jobs and high unemployment of neighborhood residents, lack of opportunities for neighborhood children and increased crime. However, students are vociferous about the Enron debacle, manipulation of earnings, the use of abstract forecasting models to beat an efficient stock market and "bandaid" solutions to fix problems in the Middle East. Consequently, graduates become unemployed in increasing numbers. Given this scenario, what vision does one have of university education and who understands the socio-economic milieu better—universities or the corporation?

Korten's (2001) also joins McClane (1998) in his seminal work, "When Corporations Rule the World" which has become a modern classic with a message of pessimism. He contends that the global economy has become like a malignant cancer, advancing the colonization of institutions for the benefit of powerful corporations and financial institutions. It has turned these once useful institutions into instruments of a market tyranny that is destroying livelihoods, displacing people, and feeding on life in an insatiable quest for money. It forces one to act in ways destructive of oneself, one's families, one's communities, and nature. However, he softens and suggests that human survival depends on a community-based, people-centered alternative beyond the failed extremist ideologies of communism and capitalism. The central idea of his work is a clear and unequivocal wake up call to humanity. The entrepreneurial university during this Age of Learning will both force and require a transformation of higher education to a point to which virtually all stakeholders agree. The challenge is to create the infrastructure—physical, human, intellectual, financial, organizational, and virtual—that harnesses the power of technology to meet the strategic needs of the country, businesses, organizations, and communities, while also taking advantage of global opportunities. Historically institutions of higher education have been able to control its own destiny. Higher education has been held in high regard and has been free from much outside interference. Since the environment in which higher education institutions operate has changed significantly over the years and outside influence have exerted more and more control over campus decisions at all levels. Changes in the organization of higher education internationally have significant implications for the role of leadership in higher education institutions.

Objections to the validity and legitimacy of the concept of entrepreneurial university on the grounds that universities' would come to serve economic objectives at the expense of classical research suggest that objectors have not considered their objections beyond the short range. To claim that the pursuit of social objectives would be contravened in an entrepreneurial university is rather too simplistic. Ever since 1953 there was a heightened tendency for corporations to assume the goal of public service and social responsibility which really was the domain of universities. (Bernstein, 1953). There were no complaints from universities. When there is a heightened interest in entrepreneurial education, the irony is that while corporations are welcoming the move but universities are becoming agitated. Freedom from worries is a non economic goal of all faculty. There are numerous economic ways that would increase this freedom. Gerstner (1998) likens the changes taking place in education to American businesses who were once faced with a stark choice—change or close. They began to invest, amongst others, in a transformation process, new methods of production, new kinds of worker training. Importantly, they continually benchmarked performance against one another and against international competition.

University Governance within the Changed Paradigm

When the corporate sector was criticized dearly for not understanding its mandate, the issue of governance immediately gained prominence. Universities were the most vociferous in the criticisms. Currently, universities are struggling to understand their universal mandate, namely, to consider variable public issues, to examine resistance to tuition, to evaluate dissatisfaction with various aspects of university life, to adjust to competition and to assess other challenges. Universities are finding themselves ever more essential to students' understanding of the good life. Research studies demonstrate that a university education is a minimum prerequisite for access to reasonable middle class standing in society. Parents are seeking educational advantages for their children at all levels, and competition for places at prestigious institutions remains at an all time high. The market is demanding the continued production of university research to drive economic competitiveness. Within this context, the management of universities is being challenged towards creativity and commitment. Faculty are seeking higher pay, greater security, and more autonomy. Student clients and customers are demanding higher quality, lower cost, and greater attention to their needs. Governments and the public are seek better education for lower cost and with a higher yield. Finally, alumni and donors expect high achievement and competitive programs in all areas.

Within the tremendous diversity of demands, universities share a common source for most of their difficulties and their success, namely, finances. While all institutions struggle with issues of definition, purpose, goals, values, and quality, the solutions appear constrained less by the imagination and commitment of university people than they do by limited resources, expanding costs, and rising expectations. Governance is ultimately an issue of finance, not because finance defines the purpose of the university, not because finance creates its values and culture, but because the management of the finances reflects an institution's values and culture and limits its ability to fulfill its purpose. If universities learn to manage their finances well, they gain the opportunity to address issues of substance. Only if they understand their finances, can universities successfully consider questions of quality, service, or values. The modern tools of corporate management, developed in the private sector to track costs, productivity, value, and improvement were rarely found welcome in universities. These institutions are insulated by bureaucracy, politics, and popular demand from the exigencies of a profit driven marketplace. Universities can no longer continue without a need for the precision tools that are becoming essential features of business management or the principles of governance as used in corporate organizations. If faculty are stressed by the imposition of external demands for accountability and performance, then in Ramsden's words "they had better get used to it as quickly as possible" (Ramsden 1998:16). Despite frequent use of the term "academic profession," academic work is organized and governed in ways that do not reflect what other groups might understand by the term "profession."

Issues of university governance have characterized the conversation about higher education (Rochford, 2001). The fundamental insights from which the field of corporate governance emanates is that there is a potential problem associated with the separation of ownership and control. Corporate governance encompasses the set of institutional and market mechanisms that induce self-interested managers to maximize the value of the residual cashflows of the firm on behalf of its shareholders (Denis, 2001). One of the difficulties experienced by both the government and higher levels of management intent upon change is the mismatch in expectation between the various stakeholders, overlaying management structures often built upon quite ancient models (Rochford, 2001). Consistent with this trend of thought, Lombard (2001) suggests that the university has lost its soul, the faculty fails to work hard enough, the administrators are wasteful, the curriculum taught are anti-intellectual or anti-American values, the quality of the academy has declined, the students are being cheated, and the taxpayers are being bilked. American higher education finds itself ill prepared to defend itself against these critics. Lombard (2001) further adds that every critic has at least one thing right, and although the subsequent analysis and self-righteous pontificating made little real contribution to either understanding or remedy, neither could the critique be dismissed as the ravings of the totally irresponsible. Universities themselves are recognizing tremendous difficulties in maintaining the integrity of all their enterprises in the face of the cost escalation and productivity stagnation. The governments accept the frame of reference of the critics (usually an attack on the values, content, and integrity of the institution) and responded in terms of values, content, and integrity rather than on the issues of cost and productivity (Subotzky, 1999).

Globally, universities enjoy the distinction of being embedded in regulatory environments that insulate it from the marketplace and make it dependent on the political tax process. As a result, in good times, universities need not heed the marketplace demand for quality at the lowest cost, and can instead simply appeal for additional state funds to increase capacity rather than adjust costs to meet demand at market prices. When adverse conditions arrive and state legislators have fewer resources to distribute and tax averse constituencies refuse to increase public revenue, universities find themselves under attack from the very legislators whose practices made cost competitive behavior unnecessary and in some cases impossible. The early 1990s saw budget crises and reductions for public universities all across the U.S. In almost every case, universities responded by reducing the scale of their operations in one or more ways, but rarely addressing the real nature of their business: governance. Many universities sought to apply business principles of cost management, but primarily to the support structures of their institutions (accounting, physical plant, financial management, admissions, registrar, financial aid and other similar functions) rather than to the academic core of the institution where the greatest costs exist. One should not forget that universities recognize all these issues, and are discussing them at length. Their leadership structures find it difficult to engage them directly. In part this stems from the peculiarity of the university's location in economic space and in part from the organizational dysfunction within universities themselves.

Based upon these criticisms, successive governments have identified the need for change in the management structures of universities. Calls were made for greater transparency, for governance structures that would command public confidence and for ethics in public life. The Hoare Commission Report (1995:44) highlights that "effective governance is a matter which needs to be reconsidered in the light of the current and developing environment for higher education. Universities can probably no longer rely on their traditional governance forms if they are to operate fully effectively."

A Stakeholder Model for University Governance

The real world is increasingly impinging upon the academic world. Within this context one needs to think carefully about the role of the university in a world where the flow of information increasingly bypasses one, where resources must increasingly be earned and where the university's worth is assessed increasingly in economic terms. These are issues that cut across disciplinary boundaries and demand that individuals from diverse areas discuss and resolve them. Developing a stakeholder model involves the establishment of relationships into strategic partnerships. Stakeholders are usually common people coming together to attain uncommon results. This is critical in creating successful universities of the future. For a complete acceptance of a corporatized university, several procedures have to be followed.

- Firstly, the institutions have to recognize their stakeholders. This recognition is vitally important in determining the vision of the university and identifying whom the university is serving.
- Secondly, the various stakeholders need to understand the mandate of the institution and need to realize that mandates change from period to period. Universities need to impact upon society's way of life.
- Thirdly, the role of each stakeholder needs to be articulated in concrete terms. What each stakeholder needs to contribute financially or otherwise must be clearly spelt out. Each stakeholder has to determine one's value added potential to the mandate of the institution.
- Fourthly, a constant evaluation of the mandate needs to be done, assessment of stakeholders and an analysis of their value adding potential.

It is fundamental that each stakeholder adds value to the mandate. The value could be a core function or a critical support function. Two categories of stakeholders can be discerned. Firstly, internal and secondly external. Internal stakeholders would typically be: students; faculty; staff; administration; support services; governing boards; faculty senate/council; and other administrative department. External stakeholders could very well be: Parents; community organizations; government; providers of funds; alumni and accrediting organizations. A typical stakeholder would be the Chief Purchasing Officer of the university. Traditionally, this position is one of transactional, where an officer merely places an order as requested by a user department. In a corporatized university, the purchasing department must assure itself that the costs of procured products and services are cost competitive and contribute to the overall cost competitive position of the university. With declining budgets, this function is called to do more with less. The task now becomes more strategic than transactional. The chief purchasing officer can be a powerful catalyst for the transformation of the university.

Each stakeholders or groups of stakeholders become a business development unit. Stakeholders examine the economic viability of programs and other offerings in the manner consistent with business. Figure 1 shows the university as a center of scholarly activity. The four basic influences are: Techno-logical forces, Socio-economic forces, Political and legal forces and Cultural and Environmental forces. These forces have varying different influences and the Chief Executive Officer the university needs to establish the significance of each force. The mandate of the university comes from a clear understanding of these forces.

As universities are working feverishly towards becoming institutions of excellence within a corporate setting, it is important for then to embrace new and innovative ways in which to accomplish the various results. Institutions that re-arrange resources and priorities in ways that have not been done previously, open up an entirely different range of possibilities. The governance of the entire university in the hands of stakeholders present opportunities that one cannot imagine. It can be freed from the criticism of maintaining an imbalance with their environments. In formulating strategies for the business development unit, stakeholders must consider the nature of the value that is going to be added. Value added may come in different forms, not necessarily in the form of economic benefits. However, the value added must lead the university to a sustainable future. Universities will now be measured in terms of dollars, devices, ideas and initiatives. The application of a stakeholder's model will satisfy the corporate governing mechanisms: legal and regulatory mechanisms, internal control mechanisms, external control mechanisms and market competition. This entails teamwork, information sharing, core competency focus, customer service emphasis, and market foresight.

Concluding Remarks

This is an exploratory study placing in context the role of universities in a changing environment. It explores recent analyses of changes in universities globally. It examines whether universities should imitate the patterns of industry leadership. The structure of governance of universities is outmoded. The most commonly cited constraint to university management is the collegial structure and decision-making patterns. The study recognizes that higher education is becoming significantly competitive and universities are becoming more dominated by market forces. Should universities remain in traditional form, they would be logged into a permanent stage of unhappy disequilibria. The current environment

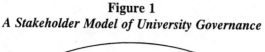

Figure 1
A Stakeholder Model of University Governance

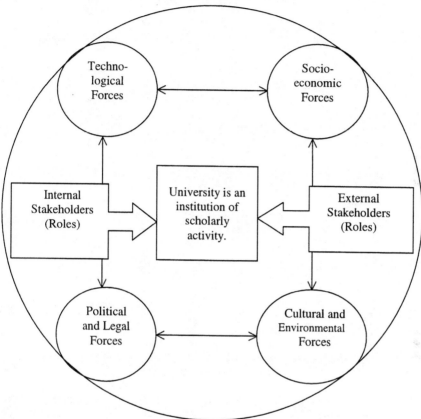

in which higher education is presented bears resemblance to the corporate environment. The study considered the issue of accountability and noted that universities are not fulfilling its mandate. As universities model themselves after corporations, it was crucial to understand how the principles of corporate culture intersect with the meaning and purpose of the university. The study further highlights that a careful constructed partnership with stakeholders can be mutually beneficial and lucrative. For the foreseeable future, increases in public funding for higher education do not appear likely. Universities must become more deliberate and creative in their efforts to attain or maintain adequate funding for the activities necessary to support it mandate.

References

Clark, B. R. (1998) *Creating Entrepreneurial Universities: Organizational Pathways of Transformation* Oxford: Pergamon/Elsevier Science.

Clarke, J. and Newman, J. (1997) *The Managerial State: power politics and idealogy in the remaking of social welfare* (London, Sage).

Currie, J. and L. Vidovich (1998) *Globalisation and Australian Universities: Policies and Practices* Paper presented at the World Congress of Comparative Education, Cape Town 12-17 July.

Dill, D. D. (1997) "Markets and higher education: an introduction" in *Higher Education Policy* 10, 3-4.

Exworthy, M. and Halford, S. (1999) *Professional and the new managerialism in the public sector* (Buckingham, Open University Press).

Grantham, M. (1999) *Accountability in higher education: Are there fatal errors embedded in current U.S. policies affecting higher education* (Unpublished paper University of Minnesota Extension Service).

Kraak, A. (1997) "Globalisation, Changes in Knowledge Production, and the Transformation of Higher Education" in N. Cloete et al (eds.) *Knowledge, Identity and Curriculum Transformation in Africa*. Cape Town: Maskew Miller Longman.

Kraak, A. and K. Watters (1995) *Investigating New Knowledge Production: A Western Cape Higher Education Case Study* Paper commissioned by Taskgroup 2 of the National Commission on Higher Education of South Africa.

Korten, D.C. (2001) *When corporations rule the world* (U.S. Publishers)

Marchese, T. (2000) *Entrepreneurial Universities* (Change Jan/Feb 2000 vol. 32 Issue 1).

McLane, S. (1998) *Should Universities imitate industry?* American Scientist—The magazine of Sigma Xi, The Scientific research society.

Orr, L. (1997) "Globalisaton and the Universities: Towards the 'Market University'?", *Social Dynamics* 23 (1): 42-64.

Palliam, R and Shalhoub, Z, (2002) *The phenomenology of earnings management within the confines of agency theory*, International Journal of value-based Management, Kluwer Academic Publishers.

Rochord, F. (2001) *Issues of university governance and management giving rise to legal liability* Journal of Higher Education Policy and management vol. 23 no. 1.

Slaughter, S. and L. Leslie (1997) *Academic Capitalism: Politics, Policies, and the Entrepreneurial University* Baltimore: Johns Hopkins University.

Tierney, W. G. (1996) "The Academic Profession and the Culture of the Faculty: A Perspective on Latin American Universities" in W. G. Tierney, and K. Kempner (eds.) *The Social Role of Higher Education* New York and London: Garland Publishing.

Tierney, W. G. (1997) (ed.) *The Responsive University: Restructuring for High Performance* Baltimore: Johns Hopkins University.

Walshock, G. (1996) *Knowledge without Boundaries: What America's Research Universities Can Do for the Economy, the Workplace, and the Community* San Francisco: Jossey-Bass.

Ward, K. and L. Wolf-Wendel (1997) *A Discourse Analysis of Community-Based Learning: Moving from "I" to "We"* Paper presented at the Annual Conference of the Association for the Study of Higher Education, Albuquerque, New Mexico, November.

Whitehead, S. and Moodley, R. (1999) *Transforming Managers: engendering change in the public sector* (London, Falmer Press).

Chapter Twenty

A New Model for Learning and Innovation in the Healthcare Industry:
The Center for Learning and Innovation of the North Shore-Long Island Jewish Health System

MICHAEL J. DOWLING
KATHLEEN GALLO
ALAN COOPER

The Business Case for Change

In the last decade the healthcare industry has experienced monumental changes. These changes include a shift in social demographics, revolutionary medical technologies, increased consumer demand for high quality, low cost care, new healthcare delivery models, and changes in organizational structures. Like organizations in all sectors of the economy, healthcare needs to be flexible and open to change. This new environment, a consumer focused-competitive driven marketplace, brings with it transformative powers that no healthcare organization will escape—if they are to be successful. A paradigm shift in organizational models needs to occur.

Traditional organizational models; hierarchical, slow, inwardly focused, were acceptable during the predictable, simpler times of the past. These models, however, are incongruent with the new marketplace that requires organizations to change as rapidly as the unpredictable marketplace itself. The question for the healthcare industry now becomes: What are the requisite skills, tools and techniques that our organizations need to embrace in order to become aligned with the new environment? How do we transform ourselves from the traditional tortoise to the contemporary hare? The North Shore-Long Island Jewish Health System (North Shore-LIJ) believes that creating a world class Learning Organization is the answer.

The Journey Begins

As the nation's third-largest not-for-profit healthcare system, and Long Island's largest employer, North Shore-LIJ has taken a proactive approach in response to the changing marketplace by building a new model for organizational learning and growth. We are an enormous people business. Currently there are 32,000 employees from diverse backgrounds with various levels of training and education. How North Shore-LIJ attracts, develops, and retains that enormous people talent will dictate future success as a healthcare leader. Organizations that foster a climate of professional growth and life long learning among their employees create a culture dedicated to excellence, innovation, teamwork, and continuous change.

The development of a white paper in 1999 that conceptualized the transformation of our Health System into a learning organization was the pivotal starting point of this journey. It was very clear that success in this rapidly evolving marketplace required a new business strategy. For this new business strategy to be successful, it required the support of a learning strategy. Understanding the complexity involved in building this learning strategy, we sought collaboration from experts outside of healthcare to join us in this endeavor.

General Electric's (GE) Leadership Institute in Crotonville, NY is considered one of the best corporate universities in the business world. The Institute is a model for promoting organizational change and leadership development at GE. Harvard University's academic reputation is unsurpassed, and the Harvard School of Public Health has designed courses for physician's and healthcare executives that are regarded as the gold standard in the industry today. We chose GE and Harvard School of Public Health as collaborators in this endeavor because they provide North Shore-LIJ with the best of the corporate sector and academia.

In June of 2000, strategy teams were formed among North Shore-LIJ, GE, and Harvard School of Public Health to begin planning efforts. The group did not set out to develop a "training program" because training is usually considered a "frill" with no link to business results. Learning, on the other hand, expands capability and capacity via experience gained through an ongoing process. It is dynamic and occurs over time in "real life," not in a classroom setting. It was our goal to have learning inseparable from work. We felt that opportunities for experimentation and best practice sharing needed to become engrained in the everyday activity of work. Therefore, learning would be driving the momentum for cultural change, thus advancing business performance. The requisite strategy for success needed to be so powerful that, over time, it would transform the DNA of the organization.

The Center for Learning and Innovation, the organization's corporate university, was created and serves as the focal point for this transformation. The Center was launched in January 2002.

What is a Learning Organization?

The notion of a learning organization emerged during the late 1980s when companies were scrambling for a magic bullet that would transform them into flat, nimble, customer-centric organizations. According to Peter Senge, author of *The Fifth Discipline, The Art and Practice of the Learning Organization* (1990), the prevailing view of "learning organizations" emphasizes increased adaptability to the accelerating pace of change that is occurring. "The organizations that will truly excel in the future will be those that discover how to tap into people's commitment and capacity to learn at all levels of an organization." However, the question was posed, would "learning organizations" go the way of most new management fads. Birth and death takes place quite rapidly with fads and they leave no long term, positive effects on the business.

Senge (1990) suggested that one way to influence the sustainability of "the learning organization" was to establish an intellectually challenging base of ideas and tools early on. He suggested that the essential building block for creating a sustainable learning organization is to include the following concepts during construction: personal mastery or proficiency, mental modeling, building a shared vision, team learning, and systems thinking. Since our goal from the beginning was to develop a learning strategy that would support and drive the organization toward achieving the business goals and objectives set forth in our business strategy, our learning initiatives where grounded in these essential building blocks.

Building Blocks of a Learning Organization

Employees that work in an environment that facilitates the application of their capabilities give meaning to what they do. Personal mastery, an exceptional level of proficiency, results in one becoming committed to their own life long learning. Changing the way people "think and interact at work" and thus fostering a sustained change in their belief system, would required both a commitment from the employees as well as one from the Health System. From the beginning, North Shore-LIJ placed a stake in the ground committed to providing opportunities for personal mastery and communicated it through the Center for Learning and Innovation's position statement to our employees:

> To all members of the North Shore-LIJ Health System committed to setting new standards in healthcare, the Center for Learning and Innovation will provide the opportunity for your ongoing growth and development while transforming us into a national healthcare leader in the 21st century. Together we will accomplish this by offering programs that are both relevant and exciting. Rediscover the benefits of learning.

An organization's commitment to learning and expanding its capacity to learn is solely dependent on its employees to do the same. Our learning initiatives take place in the classroom and are practiced in the workplace. These courses are designed to assist in the professional and personal development of the employees and physicians of the Health System. This growth and achievement is strategically linked to the business imperatives of the Health System. Our objective is to promote individual learning that is ultimately transformed into performance and measurable outcomes, thus advancing organizational learning and growth.

Learning Initiatives

Management Courses

Phase one of the Core Management courses began in February 2002. These courses are targeted toward middle line managers and supervisors. The first three classes were Human Resources, Finance, and Quality Management, sixteen hours for each topic collectively running for 7 weeks. In an effort to integrate theory, practice, and business performance, each team is assigned a Capstone project at the completion of their classroom sessions. The classes are structured so there are no more than 30 managers to a class, grouped into 6 teams. Many of them do not know each other on arrival, and enter the class with some level of anxiety that soon fades. As we begin each of the core topics a common platform prevails.

All classes begin by asking the managers "what are your heart burn issues?" about the specific topic: "What irritates you about the interviewing process or employee counseling?" All heartburn issues are documented on flip charts and by the end of the session the faculty addresses each item while delivering their course content. The faculty is comprised of the senior leadership of the Health System. Dialogue is encouraged between senior management (faculty) and the class (middle management.) An open exchange of ideas, challenging one another's assumptions and generalizations leads to mutual understanding and learning, as well as building a shared vision.

How we respond to the world and make decisions is based on our deeply engrained assumptions. These mental models influence our decision making every day at work. As the external environment has radically changed our assumptions, we need to also change to reflect the new marketplace or we will constantly be in conflict with the new strategies that are necessary for success. Newly developed business models cannot be successful if they are grounded in assumptions that reflect the outdated marketplace. The structure of our classes fosters openness and an opportunity to surface and examine assumptions that affect our attitudes and decision-making process at work. Aside of the knowledge transfer that occurs in class, the interaction between class and faculty is a value added activity to the organization as it promotes building a shared vision and necessitates the examination of assumptions that might impair organizational change and learning. Learning is promoted not only through delivery of theory and open dialogue, but by team problem solving of business cases that relate to the organization as well.

Teamwork is a core value in the Health System and a pre-requisite for today's successful organizations. Our classes are designed around teams and teamwork; in fact many of the faculty team-teach. In an effort to lay down the foundation for creating high performance teams, our first class is on team building and working in teams, and is based on the Meyers-Briggs Type Inventory. It serves as an opportunity for each individual to identify their assumptions about others, their style of taking in information, how they making decisions, and understanding how they work within a team. One of the goals of this class is for the teams to come to the conclusion that diversity within a team has clear advantages. Ideas and solutions that emerge from different points of view are far superior to single minded solutions and lead to everyone's success. Working in teams is the cornerstone of our learning strategy.

Once the classroom sessions are completed, the teams are assigned a Capstone project. The goal of the Capstone is to take all the theory and knowledge learned in the classroom and apply it to a real business problem in the Health System. The teams go back to their hospital or other system entity and are given 5 weeks to complete the project. Five weeks is necessary because they are completing the Capstone in addition to their daily work. This time period also allows for the new approach to become engrained into everyday activity. Successful completion of the Capstone requires not only teamwork and application of knowledge received during class, but movement across boundaries throughout the organization. The Capstone is designed so that a cross-functional approach is necessary to complete the project. This results in the breaking down of barriers or fiefdoms within the organization.

The teams emerge from the project with solutions based on a systems perspective, accurate data collection and analysis, individual leadership, and teamwork. We set aside a full day and have each team report-out and present their Capstone projects to the senior leadership of the organization. Some solutions have been implemented while the subsequent Capstone groups are advancing others.

We have consistently received positive feedback about this method of team based, action learning. As one employee stated during her Capstone report out, "The process of working as a team was more important than the solution to the business problem." Another team used the analogy of an orchestra working together while presenting their project. They even handed a conductor's baton to each other as the next person presented. As employees move through these learning experiences, they are clearly demonstrating the enjoyment and value of participation and teamwork.

Building a shared vision with employees at all levels is a pre-requisite for change. It not only fosters commitment but it is something that needs to be "felt"—employees need to visualize the future organization and become part of it. Building our shared vision takes place continuously throughout the organization.

Foundations

One of the first steps in changing our organizational culture was to significantly enhance the Health System's orientation process. Properly orienting new employees results in shaping the organization's culture, while research has also suggested that it increases employee retention. All new employees are oriented through the first class that they must attend called Foundations. Foundations focuses on aligning the new employees with the corporate mission, vision, values, behaviors and expectations of the organization, the history of the organization, where we are now, and the future vision is clearly illustrated. The faculty is comprised of senior leadership (CEO, CLO, VPs, etc.) This is not a one-way information session but, as with other classes, dialogue is promoted between the faculty and new employees. Small group team building exercises offer the new employee the opportunity to engage in problem solving activities that resemble actual work experiences that they will encounter.

While building a shared vision is an ongoing process, the Health System has committed to actively enlisting all 32,000 employees. Beginning on the first day of work, every new employee is enlisted to work toward the future vision of the organization. This is done through a variety of formal and informal channels such as learning initiatives, town hall and staff meetings, best practice forums, etc.

Six Sigma, CAP and FTD

The Center for Learning and Innovation has also put into practice Six Sigma process improvement and management processes that have been widely recognized in the business sector for more than two decades. General Electric and GE Medical Systems (GEMS) have a long tradition of innovative, leading edge technologies and services. GEMS has been mentoring us throughout our Six Sigma initiative. Different from traditional Six Sigma models, GE's approach to Six Sigma includes two innovative change management techniques: Change Acceleration Process (CAP) and Work-Out.

Six Sigma is a focused process that uses proven quality principles and techniques to reduce process variance, thus increasing efficiency while moving the organization towards future growth and business success. It uses rigorous statistical methods and puts control mechanisms in place in order to tie together quality, cost, process, people, and accountability.

Six Sigma begins with an understanding of the customer's needs, requirements and values. Customers can be internal (employees, departments, physicians) or external (patients, families). Once the customer's needs and values are defined, this method identifies those factors that are critical to customer satisfaction, which are then measured and analyzed. Errors that interfere with customer satisfaction are identified and the improvement phase begins with the team enlisting the front line employees to help develop and implement new, more efficient, processes. Experience has taught all organizations that some quality improvement efforts can return to their former state if not meticulously monitored. By using meticulous data collection, the control stage of six sigma ensures that any backsliding is identified immediately and corrected.

Incorporated into Six Sigma are two innovative management techniques, CAP and Fast Tract Decision-making (FTD). FTD is the equivalent to GE's Work-Out, which has been used by GE for almost 3 decades. We elected to change the name at North Shore-LIJ because we saw it as a team approach to focused, rapid problem solving, with an emphasis on involvement, decision-making and accountability, and we wanted to capture the true nature of the process in its' name. FTD allows everyone in the organization to participate and solve the everyday business problems that plague them.

CAP is a methodology that helps create and mobilize enthusiastic process teams. It is a philosophy and a toolset that creates a shared need, shapes the vision, mobilizes commitment, makes change last, and monitors progress. Once a recommended solution is ready for implementation, CAP addresses the cultural and people side of change.

We found that CAP and FTD have had such a profound affect on the employee's problem solving and change management capabilities that we have added additional Change Facilitation courses where employees learn CAP and FTD without Six Sigma. Currently we have over 90 Change Facilitators in the Health System who have integrated these new management practices into everyday work activity.

In an effort to align leadership, we have a class titled FTD for Leaders. In this class the organization's leaders are exposed to the FTD process that their Change Facilitators have been taught. The objective of the class is to make the leaders aware of the new skill set that their employees have acquired so that they recognize and can take advantage of the fact that problems can now be solved by teams of front line employees involved in the day to day activity of work. Leadership commitment is paramount to employee and organizational development. FTD should and can be used at all levels of the organization for team problem solving.

A recent example of FTD in action is a session held by one of the System's community hospitals on patient identification. The hospital identified the need for enhancement of their policy and procedure to positively identify patients prior to their being given medications or sent for procedures. The session was lead by a hospital change facilitator and included approximately 30 employees at all levels from throughout the organization. At the end of the session the group presented to senior leadership their suggestions on a policy and procedure to positively identify patients. The suggestions were accepted and the process has been put into place.

Our vision is to have as many employees as possible with change facilitation skills. If all employees are Change Facilitators, organizational transformation will emerge from empowered employees, skilled in working as a team to solve business problems and changing the way that they do work. One of the best ways to change culture is to change the behaviors that drive the culture. By instilling the CAP and FTD philosophy into our employees, thus changing the way they solve problems, the Health System has taken the first step in changing organizational culture.

Six Sigma, CAP, and FTD are an excellent fit for a learning organization because they embody the basic building blocks: personal mastery, mental modeling, building a shared vision, team learning, and systems thinking. We have just completed our first wave of Six Sigma education and projects. Six teams from various hospitals and Health System entities were enrolled in the course that ran for 6 months. The Health System now has 6 Six Sigma "Black Belts" (highly specialized full time employees), 18 Six Sigma "Green Belts" (highly trained employees that devote part of their time to six sigma) and 6 completed projects within the organization. These employees make up high performance teams and now possess a skill set that allows them to analyze and solve everyday business problems by combining systems thinking with a rigorous statistical method, FTD, and CAP.

Executive Courses

Senior leadership is responsible and accountable for the business results of their respective entities and the success of the new initiatives that drive these business results. Their success requires them to align their organizations with the future vision of the North Shore-LIJ Health System. As organizations move away from bureaucracy and a hierarchal approach to problem solving, to becoming a flat and nimble organization where front line employees have learned to solve everyday business problems quickly, the leadership cannot lag behind in their capacity to learn. As their employees acquire new proficiencies and practices, they too require a change in their assumptions about employees, the workplace, and the marketplace. Executive courses expose senior leaders to methodologies that are essential for strategic alignment, and managing and sustaining change in their new organizations. These courses are open to senior leadership by invitation, and are held off-site for two days several times a year. In addition, senior leadership is also called upon as faculty at The Center for Learning and Innovation; alignment with the learning strategy that is supporting the Health System's strategic business strategy is essential.

The faculty for this year's executive courses included national experts in the areas of leadership and organizational change: Steve Kerr, Chief Learning Officer (CLO) at Goldman Sachs (formerly CLO at GE); Dave Ulrich, Professor of Business Administration at University of Michigan and author of several books including Results-Based Leadership; David A. Shore, associate dean and executive director of the Harvard School of Public Health, a renowned authority on healthcare branding, positioning, and competitive strategies; and James Champy, author of The Arc of Ambition, Reengineering Management and coauthor of Reengineering the Corporation. These change and leadership experts described how the Health System's leaders needed to approach the future in order to guide the Health System through the upcoming environmental and organizational changes.

Executive Education for Senior Physician and Nurse Leaders

In response to the changing demands of patients and other constituents, it is critical that the clinical leadership seek new insights, perspectives and skills that enable them to respond to change at the same pace that their administrative partners do. Alignment between clinical and administrative leadership is essential for achieving our future vision.

To achieve this, Harvard School of Public Health has customized a program for our clinical leadership. The initial courses given this year were Enhancing Clinical and Management Trust in the Healthcare Environment and Building Healthcare Brands. Examples of other courses in our program that will be taught by Harvard faculty will include: Leadership, Negotiation and Conflict Resolution, Finance for Clinical Leaders, and Physician Practice Management.

This program is dynamic and will be customized as the Health System sees fit.

Enrichment Program

Our learning strategy includes creating leaders at every level of the organization. Engaging all 32,000 employees in learning initiatives is a considerable logistical challenge. We created our Enrichment program to help tackle that challenge. This program is scheduled to start January 2003 and it is open to all employees who commit their own time to attend. A diverse range of classes to enhance both personal and professional development will be offered on an ongoing basis. Classes such as Healthcare Statistics, Meyers-Briggs as the Foundation of the Team, Personal Finance, American Sign Language, Personal Wellness, Career Counseling, and Time Management will be offered on a regular basis on various days and times. The goal of the enrichment program is to expose employees at all levels of the organization to learning initiatives in an effort to build a shared vision and promote life long learning.

The Everlasting Journey

Creating a world class learning organization takes time and hard work from employees at all levels of the organization. Long lasting transformation efforts are not for the faint hearted or for those needing immediate gratification. Transformation requires a fundamental change in the belief system of all employees and therefore requires commitment, time, patience, and learning. Systems, structure, and processes that have been put in place over years reinforce organizational culture. In order to transform organizational culture, all outdated modes of reinforcement need to be eradicated and replaced with those that support and reinforce the new culture. This requires intestinal fortitude and time for long-term effectiveness.

How will we measure our efforts? While, the process of measuring learning is highly subjective, linking learning to business results and reporting them through balanced scorecards will provide a roadmap of how we are progressing toward our future vision. As illustrated, we have realized some positive business results this year as a result of our learning initiatives. However, not all results are overt. Employees that are experiencing these learning initiatives report an increase in their morale and a willingness and eagerness to help shape the future of the organization.

We are on a continuous learning curve and our learning strategy will evolve to meet the needs of the organization's business strategy. Enhancing leadership and technical skills at all levels of the organization and improving business processes through empowering front line employees will lead to an organization made up of exceptional talent. Linking our employee's growth and achievement to the business imperatives of the health system, while not easy, is the road to true organizational transformation. Our employees ARE our competitive advantage and investing in them will result in the North Shore-LIJ Health System becoming a Learning Organization.

Link to Traditional Education

Is the Center for Learning and Innovation a challenge to higher education? While some may see the rapid increase of corporate universities as a failure of the higher education system, others see it as an enhancement and refreshment of the knowledge acquired during college and graduate school. These pundits would profess that corporate universities are necessary for several reasons: first, with the decreasing shelf life of knowledge, corporate universities act as a refresher system. Second, corporate universities result in tighter control of the learning process and course content, and can therefore link educational programs to real business goals and strategies. Third, human capital has been recognized as one of the only remaining strategic advantages in most industries, therefore, investing in the development of their employees will add to the bottom line of the organization. Fourth, corporations have access to proprietary information that colleges and universities do not. And finally, a corporate university is the path to life long learning, a concept that is essential to creating a learning organization. This learning bridges the gap between academia and the corporate world.

Also, corporate universities may be picking up where traditional institutions of higher education are lagging behind or have failed. It may be easier for a corporate university to incorporate innovative learning solutions since an educational governing board does not oversee their programs. Most corporations are adept at using technology for meetings or conferences; traditional universities have only recently delved into this arena. Organizations are evolving, especially in the healthcare industry, therefore, corporate universities are an essential tool in driving change through an organization, something a traditional university could not even conceive of.

Although the Center for Learning and Innovation, like most other corporate universities, can stand on its own, a link with traditional institutions of higher education can be mutually beneficial. The number of corporate universities in the United States has grown from 400 in 1988 to well over 2,000 currently. During this same period, more than 100 four-year colleges have been forced to close. Corporate training budgets in the United States have exceeded the combined budgets of traditional universities. But are corporate universities a threat to traditional higher education? While higher education provides vetted, research-based content, corporate universities provide capital, real-world applications. Corporate universities can use the traditional institutions foundation to build a customized program of study more relevant to the organization's business goals and objectives. Many corporate universities have partnered with local colleges and universities to provide an educational program that takes advantage of the benefits of both types of education.

Due to the changing educational market place, traditional universities need to change the way they do business. The non-traditional working adult student now comprises over 44% of the educational market and is expected to be the fastest growing segment in the post-secondary education market through the twenty-first century (Meister, 1998). By forming partnerships with corporations, these institutions can transform themselves into agile organizations and meet consumer demands by providing timely, high quality, convenient education to the growing market. This transformation will resemble healthcare's response to its changing market place. These partnerships will also increase value of the traditional university's offerings by satisfying the need for life-long learning. Since the shelf life of knowledge is continuously decreasing, continuous learning must take place in order to keep up with the changing business environment. With such a partnership, the continuous value of higher education will be maintained. There is also value added to the corporate university that partners with the traditional educator. A high value is put on college credits and advanced degrees. The partnership will allow the corporation's employees that are taking classes for personal and professional development to gain these credits and work toward a degree.

The Center for Learning and Innovation currently has a relationship with the Harvard School of Public Health for its clinical executive leadership programs. We are currently researching several options for affiliation with local universities and business schools. As previously discussed, these affiliations will benefit both the Center and the traditional educational institution.

A synergistic relationship can be established between corporate universities and traditional universities that will greatly enhance the value of the programs that each has to offer. In this respect, the corporate university is not only without threat to traditional education, but may actually be an avenue for transformation and growth.

References

Meister, J. 1998. *Corporate Universities: Lessons in Building a World-Class Work Force*. New York: McGraw-Hill

Senge, P. 1990. *The Fifth Discipline: The Art and Practice of the Learning Organization*. New York: Currency/Doubleday.

Chapter Twenty One

Self-Ratings and Expectations of the U.S. President, Ideal Physician, and Ideal Automechanic

CAROLE A. RAYBURN

SUZANNE OSMAN

Introduction

Much interest has been paid to the choice of the U. S. President and the factors involved in candidate preference. To study some of these factors, the present investigation has been done, with self-ratings and ratings/expectations of the U. S. President and two other idealized workers.

Method

To study relationships between self-ratings and ratings of various expectations of the U. S. President, the ideal physician, and the ideal automechanic, and correlations between those expectations, the Bipolar Adjective RatingScale (Piedmont, 1995), State-Trait Morality Inventory (Rayburn, Birk, & Richmond, 1998), Peace Inventory (PI) (Rayburn, Handwerker, & Richmond, 1999), Inventory on Spirituality (IS) (Rayburn & Richmond, 1999), and the Life Choices Inventory (LCI) (Rayburn, Hansen, Siderits, Burson, & Richmond, 1999), and overall expectations for the President, physician, and automechanic (with subscales on spirituality, morality, life choices, organization and leadership, and peacefulness) were administered to 43 men at a university setting on the eastern coast of the USA. The men first were asked to rate themselves on all of these instruments, except the overall expectations composite measures. Then they were presented, one at a time, with a vignette of the U. S. President (asking them to describe the ideal presidential candidate), or the ideal automechanic (asking them to describe the ideal automechanic to whom they could go for long-term service), and the ideal physician) (one to whom they would want to go on a regular basis, and for whom they would like to know more than that that person had a medical degree).

For the ratings of each of these ideal persons, the men first responded to a 20 item questionnaire that was a composite of factors of organization and leadership, morality, spirituality, peacefulness, and agentic and communal life choices (yielding five subscales of four items each and a total score). Then, for each of the ideal persons, the men responded to the BARS, STMI, LCI, PI, and IS in terms of what they thought the ideal U. S. President, physician, or automechanic would answer.

The mean age of the men was 19.5349 years, with a range of 17 to 24 years. There were 41 Euro-Americans, one African-American, and one Hispanic-American. None were married. Educationally, two were graduates from a junior college, 40 had master's degrees, and one had a doctorate degree. For religious affiliation, 5 indicated "none," two "atheist," one "agnostic," one "Muslim," 17 "Protestant," 14 "Roman Catholic," and 3 "other." For religious group identity, reflecting the background of their religious groups, 20 indicated "traditional," 2 "conservative," 7 "liberal," 13 "middle-of-the-road," and one as "other." In terms of political identity, 7 indicated Independent, 15 Democrats, 13 Republicans, one Liberal, 4 Green Party, one Reform party, and 2 "other."

Self-Ratings of the 43 Men

For the self-rating, the LCI Agentic (a subscale emphasizing career-mindedness and a business orientation) and the BARS Conscientiousness were significantly related ($r = .470**$, $p = .002$). LCI Communal (focused on family-mindedness and relating to other people in a meaningful way) was significantly related to the men's view of themselves as spiritual and religious ($r = .320*$, $p = .036$), to their Spiritual Self ($r = .335*$. $p = .028$), and to their Religious Self ($r = .418**$, $p = .005$). BARS Agreeableness and IS Seeking Goodness and Truth ($r = .434**$, $p = .004$) and IS Forgiveness, Cooperation, and Peacefulness ($r = .316*$, $p = .041$) were also correlated. BARS Openness was related to the men's view of themselves as spiritual or religious ($r = -.365*$, $p = .017$), to their Religious Self ($r = -.394**$, $p = .010$), and to their Spiritual Index (several spirituality factors combined, $r = -.330*$, $p = .033$). For PI Peacefulness, the men had significant correlations with STMI Trait Morality ($r = -.548**$, $p = .000$), BARS Agreeableness ($r = .622**$, $p = .000$) and BARS Conscientiousness ($r = .575**$, $p = .000$). The STMI is scored such that high scores indicate lower morality and low scores indicate higher morality; state morality reflects thoughts and feelings of a recent nature of ideas of right and wrong, and trait morality reflects those thought and feelings that are relatively of a more permanent and general nature.

For STMI State Morality, a negative correlation was found for BARS Neuroticism ($r = .477*$, $p = .001$) and BARS Agreeableness ($r = -.344*$, $p = .026$). Trait Morality was related to BARS Neuroticism ($r = .332*$, $p = .032$), BARS Agreeableness ($r = -.412**$, $p = .007$, IS Seeking Goodness and Truth ($r = -.504**$, $p = .001$), IS Forgiveness, Cooperation, and Peacefulness ($r = -.575**$, $p = .000$), and IS seeing the equal importance of showing both Justice and Mercy ($r = -.316*$, $p = .039$), and view of oneself as spiritual or religious ($r = -.320*$, $p = .036$).

For the self-ratings in IS Caring for Others, significant findings with IS Transcendence ($r = .784**$, $p = .000$), IS Seeking Goodness and Truth ($r = .797**$, p=.000), IS Forgiveness, Cooperation, and Peacefulness (r=.780**, p=.000) the Spiritual Self (r=.563**, p=.000), and STMI State Morality (r=-.312*, p=.0420, and STMI Trait Morality (r=-.541**, p=.000). IS seeing the equal importance of Justice and Mercy was related significantly to the men's Spiritual Self (r=.385*, p=.011), Religious Self (r=.328*, p=.032), and Spiritual Index (r=.309*, p=.044).

Expectations of the U. S. President
(Rayburn & Osman, 2001)

How did the men's self-ratings correlate with their expectations of an ideal U. S. president? For BARS Extraversion and rating of the ideal President on Extraversion, r=.409**, p=.009). For BARS Openness, r=.567**, p=.000. However, the men's expectations of an ideal U. S. President was not related significantly to their ratings of themselves on these same measures for Neuroticism, Agreeableness, nor Conscientiousness. Nor were there significant relationships between self-ratings and ratings of the President on PI Peacefulness or STMI State Morality. For STMI Trait Morality, however, the correlation is significant (r=.394**, p=.011). For LCI, self-ratings and president ratings were highly significant, for Agentic (r=.492**, p=.001 and Communal (r=.407**, p=.009) Life Choices.

Significantly correlated with President Organization and Leadership were President Spirituality (r=.761**, p=.000), President Morality (r=.338*. p=.026), President Peacefulness (r=.607**, p=.000), President Extraversion (r=.335*, p=.032), President Conscientiousness (r=493*, p=.001), President Neuroticism (r=-.389*, p=.012), President Caring for Others (r=.467**, p=.002), President Transcendence (r=.346*, p=.027), President Forgiveness, Cooperation, and Peacefulness (r=.503**, p=.001), and President Seeking Goodness and Truth (r=.454**, p=.003).

President Conscientiousness was highly correlated with President Peacefulness (r=.608**, p=.000), President Caring for Others (r=.531**, p=.000), President Transcendence (r=.362*, p=.020), and President Seeking Goodness and Truth (r=.558**, p=.000).

Correlated with the U. S. President being viewed as a religious person was the respondents' self-ratings on IS Forgiveness, Cooperation, and Peacefulness (r=.363*, p=.020). Associated with the President being seen as a spiritual person were the self-ratings of the men on IS Caring for Others (r=.504**, p=.001), IS Transcendence (r=.545**, p=.000), IS Seeking Goodness and Truth (r=.453**, p=.003), IS Forgiveness, Cooperation, and Peacefulness (r=.457**, p=.003), respondents seeing themselves as spiritual (r=.617**, p=.000), and STMI Trait Morality with a negative correlation (r=-.364*, p=.019).

Perhaps now, more than ever before, the U. S. President and the candidates for U. S. President are scrutinized more carefully for character flaws as well as questionable political and personal history, intellectual ability and good decision-making. Spiritual and perhaps even religious issues have become more important, especially as these are thought to pertain to a presidential candidate's morality and genuine caring and concern for the welfare of others and of the environment. This study could help in shedding some light on how important these issues may be to voters in nominating and voting for particular candidates as they appear to fulfill voters' picture of the ideal presidential candidate.

Expectations of the Ideal Physician

The men's self-ratings on Openness were significantly related to their rating the ideal physician on Openness (r = .437**, p = .004) and physician Morality (r = -.351*, p = .026). The negative correlation between self Openness and physician Morality reflects the morality scores being in the reverse direction, so that a high score on the morality items indicates lower morality, and a lower score suggests higher morality. Ratings of self State and Trait Morality were significantly and negatively correlated with physician Caring for Others (a subscale of the Inventory on Spirituality), (with State r = -442**, p. 83)." Trait r = -578**, p = .000) and with physician Seeking Goodness and Truth (IS subscale) (with State r = -.385*, p = .012; Trait r = -.536**, p = .000). So, the higher the men rated themselves on being moral (low STMI scores), the higher they rated physicians on Caring for Others and Seeking Goodness and Truth. Self Caring for Others was significantly and positively related to physician Caring for Others (r = .555**, p = .000), physician Seeking Goodness and Truth (r = .443**, p = .003), physician Transcendence (an IS subscale: believing that there is some Higher Power outside the self that guides one's life) (r = .523**, p = .000), physician Forgiveness, Cooperation, and Peacefulness (IS subscale: seeing forgiveness, cooperation, and peace as essential to harmonious living) (r = .499**, p = .001), physician Conscientiousness (r = .328*, p = .034), and physician total Peacefulness (r = .402**, p = .008). Self Forgiveness, Cooperation, and Peacefulness was significantly related to physician Conscientiousness (r = .454**, p = .003), physician total Peacefulness (r = .503**, p = .001), Total Overall Physician Expectations (r = .315*, p = .045), Overall Physician Organization and Leadership (r = .318*, p = .043), physician Communal Life Choice (r = .340*, p = .028), physician Extraversion (r = .345*, p = .028), physician Spiritual Self (r = .377*, p = .000), and physician Religious Self (r = .550**, p = .000).

Their mother's employment/occupation was significantly related to the men's ratings of total overall physician expectations (r = .309*, p = .050) and to physician spirituality (r = .361*, p = .020). Agentic and Communal Life Choices were significantly correlated with physician Agentic (r = .434**, p = .004, and r = .305*, p = .049, respectively) and physician Communal (r = .403**, p = .008, and r = .364*, p = .018, respectively) Life Choices. Agentic life choice involves power- and career-seeking, whereas Communal Life Choice concerns family- and community-mindedness. Self Communal Life Choices were also highly correlated with physician Morality (r = .315*, p = .045).

Expectations of the Ideal Automechanic

The men's self-ratings on Seeking Goodness and Truth were significantly related to the ideal automechanic Seeking Goodness and Truth (r = .537**, p = .000), automechanic Forgiveness, Cooperation, and Peacefulness (r = .470**, p = .001), automechanic Religious Self (r = .520**, p = .000), automechanic Spiritual Self (r = .453**, p = .002), automechanic Agreeableness (r = .310*, p = .043), automechanic State (r = -.409**, p = .005) and Trait (r = -.383*, p = .011), Total Overall Mechanic Expectations (r = .328*, p = .032), Overall Mechanic Morality (r = .342*, p = .025), Overall Mechanic Organization and Leadership (r = .434**, p = .004), and Total Mechanic Peacefulness (r = .371*, p = .014).

Self Communal Life Choice was significantly related to automechanic Extraversion (r = .532**, p = .000), automechanic Openness (r = .330*, p = .031), automechanic

Agreeableness (r = .438**, p = .003), Agentic (r = .306*, p = .046) and Communal (r = .547**, p = .000) Life Choices, automechanic State (r = -.451**, p = .002) and Trait (r = -.433, p = .004), and automechanic Seeking Goodness and Truth (r = .507**, p = .001). Self Caring for Others was significantly related to automechanic Caring for Others (r = .512**, p = .000), automechanic Seeking Goodness and Truth (r = .555**, p = .000), automechanic Agreeableness (r = .319*, p = .037), automechanic Conscientiousness (r = .346*, p = .023), Automechanic State (r = -.464**, p = .002) and Trait (r = -.465**, p = .002) Morality, automechanic Transcendence (r = .501**, p = .001), and Total Overall Mechanic Expectations (r = .426**, p = .004), with a significant and negative correlation with automechanic Neuroticism (r = -.439**, p = .003).

Rank-Ordering of the U. S. President, Ideal Physician, and Ideal Automechanic on the Various Factors (See Table 1)

For the three occupational representatives, the means placed them in rank-order as follows:

Ideal U.S. President: #1 in Neuroticism, Agentic (power- and career-mindedness) and Communal (family- and community-mindedness) Life Choices, Trait (more permanent, ingrained factor) Morality (i.e., seen as least moral in terms of more characterological morality), Caring for others, Transcendence, Seeking Goodness and Truth, Forgiveness/Cooperation/Peacefulness, being concerned with Justice and Mercy, being seen as Spiritual and Religious, Total Overall Expectations (a composite measure), Overall Spirituality, Overall Morality, and Overall Organization and Leadership; #2 in State (more transitory or situational) Morality, Overall Life Choices, and Overall Peacefulness; and #3 in Extraversion, Openness, Agreeableness, Conscientiousness, and Peacefulness (PI).

The Ideal U. S. President, then, was rated as most neurotic of the three occupational representatives studied here, most power- and community-minded, least moral in terms of more permanent and ingrained ideas of right and wrong, most caring for others' well-being, most transcendent in seeing guidance as coming from a Higher Power, highest in seeking goodness and truth and in forgiveness of oneself and others and being cooperative and peaceful, most concerned with justice and mercy, first in being seen as spiritual and religious, highest in overall expectations (including more positive factors of morality and spirituality, and organization and leadership). The Ideal U. S. President occupied the middle position in terms of state (more situational) morality, and was rated as least extraverted, open, agreeable, conscientious, and peaceful (the latter in terms of not just an attitude but specific choices of being and acting more or less peaceful—such as being "hating" or "loving"). There is a question of whether some of these factors were seen as attributes of the Ideal U. S. President or what the men expected that person would be (even though the respondents were asked to answer in terms of the Ideal Candidate for the U. S. President).

Ideal Physician: #1 in Extraversion, Openness, Agreeableness, Conscientiousness, Peacefulness, Overall Life Choices, Overall Peacefulness; #2 in Agentic (power- and career-mindedness) and Communal (family- and community-mindedness) Life Choices, Caring for Others, Transcendence, Seeking Goodness and Truth, Forgiveness/ Cooperation/and Peacefulness, being concerned with Justice and Mercy, having a Spiritual and Religious Self, Total Overall (positive) Expectations, Overall Spirituality, Overall Morality, and Overall Organization and Leadership; and #3 in Neuroticism, State (transitory, situational) and Trait (general, more permanent factor) Morality (ideas of right and wrong). Thus, the Ideal Physician was seen as the least immoral, i.e., the most moral.

The Ideal Physician, then, was seen as the least neurotic and the least immoral (situational and ingrained ideas of right and wrong) of the three occupational representatives, the most extraverted, open, agreeable, conscientious, and peaceful. The ideal Physician held the middle position on agentic (power-seeking) and communal (community-mindedness) life choices, caring for others' well-being, seeking goodness and truth, being transcendent and forgiving/cooperative/peaceful, being concerned with justice and mercy, seeing themselves as spiritual and religious, in total overall expectations, and in overall organization and leadership.

Ideal Automechanic: #1 in State (transitory, situational) Morality—seen as the most immoral (i.e., least moral) in situational dealings with ideas of right or wrong; #2 in Neuroticism, Extraversion, Openness, Agreeableness, Conscientiousness, Total Peacefulness (PI), and Trait (more permanent, ingrained factor) Morality; #3 in Agentic (power- and career-mindedness) and Communal (family- and community-mindedness) Life Choices, Caring for Others, Transcendence, Seeking Goodness and Truth, Forgiveness/Cooperation/ and Peacefulness, being concerned with Justice and Mercy, having a Spiritual and Religious Self, Total Overall (positive) Expectations, Overall Spirituality, Overall Morality, overall Life Choices, Overall Peacefulness, and Overall Organization and Leadership.

The Ideal Automechanic, then, was seen as the least moral in terms of situational (state) morality, least concerned with power-seeking and communal life choices, the least caring for others' well-being, the least concerned with guidance from a Higher Power, the least apt to seek goodness and truth, to be forgiving and cooperative, the least concerned with matters of justice and mercy, the least spiritual or religious, having the lowest total overall (positive) expectations and overall organization and leadership. The Ideal Automechanic occupied a middle position in being peaceful, neurotic, extraverted, open, agreeable, conscientious, in overall peacefulness, and in more ingrained (trait) morality.

And with whom did the self-ratings of the 43 men indicate that they most identified? On four of the factors—agreeableness, conscientiousness, power-seeking, and overall peacefulness—the men identified with the Ideal Automechanic! On neuroticism (highest rating) and trait morality (highest immorality), they identified most with the Ideal U. S. President. The men identified with the Ideal Physician on extraversion and forgiveness/cooperaton/peacefulness. In general, self-ratings had significant correlations with ratings of the three occupational representatives. It is not certain how much the experience of dealing with the three ideal representatives or at least reading or hearing of their performance (as in the case of the U. S. President) entered into the rating/expectation of these representatives.

Conclusions

Although the sample size for this study was rather small, it did provide some interesting and significant findings about the relationships between self-ratings and ratings of the ideal U. S. President, ideal physician, and ideal automechanic. The study also offers interesting insight into the relationships between various ratings or perceptions of these representatives when each was described and viewed from the point of what influences there may be on such persons in terms of organization and leadership, spirituality, morality, peacefulness, agentic and/or communal lifestyles, caring for others, seeking goodness and truth, and even being forgiving and cooperative. A larger population, including female respondents, with more ethnic minority representation and a broader range of ages, preferably in many settings beside the college campus, would be the aim of a further future study on these issues. Additionally, a structured interview with perhaps ten percent of the tested population would shed additional light on the issues involved in this investigation.

References

Piedmont, R. L. (1995). Big-Five Adjective Marker Scales for use with college students. Psychological Reports, 77, 160-162.

Rayburn, C. A., Birk, J., and Richmond, L. J. (1998). State-Trait Morality Inventory (STMI). Washington, D. C.: U. S. Copyright Office.

Rayburn, C. A., Handwerker, S., and Richmond, L. J. (1999). Peace Inventory (PI). Washington, D. C.: U. S. Copyright Office.

Rayburn, C. A., Hansen, L. S., Siderits, M. A., Burson, P. J., and Richmond, L. J. (1999). Life Choices Inventory (LCI). Washington, D. C.: U. S. Copyright Office.

Rayburn, C. A., and Osman, S. (2001). Self-ratings and Expectations of the U. S. President. Paper presented at the Southeast Asia Regional Conference on Scientific and Applied Psychology, Mumbai (Bombay), India.

Rayburn, C. A., and Richmond, L. J. (1997). Inventory on Spirituality (IS). Washington, D. C: U. S. Copyright Office.

Table 1

Means for the Men's Self-Ratings, and Ratings for
Ideal U. S. President, Physician, and Automechanic (n=43)

	Self-Ratings	President	Physician	Automechanic
Neuroticism	49.3452	52.0073	38.5354	44.1904
Extraversion	50.5739	35.8885	51.2237	43.8198
Openness	51.2531	38.2708	41.8299	41.4363
Agreeableness	50.3136	36.7026	56.7562	47.7176
Conscientiousness	50.6648	28.6299	60.6605	52.4343
Agentic L. C.	79.0930	87.6750	82.0238	78.9535
Communal L. C.	76.0000	85.7000	84.0000	68.8605
Total PI	85.3721	56.9512	92.1429	82.9070
State Morality	49.5581	45.9024	40.0952	45.9535
Trait Morality	49.7209	49.1707	42.6429	48.2326
Caring for Others	53.8372	58.0488	55.7381	50.0930
Transcendence	38.3953	39.8537	37.8571	33.4884
Seeking Goodness and Truth	36.7907	40.7073	38.5714	33.5581
Forgiveness, Cooperation, Peace	31.7209	33.0244	30.1905	27.3721
Justice and Mercy	8.2093	9.0500	8.7857	8.5349
Spiritual Self	3.3488	3.6829	3.4048	3.0000
Religious Self	3.0930	3.4878	3.1667	3.0465
Total Overall Expectations		85.6744	84.8049	69.3488
Overall Spirituality		26.3488	25.7805	19.7907
Overall Morality		13.6744	13.5854	12.7674
Overall Life Choices		10.7209	10.8293	7.6047
Overall Peacefulness		12.2558	12.9756	9.4651
Overall Organization and Leadership		22.6744	21.6341	19.7209

Chapter Twenty Two

Emotional Intelligence: Applications for Education and Business

ELLEN LENT

The professional literatures in business, psychology, and education have been addressing the concept of "emotional intelligence" over the last ten years. This chapter offers an overview of this concept and how it is currently being operationalized and measured. The use of 360-degree feedback with emotional intelligence will be discussed. Finally, this chapter addresses how emotional intelligence concepts can illuminate thinking about aggressive or violent behaviors in the workplace and in educational settings.

Overview

The psychologists John D. Mayer and Peter Salovey have written extensively about emotional intelligence (EI) (cf. Mayer, 2001; Mayer & Salovey, 1997; Salovey & Mayer, 1990; Salovey, Mayer, & Caruso, 2001), as has the behavioral science and business writer Daniel Goleman (Goleman, 1995, 1998; Goleman, Boyatzis, & McKee, 2002) and others (e.g., Bar-On, 1997; Ciarrochi, Chan, Caputi & Roberts, 2001). Ciarrochi et al. (2001) defined EI as "the ability to perceive, express, understand, and manage emotions" (p. 26). Mayer and Salovey have described emotional intelligence as an intelligence based in behavior or performance: "an ability to recognize the meanings of emotions and their relationships, and to reason and problem-solve on the basis of them." (Mayer, 2001, p. 9). Mayer, Salovey, Caruso, and Sitarenios (2001) emphasized the interpersonal focus of their theoretical model by stating that emotions have to do with the interactions between people, and are not simply reactions to concepts or inanimate objects. Mayer also suggested that awareness of emotions helps to enhance other intelligences (Mayer, 2001).

Ciarrochi et al. (2001) suggested that emotional intelligence, as defined by Mayer and Salovey, predicts the ability to adapt successfully to life events, and to outcomes related to health, relationships, work, and other important arenas. They hypothesized that people high in emotional intelligence might conduct their lives in ways that help them avoid negative life events.

Mixed Models

Other models of emotional intelligence, called "mixed models" by Mayer and Salovey (Mayer, 2001, p. 9), incorporate motivation, moods, social relationship skills, and other constructs and behaviors not present in the traditional "intelligence" definition mentioned above. These models, while mentioning desirable states and behaviors, might be too crowded with various concepts to adequately predict outcomes such as better work or school performance. For instance, if a positive mood is part of the definition of emotional intelligence, it could be that people's general moods, instead of their awareness of specific emotions, contributes to their decisions not to verbally abuse someone when frustrated.

Criticisms of EI

Objections by Howard Gardner (1993; 1983) to this construct have included the charge that emotional intelligence reflects the ability to manipulate others for selfish purposes. In response to this concern, EI researchers often assert that self-awareness and/or empathy for others are basic components of emotional intelligence (e.g., Goleman, 1995).

Sternberg (2002) raised other criticisms of emotional intelligence. He pointed to the preponderance of scientific literature showing that intense emotions interfere with cognition, and wondered under what circumstances emotions could be shown to do the opposite. He also commented on the lack of convergence in different measures of EI.

Deep Brain Links to Emotion and Behavior

The study of emotional intelligence is enriched by findings from cognitive neuroscience which have located a center of emotion processing in the amygdala, a deep brain structure. Neural clusters have even been found in the digestive tract, lending new credence to the concept of "gut feelings."

If we do suspect that emotional reactions can enhance our intelligence, we must show that people can recognize those reactions and know what they mean. An essential step in any model of emotional intelligence is the ability to understand emotions. The amygdala has been shown in recent research to underlie this understanding or awareness by encoding emotional memories and making judgments based upon our feelings (Ochsner & Lieberman, 2001).

In one perspective of the amygdala's role in EI, Goleman (1995, 1998) suggests that people are susceptible to "amygdala hijacks"—exaggerated emotional reactions that are out of proportion to the situation and for which the person is regretful later. According to this view, the more primitive amygdala, without regulation from the cerebral cortex, urges impulsive behavior linked to basic survival and not attuned to modern protocols of social interaction.

The feelings behind such instinctual behavior are always valid, says Goleman: they include anger, fear, joy, grief, and other human emotions. The problem lies in the response to those feelings. Without a habit of regulating their reactions, people are prone to inappropriate displays of intense emotion that spring from more ancient parts of the brain, from a time when quick action might mean saving oneself from predators.

In present days, Goleman argues, we rarely must escape the jaws of a hungry meat-eater. But parts of our brain still argue for immediate action in the face of intense emotions. In fact, the amygdala has the capacity to override the cerebral cortex. The challenge is to avoid damaging or illegal acts while honoring the brain's intelligence in the emotional realm.

Cognition itself is being studied in relation to how thoughts can evaluate and perhaps regulate emotional reactions such as "amygdala hijacks." If we are able to identify emotions, and then use thoughts to manage how we respond to those emotions, we are more capable of self-regulation and presumably more in control of our behavior.

The process of accurately defining and measuring emotional intelligence is critical to using it effectively. A number of methods for measuring EI are presented in the next section, including a look at the usefulness of asking people to rate themselves on this ability. Some measures of EI use 360-degree feedback, which incorporates others' views of the EI of a target individual. The strengths and weaknesses of 360-degree feedback will be discussed. Finally, the use of emotional intelligence in the regulation of feelings and behavior will be addressed, with a focus on the prevention of violence in school and workplace settings.

Measurement of Emotional Intelligence

Ability Measures

A number of researchers have made efforts to reliably measure emotional intelligence, and to determine if their measures validly reflect the construct. Mayer (2001) explored how emotions inform and enhance intelligent action. He and his colleagues measured emotional intelligence using an ability model, with behavior outputs as the dependent variables. For instance, they studied peoples' capacity to identify what specific emotions mean (for instance, that sadness signifies a loss), and their capacity to manage emotions in themselves and in other people.

The *Mayer-Salovey-Caruso Emotional Intelligence Test (MSCEIT),* with 141 items, measures participants in two categories of EI: experiential and strategic. Experiential EI includes the perception and reaction to emotions; strategic EI involves actual understanding of, and cognitive management of, emotions. This test "indexes how accurately a person understands what emotions signify (e.g., that sadness typically signals a loss) and how emotions in oneself and others can be managed." (Ciarrochi et al., 2001, p. 33).

The two categories in the *MSCEIT* encompass four branches of EI. 1) Perceiving Emotions is measured by asking participants to identify different emotions and their intensity on images of peoples' faces. 2) Facilitating Thought is measured by items such as, "What is the best mood to be in if you're planning a birthday party?" 3) An item from Understanding Emotions is "Jane was angry, and an hour later was ashamed. What happened?" 4) In Managing Emotions, participants are presented with a scenario which would evoke a mood or feeling and then asked, "How would this person maintain his or her mood?"

Other researchers have operationalized emotionally intelligent behavior by testing people on their ability to link facial expressions to an emotion, to conceal inappropriate emotion, to express appropriate emotion, and to predict how someone would feel in specific situations. Lane and colleagues (1998) have found that blood flow to particular parts of the brain is significantly higher in people rated high in EI, another indicator that there is a physiological component to the recognition and processing of emotional information.

Other findings demonstrate the usefulness of emotional awareness in our daily lives. Ciarrochi et al. (2000) found that participants who were rated higher in emotional intelligence were less likely to allow their transient mood to affect their opinions or thoughts. This suggests that people can use the emotion-cognition highway in either direction: emotions can enhance thoughts or thoughts can modulate emotions.

Ability Measures with Children

Emotional intelligence in children has been assessed by several researchers. Cassidy, Parke, Butkobsky, and Braungart (1992) asked kindergarten students to look at photographs of children and identify what each child might be feeling. They were then asked if they had ever felt that way, and what would an adult important in their life do if they saw the child showing that emotion. Participants varied in how well they could respond, and higher scoring children were shown to be more accepted by their peers.

Another study (Barth & Bastiani, 1997) demonstrated that children who were more likely to see angry or negative emotions when observing photographs of faces were also more likely to have poorer social relationships over time. This implies that identification of emotional expressions might be a function of several factors, not only observable behaviors in others. Whether the skill is amenable to intervention is a separate question. Many researchers believe that emotional intelligence skills can be taught and practiced.

Self-Report Measures

Self-report measures of EI depend upon the person completing the instrument to rate themselves on the test criteria. The *Emotional Quotient Inventory (EQ-i)* (Bar-On, 1997) defines EI as an ability to cope with stress and external pressures in an adaptive way. The *EQ-i* has 12 subscales: emotional self-awareness, assertiveness, self-regard, independence, empathy, interpersonal relationship, social responsibility, problem-solving, reality testing, flexibility, stress tolerance, and impulse control. It also contains three factors that are said to facilitate EI: happiness, optimism, and self-actualization.

The *Trait Meta-Mood Scale (TMMS)* (Salovey, Mayer, Goldman, Turvey, & Palfai, 1995) includes three scales: attention to emotion, emotional clarity, and emotion repair. Except for emotion repair, the TMMS appears to measure constructs that are distinct from mood and other Big Five personality factors.

The *Toronto Alexithymia Scale (TAS-20)* (Bagby, Parker, & Taylor, 1994), originally designed to measure the condition of minimized or unavailable emotions called alexithymia, is often used by researchers on emotional intelligence. It "assesses difficulty in identifying feelings, difficulty describing feelings, and externally oriented thinking." (Ciarrochi et al., 2001, p. 40). Although the *TAS-20* cannot logically be dubbed a measure of EI, it does measure constructs that are the approximate opposite of emotional awareness and intelligent use of emotional information.

Ratings by Others

Three-hundred-sixty-degree feedback is a method of measurement that allows individuals to compare their own self-report scores to the aggregated responses of others who know them in a work or personal context. A measure of emotional intelligence that uses 360-degree feedback is the *Emotional Competence Inventory (ECI)* (Boyatzis & Goleman, 1999). Emotional intelligence is defined within four areas: Self-Awareness, Self-Management, Social Awareness, and Social Skills. The most important competency areas according to these authors are emotional self-awareness, accurate self-assessment, self-confidence, self-control, empathy, and influence skills.

Users of the *ECI* are asked to identify which skills, beyond these six, are most important for their success. In addition, results can be compared against a target level of competence based upon a database of successful leaders compiled over 30 years by Goleman's colleague and mentor, David McClelland. This provides users with a set of behavioral anchors with which to compare their level of competence as judged by their raters. Without the ability to compare measured behaviors against norms, 360-degree feedback might be perceived by some as insulated or irrelevant.

A benefit of using 360-degree feedback, of course, is the ability to compare one's own self-reported view with that of a group of others who are familiar with one's performance, such as colleagues, clients, and supervisors. Completing such a measure allows individuals to both see more clearly how others currently see them, and to establish a dialogue with their raters about their ongoing effectiveness. Since self-awareness is a relevant aspect of emotional intelligence, this process has the potential to maintain and improve individuals' abilities in this important domain. In addition, peoples' abilities to regulate their behavior might be improved if they receive updates from trusted others about their interpersonal behavior.

Measurement Challenges

As stated earlier, some models of emotional intelligence are based specifically on behavior, and others include a mixture of behavior and personality traits. Mayer (2001) warned researchers to be aware of what is being measured by different indices or inventories of EI. Self-report measures, and 360-degree feedback instruments, are especially vulnerable to this "mixture" condition. He reported that high scores on the *EQ-i* (Bar-On, 1997), for instance, are highly negatively correlated with measures of depression, anxiety, and other mental health indicators. This could mean that mood and even overall mental health are tangled up in the measurement of EI using Bar-On's instrument.

Some self-report emotional intelligence measures overlap significantly with Big Five personality factor measures, such as the NEO-PI (Costa & McRae, 1992). This is cause for great caution in studying whether measured emotional intelligence has any predictive validity for important outcomes. Big Five personality factors are 1) neuroticism (including anxiety and depression), 2) extroversion (including sensation-seeking and activity), 3) openness to experience (including absorption and authoritarianism), 4) agreeableness, and 5) conscientiousness.

In addition, Goleman (1998) pointed out that evaluating oneself on self-awareness is a tall order. Those genuinely lower in self-awareness might be especially likely to rate themselves disproportionately high. There is also a risk that raters completing a

360-degree instrument on a target individual might use biased recollections in their ratings. These possible limitations are important when considering how to measure emotional intelligence or any other relevant construct using 360-degree technology.

Self-Control and Self-Regulation:
Bullying at School and Work

Next, we turn to specific applications relevant to our discussion of emotional intelligence: findings and methods in the worlds of education and business that leverage EI concepts against aggressive behavior.

EI and Schoolchildren

For many years, school systems have focused on social-emotional learning as a method for helping students identify and practice prosocial behavior with their peers and teachers (Zinns & Prystaloski, 2002). These authors stated that social-emotional behaviors include respecting oneself and others, managing stress and anger, using communication skills, working cooperatively, resolving conflicts, and solving interpersonal problems. Recent studies have shown a relationship between these behaviors and lowered violence, prejudice, and aggression in schoolchildren (Zinns & Prystaloski, 2002).

Sims-Patterson, Latham, and Brakke (2002) found that African-American adolescents high in self-reported emotional intelligence exhibited less pro-violence attitudes than their peers lower in EI, as measured by the *EQ-i*. Salovey (2002) reported that, of 207 multiethnic participants, children higher in measured emotional intelligence engaged in less fighting and substance use, and were rated lower in aggression by peers and teachers. Those teens with lower EI scores were more likely to report using tobacco and alcohol, substances which are correlated with mood alteration. Finally, toddlers whose mothers were higher in EI were observed as more skilled in social competence with their peers (Salovey, 2002).

Bullying in School Settings

Hazler gives a two-part definition of bullying relevant for schoolchildren (italics in original): "The *repeated (not just once) harming* of another through words, social actions or physical attack. The act of bullying is *unfair* because the bully is either physically stronger or more verbally or socially skilled than the victim(s). An individual (bullying) or group (mobbing) may carry these actions out." (2001, p. 191). Outcomes for victims of bullying can range from feeling isolated to plotting suicide or homicide. Outcomes for bullies can include disciplinary actions, removal from the school setting, and other decisions which may interfere with normal school success.

Weisfeld (1994) suggests that bullying springs from dominance aggression, a tendency to overpower others for the sake of feeling superior. This type of aggression can be underidentified in school settings, since many adults view it as playful teasing. But students reported the ongoing nature of such bullying as harmful to the victims (Weisfeld, 1994). The pervasiveness of these behaviors argues for an ongoing and consistent approach toward minimizing bullying's effects. How can EI concepts address this problem in schools?

Hallmarks of emotional intelligence abilities include awareness and understanding of one's own and others' emotions, and the regulation of emotionally-tinged behaviors that are inappropriate for particular settings. When these behaviors are modeled by trusted adults, children are more likely to observe and imitate them. Teachers and staff who demonstrate empathy, self-awareness, and self-control in their own behavior repertoire therefore support the learning of emotionally intelligent choices by students. They also have the opportunity to sanction teasing behavior as a preventive step against long-term victimization.

An emotionally intelligent response by an adult to a school bullying situation could be multi-tiered. First, if applicable, disclose that you were a victim/bully/bystander in your own school career, and how you managed your feelings in that role. Second, disclose your feelings about the current problem (e.g., sad, frustrated, angry, hopeful). Third, discuss the variety of emotional responses that could occur to someone who is in a bullying situation. Fourth, identify with the student what appropriate behavioral choices exist.

Bullying in Work Settings

Unfortunately, bullying doesn't necessarily stop at the school door. The study of bullying, mobbing (group bullying), and emotional abuse in workplaces is ongoing (e.g., Hoel, Cooper, & Faragher, 2001; Hogh & Dofradottir, 2001). Bullying at the organizational level is also being explored (Liefooghe & Davey, 2001). Individual victims of workplace bullying are often defined as those who have been exposed to repeated negative acts of intimidation, embarrassment, or inappropriate power or control at least once a week over a period of six months (Hoel et al., 2001). In a study of 5,000 residents of Great Britain, the prevalence of bullying at work has been estimated as 10% victimized in the last 6 months; 25% victimized in the last five years; and 46% having observed workplace bullying in the last five years (Hoel at al., 2001).

In one U. S. study, professional staff in academic settings reported more mistreatment than academic or support staff (Price Spratlen, 1995). In another university setting, both women and men reported equal frequencies of bullying with a theme of sexual harassment (Richman et al., 1999).

Outcomes for victims of workplace bullying can include decreased self-esteem, feelings of worthlessness, and resenting having to go to the workplace. Employees can experience "ambivalence, powerlessness, and discontent" (Liefooghe & Davey, 2001, p. 387). Perpetrators are likely to have more organizational power and status than their targets, and dominance aggression may well be a motivating factor in these cases as well.

Goleman et al. (2002) described such bullies as dissonant leaders "who not only lack empathy (and so are out of synch with the group) but also transmit emotional tones that resound most often in a negative register . . . In the extreme, dissonant leaders can range from the abusive tyrant, who bawls out and humiliates people, to the manipulative sociopath." (p. 23)

As in educational settings, emotionally intelligent responses to workplace bullying should also reflect a variety of levels of thinking and feeling. Verbal disclosure of one's own emotional reactions is a skilled response, for two reasons. First, it is likely that nonverbal indicators of feelings are already visible, including facial expressions, choice of words, body posture, and skin flushing. Acknowledging with words the emotions that we are clearly experiencing helps other people trust what we have to say.

Secondly, disclosing our emotional responses gives all parties time to pause and to potentially connect with their own feelings. This process can enhance self-awareness for the bullying target, possibly increasing his or her "intelligence" about what to do next, and can potentially alter the ratio of power or control among the parties. Revealing one's own feelings in an unjust or abusive work encounter can have the effect of drawing support from bystanders, or at least catching the bully off-guard.

Borrowing from Mayer's (2002) model, the target could then choose to imagine what feelings would best facilitate a productive response. In the case of workplace bullying, love of fairness and justice might help the target focus on stating valued outcomes assertively, and asking for help from a trusted ally. This line of thought might also assist the target in avoiding an aggressive or passive response.

Emotion-Focused Coping

Much has been written on the subject of coping effectively with emotionally stressful experiences (cf. Stanton, Parsa, & Austenfeld, 2002). There is no agreed-upon definition of workplace coping, but the emotional intelligence literature suggests several ways to adaptively use emotions in situations characterized by violence or aggression.

In order to use our emotions to cope with stressors at work, we must first know what the emotions are and how they are affecting us. The self-awareness aspect of various EI models represents a necessary step in this process. In addition, Hogh and Dofradottir (2001) stated that the ability to tolerate uncomfortable or intense negative emotions in the face of workplace bullying is an example of emotion-focused coping. They cited the distinction that has been made in the literature between emotion-focused and problem-focused coping. (The latter includes generating strategies for changing the situation, which may or may not be in someone's control.)

Knowing how we are reacting emotionally, and managing our emotions in a productive way, are concepts consistent with both the coping literature and models of emotional intelligence. Using emotional awareness in responding to difficult interpersonal situations represents a skillful coping approach.

Conclusions

The growing focus on emotional intelligence in psychology, education, and business provides an exciting milieu for important questions regarding managing oneself and coping with stressful or violent situations throughout the lifespan. Care must be used in exploring this terrain; there are various "brands" of emotional intelligence and they do not correlate strongly with one another (Matthews, 2002). Users must learn whether their measure of emotional intelligence includes motivation, mood, and other constructs, or whether it is limited to specific abilities. The broader the universe of EI factors, the less likely it will be to show effectiveness if it is meant to create desired changes.

Findings from the study of emotional intelligence can be applied to the challenges of bullying and other interpersonal violence in schools and workplaces. The use of our spontaneous emotional reactions in managing our own behavior can encourage healthy responses to stressful encounters with others. Emotional self-awareness, and the open acknowledgment of normal emotional reactions, can support self-acceptance and help us maintain calm in the face of sometimes turbulent interactions with others not so emotionally intelligent.

References

Bagby, R.M., Parker, J.D., & Taylor, G.J. (1994). The twenty-item *Toronto Alexithymia Scale—I*. Item selection and cross-validation of the factor structure. *Journal of Psychosomatic Research*, 38, 23-32.

Bar-On, R. (1997). *The Emotional Intelligence Inventory (EQ-i): Technical manual*. Toronto, Canada: Multi-Health Systems, Inc.

Barth, J., & Bastiani, A. (1997). A longitudinal study of emotion recognition and preschool children's social behaviour. *Merril-Palmer Quarterly*, 43, 107-128.

Boyatzis, R., & Goleman, D. (1999). *Emotional Competence Inventory*. Boston, MA: Hay/McBer.

Cassidy, J., Parke, R., Butkobsky, L., & Braungart, J. (1992). Family-peer connections: The role of emotional expressiveness within the family and children's understanding of emotions. *Child Development*, 63, 603-618.

Ciarrochi, J., Chan, A., Caputi, P., & Roberts, R. (2001). Measuring emotional intelligence. In Ciarrochi, Forgas, & Mayer (Eds.), *Emotional intelligence in everyday life: A scientific inquiry*, pp. 25-45. Philadelphia: Taylor & Francis.

Costa, P.T., Jr., & McRae, R.R. (1992). *Revised NEO personality inventory (NEO-PI-R) and NEO five-factor inventory (NEO-FFI)*. Odessa, FL: Psychological Assessment Resources.

Gardner, H. (1993). *Multiple intelligences: The theory in practice*. New York: Basic Books.

Gardner, H. (1983). *Frames of mind: The theory of multiple intelligences*. New York: Basic Books.

Goleman, D., Boyatzis, R., & McKee, A. (2002). *Primal leadership: Realizing the power of emotional intelligence*. Boston: Harvard Business School Press.

Goleman, D. (1998). *Working with emotional intelligence*. New York: Bantam Books.

Goleman, D. (1995). *Emotional intelligence*. New York: Bantam Books.

Hazler, R. (2001). Bullying: Counseling perpetrators and victims. In E.R. Welfel & R.E. Ingersoll (Eds.), *The Mental Health Desk Reference*. New York: John Wiley & Sons.

Hoel, H., Cooper, C.L., & Faragher, B. (2001). The experience of bullying in Great Britain: The impact of organizational status. *European Journal of Work and Organizational Psychology*, 10, 443-465.

Hogh, A., & Dofradottir, A. (2001). Coping with bullying in the workplace. *European Journal of Work and Organizational Psychology*, 10, 485-495.

Lane, R.D., Quinlan, D., Schwartz, G., Walker, P., & Zeitlin, S. (1990). The levels of emotional awareness scale: A cognitive-developmental measure of emotion. *Journal of Personality Assessment*, 55, 124-134.

Liefooghe, A.P.D., & Davey, K.M. (2001). Accounts of workplace bullying: The role of the organization. *European Journal of Work and Organizational Psychology*, 10, 369-373.

Matthews, G. (2002, August). Emotional intelligence: Science and myth. In M. Zeidner & G. Matthews (Chairs), *Toward a science of emotional intelligence*. Symposium conducted at the meeting of the American Psychological Association, Chicago, Illinois.

Mayer, J.D. (2001). A field guide to emotional intelligence. In Ciarrochi, Forgas, & Mayer (Eds.), *Emotional intelligence in everyday life: A scientific inquiry*, pp. 3-24. Philadelphia: Taylor & Francis.

Mayer, J.D., & Salovey, P. (1997). What is emotional intelligence? In P. Salovey & D.J. Sluyter (Eds.), *Emotional development and emotional intelligence*, pp. 3-31. New York: Basic Books.

Mayer, J.D., Salovey, P., Caruso, D.R., & Sitarenios, G. (2001). Emotional intelligence as a standard intelligence. *Emotion*, 1, 232-242.

Ochsner, K.N., & Lieberman, M.D. (2001). The emergence of social cognitive neuroscience. *American Psychologist*, 56, 717-734.

Price Spratlen, L. (1995). Interpersonal conflict which includes mistreatment in a university workplace. *Violence and Victims*, 10, 285-297.

Richman, J.A., Rospenda, K.M., Nawyn, S.J., Fletherty, J.A. Fendrich, M., Drum, M.L., & Johnson, T.P. (1999). Sexual harassment and generalized workplace abuse among university employees: Prevalence and mental health correlates. *American Journal of Public Health*, 89, 358-363.

Salovey, P. (2002, August). Assessing emotional intelligence as a set of abilities using the *MSCEIT*. In M. Zeidner & G. Matthews (Chairs), *Toward a science of emotional intelligence*. Symposium conducted at the meeting of the American Psychological Association, Chicago, Illinois.

Salovey, P. (2001). Applied emotional intelligence and regulating emotions to become healthy, wealthy, and wise. In Ciarrochi, Forgas, & Mayer (Eds.), *Emotional intelligence in everyday life: A scientific inquiry*, pp. 168-186. Philadelphia: Taylor & Francis.

Salovey, P., & Mayer, J.D. (1990). Emotional intelligence. *Imagination, Cognition, and Personality*, 9, 185-211.

Salovey, P., Mayer, J.D., & Caruso, D. (2001). The positive psychology of emotional intelligence. In C.R. Snyder & S.J. Lopez (Eds.), *The handbook of positive psychology*, pp. 159-171. New York: Oxford University Press.

Salovey, P., Mayer, J.D., Goldman, S., Turvey, C., & Palfai, T. (1995). Emotional attention, clarity, and repair: Exploring emotional intelligence using the *Trait Meta-Mood Scale*. In J.W. Pennebaker (Ed.), *Emotion, disclosure, and health* (pp. 125-154). Washington, D.C.: American Psychological Association.

Sims-Patterson, S., Latham, T.P., & Brakke, K. (2002, August). The relationship between emotional intelligence and attitudes towards violence among African-American adolescents. Poster session presented at the annual meeting of the American Psychological Association, Chicago, Illinois.

Stanton, A.L., Parsa, A., & Austenfeld, J.L. (2002). The adaptive potential of coping through emotional approach. In C.R. Snyder & S.J. Lopez (Eds.), *Handbook of Positive Psychology*. New York: Oxford University Press.

Sternberg, R.J. (2002, August). Discussant. In M. Zeidner & G. Matthews (Chairs), *Toward a science of emotional intelligence*. Symposium conducted at the meeting of the American Psychological Association, Chicago, Illinois.

Weisfeld, G.E. (1994). Aggression and dominance in the social world of boys. In J. Archer (Ed.), *Male violence* (pp. 42-69). London: Routledge.

Zinns, J.E., & Prystaloski, D. (2002, August). Applying social-emotional learning to facilitate school success. In M. Zeidner & G. Matthews (Chairs), *Toward a science of emotional intelligence*. Symposium conducted at the meeting of the American Psychological Association, Chicago, Illinois.

Chapter Twenty Three

A Teaching Model: Controlling Violence by Building Character and Self Esteem through Creative Thinking, Music and Poetry

ANITA O. SOLOMON

Introduction

This chapter represents this author's presentation—part of a multi-disciplined six-member panel of professionals participating in this July 2002 Oxford University, England, International Conference on Social Values. This author was honored to organize and chair the panel, *Models of Teaching Character Development, While Resolving Violent Acts*.

The author utilized cognitive and related principles over many years of working with young to older persons who have experienced a wide range of problems, evidenced in the author's psychological private practice and research, as well as in school and mental health facilities. Spanning this career, the author has conducted individual and group therapies focusing on music and poetry to build self-esteem and to express and control strong feelings and manage anger.

The author has summarized the literature, including her original work on creative thinking, and contrasted this type of thinking with that of repressed thought. She outlines studies on the effects of music and poetry on the resolution of violence. Base-line data is discussed for a proposed research on the use of music with patient populations who are prone to violent acts—to calm their anger and refocus to pleasant and productive thought.

Because of the traumas and violence prevalent in our society at this time, it is important for educators and others to help develop students' character and good citizenship, which will tend to inhibit violence. The author suggests educational and psychological principles and practices for schoolteachers, counselors, and therapists in mental health settings, who are striving to enable children and adults to develop character and self-esteem, and to acquire strong value systems—so that they will be less likely to resort to angry acts of violence.

Statistics Regarding Violence

While the September 11th terrorist attacks represent a significant example, in America we have been experiencing many prior situations that illustrate our national and international problems. We are hearing about children committing violent crimes in schools. We see resolutions of problems supposedly through violent acts in a constant bombardment of stimuli through newspapers, television and the general media.

The Society for Prevention of Violence, in collaboration with the Center for Applied Research in Education, (SPV, Cleveland, Ohio, 1999) revealed the following horrifying information:

> Juvenile violence has significantly increased in the United States. . . . There are 3.6 million persons in the U.S. who are addicted to drugs. The arrest rate for violent juveniles is expected to double from current levels. Eighty-three percent of Juvenile Center inmates reported owning a gun.

The gun seems to have become a symbol of power, as

> . . . 22 percent of students attending high schools in urban areas own guns. The gang problem is chronic in urban schools.

Studies show (Gelles, 1987) "that the conditions likely to increase the risk of violence are the same, whether a person has a mental illness or not. Studies of violence and mental illness have shown that people with mental illness who come from violent backgrounds are often violent themselves, findings that echo the incidence among the general population." In one survey Estroff, Zimmer, Lachiocotte, and Benoit, (1994) found that "chaotic, violent, family environments, in which alcohol or substance abuse is common, on-going conflict among family members, and a controlling atmosphere are associated with violence with persons who do or do not have mental illness." It has been shown that stress can aggravate the symptoms of any anger-prone individual.

Thus, the tendency to act in violent ways has become a major problem for all of us, not only among patients who have been hospitalized, (APA Statement on Prediction of Dangerousness, March 1983) but also among outpatients and the general population. These statistics demonstrate the critical need to foster and support individual critical thought and creative solutions to problems, to encourage the understanding of self, and the appreciation of diversity (Ten Ways to Fight Hate, Southern Poverty Law Center, 1999). Thus, the teacher teaches students to feel empathy and compassion toward others.

The author's experience as a mental health practitioner demonstrates that although people are generally well meaning, there is also an inclination towards evil. No man or woman should believe that they could never entertain or carry out violent concepts or acts. It is part of the educators' task to help individuals to recognize this potential (guard my inclination to do evil, as stated in The Bible in Ecclesiastes) and to be able to curb or redirect, and refocus their energies creatively and appropriately to prevent this evil. Cognitive psychology and the other suggestions in this chapter can help to deal with these problems.

The author discusses strategies for alleviating violence. Using the Oxford Dictionary definition for evil or the motive behind the word violent acts, the author has chosen to define violence as "that which is bad, harmful, and all that causes suffering in self and others." The author also agrees with Dr. Daniel Goleman, (1998) who emphasizes control of emotions. Dr. Goleman defines "self regulation," as "learning how to manage impulses, as well as distressing feelings." Paraphrasing Goleman's principles, "self regulation depends on the working of the emotional centers in tandem with the brain's executive centers in the prefrontal areas. These two primal skills—handling impulses and dealing with upsets—are at the core of the five emotional competencies which are self control, trustworthiness, conscientiousness, adaptability, and innovation."

This chapter focuses on the management of anger and impulsive feelings—to stay composed, to think clearly and in a positive manner, to stay focused under pressure. The following materials are organized according to three basic concepts.

I.   Building Self Esteem and Managing Anger using Beck's and others' Cognitive Psychology

II.   Building Character by Encouraging Creative Thinking

III. Music and Poetry to Foster Effective Learning Experiences and Encourage Healthy Expression of Feelings

Building Self Esteem using Beck's Cognitive Psychology

To develop character, to increase self-esteem, and to establish controls over angry feelings and acts, the author draws upon the techniques and methodologies of Dr. Aaron T. Beck (1996, 1989, 1986, 1985, 1976). These cognitive principles are based on a "theory of personality, which maintains that how one thinks, largely determines how one feels and behaves. This therapy is a collaborative process of empirical investigation, reality testing, and problem solving between therapist and patient." It has been demonstrated that with repeated reinforcements and readiness to think about positive experiences, patients will be more likely to exhibit meaningful and positive behaviors by his/her words or deeds, i.e., reduction in threats and violent acts.

"By dwelling upon individuals' ineptitude and insufficiencies, those low in self-esteem are exacerbating their point of greater sensibilities, and at the same time reducing their opportunity for obtaining success" (Coopersmith, 1969). On the other hand, the awareness of self is improved through attitude and appreciation of one's own ethnic values and those of others, particularly those social values of healthy family life, encouraging positive messages of self-affirmation, e.g., "I am a warm and loving person, ever-growing in wisdom and love" (Barksdale, 1972).

Educators become the central players in enhancing an individual's sense of self-worth. Ultimately, these individuals take on the actions of ". . . developing roles of positive self-evaluation. Just as children internalize the expectations of their parents or significant others, students learn to judge themselves by the same standards" (Coopersmith, 1969).

Strategies Proposed for Anger Management

Many strategies have been noted for managing violent behavior in various situations, such as for examples, on psychiatric units on which this writer is a team member. It is believed that such strategies can also help, by analogy, in educational situations.

One model which accords with the author's principles and practices is outlined in an article on the Internet, "Guiding Principles for the management of disturbed and violent patients are the same whatever the institution or setting." This article stresses the "least restrictive and controlling" setting . . . requiring a "multidisciplinary approach," which should be monitored and audited. When an event of angry feelings occurs and is unrecognized, it is the problem of the staff to recognize early signs. The article suggests that the likelihood of violence should be defined for all individuals and care should include "clear indications of any previously known antecedents and effective interventions." The article also mentions the importance of patients being "listened to and consulted regarding their own needs and goals and they should be given positive feedback about their achievements and coping strategies for dealing with the correction. In this regard, the article refers to several codes of practice (Code of Practice, Paragraphs 26, 1-26.5) and (Access to Help Records Act, 1990 and Complaints Procedure). Regarding psychology staff, relating to these strategies in the management article, it is noted that "the clinical psychologist has an important part to play in the multidisciplinary approach to case management." They can analyze disturbed behavior and take into account environmental, situational, and relationship factors regarding violent acts.

In this regard, this psychologist, drawing from her career of working with various age groups from children to adults, has chosen to interject music and poetry, sometimes as separate subjects, only music and/or only poetry—sometimes music and poetry together, used before, during, and after group therapy sessions. General aspects of music and poetry as well as specific examples are discussed Section III below.

The author is developing procedures and will conduct brief segments offering 15 minutes of music to see the effects on patients' moods, e.g., to see if characteristics such as agitation, hyperactivity, hypervigilance, or the opposite, withdrawn and/or isolated patients' behavior would be changed after the music. The exact effects would be analyzed.

Currently baseline data collection is proposed and graphs will be made at the end of each session on the frequencies of responses and the nature of these responses. Two raters will rate each patient on the following items, which represents the behavior of any one patient on a scale of "never" (1) to "several times an hour" (7). The purpose of this scale would be to see if there would be any effects of specific music or poetry that would reduce the frequency of these behaviors following the group over several hours immediately following the group for a certain period of time. A brief screening on the Cohen Mansfield Agitation Inventory is given before each group starts. To mention only a few of the items in this inventory, that relate particularly to violent acts: Item number 4, "hitting self or others; . . . Item number 9, grabbing people; . . . Item number 11, throwing things; . . . Item number 13, screaming or loud shrills; . . . Item number 25, tearing or destroying property; and . . . Item number 28, making physical, sexual advances." Clara E. Hill, et al (May 2001), suggest procedures to be followed when staff's uncomfortable feelings come about or counter transference develops during their patients' angry periods: help the client to express and explore their anger, to admit any responsibility for their feelings, and to apologize for their errors, and the therapist should not take the patient's anger personally. In other words, don't act out on the patient. Students /patients believe that when they are listened to, understood and responded to with care and sensitivity, they can reduce their need to act defensively.

In the author's work of conducting group therapies in in- and out-patient populations, she trains patients to make their own selections about positive ideations. She reinforces abilities of these patients to have "upbeat feelings" and to improve their self-esteem. For example, the author draws a picture of the brain showing these prefrontal or executive centers and the hypothalamus, thalamus, and amygdala-emotional centers of the brain. This illustration helps students to recognize the specific pathways of brain functioning when perceiving situations and problems.

She then gives them bibliotherapy or poetry and many books that have illustrations of pictures especially appealing to each individual, such as calming pictures of flowers, lakes, trees, nature scenes or poetry depicting scenes of nature. These scenes present possible future pictures to have ready for the prefrontal areas of the brain to utilize when the angry feelings seem to emerge, before escalations in feelings become so angry that these feelings are difficult to control.

It therefore helps to have preventive measures ready in the thinking process to offset that which is perceived as upsetting. In this way she asks her students/clients to have a picture ready in their mind, to have memories at hand, such as being with their grandmothers/grandfathers doing something pleasant together. Other examples of percepts are "thinking of your mother/father's vegetable soup—substitute chili, matza ball soup, meatballs, etc.," depending on the cultural and ethnic background that was given to them in their kitchens.

Other examples of percepts are imagining sitting in a room with your favorite person, or being with your pet, and seeing yourself as being appreciated and enjoyed just for yourself. This is a way of building self-esteem and countering feelings of self-pity, neglect, perceived hurts or rejection. The idea of choice is also instilled in this exercise. Individuals have the power to think of that which they choose to think about. Individuals may think of pleasant experiences if they wish to make these choices. In working with persons in individual or group therapies, this psychologist stresses that the mind is like a tape recorder or disc player. Individuals may place in their brain's the tapes/discs they wish to play. They may choose pleasant music or poetry, scenes of calming natural pictures, if they so desire, rather than ideas of ways that people have hurt them or thoughts of retaliation.

The author then suggests to teachers that in order to develop self-control, it is important to manage one's thoughts—the cognitive processing before the emotions are expressed, and then the impulses to act aggressively and hurtfully are restrained.

There is also a special understanding required for problem solving, which involves compassion, listening, respecting others' opinions, questioning, achieving self-identity, and awareness of themselves within the context of the community at large. Respect for diversity may be taught in the context of other subjects, such as music and the arts (Aranha, 2002), using Peter Yarrow's song, "Don't Call Me Names," and others that help children meet diversity.

Building Character by Encouraging Creative Thinking

The author has conducted independent research in the study of creative thinking (Solomon, 1985), drawing from the work of Dr. E. Paul Torrance (Torrance, 1966 and

2000), who stresses that "dimensions of creative thinking" can be taught. By emphasizing abilities to think fluently, flexibly—with originality and elaboration of ideas, children and adults can utilize their inner resources in solving problems, and thus use alternative actions.

The author also draws upon the work of Willis Harmon and Howard Rheingold (1984), citing their work on "Higher Creativity: Liberating the Unconscious for Breakthrough Insights," who emphasize the potentialities of discovering creative depth within individuals. "Almost everyone has had some experience of a channeling of a creative insight, a breakthrough of deeper intuition, a moment of knowledge recognizable as something beyond the usual reach of the cognitive mind. Some people find such experiences to be commonplace. The insight relates to daily life or to one's professional problems, i.e., the arts, science, business, etc.,) or to social or to spiritual matters."

Carl R. Rogers (1961) "On Becoming a Person," also spoke of this unconscious creativity, as did John C. Gowan (1960). "Creativity is like a spring, issuing forth from the porous rock of the preconscious, under the hydrostatic pressure of the mountain of the conscious accretion. A spring of fresh water often is a nuisance when it first develops, starting in as a muddy quagmire until the dirt and debris has cleared the way and a channel has been dug for the runoff. But when this is done and the bedrock exposed, the spring will run clear and increase in volume and will become a source of life for all in the vicinity."

Our task as psychologists and educators is to discover the flowing springs of life and creativity within our patients or students and us. The author's interpretation of the process of finding these springs is related to the belief that the creativity process can be understood by teaching how to think creatively; to encourage the un-muddying or the bringing to consciousness, that educators can teach how to use our integrating techniques that are developed through the process of discovery and inquiry in the child's earliest years of life. These ideas "spring forth," to use a double meaning, when you are least aware, when you are most relaxed, daydreaming, or in a semi-state of consciousness. These ideas will come about when listening to music and in dreaming, in utilizing the free association techniques in self-analysis—the ideas not only spring from the source upward but from the top downward. Layers are uncovered as you start to inquire until you reach the source of the spring in the unconscious mind. Educators can inspire others to become aware of their own original ideas, their uniqueness, their own meanings, and their own identifications of their ideas coming from the spring of their minds. The goals of the cognitive educator, therefore, whether in individual or group sessions, are to help others to appreciate their ideas, to nurture them, perhaps almost to admire them and once they are identified, to work on them further.

Creative Thinking versus Destructive Cult Thinking

In studying and developing improved therapeutic techniques for developing character and problem solving skills for patients, it was noted that these techniques were in complete opposition to the thinking of former members of destructive cults who had received cult indoctrination (Solomon 1991). After leaving these groups, these individuals spoke of the repressed thinking imposed on its members. While creativity encourages self-analysis and the growth of the mind, cult involvement or any autocracy forces the individual to be dependent and non-thinking. While healthy problem solving stirs the imagination and challenges the intellect, destructive despotism completely destroys the self-image by mental control and enslavement by their leaders. Destructive mind control, as in societies that promote terrorism, attempts to rob individuals of their mental resources. While creative problem solving encourages mental and physical well-being, the destructive cult can lead to malnutrition, disease, and psychosomatic illnesses. While building character is a healthy aspect of total development of a person, negative conditioning techniques in cults can tend to produce schizophrenic-like conditions and destroy the thinking processes of individuals. In Dr. Robert Lifton's "Thought Reform and the Psychology of Totalism," (1961), eight steps in repressive thought are discussed: "Milieu control, mystical manipulation, demand for purity, confession, sacred science, loading the language, doctrine over person, and the dispensing of existence." These processes are definitely in opposition to Torrance's dimensions of creative thinking, which promote healthy thoughts and acts.

Music and Poetry to Foster Effective Learning Experiences and Encourage Healthy Expression of Feelings

Music Enabling Effective Learning Experiences

Diana Deutsch, (1990), University of California at San Diego, is a leading researcher on the brain's musical powers. Dr. Deutsch is editor of *Music Perception,* and has demonstrated how "music calms and integrates the brain's messages through the process of either listening and/or singing various classical and popular pieces." She emphasizes using sensory awareness to heighten integration of thinking.

In hospital populations, brief baseline studies are proposed by the author to offer small segments of music to encourage improved mood. The author has found that in working with hospitalized patients, music tends to reduce agitation, calm mood states, and if communication has been infrequent, increase the number of verbal responses. Classical music played in the background of conversations or activities, also focuses the patients on the topic at hand, e.g., baseball or current events. Variables of time periods, types of music and other varieties of music styles used, need to be studied to determine specific differences of effects.

Recent journal articles have emphasized the importance of music in integrating thought, by uplifting depressed feelings, and in resolving agitation and inappropriate aggressive acts (Solomon, in Natale, 1998 and 2000). Weinberger (1998) writes in *MuSICA Research Notes,* Vol. 12, Spring 1998: "Creativity, while highly desirable, is popularly regarded as an elusive, subjective characteristic. Within music, it is reflected largely in compositions. However, creativity can be measured objectively and its involvement of music is not limited to composing. Accumulating findings indicate that musical training enhances intellectual creativity in general."

Weinberger also writes, "Music has the enormous power to cause emotions to well-up within us. These compelling, even overwhelming feelings, emerging seemingly from nowhere, color our moods, affect our perceptions, and can alter our behavior. The mystery of this power of music is yielding to scientific investigation." Weinberger's studies point to the "interaction of two factors through which music operates: how much we like a piece, which might be expected, and the magnitude of its arousal potential, which is not." Weinberger's *The Coloring of Life: Music and Mood,* notes relevant findings of Furnham and Bradley of University College, London—particularly relating the effects of music on the dimensions of "extraversion and introversion." He first assessed this aspect of personality in college students. Subjects read a 400-page passage in text either in silence or in the presence of a taped radio segment of pop music, and later were asked questions about their reading material. It was found that introverts remembered significantly less than the extraverts. In other words, the music may not always have the same effect for all people, but depends upon several factors, including whether they are introverts or extraverts. In the case of patients in inpatient settings, it is the author's conjecture that effects may differ between withdrawn patients versus aggressive, outgoing patients. Weinberger notes that additional research by investigators is much needed on how there are individual differences in how people react to sounds. However, Weinberger summarizes the findings, and he lists 16 references, "that to date provide solid support for the claim that music increases creativity."

Sherry Small Sundick's poem expresses the wonderful *Company of Music* that facilitates learning and calms strong feelings.

Music is Good Company
The serenity of ethereal harps,
Wonderous sonatas on pianos soothing violins.
Dulcet tunes on a lute,
Resounding through the air
Mandolin melodies,
Humanity in harmony.

There are many studies on how music is facilitating learning. "Overall, the research literature shows that background music, itself not a part of conscious learning task, enters into memory for the material learned. Moreover, recall is better when the music present during learning is also present during recall. Furthermore, tempo appears to be an important component of music's intrusion into memory. Finally, music's effect in altering mood plays a key role." (Weinberger 1997)

Poetry as a Reduction of Violence

Poetry has both a stimulating and relaxing effect in promoting self-esteem, improving communication, increasing socialization, and expanding alertness—thus, reducing agitation and aggression.

In the often-studied *Stopping by Woods on a Snowy Evening*, Robert Frost brings to mind calming images of natural scenes used in group therapies.

Whose woods these are I think I know.
His house is in the village, though;
He will not see me stopping here
To watch his woods fill up with snow.
My little horse must think it queer
To stop without a farmhouse near
Between the woods and frozen lake
The darkest evening of the year.

He gives his harness bells a shake
To ask if there is some mistake.
The only other sound's the sweep

Of easy wind and downy flake.
The woods are lovely, dark and deep,
But I have promises to keep,
And miles to go before I sleep,
And miles to go before I sleep.

The following poem by Sherry Small Sundick in her book of poems, "Choose Life" seems to have the effect of both relaxing and refocusing by highlighting scenes of nature.

All Living Things
Listen to sounds of all living things,
The crickets, cardinals, wrens, and starlings.
Peaceful and graceful are these living things:
Evergreens, poplars, oaks and saplings. . .

Audrey Olberg's Haiku helps to frame concepts of peaceful images in

Dawn at the beach
new splendors from the sea
Shells, like upturned palms.

Two additional Olberg verses suggest starting acts of courage to defend against the fears of meeting new challenging situations.

Envying their courage
I watch the fearless surfers
Then wade to my knees.

Guests on the back porch
Summer's first gasps of delight
For the budding roses

Using a multi-sensory approach helps further a positive image to reduce tendencies toward violence as suggested in Olberg's:

Scents of Cinnamon
In my grandmother's kitchen
Nothing storebaked here.

Natural, even spiritual scenes, are noted in *Who Has Seen the Wind?* By Christina Rossetti:

Who has seen the wind?
Neither I nor you? But when the leaves hang trembling,
The wind is passing through
Who has seen the wind? Neither you nor I:
But when the trees bow down their heads,
The wind is passing by.

These poems increase awareness of nature through the focus on all living things.

In his uplifting poem, called *Weary*, Mr. Rubin's high self-esteem is defended despite hard times:

> *. . . Never allow man's despise*
> *To depreciate your life's worth*
> *But reach inside your soul*
> *And beckon the father*
> *To make you whole*
> *Do not bear witness to naysayers*
> *Or pay homage to detractors*
> *Shake loose those evil chains*
> *Rise to a new dawn . . . from a sleepless slumber*
> *Take wings . . .*
> *And start living again.*
> *Your future is among the stars.*

Creative Problem Solving through Recognition of Diversity

The author was privileged to participate in a program in Israel, similar to the *Seeds of Peace* program, founded by John Wallach, a former Washington, DC based foreign editor of the Hearst newspaper chain. Wallach's program brought together Arab and Israeli teenagers, where children were going to summer camp in Maine, learning how to share ideas and play together in peace and harmony. These children, who are adults today, had the opportunity to learn the concept of peace. This program brought to mind the importance of the concepts of peace, essential to development in children and adults. In order to reinforce the principles of peace, individuals must bond together and "become the seeds from which an enduring peace will grow" (Wallach 1995).

Summary and Conclusions

This chapter sets out important and practical concepts and strategies representing educational principles gained from the author's life work as a psychologist and educator, as well as from leaders in various professions, who have themselves effected great changes for the betterment and welfare of children and adults. It focuses on major goals toward building self-esteem, and encouraging and developing positive emotional and creative thinking. The author emphasizes the healthy expression of feelings through music, poetry and positive visualization of natural scenes. In this age, when significant violence is prevalent in all areas of life, on the local, national and international scene, our educational, religious and psychosocial systems must work together as inter-disciplinary teams to meet the challenges of developing character.

To transfer the idea of world peace to our present situation of excessive violence in schools and other settings, the concept must start early in children's lives in environments that are relaxed and supportive. It requires learning the principles of coexistence, tolerance for diversity, reaching across national and international boundaries to "sow the seeds of peace," in order to resolve the hatred and hostility between people and nations. An effective teaching model promotes the training of teachers to enable students to redirect destructive and hostile ideas and feelings into creative problem solving and constructive acts.

In closing, the author cites the words of William Ernest Henley (1888), English Poet and Dramatist, on his words of courage and self esteem under disabling times, "Invictus"

> *Out of the night that covers me,*
> *Black as the Pit from pole to pole,*
> *I thank whatever gods may be*
> *For my unconquerable soul*
> *In the fell clutch of circumstance*
> *I have not winced nor cried aloud.*
> *Under the bludgeonings of chance*
> *My head is bloody, but unbowed.*
> *Beyond this place of wrath and tears*
> *Looms but the Horror of the shade,*
> *And yet the menace of the years*
> *Finds, and shall find, me unafraid.*
> *It matters not how strait the gate,*
> *How charged with punishments the scroll,*
> *I am the master of my fate:*
> *I am the captain of my soul.*

And, the last lines in Ecclesiastes 3:1-8:

> *. . . A time to love, and a time to hate;*
> *a time of war, and a time of peace. . . .*

And for the latter, the time to stop the violence and to "sow the seeds of peace" is now.

References

American Psychiatric Association (1983, March 18): *Statement on Prediction of Dangerousness.*

Aranha, M.C. (2001) *Character Education Program,* Maryland State Department of Education.

Aranha, M.C. (2000, January 26) in videotape—*Building Sound Character Traits.* National Professional Resources, Inc., Port Chester, NY.

Barksdale, L.S. (1972) *Building Self Esteem,* Lilburn S. Barksdale Publisher, Idyllwild, CA.

Beck, A.T. & Butler, A.C. (1996, Summer). *Cognitive Therapy for Depression. The Clinical Psychologist* 49(3), 6. Beck Institute for Cognitive Therapy and Research and University of Pennsylvania School of Medicine.

Beck, A.T. & Weishar, M.E. (1989). Cognitive therapy in Raymond J. Corsini and Danny Wedding, *Current Psychotherapies,* 4th Edition, F.E. Peacock Publishers, Inc., Itasca, IL.

Beck, A.T. & Young, J.E. (1985). Cognitive Therapy of Depression. In D. Barlow (Ed.), *Clinical Handbook of Psychological Disorders: A Step-by-Step Treatment* (pp. 206-244). NY: Guilford Press.

Beck, A.T. (1986). Cognitive therapy: a sign of retrogression or progress. *The Behavioral Therapist,* 9, 2-3.

Beck, A.T. (1976). *Cognitive Therapy and the Emotional Disorders,* NY, International Universities Press.

Bednar, R.L. (1989). *Self Esteem: Paradoxes and Innovations in Clinical Theory and Practice.* American Psychological Association, Hyattsville, MD, p. 46.

Bellack, A.S., Mueser, K., Seison, G. & Agresta, J. (1997). *Social Skills Training for Schizophrenia.* Guilford Press.

Coopersmith, S. (1969 Feb.), *Implications of Studies on Self-Esteem for Education Research Practice.* Paper presented at the American Educational Research Association Convention, Los Angeles, CA.

Coopersmith, S. (1967). *The Antecedents of Self-Esteem.* Freeman Publishers, San Francisco, CA.

Deutsch, D. (1990, June 11) Music Perceptions, cited in *"The musical brain, studies of pitch and melody reveal the inner workings of the mind, from basic perception to appreciating beauty"* U.S. News and World Report.

Estroff, Zimmer, Lachiocotte, Boit (1994). *The influence of Social Networks and Social Support on Violence by Persons with Serious Illness.*

Ferguson, J.S. & Smith, A. (1996). Aggressive behavior on an inpatient geriatric unit. *Journal of Psychosocial Nursing and Mental Health Services.* 34(4), 27-32.

Flannery, Jr., R.B. (1999). *Preventing Youth Violence: A Guide for Parents, Teachers, and Counselors.* The Continuum Publishing Company.

Frost, Robert. (1923) *Stopping by Woods on a Snowy Evening.* New Hampshire

Gelles, R. (1987). Violence in the Family, a Review of the Research. *Family Violence,* 2nd Edition, Sage Publishing, London.

Goleman, D., Boyatzis, R. & McKee, A. (2002). *Primal Leadership: Realizing the Power of Emotional Intelligence.* Harvard Business School Press.

Goleman, D. (1995). *Working with Emotional Intelligence,* Bantam Books, New York, NY.

Gowan, J. C., (1960). *Factors of Achievement in High School and College.* Journal Counsel Psychology V 7, 91-95.

Harmon, W. & Rheingold, H. (1984) Higher Creativity—Liberating the Unconscious for Breakthrough Insights, *Jeremy P. Tarcher, Inc., Los Angeles, CA.*

Hill, Clara, E. (2001). *Presentation to the Association of Practicing Psychologist,* Maryland, University of Maryland, College Park. Unpublished paper.

Horton (2002) "Neuropsychology of Violent Acts," in *Natale's Sixth International Conference on Social Values, 2002,* University of Oxford, England.

Lifton, R.J. (1961) *Thought Reform and the Psychology of Totalism: A Study of Brainwashing in China.,* W.W. Morton, New York.

Mitchell, E. W. (1999) *Does psychiatric disorder affect the likelihood of violent offending? A review and critique of the major findings.* Medicine, Science and the Law, 39 (1), pp. 23-30.

Natale, S.N., Editor, (2000) Chapter 23, Solomon, A.O. Changing concepts in treatment of the elderly mentally ill (EMCI). *Business Education and Training: On the Threshold of the Millennium:* Volume VI, University Press of America, pp. 299-31.

Natale, S.N., Editor, (1998) Chapter 15, Solomon, A.O. Changing psycho-social values, concepts, and language in the treatment of the elderly who chronically mentally ill.

Business Education and Training: A Value-Laden Process, Volume IV, Corporate Structures, Business and the Management of Values, University Press of America, Inc. pp. 239-250.

Rogers, C. (1961) *On Becoming a Person.* Houghton Mifflin, Boston, MA.

Rogers, C. (1951) *Client-centered therapy: Its Current Practice, Implications and Theory.* Boston Houghton Mifflin, Boston, MA.

Ross, J. and Langone, M. (1957). *Battle for the Mind: A Physiology of Conversion and Brainwashing.* Harper and Row. New York

Ross, J. and Langone, M. (1975). *The Mind Possessed.* Penguin Press. New York.

Rubin, R. (2001). *Weary,* Maryland. Self-published.

Sacks, O. (2002, March 31). *When Music Heals,* Washington Post Parade Magazine, pp. 4–5.

Shapiro, E., (1977) *Destructive Cultism.* American Family Physician. February, 15(2), 80–83. American Academy of Family Physicians. Kansas City, MO.

Shapiro, E. (1987) *Group Psychodynamics.* The Merck Manual of Diagnosis and Therapy, 15th ed. Merck, Sharp & Dohme Research Laboratories. Rahway, NJ.

Shapiro, E. (1978) *Therapy with Ex-cult Members.* Journal of the National Association of Private Psychiatric Hospitals, 9, 13.

Solomon, A.O., Chair (2002) Six-Member Panel Presentation: Sixth International Conference on Social Values, 2002 University of Oxford, Oxford, England.

Lent, E. (2002), *Emotional Intelligence, Applications for Professionals in Education.*

Levin, William. *Psychospiritual Blindness, Transcendent Vision, and Reduced Violence.*

Lorenz, Valerie, *A Psychological Day of Compulsive Gambling.*

MacNeill Horton, Jr. Arthur, *The Neuropsychology of Violent Behavior*

Rosedale, Herbert. *Perspectives on Destructive Cults as Affected by the September 11th Tragedy.*

Solomon, A., *A Teaching Model: Controlling Violence by Building Character and Self Esteem through Creative Thinking, Music and Poetry.*

Solomon, A.O. (January 26, 2000) on videotape—*Building Sound Character Traits.* Character Development by Aranha. Produced by National Professional Resources, Inc., Port Chester, NY.

Solomon, A.O. (1999, July 6-9). Paper presented at Oxford University, England, U.K. *Changing concepts in treatment of the mentally ill (ECMI),* Fifth International Conference on Social Values.

Solomon, A.O. (1992). Paper presentation to the American Psychological Association Annual Meeting, San Francisco, CA. *Psychotherapy of Former Victims of Destructive Groups and Cults: A Suggested Guide for Therapists,* Resources in Education, ERIC/CAPS Clearinghouse, ED 343067, RIE.

Solomon, A.O. (1989). *Psychotherapy of a Casualty from a Mass Therapy Encounter Group: A Case Study.* Cultic Studies Review, Vol. 5, No. 2, pp. 211-227.

Solomon, A.O. (1975). Analysis of creative thinking of disadvantaged children. *Journal of Creative Behavior,* 8, 4, p. 295.

Sundick, Small, S. (1987) "Choose Life" Author, Washington, D.C.

Torrance, E. Paul. (1966) *The Torrance Test of Creative Thinking: Norms-Technical Manual,* Lexington, MA. Personal Press.

Torrance, E. Paul. (1965) *Problems of Highly Creative Children.* Psychology and Education of the Gifted. Appleton Century Crofts, Meredith Publishing, NY, NY.

Wallach, J. (1995). *Seeds of Peace: An Arab-Israeli Summer Program,* Washington, D.C. Published according to Rev. Proc. 89-23, Cumulative Bulletin, 1989, 1:844.

Weinberger, N.M. (1998). *Understanding Music's Emotional Power,* Regents of the University of California.

Weinberger, N.M. (1997) The Musical Infant and the Roots of Consonance. Regents of the University of CaliforniaWeltmann, Begun, R. and Huml, F.J., Ed., (1999). *Violence Prevention Skills Lessons & Activities.* The Center for Applied Research in Education. New York.

Weinberger's (1996) *The Coloring of Life: Music and Mood.* Regents of the University of California.

West, L. J. and Delgado, R. (1978, November 26) *Psyching Out the Cults a Collective Mania.* Los Angeles Times Opinion, VII, page 1.

Yarrow, P. (taped 2001) "Don't Call Me Names." School Program Songs.

Violence and Mental Illness. http://www.hallym.ac.kr/ ~ neuro/kns/tutor/medical/violence.html

Chapter Twenty Four

The Neuropsychology of Aggressive Behavior: An Introductory Overview

Arthur MacNeill Horton, III

Introduction

As luck would have it for an expedition of Spanish soldiers enjoying a picnic breakfast in the early Americas, the nearby riverbed contained whetstones. Taking advantage of their fortune, the soldiers under the command of Narvaez used the stones to sharpen their swords and thus required proof of their sharpness. A village in close proximity provided an excellent testing ground. In his *History of the Indies* Las Casas recounts the tragic events that subsequently unfolded:

> A Spaniard in whom the devil is thought to have clothed himself, suddenly drew his sword and began to rip open the bellies, to cut and kill those lambs— men, women, children, and old folk, all of whom were seated—off guard and frightened they wielded their weapons upon stark naked bodies and this delicate flesh, they cut a man quite in half with single blow (Class notes1).

The atrocity as witnessed lacks one salient feature, an explanation more substantial than the desire to test the newly sharpened swords.

Instances of aggression and violence are commonplace throughout nature, though Homo sapiens seem to possess an extreme capacity. The manifestations of violent or aggressive behavior take on a multiplicity of forms that defy clean scientific definitions. Questions of intention, victimization, social and moral norms, and completion of the act led to disputes concerning the aggressive natures of specific cases. For the purpose of this chapter, working definitions will suffice. Paramount in the present explication is the instances of clear-cut aggression excluding for the time being vague cases. The initial story exemplifies the type of behavior to be examined.

Aggression for this chapter will thus be defined as active and intentional acts, which if successful would cause harm to some sort of victim, while violence will refer to severe aggression directed at another human being. Recent avenues of exploration into the underlying brain structures point to several areas of cortical and sub-cortical interest. Specifically, the frontal lobes, temporal lobes, and structures integral in both habit and learned, conditioned responses correlate to aggressive or violent behavior. Along the same lines several neurotransmitters and hormones active within these areas appear to participate in aggressive behavior and conversely in the inhibition of such behavior. Although the majority of research investigating aggression uses animal models allowing for more invasive exploration, modern technological advances allow for more quantifiably exact research upon human subjects.

A brief overview of the psychology attributed to aggression will help contextually. The classification of aggressive acts differentiates six major types of individuals: those who are drive to aggression by extreme circumstances, those who suffer from psychopathology, those who belong to a culture or subculture accepting particular types of aggression, those for whom aggression is intractable part of their job, those who live continuously with rage on anger, and those who are extremely inhibited (Magargee, 1993).

Edwin Megargee reviewed the factors associated with instigation to aggression. Physiologically, heredity, CNS pathology, endocrinological influences, neurotransmitters, physical illness, drugs, fatigue, and generalized arousal can be involved in instigating or inhibiting aggressive behavior (Megargee, 1993). A variety of interplaying factors in the physical and social environment may encourage or diminish aggressive behavior. In terms of psychological motivation, aggression results in either the hopes of achieving a goal so that aggression is used instrumentally or it comes about through frustration and anger (Megargee, 1993).

Genetics, Hormones, and Neurotransmitters

Determining the genetic influence in aggressive behavior is a tricky endeavor. The previously mentioned litany of factors confounds researchers ability to ascertain a distinct and clear role for genetics. In a study performed on mice that deleted the gene for the serotonin 1B receptor, mice without the receptor exhibited increased aggression in both frequency and intensity (Kandel, 2000). This study not only highlights the role played by genetics, but also the interplay between the chemical conditions of the brain and the genetic make up organism. To add another level of complexity, various stressful social conditions in lowering the inhibition against aggression also lower serotonin levels in the brain. Serotonin levels in no way represent the definitive neurotransmitter in predicting the occurrence of aggression behavior, rather they are one among many acting in a variety of brain areas and systems. A Dutch study discovered in a family with high incidences of aggression behavior and mental retardation a problem with the gene for monoamine oxides A (Kandel, 2000). This enzyme metabolizes several prevalent neurotransmitters including serotonin, norepinephrine, and dopamine (Kandel, 2000).

Research has identified certain hormones thought to be important in displays of aggression. One study from the University of Chicago found low levels of cortisol in the saliva of boys who were abnormally aggressive. The researchers explained that salivary cortisol was, strongly and inversely related to aggressive conduct disorder, peer aggression nominations, and oppositional defiant disorder (University of Chicago

Medical Center). A lack of cortisol may reflect a difference in the way aggression adolescences handle stressful situations (University of Chicago Medical Center). Put simply, aggressive individual may not be as stressed under conditions that are normally considered stressful. Another hormone believed to affect aggression is testosterone. Evidence for a link between testosterone and aggression comes from the fact that males perpetrate a significantly larger number of aggressive acts. In a survey of aggression, a correlation was found between reported measures of aggression and testosterone as well as adrenaline (Megargee, 1993). The exact role, however, of hormones still remains unclear as to a casual effect. Differences in hormone levels may result from other factors located in the brain and would be merely be caused as a response for the body to be physiologically ready for aggressive behavior.

Neuroanatomy

In looking at specific systems and structures, the role of fear and fear conditioned learning can either provoke or inhibit aggression. Primary to fear is the amygdala.

Without the amygdala fear conditioning is absent and the perception of fear is at least distorted. Perceived fear initiates the physiological responses needed for aggression under the necessary environment conditions. The outcome of the subsequent aggression is a rewarding if it is successful. For example a threat is removed, feelings of rage are quelled, or an object in disputes is obtained. Likewise, for unsuccessful aggression, e.g., the initiator is physically harmed himself or there are social consequences for ones actions, the outcomes serves as punishment inhibiting future aggression through further fear of reprisal. Frequent rewarding encouragement of aggression causes aggressive action to form as habits. Habit learning has been with the striatum, whereby aggression occurs in situations that would not have previously precipitated aggression (Class notes 2).

Near to amygdala geographically, the temporal lobe shows abnormal functioning in individuals who suffer from problems with aggression. In a review of seven case studies, the left temporal lobe consistently exhibited either an increase or decrease in activity (Brainplace.com).

This trend has led some to posit the left temporal lobe as the area predominantly involved in aggressive thought. Treatment of aggression stemming from this lobe seeks to stabilize serotonin levels (Brainplace.com). SPECT scans are often employed to verify abnormal activity and pinpoint its location. Although mainly in the left temporal lobe, dysfunction of both lobes is demonstrated in many with aggression (Brainplace.com). More medial parts of the temporal lobe dysfunction are though to reflect a quick temper (Brainplace.com).

Monkeys in which the temporal lobe has been removed including the amygdala and hippocampus show no signs of fear or anger becoming quite passive (Class notes 2). Conjunctly, They will approach animals like snakes usually associated with fearful reaction and explores objects orally. Conversely, stimulation to the amygdala or hippocampus causes aggressive outbursts (Sturb, 1981). These structures along with the hypothalamus compose the limbic system, which is responsible for much instinctive behavior. Other organisms requiring aggression for sustenance also make use of the connection between the olfactory system and the amygdala, whereby the smell of prey acts as the stimulus setting of the limbic and physiological responses that manifest in aggression (Sturb, 1981). Through its interconnection with the hypothalamus, the limbic system produces the desired physiological states to respond to specific situations. Moreover, some people with lesion to the ventrtomedial hypothalamus have been documented to produce aggressive behavior (Sturb, 1981).

Along with the limbic-temporal structures, several structures in the frontal cortex also participate in the expression of aggression. Of particular interest are the prefrontal cortex, anterior in the cingulated gyrus, and the orbital frontal gyrus. These areas relate to the initiation, planning, and evaluation of social and moral consequences. Early hints for the role of the frontal cortex in aggressive behavior come from the head trauma suffered by Phineas Gage. Gage was injured when a metal rod penetrated Gages head leaving a lesion to the ventromedial section of the frontal lobe. While Gage fortunately survived the ordeal, very noticeable changes occurred in his behavior. Gage lost the ability to inhibit inappropriate social behavior, plan for the future, and had difficulty making decisions. With these deficits Gage whose colleagues previously regarded with high esteem became extremely difficult to work with. He drank excessively and was aggressive towards others, eventually becoming a drifter.

More recent studies concerning damage to specific areas of the frontal lobe examine lesions to the prefrontal cortex, which impair a persons ability to behavior in a socially acceptable and moral way (Anderson, 1999). The participation of the prefrontal cortex again highlights the intersection of seemingly divergent factors, typified here by the relation between brain function and environment. While lesions developing in adults do damage their ability to behave appropriately, those suffering still maintain the intellectual capacity to evaluate hypothetical situations in terms of moral and social code (Anderson, 1999). Lesions which appear early in a childs development; however, effect even the individuals ability to discern the rules for a given situation (Anderson, 1999). Anderson investigates early-onset lesion in two case studies. At the time of the study both subjects, a male and female, were in their early twenties, but their lesions were present from infancy. Both showed inability to manage their personal affairs in any competent manner (Anderson, 1999). Both were physically and verbally aggressive towards others throughout their childhood and into adulthood, as well as being arrested on multiple occasions (Anderson, 1999). Ultimately, both became reliant upon their parents and social services for care (Anderson, 1999). Anderson compared both cases as resembling psychopaths.

Another area within the frontal lobe of interest to research on aggression is the orbitofrontal cortex. Generally, this portion is thought to help establish the cognitive dimension of fear. The occurrence of lesions to the orbitofrontal cortex blunts responses to emotional stimuli, concurrently reducing aggression. A study done on juvenile psychopaths found a deficit that the researchers attributed to a difficulty in inhibiting behavior (Roussy, 2000).

Continuous problems with aggressive behavior are commonly accompanied by abnormally high activity in the anterior cingulated gyrus (Brainplace.com). Its relation to aggression; however, appears to be more indirect. Rather then mediating any particular component of emotional, cognitive, or physiological aggression, the activity viewed in the anterior cingulated gyrus connets to patterns of repeated thought and an inability to shift attention (Brainplace.com).

With the recent turmoil throughout the world understanding the root causes of aggression becomes ever more pressing. From the holy lands of India and Pakistan, aggression and violent pervade our present situation. A more comprehensive picture of the dynamic relations that yield aggressive behavior represents a viable course for resolution or improvement of the current state of affairs. The hope and expectation of this chapter is that in some way it may serve to emulate this weighty problem confronting modern times.

References

Anderson, S.W., *et al.* (1999). Impairment of social and moral behavior related to early damage in human prefrontal cortex. *Neuroscience, 2 (11)*. Nature America Inc. http://neurosci.nature.com. 1032-1037.

BRAINPLACE.com Images of Violence. http://www.brainplace.com/bp/atlas/cht4.asp.

Class Notes 1. Great Philosophers: Nietzsche. The College of William and Mary.

Class Notes 2. Functional Neuroanatomy. The College of William and Mary.

Kandel, E.R., Schwartz, J.H., & Jessell, T.M. (Eds.). (2000). *Principles of Neural Science* (4th ed.), New York: McGraw-Hill, p. 50.

Low Levels of Salivary Cortisol Associated with Aggressive Behavior. (2000). University of Chicago Medical Center. http://www.sciencedaily.com/releases/2000/01/00120073039.

Megargee, E.I. (1993). Aggression and Violence. In P.B. Sutker & H.E. Adams (Eds.), *Comprehensive Handbook of Psychopathology* (2nd ed.), New York: Plenum Press, pp. 617-641.

Pietrini, P. *et al.* Neural Correlates of Imaginal Aggressive Behavior Assessed by Positron Emission Tomography in Healthy Subjects. *Abstract.*

Raine, A. *et al.* (2001). Reduced right hemisphere activation in severely abused violent offenders during a working memory task: An fMRI study. *Aggressive Behavior,* 27:111-129.

Roussy, S., Toupin, J. (2000). Behavioral inhibition deficits in juvenile psychopaths. *Aggressive Behavior, 26:* 413-424.

Strub, R.L., Black, F.W. (1989). *Neurobehavioral Disorders: A Clinical Approach.* F.A. Davis Company, Philadelphia, pp. 24-27.

Chapter Twenty Five

A Psychological Day of Compulsive Gambling

VALERIE C. LORENZ

This author has specialized in the study and treatment of pathological gambling since 1972 (Pathological Gambling is synonymous with Compulsive Gambling and Gambling Addiction). Treatment at that time was limited to the 12-Step self-help group of Gamblers Anonymous (GA), which was started in 1956. Twenty years later there were approximately 200 chapters of Gamblers Anonymous in the United States. Very few countries had even one chapter. The only professional treatment program was in the Veterans Administration Medical Center in Cleveland.

Compulsive gamblers were viewed as being of weak character, selfish, greedy, and dishonest. They wasted money and when legal access to money was no longer available to them, they began to commit non-violent, financial crimes to support their addiction. This sudden aberrant behavior of the once-honest gambler is not understood— not by the legal community, clinicians, or even members of the gamblers' families.

Punishment, such as incarceration, was viewed as a means of curing the gambling addiction. Unfortunately this is rarely true, yet it is an attitude which prevails to this day. Take, for example, the federal criminal case of U.S. v. Saul Glickstein (District Court of Delaware), in which this author served as expert witness and testified to the pathological behavior of gambling addiction. The outcome was tragic and yet not surprising, given the lack of knowledge and psychological understanding of this "hidden" psychiatric disorder. "The Failure of American Justice, 1999" illustrates the case.

The Failure of American Justice, 1999
  The Crime of Punishment
  The Death of Compassion
  Jails as Substitutes for Hospitals

Compulsive Gambling is the name
Horses, slots—whatever's the game.
    "A mental illness." Can it be so?

Saul's diagnosis: Gambling Addiction
"I can win," was his conviction.
    A mental illness does not show.

Saul lost his money, every penny
And yet his "friends" would lend him money
    They hoped, but did not know.

At last, through anger, fear and sorrow
They realized he would always borrow
    And not a soul would lend him more.

He turned to crime to pay his debts
And used the funds to place more bets.
    The "Big Win" was his goal to score.

The prosecution saw a chance
To take a loud and public stance.
    The legal system did not know.

"It's greed, he's guilty," sought conviction,
"Don't tell us about addiction,
    The place for him is prison."

The doctors spoke and pled their case
The mighty judge just turned his face.
    Why would he not listen?

The doctors pleaded, "Jail can't cure
He needs Treatment, heal his mind,
    Let our justice not be blind."

"To deter others, and punish all,
To keep the city safe from Saul."
    He needed therapy, that's all.

His mother cried, "Where did I fail?"
She was old, her health was frail.
    She begged, "don't send my son to jail."

To care for Mom had been Saul's mission.
With heavy heart he left for prison.
    Was there no other way?

He sat in jail, day after day,
To help his mind he turned to pray.
    The doctor's help was far away.

At last his prison time was done,
Saul hurried home to see his mom.
 "I'm back to care for you."

He found his mother on the floor:
She'd left this world an hour before.
 And Saul cried out in pain.

"Mom," he screamed, his pain so great,
He held her in his arms, afraid,
 To let her be alone again.

"Compulsive gambling is the name.
That broke my mind, and broke your heart,
 No more will it keep us apart."

And put a bullet through his head.

Compulsive gambling (Pathological Gambling, APA 1980) has increased dramatically in the past twenty years, not just in the United states but worldwide. How, one may ask, did this come to pass? One only needs to look at the unparalleled expansion of legalized gambling, from casinos in Las Vegas to London, horse and dog tracks with simulcasting, betting parlors, and home betting; from state lotteries to multi-state and national lotteries; and video games and slot machines which accept paper currency and credit cards. More recently began a trend in the United States of mergers between casinos, race tracks, and lotteries, all with the most addictive form of gambling, slots; thus a new term has been coined, "racinos."

There are also the many other forms and styles of gambling, such as bingo, instants lotteries, Asian games, card games, options trading, and sports betting. Access is easy, in person, over the phone, through the mail, and the Internet, with cash or on credit.

Society's general belief is that the compulsive gambler will bet on anything, enjoys every minute of gambling, and does not care about anyone or anything else. Nothing could be further from the truth. The addict's gambling becomes chronic and progressive, with tolerance levels, an intolerance for losing, the commission of crimes, a disregard for the consequences, futile attempts to stop, withdrawal symptoms, and failure to learn from experience (Graham, 1990, Lorenz, 1997b). Pathological Gambling is not an act of hedonism and disregard for others, but rather a disorder that has been recognized by the American Psychiatric Association and the World Health Organization since 1980. It is similar to other severe psychiatric disorders in that it is a behavioral response to psychological injuries suffered in childhood, reinforced with a number of emotionally unresolved critical life events in adult life, leading to affective disorders and a pressing need to avoid the uncomfortable feelings associated with these life events (van der Kolk, 1996).

Compulsive gambling requires mental health treatment, yet how can treatment be effective if the psychology of the gambler's addiction is not understood? This author struggled with the gambler's conviction of "I gamble for the rush, for the action, for the high," yet she realized that these words had different meanings for these gamblers, and the consequences of compulsive gambling were, instead, devastating. Thus she developed the *Compulsive Gambling "Action" Inventory* (Lorenz, 1995) as the instrument for a research study. The "Action" Inventory identified the psychological turmoil during one day of active compulsive gambling. The Inventory had the unexpected result of being useful as a clinical tool in treating the compulsive gambler and family members.

The Inventory has 16 steps, from the first thoughts upon awakening to the last thoughts before falling asleep. The therapist explains the Inventory, and at each step asks "What were you thinking, what were you feeling, how strong was that feeling (from 0 % to 100 %), what body part was affected (your head, upper back, stomach, etc.), and what did you do then?" A response of "I felt relief" or "I felt powerful" was followed with the question, "For how long?" The two final questions are, "Who could have stopped you, and when?" and "At what stage could you have stopped yourself?" The answers to each step are written down by the therapist, who then reviews these answers with the patient and others participating in the session. Below is an example of a compulsive gambler who bets on horse races.

1. *First thoughts upon waking up*: It goes on from the night before. I wake up thinking about yesterday, losing, and I have to win it back. I feel myself getting tense, hyper alert, I want to calm down, but the battle starts: I don't want to go, but I have to, yes, no, yes, no. I get itchy, tense, anticipation, it's in my head and shoulders (40%).

2. *Planning to gamble*: I sneak out pretending to jog, but get the paper instead and read the racing news. Ah, there's a horse I like. How am I gonna get there, without them finding out about it? Pretend I'm sick, the car broke down, I have to go to a funeral. Sometimes it's pretty tough to remember the lies, you don't want to get caught.

3. *Getting the money*: I already know where to get it, the same place I got it yesterday. If I have some, I use that. Or I write a check. I know I'll win, and the check won't bounce. Sometimes I have to borrow money from work. I handle the company accounts, so I can set up a phony loan and pay it back when I win.

4. *Going to the gambling place*: I'm racing. I drive 90 mph, I'm on automatic pilot, it's the anticipation (70%), knowing I'm going to win, then calling myself stupid and I should turn around (anxiety 70%). But all of me, everything is on high speed (tension 80%). I race to get there. I run. I get mad when people get in my way (irritation 60%). I push them. Why did I do that? I never do that. All these thoughts run in your head (confusion, disgust with self 75%). I'm afraid I'll miss a race (anxiety 90%).

5. *Studying the racing form*: I already know the horses and the jockeys. But I look at the form anyway. I pick the horses. If the line is too long I can't stand still, I'm like a jumping jack, what if I can't get to the teller in time? It's panic (90%) my muscles are in knots. I'm totally zoned out except for the gambling, no other thoughts, I feel alive (80%).

6. *Placing the bet*: I plan on an exacta, but bet a trifecta. I've gotta get the money. I used to go the track with my dad. That was the only time I ever saw him, and then he died. I couldn't even cry at his funeral.

7. *Watching the race*: I don't even watch the race. What if I lose? I didn't come to watch the horses, I came to bet on them. I go to the TVs, I can bet all twelve races, one time I didn't even have my glasses with me, I couldn't see, but I bet anyway. I just had to gamble (being driven 80%).

I run from one TV to the other, start chain smoking. The pressure hits me in the chest, I can't stand it (anxiety, nervousness 95%). I zone out some more, like I'm watching myself.

8. *Winning a bet*: I won, now I can bet more, what a relief. For 6 seconds, I can relax, but then it's on to the next bet. I can't stop. You gamble with their money. That's the rule, that's the smart way to gamble.

9. *Losing a bet*: Now I have to get it back. My dad used to call me a loser, nothing I did was good enough. He said I would never amount to anything (miserable, sad 90%), I hate that feeling, it gets me in the stomach, all tied up in knots, and in my eyes.

10. *Out of time, end of game*: It's over, I've gotta go home. I don't want to quit, but the track is closing. I get mad (90%), why do I have to stop? Sometimes I drive to Atlantic city, play some black jack, just to keep going Stopping is bad, it makes you feel worse.

11. *Overall win*: That's just like a single win, now I have the money, I have to go back tomorrow even if I don't want to. If I'm at the casino, I tip everybody, I feel powerful. I act like a big shot, a winner with an inferiority complex. What a joke.

12. *Overall loss*: I can't believe it, how stupid can you be (disgust 90%)! I'm scum (contempt 90%), why do I always hurt people (guilt 100%)? I can't walk, my legs are numb, I can't lift my leg, I just stand there. Sometimes I vomit, I puke in the trash can or on the road (disgust, 100%). My dad was right, I'm just a loser.

13. *Going home to spouse or family*: That's the worst, what excuse do I give her, she's going to be mad, she's always mad or she cries (guilt 100%), she'll leave me (terror 100%) I feel so empty, so lonely 95%, why do I do it, again and again (depressed 100%)? It's torture, plain torture, I just want to get off the world. It would be so easy to crash the car, get the insurance money. Then it would be all over.

14. *Last thought before going to sleep*: Back and forth, I just had a bad day, I should have played the other horse, I should have bet more on that horse, I should have bet less on the other one (angry with self 100%), how will I get it back, she won't be so mad at me if I do (despair 90%). I'll make it up tomorrow. I'll play better, my luck will turn (hopeful, determined 75%). My head is killing me, I can't move, my whole back hurts, all my muscles are stiff. I can't sleep.

15. *Who could have stopped you, and when?* Who? Nobody. They couldn't.

16. *At what stage could you have stopped yourself?* I couldn't. I tried, but I couldn't stop myself. I hate myself for it, but I couldn't.

A gambler's typical response upon completing the Inventory is one of surprise and disbelief that the actual "relief" or "high" lasted only six seconds, that virtually every stage resulted in intense troublesome emotions, and that the gambling was the source of the many bodily aches and pains suffered during this active phase of compulsive gambling. In this sample the gambler also realizes the connection between the gambling, father's abuse, and the low self-esteem in failing to meet father's expectations.

During the clinical discussion of the "Action" Inventory, the gambler and family members begin to understand that the disorder is reflective of childhood traumas and other critical life events. They learn that gambling is a means of avoiding the unbearable psychological impact of past events and that the need to avoid is greater than the inability to control unacceptable behaviors.

As is evidenced by this single case study, which is similar to hundreds of others, this psychiatric disorder is not an example of gambling for "the rush" or "for the high," but rather "being in action" is a desperate means of escaping emotional and financial problems. It is the gambler's futile attempt to escape childhood abuse, an inability to gain acceptance from a significant other, in this case the father, and a lifelong history of depression and/or anxiety, low self-esteem, poor coping skills, and a sense of vulnerability in reaching out to others for support. The compulsive gambler's daily reality that has become too painful to bear, thus gambling serves as that temporary escape.

Pathological Gambling emulates many of the symptoms of Post Traumatic Stress Disorder (van der Kolk, 1996), with its resultant depression, anxiety, and intrusive thoughts. "Staying in action" is a means of elevating a constant state of dysphoria brought on by emotionally unresolved stressful experiences in childhood, leading to an early onset of dysthymic depression. This author has learned that the early life dysphoric mood state (Jacobs, 1986) of the potential compulsive gambler is exacerbated in later life by a cluster of critical life events, generally occurring within a time span of two to three years, which then give the impetus for a gambling addiction. Gambling serves as a means of avoiding this psychologically stressed and intolerable reality (Lorenz, 1977a). Magical thinking, a trance-like state, and dissociation brought on by pathological gambling temporarily heal these psychological wounds. Co-addiction, such as heavy smoking, is common. Over sixty percent consider suicide, most often by crashing their cars, others by gun (Lorenz, 1999), pills, or drowning (Lorenz & Politzer, 1990).

Compulsive gamblers may recognize at this stage that they need help, but going "to a shrink or the loonie bin" is just a sign of "being weak, being a loser. They can't help me, anyway, they don't understand." The resistance to treatment and fear of discovery of today's compulsive gambler is akin to the alcoholic's attitudes some thirty years ago. It took much effort on the part of many people to change that attitude. A similar situation exists with compulsive gambling.

While the gambling industry is lobbying for more gambling, and legislators are convinced that gambling monies are preferable to increased taxes, the number of gamblers and compulsive gamblers increases. Community education, prevention, and early intervention programs are essential to combat the growth of this addiction. Training of mental health professionals and access to professional treatment are required to combat the personal devastation and the related consequences of this national health problem. The "Action" Inventory is one step in the treatment process. Perhaps it can serve as a means of avoiding another crime and suicide, brought on by compulsive gambling.

References

American Psychiatric Association. (1980). *Diagnostic and statistical manual of mental disorders* (3rd ed.). Washington, DC: Author.

Graham, J.R. (1990). *MMPI-2: Assessing personality and psychopathology*. New York: Oxford University Press.

Jacobs, D.F. (1986). A general theory of addictions: A new theoretical model. *Journal of Gambling Behavior, Vol. 2(1)*, 15-31.

Kelly, T. (ed.). (1999). Final Report: National Gambling Impact Study Commission. Washington, D.C.: U.S. Government Printing Office.

Lorenz, V.C. (1995). Compulsive Gambling *"Action"* Inventory. Baltimore: Author.

Lorenz, V.C. (1997a). Compulsive Gambling and Dissociation: Hitting the "O-Zone" or the Point of No Return." Presented at the 10th International Conference on Gambling and Risk-Taking, University of Nevada/Reno, in Montreal, Quebec, June 12, 1997.

Lorenz, V.C. (1997b). Compulsive Gambling: Patients' Criminal Charges and MMPI Subscales. Presented at the 2nd Bi-Annual Ontario Conference on Problem and Compulsive Gambling, Ontario, June 5, 1997.

Lorenz, V.C. (1999). *The failure of American justice, 1999: The crime of punishment, the death of compassion, jails as substitutes for hospitals*. Baltimore: Author.

Lorenz, V.C. & Politzer, R.M. (eds.) (1990). Task Force on Gambling Addiction in Maryland: Final Report. Baltimore: Maryland Department of Health and Mental Hygiene.

Rosenthal, R.J. (Fall/Winter, 1986). The pathological gambler's system of self-deception. *Journal of Gambling Behavior, 2(2)*, 108-120.

Van der Kolk, B.A., McFarlane, A.C., and Weisaeth, L. (Eds.). (1996). Traumatic stress: The effects of overwhelming experience on mind, body, and society. New York: The Guilford Press.

COMPULSIVE GAMBLING *"ACTION"* INVENTORYⓒ

This inventory is to be completed by the therapist while interviewing the compulsive gambler. It should be conducted in the presence of the spouse or other significant person in the gambler's life. This will promote understanding of the gambler's thought processes and feelings throughout a day of compulsive gambling. Fill in the data, then review the instructions.

		# Years	# Years out
Name_____	Sex___ Age____	Gambled____	of control____
Type of	Date last	Today's	
Gambling_____ Where_____	Gambled_____	Date_____	

Instructions

"This interview is to determine how you think, feel, and act from the moment you wake up in the morning until you go to bed at night, during the out-of-control period of your gambling. I will go from step to step. Tell me all of your thoughts during each of the various time periods or stages. Then tell me what feelings you are experiencing, how strong each feeling is, from 0% to 100%, and then in what part of your body you experience that feeling – in your head, your heart, stomach, etc. Please look at the form to familiarize yourself with this process. Feel free to add additional feelings that you may have experienced."

Accepted	Anticipation	Escape	Fear	Lost	Rush	Trance
Action	Anxiety	Euphoric	Guilty	Oblivious	Sedated	Watching myself
Alive	Depressed	Excitement	Impatient	Racing	Tense	Zoned out
Angry	Empty	Exhaustion	Important	Relief	Tension building	Other

Gambling or Related Acts	All Thoughts All Behaviors	All Feelings	0-100 %	Body Parts Affected
1. First thoughts upon waking up				
2. Planning to gamble				
3. Planning or getting the $				
4. Going to the gambling site				
5. Study the line, form, #s, slot				
6. Placing the bet				
7. Watch the race, game, #s, reels				
8. Winning the bet				
9. Losing the bet				
10. Out of $$, time or site closes				
11. Overall Win				
12. Overall Loss				
13. Going home				
14. Last thoughts before sleep				

15. Who could have stopped you, and when?	16. At what stage could you have stopped yourself?

This survey instrument was developed by Valerie C. Lorenz Ph.D., Compulsive Gambling Center, Inc , Baltimore. Administration requires brief training. It is recommended that data be collected and presented to the field. The Inventory and author must be referenced in writings.   © 1995

Chapter Twenty Six

Psychospiritual Blindness, Transcendent Vision and Reduced Violence

WILLIAM J. LEVIN

Introduction

The numeric designation 9/11 has ruthlessly commandeered our collective consciousness. On that day devastating, incomprehensible violence crashed into psychological living rooms without warning, painfully shattering window dressing invulnerability. Despite the human proclivity for screening out distasteful reality, the horror and unpredictability of that infamous day exposed our naked frailty just below a thin cover of insulating complacency. Telltale signs of recovery are manifest, yet an unsettling apprehension perks up to the surface of awareness: *We will never be the same.*

Before our pre-9/11 oblivion shrouds us anew in delusive invincibility, can we be brave enough to check out, and learn from, our compromised perception of tranquillity and control? In so doing, perhaps we can gird ourselves in truly protective psychospiritual armor: humbling, honest self-appraisal; the compassionate embrace of diversely-expressed universal oneness; and wide-eyed, mindful intimations of a transcendent reality in which the "lions and lambs" (Isaiah 11:16) of human potentiality lie down together in harmony and peace, awakening with vigor, restoring and safeguarding the world for ourselves and posterity.

The author contends that by linking our arms, hearts, minds, and souls we can undercut violence as a solution to conflict. Given the persistence, prevalence, and perverse attractiveness of violence, this is a daunting task. Recalling that the source of mighty rivers is often a trickle of water gaining strength incrementally over a long course of space and time, so, too, a major social movement begins modestly, adding voices one by one until a critical mass is reached, breaking through the dammed up resistance to necessary change. To think that entrenched, passionately motivated violence will yield easily to pacific good intentions would be naive. However, to presume that violence cannot ultimately be defeated blinds us to the incredible human potential for life-affirming, magnanimous, altruistic endeavors (Maslow, 1971; Fromm, 1973; Kohn, 1990). By purposely pooling our talents and energy, guided by the collective wisdom of our species refined by hard experience over so many centuries, as well as a humble sense of our perceptual and psychological limitations, who can, with certainty, deny that we could co-create a safer world in which far more human beings could flourish? To realize this important goal, which has become so much more compelling since 9/11, we must open up our eyes and see beyond what is familiar, comforting, and self-justifying. Then, together, we might see our way out of the violent darkness hovering over us so menacingly, expediting the reappearance of the warming sunshine of more-evolved human development conducive to world peace.

Psychospiritual Blindness

I pitied him in his blindness
But can I boast, "I see"?
Perhaps there walks a spirit
Close by, who pities me (Kemp, 1955).

A number of years ago the author heard a stunning news item on the radio. It had been reported that a car was swerving recklessly all over the Delaware Memorial Bridge. A state trooper was dispatched to head off the out-of-control driver. Pulling the car over, the steamed-up officer demanded an explanation for such extraordinarily dangerous driving. He became momentarily speechless as he realized that the driver was BLIND. Suddenly noticing that there was another passenger in the front seat of the car, the utterly confused policeman could barely articulate the obvious question, "Since you're blind, why isn't your friend at the wheel?" Quick on the draw, the sightless driver fired off a snappy retort: "Oh, I couldn't do that, officer. He's drunk!"

The author invites you to consider the possibility that the hapless, blind driver could just as easily be you or me.

The consequences of our limited psychospiritual vision, as opposed to neurological or structural impairment, are far from trivial. As we shall soon see, blindness to the less-than-noble aspects of our character and coping, as well as the attributes of those who differ significantly from ourselves, can potentiate violence.

The widespread assumption ripe for challenging vis-à-vis psychospiritual blindness is our conviction that we see reality exceptionally well. Despite copious evidence to the contrary, the overwhelming majority of human beings —women, men, boys, and girls —seem to believe that, with few exceptions, everyone else is off the mark. Too often to count we shake our heads in amused disbelief that yet another supposedly intelligent person has acted stupidly right in front of our infallible eyes. That generally means that the miscreant behaved differently than we believe we would have under the same conditions. But, when was the last time we voluntarily scrutinized our own questionable actions, concluding that, perhaps we had fallen a few standard deviations below Average on the IQ scales? Moreover, can you imagine a major celebrity, maybe a national politician, addressing the general populace in this manner?: "My fellow citizens, I want to admit that I have made several disastrous mistakes this year that have harmed you catastrophically. It was all my fault. Regrettably, I cannot promise that this will not recur in the future. Furthermore, as you have long suspected, 80% of my decisions have been politically motivated." As a result, being inundated with instantaneous myocardial infarctions, emergency rooms would have to shut their doors on the spot!

Following Baumeister's recommendation (Baumeister, 1991), representative nuggets of cross-disciplinary inquiry have been assembled to buttress the assertion that we humans are blind about ourselves. A logical place to begin is with Sigmund Freud (1960), who alerted us startlingly to the insidious, subversive undertow of irrational, subconscious forces drowning rational thought. While the details of psychoanalysis remain controversial, many of Freud's fundamental discoveries have become self-evident tenets of everyday discourse. Yet, outside of psychotherapy relatively few people appear to be engaged in rigorous psychological self-examination. Long before Freud shed light on our customary self-delusion, sound warnings about self-blindness resounded across multi-century wide chasms to little avail (Isaiah 42:18). St. Augustine rued the observable fact that humans tend to be indifferent to self-discovery (Buzan, 2001) and Sir John Davies confessed that his own soul was "blind" (Davies, 1596).

Philosophers and theologians have been cautioning us for ages about the seductive trap of equating appearance with reality, which blindsides us quite regularly (Russell, 1959); man's "near-sightedness" (Emerson, 1990); and the illusory "veils of maya" (Mishra, 1974; Democratus, 1991). The saliency of subjectivity underlying perception was underscored by the philosopher/psychologist William James (1991) who opined: "As a rule we disbelieve all facts and theories for which we have no use."

Many modern scientists, epitomized by Ilya Prigogine, a Nobel laureate in chemistry (Csikszentmihaly, 1993), along with philosophers (e.g., Kant, 1959), and psychologists (e.g., Kelly, 1955) have called attention to the personal construction of experience that complicates even further the question of objective apprehension of reality. To be unaware of, or minimally acquainted with, one's personal contruct system, utilized to measure and cope with reality, is to stagger through life with a bag over one's head, creating functional blindness.

Evolutionary biologists have also contributed profound insights into personal blindness. To illustrate, Stephen Jay Gould (2002), in his recent monumental tome, applauded structuralist theory's explication of the survival value of dichotomous thinking. Under highly stressful circumstances when making a quick decision could save one's life, black-and-white thinking is efficient. Unfortunately, as Gould indicated, this process is also notoriously inaccurate. Similarly, Goleman (1995) pointed out that all-or-nothing, "emotionally hijacked," shoot-from-the-hip problem solving can be extremely irresponsible, inducing indiscriminate violence.

Dating back to the early post-World War II days, social psychologists have provided bountiful evidence of the enormous impact of contextual factors on human perception (e.g., Postman *et. al.*, 1948; Bruner *et. al.*, 1955; Bruner, 1958; and Aronson, 1976). The upshot of that research, supplemented by more recent investigations conducted by neuroscientists (e.g., Ratey, 2002), is that humans are extremely vulnerable to misperception, distortion, and misinterpretation of sensory input.

It is tempting to attribute such aberrant perception to abnormal people. For example, when a floridly psychotic person ascribes evil intent to his genuinely friendly, benign neighbor, we might readily and accurately characterize such behavior as "paranoid." But, as another social psychologist has discovered (Myers, 2000): "Most people perceive themselves as more intelligent than their average peer, as better looking and as less prejudiced than others in their communities." Here is a mundane but excellent illustration of Myers' hypothesis. The most recent issue of the American Automobile Association magazine (AAA World, July/August, 2002) contained this headline:

> 7 out of 10 parents think it's easy to install a child safety seat.
> 8 out of 10 safety seats are installed incorrectly.

The author believes that what is far more problematic with respect to the problem of violence is that throughout history "normal" humans, with absolute certainty of their rationality and moral correctness, have sincerely and fervently prayed to God to eradicate their "heathen," "infidel," or otherwise misguided and despicable enemies, who have been perceived as immediate, tangible threats to their survival (see Dostoyevsky (1991) for a similar viewpoint). We usually do not pause to recognize the ironic and nettlesome theological problem associated with importuning a universal God to eviscerate our dangerous counterparts—also God's children—who may be simultaneously offering mirror image prayers to eliminate the previously mentioned threatened ones, also construed as evil incarnate—and violence begets more violence on and on.

In 2002 parlance, what terrorist, homicidal bomber, or tyrannical dictator would regard him/herself as a "terrorist?" Conversely, no one who vows, with all the righteous power one can muster, to destroy terrorism, considers him/herself to be a "terrorist." To an impartial observer, however, the absolute difference between a "freedom fighter" and a "terrorist"—seemingly polar opposite character types—may become blurred. Ordinarily, in our minds, we are the "good guys" no matter what side we represent or what methods we employ to pursue our self-evidently holy cause. When we unquestioningly conclude that we are, by definition, always in the right, the ends justify the means.

This potentially quite inaccurate self-assessment strongly correlates with devaluation and oppression of others (Carnegie, 1936; Fromm, 1973; Calvin, 2000; and Johnson, 2000). It is only a short step from derogating others to considering them as enemies when we feel threatened (see Lazarus and Folkman, (1984) for careful documentation of the linkage between perceived threat and stress). Thus, those who may have begun with the best of intentions, but with complete blindness to their participation in this deleterious process, may, nevertheless, extend the historical cycle of violence. Is it really surprising, then, that hyper-patriotic, God-is-only-on-our-side psychospiritual blindness is alive and well?

Francis Cardinal Arinze (2002) has courageously applied this type of analysis to organized religion. Steeped in salvation ideology and understandably committed to self-preservation and propagation, these hallowed institutions can unwittingly abet destructiveness. Obviously, the eminent Cardinal, who is on the Pope's staff in Rome, is not antagonistic to organized religion. Rather, Cardinal Arinze has advocated that organized religions acknowledge their periodic short-sightedness and errors of judgment that have sometimes fanned the existing flames of hatred and violence. Laudably, as an informed insider, he admits that even our beloved major religious institutions are subject to the same social psychological variables individuals typically face. It would be laughable for any person or organization to insist that it is immune from such influences. As Dr. George Kelly (1969) sagely observed:

> Beware of the obvious. There is something about the obvious things in this world that repeatedly rises to plague me . . . those things I once thought I knew for sure, those are what get me into hot water, time after time.

Cardinal Arinze had initiated a promising interfaith dialogue. Perhaps, it will catalyze the coordinated application of the enormous goodwill, resources, and influence of the major religions that could contribute significantly towards the reduction of violence. Transcendent vision is needed to attain that essential goal.

Transcendent Vision

How odd it is that physically blind people can be proficient at recognizing different species (Gardner, 1999) while most sighted individuals cannot even recognize their scanty self-insight. Unlike the Portuguese Nobel laureate in literature, Jose Saramago, we do not usually realize how compromised we are psychospiritually (Saramago, 1995, p. 326): "I think we are blind, Blind but seeing, Blind people who can see, but do not see."

Sequing to physics, Saramago's somber assessment is reminiscent of Werner Heisenberg's "uncertainty principle" (Heisenberg, 1927), a major construct in quantum mechanics, which held that it is impossible to measure anything perfectly. Accuracy requires a qualifier. Another Nobel prize winner in physics, Niels Bohr, challenged Heisenberg's theoretical position (see Baggott, 1992). Although Heisenberg's innovation is very instructive, one might question its pertinence to the current theme of psychospiritual blindness. Juxtaposing the humanistic mantra, "Man is the measure of all things" (Protagoras, 1959) with the two concepts of psychospiritual blindness and Heisenberg's "uncertainty principle," the following syllogism emerges:

1. Man (in a generic sense) is the uncertain measure of all things.
2. Man is blind to his inherent limitations.
3. Man is the blind measure of all things who is certain that he is accurate which is certainly wrong, leaving Man blind to his BLINDNESS!

It is reasonable to ask how one can effectively respond to psychospiritual blindness. Fortunately, there are some provocative, kite-like possibilities in sight, uplifted by solicitous winds of growing consensus that new orientations are needed to nullify violence. One such idea floated recently by Danah Zohar, who teaches at Oxford University, and her psychiatrist husband, Dr. Ian Marshall (Zohar and Marshall, 2000, p. 23) lays bare the root cause of psychospiritual blindness:

> We are blind to the deeper levels of symbol and meaning that place our objects, our activities, and ourselves in a larger existential framework. We are not colour blind, but meaning blind.

Once the cause of a problem is identified, attention can be redirected toward solving it. To illustrate, Zohar and Marshall are proponents of "spiritual intelligence" (SQ) which is centered on meaningful action. They regard SQ as the "necessary foundation (Zohar and Marshall , 2000, p. 3) for both IQ and EQ (Emotional Intelligence). Spiritual intelligence is concerned with ultimate values and transformative experience. In the same vein, Winifred Gallagher (2001) has coined the term, "spiritual genius," which she defines as the "uniquely human ability to seek life's meaning" (for a fair-minded critique of spiritual intelligence, see Gardner, 1999). The convergence of like-minded thinkers from many disciplines, lifestyles, and beliefs who advocate personal and collaborative transformational ventures to enhance meaningful human interaction is encouraging (e.g., James, 1958, 1991; Frankl, 1985; Maslow, 1971; Aronson, 1976; Wilber, 1979; Moses, 1989; Kohn, 1990; Ury, 1990; Einstein, 1991; Kierkegaard, 1991; Ram Dass and Bush, 1992; Capra, 1993; Csikszentmihaly, 1993; Walsh and Vaughn, 1993; The Dalai Lama, 1995; Houston, 1997; Hanh, 2000; Chah, 2001; Dostoyevsky, 2001; Gallagher, 2001; Kushner, 2001; Smith, 2001; Arinze, 2002; and Redfield and Murphy, 2002). Given the pervasive dissatisfaction with vacuously materialistic modern culture and its attendant alienation, depersonalization, and despair (Smith, 2001), it is likely that this international, interdisciplinary search for more meaningful living will continue to attract more fellow travelers.

It is also hopeful that Ajahn Chah, a Buddhist scholar, has noted that psychospiritual blindness can be reversed: "If there is delusion, knowledge ceases. If there is seeing, blindness ceases" (Chah, 2001). The kind of seeing to which Chah alludes is transcendent in nature, reflecting the deeper layers of reality that typically elude most people, but which one knows with certainty exist during "peak experiences" (Maslow, 1971). These transcendent experiences have been cross-validated by countless other people in their everyday lives.

Central to this "transpersonal" world view is the appreciation of multiple realities that are apprehendable through heightened consciousness (Mack, 1993). Thus, transpersonal theorists emphasize the importance of enhanced consciousness (e.g., see Langer, 1989). This approach may expose one to greater discomfort and psychological pain, but also to intensified gratification associated with living more fully, honestly, realistically, spontaneously, freely, and ethically.

John Ratey (2002, p. 14), a Harvard Medical School psychiatrist, has succinctly captured the ethos of this alternative approach transcending shallow, disconnected, self-centeredness in favor of a personally-evolving consciousness:

> Becoming more conscious would certainly improve our abilities as social animals. It would help us focus more on decisions and consequences, on associations, so that we are more keenly aware of our connectedness to others. . . . As we gain more attention and consciousness we can better evaluate actions and consequences and be less impulsive than our current selves (also see Wilber, 1993, pp. 214–222 and Goleman, 1995).

Perhaps, Ratey's perspective can serve as a sensible, state-of-the-art counterpoint to Tennyson's (1955) sobering depiction of human behavior besotted with ignorance leading to violence:

> Blind and naked Ignorance
>   Delivers brawling judgments un-
>   Ashamed,
> On all things all day long.

With this overview in mind, the author will offer suggested directions for reducing violence.

Reducing Violence

In this concluding section the three constituent elements of the psychospiritual armor identified in the INTRODUCTION will be described in more detail. Practical steps will be articulated to jumpstart personal contributions to the formidable challenge facing humanity of transforming violence into collaborative problem solving for the betterment of mankind.

Element #1: Honesty

1.   **Accurate Self-Assessment**: Mother Theresa reportedly characterized herself as having a "Nazi in my heart." Lesser mortals are not as good as we like to think we are. In this regard, people all over the world can benefit from the knowing advice of Lao Tzu in the *Tao Te Ching* (Ram Dass and Bush, 1992): "Knowing others is wisdom; knowing the self is enlightenment." Individuals are not as powerless as is frequently thought to stimulate major change in the world. To get started, with the help of trusted friends and loved ones who see what we cannot see clearly about ourselves, individuals can identify true personal strengths and weaknesses. Leading with those strengths and doing the best one can over and over again, it is possible to at least neutralize weaknesses and hone the strengths, greatly augmenting successful peacemaking.

2.   **Muscular Spirituality**: By this term the author means an active, engaged, self-assured spirituality that is informed by all the wisdom of its day. Albert Einstein's (1996) pithy comment is applicable: "Science without religion is lame, religion without science is blind." Muscular spirituality easily accommodates Dr. John Ratey's astute integration of brain function expertise and religious experience. In the following quotation Ratey makes reference to vastly different orientations towards God—left-brained legalistic and ritualistic approaches and right-brained personal, experiential ones—which can be meaningfully synthesized.

Instead of arguing about and in some cases killing each other over our different conceptions of God, we might try bringing both deities—both hemispheres—together. Then we might at least find a better way to think about the Almighty, and about the universe and our place in it"(Ratey, 2002, p. 375).

Muscular spirituality is not content to proffer bromides and it is not equivalent to the "lowest-common denominator religion" (Arinze, 2002).

In addition, the utilization of muscular spirituality could indirectly stimulate peace by empowering others. Our lives have rippling effects on other people. By knowledgeably offering vital support and encouragement from the sidelines, we can potentiate other people's major contributions towards peace.

3.   **Artistic Challenge To The Lies Underlying Violence**: Solzhenitsyn, the Russian Nobel prize winner in literature, has passionately extolled the crucial role of the artist in emasculating violence (Solzhenitsyn, 1991):

Once someone has proclaimed violence as his METHOD, he must inexorably select the lie as his PRINCIPLE . . . Writers and artists have a greater opportunity: TO CONQUER THE LIE! . . . And as soon as the lie is dispersed, the repulsive nakedness of violence is exposed, and violence will collapse in impotence.

Element #2: Compassion

1.   **Oneness**: Beginning with the "Great Chain of Being" (Wilber, 1969) linking all living creatures, one can advance phenomenologically to a sense of oneness with others regardless of their beliefs. Moreover, the congruence of principles and values across the major religions (e.g., "sparks of divinity"; "the golden rule"; "blessed are the peacemakers") is impressive (Moses, 1989). What the author finds more compelling is the commonality in the experiential reality of awesome wonder, universal connectedness, and peacefulness underlying religious belief (Smith, 2001). Once we sense commonality it becomes easier to empathize with, and feel compassion for, others. Then, discrepant beliefs may become secondary to the perception of brotherhood and sisterhood in God's dominion, or for non-deists, to a sense of family interrelatedness as human beings.

2.   **Suffering**: Pain hurts no matter who feels it. Who can completely avoid pain in this life? We are inextricably linked in exposure to suffering and the relentless seeking of relief from it (Rinpoche, 1994). Once again, apprehending this fact of life and remaining focused on it—a harder task—can help us immeasurably, removing artificial psychological barriers between others and ourselves. The net result could be more peaceful interpersonal relationships built one at a time.

3.   **Understanding** the viewpoints of other people, whether one agrees or disagrees with them, may lead to greater comfort with, and tolerance of, those positions. Increased understanding and tolerance often result in improved social relating and sometimes, forgiveness—essential ingredients to escape the perennial cycle of retributive justice-based violence (Moses, 1989).

More psychologically balanced historical accounts facilitate this process. Exemplifying this point, the historian Herodotus (1987) presented many sides of an epic Greek-Persian struggle. He was deeply concerned with the perceived flesh-and-blood perceived truths of the competing protagonists rather than merely the bland, "objective" reporting of "facts." (see James, 1991). It would be inane to argue that Herodotus was a better historian than the more factually-centered Thucydides (1972). They both exhibited great, but vastly different, competencies serving different purposes. From Herodotus we can learn that by understanding the reasons for violence held by the perpetrators of violence—even if those reasons are unconvincing, absurd, and/or evil-minded—one can increase the probability of countering them successfully (Aronson, 1976).

4.   **Challenging "cultural and religious myopia"** (Arinze, 2002, p. 133): This can reduce prejudice, indirectly decreasing violent outbreaks. Expanding one's general awareness of other cultures and religions effectively undermines the formation, maintenance, and application of stereotyped thinking to individuals representing those cultures and/or religions that may be unfamiliar.

5.   **Collaborative Efforts**: Studying, praying, and problem solving together in ways that are respectful to the respective religious traditions are examples of collaborative interfaith efforts (For a large inventory of such interfaith programs and charitable projects, see Beversluis, 2000). Just how far we are from accomplishing this goal was demonstrated by a recent *Washington Post* article (July 9, 2002) which reported that a minister had

been suspended by church officials merely for participating in an interfaith service following the tragic 9/11 event. On the other hand, on a more positive note, to show support for peace efforts in the Middle East that would fairly and realistically meet the needs of both the Palestinians and the Israelis, a spirited, synergistic, meaningful, and well-attended interfaith service, sponsored by Christian, Jewish, and Muslim organizations, was conducted at the National Cathedral in Washington, D.C.

Element #3: Transcendence

1. **Beyond the Ego**: Somewhere over the ego's rainbow radiant transpersonal realities beckon individuals to move beyond their limitations (Maslow; 1971; Csikszentmihalyi, 1993; Redfield and Murphy, 1993; Walsh and Vaughn, 1993; Zohar and Marshall, 2000). This is not meant to imply that it is always desirable to abandon one's ego. Instead, what is intended is actualization of more of our latent abilities, including the capacity to perceive consensual reality in more vivifying ways. As a result, appreciating the wondrous diversity right in front of our eyes, rather than being threatened and angered by it, we can give peace a greater chance to prevail.

2. **Beyond The "Man Is Inherently Violent" Assumption**: This assumption provides a rationale for ongoing violence—*"We can't help it. It's in our nature."* This line of reasoning has not been proven. On the other hand, many theorists have convincingly argued against it (e.g., Fromm, 1973; Aronson, 1976; Ury, 1999). Instead of blind acceptance of this dangerous, self-fulfilling assumption, individuals can implement what works to reduce violent acts. For example, Aronson (1976) enumerated various effective violence-reducing steps including positively reinforcing non-violent behavior and modeling peacefulness and cooperation. Kelman (1973) and Goleman (1995) have advocated raising the threshold for violence. In addition, establishing the inevitability of salutary, but perhaps unwanted change, tends to let the air out of the violent balloon. An outstanding illustration of this approach can be found in the groundbreaking work of Pettigrew (1959). His investigation demonstrated the influence of perceived inevitability in the increased acceptance of integration in the United States following the revolutionary 1954 *Brown v. Board of Education* Supreme Court case.

3. **Combating The "Common Enemy": Indifference** (Menninger, 1970): Elie Wiesel (2002), also cites indifference to evil as a major obstacle to eliminating oppression:

> Indifference to evil is the enemy of good, for indifference is the enemy of everything that exalts the honor of man. We fight indifference through education, we diminish it through compassion. The most effective remedy? Memory.

4. **Advocating For The "Third Side"**: In marital therapy psychotherapists often represent the "We" aspect of the relationship which is frequently malnourished. Similarly, in a broader context, William Ury (1999) champions the "third side"—the "surrounding community which serves as a container for any escalating conflict." The third side reflects a superordinate, transcendent possibility. Two wonderful examples pertaining to the heartbreaking Israeli-Palestinian conflict dramatize the peacemaking potential of the third side.

The first instance concerns an ad in the *Washington Post* (June 20, 2002) run by a group of moderate Palestinian leaders which renounced the murder of civilians as a means of obtaining political goals. This is a spectacular step which deserves great praise from peace-loving people everywhere. The other example relates to a talk radio program (National Public Radio, May 4, 2002) in which Laura Blumenfeld, an American journalist, described her determination to argue in an Israeli court on behalf of a Palestinian man. What was astounding was the identity of that man: ten years previously he had shot and nearly killed her father who had been visiting Israel at that time. Subsequent to the shooting, Laura became friends with the shooter and his family, but did not reveal to them that she was the daughter of the man whom he had tried to kill simply because he was a Jew in Israel. Upon seeing Laura plead with the Israeli judge for mercy for him, the attempted murderer swore that he would never again commit violence. The author believes that more third side champions "taking the high road" can accelerate the cause of peace.

5. **Are You God In Hiding?** (Houston, 1997): Within just a few minutes, this group exercise can transform a throng of strangers into open-minded truth seekers suddenly filled with the exciting, awe-inspiring possibility of divinity within their midst. Therefore, the author wonders if the perceived imminent/immanent presence of God affects how we treat others. In particular, can it persuade everyday people to accord others dignity and interact with them peacefully?

6. **Affectionate Laughter At Our Foibles**: This lighthearted, self-accepting attitude could generate increased relaxation, openness, joy, and acceptance of others. As humans laugh at themselves they are more likely to transcend fixed viewpoints. This can facilitate the development of broader, deeper, and richer perspectives consistent with creative problem resolution and the manifestation of peace of the inner and outer varieties.

7. **Reverence For Life**: Being mindful of Dr. Albert Schweitzer's impassioned call for reverential treatment of other living creatures, even today, one can think anew how to individually and collectively do something to hasten the arrival of that glorious day when *violence* will be cut down to size, silenced, and eventually extinguished (Schweitzer, 1991, pp. 240-241):

> But this goal cannot be reached unless countless individuals will transform themselves from blind men into seeing ones and begin to spell out the great commandment which is Reverence for Life . . . It is the source of constant renewal for the individual and for mankind.

In closing, it is important to remember that reducing violence depends not only on decreasing the frequency and intensity of violent acts, but also on *minimizing the psychological presence of violent mind sets that precondition us to violent acting out.* History suggests that this may be a long-term undertaking. In doing one's part to shorten that process, the author proposes that we consider clothing ourselves in humility and knowing smiles of genuine thanksgiving that one can meaningfully choose to be transcendently, compassionately, and ironically "blind" to the shortcomings of others as recommended by Edgar Albert Guest (1955):

Let me be a little kinder
Let me be a little blinder
To the faults of those around me.
Let me praise a little more.

Psychospiritual blindness can be remedied, transcendent vision is attainable, and, yes, violence could be reduced to an "Emperor's New Clothes" foolhardy strategy. As we honestly reappraise ourselves, surprisingly, we might find ourselves skipping a felicitous stone of realistic hopefulness into a nearby river of opportunity, engendering and witnessing concentric circles of widening, proactive influence in the transcendent-yet-palpable evolving, compassionate, human journey towards peace.

*****

The author would like to acknowledge four people who offered valuable assistance in the preparation of this chapter. His friends and colleagues in the Maryland Psychological Association Writers' Group—Anita Solomon, Ph.D., Ellen Lent, Ph.D., and Valerie Lorenz, Ph.D.—offered wonderful support and excellent editorial comments. Dr. Levin is also grateful to his inspiring rabbi, Dr. Philip Pohl of congregation B'nai Shalom of Olney (Olney, Maryland), for his ongoing wise counsel regarding spiritual matters.

Chapter Twenty Seven

What Does it Mean to Orient Oneself in Thinking? The New Old Crisis of the University from a Continental Perspective

ACHIM D. KÖDDERMANN

"Was heißt, sich im Denken zu orientiren?" (Kant *WDO*: 131; *Richardson*: 87 "What means, to orient one's self in thinking?"). To understand the current global crisis of the university, it is necessary to orient oneself where it all started in the early 12th century: the new old crisis of the university has to include a view from a continental perspective.

What does it mean to orient oneself in thinking? This was the question Kant answered by pointing to one of the essential functions of higher education; the capacity to help us to orient ourselves in a more and more complex reality. Before him, Moses Mendelssohn had already pointed out that orientation is necessary for the condition of enlightenment (Mendelsohn). Orientation allows us to place knowledge, and to find a way to autonomy.

Kant's successor at Königsberg addressed the need for orientation in his philosophical dictionary: "Orientiren (sich) heißt eigentlich den Orient oder den Ort im Horizonte suchen, wo die Sonne zur Zeit der Tag—und Nachtgleiche aufgeht, wodurch dann auch die übrigen Weltgegenden leicht bestimmbar sind" (Krug; Orth: 31). ("To orient oneself means to find the orient or place on the horizon where the sun rises at the time of the solstice, hence, we can determine the other world regions.")

This definition of orientation can be interpreted allegorically. Knowledge of the place and time allows finding the way. Applied to universities, it can be said that knowledge as produced by institutions of higher learning allows orientation. It reaches from the determination of the solstice by ancient civilizations to the more and more refined measurements of time. Its application, be it through a sun dial, a water clock, or more modern forms of time measurements, is linked to non-applied academic research about the nature of time. Applications such as the integration of a pendulum in watch making demonstrate that fundamental research can lead to, at first unintended, applications. It is a necessary precondition for commercial orientation.

The direct benefit of orientation fell back on society as a whole, not on the providers of knowledge. In exchange, those in charge of the finding and teaching of knowledge gained academic freedom, respect by society, and autonomy. Such autonomy, not only for a small elite, but also for society as such, is necessary. It inspired Humboldt's attempt to reform the state via a fundamental reform of the university (Natale: 86): "Der Gang der Wissenschaft ist offenbar auf einer Universität, wo (sie) immerfort in einer großen Menge und zwar kräftiger, rüstiger jugendlicher Köpfe herumgewühlt wird, rascher und lebendiger" (Humboldt: 257). ("At a university, which constantly rummages through a large number of strong, able bodied youthful heads, the progress of science is faster and more lively.")

The problem of the Germanic university is that it has a tendency to rely on old structures, which has led to less innovation and more stasis. In Germany, this tendency became stronger than in other countries. Century old institutions kept a reputation that was not tainted by the recent Nazi past (Neuhaus). Indeed, of the about 85 institutions which have endured for the last 500 years such as the Catholic church, some Swiss cantons, etc., 70 are universities (Kerr, Mathy). And the "ideal" university, as reformulated by Humboldt, has indeed become the pattern or model for worldwide admiration and imitation.

Its roots are documented in Fichte's attempts at a new foundation in the "Wissenschaftslehre" which is seen as an alternative to the purely traditional, repetitive form of learning. Learning is thereby seen as productive, thus bridging the gap between theory and practice deplored in the rift between universities and universities of applied sciences. Schelling follows the movement with his "Vorlesungen über die Methode des akademischen Studiums" in 1802: studies are to form an organic whole of knowledge and application. Friedrich Schleiermacher and H. Steffens ("Über die Idee der Universität," 1809) complete the revised paradigm of the German university (Spranger). Wilhelm von Humboldt coins its applied form in his drafts for educational reform (Humboldt 1920: 279). In 1802, Humboldt argued against the old form of specialized training, which he encountered in the French system of higher education: "Sie ertöteten durch die enge ihres Gesichtskreises jeden wissenschaftlichen Geist und waren schließlich nichts anderes als Schulen der empirischen Praxis" (Spranger: 200 f., "Through the narrowness of its horizon they eliminated all forms of scientific spirit and became nothing else but schools of empirical practice.")

Humboldt and his foundation of the free university in Berlin created the model of worldwide university reform. Jefferson imported the enlightenment inspired Germanic model of higher education to the U. S., and the Ph.D. in its current U. S. form is a copy of the Germanic doctorate (Jefferson). Early resistance against this Germanic influence came in the U. S. from William James, who deplored "The Ph.D. Octopus" (James) as form of elitism. In Germany, it became clear in the years after the World War II that century old structures did not provide the right framework. Lacking the vivid spirit of Humbold's reforms, the structure of the German post-war university crumbled in the student riots of 1968. A trendy prediction of a "catastrophe of education," made by a religious philosopher in 1964, finally became true (Rüthers: 16). Rioting students addressed the antiquated structures symbolized by old forms "Unter den Talaren der Muff von 1000 Jahren" (Under academic gowns the musty air of 1000 years). Protesting students were joined by (American-trained emigrant returnees) Adorno and Habermas

(Hammerstein). The authorities responded to the public demand for innovation by a loosening of the old, hierarchical structure; the new mass university, with its anonymity and a lack of belief in itself was born. Access to higher education by all became the goal of higher education, and its structure was revised, professors had to share power with students and assistants ("Mittelbau"). For this purpose, the preparatory high school system (Abitur in Germany, Matura in Austria, Baccalaureat in France) was opened to more and more students, allowing wider access to universities than ever before. The apparent problems of the old, elitist higher education system (Köddermann) were addressed by the invention of a new, parallel track of university-like education, the universities of applied sciences: "Fachhochschulen."

There is a fundamental difference between the old idea of the university as institution of higher learning and its counterpart, the university of applied sciences. In the Austro-Germanic educational system, this difference is clearly formulated as a different approach to praxis and research (Mische: 16 f.). The intended outcome of the revised mission statements for universities and universities of applied sciences was to allow for competition among universities, both within each category and between university systems. "Gleichwertigkeit," equivalence, was the goal formulated by a large political majority. The intended short-term outcome was to regulate the competition in such a way that a specific flaw of the Germanic university, the long duration of studies, could be addressed. The university of applied sciences was supposed to compete with the purely theoretical knowledge of long standing, offered by the traditional universities. The focus on organized, well-structured studies with an intended outcome allowed these to shorten while still allowing applied universities to remain within the realm of science. (The untranslatable Germanic word used in this context is "Wissenschaftlichkeit" which applies to the natural and the "humanistic" sciences, the humanities, alike.)

Universal comparisons are necessary to ensure the compatibility of knowledge. For this purpose, the originally absolute independence of the university (see the title, "Freie Univerität" in Berlin) was sacrificed. Parallel to the development of the U. S. educational system, the quantification of results in a uniform pattern became necessary to allow standardized testing. The standardization is supposed to allow a comparison of the competing systems, notwithstanding the differences in their original missions. In 2001, the so-called "Pisa Study" which compared school systems internationally, led to a spurt of reform in Europe.

Both forms of universities are supposed to prepare the student for professional life. Traditional universities focus on the teaching of methods. For the universities of applied sciences however, the mission is reduced to the application of knowledge; thus, professors for the latter category will have to have demonstrated skills beyond the academic realm in at least five years of praxis and to have shown the capacity to transfer academic knowledge to successful application (Mische: 17).

The traditional condition of tenure at a Germanic traditional university is still the habilitation, a form of second doctorate, which adds an average of five more years to the already lengthy studies of most applicants for continued employment. Since the goal of applicability gained weight, and when it became obvious that the teaching skills and innovative tendencies of younger faculty could not be developed in the traditionally rigid system, so called "junior professorships" were introduced. In principle, they will adapt the Germanic system to U. S. standards. The assistant professor is introduced and lifelong tenure in the automatic form of the current university system is replaced by a conditional tenure system. Implemented from "above" by the federal ministry of education, with financial incentives for the complying federal states, it still has many flaws. For the position called "Junior Professor" tenure track is optional. It allows a career in the home institution, thus fostering intellectual inbreeding. It includes some teaching responsibilities as compared to the purely scholarly habilitation (Bulmahn). In Austria, the attempt to commercialise the university by outcome measurements has led to mass resignations of the self-administered university faculty in 2002.

The ability to react quickly to the job market, the ability to form alliances, and the internationalisation of their curriculum have shown that in many respects the universities of applied sciences have sharpened their profile to such a degree that they are the clear winners of the competition. In a way, the European applied universities are following the example of the old English Royal Academy which described its mission under the experimental scientist Robert Hook in 1663 as follows: "To improve the knowledge of natural things, and all useful Arts, Manufactures, Mechanic Practices, Engines and Inventions by Experiments" (Weld).

Since nobody will accuse the Royal Society of a lack of scientific rigor and standard, it can be seen that the reforms of the continental university systems are a late adaptation of old structures to new realities, with applicability included in the mission of fundamental research. Jean Jacques Rousseau addressed the problem in his *Second Discourse on the Origins of Inequality Among Men*. The sciences are reproached for not having fostered the benefit of humanity but only that of the privileged few. However, today's reforms of the continental university system, with the introduction of bachelor degrees and a separation of graduate and undergraduate studies, are more interested in the applicability of knowledge and the reduction of cost than in the fostering of a link between research and application. As in all Platonic cases, the Germanic copy is even less desirable than the U. S. original.

Students of universities of applied sciences are winners and losers of the competition between the university systems. At first highly employable graduates receive no systematic overview beyond the limits of their original field of studies. They lack time and space to gain such knowledge. The structure of their studies is in the hands of others; they remain within a school-like structure. As tradeoff for the loss of freedom and choice, they gain fast access to the job market. Their employability is far superior to the average applicant from traditional mass universities. In principle, their professors stand with both legs in a practical life that prepares the students well. They spend their time primarily in teaching and not in research; the student being the sole purpose of such institutions, and the application of knowledge dominates all other aspects of academic life. From a career oriented point of view, one could argue that such focused studies are a full success since even the classical continental universities are unable to offer the alternative: traditional liberal arts degrees as *Studium Generale*, based since 12th century Salerno, Bologna and Paris on universal knowledge.

It can be argued that our complex reality needs more broadly spread knowledge, and that the half-life of the claimed applicability is declining: to teach skills successfully does not mean that the student will be able to develop the necessary transfer skills, and the "anthropological premise" of all studies, the view of the whole and the Kantian hope for an exit from self inflicted tutelage, is pushed to the background. Plato and Aristotle agreed on the necessity to gain knowledge in such a way that we are able to see the "holon" (Wirth: 105), the whole: In the above quoted text on the need for orientation, Kant claims that abstract, not applied, "Denken" ("Thinking") is necessary to combine logically. The freedom to think becomes the last probing stone of truth (Kant *WDO*: 146; *Richardson*: 407 "The chief touchstone of truth of one's self").

Since the times of the medieval university, it was not clear whether the whole or the parts are more important, and the quarrel of the Universals is revived today in the competition between universities and universities of applied science. What is beyond debate is the complexity of systems, which the university of applied science, and more and more, the university as such, have declined the responsibility to address. Instead, that study has been relegated to specialized fields such as system theory or cybernetics.

The goal of the university, in its newly revised mission, has to become or remain to understand relationships: "die Bedingtheit begreifen lernen" (to understand conditionality). All knowledge is mediated, conditioned by words, concepts, myths (Bösch). In this sense, we have to address the same problem Aristotle and Plato faced: the belief in easy applications, the "for sale" sign on knowledge, are not new: they have threatened education since sophistry became a trade, not an art.

However, the trademark university in its privatised, for profit shape as mentioned by Natale is not the true threat for the Germanic or Continental university: here, the "for free" (Joffe) public support for the public institutions of higher learning has so far prevented the success of institutions such as the University of Phoenix (Natale: 39 ff). However, in anticipation to the same needs as addressed by commercial institutions such as the said University of Phoenix, the European flagship universities have started to engage themselves in a process of self-commercialisation. Thus, both American and Continental institutions face different symptoms of the same phenomenon. The sophistication of studies has led to a spread of sophistry. . . . And those engaged in non-applicable liberal arts education have contributed their own share to the trend: since the appearance of objectivity has been deconstructed. The appearance of Truth was denounced by those defending it, leading to a general feeling of disorientation. It is understandable that applicable job skills need no immediate in depth study of theory, and lead to less doubt; therefore, more focus and more immediate happiness than could be achieved through lengthy sophisticated studies of what turned out to be nothing but sophistry: to study ideas without believing in them is not the most promising antidote to the new concept of applied, corporative studies. The intellectual infighting between different schools of thought has shifted the focus from a university that leads society intellectually to a university that, at best, reports on it, and that cannot agree on the validity of its reports. In most continental philosophy, for example, the study of past knowledge has become a pure intellectual exercise in glass pearl playing. No practical results are expected, and the less practical the thesis, the more elaborate the vocabulary, the higher the assumed level of scholarship. It is understandable that the goal of such studies will not be the understandability of the findings. It is also understandable that such news will never be shared with a general public (Bauer). This outdated model of high-priesthood, which confers a form of nobility on the bearers of titles, is partly to be blamed for the current downfall of the classical university. When universities confer titles to their own governing bodies or to donors, even their intellectual integrity is in question. Titles loose their respectability, and the conferring universities their role of choice in society. Respect could then be reduced to the admiration of power and money. In the field of non-applicable education by public institutions, private commercial enterprises can gain space: the Bank academies in Europe are part of a growing field of parallel educational systems of higher learning. They introduce corporate knowledge and skill in the curriculum, heightening the applicability. Such commercial academies are comparable to the educational systems of distant learning as described by Natale for the U. S. (27 f.). However, in the sense of the original institutions, they are no true universities.

Since the commercial success of such institutions and educational systems in the U. S. seems apparent, and since the Continental systems are prone to imitate any U. S. development in order to stop the apparent "brain drain" and educational advantages of the U. S., why should one oppose such a trend?

Lack of orientation by those formed in such a system is the answer to this rhetorical question, since education is not a good like all the others. Unlike commercial commodities, such as grain, it is the one grain that stands out of the mass that yields the hidden value: qualitative measurements, and systems of mass production of knowledge at lower cost, will miss the chance to find this grain. In a way, the commercial streamlining of the output-oriented modern university in all its forms threatens our intellectual freedom more than direct censorship of freedom of speech would have threatened a democracy: such a commercial entity leaves no space for the elaboration of new answers, and it will not be possible to find a forum for the discussion of such answers.

We also have to consider classical warning voices against all trends of focused output measured study: if an educational system fails, Plato's Republic (VIII) shows how *tyrannis* can develop out of a democracy that has failed to educate its elites and population. Karl Jasper saw some of the same signs Natale calls "The corporate eclipse of the university": "Durch die Ausbildung der Arbeitskräfte für die Zwecke der in ganz ziellose, immer nur an partikulare Zwecke gebundenen technischen Massengeschäft wird der Aufgabe der Universität nicht genug getan" (Jaspers). ("The education of workers for particular purposes to satisfy specific needs of technological mass production does not fulfil the original task of the university.")

The limitation of the scope of the university to such short-term goals, which today's corporatization demands, eliminates the search for non-tangible long-term goals. "Mit der Universität sinken Gesellschaft und Staat ab" (Jaspers, Hoffacker). ("Society and state fall with the university.")

Society and the university are linked: without universal scope of its mission, the institution is reduced to a corporate entity like all the others. However, corporate goals are short term, quantitative goals, which are measured by financial outcome. The goals of a university can be reduced to such corporate goals with streamlined, more efficient corporate structures. However, the university will then have to loose one essential part of its mission for society: to provide meaning, to search for meaning, and to define the guidelines for society. The essence of its mission is not the teaching of survival skills alone. Only in the framework of a free academic institution can we expect to gain orientation in more than the literal sense. The teaching of skills alone outdates quickly. It does not live up to the expectations of the new clients, industry (interested in a skilled workforce) and students (interested in stable, well numerated employment). The sense and meaning giving capacity of a free, independent, not financially restrained university is a condition for the further development of society: it is not astonishing to see that the German university through its students was the father of the first democratic movements in Germany. Students in such institutions of higher learning led the change of society, and they resisted attempts of corporatisation successfully in the France of the sixties through the nineties of the last century. Devaquet could not implement modest reforms of the curriculum. Such intellectual and political independence which forced structural change will be impossible in a commercialised university system when the students are reduced to the role of paying clients or potential donors, and the faculty are following the work for hire concept of employment. Without an idealistic core of studies, that allows to search for orientation in world which is less and less easy to decipher, the individual, be it student or professor, will lack the necessary educational background to orient her/himself. Without such non-focused liberal arts training, the necessary intellectual maturity to confront future problems, to continue education, is not provided.

To find a way out of this dead end scenario, universities have to play a dominant role: Orientation is only possible if the universities can provide more than a belief that "anything goes." Natale calls this current activity "bobbing aimlessly in a sea of cultural relativism in which it seems that anything can count as knowledge" (Natale: 29). A "one fits all" educational answer cannot be found. The challenge to be addressed after elitist education is mass education. Corporatisation as the current trend can offer commercialised, partially good results. It is natural that large organizations offer their own, corporate forms of carrier management. Only when this form of qualification starts to threaten and replace the non-for-profit forms of education is society as such in danger (Luhmann).

To help future generations of students to "orient themselves" in a more and more diverse reality, certain ground rules for general education have to be reintroduced in all forms of higher learning: a core, not in the sense of a strictly defined body of knowledge, but in the sense of a skill transcending form of classical, root oriented "Bildung." Such a form of education in the own tradition has to be complemented by the study of other traditions, in other languages, which will allow an objective view of the own background, and a conversation beyond the own background. In the latter respect, the Continental universities are able to show a growing proficiency in foreign languages, and are well ahead of their U. S. counterparts. However, as far as "study abroad" are concerned, private institutions of higher learning such as the Fontainebleau-based *INSEAT* are leading the phalanx, followed by universities of applied sciences which offer instruction in English. However, one of the oldest and most venerated institutions of higher learning in Belgium, the University of Löwen/Leuven has successfully introduced an international track in its curriculum, offering the view of a foreign yet related culture (in English language) to students from abroad, with a large constituency from the U. S.

Further, such a "public interest" curriculum would have to make space a moral education of students: a modern society without communally shared and reflected values cannot expect its members to bear responsibility beyond their own immediate interests.

"Aufklärung in einzelnen Subjekten durch Erziehung zu gründen, ist also garleicht, man muß nur früh anfangen, die jungen Köpfe an diese Reflexion zu gewöhnen" (Kant *WDO*: 146). "To found enlightenment in single subjects by education is therefore very easy; one has nothing to do but do begin early to accustom young understanding to this reflection" (*Richardson*: 407).

As a response to the "customized approach to education," (Natale: 42) that is offered by corporate for profit educational models, the financial balance has to be tilted in the direction of non-for profit institutions, be they state sponsored or private (Such as the Jesuit institutions of higher learning in Germany which are only co-financed up to 18 percent [Hochschule für Philosophie München] by public sources). For the sake of sound finances, in view of the need for widespread affordable access to education in the 21st century, the tuition question has to be addressed: it is fundamentally unfair to allow all students to study without contribution to the cost of studies. The current no or low tuition model supports the strongest in studies and research, without the necessary redistribution of resources to support the weaker parts of the system. The old tutorial system of the British flagship institutions is equally unaffordable and unfair, since it limits the best instruction to a small minority. Even land grants cannot support mass education, and continental universities lack endowments of any form.

However, the "good deal" offered to society by students from public institutions has its price. Supplementing the tuition to be raised from those who can afford it, the state will have to finance the difference to the cost of private education, thus offering the incentives for the non-job related training in values, meaning and orientation. The classical liberal arts education in public institutions has to be revived with the help of public funding, yielding a long-term benefit to society as a whole. For this purpose, it will also be necessary to further include all teaching faculty in the general mission of the university, thus offering a valid alternative to corporate, for profit models of education. This faculty-involvement in the changes of society made the German universities of the 19th century to the engine of societal change. Through the "Göttingen Five," it also provided a forum for democratic reform or resistance to tyranny.

Such an alternative to vocational training cannot be solely based on the radical liberal arts concept as presented by Bishop Newman and others (Natale: 88). "Vocational" training cannot be entirely dismissed from a modern university: the mediated form of knowledge which removes us further and further from the culture of scripture alone demands more training in vocational skills than offered by classical grammar or high schools. The use of body extending devices such as computers is necessary, and requires further training than penmanship. Those Germanic universities that have not been willing to accept this necessity of modern academia will remain the losers of the international competition for the best educational system. Less and less foreign students are enrolled in German universities. However, the strategic alliances forged to keep up with technological change are a dangerous first step in the direction of corporatization of a genuinely not-for-profit field. Again, a balance is needed, with state funding for value education, fundamental research and liberal arts education, supplemented with focused financing of specific projects ("Drittmittelforschung") and tuition.

Specialization and relevance of studies play a legitimate role in the choice of future careers (Natale: 96 f). However, a general curriculum that includes cultural literacy does not contradict vocational requirements of future employers. It is one of the major flaws of the European university system that it prepares its students badly for life after academia, and that the students graduate at an advanced age which makes it difficult to include them in corporate structures. The competition with the more flexible universities of applied sciences will allow to sharpen both profiles. However, a general re-orientation, away from the current, financially tempting trend of corporatisation is needed.

To act, all agents have to have a minimum of knowledge of their actions. Without any contact with "real" life beyond academia, such orientation will be impossible. Orientation is always orientation about orientation. Orientation is determined by previous orientation, which means that, in the sense of Kant's work cited above, we can only orient ourself if we are able to determine our horizon. For this successful application of knowledge, it is necessary to master the media: what we need is further media literacy. Lack of orientation, as deplored widely in society, cannot be overcome by vocational training alone. Liberal arts training that allows such orientation complements application of knowledge: it is its precondition, if the skills have to be updated at a later point in life. Lifelong learning is only successful if the foundations are solid: quantitative and qualitative knowledge has to be conveyed in a value-building environment. These goals of society transcend corporate needs and corporate mission.

They form the context, in which a healthy corporate environment can grow. Without direction, skills cannot be applied. The finding and defining of meaning oscillates between the satisfaction of needs (applied science, vocational training) and the desire to find meaning (Orth: 21 ff.). Even the sensualist Abbé de Condillac is aware that there is more to experience than senses alone: Economy is seen as the science of needs. Such needs can only be determined with a view beyond the scope of the immediate application. Philosophy, in the sense of the old "philosophicum," can reconciliate theoria and praxis. It has to help to orient the orientation, to find direction, to define standpoints, and to develop alternatives.

"Es wird aber dieser Ausdruck auf das Gebiet der Erkenntniß übertragen, und da heißt sich orientieren soviel als sich auf jenem Gebiete zurecht finden, und zwar dadurch, daß man die Gesetze der Erkenntniß aufsucht. Da nun dieß bloß durch Philosophieren möglich ist, so ist die Philosophie gleichsam die Orientierungs-Wissenschaft in Bezug auf alle übrige Wissenschaften. Soll sie aber dieß sein, so muß sie freilich vorher ihren eigenen Orient oder Aufgangspunct gefunden haben. Ob sie diesen bereits gefunden, ist zur Zeit noch problematisch (Krug: 131; "Transferred to the field of knowledge, orientation means finding one's way of seeking the laws of knowledge. Since this is only possible through philosophising, philosophy alone can help to guide us as the orientational science of the sciences. If philosophy endeavours to be just that it first has to find its own horizon, or starting point. Whether it has found it is difficult to say at this time.").

It is indeed questionable if philosophy has found its own standpoint. However, it can depict alternative ways of seeing, without judging. That these alternatives can be evaluated as corporate planning makes them applicable, yet they are not part of corporate planning. They are the condition of the development of future applications.

To orient oneself means to find one's place, but also to be able, figuratively, to know. Curriculae that help orientate allow preparing the necessary choices in a society where compromise has informed consent as a precondition. It further means that we are orientating ourselves in different dimensions, in different cultural fields. We can define goals only if we are able to bridge the gap between theory and praxis. Disorientation, a lack of knowledge or a lack of acceptance of common sense, can be mediated via liberal arts education (Lübbe, Orth: 30). The danger of purely applied education and purely vocational training is that it provides the illusion of orientation, whereas it only offers an unreflected standpoint. Training does not prepare for change. In the platonic sense, it is not an art. Since change occurs faster than ever, higher education has to offer the necessary resting place for fundamental reflection that prepares for faster adaptation in the future. Time is of the essence and the reflective capacity, the look back in order to find the way, is in danger. Kant: "To *orientate* oneself, in the proper sense of the word, means to use a given direction—and we divide the horizon into four of these—in order to find the others, and in particular that of *sunrise.*" (*Reiss* 238, *AA* VIII 134) Orientation needs knowledge here and now, but also a sense of direction.

Kant is aware of this problem: "Ein Zeitalter aber aufzuklären, ist sehr langwierig." (*Reiss:* 249 "To enlighten an era, however, is a very protracted process;" *Richardson*: 407 "But to enlighten an age, is very wearisome").

The solution for education has to be a structure that allows both the applied and the traditional university structure to provide the necessary space and time to find the way.

In a purely corporate educational environment, this will not be achievable. In a short-term election based state run system, this will equally be impossible. As Steffens found, the state and science have fundamentally different interests. So do corporate entities. Only society has the right and duty to define its goals by balancing the present and future interests of all. A balance between all the parts is needed to define the new, old, re-oriented university. Re-orientation means that not all can do everything at the same time: redefinition of mission and specific "niche" service to society that allows positioning all the players (Natale: 208). If society defines itself as a marketplace, it has also to present itself in terms of the marketplace. A re-oriented university will have no problem presenting its long-term achievements and will demonstrate potential for such achievements. Yet we cannot assess them with the same short-term quantitative tools we use in economics. Some symbols transcend their prize. A flag has little or no commercial value, and yet it is symbol for all values of a society or group. Universities are flagships of value finding and symbols of orientation in a disoriented time. They are society's only tools to master the mediated, media-driven information age. The defence of the salient place of the university as *universitas magistrorum et scholarium* was possible through independence from state and church from the 13th century. Today it needs to guard its independence from commercial and immediate needs to remain the orienting institution of society. The university needs its autonomy to achieve its goal with knowledge: "denn über Gelehrte als solche können nur Gelehrte urtheilen" ("since only genuine scholars can judge about scholars." *A* VII, 17, *The Contest of the Faculties* (*CF*), introduction, not translated). Finally, orientation has to be disinterested, neutral and knowledgeable, as Kant claimed: "Rational inquiry and moral conduct can be practised properly only in a society governed according to principles of politics based on the idea of freedom." (*Reiss:* 236)

References

Unless stated otherwise, translations from German are my own, in brackets. Page references to Kant's works in the text and in endnotes refer to the relevant volumes of the Prussian Academy edition (*Kant's gesammelte Schriften.* 27 volumes. Edited by the Königlichen Preußischen (later Deutschen) Akademie der Wissenschaften. Berlin, Reimer (later de Gruyter), 1900-, quoted as *AA* and according to the abbreviation key of the Kantbibliographie).

Bauer, Elizabeth-Maria, *Die Hochschule als Wirtschaftsfaktor*, Münchner Studien zur Sozial—und Wirtschaftsgeographie, vol. 41, Lassleben Kallmütz, Regensburg 1997, pp. 20-21.
Bleek, Wilhelm, *Von der Kameralausbildung zum Juristenprivileg*, Berlin 1972.
Bösch, Michael, "Symbolische Prägnanz und Passive Synthesis", *Philosophisches Jahrbuch # 109*, I, 2002, pp. 148-161.
Bulmahn, Edelgard (ed.), *Antworten auf Fragen zur Juniorprofessur*, Bundesministerium für Bildung und Forschung, Berlin 2002.
Fallon, Daniel, *The German University, A Heroic Ideal in Conflict with the Modern World*, Colorado Associated Press, Boulder 1980, p. 6.

Glotz, Peter, *Im Kern Verrotted, Fünf vor Zwölf and Deutschlands Universität*, Deutsche Verlagsanstalt, Stuttgart 1996.

Habermas, Jürgen, *Protestbewegung und Hochschulreform*, Suhrkamp, Ffm 1969, p. 121.

Hammerstein, N., Universität, in *Historisches Wörterbuch der Philosophie*, ed. Ritter ed al., vol. XI, Schwab, Basel 2001, p. 215.

Hoffacker, Werner, *Die Universität im 21. Jahrhundert*, Dienstleistungsunternehmen, öffentliche Einrichtung, Luchterhand, Neuwied 2000.

von Humboldt, Wilhelm, *Gesammelte Schriften*, 17 Vols, Berlin 1903-36, vol. X, p. 257.

—*Unmaßgebliche Gedanken zur Einrichtung des Litauischen Schulwesens*, 1809, Akadademie Ausgabe, vol. XIII, 1920, p. 279.

James, William, "The PhD Octopus," *Harvard Monthly*, vol. 36, 1903, pp. 1-3.

Jaspers, Karl, "Das Doppelgesicht der Universitätsreform," in *Deutsche Universitätszeitung* 1960, # 3, vol. 15, p. 8.

Joffe, Josef, "Das Gestern als Gesetz," Linkes Projekt, (unge) rechte Folgen, in *Die Zeit*, 18, 25. April 2002, p. 1.

Kant, Immanuel, *Gesammelte Schriften*:

—Beantwortung der Frage: Was ist Aufklärung? (1784) *AA* VIII

—An answer to the question: What is Enlightenment? in *Kant's Political Writings*, transl. H. B. Nisbet, edited by Hans Reiss, Cambridge, Cambridge University Press, 1970, 2nd ed. 1990.

—*Der Streit der Fakultäten, AA* VII

—Verkündigung des nahen Abschlusses eines Tractats zum ewigen Frieden in der Philosophie (1796) In: *AA* VIII 421 f.

—Was heißt: Sich im Denken orientiren? (1786, modern spelling: orientieren). *AA* VIII, 131-47. First published in *Berlinische Monatsschrift*, VIII (October 1786), 304-30.

—What is Orientation in Thinking? In (*Reiss*)

The first translation by William Richardson (London, Royal Exchange, 1798) calls the text: "What means, to orient one's self in thinking"

—Zum ewigen Frieden (1795), *AA* VIII

Kerr, Clark, *Postscipt 1982, The Uses of the University*, 3rd edition, Harvard University Press, Cambridge 1982, p. 152 f.

Köddermann, Achim D., "Why the Medieval Idea of the University is still modern," *Educational Change*, 1995, I, pp. 78 f. and 96.

Krug, Wilhelm Traugott, *Allgemeines Wörterbuch der Philosophischen Wissenschaften nebst ihrer Literatur und Geschichte*, vol. 3, 2nd ed., Leipzig 1833, p. 131.

Lübbe, Hermann (ed), *Der Mensch als Orientierungsweise*, Alber, Freiburg/München 1982.

Luhmann, Niklas, *Das Erziehungssystem der Gesellschaft*, Suhrkamp, Ffm 2002,

Mathy, Helmut, *Die Universität Mainz, 1477-1977*, Krach, Mainz 1977.

Mendelsohn, Moses, *Morgenstunden oder Vorlesungen über das Daseyn Gottes*, Berlin 1785, *Jubiläumsausgabe* vol. 2/3, Stuttgart-Bad Cannstatt 1974, p. 82.

Mische, Wilfried, and Agathe Odinius, *Die Fachhochschule in Deutschland*, FH Aachen, FB Wirtschaft, Siebengebirgsverlag Wienands, Bad Honnef 1998, pp. 16-17.

Natale, Samuel M., Anthony F. Libertella, and Geoff Hayward, *Higher Education in Crisis*, The Corporate Eclipse of the University, Global Publications, Binghamton 2001.

Neuhaus, Ralf, *Dokumente zur Hochschulreform*, 1961, p. 264: "Blaues Gutachten", 1948: the universities carry on an in its core healthy tradition: "Hochschulen als Träger einer alten und im Kern gesunden Tradition." Justification is that they educate more than specialists: "nicht nur als Spezialist, sondern auch als Mensch tauglich."

Orth, Ernst Wolfgang, *Was ist und was heißt "Kultur?"*, Königshausen und Neumann, Würzburg 2000, pp. 32 f.

Jefferson Papers, Library of Congress Microfilm, series T, Doc. 18172, reel 22, quoted in Robert R. Riegel, *Young America*, Norman, University of Oklahoma Press, 1949.

Rüthers, Bernd, *Universität und Gesellschaft*, Thesen zu einer Entfremdung, Universitätsverlag Konstanz, Konstanz 1980, p. 16.

Seelbach, Ralf, *Staat, Universität und Kirche*, Die Instititutionen—und Systemtheorie Immanuel Kants, Peter Lang, Ffm 1993.

Spranger, Eduard, *Wilhelm von Humboldt und die Reform des Bildungswesens*, 1919, 2nd edition Tübingen 1965, pp. 200-204.

Weld, C. R., *A History of the Royal Society*, vol. I, J. W. Parker, London 1848, p. 146.

Chapter Twenty Eight

Ways of Knowing—Confucian and Daoist Perspectives

HYUN HÖCHSMANN

The feet of man on the earth is but on a small space, but going on to where he has not trod before, he traverses a great distance easily; so his knowledge is but small, but going on to what he does not already know, he comes to know what is meant by Heaven (*Zhuangzi* 24, Legge II. 112).[1]

Harmony as the Ethical Goal

The tradition of moral philosophy is the great legacy of philosophical thought in China. In reading the ancient texts, the precise terms of the explanations may appear remote from the present, but the essential ideas are timeless and ever present at the centre of all philosophical activity. We join Confucius in his persistent effort at living ethically. With Zhuangzi we strive for moral autonomy, freedom, and equality of all. Zhuangzi emphasized that the right way to live is not laid out for all eternity by the ancient sages nor does it consist in pursuing the straight path of virtue but is to be discovered by those who question everything and dare to go beyond the traditions of ceremony and ritual.

While the conception of human nature, proposals, strategies, and the specific aims varied greatly, the goals that all divergent thinkers of China agree on are the cultivation of the moral life of the individual and harmony within the society.[2] Harmony is the pervasive ideal and the ultimate goal of all activity in all spheres. All schools of thought have presented conceptions of harmony and ways of achieving it. From Laozi, Zhuangzi, Confucius, and Mencius to the Neo-Confucian philosophers, every major thinker sought to chart the moral path of man in the constantly changing world. The Confucian and the Daoist approaches differ on how to cultivate the individual life but the aims are the same. The ethical goals for Confucius and the Daoist converge on the point of concern for the well-being of the people. Both arise from an intense awareness of the moral desire for the good life for all. While Confucius and Mencius emphasize the study of the classics and fulfillment of the duties of benevolence and righteousness and observation of rites and propriety in personal and political relations, Laozi and Zhuangzi advocate renouncing learning and focus on the natural development of all beings. The Daoist philosophers seek to derive a pattern of life from the way of nature. Zhuangzi advocates spontaneity and authentic self-development. The conception of a person in Confucian ethics is essentially a social being while Zhuangzi conceives the individual as an autonomous being. For philosophers in the Confucian tradition, harmony is achieved by realizing the love of humanity (*ren*) in action, guided by knowledge of the classics and proper conduct (*li*) and emulating the paradigms of virtue of the sage rulers of antiquity. The goal of study is a harmonious self-cultivation which consists in striving for intellectual, moral, and aesthetic virtues simultaneously.

The same virtues—benevolence, altruism, righteousness, and sincerity, and rules of propriety—apply in personal ethics and political morality. Both for the individual and society the harmonious cultivation of human relation in all spheres of action is the goal. Politics is understood primarily as a matter of human relations based on virtue rather than an impersonal institution based on a contractual agreement or on government by law.[3] Philosophers in China were primarily concerned with practical ethical questions. The crucial question was "What is the way to order the state and conduct personal life?"[4] The most influential person in the entire civilization in China was not a conqueror of territories or men but a philosopher, the first teacher of the people and the rulers, Confucius (551-479 BCE).

Confucius

I make no complaint against Heaven, nor blame men, for though my studies are lowly my mind soars aloft (*Analects* 14.37).[5]

With his love of learning Confucius sought to guide all people, from the emperor to the people of the land, to live ethically. Confucius, the most renowned of all philosophers in China, was a person of deep intellectual and moral humility. Through the sheer range and clarity of his ideas he was able to bring together the ways of thought and connect the customs of a vast and complex civilization with moral principles acceptable by all. Confucius' ideas have shaped the moral values and practices and formed the foundation of political thought and institutions in China and East Asia. It might be argued that it was not the intrinsic merit of his ideas but the force of an imperial edict which established the ideas of Confucius as a state religion. In the Han Dynasty during the reign of Emperor Wu (141-87 BCE), as the Confucian scholar officials gained political power, Confucianism became established as state orthodoxy. But a way of life and a moral perspective accepted by the people are unlikely to be the result of laws enforced by political authority especially when "the mountains are high and the emperor is far away."

Drawing upon his intensive study of the classics, Confucius provided the one universal standard with which philosophers and rulers sought to reconcile conflicting claims and interests. Confucius was a pioneer in philosophical thought. There was no established tradition of systematic philosophical schools when Confucius began his philosophical activity. There is no direct reference to a philosopher or a thinker by a specific name. All Confucius had before him were the *Book of Odes*, the *Book of History*, the *Book of Changes*, the *Spring and Autumn Annals*, and the *Book of Music*, which became the basis of Confucian learning. In studying the writings and recorded conversations of Confucius, we encounter the classics of Chinese thought.

At the center of the power of his philosophy and achievement was his great ability to bring to a synthesis the entire learning and art up to his time. During the period of the decline of the traditions, there was a movement to preserve the lessons of antiquity, and the philosophers proposed a wide range of solutions to restore justice and end conflict. Confucius differed from the philosophers who focused on specific doctrines of the particular schools. Setting the goal of education to be the cultivation of the whole person for the whole of life, Confucius taught his disciples a wide range of subjects. In the *Analects*, a disciple says of him, "He has broadened me by culture and restrained me by the usage of good conduct" (*Analects* 9. 10). This broad range of knowledge is reflected in the differing interests of Confucius' disciples in the *Analects*. Confucius sought to bring about the cultivation of the individual through the study of poetry, history, and music. He turned to rites and ceremony to guide human relations in personal life and in the political domain. Music was an integral part of the cultivation of personal life. Confucius played on the Zither and sang the three hundred and five pieces which comprise the present *Book of Odes*. He refers to the *Book of History* for moral instruction and wishes that he could devote fifty years to the study of the *Book of Changes*. He studied the *Book of Odes* and the *Book of History* to re-assemble and restore them, carrying his research into the study of the rites of the three dynasties, Xia, Shang, and Zhou. Confucius was the first to methodically study the classics and make them into the foundation of systematic learning and the basis of education for the common people. From the *Historical Records* (*Shi Ji*) we know of his activities as a teacher. Confucius believed that "in teaching there should be no class distinctions," and initiated the dissemination of learning among the general population. Confucius' completely egalitarian approach to teaching became established as a central tenet in the Confucian tradition.

What were the ideas conceived in the mind of Confucius that came to be developed into a continuous unbroken tradition from his time, the sixth century BCE to the present, spanning over two thousand and five hundred years? Confucius' moral and political philosophy is clearly set forth in the *Analects*. It is a simple and abbreviated record of Confucian sayings and conversations with the disciples. The familiar view of Confucius portrays him as contentedly conforming to the conventions. But this overlooks the innovations which are at the core of Confucius' philosophy: the Principle of Reciprocity— "Do not do to others what you do not like yourself"—and the ideas *ren* (love), *de* (virtue), and *li* (right action). Conscientiousness (*zhong*) and altruism (*shu*) are the expressions of *ren* in social contexts. The Principle of Reciprocity, as first formulated by Confucius, captures the common starting point in ethics (*Analects* 12.2). In the ethical traditions of Hinduism, Judaism, and Christianity we find analogous formulations of the Principle of Reciprocity, also known as the Golden Rule.[6] From the Indian epic *Mahabharata*, we have "Let no man do to another that which would be repugnant to himself." "What is hateful to you do not do to your neighbour," said Rabbi Hillel. Christianity advocates "Love your neighbour as yourself." In not doing to others what we do not wish for ourselves, we exercise moral empathy. The first step in ethical thinking is to expand the sphere of concern beyond our own domain of interests. In this sense then, the origin of *de* (virtue) is in setting aside self-interest. The Principle of

Reciprocity requires that in our actions we take into consideration our well-being as well as that of others.

Confucius launches ethics from a new point of departure. For Confucius *li* (propriety, right actions or rules for appropriateness of actions) and *ren*, as love which is the essence of humanity, form the basis of ethics simultaneously. Prior to Confucius morality was a matter of emulating the actions of particular revered personalities upheld as moral paradigms for all occasions. *Li* meant something entirely external and objective applying to acts which are concordant with circumstances, in compliance with tradition and custom.[7] In Confucius' conception, *li* becomes an internal moral sense which can be cultivated and called upon in action. Confucius invents the inner moral life of man. The Confucian revolution was to set the course of the moral life in society on the development of the moral character and action of the individual.

Li, conceived as the rules of right conduct, guides our actions as objective criteria of ethics. Confucius sees the interconnectedness of human development. *Li* is not restrictive but expands the individual as well as others. By developing ourselves we create an environment in which others may also flourish. In Confucius' thought the two pillars of ethics, *ren* and *li*, build the bridge between the individual and the world. *Ren* and *li* permeate the individual moral life and social relations. The five relations among all human beings—parent and child, husband and wife, friends, old and young, ruler and subject—are associated both with *ren* and *li*. Each relation is guided by *li* as an expression of *ren* appropriate to it. Acting in accordance with *li* creates social order and acting from *ren* creates kindness and charity.

How long should education continue?

> At fifteen I set my heart upon learning, At thirty, I had planted my feet firm upon the ground. At forty I no longer suffered from perplexities. At fifty, I knew what were the biddings of Heaven. At sixty I heard them with docile ear. At seventy I could follow the dictates of my own heart, for what I desired no longer overstepped the boundaries of right (*Analects* 2.4).

Confucius' dictum "Spare no effort in learning" is developed in the later text, *the Doctrine of the Mean*. Where there is anything not yet studied, or studied but not yet understood, do not give up. Where there is any question not yet asked, or asked but its answer not yet known, do not give up. Where there is anything not yet thought over, or thought over but not yet apprehended, do not give up.

> When there is anything not yet practiced, or practiced but not yet earnestly, do not give up. If another man succeeds by ten efforts, we will use a thousand efforts. If we really follow this course, though unintelligent, we will surely become intelligent, and though weak, will surely become strong.[8]

Who then is the Confucian Sage? A student of philosophy, a lover of knowledge, and not an authority.

> Am I indeed a man with innate knowledge? I have no such knowledge; but when an uncultivated person, in all simplicity, comes to me with a question, I think out its pros and cons until I fathom it (*Analects* 9.7).

Confucius confesses that he has not succeeded in treating his brothers as he would like to have been treated himself. He has not succeeded in putting the Principle of Reciprocity into action. Confucius stresses the constant awareness of his own moral imperfection and ignorance and the need for persistent effort in correcting his mistakes through critical self-examination and the "unwavering pursuit of wisdom." "In literature perhaps I may compare with others, but as to my living the noble life, to that I have not yet attained" (*Analects* 7.32).

> Neglect in the cultivation of character, lack of thoroughness in study, incompetence to move towards recognized duty, inability to correct my imperfection . . . these are what cause me solicitude (*Analects* 7.3).

Confucius' prominence in the history of Chinese philosophy and the vast influence of his thought frequently led to an uncritical admiration of the man and his ideas. The epithets, "the most perfect sage," "the first teacher," and the subsequent veneration of Confucius was detrimental to an open-minded inquiry and also contrary to Confucius' own view of his arduous attempt at learning. Confucius as the historical personage is distinct from the legendary and idealized representative of the Confucian school of thought.

There is a general impression that philosophy in the East is less philosophical in the sense that it emphasizes the preservation of scholarly tradition, whereas philosophy in the West is practiced as independent rational inquiry. Not only in the field of knowledge but also in the moral and political realms, the Eastern sensibility may appear to be more prone to veneration than to disputation. With its emphasis on filial piety, reverence of ancestors, and performance of rites, it has been frequently observed that in China the individual is subsumed in a social matrix of relations and obligations. It is nevertheless true that Confucius' emphasis on the cultivation of personal life is a clear indication of the importance of the individual. Conformity to social convention is nowhere upheld as a desirable means or ends. If Confucius came revered as "sage and serious" and his utterances were subsequently engraved into stone tablets in later centuries, these developments do not reflect the frank skepticism and the challenge of the disciples in the *Analects*, who were not unthinking followers but active participants in an ongoing dialogue.

The veneration of Confucius as not as a mortal but as though he were born of a dragon, certainly it is contrary to his view of himself. Confucius is almost always seen as an upholder of tradition, and his assertion that he is "a lover of antiquity" reinforces the received view. But Confucius emphasizes the study of classics not as ends in themselves but as an approach to achieving moral and intellectual virtue. Confucius does not value knowledge for its own sake but for its practical application.

> A man may be able to recite the three hundred Odes, but when given a post in the administration, he proves to be without practical ability, or when sent on a mission he is unable himself to answer a question, although his knowledge is extensive, of what use is it? (*Analects* 13.5)

There is a continuity of knowledge between intellectual and moral virtue. In the Confucian text, the *Great Learning*, the purpose of education is to strive for "cultivation of personal life, harmony in the family and order in the state" not as ends in themselves but as intermediate stages to peace in the world.[9]

Confucius' view of himself as the "one who is fond of learning" and Socrates' characterization of a philosopher as a lover of knowledge are parallel. There is a striking similarity between Socrates' view that wisdom begins with knowing that one does not possess knowledge and Confucius' view of knowledge. Confucius announces:

> Shall I teach you the meaning of knowledge? When you know a thing, to recognize that you know it; and when you do not, to know that you do not know,—that is knowledge (*Analects* 2.17).

Confucius' humility is akin to Socratic humility. Confucius believed that he is a transmitter and not an originator of knowledge. Socrates confesses that he has no knowledge of his own to impart and that he is like a "mid-wife" who assists in the birth of knowledge. While Confucius sought to preserve and restore what he regarded as great and true, Socrates inquired and strove to create a new conception of the life worth living since there were no precedents which satisfied his search for truth.

Unlike the writings of Plato, the *Analects* which is a discursive record of Confucian sayings is neither a consummate literary composition nor a series of compelling arguments sustained in a philosophical dialogue. Its fragmentary nature and the conversational style have been compared to pre-Socratic writing. We need to piece together the statements and the questions to construct arguments. But once such a reconstruction is made the similarity in the flow of thought and expression to the Socratic dialogues emerges. Socratic method and Confucian method are similar. Initially both are destructive. There is a common core of scepticism in their approach regarding the reliability of general experience and sense perception. Confucius is described as being entirely without preconceptions. Neither Socrates nor Confucius can resist the urge to question what is customarily taken for truth. The sophists, relativists, and subjectivists of ancient China and Greece questioned the objectivity of knowledge while being certain of the relative merits of each individual's claim to knowledge. The scepticism of Confucius and Socrates, on the other hand, is about their own individual ability to know the truth. Both Socrates and Confucius are certain about the possibility of objective knowledge and the mind's ability to acquire it. Socratic doubt and Confucian uncertainty are about the unreliability of the general claim to knowledge based on individual experience and not about the capacity of human mind, reason, and intellect to know the nature of things.

Confucius includes the rectification of names as an integral part of moral education, together with the study of the classics, poetry, history, rites, and music. Confucius is acutely aware of the deficiency of language to express truth. Confucius bursts out, "I wish I could do without speaking." To the response "If you did not speak, what should we disciples pass on to others?" Confucius replies, "What speech has Heaven? The four seasons run their course and all things flourish; yet what speech has Heaven?" (*Analects* 17.19) But below in the fallen world, during the period of chaos of the Warring States, when the possessors of names no longer corresponded to their appropriate names— when the ruler was not a ruler, the minister not a minister—Confucius stressed the importance of definitions and correct usage of language. Like Confucius Plato also emphasized the central place of definitions and clear understanding of language. Confucius matches Socratic tenacity in his persistence in seeking to clarify the meaning of the fundamental ethical concepts.

The goal of political life for Socrates and Confucius was not an exercise of individual liberty but a harmonious society. Both Socrates and Confucius regarded politics as a science requiring an expert knowledge, high moral character, and above all, the utmost concern for the common good. The strength of Confucian ideals emerged in their ability to set clear guidelines for the rulers and the people. In his conception of the moral person, *junzi*, Confucius does not regard the aim of moral education to produce a duty-bound citizen or a member of a committee but a person who has inner qualities of honesty, self-criticism, self-reflection, sincerity of will, and rectitude of mind. Confucius' view of the role of the emperor is not that of a supreme ruler with absolute power. Nor is it that of the world-historical individual who carries out the grand schemes of history outside the bounds of ordinary moral standards. From the moral point of view, equality prevails. The moral obligations of the emperor to his parents are the same as that of the people to their parents. From the people to the ruler, all have the same duty of benevolence and righteousness, and the same virtues of altruism and conscientiousness are to be cultivated. Confucius believed that all can acquire virtue through knowledge and emphasized that all are to abide by the same standard of righteousness.

In a world of continual strife and conflict how can harmony be achieved? When he is asked how one can excel in virtue and eliminate ingrained evil, Confucius responds enthusiastically,

> Truly a good question! If we first do what is to be done and only then be concerned about success—isn't this the way to excel in virtue? To attack evil that is within oneself and not to attack the evil of others—isn't this the way to correct evil? (*Analects* 12. 21)

Confucius emphasizes that when we see good conduct we ought to seek to learn from it and when we encounter flawed actions we should look within ourselves to correct our own shortcomings (*Analects* 12. 16).

> The moral person seeks to perfect the good qualities of men, and does not call attention to their bad qualities. The small man does the opposite of this.

Confucius' response to the problem of evil calls for not punishment of wrongdoing but self-reflection and the cultivation of virtue in those who have political authority. When he is asked, "What do you say to killing the unprincipled for the good of the principled?" he replies,

> On carrying on your government, why should you use killing at all? Let your evinced desires be for what is good, and the people will be good. The reaction between superiors and inferiors is like that between the wind and the grass. The grass must bend, when the wind blows over it! (*Analects* 12. 19)

Confucius stresses that the rulers need to be just for there to be justice among people. The cause of social evil is an unjust government of corrupt ministers. "How true is the saying: 'If good men ruled the country for a hundred years, they would . . . abolish capital punishment'" (*Analects* 13.11). The view of justice as benevolence was not restricted to Confucius. Laozi also argues against capital punishment. The laws enforcing justice as retribution and punishment were seen as having originated in the time of decay.

When Confucius' ideas became ossified as static icons of state religion, the inward momentum of cultivation of virtue and initiative of changing the world for the better were lost. But the insight expressed in the two Confucian ideas, "Love *all* men" and "Do not do to others what you do not wish for yourself"—are as timeless as the injunctions of Delphi in ancient Greece—"Know thyself" and "Nothing in excess"—and have persisted throughout all political upheavals and natural calamities. Again and again, the moral insights of Confucius, the ideals of love of humanity, moral development, and just society have resonated across vast stretches of time and space.

Laozi

To know non-knowledge is the highest good. Not to know what knowledge is a kind of suffering. Only if one suffers from this suffering does one become free from suffering (*Dao De Jing* 71).[10]

Laozi urges that we seek knowledge until we reach the limit of our knowledge. To know that we do not possess complete knowledge is the beginning of true knowledge—Socrates would concur with Laozi. *Dao De Jing* of Laozi (551-479 BCE) is the foremost text of Daoist thought.[11] It is a collection of aphorisms of varying length and subjects but unified under the theme of the book itself: the way and its power. It consists of eighty-one short stanzas. Each stanza expresses a philosophical reflection in bold summary, often drawing upon well-known proverbs to make a fresh point. The brief text of *Dao De Jing* has exerted a significant influence. In the West since its first translation in 1788, the knowledge of Laozi's writing has become widespread. *Dao De Jing* (literally, "way—virtue—a work of standard authority, a classic") has been translated as *The Way and Its Power*, *The Book of Tao*, and *The Book of the Way*. It is the most frequently translated text of the classics of China. Unlike the Confucian texts where lucidity prevails throughout, there is a penchant for paradoxes and contradictions. This is a distinct characteristic in the writings of the Daoist philosophers in which the intended meaning is shrouded in an elliptical expression inviting us to penetrate the cryptic constructions. The Daoist thinkers do not conceive the task of philosophy as showing the fly its way out of the fly-bottle but to entice and bewilder the mind and to take us into the labyrinth of philosophical imagination at the center of which we find the way to soar above with the *dao*.[12] If the text is on occasion less than transparent, it is not because there is a deliberately enigmatic hidden meaning to be deciphered or esoteric teaching open only to the initiates. The epigrammatic sayings in the *Dao De Jing* are frequently new renderings of inherited maxims whose initial clarity has been blurred by time. Laozi glides effortlessly from one stanza on the metaphysics of the *dao* to concrete objections against war, violence, and retributive justice.

Laozi criticizes the excessive scholasticism of his day, which was not efficacious in changing the world for the better. Laozi seems to point to the antithesis of the Confucian love of learning: "When we renounce learning we have no troubles" (*Dao De Jing* 19). The intent of the *Dao De Jing* is frankly didactic. For a text which calls for renouncing all learning, it insists on a more direct pedagogical approach and active strategy of learning than the *Analects*. Even when knowledge and excessive reliance on book learning are criticized by Laozi and Zhuangzi—as they are seen to stifle spontaneity and freedom of thought—it is by argumentation and not by jettisoning reason in favour of mystical insight that the man of the *dao* is upheld as the paradigm of virtue to be emulated.

Laozi explains that wisdom consists in self-knowledge and true strength consists in self- discipline.

> Whosoever knows others is clever; whosoever knows himself is wise. Whosoever conquers others has force; whosoever conquers himself is strong (*Dao De Jing* 33).

The *Dao De Jing* is concerned with practical ethics—a subject as much in urgent need of philosophical reflection in the present as it was in Laozi's time.

> Weapons are instruments of bad omen, not the instruments of the noble. He uses them only when he cannot help it. Quietness and peace are his highest values. He gains victory but he does not rejoice in it. Whosoever would rejoice in it would, in fact, rejoice in the murder of men. Whosoever would rejoice in the murder of men cannot achieve his goal in the world. . . . He who has killed a multitude of men should weep for them with the bitterest grief (*Dao De Jing* 31).[13]

In Daoist thought it is taken as being self-evident that violence of any kind is contrary to the principle of *dao*. Laozi argues that putting people to death as a punishment for crimes does not work as a deterrent. When people are driven to desperation they do not fear death and it inevitably brings harmful consequences upon those who destroy lives to achieve their ends.

> If people do not fear death, how can one frighten them with death? But if I keep the people constantly in fear of death and if someone does strange things, should I seize him and kill him? Who dares do this? There is always a power of death that kills. To kill instead of leaving killing to this power of death is as if one wanted to use the axe oneself instead of leaving it to the carpenter. Whosoever would use the axe instead of leaving it to the carpenter shall rarely get away without injuring his hand (*Dao De Jing* 74).

We may concede that the threat and the infliction of violent punishment make people prudent but not moral and incite impulses of retaliation. But since neither the individuals nor governments have yet succeeded in eliminating the causes of harmful actions what is the just way to remedy the ills of society? Laozi urges that we work to eliminate exploitation and poverty which cause crime (*Dao De Jing* 19). The way to lead people is not to put them to death for wrong actions but to reform the government (*Dao De Jing* 75).

> When the people go hungry, this comes from too much tax being devoured by the high and mighty. . . . When the people take death too lightly, this comes from life's abundance being sought too greedily by the high and mighty.

In the *Dao De Jing* there is an implicit belief in the inherent goodness of human nature. Daoist philosophers turn to the receptivity of the human mind to the good as the best and most reliable incentive instead of inculcation of virtues by following the rules of morality.

Zhuangzi

It is with the arrival of Zhuangzi (ca. 369-286 BCE) that the ideas of Laozi become imbued with a deeper philosophical significance. With Laozi, Zhuangzi is regarded as the founder of Daoism as a philosophical school. Zhuangzi's philosophical contribution consists in his conception of the equality of all forms of life and the affirmation of freedom.[14] While preserving the moral ideal of living in harmony with the entire universe, Zhuangzi emphasizes the importance of individual freedom in thought and action and seeks to show how it is possible to achieve this freedom for all.

Equality of all things is the basis of Zhuangzi's ethics (Legge I. 184). Zhuangzi challenges Confucius' conception of the morally superior person who cultivates the virtues of benevolence and righteousness. Zhuangzi startles us by insisting that a robber adopts the same principles as the sage. By putting the robber and the scholar on the same level Zhuangzi seeks to show that it is in exalting one and condemning the other that we may fall into an error of judgment. Zhuangzi urges that we set aside the conduct of the sage emperors and scholars as paradigms of moral excellence. But surely it is just to reward the scholar and condemn the robber? Zhuangzi has an impassioned response to this.

> Here is one who steals a hook (for his girdle) and he is put to death for it. Here
> is another who steals a state and he becomes a prince. But it is at the gates of
> the princes that we find benevolence and righteousness professed.

Zhuangzi is critical of the conventional dispensation of justice. Instead of punishing the robber and rewarding the scholar according to the whim of the prince, who also is a robber (and even worse because he steals entire states), we need to work on eliminating the cause of theft: poverty, greed, and exploitation. It is injustice that leads to social evil and not any flaw or defect in man or lack of knowledge. Zhuangzi advocates reforming the government of corrupt rulers. Zhuangzi believes that the source of good government resides in the people, and the rulers should seek to avoid violence even when it means giving up their political power.

Zhuangzi criticizes the use to which the doctrines of the scholars are put to sanctify the conduct of unjust rulers. "When sages are born great robbers arise" (Legge I. 284). Zhuangzi criticizes the "versatility shown in artful deceptions" and the ingenious discussions of the sophists which leave the people perplexed and lead to "great confusion and disorder" (Legge I. 289). He is unsparing in his criticism of "the error of sagely men": "If an end were put to sageness and wisdom put away, the great robbers would cease to arise" (Legge I. 286). Granted that Zhuangzi's criticism is aimed at the apologists who justify aggression and plunder which were at the basis of political power, isn't it going too far to disparage all learning and claim that scholars are no better than robbers? The robbers who cause harm to material goods are acting from greed but those who affect learning are afflicted by deeper corruption of the good of the intellect.[15] What we praise in the scholar—intelligence, perseverance and determination—are also the virtues possessed by the robber. The moral potential of man is not increased or diminished by the failure or success of his actions. All distinctions between superior and inferior man must be set aside. For Zhuangzi equality is not a remote ideal but an actuality that has been forgotten in our preoccupation with individual differences. Once we become aware of the real equality of all beings underlying the different approaches of life, we will be able to embrace all ways of life.

In equating the scholar and the prince with the robber Zhuangzi is questioning the standard by which actions are evaluated. Zhuangzi's point is not that there are no distinctions between right and wrong conduct but that we must discard the inequality of prevailing standards to recognize that what is moral for one is moral for all. Zhuangzi traces the causes of theft to the institution of rank and property.[16] "If jade were put away and pearls broken to bits, the small thieves would not appear" (Legge I. 286). If all were to cultivate the land side by side there would be no alienated labour and class distinctions between princes and paupers. Zhuangzi urges that we do away with the hierarchy of moral standards established by social conventions. But is it possible or desirable to do away with all distinctions? What would happen to personal and social relations which are based on distinctions? Zhuangzi challenges us to examine the basis of our claims regarding the distinctions among things and inquires, "How have they become so?" He argues that conventional distinctions are based on custom and habitual usage which may be arbitrary: "They have become so because people say they are so" (*Zhuangzi* 2). Zhuangzi searches for foundations of morality beyond events of history or social institutions circumscribed by particular individual human relations.

Zhuangzi affirms the unity of all life in the universe.

> All things may be comprehended in their unity. It is only the far reaching in thought that know how to comprehend them in this unity (Legge I. 184).

The beginning of ethics is an awareness that there is a point of view from which the well-being and interests of others are taken into consideration in all our actions.

As a defender of individual freedom against the imposition of authority and tradition, Zhuangzi is unparalleled. Even if we were to regard any constraint as an evil to be avoided from the standpoint of upholding individual freedom as an absolute value, freedom consists in more than following wherever our nature takes us. When we are following our inclinations without rational reflection and real knowledge of genuine alternatives for actions we cannot be said to be free. What Zhuangzi values is not simply freedom from constraints of conventions and rules but freedom of thought and action vital for authentic existence and self-development. Zhuangzi's discussion of letting nature take its own course may appear simply as "being at ease with oneself."

> When one is at ease with oneself, one is near the dao. This is to let nature take its own course. This is because he relies on the dao and stops at this. This is the dao (*Zhuangzi* 2).

But inquiring how we may come to be at ease with ourselves we realize that it requires an energetic exertion. It will not suffice to investigate the needs of the self.

> If we are to follow what is formed in our mind as a guide, who will not have such a guide? Not only those who know the succession of night and day and choose them by exercising their own minds have them. Ignorant people have theirs too (*Zhuangzi* 2).

Relying on one's own opinion is hazardous at best since all have opinions regardless of whether one possesses knowledge or not. What does Zhuangzi propose in place of justification of beliefs based on a sharp delineation of things? Zhuangzi describes the way of the sage which looks for the commonality among things. Instead of putting forth novel doctrines, he sees things as they are without imposing a narrow individual interpretation.

> The sage aims at removing the confusions and doubts that dazzle people. Because of this he does not use his own judgement but abides in the common principle. This is what is meant by using the light of nature (*Zhuangzi* 2).

To stand forth in our natural attributes means not forming isolated judgements but seeking out "the common principle": Only the wise person knows how to identify all things as one. Therefore he does not use his own judgement but abides in the common principles (*Zhuangzi* 2). We discover that the moral significance of being at ease with oneself and letting nature take its course consists in expanding the conception of the self until one can identify oneself with the whole of existence.

The relevance of the moral philosophy of Confucianism and Daoism to present and future is in the area of practical ethics: preservation of the environment, elimination of death penalty, prevention of suffering caused by poverty, and peace as the goal of politics. Daoism offers a viable ethical perspective for the future as it can be interpreted as advocating setting the boundaries to prevent accelerated encroachment on the natural environment.

> The knowledge shown in the making of bows, cross-bows, hand-nets, stringed arrows, and contrivances with springs is great, but the birds are troubled by them above. The knowledge shown in the hooks, baits, various kinds of nets, and bamboo traps is great, but the fishes are disturbed by them in the waters. The knowledge shown in the arrangements for setting nets, and the nets and snares themselves, is great but the animals are disturbed by them in the marsh grounds (*Zhuangzi* 9, Legge I. 288).

Zhuangzi is critical of the shortsightedness of human contrivance which "disrupt the quietness in the mountains and the rivers" and interrupt the round of the four seasons. Zhuangzi refers to the state of nature in which harmony prevailed.

> At that time, in the hills there were no footpaths, nor excavated passages, nor dams. Birds and beasts multiplied. Yes, in the age of perfect virtue, men lived in common with birds and beasts, and were on terms of equality with all creatures, as forming one family (*Zhuangzi* 10, Legge I. 278).

Zhuangzi's regard for the natural environment and all life is directly linked to the contemporary moral issues of the protection of the environment as the habitat of sentient life. Zhuangzi's moral philosophy emphasizes the equal treatment of all sentient beings, nonviolence, global justice, and preservation of the environment. The moral point of view, which urges us to view the whole of nature from an impartial standpoint, provides a foundation for our moral responsibility to bring about the harmony of all life. Zhuangzi regards human life as a part of the continuum of life, and not as having dominion over nature.

Zhuangzi celebrates the life of freedom and equality of all. But unless we have good reasons to have an unshakable confidence in the principle of pre-established harmony, we need to concede that subjective freedom is more frequently the cause of conflict. Zhuangzi can defend freedom not as a natural right but on the grounds of the common interests of all. Zhuangzi, in upholding individual freedom, is not a champion of anarchy of feeling and individual will. Citing the ancient worthies, Zhuangzi states that they all did "service for other men and sought to serve for them what they desired, not seeking their own pleasure." General well-being is possible when individuals have the possibility of full self-realization. The autonomy of the individual and the concern for the shared interests are not in conflict. Zhuangzi's aim is to bring contending positions into a comprehensive, universal and an objective point of view beyond shifting opinions. When contradictory views are in collision we need to seek out that which is found not in one isolated standpoint only but what is held in common.

> A human being is a part of the whole, called by us "the universe," a part limited in time and space. He experiences himself, his thoughts and feelings, as something separate from the rest—a kind of optical delusion of his consciousness. This delusion is a kind of prison for us restricting us to our personal decisions and to affection for a few persons nearest to us. Our task must be to free ourselves by widening our circle of compassion to embrace all living creatures and the whole of nature in its beauty.[17]

These words of Einstein, who believed that "one exists for other people—first of all for those upon whose smile and well-being our own happiness is wholly dependent and then for the many unknown to us, to whose destinies we are bound by the ties of sympathy," embody the ideas of Zhuangzi. With the "proper light of the mind" we can find "the pivot of the *dao*." (*Zhuangzi* 2, Legge I. 183)

> Therefore the scintillations of light from the midst of confusion are indeed valued by the sagely man. Not to use one's own views and to take his position the ordinary views is what is called using the proper light (Legge I. 187).

The sage makes the mind of the people his mind. By following one's given nature Zhuangzi does not mean following individual inclinations disregarding all else. The still point of the turning world is not the self but the point of view of Heaven. To affirm everything and to say "Yes!" to the universe—that is the knowledge of the *dao*.[18]

Notes

1. James Legge, trans., *The Texts of Taoism, The Tao Te Ching of Lao Tzu, The Writings of Zhuangzi*, New York: Dover, 1962.
2. I have developed these ideas in further in *On Philosophy in China*, Wadsworth Publishers, 2002 (forthcoming).
3. This point is made by Dawson in *The Chinese Experience*, London: Phoenix Press, 1978, p. 17. See Jacques Gernet's discussion *A History of Chinese Civilization*, Cambridge: Cambridge University Press, 1999, p. 106.
4. A. C. Graham, *Disputers of the Dao*, Chicago: Open Court Publishing Co., 1997, p. 3.

5. James Legge, trans., *Confucius—the Confucian Analects, the Great Learning, and the Doctrine of the Mean*, New York: Dover 1971.
6. Peter Singer has pointed this out. *How are We to Live?* Melbourne: Text Publishing, 1993, p. 230.
7. Arthur Waley, *The Way and Its Power*, London: Allen & Unwin, 1934, pp. 60-62.
8. James Legge, trans., *Confucius—the Confucian Analects, the Great Learning, and the Doctrine of the Mean*.
9. *Ibid.*
10. James Legge, trans., *The Texts of Taoism, The Tao Te Ching of Lao Tzu, The Writings of Zhuangzi*. New York: Dover, 1962.
11. I have drawn from Richard Wilhelm's translation of *Dao De Jing, Tao Te Ching: The Book of Meaning and Life*, Harmondsworth: Penguin Books, 1989.
12. To paraphrase Wittgenstein's famous fly-bottle of philosophy.
13. The Duke of Wellington remarked that wining a battle was the saddest thing next to losing it. Legge, *The Texts of Taoism*, I, p. 74.
14. I have developed these ideas in further in *On Chuang Tzu*, Wadsworth Publishers, 2000.
15. Dante who condemns the hypocrites to the lower circle of the Inferno than the thieves would agree with Zhuangzi.
16. Graham, *Chuang Tzu*, p. 188.
17. Albert Einstein, *Ideas and Opinions*.
18. A. C. Graham, trans., *Chuang Tzu*, Indianapolis: Hackett, 2001, p. 60.

Chapter Twenty Nine

The Role of Culture in Radical Change

ROBERT ALBRIGHT
DAVID RAINEY

In this discussion, David Boyd and Thomas Begley explicitly examine the concept of corporate culture. Their study of executive viewpoints regarding the corporate cultures of a robust sample of U.S. high technology firms is enlightening. It provides evidence that supports the contention that senior executives believe culture directly contributes to the furtherance of company goals. Indeed, the interview results reported in the paper indicate active attention to the management of culture due to its ability to facilitate change and drive performance. Such a proactive use of culture may be an especially important tactic for firms operating in globalized, time compressed industries where leading technological innovation is critical to success.

This chapter will attempt to further the discussion of culture as a managed enabler of corporate performance by hypothesizing that certain cultural characteristics are essential to firms that must consistently lead and deal with radical change within their industry. Here we contend that culture is an essential piece of the uncommon organizational architecture needed to lead technological innovation. Culture can facilitate the constant re-organizations required by today's business drivers. It can also encourage the introspective and adaptive processes essential to organizational learning and change. Simultaneously, culture can ensure the organization focuses on core values that allow continuity in the face of rapid change and uncertainty. Thus, we contend that corporate culture increasingly plays both a stabilizing and a disruptive role. It can provide a sense of stability by providing a recognized set of organizational anchors *and* promote rapid organizational evolution. We will begin by discussing the concept of radical change and its implications for the management models and systems used by the modern organization. Subsequently, we will discuss the uncommon organizational architecture required to manage radical change, and the central role culture plays within that architecture.

The Traditional Management Model

Traditional management models were straightforward constructs focusing on hierarchical organizational structures. Senior management provided the strategic direction, and functional management (through the chain of command) provided the operational decision making. The hierarchical models worked reasonably well as long as management had adequate time to make decisions. In the relatively slow-paced world of the early 20th century, the hierarchical organizational models functioned adequately because most businesses had similar constructs and were able to deal with the burden of time-consuming decision-making.

However, the business environment changed radically during the early 1970s. With the oil crisis of 1973 and a similar situation in 1979, along with high inflation, stagnation, and high interest rates, business conditions were substantively altered. Business conditions became less predictable. The rate of change increased significantly as business entities around the world discovered new opportunities and corresponding challenges. Change became an ever-present phenomenon.

Based on the changing landscape, the early vestiges of globalization took hold. Competition expanded dramatically as powerful producers in regional markets sought opportunities in distant locations. The automobile industry in the United States illustrates the phenomenon. The insular "Big Three" were ill-prepared to respond to the onslaught of the Japanese and European automobile companies. The world had radically changed, demanding products and technologies commensurate with the new realities; but General Motors, Ford, and Chrysler were unable to keep pace. Managers increasingly became aware that in a global business environment, success is measured based on world-class attributes, not local practices.

Based on the radical new world of global events and global impacts, strategic business planning models of the 1970s drastically changed conventional management thinking. Strategies and objectives became more important than action plans and activities. Management reached out to identify and incorporate new opportunities and to respond to threats. Management constructs evolved from organizational models to management systems that included strategic planning, strategic management, and the operating level. Total quality management (TQM) and similar constructs were key drivers in the evolution toward more horizontal models that replaced the vertical approach of the hierarchical organizational models. However, the focus was on continuous improvement, not continuous change.

During the 1980s, Michael Porter's famous Value Chain and Value System were truly revolutionary perspectives about management systems (Porter, 1985). Porter changed the basic construct from focusing on organizational linkages in decision making to a process-management construct of managing deliverables and achieving customer satisfaction. It embodied the philosophies of quality, customer satisfaction, and value. Porter's models focused on the system and its essential elements. They examined the interrelationships between suppliers, the producer, value networks, customers, and competitors and how those relationships created value. While new entrants and substitution were explored, the focus was on the prevailing situation. The dynamics of time and the impacts of change were tangential rather than central to the construct.

During the 1990s, management systems became even more sophisticated as business leaders made significant improvements in integrating their business strategies and operations, creating innovation, and improving overall business performance. The management system became the pivotal construct. The management systems represented the integration of all of the essential elements of the internal and external dimensions for managing in the present as well as the future.

Enterprise Management constructs are recent developments that are still evolving. They incorporate a holistic view of business that addresses globalization, the intensity of competition and technological change. In their article, "Converging Innovation, Integration and Leadership to Manage Business Enterprises in the 21st Century," David Rainey and Edward Arnheiter discuss enterprise management and its implications (Rainey & Arnheiter, 2000).

> Enterprise management is the full integration of the internal functional areas and the strategic position of the organization with all of the external factors influencing the business. It encompasses the whole, both internal and external, and the present and the future. The power of enterprise management is that it is inclusive of all of the essential dimensions in managing and leading an organization.

> While enterprise management focuses on the integration of the business environment and is a comprehensive model of the prevailing conditions and trends, the dynamics of the business environment requires a construct that includes innovation and change.

An ever-increasing number of contemporary business entities are finding themselves confronted with an environment that demands continuous innovation and change. Vision is essential to survival in this environment, as are forward thinking business strategies and the supporting objectives that the strategies spawn. However, these generally accepted management constructs need to be drastically supplemented if today's firms are to systematically exploit radical change and innovation. Exploiting radical change so that firms can better create customer value requires enhanced attention to several increasingly important dimensions of organizational management. The remainder of this chapter will discuss several of these key elements.

First and foremost, turbulent environments and radical change require an uncommon organizational architecture. This architecture (which encompasses the organization's structure, processes, values and culture) determines the organization's ability to manage and take advantage of radical change. Among other things, the architecture must provide seamless cross-functional integration and synergy. It must promote and facilitate constant reorganization and flexibility, and it must assure a sense of stability for its human resources by providing a relatively constant set of core values that are consistently applied as it pursues its objectives. The multiple competencies required of organizational leaders and teams that foster the development of radical change are different than the competencies required of our organizational leaders of the past. The contemporary leaders that can proactively manage radical change must excel at the construction of the organizational architecture mentioned above and be a master with the tools that provide the strategic linkages and interfaces with other entities. In addition, they must be able to concurrently manage some of our time-honored tradeoffs. They must excel at concurrently managing efficiency and adaptability, be able to pay attention to both the short and the long run, and carefully provide organizational stability while implementing disruptive change. Structural reorganizations, integrative and adaptive processes and shared corporate values are emerging as indispensable tools for contemporary leaders as they attempt to achieve these seemingly incongruous objectives.

Figure 1
The Ability to Foster Radical Change Necessitates an
Uncommon Organizational Architecture and Culture

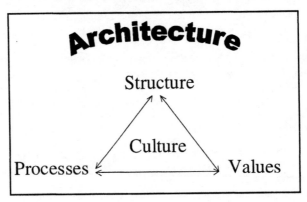

Structure

The organic organization first conceptualized by Burns and Stalker has long been considered the organizational type most appropriate for firms that find themselves in rapidly changing environments. These adaptive organizations presumable derive their flexible characteristics from a loose hierarchy of authority, decentralized decision making, jobs without much formal definition and a control system located anywhere in the organization (Burns & Stalker, 1961). More recently, Claudia Bird Schoonhoven and Marian Jelinek note that the logic maintaining that the organic organization is essential to firms that consistently manage high technological change is unsatisfactory. (Schoonhoven & Jelinek, 1990). After interviewing more than 100 high technology managers and engineers, Schoonhoven and Jelinek report that successful high technology firms most often display well-articulated structures, definite reporting relationships and clear job responsibilities. This type of architecture is essential, for in addition to constantly innovating their products and manufacturing processes, high technology firms must most often manufacture their new products in an efficient high volume manner. This manufacturing efficiency is more commonly accepted as being best achieved by a mechanistic organization where a clear structure, job definition and reporting hierarchy are the norm.

The Ability to Reorganize Frequently

This complex set of demands on contemporary firms is not well addressed by any of the popular existing structural models (e.g., functional, matrix, etc.) The demands are better addressed not by a relatively permanent structure but instead by a new organizational competency: the ability to reorganize frequently based upon the environmental conditions and business drivers at hand. This notion contrasts with the traditional organic organization concept. It maintains that a flexible and responsive organization may have the qualities traditionally associated with the mechanistic organization (a strict chain of command, definitive policies and procedures, etc.) for long or short periods of time. The organizational flexibility and responsiveness necessary to deal with a changing environment is derived via the entity's willingness and ability to reorganize often, not through the organizational characteristics such as dispersed decision-making and loose control mechanisms.

Essential to this "reorganization competency" is the willingness and ability of a skilled and retainable work force to work for relatively short periods of time within the structure most appropriate for the time. This notion, while easy to state, is much more difficult to achieve. Management has traditionally found reorganizations to be exceptionally difficult (Marshall & Lyles, 1994). Human resistance to change, together with the plethora of system adjustments that must be made when any organizational structure is modified, almost inevitably creates the conditions for a high stress and exhausting maneuver. Thus, a number of managerial capabilities have become essential to firms that must reorganize on a continuous basis:

- Management talent must be able to engage a wide variety of stakeholders in continuous strategic analysis (of changing external conditions, business drivers and the firm's ability to address the same.)
- Management must be capable of designing the optimal organizational structure and the set of processes that best address current problems and business drivers. This requires knowledge of the strengths and weaknesses associated with different structural designs, a thorough understanding of the technical core of the business, as well as knowledge regarding how the organization's core processes will be facilitated or hampered by the envisioned structure.
- Management must excel at the optimal deployment and re-deployment of the firms' human resources. The human tendency to resist change has been a well documented and thorny problem for managers throughout history. Few organizational maneuvers raise employee anxieties as quickly as restructuring. Fears associated with potential losses of responsibility or status, new bosses and new reporting relationships, etc. make for a high stress work context not conducive to productivity. Although the literature abounds with methodologies and advice regarding how to overcome this human resistance to change, the complexity of the task often thwarts many an organizational development effort. Thus, managerial competencies associated with change management and communication are essential to those that must successfully deal with the demands of constant re-organization.
- Lastly management must be able to quickly re-new and re-vitalize the organization following any re-organization. New roles and responsibilities must be quickly established that focus the organization's efforts on the new strategies and tactics that will enable the achievement of the new vision. Focusing the organization on its new set of desired outcomes through mechanisms such as goal setting, the generation of "quick wins" and the celebration of the same is essential.

The understandable tendency for organizations to attempt to use their current structures and processes (albeit with minor modifications) in the face of changing environmental conditions is no longer satisfactory. Firms that can successfully and continuously restructure in order to meet environmental conditions must retain managerial talent that is expert in implementing change. In addition, the firms must foster and embrace a number of cross-functional processes that actually promote the acceptance of a constant string of reorganizations.

Processes

Change facilitating processes would include the methods and activities that allow the aforementioned strategic restructuring. Among these processes are those associated with strategic analysis. The firm must be capable of constant strategic analysis that assesses whether the current structure optimizes the organization's ability to meet the extant business drivers. This strategic analysis may often be conducted by quasi-formal structures of organizational employees supplemented by external expertise. These ad-hoc teams, task forces or committees would typically operate for temporary periods of time as a parallel structure to the existing organization (Lawler, Ledford, Mohrman, & Albers, 1989). They augment the formal structure and help create cultural norms associated with the acceptance of organizational learning and growth. The impetus for the formation of the group might be the need to resolve a problem, or the need to address an emergent market opportunity. The important point to note is that organizations with the ability to re-organize to meet environment conditions do not hesitate to establish mechanisms that allow open strategic analysis of the organization's ability to optimally achieve the critical success factors within the relevant industry.

In addition to processes that allow the continuous strategic analysis that directly facilitates enterprise management, other processes must continuously engage people from diverse organizational elements and foster multiple collegial interactions. Processes that allow for problem-based interactions, expertise-based interactions and interest-based interactions must abound and be readily accepted by all. Colleague-based problem-solving groups need to produce achievable continuous improvement ideas. Expertise-based groups can contribute to technological breakthroughs and the rapid deployment of the same. Interest-based groups can play a key role in any strategy or change implementation effort. These processes are not hierarchical interactions but they must be accorded an organizational status that allows their outputs to be seriously considered and adopted by management.

Values

Lastly, values play an important role in assuring employees some stability in the face of constantly changing working conditions. A consistent set of commonly espoused core values can help guide the plethora of organizational decisions that must be continuously made. Additionally, the values can help assure some constancy in terms of the way change decisions are implemented. Common core values such as integrity, openness, respect for people, customer focus, etc. can provide guidance in any change implementation effort, as well as assurance to the stakeholders affected by the change that the change will be implemented in a manner that makes it acceptable.

A strong and widely held set of core values can even be considered a source of competitive advantage. The common understanding and behavioral control that stems from core values influence the tactical decisions made by the workforce and therefore reduces the need for bureaucratic controls (e.g., policies, rules, procedures, etc.) that quickly become outdated and dysfunctional as conditions change. An essential competency for leaders managing radical change deals with integrating current events and organizational evolution with the established organizational anchors (e.g., the core values.)

Culture

Core values as just discussed are an integral, and perhaps indistinguishable, piece of the corporate culture. Here we describe corporate culture as a powerful multi-dimensional construct that is derived from the organization's history, its values, structure and processes. Culture plays a central role in the management of radical change. It plays an important and enabling role in the processes just discussed, as well as in the continuous strategic assessment and restructuring mentioned earlier. Some of the more salient aspects of the culture of firms that thrive while managing radical change follow:

The culture must allow organizational self-criticism. This self-criticism is needed if the firm is to be capable of continuously evaluating its ability to flourish given the state of the industry. This requires a collective effort to stay focused on the outcomes the firm is attempting to achieve within the external environment. The organization's managers must be constantly vigilant and always cognizant of developments in the external environment. External developments and trends must be quickly processed and understood. Valid and intense organizational assessments have to be constantly conducted in order to determine whether the firm is optimally organized to address external developments and trends. The conflict that such assessments and self-criticisms spawn must be considered by all organizational members as healthy and acceptable. This "interactionist" view of conflict must be a part of the organization's prevailing culture. Conflict that is an outgrowth of divergent approaches championed vigorously in the pursuit of mutually held goals must not only be accepted but even encouraged (Masters & Albright, 2002).

While conflict stemming from the passionate championing of approaches is essential, seamless cross-functional integration and synergy must be the norm once decisions have been made to pursue a particular strategy or to take a particular approach. Such integration must be demanded and supported by the prevailing organizational culture. There can be little tolerance for the sub-optimization, the turf battles or the defensiveness so commonly found in organizations that remain relatively static and re-organize on an infrequent basis. Thus, a culture that both promotes organizational conflict for some purposes, while discouraging other forms of conflict is required. Conflict in the form of collegial debate regarding strategic approaches to the organization's outcomes and process improvements must be encouraged by the prevailing culture. Simultaneously, the dysfunctional sub-optimizing behaviors so often found in traditional organizations must be prevented and controlled by a strongly held culture.

Second, the organization's culture must promote the notion of the "boundaryless" organization so often articulated by General Electric's Jack Welch. The organization must have the capability to proactively manage multiple linkages and interfaces between the enterprise and other organizations (suppliers, customers, collaborators, the makers of complementary products, regulators and even competitors!) Myopic and inwardly focused behavior becomes especially damaging in a turbulent environment. The corporate culture can help ensure that linkages and alliances with other firms are viewed as positive arrangements that can build competitive advantage. In enterprise management, alliance partners can provide an array of value-adding capabilities. They may provide market access, critical technologies, expertise in management and operational disciplines or creative product and market ideas. All of the above can be used to synergistically complement a firm's internal capabilities. It goes without saying that the organizational learning that accompanies these linkages and alliances is a way to build and perhaps eventually internalize new and value adding core competencies.

Lastly, the culture must accept organizational upheaval and discontinuity. As mentioned earlier, constant re-organizations must be accepted as the norm. The constant calls for strategic analysis and reorganization cannot be interpreted by the organization as a failure of the previous management team or the previous structure. Instead, the culture must support reorganization as a means to continuously adapt the organization to the changing external environment. Inherently, this type of culture needs to minimize perceptions of individual rank and status based on the position held in the organizational hierarchy. Since positions, and the people within them change so often, organizational status needs to be accorded in a non-traditional fashion. Individuals will need to readily change their reporting relationships—at the extreme, rank inversions where direct reports and bosses even change places from year to year may be conceivable. Status based on function, past accomplishments and the contributions individuals make towards the achievement of organizational outcomes must become the norm.

To summarize, firms that must consistently lead and deal with radical change need to adopt an organizational architecture that enables them to be continuously adaptive. This architecture comprised of a progressive culture, integrative and adaptive processes and a continuously evolving structure will become the norm for the firms that flourish in the technologically powered environment of the future.

References

Burns, T., and Stalker, G. M., 1961. *The Management of Innovation* (London: Tavistock,)

Marshall, R., and Lyles, L., 1994. "Planning for a Restructured, Revitalized Organization" *Sloan Management Review* 35: 81-91.

Masters, M. and Albright, R. 2002. *The Complete Guide to Conflict Resolution in the Workplace*. AMACOM, American Management Association.

Lawler, E., Ledford, G., Morhman, S. and Albers, S., 1989. *Employee Involvement in America: A Study of Contemporary Practices*. Washington, D. C.: American Productivity and Quality Center.

Porter, M., 1985. *Competitive Advantage, Creating and Sustaining Superior Performance*, Free Press.

Rainey, D., and Arnheiter, E., 2001. *Converging Innovation, Integration and Leadership to Manage Business Enterprises in the 21st Century*, Unpublished Working Paper, p. 12.

Schoonhoven, C. B. & Jelinek, M. 1990. "Dynamic Tension in Innovative High Technology Firms: Managing Rapid Technological Change Through Organizational Structure," in M. Von Glinow & S. Mohram (Eds.), *Managing Complexity in High Technology Organizations*, Oxford University Press, 1990.

Chapter Thirty

Selling Change Inside Organizations: Value Based Techniques

Timm L. Kainen

Introduction

Many of the traditional firms of the industrial age are giving way to the more fragmented companies and network structures now dotting the landscape of the global information/service economy (Drucker, 1993), (Handy, 1995), (Toffler, 1991). These companies depend on knowledge, speed and flexibility to move in and out of complex technologies and market niches. This is particularly true for so many of the entrepreneurial start-up and high-tech firms. The structures of these companies are less hierarchical and the management processes within are typified by more ad hoc collegial interactions.

Middle managers in these organizations spend a good deal of time carrying out team and project-based assignments. In these situations, where individual expertise distributes power horizontally, and conflict is a normal part of problem solving, managers have less established authority for directing the activities of others toward desired ends. Without such authority, gaining the cooperation of colleagues is more difficult. When it comes to working out day-to-day matters, a manager can expect a certain amount of cooperation by simply having an up-to-date membership in the culture of shared values.

However, when it comes to getting support for new goals or projects managers often find that their organization begins to look a lot like an internal marketplace; one where gaining support for ideas and the resources to fund them is a highly competitive process. In this arena cooperation must be achieved through a more complex influence process. This requires the negotiation of new working partnerships with existing colleagues or other members of the organization who may not be well known to the change agent. Finding techniques that effectively facilitate this process presents challenges.

This chapter explores how shared beliefs, core values and cultures within organizations can have an impact on gaining support for ideas and projects inside the new organization forms such as network structures. It focuses on the concept of "influence without authority" and the role of negotiating working partnerships in helping that process. It also explores the utility of a new management tool derived from an unusual source.

Influence *With* Authority

A traditional approach to getting "buy-in" can be observed in general paradigms for change. A classical, and well known model used by Kotter (1996) recommends that managers wanting to accomplish change should: 1.) establish a sense of urgency, 2.) form a guiding coalition, 3.) create a vision, 4.) communicate the vision, 5.) empower others to act on the vision, 6.) plan for (and create) short term wins, 7.) consolidate improvements, 8.) institutionalize the new approaches. This model may be well suited for making change from a managerial position of power, but it is much more difficult to implement for middle managers trying to influence colleagues.

We do not see anything close to a paradigm shift if we look at a typical influence model for middle managers. Such models are similar in assumptions and recommendations to those for making change from positions of power. They do seem to recognize a diminished power base but, at the same time, are animated by a desire to re-establish it. A typical pattern would include: 1.) have a compelling vision, 2.) secure a clear mandate from a source of authority, 3.) develop a workable technological solution, and 4.) communicate the idea clearly to the other parties (Sebenius, 1995).

This approach focuses on the goals of the initiating manager, facility with the numbers and strong presentation skills. The power to influence is based on personal expertise. The interaction pattern is aimed at convincing the other players of the idea logic. Preparedness, persistence and motivation to achieve are the individual qualities often considered to be critical for success. Others would say that healthy doses of wit, charm and guile also help move the process along. These skills are not unlike those associated with the old influence models of the sales profession. These sales models would traditionally include: 1.) find the decision-maker, 2.) gain access, 3.) make a presentation, 3.) handle objections, and 4.) close the sale with concession-trading.

Influencing *Without* Authority

Another approach to getting "buy-in" depends on understanding the softer side of the organization. Here, within the culture of an organization, shared sets of core values can either support or reject change ideas—and regularly do so without apparent authority. Access to this system by a change agent is based on the informal sets of relationships that emerge over long periods of interaction and the friends and favors that accompany them.

The core values of culture, and the rituals attached to them are important because they often act as a psychic shock absorber to unanticipated events. In modern organizations these core values also provide operational flexibility as they interact with the structural components. For example, large mass production firms capture the economies of scale to generate impressive output. But, because they need predictability to accomplish this feat they often build organizational structures that tend toward rigidity. The internalized shared beliefs of well-established cultures provide a library of past practices, acceptable shortcuts and ranges of individual initiatives that allow employees to bend the formal rules enough to make the system work at the lower levels of the organizations.

Core Values, Influence And Leadership

Core values and shared beliefs also provide operational flexibility at the leadership level in an organization. Here collectively internalized beliefs allow managers to interpret unforeseen circumstances, make exceptions to established rules and regulations and make adjustments to strategy. They allow leaders to lead. These core values become the center of gravity for the organization should it become lost in the passions of competition. However, there is a potential problem in this. When the core values are weak, or not well internalized by leaders, organizations can become subject to an influence process that can push them in the wrong direction.

When leaders do not have the subjective good judgment to adjust and direct organizations properly, those organizations can become runaway trains. Very recent events in corporate America attest to this fact. In its citation of a University of Michigan speech given by former Secretary of State James A. Baker III, Business Week quotes him as follows: "the genius of capitalism is to pacify a destructive human characteristic, greed, into benign self-interest—something we know as 'incentive.'" It goes on to note that . . . "in the anything-goes 1990s greed overwhelmed the system because there were no counter forces to keep it in check (Byrne, 2002).

John C. Bogle, founder of The Vanguard Group, said that "investing is an act of faith." Joseph Nocera (2002) uses this quote to make his own point that: "Without that faith [that reported numbers reflect reality, that companies are being run honestly, that Wall Street is playing it straight, and that investors aren't being hoodwinked] our capital markets simply can't function." Our faith must ultimately reside in managers who have a set of values that enables them to take personal responsibility for guiding the system correctly. Whenever managers have become unwilling or unable to do so, history shows that new laws and regulations and additional layers of bureaucratic control become the alternative to their lack of leadership.

When it came to evaluating leadership for hiring and promotion decisions Jack Welch, the now retired CEO at General Electric Corporation, placed *values* at the top of his list. He saw executives as being in one of four categories in his values paradigm: 1.) the first type of executive was one who could both deliver financial results and who shared the values of the company. This was the most sought after manager. 2.) the second type was one who did not meet financial goals and did *not* share the values. This manager did not fit. 3.) The third type was one who fell short of financial targets but did share the values. This manager would be given second and third chances [and training]. 4.) The fourth type was the executive who delivered financial results, but did not share the values of the firm and what it was trying to accomplish. For Welch this was the most dangerous manager and the one to be least tolerated. These managers are willing to grind up people and resources to get short-term results. In the process they break faith with the belief system and the reason for doing anything at all. Welch noted that:

> Too often all of us have looked the other way in tolerating these "type 4" managers because they always deliver—at least in the short term. And perhaps this type was more acceptable in the easier times, but in an environment where we must have every good idea from every man and woman in the organization, we cannot afford management styles that suppress and intimidate. Whether we can convince and help these managers change—recognizing how difficult *that can be—or part company with them if they* cannot, *will be the* ultimate test of our commitment to the transformation of this Company and will determine

the future of the mutual respect and trust we are building. . . . (Tichey & Sherman, 1993)

Welch's beliefs are time tested. They also hold particular resonance for organizations on the current business landscape that have adopted hybrid control systems that combine elements of hierarchy with cultural core values.

Core Values and Network Structures

While there are still a wide variety of organization designs in use, the less hierarchical forms are clearly in ascendance. The most sophisticated of these structures are referred to as *network structures*. Networks are recognized groups of managers that can be assembled across functional units, business divisions, geographical locations and/or different levels of hierarchy. What the members hold in common is experience, judgment, and a shared set of core values about the company's purpose. They control resources and information flows. They make decisions and take actions that shape corporate strategy and form sub-networks that make the linkages even more complicated.

Networks form and affect the patterns of interactions by encouraging managers to talk openly, test each other's decisions and build relationships (Charan, 1991). Networks are generally referred to as types of structures, but they act more like cultures. The controls in these systems are: 1.) shared belief systems or core values, 2.) Boundary systems that set limits on freelancing, 3.) Interactive control systems that distribute and share information, and 4.) Diagnostic control systems that continuously monitor key performance variables (Simons, 1995). Above all networks are systems of relationships built on trust and reciprocity with highly developed sets of shared core values.

An unfortunate *negative* example of a network in full operating mode can be seen in the now infamous "Al Qaeda Network. This worldwide terrorist organization was able to plan and carry out the September 11, 2002 attacks on the New York World Trade Center Towers without a formal recognizable structure to guide the process. However, its members' participation in a shared mission statement, core belief system and information sharing gave it the coordination capabilities to perform with lethal results.

On the other side of the conflict, the United States planned and implemented a strategy for eliminating that same Al Qaeda Network with the realization that the organizational form of its adversary did not allow for a traditional military frontal assault. As such, the strategy for winning began to focus on the clandestine penetration of Al Qaeda's information system and decision-making processes. Defeating the network would require taking it apart piece-by-piece from the inside. That meant leaving it intact and dealing with it by using techniques of intelligence gathering in combination with military tactical operations. Uncoordinated "old-style" military battles, even if won, could cause pieces of the network to shut down prematurely. This could make it more difficult to access and destroy the leadership cells in the specific sequences that would keep them from regenerating (Izaz, 2002). The fact that this is such a daunting task speaks clearly to the power of network designs. However, it is important to note that networks are effective because of the functional appropriateness of their design. Their effectiveness does not require that they operate in secret, even though some may do so.

Influence *Without* Authority In Network Structures

To maintain their flexibility and speed, effective network organizations expect their sub-unit operations to act independently. This keeps them close to their markets and technologies and encourages creative problem solving. This, in turn, requires that the coordination activity within each unit and with other units have communications and relationships that are open. Interaction processes must be overt. Participants in these systems are both the actors and directors, freelancing within prescribed limits. The organization is not something they have to work around. In fact, they, and their patterns of interaction, are the organization. The patterns and parameters are carried in their heads as a shared value system.

In these networks the substance of an idea gains importance because it intertwines with day-to-day company business. Trying to "hard sell" an idea on technical merits or financial logic alone can actually be dysfunctional. It is the ongoing nature of the influence process itself and its long-term impact on relationships that is just as important as the idea or project at hand. Consequently, the interactions themselves cannot regress to clandestine favor trading or depend solely on managing personal relationships.

A New Influence Model From An Old Source

If technical and financial logic alone is "too hard" and relationship management alone is "too soft," then what kind of influence process may be "just right"? One answer to this question has appeared from a rather unexpected source: Salespeople. This source is unexpected because the sales profession still bears the weight of its own stereotype ingrained in western culture and reinforced for decades in literature and pop-culture. We only need to read Arthur Miller's *Death Of A Salesman,* or watch Robert Preston hustle non-existent musical instruments to the unsuspecting citizens of "River City" in the movie *Music Man* to be reminded of how salespeople are perceived.

However, because of changes in the economy, business practices and organization structures, many sales processes now involve abstract ideas, sophisticated technologies and multi-party transactions, over long sell cycles. This level of deal-complexity requires the development of long-term interactive relationships with buyers, *not* high-pressure tactics.

Not too many years ago, sales managers realized that they needed to find more effective techniques for selling their own increasingly sophisticated products and services into the more intricate conditions of new information age companies. In analyzing their customers, they began to understand and appreciate the complexities that managers in those organizations were facing. Selling into these flatter matrix and network designs would require a more sophisticated influence process. Good technical product knowledge and "people skills" would not be enough.

To deal with the problem, sales managers developed a number of sales models that focused on building trust through sincerity and competence. The primary interest was in developing long-term relationships. Most importantly, these models also focused on the development of specific and learnable techniques for managing the interaction process itself. What they wanted was a system for negotiating the working partnerships that are necessary to move ideas forward and across boundaries in organizations; even where those boundaries are not always clear.

Some of the more significant innovations in the sales process have been developed by Holden (1990) who focuses on identifying and establishing the appropriate individual as the target of the interaction; Bosworth (1995), Hanan (1995) and Rackham (1988) who focus on managing the middle stages of the interaction; and the work of Miller & Heiman (1987) who focus on preserving the long-term working relationships with strategic linkages and developing them into additional joint projects.

A compilation of these sales models includes the following elements: 1.) identify, and gain access to, individuals with a specific problem that could be solved by your new product or service, 2.) conduct early meetings to help those individuals confess the problem, 3.) jointly develop a hypothetical solution, 4.) get them involved in developing a proposal to solve the hypothetical solution, and 5.) conduct follow up meetings to show how the idea or project solves their problem.

An adaptation of these models for managers selling change inside the organizational marketplace would be outlined as follows. The first and most critical step is to correctly identify the person/s who could most benefit from the seller's idea. The operational definition for "who could benefit" is: the person who has a problem that you can help them solve. This is what salespeople call a "qualified lead." It means that the best potential customer is someone experiencing pain. Beginning the process with this orientation immediately places the emphasis on the other person's critical issues rather than on what the seller may think is the "genius" and/or logic of his own idea. It also reminds the change agent (seller) that his idea has no real "value" until it represents a solution for someone else. The process of identifying the qualified lead requires high doses of one key element: homework.

The second step in the process is to engage the "buyer" in a forthright discussion about the problem. The goal of this interaction is to explore the problem and clearly understand all the details associated with it. The focus is on using a well thought out questioning and listening protocol to accomplish an accurate diagnosis only. Solutions or costs are not topics of discussion. A critical hurdle at this stage is to gain the trust of the "buyer." If the questions are well thought-out and if there is sincere interest demonstrated in the buyer's issues, the chance for building trust increase. One signal of trust is when the buyer is willing to disclose his problems (the "dirty laundry") and "take ownership" of them. Trust is what allows the "working partnership" to develop. The idea is to let the relationship develop along a well-known sequence: strong relationships invite cooperation; cooperation produces creative solutions; creative solutions solve problems; solved problems create value; and value trumps price. And, price is usually the last hurdle to getting an idea or change accepted. An important note here is that the person being engaged may or may not be the final decision maker. However, in either case s/he must end up as a partner with the change agent (seller). This stage of the internal sales process will often involve multiple meetings with multiple players. As the number of these interactions increases, so do the number of negotiated partnerships in the project. This also increases the probability of access to the final decision maker/s.

The third stage of this influence process is focused on developing potential solutions. The critical element here is that the solutions being developed are those that the working partners have identified and accepted as having good potential for fixing the problem. Even more importantly, the working partner has taken "ownership" of the process by explicitly agreeing to a more detailed search for a solution. The process has now become an exercise in creative problem solving being carried out jointly or collectively. At this point, the interaction pattern begins to match the interaction patterns that we say are necessary, and expect to see, in network organizations.

The fourth stage of the process becomes the final presentation of the proposed solution (which has the seller's original idea wrapped inside it). However, at this point the solution is being presented by a team of people who are mutually invested in carrying out the new idea and/or change. The critical concept is to make this a non-confrontational meeting. It should be just another step in the creative problem-solving process. This allows "ownership" by as many members as possible and solidifies the shared core values of open cooperation. The trust that comes from successful and substantive joint problem solving creates a condition that allows the pattern to recycle.

The dilemmas faced by many middle managers within their new organizations are similar to those faced by the vendors learning to sell to them. By adapting these new sales models, middle managers inside network organizations may improve their ability to sell new ideas or make changes. This would be especially true if they approached their organizations as marketplaces of competing ideas.

References

Byrne, John A. 2002. *Restoring Trust In Corporate America*. Business Week, (June 24)

Bosworth, Michael, T. 1995. *Solution Selling*. New York: Irwin

Charan, Ram. 1991. *How Networks Shape Organizations—For Results*. Harvard Business Review. (September-October)

Drucker, Peter F. 1993. *Post-Capitalist Society*. Harper Business.

Hanan, Mack. 1995. *Consultative Selling (5th edition)*. New York: Amacom

Handy, Charles. 1995. *The Age of Unreason*. Boston: Harvard Business School Press

Holden, Jim. 1990. *Power Base Selling*. New York: John H. Wiley & Sons Inc.

Izaz, Mansour. 2002. *On the Record with Greta Van Susteren*. New York: The Fox News Channel, (July 16)

Kotter, John P. 1996. *Leading Change*. Boston: Harvard Business School Press.

Miller, Robert B. & Heiman, Stephen E. 1987. *Strategic Selling*. U.S.A.: Miller Heiman Inc.

Nocea, Joseph. 2002. System Failure. *Fortune*, (July 1)

Page, Charles 1951. The Other Side of Bureaucracy

Rackham, Neil. 1988. *Spin Selling*. New York: McGraw Hill.

Sebenius, James K. 1995. *Negotiating Corporate Change* (videotape) Harvard Business School

Simons, Robert. 1995. *Control In The Age Of Empowerment*. Harvard Business Review. (March-April)

Tichey, Noel M. & Stratford Sherman. 1993. *Control Your Destiny or Someone Else Will: How Jack Welch is Turning General Electric Into The World's Most Competitive Corporation*. New York: Currency/Doubleday (273-274)

Toffler, Alvin. 1991. *Powershifts: Knowledge, Wealth and Violence At the Edge of The 21st Century*. Bantam Books.

Chapter Thirty One

Maturity and Leadership:
Defining Qualities of Society

CAJETAN SALEMI
MARY BRADY SERVICE

In a previous paper, the authors presented ideas concerning the gradual but noticeable destruction of societal linchpins and the effect on government, business, education, and the family. We proposed that individual, evolutionary forces operating in society direct growth and development, while opposing togetherness forces promote regression and unraveling. This chapter attempts to describe the individual evolutionary force, more commonly known as the self, which accounts for the leadership quota in any society. We examine leadership in light of the late Dr. Murray Bowen's concept of self and differentiation-of-self scale (comparable to a scale of emotional maturity)[1] and propose an explanation for the paucity of leaders.

Leaders recognize the association between actions and consequences, are willing to take on responsibility, and have the capacity to move beyond their own needs and wants toward a goal. As a result, they motivate—indeed, some may inspire—followers to seek and realize a better way of living. Certainly, in Bowen's scheme, leaders are those who demonstrate an exceptional ability to differentiate feeling and thinking. We will discuss how leaders flourish (or not) in business, education, and religion.

In examining the elements of leadership, we discovered similarities to current business thinking about the essential makeup of leaders, even though there is no consensus in any field about the genesis of leadership. While *leadership* is a current buzz word— witness the numbers of books, articles, meetings, and Web sites devoted to the subject, as well as 900 studies[2]—the topic was an equally "hot" one for the ancient Greeks, as well as many thinkers and writers in succeeding centuries.

The Actual Self

It is the contention of this chapter that the principles found in all leaders flow from the "actual self" rather than the "pretend self." The writers have chosen to define the principle that they believe links leadership qualities to the actual or authentic self.

In confronting a crisis, an authentic self is not deterred by unforeseen forces; rather, it is invincible. A true self can be silenced for a time and even destroyed, but its potential to influence and inspire others remains. The same can be said of a leader, although it is still uncertain whether a leader is born or made; in the Bowen schema, those few who would be leaders are born, not developed. Even an authority such as E.O. Wilson, in his discussion of the leadership qualities that are found in much earlier societies, posits that humans are born with a disposition for leadership.[3] Many current business theorists, however, emphasize that leaders can be nurtured and trained, as in "On Mission and Leadership," part of *The Drucker Foundation Leader-to-Leader Guide*.[4] These writings raise the tantalizing question: to what extent can leadership be learned?

The actual self embodies the following values or "ethical axioms," as expressed by Melvin Konner: "truth, respect for self, respect for others, and respect for something larger and more embracing than one's own immediate experience . . . a built-in predisposition toward certain ethical values, which have the same degree of general relevance to human society as do the Euclidean axioms of geometry to the material world."[5] These elements are all essential components in the makeup of a leader, but they embody more than respect. The importance of Konner's observations lies in his inclusion of "predisposition toward ethical values."

The authors assert that leadership is in short supply because too few people (i.e., leaders) are capable of personalizing and internalizing values in such a way that they become part of one's inner core or character. A leader would be willing to sacrifice his [or] her life rather than compromise a carefully nurtured and internalized value system. For example, respect for others may be easily assumed (as clothing is put on), learned from one's family, or adapted from cultural or social interactions. If the person is asked to denigrate the worth of this respect for others and does so, this value system is obviously easily compromised or denied. But if respect for others is a profound experience of affirming the other as a peer or an equal or even a superior person, this value, having become second nature, cannot be compromised without destroying the authentic self.

The authentic or actual self is constantly and actively thinking and rethinking, applying and experiencing the stated values in all kinds of relationships: business, academic, and religious—even in family circles. A value mentioned by another person starts a mental process. Experiencing this value in real-life situations, the authentic self is forced to own it personally; this process, however, may take as long as four years.

Looking at these newly acquired values through a series of situations, the authentic self so encapsulates the value that it now becomes part and parcel of its being. In this way, one's inner core or character accumulates axioms for living. The authors say, therefore, that any given leader is filled with "I" statements, not selfish declarations of wants and needs (much less the self-focused, narcissistic "I"), but "I" statements of purposeful direction and execution that do not attack another person or require defense of one's own value system. "Here I stand" is the definitive statement of an authentic self.

Any human being confronting a crisis can become paralyzed by fear and rendered incapable of utilizing one's thinking brain. The urge to flee the situation is an immediate response to the present danger. The stimulus-response mechanism is a proven psychological principle found in all natural systems. Among humans, a leader is able to inject a thinking action between a stimulus and a response. The natural reaction to flee, therefore, is removed, and the higher faculty of thought commands the situation. Through this intervening thinking action, the self takes charge.

An example of such leadership in action was shown during the Apollo XIII mission to the moon 32 years ago.[6] All systems were dead or nearly dead when Mission Control Director Eugene Kranz took decisive action to guide the crippled spacecraft to earth. He told his ground personnel not to guess at what might be happening, not to panic—but to "stay cool." Through his words and actions, Kranz took control of the situation and the lives of the astronauts. Even in such extreme difficulty, a leader refuses to let anxiety or fear take over. Those feelings are hallmarks of the operating forces that dominate people at the lower end of Bowen's differentiation-of-self scale. The higher functioning capacity to think—in particular, to think clearly and quickly in a crisis—is a sign of a leader. Therefore, the authors propose that the current absence of leaders is the result of an inability to control fear and anxiety, as well as the inability to move beyond basic wants and needs. Too few people have a sufficiently developed inner character or authentic self. Because thinkers (those individuals who act accountably and decisively after consideration of risks) are in short supply, so are leaders.

The Levels of Self

What follows is an educated attempt to identify the elements of leadership necessary to inspire positive growth in society; an examination of the self and the pretend self will then yield an explanation for the lack of world-class leaders.

Maturity and integrity, the linchpins of leadership, come from a self well-positioned to think and act, braving the negative voices in a way that maintains respect for the opposing parties but do not obscure the individual's goal, however; that may be defined by the leadership.

The human phenomenon is composed of two parts, a self and a pretend or pseudo-self. Dr. Murray Bowen (a professor in family psychiatry at Georgetown Medical School in the 1960s) devised what he termed a differentiation-of-self scale, one that he said was "comparable to a scale of emotional maturity."[1] In describing the level of self and pretend self in the human, Bowen suggests that lack of leadership results mainly from the absence of a "authentic self" pool. The authors (one, having spent the last 30 years writing and thinking as a therapist, counselor, and minister; the other, a writer and editor of 20 years) confidently state that the number of pretend selves is greater than that of authentic or actual selves. When the weight of "pretend self" is greater than that of the "authentic self" pool, the result will be fewer leaders from the high end of the scale, where one ordinarily finds the most mature and best-integrated people. If all leaders come from the lowest end of the scale, countries and businesses will fall into serious disarray—politically, culturally, and financially. Society cannot operate on the low end of this scale without disintegrating, which has happened in Russia, Bosnia, and some African nations, such as Burundi. Educational and church systems are not immune to the disintegration that results from lower-level leadership. The recent revelations of sexual scandals in the American Catholic Church and the controversy concerning the role of homosexuals in the priesthood are world-wide phenomena. Regarding the sexual scandals, editor Tom Roberts of *National Catholic Reporter*, stated that 17 years after first reporting the problem, he was unable to identify "one leader, one bishop or cardinal, who has exhibited courage in confronting this crisis."[7]

One level of self is the pretend self, or pseudo-self, which is formulated by latching onto the ideas, opinions, and beliefs of others. This self is malleable, forming and re-forming according to outside influences alone. It does not develop an individually formed core of principles or ideas.

The pretend self is easily negotiable. This loose—indeed, shapeless—collection of feelings, opinions, random thoughts, and eclectic insights garnered from philosophy, literature, science, and religious systems becomes the façade for functioning in society. Operating as a giant vacuum cleaner, the pretend self sucks in—without a conscious effort to discriminate. These easily acquired thoughts, feelings, opinions, and insights can be spewed out as quickly as they were swept up. Thus, the operating method of the pretend self is summed up as a "good show," a concern only with impressions, false security, and getting to the higher ground of any argument, discussion, or crisis.

The actual self could not provide a greater contrast. This level of self is not as expansive as the pretend self and is certainly not out to impress, cajole, or otherwise entertain. Here are carefully considered insights, beliefs, opinions, and feelings. When the self declares, "Here I stand," "This is my belief," "This is my insight," "This is my idea," he or she performs an act of differentiation, consciously distinguishing one's thoughts, ideas, feelings, and opinions from those of others people. This discrimination is made by a clearly defined person who has integrated his or her life experiences, knowing when to choose a position and argue for its acceptance—or when to opt for a strategic verbal retreat as the better alternative. This self accepts responsibility for actions, understands that every action has a consequence, and willingly puts reputation, position, and class to the test. In other words, this self exhibits a mature and integrated character.

Differentiation-of-Self Scale

Bowen outlined a scale from 0 (no self) to 100 (the true self), as a means to classify all human activity on a single continuum. The scale provides a measure of maturity; quantifying this concept has challenged the analytical sciences. Bowen's attempt is the best example, as far as the authors are aware, of measuring human activity in the public domain. (Work done by Daniel Goleman in *Emotional Intelligence* and by Goleman, Annie McKee, and Richard E. Boyatzis in *Primal Leadership* describing their research on effective leaders offers an approach to measuring leadership components.)[8,9]

People in the range of 0 to 25 have fused feeling and thinking to such an extreme that they can no longer distinguish between the two functions. This level of self is so minute that it cannot be measured, if it exists at all. This group includes those who seek a good time as the be-all and end-all of life, clearly putting all their efforts into feeling good, which is their main preoccupation.

The range between 25 and 50 represents a different class of people, who have struggled to distinguish feeling from thinking. Those closer to the upper level of 50 in this group make a strong effort, sometimes lasting a lifetime, to create a self out of the existing sources of wisdom, knowledge, literature, and the arts. These individuals are characterized by strong beliefs and opinions, and may occasionally be vocal in disputing others, passionate about treasured customs, unwilling to let go of a worthy idea. Those at the higher end of this group are individuals who are very much like the present leaders in business, education, and religious institutions.

In the third group, from about 50 to 75 on the scale, are individuals who have no difficulty distinguishing between feeling and thinking. Many people in the lower second quadrant misuse "I think" for "I feel." The members of the group in the third quadrant do not make that mistake. When they say, "I think," they mean it. They have assessed situations, investigated sources, and researched their subjects in an intelligent and planned manner. As a result, they have reached a solid conclusion as to the value, merit, and feasibility of a course of action and are willing to implement it.

The authors are unaware of anyone who belongs in the fourth quadrant (75 to 100). Operating at peak efficiency, using all available resources, enjoying both an emotional life and a distinct intellectual effort, never confusing the two selves—all these factors characterize this group, but only as a theoretical construct.

If drawn, Bowen's scale would resemble a bell curve, with a rounded peak that tapers away at either end. In other words, fewer people are at the top (near 100), a majority of people are found in the middle range, and the remainder are at the bottom (near 0).

Applying the Scale

Business

When corporations declare bankruptcy, they leave their employees personally and financially devastated. In every Enron, the giant corporation that imploded spectacularly in early 2002, one can discern the goal of greed and the aim of the good life that can only be achieved by abandoning principle and a sense of rightness. How else does one explain the excessive amounts of money made and spent, other than by characterizing those who made it and spent it as being consumed by "infectious greed?"[10] Leaders in that company either did not know or did not care whether business was conducted on a level playing ground or whether any benefit was to be shared with lower-level employees. Here is a classic case of selfish behavior.

In a 1997 interview, Max De Pree, the chairman emeritus of Herman Miller (the office furniture manufacturer), described the type of behavior that company executives should avoid.[11] His terms bear little resemblance to the behavior exhibited by Enron executives or many others caught up in the fast-wheeling, high-spending excesses of the 1990s: "When leaders indulge themselves with lavish perks and trappings of power, they're not showing appropriate restraint, and they're damaging their standing as leaders." In describing the role of a leader, De Pree emphasized the importance of accountability, "visibility and personal engagement," and the respect that every leader owes those people who would be followers. For the authors of this chapter, all of De Pree's terms reinforce this point: that only a small group is capable of exhibiting these leadership qualities—and those qualities are found only among people at the upper end of Bowen's scale. These are leaders who are capable of thinking about the best for others, not the type of leaders, exemplified by Enron executives, whose primary focus appeared to be "I want."

Another corporation, however, grew steadily and handsomely due to excellent leadership, when most business experts questioned whether the company had a future. Louis Gerstner, Jr. became chairman and chief executive of IBM in 1993, when the best way to manage the company appeared to be "balkanizing" it. Further, while Gerstner's abilities as a manager were praised, he had no experience in the computer industry. How, many asked, could he run "Big Blue"?

In an extensive interview,[12] Gerstner related how he read thousands of pages of corporate plans and decided in his first 90 days on the job to keep the company intact. In doing so, Gerstner said, "I knew it was a big risk, but I never doubted that it was the right thing to do at IBM." Can there be a clearer demonstration of leadership qualities? He studied the situation, listened to employees and customers, devised strategies to change the company and its workers, and implemented the plans. In determining a course of action, he spent little energy on feeling good. Instead, Gerstner made demands, set rigorous policies, and established standards to measure performance. The result was an exceptional company, healthy in many respects, with all levels of leadership apparently performing well—largely due to the leadership provided by Gerstner.

Gerstner would fall at the higher end of Bowen's scale. In the terms of Warren Bennis, author of *Leaders*,[13] and Distinguished Professor of Business Administration at the University of Southern California, Gerstner exhibited the qualities of management of attention (in his vision of what the company could be) and of self (in his commitment to goals and his ability to take a risk), two essential characteristics of leaders. (For a discussion of the leadership qualities of humility and charisma, Patrick Lencioni's "What Kind of Leader Are You?" offers many valuable insights.[14])

Education

Nowhere is lack of leadership more evident than in the field of education. Although major and minor financial skirmishes are not unusual in suburban school districts, budgets are more likely to be approved in affluent areas that understand the implications of supporting the best educational system. In urban schools, money is only one of a long list of troubling considerations.

A far more disturbing scenario is unfolding in higher education, according to Jeffrey Hart, professor emeritus of English at Dartmouth and senior editor of *National Review*. His scathing critique of US colleges, which he terms the "triumph of nescience," is contained in *Smiling Through the Cultural Catastrophe: Toward the Revival of Higher Education*.[15]

Hart outlines the catastrophe facing colleges today in his carefully considered book. In his view, universities and colleges have dismissed as irrelevant the collected wisdom of the ages by no longer requiring a basic, one-year freshman- or sophomore-level course. Such a course could be modeled on Humanities I or II taught by the author at Columbia University.

As Hart says, "the catastrophe is evident to anyone with eyes to see and ears to hear."[16] When professors do not claim ownership or even familiarity with the essential knowledge of civilization collected in stories, epic poems, and other forms of literature, something is missing in their educations and in that of their students, as well. The supposed philosophical basis for dismissing these ancient and modern sources is a seemingly innocuous proposition: "All things are created equal, more or less. Therefore, one century is as good as another; one idea is as good as another." This perspective has created a growing incoherence in the university curriculum, "leading to a proliferation of whimsical and shallowly ideological courses, conferring on these students the degree of 'nescience.'"[17]

A turnaround in higher education is necessary, therefore, if we are to avoid the furtherance of intellectual wastelands. The collected wisdom of the ages found in the literature of many cultures contributed a great deal to society, as Hart makes clear:

"Indeed, Western civilization has flourished to a considerable degree because of its eclecticism, its ability to absorb and make use of what it has found to be valuable outside itself."[18] Through such broad study, the human race is confronted with images and aspirations of the grand themes of life—honor, integrity, compassion, courage, failure, violence, anger, and death. All these characteristics and emotions found in the great men and women of the past continue to have value. Hart, however, declares that we are cavalierly dismissing the past, shelving its learning and lessons to allow inclusion of allegedly more practical courses that appear to have the potential of more immediate, financial gain.

Yet another educational theorist, Diane Ravitch, a visiting fellow at the Hoover Institution and the author of many educational books and articles, in discussing school choice and multiculturalism, follows a path similar to that of Hart.[19] While acknowledging that the common culture transmitted to her and her classmates in the late 1940s and early 1950s in the Houston, Texas, school system was simplistic, Ravitch decries the far swinging educational pendulum that has produced the particularism that predominates in many schools. As she says, "The American story—warts and all, but not warts alone—is a great story, and it should be told. It is a story of many people from many different backgrounds, races, religions, and starting points learning to live together and creating something new in the world. Children should be introduced to great and inspiring literature, not to the scraps compiled in commercial textbooks or the political doggerel of our times." One idea, one book *may not* be as good as another idea or book.

We can only ask: Is there a leader who has the capacity to identify and promote the teaching of the most significant educational values—in grammar schools as well as in colleges—in such a way as to satisfy the diverse political, cultural, and racial components of the United States in the 21st century? Such a person could only be found at the highest end of Bowen's differentiation-of-self scale.

Religion

Recent revelations of illicit sexual activity have caused much discussion in the Roman Catholic Church. Certainly, the prevalence of pedophilia in the American Catholic priesthood has been thoroughly reported in the press. As we have already noted, the editor of *National Catholic Reporter* has been unable to identify a leader at any level of the hierarchy who has been willing to take on the crisis.[7] Amidst negative reports and apparently secret strategic sessions, Pope John Paul II remained officially silent until American bishops convinced him that these sexual issues were explosive ones for the church worldwide. An unprecedented meeting of American bishops held with the Pope the week of April 22, 2002, resulted in a declaration of non-tolerance (but not zero tolerance) for priests who engaged in illicit sexual behavior.[20] Some of the participants called for a reexamination of the rule of celibacy, with the Cardinal of Los Angeles, Roger Mahony, suggesting that it may be time to consider a married clergy.[21] Other people have demanded resignations by bishops and apologies, especially to victims and to the wider community of loyal followers.

In contrast to the monolithic institution of the Roman Catholic Church and its structural inability to tolerate public dissension is the Anglican Church, which does not demand uniformity of theological thought and action. Consequently, the Anglican leader, Dr. George Carey, Archbishop of Canterbury, was able to oversee the ordination of women priests (beginning in 1994) while coping with the divisions such action created within the Church of England. Dr. Carey's leadership will be greatly missed following his proposed retirement in autumn 2002.

The hierarchy of the Roman Catholic Church has refused to reconsider the question of ordaining women to the priesthood. Pope John Paul II discounted the weighty conclusions of distinguished scripture scholars who found no prohibition in the New Testament regarding the ordination of women.[22] Indeed, the Pope has prohibited discussion of the topic, although his strictures have been ignored. In doing so, he violated the basic principle of an open system necessary for leaders to emerge: All voices must be heard, and all ideas must be evaluated. To choose a path because of a prejudice of culture or race rather than according to the inherent value of an action is indicative of leadership dominated by external, feeling forces.

Historical evidence demonstrates that a closed system—and this applies to all natural systems of life—will destroy itself. In writing about open and closed systems, Ludwig von Bertalanffy observed that real systems interact with their environments and are transformed through a process of continual evolution.[1, 23] We would argue that the recent worldwide sexual scandals and the reaction of the Roman Catholic Church present evidence of a closed system. "Don't make a fuss, and we will pay you" has been the axiom for handling many of the sexual abuse cases. In a few months in 2002, the centuries-held habit of secrecy and not talking openly about problems has proved explosively disastrous for the Roman Catholic Church.

Charismatic though the present Pope may be, neither he nor anyone in the American hierarchy appears willing to be held accountable—as the best leaders are—nor to be a risk taker or visionary in leading clerics and laity to more worthy goals. The authors assert that future leaders of the Roman Catholic Church will not come from the top but will rise from within the ranks of the church membership.

Conclusion

Leadership as defined in this chapter is related to initiative, imagination, insight, and the implementation of plans and programs that will raise levels of satisfaction, life, and cooperation among all people. Essential in the composition of leaders is a concern for others. Such leadership is in short supply, we believe, because the available pool is not large at any period. Today's most respected leaders, i.e., those who exhibit the greatest leadership qualities, are relinquishing their power (e.g., Archbishop of Canterbury and Louis Gerstner of IBM).

What of leadership in the 21st century? If educators can instill a sense of mystery, purpose, and self-worth in students, training them to be critical, encouraging them to form judgments about societal events, encouraging research in their fields of interest and the necessity of owning ideas as personal decisions, then the atmosphere in which leaders can thrive will have been created. This process, however, begins in the schools and is disseminated ultimately to other societal components, such as business, religious, and government communities—and to the most personal arena, one's conscience and one's God.

References

Bennis, Warren and Nanus, Burt. *Leaders: The Strategies for Taking Charge*. New York: Harper Business, 1997.

Bowen, Murray, MD. *Family Therapy in Clinical Practice*. New York: Jason Aronson, 1978.

Collins, Jim. *Good to Great: Why Some Companies Make the Leap . . . and Others Don't*. New York: HarperCollins Publishers, 2001.

De Pree, Max. "A Leader's Legacy: A Conversation With Max De Pree." *Leader to Leader*, no. 6, Fall 1997.

Eakin, Emily. "Looking for X in the Algebra of Leadership; Is Impact the Criterion or Charisma? Experts Ransack Leaders' Psyches." *The New York Times*. June 29, 2002.

Goleman, Daniel. *Emotional Intelligence*. New York: Bantam Books, 1997.

Goleman, Daniel, Annie McKee, and Richard E. Boyatzis. *Primal Leadership: Realizing the Power of Emotional Intelligence*. Boston: Harvard Business School Publishing, 2002.

Hart, Jeffrey. *Smiling Through the Cultural Catastrophe*. New Haven, Conn: Yale University Press, 2001.

Henneberger, Melinda. "Scandals in the Church; The Overview; Pope Offers Apology to Victims of Sex Abuse by Priests." *The New York Times*. April 24, 2002.

Konner, Melvin. *The Tangled Wing*. New York: Harper Colophon Books, 1983.

Lencioni, Patrick. "The Trouble With Humility." *On Mission and Leadership*, A Leader to Leader Guide, A Drucker Foundation Leaderbook. Hesselbein, Frances and Johnston, Rob, eds. San Francisco, Cal: Jossey-Bass, 2002.

Lohr, Steve. "He Loves to Win. At I.B.M., He Did." *The New York Times*. March 10, 2002, section 3, 1.

On Mission and Leadership, A Leader to Leader Guide, A Drucker Foundation Leaderbook. Hesselbein, Frances and Johnston, Rob, eds. San Francisco, Cal: Jossey-Bass, 2002.

Ravitch, Diane. "Ex Uno Plures." *Education Next*. Vol. 1, no 3, Fall 2001.

Roberts, Tom. "Editorial." *National Catholic Reporter*. March 22, 2002, 2.

Stevenson, Richard W. and Oppel, Jr, Richard A. "Fed Chief Blames Corporate Greed; House Revises Bill." *The New York Times*. July 17, 2002.

Swidler, Arlene and Swidler, Leonard. *Women Priests*. Ramsey, NJ: Paulist Press, 1977: 338-346.

Useem, J. "What It Takes." *Fortune*, November 12, 2001.

von Bertalanfy, Ludwig. *General System Theory*. New York: George Braziller, 1980.

Wakin, Daniel J. "Scandals in the Church: The Bishops; Pope's Words to Cardinals Reach Past U.S." *The New York Times,* April 28, 2002.

Wilson, Edward O. *Of Human Nature*. Cambridge, Mass: Harvard University Press, 1978.

Notes

1. Bowen, Murray, MD. *Family Therapy in Clinical Practice*. New York: Jason Aronson, 1978; 472-480.
2. Eakin, Emily. "Looking for X in the Algebra of Leadership; Is Impact the Criterion or Charisma? Experts Ranscak Leaders' Psyches." *The New York Times*, June 29, 2002, B7.
3. Wilson, Edward O. *Of Human Nature*. Cambridge, Mass: Harvard University Press, 1978; 86.
4. *On Mission and Leadership*, A Leader to Leader Guide, A Drucker Foundation Leaderbook. Hesselbein, Frances and Johnston, Rob, eds. San Francisco, Cal: Jossey-Bass, 2002.
5. Konner, Melvin. *The Tangled Wing*. New York: Harper Colophon Books, 1983; 428.
6. Useem, J. "What It Takes." *Fortune*, November 12, 2001; 130.
7. Roberts, Tom. "Editorial." *National Catholic Reporter*. March 22, 2002, 2.
8. Goleman, Daniel. *Emotional Intelligence*. New York: Bantam Books, 1997.
9. Goleman, Daniel, Annie McKee, and Richard E. Boyatzis. *Primal Leadership: Realizing the Power of Emotional Intelligence*. Boston: Harvard Business School Publishing, 2002.
10. Stevenson, Richard W, and Oppel, Jr, Richard A. "Fed Chief Blames Corporate Greed; House Reverses Bill," *The New York Times*, July 17, 2002, A1.
11. De Pree, Max. "A Leader's Legacy: A Conversation With Max De Pree." *Leader to Leader*, no. 6, Fall 1997.
12. Lohr, Steve. "He Loves to Win. At I.B.M., He Did." *The New York Times*. March 10, 2002, section 3, 1.
13. Bennis, Warren and Nanus, Burt. *Leaders: The Strategies for Taking Charge*. New York: Harper Business, 1997.
14. Lencioni, Patrick. "The Trouble With Humility." *On Mission and Leadership*, A Leader to Leader Guide, A Drucker Foundation Leaderbook. Hesselbein, Frances and Johnston, Rob, eds. San Francisco, Cal: Jossey-Bass, 2002.
15. Hart, Jeffrey. *Smiling Through the Cultural Catastrophe*. New Haven, Conn: Yale University Press, 2001; p xii.
16. Ibid.
17. Ibid.
18. Ibid, p. 9.
19. Ravitch, Diane. "Ex Uno Plures." *Education Next*. Vol. 1, no 3, Fall 2001.
20. Wakin, Daniel J. "Scandals in the Church: The Bishops; Pope's Words to Cardinals Reach Past U.S." *The New York Times*, April 28, 2002, 47.
21. Henneberger, Melinda. "Scandals in the Church; The Overview; Pope Offers Apology to Victims of Sex Abuse by Priests." *The New York Times*, April 24, 2002, 1.
22. Swidler, Arlene and Swidler, Leonard. *Women Priests*. Ramsey, NJ: Paulist Press, 1977: 338-346.
23. von Bertalanfy, Ludwig. *General System Theory*. New York: George Braziller, 1980.

About the Authors

Dr. Susan E. Morey is an Intercultural Training and Global HRD Consultant to education, business and NGO's. Recently, she was appointed by the U.S. Department of State, Cultural Affairs Division as a Senior Fulbright Specialist (2001-2006) to consult on short-term international projects. She holds dual citizenship with Canada and the USA, and served as a Fulbright Scholar to Romania in 1991 and to Hungary in 1992.

Alison Fuller is a Senior Research Fellow at the Centre for Labour Market Studies, University of Leicester. She has published widely on vocational education, and apprenticeship. She is currently working on a project ("Improving Incentives to Learning in the Workplace") funded by the ESRC's teaching and learning research programme.

Bruce Cutting recently retired from the Senior Executive Service in the Australian Commonwealth Department of Finance. He worked in the area providing budgetary policy advice to Cabinet. He has degrees in Engineering, Science and Economics and has just completed a PhD (Management) thesis titled, *Refounding Governance: Transforming the Science to Master the Art.*

Alexander Kouzmin holds the Chair in Organizational Behaviour at the Cranfield School of Management. His recent books are (with J. Garnett) *Handbook of Administrative Communication* (Marcel Dekker, 1997) and (with A. Hayne) *Essays in Economic Globalization, Trans-national Policies and Vulnerability* (IOP Press, 1999). He has published, to date, some 260 papers and chapters and is a founding co-editor of the international *Journal of Contingencies and Crisis Management,* published quarterly since 1993.

Dick Ottaway is Professor Of Management at Fairleigh Dickinson University, Madison, NJ. His PhD is in organizational psychology from University of Manchester (UK). Also an Episcopal priest with an MDiv from Virginia Theological Seminary, he designed the business ethics course at FDU, which is required of undergraduates in the College of Business.

Anna-Maija Lämsä, Ph.D, is currently a senior lecturer of management and leadership at the University of Jyväskylä, School of Business and Economics, Finland. Her research interests are managerial and leadership ethics, gender issues, and business education development. She has recently published in the *Journal of Business Ethics, Business Ethics: A European Review* and *Leadership and Organization Development Journal*. She has also published books in Finland and professional articles widely in Finnish media.

Pirkko Turjanma, Ph.Lic., is a principal lecturer of research and development projects at Oulu Polytechnic, Business School, Finland. She is also a vice rector of Oulu Business School. Her research interests are quality and learning. She has previously published in the *International Journal of Value-Based Management*. She has also written articles about business education in professional magazines in Finland.

Aila Säkkinen, Ph.Lic., is a principal lecturer of information technology at Oulu Polytechnic, Business School, Finland. She is also a manager of Information Technology degree programme. Her research interest is e-learning. She has previously published in the *International Journal of Value-Based Management*. She has also written articles about virtual and business learning in professional articles in Finland.

F. Byron Nahser, Ph.D., is Chairman and CEO of The Globe Group (Strategic Pathfinder, Marketing/Communication and Graphic Solutions) and Managing Director of Corporantes, Inc. He holds a B.A. degree from Notre Dame University, an M.B.A. from Northwestern University's Kellogg Graduate School of Management, an M.A. in Religious Studies from Mundelein College and a Doctorate in Philosophy, from DePaul University concentrating on American Business Philosophy. Dr. Nahser is the author of *Learning to Read the Signs: Reclaiming Pragmatism in Business*, as well as numerous articles for journals such as the *Value Inquiry Book Series*; *Praxiology: The International Annual of Practical Philosophy and Methodology*; *Perspectives: The Journal of the World Business Academy*; and the *Journal of Business Ethics*.

Dr. Cécile Deer is Research Fellow at SKOPE (Skills, Knowledge and Organisational Performance), a multi-disciplinary research centre at the Department of Economics, Oxford University and lectures at Balliol College on French institutions and society. Educated in France and in England, she has worked on the history of education and on comparative higher education policy. Her book, *Higher Education in France and England since the 1980s* is to be published by Symposium Books in 2003. She has forthcoming articles in the *British Journal of Sociology of Education on Pierre Bourdieu* and recent higher education reforms and in *Sciences de la Société* on evolving governance practice in higher education.

Herbert Rosedale—Biographical information not available

Jan Thomas MA, born in 1968, has studied Education, Humanities and Theology at Hamburg, Passau and Vienna Universities and holds Master level degrees in Education and Linguistics. Jan is currently working as a part-time lecturer at the Institute of Education, Vienna, Austria (PI Wien) and as a freelance consultant in the field of e-learning. Contact: jan.thomas@web.de

Yi-Ying Huang, Ph.D. of the Ohio State University, is Associate Professor at the Institute of Teacher Education, National Chengchi University, Taiwan. Papers published for the past years deal with curriculum theory, systems paradigm, and knowing change. With various interests, Yi-Ying's research efforts focus on transdisciplinary themes and the connections between.

David Boyd is Professor of Human Resources in Northeastern University's College of Business where he served as dean from 1987 to 1994. He has published more than seventy papers on organizational psychology and entrepreneurial leadership. Professor Boyd holds a BA from Harvard University and a D.Phil. from Oxford University, England.

Thomas Begley is Associate Professor of Human Resources at Northeastern University. His research on cross-cultural management and entrepreneurship has appeared in outlets such as the *Journal of Applied Psychology*, the *Journal of International Business*, and the *Journal of Management*. Professor Begley holds a BA from Seton Hall University and MA and PhD degrees from Cornell University.

Ronald C. Arnett does managerial communication and communication ethics, informed by philosophical hermeneutics. His work examines the presuppositions and the implications of philosophy of communication authors such as Martin Buber, Emmanuel Levinas, Hans Gadamer and Paul Ricouer in applied communication contexts. Dr. Arnett is the author of four books and two edited books. He is the recipient of two article awards, one book award and awards related to service and ethics.

S. Alyssa Ritz is an instructor in the Department of Communication & Rhetorical Studies at Duquesne University. Her research and teaching focus on connecting the rhetoric and philosophy of integrated marketing communication to practical application in the marketplace. Her interests link advertising and public relations to communication ethics, especially related to issues of responsibility and accountability in public discourse.

Dr. Joseph W. Sora is currently an assistant professor in the department of Communication & Rhetorical Studies at Duquesne University in Pittsburgh, Pennsylvania. Prior to receiving his doctor of arts in English literature from St. John's University he worked in the publishing industry as a managing editor.

Dr. Alison Sheridan and **Gina Milgate** work together in the School of Marketing & Management at the University of New England and have an ongoing research interest in women's experiences of corporate governance.

Diana D'Amico Juettner brings the experience of a legal studies program director, a practicing lawyer, and a volunteer mediator and arbitrator. She is involved in campus governance and in teaching a broad-based undergraduate legal studies curriculum.

Dorothy Cali Balancio, a sociologist, is a senior trainer with consulting experience in many private and public environments. She has provided career and outplacement counseling in individual as well as group formats in addition to teaching a wide variety of behavioral science courses.

Arthur Lerman, political scientist, began studying conflict management and democracy in the 1960's in his dissertation research on legislatures in Taiwan. He teaches a wide range of history and political science courses and is involved in campus governance, ethnic and civic societies and is certified as a New York State Community Mediator.

Ronald Black is the Vice President for Technology and Distance Learning/Chief Information Officer at Dowling College located in Oakdale, New York. Dr. Black has been a higher education senior administrator and faculty member since 1970 with a specific focus on technology. He received his Ed.D from Nova Southeastern University with a concentration in Higher Education Administration. Specific research interests include distance learning, technology transformation in higher education and technology project management.

Dr. Faith M. Pereira has degrees in Science and Business, with experience in academia and corporate management in the developed and developing worlds, in the private and the public sectors. She is also Faculty Advisor of the Dowling College Delta Pi Chapter of the National Business Honor Society, Delta Mu Delta; member of the Board of Trustees of Briarcliffe College, and Chairperson, Faculty & Academic Affairs Committee; recipient of Awards for Excellence in Teaching and Student Dedication; teacher of graduate and undergraduate classes; and presenter of papers, domestically and internationally, with several publications to her credit.

Ralph Palliam—Biographical information not available

Zeinab Shaloub—Biographical information not available

Michael J. Dowling is President and Chief Executive Officer, North Shore-Long Island Jewish Health System. Before that, Mr. Dowling served as executive vice president and chief operating officer. He came to the North Shore-LIJ Health System in July 1995 from Empire Blue Cross/Blue Shield, where he was a senior vice president. Prior to that, Mr. Dowling served in New York state government for 12 years.

Kathleen Gallo RN, Ph.D., MBA, is the Senior Vice President and Chief Learning Officer at North Shore-Long Island Jewish Health System. As the Chief Learning Officer, Dr. Gallo has worked with Harvard University and General Electric in creating the Center for Learning and Innovation. She is also responsible for Corporate Human Resources as well as Service Excellence for the Health System. Dr. Gallo has over 25 years experience in Emergency Nursing comprising of a variety of clinical and administrative roles in tertiary care hospitals on Long Island.

Alan H. Cooper, Ph.D., is Vice President, North Shore-Long Island Jewish Health System. Dr. Cooper has been with the Health System for 12 years, most recently with the Center for Learning and Innovation, the Health System's corporate university. In this role he also serves as the Health System's Corporate Director for Six Sigma Operations. Dr. Cooper was instrumental in the establishment of the Center for Learning and Innovation. He also holds an adjunct faculty position at Adelphi University in New York.

Carole A. Rayburn, Ph.D., M. Div., clinical, consulting, and research psychologist, is a past-president of the American Psychological Association Division on the Psychology of Religion, the Section on the Clinical Psychology of Women (of APA's Division on Clinical Psychology), and of the Maryland Psychological Association. She is a co-creator of theobiology, the interfacing of theology and the sciences.

Suzanne L. Osman, Ph.D., is an assistant professor of social psychology at Salisbury University (Salisbury, Maryland, USA). Her research interests include gender, sexuality, and related issues.

Ellen Lent is a licensed psychologist and member of the adjunct doctoral faculty in counseling psychology, University of Maryland, College Park (USA). She has over 30 years' experience in workplace consulting, career and personal counseling, training, and executive coaching. Her interests include job satisfaction, excellent workplace performance, career management, and regulating emotional expression.

Anita O. Solomon, Ph. D., ABPP, APA Fellow, Diplomate Clinical Psychologist; Honors: Maryland Psychologists Board of Examiners, federal grant researching intelligence and creativity; APA Karl F. Heiser Award, Legislative Advocacy; Public Service Awards, DC, Maryland Psychological Associations; Montgomery–PG Counties Practicing Psychologists presidencies; Maryland Governor's Mental Hygiene Advisory Council.

Arthur MacNeill Horton, III graduated from the College of William and Mary in 2002 with a double major in Biological Psychiatry and Philosophy. Currently he is travelling.

Arthur MacNeill Horton, Jr. earned his Ed.D. in 1976 from the University of Virginia. He holds Diplomates in Clinical Psychology and Behavioral Psychology from the American Board of Professional Psychology and in Neuropsychology from the American Board of Professional Neuropsychology.

Valerie C. Lorenz, Ph.D. has specialized in research and treatment of Pathological Gambling since 1972. Her master's thesis (Pennsylvania State University) and her doctorate dissertation (University of Pennsylvania) were on pathological gambling. She has conducted seminal research, is a prolific author, and operates the oldest (1986) residential treatment program in the world for compulsive gamblers and their families. Dr. Lorenz is considered a pioneer and expert by her colleagues.

Dr. Bill J. Levin is a licensed psychologist with over thirty years of professional experience. He maintains a psychotherapy practice with children adolescents, and adults and provides psychotherapy and staff training in nursing homes with a focus on improving the quality of life in those settings. He is writing a self-help book highlighting a biopsychosocial/spiritual model of personal evolution.

Achim D. Köddermann studied philosophy, the Laws and Comparative Literature at Dijon (universite de Bourgogne), Heidelberg University and Mainz University before receiving his Ph.D. in Philosophy from Johannes Gutenberg University, Mainz, in 1990. He also worked as corporate planner for German Public Television (ZDF), and held visiting appointments at Denver University and Sripatum University, Bangkok. He is associate professor of philosophy at the State University of New York, College at Oneonta, and associate member or CEMERS (Centre for Medieval and Renaissance Studies) at Binghamton University. The focus of his research lies in applied philosophy (Media-, Business- and Environmental Ethics) and philosophy of culture (History of Ideas, Hermeneutics, Aesthetics).

Hyun Höchsmann—Biographical information not available

Robert Albright is an Associate Professor at Rensselaer. His expertise includes Strategy and Organizational Behavior. Bob received his Ph.D. in Human Resource Management from the University of Pittsburgh in 1994. Bob has published in an array of journals and received fellowships from the American Council of Education and Yale.

David Rainey is also an Associate Professor at Rensselaer. He also serves as the Department Chair of the Lally School of Management at Rensselaer at Hartford. His expertise includes Technological Change and Innovation. David received his Ph.D. from Rensselaer in 1992.

Timm Kainen is a professor of management at the University of Massachusetts, Lowell. He has had previous corporate management experience and is an active business consultant. He specializes in Organization Design, Change and Negotiation. His research on negotiating complex, long-cycle sales is focused on developing new techniques for managing change inside organizations.

Cajetan Salemi, a parish priest since 1961, has taught high school courses in marriage and family life. A licensed counselor, he studied under Dr. Murray Bowen at Georgetown University Medical School. He is presently assigned to a Woodcliff Lake, New Jersey, parish.

Mary Brady Service received a BA from Marymount Manhattan College, New York City, and an MPA from the University of Missouri. An award-winning journalist, she has spent 20 years in publishing and in medical education. She is currently editorial director, Fallon Medica, Red Bank, New Jersey.

About the Editors

Samuel M. Natale is Professor of Strategic Management, School of Business, Adelphi University, Garden City, New York, and, concurrently, Senior Research Associate, Department of Educational Studies, University of Oxford, England. Natale is editor-in chief of three international journals which include *International Journal of Value-Based Management; Cross-Cultural Management* and co-editor of the *International Journal of Effective Board Performance*. His current research focuses on institutional board performance and strategic models for universities and colleges. He is a graduate of the University of Oxford.

Anthony F. Libertella is Dean of the School of Business and Special Assistant to the President for Business Development at Adelphi University. He is editor-in-chief of the *Northeast Journal of Legal Studies*, the co-editor of *International Journal of Effective Board Performance*, and managing editor for the *International Journal of Value-Based Management*. His current research focuses on strategic models for universities and colleges and university governance. He received his B.A. degree from Iona College and his M.A. and Ph.D. degrees from The Ohio State University. In addition, he received his J.D. degree from St. John's University School of Law.